THE GUINNESS
FOOTBALL
FACT BOOK

Second Edition

Jack Rollin

GUINNESS PUBLISHING

CONTENTS

BRITISH FOOTBALL

A–Z English League clubs 5
Season by season League record
League football 82
FA Premier League 84
FA Cup 94
League Cup 103
Other domestic cups 105

A–Z Scottish League clubs 106
Season by season League record
Scottish League 141
Scottish Cup 145
Scottish League Cup 148

Welsh football 149
Irish League 150
League of Ireland 152

Goalscoring 153
Managers 155
British Isles in Internationals 156

Major British records 162

EUROPEAN FOOTBALL

European Championship 166
European Cup 166
Cup-Winners' Cup 170
UEFA Cup 172
Super Cup 173

European club competition records 174
British clubs in Europe 175
European Footballer of the Year 224
Golden Boot award 225

FOOTBALL IN OTHER CONTINENTS

South American Championship 227
(*Copa America*)
South American club championship 228
(*Copa Libertadores*)
Africa 228
USA & World Cup 1994 230

WORLD FOOTBALL

World Cup 232
World Club Championship 235
World goalscoring records 236
International team coaches 237
International appearances 238
World Footballer of the Year 239
FIFA Fair Play award 239

Rules 239
Tactics 241
Transfers 242

Extra Time 244

Index 252

INTRODUCTION

This book includes much of the spirit and substance of the *Soccer Facts and Feats* series but also features several new concepts as well as combining items from *Soccer – The Records*; *Soccer Records, Facts and Champions*; and the previous edition of *The Football Fact Book*.

There are new factual stories covering not only Premier League, Football League and Scottish League clubs, but those who appeared in these competitions in the past.

Also for the first time, there is the complete record of all clubs who have played in them. Their previous names are given if they appeared in either competition under a different one.

The complete record of results and scorers for all British and Republic of Ireland clubs who have competed in Europe is also given.

Each winner of the FA Cup has a summary of its achievements and the same principle is applied to the European Cup and the World Cup.

At international level there is a full record of the respective national teams from the British Isles, the three major European cup competitions are detailed and there are articles on Wales, Ireland, the Republic of Ireland, goalscoring achievements and managers.

The Football League Cup, Scottish League, Scottish Cup, Scottish League Cup and other domestic competitions are covered as well.

Special features include transfers, United States and the 1994 World Cup, International appearances, tactics, the new Premier League in England, an update on Rules of the Game and the emerging continent of Africa.

World champions Germany celebrating a goal by Jurgen Klinsmann against Holland in the 1990 World Cup (Popperfoto)

BRITISH FOOTBALL

A–Z ENGLISH CLUBS

Season by season League records

ABERDARE

Year	Div	P	W	D	L	F	A	Pts	Pos
1921–22	IIIS	42	17	10	15	57	51	44	8th
1922–23	IIIS	42	9	11	22	42	70	29	21st
1923–24	IIIS	42	12	14	16	45	58	38	12th
1924–25	IIIS	42	14	9	19	54	67	37	18th
1925–26	IIIS	42	17	8	17	74	66	42	9th
1926–27	IIIS	42	9	7	26	62	101	25	22nd

During 1926–27, Arthur Brown and Len Evans competed for the first team goalkeeping position with **Aberdare Athletic**. Both were Welsh Internationals.

ACCRINGTON STANLEY

(Accrington, separate club, withdrew 1893)

Year	Div	P	W	D	L	F	A	Pts	Pos
1888–89	FL	22	6	8	8	48	48	20	7th
1889–90	FL	22	9	6	7	53	56	24	6th
1890–91	FL	22	6	4	12	28	50	16	10th
1891–92	FL	26	8	4	14	40	78	20	11th
1892–93	I	30	6	11	13	57	81	23	15th
1921–22	IIIN	38	19	3	16	73	57	41	5th
1922–23	IIIN	38	17	7	14	59	65	41	8th
1923–24	IIIN	42	16	8	18	48	61	40	13th
1924–25	IIIN	42	15	8	19	60	72	38	17th
1925–26	IIIN	42	17	3	22	81	105	37	18th
1926–27	IIIN	42	10	7	25	62	98	27	21st
1927–28	IIIN	42	18	8	16	76	67	44	9th
1928–29	IIIN	42	13	8	21	68	82	34	18th
1929–30	IIIN	42	14	9	19	84	81	37	16th
1930–31	IIIN	42	15	9	18	84	108	39	13th
1931–32	IIIN	40	15	6	19	75	80	36	14th
1932–33	IIIN	42	15	10	17	78	76	40	13th
1933–34	IIIN	42	13	7	22	65	101	33	20th
1934–35	IIIN	42	12	10	20	63	89	34	18th
1935–36	IIIN	42	17	8	17	63	72	42	9th
1936–37	IIIN	42	16	9	17	76	69	41	13th
1937–38	IIIN	42	11	7	24	45	75	29	22nd
1938–39	IIIN	42	7	6	29	49	103	20	22nd
1939–46	Regional Leagues operating								
1946–47	IIIN	42	14	4	24	56	92	32	20th
1947–48	IIIN	42	20	6	16	62	59	46	6th
1948–49	IIIN	42	12	10	20	55	64	34	20th

Year	Div	P	W	D	L	F	A	Pts	Pos
1949–50	IIIN	42	16	7	19	57	62	39	13th
1950–51	IIIN	46	11	10	25	42	101	32	23rd
1951–52	IIIN	46	10	12	24	61	92	32	22nd
1952–53	IIIN	46	8	11	27	39	89	27	24th
1953–54	IIIN	46	16	10	20	66	74	42	15th
1954–55	IIIN	46	25	11	10	96	67	61	2nd
1955–56	IIIN	46	25	9	12	92	57	59	3rd
1956–57	IIIN	46	25	8	13	95	64	58	3rd
1957–58	IIIN	46	25	9	12	83	61	59	2nd
1958–59	III	46	15	12	19	71	87	42	19th
1959–60	III	46	11	5	30	57	123	27	24th
1960–61	IV	46	16	8	22	74	88	40	18th

Accrington failed to fulfil their fixtures in the Lancashire Combination during 1895–96 after just five matches. But they did play one more game, in the Lancashire Senior Cup on 18 January, losing 12–0 to Darwen at Barley Bank.

George Stewart scored the first five goals for **Accrington Stanley** against Gateshead on 27 November 1954 in a 6–2 win in Division Three (North). On 16 November 1935, Billy Harker had achieved a similar feat in a 6–1 win over Gateshead.

ALDERSHOT

Year	Div	P	W	D	L	F	A	Pts	Pos
1932–33	IIIS	42	13	10	19	61	72	36	17th
1933–34	IIIS	42	13	12	17	52	71	38	14th
1934–35	IIIS	42	13	10	19	50	75	36	18th
1935–36	IIIS	42	14	12	16	53	61	40	11th
1936–37	IIIS	42	7	9	26	50	89	23	22nd
1937–38	IIIS	42	15	5	22	39	59	35	18th
1938–39	IIIS	42	16	12	14	53	66	44	10th
1939–46	Regional Leagues operating								
1946–47	IIIS	42	10	12	20	48	78	32	20th
1947–48	IIIS	42	10	15	17	45	67	35	19th
1948–49	IIIS	42	11	11	20	48	59	33	21st
1949–50	IIIS	42	13	8	21	48	60	34	20th
1950–51	IIIS	46	15	10	21	56	88	40	18th
1951–52	IIIS	46	18	8	20	78	89	44	12th
1952–53	IIIS	46	12	15	19	61	77	39	19th
1953–54	IIIS	46	17	9	20	74	86	43	17th
1954–55	IIIS	46	16	13	17	75	71	45	14th
1955–56	IIIS	46	12	16	18	70	90	40	15th
1956–57	IIIS	46	15	12	19	79	92	42	19th
1957–58	IIIS	46	12	16	18	59	89	40	19th
1958–59	IV	46	14	7	25	63	97	35	22nd
1959–60	IV	46	18	9	19	77	74	45	13th
1960–61	IV	46	18	9	19	79	69	45	10th

Year	Div	P	W	D	L	F	A	Pts	Pos
1961–62	IV	44	22	5	17	81	60	49	7th
1962–63	IV	46	15	17	14	73	69	47	11th
1963–64	IV	46	19	10	17	83	78	48	9th
1964–65	IV	46	15	7	24	64	84	37	18th
1965–66	IV	46	15	10	21	75	84	40	17th
1966–67	IV	46	18	12	16	72	57	48	10th
1967–68	IV	46	18	17	11	70	55	53	9th
1968–69	IV	46	19	7	20	66	66	45	15th
1969–70	IV	46	20	13	13	78	65	53	6th
1970–71	IV	46	14	17	15	66	71	45	13th
1971–72	IV	46	9	22	15	48	54	40	17th
1972–73	IV	46	22	12	12	60	38	56	4th
1973–74	III	46	19	11	16	65	52	49	8th
1974–75	III	46	14	11	21	53	63	38	20th
1975–76	III	46	13	13	20	59	75	39	21st
1976–77	IV	46	16	11	19	45	59	43	17th
1977–78	IV	46	19	16	11	67	47	54	5th
1978–79	IV	46	20	17	9	63	47	57	5th
1979–80	IV	46	16	13	17	62	53	45	10th
1980–81	IV	46	18	14	14	43	41	50	6th
1981–82	IV	46	13	15	18	57	68	54	16th
1982–83	IV	46	12	15	19	61	82	51	18th
1983–84	IV	46	22	9	15	76	69	75	5th
1984–85	IV	46	17	8	21	56	63	59	13th
1985–86	IV	46	17	7	22	66	74	58	16th
1986–87	IV	46	20	10	16	64	57	70	6th
1987–88	III	46	15	8	23	64	74	53	20th
1988–89	III	46	8	13	25	48	78	37	24th
1989–90	IV	46	12	14	20	49	69	50	22nd
1990–91	IV	46	10	11	25	61	101	41	23rd
1991–92	Expelled from League 25.3.92								

Aldershot began the 1991–92 season with a friendly against Leeds United at Elland Road, Leeds winning 3–1. At the end of the season Leeds were Football League champions, but Aldershot did not complete their fixtures, being forced to withdraw through financial problems. Re-formed as Aldershot Town, they won promotion from the Diadora League, Division Three exactly one year and two days after their demise.

ARSENAL

(Woolwich Arsenal until 1914)

Year	Div	P	W	D	L	F	A	Pts	Pos
1893–94	II	28	12	4	12	52	55	28	9th
1894–95	II	30	14	6	10	75	58	34	8th
1895–96	II	30	14	4	12	59	42	32	7th
1896–97	II	30	13	4	13	68	70	30	10th
1897–98	II	30	16	5	9	69	49	37	5th
1898–99	II	34	18	5	11	72	41	41	7th
1899–1900	II	34	16	4	14	61	43	36	8th
1900–01	II	34	15	6	13	39	35	36	7th
1901–02	II	34	18	6	10	50	26	42	4th
1902–03	II	34	20	8	6	66	30	48	3rd
1903–04	II	34	21	7	6	91	22	49	2nd
1904–05	I	34	12	9	13	36	40	33	10th
1905–06	I	38	15	7	16	62	64	37	12th
1906–07	I	38	20	4	14	66	59	44	7th
1907–08	I	38	12	12	14	51	63	36	14th
1908–09	I	38	14	10	14	52	49	38	6th
1909–10	I	38	11	9	18	37	67	31	18th
1910–11	I	38	13	12	13	41	49	38	10th
1911–12	I	38	15	8	15	55	59	38	10th
1912–13	I	38	3	12	23	26	74	18	20th
1913–14	II	38	20	9	9	54	38	49	3rd
1914–15	II	38	19	5	14	69	41	43	5th
1915–19	Regional Leagues operating								
1919–20	I	42	15	12	15	56	58	42	10th
1920–21	I	42	15	14	13	59	63	44	9th
1921–22	I	42	15	7	20	47	56	37	17th
1922–23	I	42	16	10	16	61	62	42	11th
1923–24	I	42	12	9	21	40	63	33	19th
1924–25	I	42	14	5	23	46	58	33	20th
1925–26	I	42	22	8	12	87	63	52	2nd
1926–27	I	42	17	9	16	77	86	43	11th
1927–28	I	42	13	15	14	82	86	41	10th
1928–29	I	42	16	13	13	77	72	45	9th
1929–30	I	42	14	11	17	78	66	39	14th
1930–31	I	42	28	10	4	127	59	66	1st
1931–32	I	42	22	10	10	90	48	54	2nd
1932–33	I	42	25	8	9	118	61	58	1st
1933–34	I	42	25	9	8	75	47	59	1st
1934–35	I	42	23	12	7	115	46	58	1st
1935–36	I	42	15	15	12	78	48	45	6th
1936–37	I	42	18	16	8	80	49	52	3rd
1937–38	I	42	21	10	11	77	44	52	1st
1938–39	I	42	19	9	14	55	41	47	5th
1939–46	Regional Leagues operating								
1946–47	I	42	16	9	17	72	70	41	13th
1947–48	I	42	23	13	6	81	32	59	1st
1948–49	I	42	18	13	11	74	44	49	5th
1949–50	I	42	19	11	12	79	55	49	6th
1950–51	I	42	19	9	14	73	56	47	5th
1951–52	I	42	21	11	10	80	61	53	3rd
1952–53	I	42	21	12	9	97	64	54	1st
1953–54	I	42	15	13	14	75	73	43	13th
1954–55	I	42	17	9	16	69	63	43	9th
1955–56	I	42	18	10	14	60	61	46	5th
1956–57	I	42	21	8	13	85	69	50	5th
1957–58	I	42	16	7	19	73	85	39	12th
1958–59	I	42	21	8	13	88	68	50	3rd
1959–60	I	42	15	9	18	68	80	39	13th
1960–61	I	42	15	11	16	77	85	41	11th
1961–62	I	42	16	11	15	71	72	43	10th
1962–63	I	42	18	10	14	86	77	46	7th
1963–64	I	42	17	11	14	90	82	45	8th
1964–65	I	42	17	7	18	69	75	41	13th
1965–66	I	42	12	13	17	62	75	37	14th
1966–67	I	42	16	14	12	58	47	46	7th
1967–68	I	42	17	10	15	60	56	44	9th
1968–69	I	42	22	12	8	56	27	56	4th

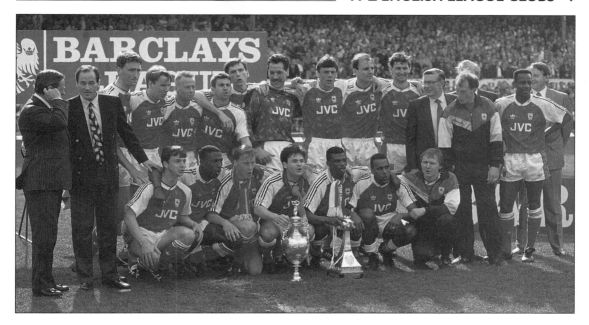

The Arsenal side which won the Championship in 1991 and lost only once in the League that season, celebrating their title win in front of a happy Highbury crowd (Bob Thomas)

		P	W	D	L	F	A	Pts	Pos
1969–70	I	42	12	18	12	51	49	42	12th
1970–71	I	42	29	7	6	71	29	65	1st
1971–72	I	42	22	8	12	58	40	52	5th
1972–73	I	42	23	11	8	57	43	57	2nd
1973–74	I	42	14	14	14	49	51	42	10th
1974–75	I	42	13	11	18	47	49	37	16th
1975–76	I	42	13	10	19	47	53	36	17th
1976–77	I	42	16	11	15	64	59	43	8th
1977–78	I	42	21	10	11	60	37	52	5th
1978–79	I	42	17	14	11	61	48	48	7th
1979–80	I	42	18	16	8	52	36	52	4th
1980–81	I	42	19	15	8	61	45	53	3rd
1981–82	I	42	20	11	11	48	37	71	5th
1982–83	I	42	16	10	16	58	56	58	10th
1983–84	I	42	18	9	15	74	60	63	6th
1984–85	I	42	19	9	14	61	49	66	7th
1985–86	I	42	20	9	13	49	47	69	7th
1986–87	I	42	20	10	12	58	35	70	4th
1987–88	I	40	18	12	10	58	39	66	6th
1988–89	I	38	22	10	6	73	36	76	1st
1989–90	I	38	18	8	12	54	38	62	4th
1990–91	I	38	24	13	1	74	18	83	1st
1991–92	I	42	19	15	8	81	46	72	4th
1992–93	PL	42	15	11	16	40	38	56	10th

Arsenal were forced to fulfil a Division Two fixture and an FA Cup tie on the same day, 12 December 1896. The reserves took on Leyton at home in the Cup, winning 5–0, but the first team lost 8–0 away to Loughborough Town. This represents the club's heaviest defeat.

ASHINGTON

Year	Div	P	W	D	L	F	A	Pts	Pos
1921–22	IIIN	38	17	4	17	59	66	38	10th
1922–23	IIIN	38	11	8	19	51	77	30	19th
1923–24	IIIN	42	18	8	16	59	61	44	8th
1924–25	IIIN	42	16	10	16	68	76	42	10th
1925–26	IIIN	42	16	11	15	70	62	43	9th
1926–27	IIIN	42	12	12	18	60	90	36	16th
1927–28	IIIN	42	11	11	20	77	103	33	18th
1928–29	IIIN	42	8	7	27	45	115	23	22nd

George Johnson set a club record 23 goals for **Ashington** in 1927–28. A local discovery, he subsequently played for Sheffield Wednesday before being converted from centre-forward to right-half with Reading and then Watford.

ASTON VILLA

Year	Div	P	W	D	L	F	A	Pts	Pos
1888–89	FL	22	12	5	5	61	43	29	2nd
1889–90	FL	22	7	5	10	43	51	19	8th
1890–91	FL	22	7	4	11	45	58	18	9th
1891–92	FL	26	15	0	11	89	56	30	4th
1892–93	I	30	16	3	11	73	62	35	4th
1893–94	I	30	19	6	5	84	42	44	1st
1894–95	I	30	17	5	8	82	43	39	3rd
1895–96	I	30	20	5	5	78	45	45	1st
1896–97	I	30	21	5	4	73	38	47	1st
1897–98	I	30	14	5	11	61	51	33	6th
1898–99	I	34	19	7	8	76	40	45	1st
1899–1900	I	34	22	6	6	77	35	50	1st

Aston Villa's Double-winning side of 1897. Villa were the second team to do the Double since the introduction of the Football League, but would be the last for over sixty years (Popperfoto)

1900–01	I	34	10	10	14	45	51	30	15th
1901–02	I	34	13	8	13	42	40	34	8th
1902–03	I	34	19	3	12	61	40	41	2nd
1903–04	I	34	17	7	10	70	48	41	5th
1904–05	I	34	19	4	11	63	43	42	4th
1905–06	I	38	17	6	15	72	56	40	8th
1906–07	I	38	19	6	13	78	52	44	5th
1907–08	I	38	17	9	12	77	59	43	2nd
1908–09	I	38	14	10	14	58	56	38	7th
1909–10	I	38	23	7	8	84	42	53	1st
1910–11	I	38	22	8	8	72	40	52	1st
1911–12	I	38	17	7	14	76	63	41	6th
1912–13	I	38	19	12	7	86	52	50	2nd
1913–14	I	38	19	6	13	65	50	44	2nd
1914–15	I	38	13	11	14	62	72	37	14th
1915–19	Regional Leagues operating								
1919–20	I	42	18	6	18	75	73	42	9th
1920–21	I	42	18	7	17	63	70	43	10th
1921–22	I	42	22	3	17	74	55	47	5th
1922–23	I	42	18	10	14	64	51	46	6th
1923–24	I	42	18	13	11	52	37	49	6th
1924–25	I	42	13	13	16	58	71	39	15th
1925–26	I	42	16	12	14	86	76	44	6th
1926–27	I	42	18	7	17	81	83	43	10th
1927–28	I	42	17	9	16	78	73	43	8th
1928–29	I	42	23	4	15	98	81	50	3rd
1929–30	I	42	21	5	16	92	83	47	4th
1930–31	I	42	25	9	8	128	78	59	2nd
1931–32	I	42	19	8	15	104	72	46	5th
1932–33	I	42	23	8	11	92	67	54	2nd
1933–34	I	42	14	12	16	78	75	40	13th
1934–35	I	42	14	13	15	74	88	41	13th
1935–36	I	42	13	9	20	81	110	35	21st
1936–37	II	42	16	12	14	82	70	44	9th
1937–38	II	42	25	7	10	73	35	57	1st
1938–39	I	42	15	11	16	71	60	41	12th
1939–46	Regional Leagues operating								
1946–47	I	42	18	9	15	67	53	45	8th
1947–48	I	42	19	9	14	65	57	47	6th

1948–49	I	42	16	10	16	60	76	42	10th
1949–50	I	42	15	12	15	61	61	42	12th
1950–51	I	42	12	13	17	66	68	37	15th
1951–52	I	42	19	9	14	79	70	47	6th
1952–53	I	42	14	13	15	63	61	41	11th
1953–54	I	42	16	9	17	70	68	41	13th
1954–55	I	42	20	7	15	72	73	47	6th
1955–56	I	42	11	13	18	52	69	35	20th
1956–57	I	42	14	15	13	65	55	43	10th
1957–58	I	42	16	7	19	73	86	39	14th
1958–59	I	42	11	8	23	58	87	30	21st
1959–60	II	42	25	9	8	89	43	59	1st
1960–61	I	42	17	9	16	78	77	43	9th
1961–62	I	42	18	8	16	65	56	44	7th
1962–63	I	42	15	8	19	62	68	38	15th
1963–64	I	42	11	12	19	62	71	34	19th
1964–65	I	42	16	5	21	57	82	37	16th
1965–66	I	42	15	6	21	69	80	36	16th
1966–67	I	42	11	7	24	54	85	29	21st
1967–68	II	42	15	7	20	54	64	37	16th
1968–69	II	42	12	14	16	37	48	38	18th
1969–70	II	42	8	13	21	36	62	29	21st
1970–71	III	46	19	15	12	54	46	53	4th
1971–72	III	46	32	6	8	85	32	70	1st
1972–73	II	42	18	14	10	51	47	50	3rd
1973–74	II	42	13	15	14	48	45	41	14th
1974–75	II	42	25	8	9	69	32	58	2nd
1975–76	I	42	11	17	14	51	59	39	16th
1976–77	I	42	22	7	13	76	50	51	4th
1977–78	I	42	18	10	14	57	42	46	8th
1978–79	I	42	15	16	11	59	49	46	8th
1979–80	I	42	16	14	12	51	50	46	7th
1980–81	I	42	26	8	8	72	40	60	1st
1981–82	I	42	15	12	15	55	53	57	11th
1982–83	I	42	21	5	16	62	50	68	6th
1983–84	I	42	17	9	16	59	61	60	10th
1984–85	I	42	15	11	16	60	60	56	10th
1985–86	I	42	10	14	18	51	67	44	16th
1986–87	I	42	8	12	22	45	79	36	22nd
1987–88	II	44	22	12	10	68	41	78	2nd
1988–89	I	38	9	13	16	45	56	40	17th
1989–90	I	38	21	7	10	57	38	70	2nd
1990–91	I	38	9	14	15	46	58	41	17th
1991–92	I	42	17	9	16	48	44	60	7th
1992–93	PL	42	21	11	10	57	40	74	2nd

Aston Villa scored 128 League goals in the 1930–31 season. They scored in every home game and in all but three away: at Newcastle, Portsmouth and Sheffield Wednesday. Four players contributed all but 20 of the goals: Pongo Waring 49, Eric Houghton 30, Billy Walker 15 and Joe Beresford 14. But Villa only finished second to champions Arsenal who scored one goal fewer.

Villa scored four or more goals on 20 occasions including losing one game 6–4 at home to Derby County and drawing 5–5 away to West Ham United. On only six occasions at home did they score less than four and yet managed seven fewer points than the champions.

BARNET

Year	Div	P	W	D	L	F	A	Pts	Pos
1991–92	IV	42	21	6	15	81	61	69	7th
1992–93	III	42	23	10	9	66	48	79	3rd

Barnet made television history when on Saturday 19 October 1946, their Athenian League home game with Tooting & Mitcham was the first football match to be transmitted live on BBC TV.

BARNSLEY

Year	Div	P	W	D	L	F	A	Pts	Pos
1898–99	II	34	12	7	15	52	56	31	11th
1899–1900	II	34	8	7	19	46	79	23	16th
1900–01	II	34	11	5	18	47	60	27	15th
1901–02	II	34	12	6	16	51	63	30	11th
1902–03	II	34	13	8	13	55	51	34	8th
1903–04	II	34	11	10	13	38	57	32	8th
1904–05	II	34	14	5	15	38	56	33	7th
1905–06	II	38	12	9	17	60	62	33	12th
1906–07	II	38	15	8	15	73	55	38	8th
1907–08	II	38	12	6	20	54	68	30	16th
1908–09	II	38	11	10	17	48	57	32	17th
1909–10	II	38	16	7	15	62	59	39	9th
1910–11	II	38	7	14	17	52	62	28	19th
1911–12	II	38	15	12	11	45	42	42	6th
1912–13	II	38	19	7	12	57	47	45	4th
1913–14	II	38	19	7	12	51	45	45	5th
1914–15	II	38	22	3	13	51	51	47	3rd
1915–19	Regional Leagues operating								
1919–20	II	42	15	10	17	61	55	40	12th
1920–21	II	42	10	16	16	48	50	36	16th
1921–22	II	42	22	8	12	67	52	52	3rd
1922–23	II	42	17	11	14	62	51	45	9th
1923–24	II	42	16	11	15	57	61	43	11th
1924–25	II	42	13	12	17	46	59	38	15th
1925–26	II	42	12	12	18	58	84	36	18th
1926–27	II	42	17	9	16	88	87	43	11th
1927–28	II	42	14	11	17	65	85	39	13th
1928–29	II	42	16	6	20	69	66	38	16th
1929–30	II	42	14	8	20	56	71	36	17th
1930–31	II	42	13	9	20	59	79	35	19th
1931–32	II	42	12	9	21	55	91	33	21st
1932–33	IIIN	42	19	8	15	92	80	46	8th
1933–34	IIIN	42	27	8	7	118	61	62	1st
1934–35	II	42	13	12	17	60	83	38	16th
1935–36	II	42	12	9	21	54	80	33	20th
1936–37	II	42	16	9	17	50	64	41	14th
1937–38	II	42	11	14	17	50	64	36	21st
1938–39	IIIN	42	30	7	5	94	34	67	1st
1939–46	Regional Leagues operating								
1946–47	II	42	17	8	17	84	86	42	10th
1947–48	II	42	15	10	17	62	64	40	12th
1948–49	II	42	14	12	16	62	61	40	9th
1949–50	II	42	13	13	16	64	67	39	13th
1950–51	II	42	15	10	17	74	68	40	15th
1951–52	II	42	11	14	17	59	72	36	20th
1952–53	II	42	5	8	29	47	108	18	22nd
1953–54	IIIN	46	24	10	12	77	57	58	2nd
1954–55	IIIN	46	30	5	11	86	46	65	1st
1955–56	II	42	11	12	19	47	84	34	18th
1956–57	II	42	12	10	20	59	89	34	19th
1957–58	II	42	14	12	16	70	74	40	14th
1958–59	II	42	10	7	25	55	91	27	22nd
1959–60	III	46	15	14	17	65	66	44	17th
1960–61	III	46	21	7	18	83	80	49	8th
1961–62	III	46	13	12	21	71	95	38	20th
1962–63	III	46	15	11	20	63	74	41	18th
1963–64	III	46	12	15	19	68	94	39	20th
1964–65	III	46	9	11	26	54	90	29	24th
1965–66	IV	46	15	10	21	74	78	40	16th
1966–67	IV	46	13	15	18	60	64	41	16th
1967–68	IV	46	24	13	9	68	46	61	2nd
1968–69	III	46	16	14	16	58	63	46	10th
1969–70	III	46	19	15	12	68	59	53	7th
1970–71	III	46	17	11	18	49	52	45	12th
1971–72	III	46	9	18	19	32	64	36	22nd
1972–73	IV	46	14	16	16	58	60	44	14th
1973–74	IV	46	17	10	19	58	64	44	13th
1974–75	IV	46	15	11	20	62	65	41	15th
1975–76	IV	46	14	16	16	52	48	44	12th
1976–77	IV	46	23	9	14	62	39	55	6th
1977–78	IV	46	18	14	14	61	49	50	7th
1978–79	IV	46	24	13	9	73	42	61	4th
1979–80	III	46	16	14	16	53	56	46	11th
1980–81	III	46	21	17	8	72	45	59	2nd
1981–82	II	42	19	10	13	59	41	67	6th
1982–83	II	42	14	15	13	57	55	57	10th
1983–84	II	42	15	7	20	57	53	52	14th
1984–85	II	42	14	16	12	42	42	58	11th
1985–86	II	42	14	14	14	47	50	56	12th
1986–87	II	42	14	13	15	49	52	55	11th
1987–88	II	44	15	12	17	61	62	57	14th
1988–89	II	46	20	14	12	66	58	74	7th
1989–90	II	46	13	15	18	49	71	54	19th
1990–91	II	46	19	12	15	63	48	69	8th
1991–92	II	46	16	11	19	46	57	59	16th
1992–93	I	46	17	9	20	56	60	60	13th

In the 1932–33 season, **Barnsley** signed an inside-forward from West Stanley named Jackie Smith. He was barely 5ft 3in tall and nicknamed 'Peter Pan' or 'Tiny'. Despite his lack of height he scored 12 goals in each of his two seasons with the club, many of them with his head.

BARROW

Year	Div	P	W	D	L	F	A	Pts	Pos
1921–22	IIIN	38	14	5	19	42	54	33	15th
1922–23	IIIN	38	13	4	21	50	60	30	18th
1923–24	IIIN	42	8	9	25	35	80	25	22nd

Year	Div	P	W	D	L	F	A	Pts	Pos
1924–25	IIIN	42	16	7	19	51	74	39	14th
1925–26	IIIN	42	7	4	31	50	98	18	22nd
1926–27	IIIN	42	7	8	27	34	117	22	22nd
1927–28	IIIN	42	10	11	21	54	102	31	19th
1928–29	IIIN	42	10	8	24	64	93	28	20th
1929–30	IIIN	42	11	5	26	41	98	27	22nd
1930–31	IIIN	42	15	7	20	68	89	37	16th
1931–32	IIIN	40	24	1	15	86	59	49	5th
1932–33	IIIN	42	18	7	17	60	60	43	9th
1933–34	IIIN	42	19	9	14	116	94	47	8th
1934–35	IIIN	42	13	9	20	58	87	35	17th
1935–36	IIIN	42	13	12	17	58	65	38	15th
1936–37	IIIN	42	13	10	19	70	86	36	16th
1937–38	IIIN	42	11	10	21	41	71	32	21st
1938–39	IIIN	42	16	9	17	66	65	41	13th
1939–46	Regional Leagues operating								
1946–47	IIIN	42	17	7	18	54	62	41	9th
1947–48	IIIN	42	16	13	13	49	40	45	7th
1948–49	IIIN	42	14	12	16	41	48	40	13th
1949–50	IIIN	42	14	9	19	47	53	37	15th
1950–51	IIIN	46	16	6	24	51	76	38	19th
1951–52	IIIN	46	17	12	17	57	61	46	12th
1952–53	IIIN	46	16	12	18	66	71	44	19th
1953–54	IIIN	46	16	12	18	72	71	44	12th
1954–55	IIIN	46	17	6	23	70	89	40	17th
1955–56	IIIN	46	12	9	25	61	83	33	22nd
1956–57	IIIN	46	21	9	16	76	62	51	10th
1957–58	IIIN	46	13	15	18	66	74	41	18th
1958–59	IV	46	9	10	27	51	104	28	23rd
1959–60	IV	46	15	11	20	77	87	41	18th
1960–61	IV	46	13	11	22	52	79	37	22nd
1961–62	IV	46	17	14	13	74	58	48	9th
1962–63	IV	46	19	12	15	82	80	50	9th
1963–64	IV	46	6	18	22	51	93	30	24th
1964–65	IV	46	12	6	28	59	105	30	21st
1965–66	IV	46	16	15	15	72	76	47	12th
1966–67	IV	46	24	11	11	76	54	59	3rd
1967–68	III	46	21	8	17	65	54	50	8th
1968–69	III	46	17	8	21	56	75	42	19th
1969–70	III	46	8	14	24	46	81	30	23rd
1970–71	IV	46	7	8	31	51	90	22	24th
1971–72	IV	46	13	11	22	40	71	37	22nd

In the 1931–32 FA Cup first round **Barrow** drew 3–3 at home with Doncaster Rovers. The replay at Doncaster finished at 1–1 as did the second replay at Maine Road. A third replay at Leeds saw Doncaster win 1–0. But in 1933–34 and 1934–35, Barrow gained revenge winning 4–2 at home in the first season and 2–0 at Doncaster in the second when the teams again met in the competition.

BIRMINGHAM CITY

(Small Heath until 1905 and added 'City' 1945)

Year	Div	P	W	D	L	F	A	Pts	Pos
1892–93	II	22	17	2	3	90	35	36	1st
1893–94	II	28	21	0	7	103	44	42	2nd
1894–95	I	30	9	7	14	50	74	25	12th
1895–96	I	30	8	4	18	39	79	20	15th
1896–97	II	30	16	5	9	69	47	37	4th
1897–98	II	30	16	4	10	58	50	36	6th
1898–99	II	34	17	7	10	85	50	41	8th
1899–1900	II	34	20	6	8	78	38	46	3rd
1900–01	II	34	19	10	5	57	24	48	2nd
1901–02	I	34	11	8	15	47	45	30	17th
1902–03	II	34	24	3	7	74	36	51	2nd
1903–04	I	34	11	8	15	39	52	30	11th
1904–05	I	34	17	5	12	54	38	39	7th
1905–06	I	38	17	7	14	65	59	41	7th
1906–07	I	38	15	8	15	52	52	38	9th
1907–08	I	38	9	12	17	40	60	30	20th
1908–09	II	38	14	9	15	58	61	37	11th
1909–10	II	38	8	7	23	42	78	23	20th
1910–11	II	38	12	8	18	42	64	32	16th
1911–12	II	38	14	6	18	55	59	34	12th
1912–13	II	38	18	10	10	59	44	46	3rd
1913–14	II	38	12	10	16	48	60	34	14th
1914–15	II	38	17	9	12	62	39	43	5th
1915–19	Regional Leagues operating								
1919–20	II	42	24	8	10	85	34	56	3rd
1920–21	II	42	24	10	8	79	38	58	1st
1921–22	I	42	15	7	20	48	60	37	18th
1922–23	I	42	13	11	18	41	57	37	17th
1923–24	I	42	13	13	16	41	49	39	14th
1924–25	I	42	17	12	13	49	53	46	8th
1925–26	I	42	16	8	18	66	81	40	14th
1926–27	I	42	17	4	21	64	73	38	17th
1927–28	I	42	13	15	14	70	75	41	11th
1928–29	I	42	15	10	17	68	77	40	15th
1929–30	I	42	16	9	17	67	62	41	11th
1930–31	I	42	13	10	19	55	70	36	19th
1931–32	I	42	18	8	16	78	67	44	9th
1932–33	I	42	14	11	17	57	57	39	13th
1933–34	I	42	12	12	18	54	56	36	20th
1934–35	I	42	13	10	19	63	81	36	19th
1935–36	I	42	15	11	16	61	63	41	12th
1936–37	I	42	13	15	14	64	60	41	12th
1937–38	I	42	10	18	14	58	62	38	18th
1938–39	I	42	12	8	22	62	84	32	21st
1939–46	Regional Leagues operating								
1946–47	II	42	25	5	12	74	33	55	3rd
1947–48	II	42	22	15	5	55	24	59	1st
1948–49	II	42	11	15	16	36	38	37	17th
1949–50	II	42	7	14	21	31	67	28	22nd
1950–51	I	42	20	9	13	64	53	49	4th
1951–52	II	42	21	9	12	67	56	51	3rd
1952–53	II	42	19	10	13	71	66	48	6th
1953–54	II	42	18	11	13	78	58	47	7th

Year	Div	P	W	D	L	F	A	Pts	Pos
1954–55	II	42	22	10	10	92	47	54	1st
1955–56	I	42	18	9	15	75	57	45	6th
1956–57	I	42	15	9	18	69	69	39	12th
1957–58	I	42	14	11	17	76	89	39	13th
1958–59	I	42	20	6	16	84	68	46	9th
1959–60	I	42	13	10	19	63	80	36	19th
1960–61	I	42	14	6	22	62	84	34	19th
1961–62	I	42	14	10	18	65	81	38	17th
1962–63	I	42	10	13	19	63	90	33	20th
1963–64	I	42	11	7	24	54	92	29	20th
1964–65	I	42	8	11	23	64	96	27	22nd
1965–66	II	42	16	9	17	70	75	41	10th
1966–67	II	42	16	8	18	70	66	40	10th
1967–68	II	42	19	14	9	83	51	52	4th
1968–69	II	42	18	8	16	73	59	44	7th
1969–70	II	42	11	11	20	51	78	33	18th
1970–71	II	42	17	12	13	58	48	46	9th
1971–72	II	42	19	18	5	60	31	56	2nd
1972–73	I	42	15	12	15	53	54	42	10th
1973–74	I	42	12	13	17	52	64	37	19th
1974–75	I	42	14	9	19	53	61	37	17th
1975–76	I	42	13	7	22	57	75	33	19th
1976–77	I	42	13	12	17	63	61	38	13th
1977–78	I	42	16	9	17	55	60	41	11th
1978–79	I	42	6	10	26	37	64	2	21st
1979–80	II	42	21	11	10	58	38	53	3rd
1980–81	I	42	13	12	17	50	61	38	13th
1981–82	I	42	10	14	18	53	61	44	16th
1982–83	I	42	12	14	16	40	55	50	17th
1983–84	I	42	12	12	18	39	50	48	20th
1984–85	II	42	25	7	10	59	33	82	2nd
1985–86	I	42	8	5	29	30	73	29	21st
1986–87	II	42	11	17	14	47	59	50	19th
1987–88	II	44	11	15	18	41	66	48	19th
1988–89	II	46	8	11	27	31	76	35	23rd
1989–90	III	46	18	12	16	60	59	66	7th
1990–91	III	46	16	17	13	45	49	65	12th
1991–92	III	46	23	12	11	69	52	81	2nd
1992–93	I	46	13	12	21	50	72	71	19th

When **Birmingham City** were still known as Small Heath they scored 103 goals in 28 Division Two matches in 1893–94 for an average of 3.67 goals per game, easily the best in League matches. It was not enough to win the championship, Liverpool finishing eight points in front of them.

BLACKBURN ROVERS

Year	Div	P	W	D	L	F	A	Pts	Pos
1888–89	FL	22	10	6	6	66	45	26	4th
1889–90	FL	22	12	3	7	78	41	27	3rd
1890–91	FL	22	11	2	9	52	43	24	6th
1891–92	FL	26	10	6	10	58	65	26	9th
1892–93	I	30	8	13	9	47	56	29	9th
1893–94	I	30	16	2	12	69	53	34	4th

Year	Div	P	W	D	L	F	A	Pts	Pos
1894–95	I	30	11	10	9	59	49	32	5th
1895–96	I	30	12	5	13	40	50	29	8th
1896–97	I	30	11	3	16	35	62	25	14th
1897–98	I	30	7	10	13	39	54	24	15th
1898–99	I	34	14	8	12	60	52	36	6th
1899–1900	I	34	13	4	17	49	61	30	14th
1900–01	I	34	12	9	13	39	47	33	9th
1901–02	I	34	15	6	13	52	48	36	4th
1902–03	I	34	12	5	17	44	63	29	16th
1903–04	I	34	11	6	17	48	60	28	15th
1904–05	I	34	11	5	18	40	51	27	13th
1905–06	I	38	16	8	14	54	52	40	9th
1906–07	I	38	14	7	17	56	59	35	12th
1907–08	I	38	12	12	14	51	63	36	14th
1908–09	I	38	14	13	11	61	50	41	4th
1909–10	I	38	18	9	11	73	55	45	3rd
1910–11	I	38	13	11	14	62	54	37	12th
1911–12	I	38	20	9	9	60	43	49	1st
1912–13	I	38	16	13	9	79	43	45	5th
1913–14	I	38	20	11	7	78	42	51	1st
1914–15	I	38	18	7	13	83	61	43	3rd
1915–19	Regional Leagues operating								
1919–20	I	42	13	11	18	64	77	37	20th
1920–21	I	42	13	15	14	57	59	41	11th
1921–22	I	42	13	12	17	54	57	38	15th
1922–23	I	42	14	12	16	47	62	40	14th
1923–24	I	42	17	11	14	54	50	45	8th
1924–25	I	42	11	13	18	53	66	35	16th
1925–26	I	42	15	11	16	91	80	41	12th
1926–27	I	42	15	8	19	77	96	38	18th
1927–28	I	42	16	9	17	66	78	41	12th
1928–29	I	42	17	11	14	72	63	45	7th
1929–30	I	42	19	7	16	99	93	45	6th
1930–31	I	42	17	8	17	83	84	42	10th
1931–32	I	42	16	6	20	89	95	38	16th
1932–33	I	42	14	10	18	76	102	38	15th
1933–34	I	42	18	7	17	74	81	43	8th
1934–35	I	42	14	11	17	66	78	39	15th
1935–36	I	42	12	9	21	55	96	33	22nd
1936–37	II	42	16	10	16	70	62	42	12th
1937–38	II	42	14	10	18	71	80	38	16th
1938–39	II	42	25	5	12	94	60	55	1st
1939–46	Regional Leagues operating								
1946–47	I	42	14	8	20	45	53	36	17th
1947–48	I	42	11	10	21	54	72	32	21st
1948–49	II	42	15	8	19	53	63	38	14th
1949–50	II	42	14	10	18	55	60	38	16th
1950–51	II	42	19	8	15	65	66	46	6th
1951–52	II	42	17	6	19	54	63	40	14th
1952–53	II	42	18	8	16	68	65	44	9th
1953–54	II	42	23	9	10	86	50	55	3rd
1954–55	II	42	22	6	14	114	79	50	6th
1955–56	II	42	21	6	15	84	65	48	4th
1956–57	II	42	21	10	11	83	75	52	4th
1957–58	II	42	22	12	8	93	57	56	2nd
1958–59	I	42	17	10	15	76	70	44	10th
1959–60	I	42	16	5	21	60	70	37	17th

1960–61	I	42	15	13	14	77	76	43	8th
1961–62	I	42	14	11	17	50	58	39	16th
1962–63	I	42	15	12	15	79	71	42	11th
1963–64	I	42	18	10	14	89	65	46	7th
1964–65	I	42	16	10	16	83	79	42	10th
1965–66	I	42	8	4	30	57	88	20	22nd
1966–67	II	42	19	13	10	56	46	51	4th
1967–68	II	42	16	11	15	56	49	43	8th
1968–69	II	42	13	11	18	52	63	37	19th
1969–70	II	42	20	7	15	54	50	47	8th
1970–71	II	42	6	15	21	37	69	27	21st
1971–72	III	46	19	9	18	54	57	47	10th
1972–73	III	46	20	15	11	57	47	55	3rd
1973–74	III	46	18	10	18	62	64	46	13th
1974–75	III	46	22	16	8	68	45	60	1st
1975–76	II	42	12	14	16	45	50	38	15th
1976–77	II	42	15	9	18	42	54	39	12th
1977–78	II	42	16	13	13	56	60	45	5th
1978–79	II	42	10	10	22	41	72	30	22nd
1979–80	III	46	25	9	12	58	36	59	2nd
1980–81	II	42	16	18	8	42	29	50	4th
1981–82	II	42	16	11	15	47	43	59	10th
1982–83	II	42	15	12	15	58	58	57	11th
1983–84	II	42	17	16	9	57	46	67	6th
1984–85	II	42	21	10	11	66	41	73	5th
1985–86	II	42	12	13	17	53	62	49	19th
1986–87	II	42	15	10	17	45	55	55	12th
1987–88	II	44	21	14	9	68	52	77	5th
1988–89	II	46	22	11	13	74	59	77	5th
1989–90	II	46	19	17	10	74	59	74	5th
1990–91	II	46	14	10	22	51	66	52	19th
1991–92	II	46	21	11	14	70	53	74	6th
1992–93	PL	42	20	11	11	68	46	71	4th

Because of a clash of blue and white colours in the 1890 FA Cup Final with Sheffield Wednesday, **Blackburn Rovers** played in white evening dress shirts which they bought after their arrival in London. Rovers won 6–1.

BLACKPOOL

Year	Div	P	W	D	L	F	A	Pts	Pos
1896–97	II	30	13	5	12	59	56	31	8th
1897–98	II	30	10	5	15	49	61	25	11th
1898–99	II	34	8	4	22	49	90	20	16th
1899–1900	Failed re-election								
1900–01	II	34	12	7	15	33	58	31	12th
1901–02	II	34	11	7	16	40	56	29	12th
1902–03	II	34	9	10	15	44	59	28	14th
1903–04	II	34	11	5	18	40	67	27	15th
1904–05	II	34	9	10	15	36	48	28	15th
1905–06	II	38	10	9	19	37	62	29	14th
1906–07	II	38	11	11	16	33	51	33	13th
1907–08	II	38	11	9	18	51	58	31	15th
1908–09	II	38	9	11	18	46	68	29	20th
1909–10	II	38	14	8	16	50	52	36	12th

1910–11	II	38	16	10	12	49	38	42	7th
1911–12	II	38	13	8	17	32	52	34	14th
1912–13	II	38	9	8	21	39	69	26	20th
1913–14	II	38	9	14	15	33	44	32	16th
1914–15	II	38	17	5	16	58	57	39	10th
1915–19	Regional Leagues operating								
1919–20	II	42	21	10	11	65	47	52	4th
1920–21	II	42	20	10	12	54	42	50	4th
1921–22	II	42	15	5	22	44	57	35	19th
1922–23	II	42	18	11	13	50	43	47	5th
1923–24	II	42	18	13	11	72	47	49	4th
1924–25	II	42	14	9	19	65	61	37	17th
1925–26	II	42	17	11	14	76	69	45	6th
1926–27	II	42	18	8	16	95	80	44	9th
1927–28	II	42	13	8	21	83	101	34	19th
1928–29	II	42	19	7	16	82	76	45	8th
1929–30	II	42	27	4	11	98	67	58	1st
1930–31	I	42	11	10	21	71	125	32	20th
1931–32	I	42	12	9	21	65	102	33	20th
1932–33	I	42	14	5	23	69	85	33	22nd
1933–34	II	42	15	13	14	62	64	43	11th
1934–35	II	42	21	11	10	79	57	53	4th
1935–36	II	42	18	7	17	93	82	43	10th
1936–37	II	42	24	7	11	88	53	55	2nd
1937–38	I	42	16	8	18	61	66	40	12th
1938–39	I	42	12	14	16	56	68	38	15th
1939–46	Regional Leagues operating								
1946–47	I	42	22	6	14	71	70	50	5th
1947–48	I	42	17	10	15	57	41	44	9th
1948–49	I	42	11	16	15	54	67	38	16th
1949–50	I	42	17	15	10	46	35	49	7th
1950–51	I	42	20	10	12	79	53	50	3rd
1951–52	I	42	18	9	15	64	64	45	9th
1952–53	I	42	19	9	14	71	70	47	7th
1953–54	I	42	19	10	13	80	69	48	6th
1954–55	I	42	14	10	18	60	64	38	19th
1955–56	I	42	20	9	13	86	62	49	2nd
1956–57	I	42	22	9	11	93	65	53	4th
1957–58	I	42	19	6	17	80	67	44	7th
1958–59	I	42	18	11	13	66	49	47	8th
1959–60	I	42	15	10	17	59	71	40	11th
1960–61	I	42	12	9	21	68	73	33	20th
1961–62	I	42	15	11	16	70	75	41	13th
1962–63	I	42	13	14	15	58	64	40	13th
1963–64	I	42	13	9	20	52	73	35	18th
1964–65	I	42	12	11	19	67	78	35	17th
1965–66	I	42	14	9	19	55	65	37	13th
1966–67	I	42	6	9	27	41	76	21	22nd
1967–68	II	42	24	10	8	71	43	58	3rd
1968–69	II	42	14	15	13	51	41	43	8th
1969–70	II	42	20	13	9	56	45	53	2nd
1970–71	I	42	4	15	23	34	66	23	22nd
1971–72	II	42	20	7	15	70	50	47	6th
1972–73	II	42	18	10	14	56	51	46	7th
1973–74	II	42	17	13	12	57	40	47	5th
1974–75	II	42	14	17	11	38	33	45	7th
1975–76	II	42	14	14	14	40	49	42	10th

1976–77	II	42	17	17	8	58	42	51	5th
1977–78	II	42	12	13	17	59	60	37	20th
1978–79	III	46	18	9	19	61	59	45	12th
1979–80	III	46	15	11	20	62	74	41	18th
1980–81	III	46	9	14	23	45	75	32	23rd
1981–82	IV	46	15	13	18	66	60	58	12th
1982–83	IV	46	13	12	21	55	74	49	21st
1983–84	IV	46	21	9	16	70	52	72	6th
1984–85	IV	46	24	14	8	73	39	86	2nd
1985–86	III	46	17	12	17	66	55	63	12th
1986–87	III	46	16	16	14	74	59	64	9th
1987–88	III	46	17	14	15	71	63	65	10th
1988–89	III	46	14	13	19	56	58	55	19th
1989–90	III	46	10	16	20	49	73	46	23rd
1990–91	IV	46	23	10	13	78	47	79	5th
1991–92	IV	42	22	10	10	71	45	76	4th
1992–93	II	46	12	15	19	63	75	51	18th

When George Farm signed for **Blackpool** from Hibernian in September 1948, he was only third choice at Easter Road. He cost £2,700 but went on to play 500 senior games including 47 consecutive FA Cup appearances in goal. He was sold to Queen of the South for £3,000 in 1960 after 465 League appearances out of 512 League and Cup games.

BOLTON WANDERERS

Year	Div	P	W	D	L	F	A	Pts	Pos
1888–89	FL	22	10	2	10	63	59	22	5th
1889–90	FL	22	9	1	12	54	55	19	9th
1890–91	FL	22	12	1	9	47	34	25	5th
1891–92	FL	26	17	2	7	51	37	36	3rd
1892–93	I	30	13	6	11	56	55	32	5th
1893–94	I	30	10	4	16	38	52	24	13th
1894–95	I	30	9	7	14	61	62	25	10th
1896–97	I	30	12	6	12	40	43	30	8th
1897–98	I	30	11	4	15	28	41	26	11th
1898–99	I	34	9	7	18	37	51	25	17th
1899–1900	II	34	22	8	4	79	25	52	2nd
1900–01	I	34	13	7	14	39	55	33	10th
1901–02	I	34	12	8	14	51	56	32	12th
1902–03	I	34	8	3	23	37	73	19	18th
1903–04	II	34	12	10	12	59	41	34	7th
1904–05	II	34	27	2	5	87	32	56	2nd
1905–06	I	38	17	7	14	81	67	41	6th
1906–07	I	38	18	8	12	59	47	44	6th
1907–08	I	38	14	5	19	52	58	33	19th
1908–09	II	38	24	4	10	59	28	52	1st
1909–10	I	38	9	6	23	44	71	24	20th
1910–11	II	38	21	9	8	69	40	51	2nd
1911–12	I	38	20	3	15	54	43	43	4th
1912–13	I	38	16	10	12	62	63	42	8th
1913–14	I	38	16	10	12	65	52	42	6th
1914–15	I	38	11	8	19	68	84	30	17th

1915–19	Regional Leagues operating								
1919–20	I	42	19	9	14	72	65	47	6th
1920–21	I	42	19	14	9	77	53	52	3rd
1921–22	I	42	20	7	15	68	59	47	6th
1922–23	I	42	14	12	16	50	58	40	13th
1923–24	I	42	18	14	10	68	34	50	4th
1924–25	I	42	22	11	9	76	34	55	3rd
1925–26	I	42	17	10	15	75	76	44	8th
1926–27	I	42	19	10	13	84	62	48	4th
1927–28	I	42	16	11	15	81	66	43	7th
1928–29	I	42	14	12	16	73	80	40	14th
1929–30	I	42	15	9	18	74	74	39	15th
1930–31	I	42	15	9	18	68	81	39	14th
1931–32	I	42	17	4	21	72	80	38	17th
1932–33	I	42	12	9	21	78	92	33	21st
1933–34	II	42	21	9	12	79	55	51	3rd
1934–35	II	42	26	4	12	96	48	56	2nd
1935–36	I	42	14	13	15	67	76	41	13th
1936–37	I	42	10	14	18	43	66	34	20th
1937–38	I	42	15	15	12	64	60	45	7th
1938–39	I	42	15	15	12	67	58	45	8th
1939–46	Regional Leagues operating								
1946–47	I	42	13	8	21	57	69	34	18th
1947–48	I	42	16	5	21	46	58	37	17th
1948–49	I	42	14	10	18	59	68	38	14th
1949–50	I	42	10	14	18	45	59	34	16th
1950–51	I	42	19	7	16	64	61	45	8th
1951–52	I	42	19	10	13	65	61	48	5th
1952–53	I	42	15	9	18	61	69	39	14th
1953–54	I	42	18	12	12	75	60	48	5th
1954–55	I	42	13	13	16	62	69	39	18th
1955–56	I	42	18	7	17	71	58	43	8th
1956–57	I	42	16	12	14	65	65	44	9th
1957–58	I	42	14	10	18	65	87	38	15th
1958–59	I	42	20	10	12	79	66	50	4th
1959–60	I	42	20	8	14	59	51	48	6th
1960–61	I	42	12	11	19	58	73	35	18th
1961–62	I	42	16	10	16	62	66	42	11th
1962–63	I	42	15	5	22	55	75	35	18th
1963–64	I	42	10	8	24	48	80	28	21st
1964–65	II	42	20	10	12	80	58	50	3rd
1965–66	II	42	16	9	17	62	59	41	9th
1966–67	II	42	14	14	14	64	58	42	9th
1967–68	II	42	13	13	16	60	63	39	12th
1968–69	II	42	12	14	16	55	67	38	17th
1969–70	II	42	12	12	18	54	61	36	16th
1970–71	II	42	7	10	25	35	74	24	22nd
1971–72	III	46	17	16	13	51	41	50	7th
1972–73	III	46	25	11	10	73	39	61	1st
1973–74	II	42	15	12	15	44	40	42	11th
1974–75	II	42	15	12	15	45	41	42	10th
1975–76	II	42	20	12	10	64	38	52	4th
1976–77	II	42	20	11	11	74	54	51	4th
1977–78	II	42	24	10	8	63	33	58	1st
1978–79	I	42	12	11	19	54	75	35	17th
1979–80	I	42	5	15	22	38	73	25	22nd
1980–81	II	42	14	10	18	61	66	38	18th

1981–82	II	42	13	7	22	39	61	46	19th
1982–83	II	42	11	11	20	42	61	44	22nd
1983–84	III	46	18	10	18	56	60	64	10th
1984–85	III	46	16	6	24	69	75	54	17th
1985–86	III	46	15	8	23	54	68	53	18th
1986–87	III	46	10	15	21	46	58	45	21st
1987–88	IV	46	22	12	12	66	42	78	3rd
1988–89	III	46	16	16	14	58	54	64	10th
1989–90	III	46	18	15	13	59	48	69	6th
1990–91	III	46	24	11	11	64	50	83	4th
1991–92	III	46	14	17	15	57	56	59	13th
1992–93	II	46	27	9	10	80	41	90	2nd

Harold Blackmore scored two goals for Exeter City in their 3–2 win over **Bolton Wanderers** during a benefit match in March 1927 for Exeter's Robert Pollard. Bolton immediately signed him for £2,150 and he made 165 League and Cup appearances and scored 122 goals before moving on to Middlesbrough, Bradford Park Avenue and Bury.

BOOTLE

Year	Div	P	W	D	L	F	A	Pts	Pos
1892–93	II	22	8	3	11	49	63	19	8th

Bootle lost their initial Division Two match 7–0 at Ardwick (later Manchester City) on 3 September 1892. The attendance was 4000.

AFC BOURNEMOUTH

Year	Div	P	W	D	L	F	A	Pts	Pos
1923–24	IIIS	42	11	11	20	40	65	33	21st
1924–25	IIIS	42	13	8	21	40	58	34	20th
1925–26	IIIS	42	17	9	16	75	91	43	8th
1926–27	IIIS	42	18	8	16	78	66	44	7th
1927–28	IIIS	42	13	12	17	72	79	38	14th
1928–29	IIIS	42	19	9	14	84	77	47	9th
1929–30	IIIS	42	15	13	14	72	61	43	10th
1930–31	IIIS	42	15	13	14	72	73	43	10th
1931–32	IIIS	42	13	12	17	70	78	38	15th
1932–33	IIIS	42	12	12	18	60	81	36	18th
1933–34	IIIS	42	9	9	24	60	102	27	21st
1934–35	IIIS	42	15	7	20	54	71	37	17th
1935–36	IIIS	42	16	11	15	60	56	43	8th
1936–37	IIIS	42	20	9	13	65	59	49	6th
1937–38	IIIS	42	14	12	16	56	57	40	13th
1938–39	IIIS	42	13	13	16	52	58	39	15th
1939–46	Regional Leagues operating								
1946–47	IIIS	42	18	8	16	72	54	44	7th
1947–48	IIIS	42	14	9	9	76	35	57	2nd
1948–49	IIIS	42	22	8	12	69	48	52	3rd
1949–50	IIIS	42	16	10	16	57	56	42	12th
1950–51	IIIS	46	22	7	17	65	57	51	9th

1951–52	IIIS	46	16	10	20	69	75	42	14th
1952–53	IIIS	46	19	9	18	74	69	47	9th
1953–54	IIIS	46	16	8	22	67	70	40	19th
1954–55	IIIS	46	12	18	16	57	65	42	17th
1955–56	IIIS	46	19	10	17	63	51	48	9th
1956–57	IIIS	46	19	14	13	88	62	52	5th
1957–58	IIIS	46	21	9	16	81	74	51	9th
1958–59	III	46	17	12	17	69	69	46	12th
1959–60	III	46	17	13	16	72	72	47	10th
1960–61	III	46	15	10	21	58	76	40	19th
1961–62	III	46	21	17	8	69	45	59	3rd
1962–63	III	46	18	16	12	63	46	52	5th
1963–64	III	46	24	8	14	79	58	56	4th
1964–65	III	46	18	11	17	72	63	47	11th
1965–66	III	46	13	12	21	38	56	38	18th
1966–67	III	46	12	17	17	39	57	41	20th
1967–68	III	46	16	15	15	56	51	47	13th
1968–69	III	46	21	9	16	60	45	51	4th
1969–70	III	46	12	15	19	48	71	39	21st
1970–71	III	46	24	12	10	81	46	60	2nd
1971–72	III	46	23	16	7	73	37	62	3rd
1972–73	III	46	17	16	13	66	44	50	7th
1973–74	III	46	16	15	15	54	58	47	11th
1974–75	III	46	13	12	21	44	58	38	21st
1975–76	IV	46	20	12	14	57	48	52	6th
1976–77	IV	46	15	18	13	54	44	48	13th
1977–78	IV	46	14	15	17	41	51	43	17th
1978–79	IV	46	14	11	21	47	48	39	18th
1979–80	IV	46	13	18	15	52	51	44	11th
1980–81	IV	46	16	13	17	47	48	45	13th
1981–82	IV	46	23	19	4	62	30	88	4th
1982–83	III	46	16	13	17	59	68	61	14th
1983–84	III	46	16	7	23	63	73	55	17th
1984–85	III	46	19	11	16	57	46	68	10th
1985–86	III	46	15	9	22	65	72	54	15th
1986–87	III	46	29	10	7	76	40	97	1st
1987–88	II	44	13	10	21	56	68	49	17th
1988–89	II	46	18	8	20	53	62	62	12th
1989–90	II	46	12	12	22	57	76	48	22nd
1990–91	III	46	19	13	14	58	58	70	9th
1991–92	III	46	20	11	15	52	48	71	8th
1992–93	II	46	12	17	17	45	52	53	17th

At Merthyr on 5 March 1927, **Bournemouth** were at 4–4 with 20 minutes remaining. But Bournemouth centre-forward Ronnie Eyre completed a hat-trick and helped his team to a 6–4 win, in Division Three (South).

BRADFORD CITY

Year	Div	P	W	D	L	F	A	Pos	Pts
1903–04	II	34	12	7	15	45	59	31	10th
1904–05	II	34	12	8	14	45	49	32	8th
1905–06	II	38	13	8	17	46	60	34	11th
1906–07	II	38	21	5	12	70	53	47	5th
1907–08	II	38	24	6	8	90	42	54	1st

Year	Div	P	W	D	L	F	A	Pts	Pos
1908–09	I	38	12	10	16	47	47	34	18th
1909–10	I	38	17	8	13	64	47	42	7th
1910–11	I	38	20	5	13	51	42	45	5th
1911–12	I	38	15	8	15	46	50	38	11th
1912–13	I	38	12	11	15	50	60	35	13th
1913–14	I	38	12	14	12	40	40	38	9th
1914–15	I	38	13	14	11	55	51	40	11th
1915–19	Regional Leagues operating								
1919–20	I	42	14	11	17	54	63	39	15th
1920–21	I	42	12	15	15	61	63	39	15th
1921–22	I	42	11	10	21	48	72	32	21st
1922–23	II	42	12	13	17	41	45	37	15th
1923–24	II	42	11	15	16	35	48	37	18th
1924–25	II	42	13	12	17	37	50	38	16th
1925–26	II	42	13	10	19	47	66	36	16th
1926–27	II	42	7	9	26	50	88	23	22nd
1927–28	IIIN	42	18	12	12	85	60	48	6th
1928–29	IIIN	42	27	9	6	128	43	63	1st
1929–30	II	42	12	12	18	60	77	36	18th
1930–31	II	42	17	10	15	61	63	44	10th
1931–32	II	42	16	13	13	80	61	45	7th
1932–33	II	42	14	13	15	65	61	41	11th
1933–34	II	42	20	6	16	73	67	46	6th
1934–35	II	42	12	8	22	50	68	32	20th
1935–36	II	42	15	13	14	55	65	43	12th
1936–37	II	42	9	12	21	54	94	30	21st
1937–38	IIIN	42	14	10	18	66	59	38	14th
1938–39	IIIN	42	22	8	12	89	56	52	3rd
1939–46	Regional Leagues operating								
1946–47	IIIN	42	20	10	12	62	47	50	5th
1947–48	IIIN	42	15	10	17	65	66	40	14th
1948–49	IIIN	42	10	9	23	48	77	29	22nd
1949–50	IIIN	42	12	8	22	61	76	32	19th
1950–51	IIIN	46	21	10	15	90	63	52	7th
1951–52	IIIN	46	16	10	20	61	68	42	15th
1952–53	IIIN	46	14	18	14	75	80	46	16th
1953–54	IIIN	46	22	9	15	60	55	53	5th
1954–55	IIIN	46	13	10	23	47	55	36	21st
1955–56	IIIN	46	18	13	15	78	64	49	8th
1956–57	IIIN	46	22	8	16	78	68	52	9th
1957–58	IIIN	46	21	15	10	73	49	57	3rd
1958–59	III	46	18	11	17	84	76	47	11th
1959–60	III	46	15	12	19	66	74	42	19th
1960–61	III	46	11	14	21	65	87	36	22nd
1961–62	IV	44	21	9	14	94	86	51	5th
1962–63	IV	46	11	10	25	64	93	32	23rd
1963–64	IV	46	25	6	15	76	62	56	5th
1964–65	IV	46	12	8	26	70	88	32	19th
1965–66	IV	46	12	13	21	63	94	37	23rd
1966–67	IV	46	19	10	17	74	62	48	11th
1967–68	IV	46	23	11	12	72	51	57	5th
1968–69	IV	46	18	20	8	65	46	56	4th
1969–70	III	46	17	12	17	57	50	46	10th
1970–71	III	46	13	14	19	49	62	40	19th
1971–72	III	46	11	10	25	45	77	32	24th
1972–73	IV	46	16	11	19	61	65	43	16th
1973–74	IV	46	17	14	15	58	52	48	8th
1974–75	IV	46	17	13	16	56	51	47	10th
1975–76	IV	46	12	17	17	63	65	41	17th
1976–77	IV	46	23	13	10	71	51	59	4th
1977–78	III	46	12	10	24	56	86	34	22nd
1978–79	IV	46	17	9	20	62	68	43	15th
1979–80	IV	46	24	12	10	77	50	60	5th
1980–81	IV	46	14	16	16	53	60	44	14th
1981–82	IV	46	26	13	7	88	45	91	2nd
1982–83	III	46	16	13	17	68	69	61	12th
1983–84	III	46	20	11	15	73	65	71	7th
1984–85	III	46	28	10	8	77	45	94	1st
1985–86	II	42	16	6	20	51	63	54	13th
1986–87	II	42	15	10	17	62	62	55	10th
1987–88	II	44	22	11	11	74	54	77	4th
1988–89	II	46	13	17	16	52	59	56	14th
1989–90	II	46	9	14	23	44	68	41	23rd
1990–91	III	46	20	10	16	62	54	70	8th
1991–92	III	46	13	19	14	62	61	58	16th
1992–93	II	46	18	14	14	69	67	68	10th

In 1988–89 **Bradford City** defeated First Division opponents in two consecutive Cup ties at Valley Parade. Everton were beaten 3–1 in the League Cup 4th round and Tottenham Hotspur 1–0 in the 3rd round of the FA Cup.

BRADFORD PARK AVENUE

Year	Div	P	W	D	L	F	A	Pts	Pos
1908–09	II	38	13	6	19	51	59	32	16th
1909–10	II	38	17	4	17	64	59	38	10th
1910–11	II	38	14	9	15	53	55	37	12th
1911–12	II	38	13	9	16	44	45	35	11th
1912–13	II	38	14	8	16	60	60	36	13th
1913–14	II	38	23	3	12	71	47	49	2nd
1914–15	I	38	17	7	14	69	65	41	9th
1915–19	Regional Leagues operating								
1919–20	I	42	15	12	15	60	63	42	11th
1920–21	I	42	8	8	26	43	76	24	22nd
1921–22	II	42	12	9	21	46	62	33	21st
1922–23	IIIN	38	19	9	10	67	38	47	2nd
1923–24	IIIN	42	21	10	11	69	43	52	5th
1924–25	IIIN	42	19	12	11	84	42	50	5th
1925–26	IIIN	42	26	8	8	101	43	60	2nd
1926–27	IIIN	42	24	7	11	101	59	55	3rd
1927–28	IIIN	42	27	9	6	101	45	63	1st
1928–29	II	42	22	4	16	88	70	48	3rd
1929–30	II	42	19	11	12	91	70	50	4th
1930–31	II	42	18	10	14	97	66	46	6th
1931–32	II	42	21	7	14	72	63	49	6th
1932–33	II	42	17	8	17	77	71	42	8th
1933–34	II	42	23	3	16	86	67	49	5th
1934–35	II	42	11	16	15	55	63	38	15th
1935–36	II	42	14	9	19	62	84	37	16th
1936–37	II	42	12	9	21	52	88	33	20th
1937–38	II	42	17	9	16	69	56	43	7th
1938–39	II	42	12	11	19	61	82	35	17th

Year	Div	P	W	D	L	F	A	Pts	Pos
1939–46	Regional Leagues operating								
1946–47	II	42	14	11	17	65	77	39	16th
1947–48	II	42	16	8	18	68	72	40	14th
1948–49	II	42	13	11	18	65	78	37	17th
1949–50	II	42	10	11	21	51	77	31	22nd
1950–51	IIIN	46	23	8	15	90	72	54	6th
1951–52	IIIN	46	19	12	15	74	64	50	8th
1952–53	IIIN	46	19	12	15	75	61	50	7th
1953–54	IIIN	46	18	14	14	77	68	50	9th
1954–55	IIIN	46	15	11	20	56	70	41	16th
1955–56	IIIN	46	13	7	26	61	122	33	23rd
1956–57	IIIN	46	16	3	27	66	93	35	20th
1957–58	IIIN	46	13	11	22	68	95	37	22nd
1958–59	IV	46	18	7	21	75	77	43	14th
1959–60	IV	46	17	15	14	70	68	49	11th
1960–61	IV	46	26	8	12	84	74	60	4th
1961–62	III	46	20	7	19	80	78	47	11th
1962–63	III	46	14	12	20	79	97	40	21st
1963–64	IV	46	18	9	19	75	81	45	13th
1964–65	IV	46	20	17	9	86	62	57	7th
1965–66	IV	46	21	5	20	102	92	47	11th
1966–67	IV	46	11	13	22	52	79	35	23rd
1967–68	IV	46	4	15	27	30	82	23	24th
1968–69	IV	46	5	10	31	32	106	20	24th
1969–70	IV	46	6	11	29	41	96	23	24th

Bradford Park Avenue provided the leading scorer in the Football League in 1965–66 when Kevin Hector scored 44 goals. During his service with the club he scored 113 in 176 League matches.

BRENTFORD

Year	Div	P	W	D	L	F	A	Pts	Pos
1920–21	III	42	9	12	21	42	67	30	21st
1921–22	IIIS	42	16	11	15	52	43	43	9th
1922–23	IIIS	42	13	12	17	41	51	38	14th
1923–24	IIIS	42	14	8	20	54	71	36	17th
1924–25	IIIS	42	9	7	26	38	91	25	21st
1925–26	IIIS	42	16	6	20	69	94	38	18th
1926–27	IIIS	42	13	14	15	70	61	40	11th
1927–28	IIIS	42	16	8	18	76	74	40	12th
1928–29	IIIS	42	14	10	18	56	60	38	13th
1929–30	IIIS	42	28	5	9	94	44	61	2nd
1930–31	IIIS	42	22	6	14	90	64	50	3rd
1931–32	IIIS	42	19	10	13	68	52	48	5th
1932–33	IIIS	42	26	10	6	90	49	62	1st
1933–34	II	42	22	7	13	85	60	51	4th
1934–35	II	42	26	9	7	93	48	61	1st
1935–36	I	42	17	12	13	81	60	46	5th
1936–37	I	42	18	10	14	82	78	46	6th
1937–38	I	42	18	9	14	69	59	45	6th
1938–39	I	42	14	8	20	53	74	36	18th
1939–46	Regional Leagues operating								
1946–47	I	42	9	7	26	45	88	25	21st
1947–48	II	42	13	14	15	44	61	40	15th
1948–49	II	42	11	14	17	42	53	36	18th
1949–50	II	42	15	13	14	44	49	43	9th
1950–51	II	42	18	8	16	75	74	44	9th
1951–52	II	42	15	12	15	54	55	42	10th
1952–53	II	42	13	11	18	59	76	37	17th
1953–54	II	42	10	11	21	40	78	31	21st
1954–55	IIIS	46	16	14	16	82	82	46	11th
1955–56	IIIS	46	19	14	13	69	66	52	6th
1956–57	IIIS	46	16	16	14	78	76	48	8th
1957–58	IIIS	46	24	10	12	82	56	58	2nd
1958–59	III	46	21	15	10	76	49	57	3rd
1959–60	III	46	21	9	16	78	61	51	6th
1960–61	III	46	13	17	16	56	70	43	17th
1961–62	III	46	13	8	25	53	93	34	22nd
1962–63	IV	46	27	8	11	98	64	62	1st
1963–64	III	46	15	14	17	87	80	44	16th
1964–65	III	46	24	9	13	83	55	57	5th
1965–66	III	46	10	12	24	48	69	32	23rd
1966–67	IV	46	18	13	15	58	56	49	9th
1967–68	IV	46	18	7	21	61	64	43	14th
1968–69	IV	46	18	12	16	64	65	48	11th
1969–70	IV	46	20	16	10	58	39	56	5th
1970–71	IV	46	18	8	20	66	62	44	14th
1971–72	IV	46	24	11	11	76	44	59	3rd
1972–73	III	46	15	7	24	51	69	37	22nd
1973–74	IV	46	12	16	18	48	50	40	19th
1974–75	IV	46	18	13	15	53	45	49	8th
1975–76	IV	46	14	13	19	56	60	41	18th
1976–77	IV	46	18	7	21	77	76	43	15th
1977–78	IV	46	21	14	11	86	54	56	4th
1978–79	III	46	19	9	18	53	49	47	10th
1979–80	III	46	15	11	20	59	73	41	19th
1980–81	III	46	14	19	13	52	49	47	9th
1981–82	III	46	19	11	16	56	47	68	8th
1982–83	III	46	18	10	18	88	77	64	9th
1983–84	III	46	11	16	19	69	79	49	20th
1984–85	III	46	16	14	16	62	64	62	13th
1985–86	III	46	18	12	16	58	61	66	10th
1986–87	III	46	15	15	16	64	66	60	11th
1987–88	III	46	16	14	16	53	59	62	12th
1988–89	III	46	18	14	14	66	61	68	7th
1989–90	III	46	18	7	21	66	66	61	13th
1990–91	III	46	21	13	12	59	47	76	6th
1991–92	III	46	25	7	14	81	55	82	1st
1992–93	I	46	13	10	23	52	71	49	22nd

When **Brentford** won promotion to Division One in 1934–35, the first club to congratulate them was Arsenal, who sent the following telegram: The League Champions congratulate the Division Two Champions. Stop. Come up and see us sometime next season. Stop. A warm welcome awaits you – Arsenal.

BRIGHTON & HOVE ALBION

Year	Div	P	W	D	L	F	A	Pts	Pos
1920–21	III	42	14	8	20	42	61	36	18th
1921–22	IIIS	42	13	9	20	45	51	35	19th
1922–23	IIIS	42	20	11	11	52	34	51	4th
1923–24	IIIS	42	21	9	12	68	37	51	5th
1924–25	IIIS	42	19	8	15	59	45	46	8th
1925–26	IIIS	42	19	9	14	84	73	47	5th
1926–27	IIIS	42	21	11	10	79	50	53	4th
1927–28	IIIS	42	19	10	13	81	69	48	4th
1928–29	IIIS	42	16	6	20	58	76	38	15th
1929–30	IIIS	42	21	8	13	87	63	50	5th
1930–31	IIIS	42	17	15	10	68	53	49	4th
1931–32	IIIS	42	17	12	13	73	58	46	8th
1932–33	IIIS	42	17	8	17	66	65	42	12th
1933–34	IIIS	42	15	13	14	68	60	43	10th
1934–35	IIIS	42	17	9	16	69	62	43	9th
1935–36	IIIS	42	18	8	16	70	63	44	7th
1936–37	IIIS	42	24	5	13	74	43	53	3rd
1937–38	IIIS	42	21	9	12	64	44	51	5th
1938–39	IIIS	42	19	11	12	68	49	49	3rd
1939–46	Regional Leagues operating								
1946–47	IIIS	42	13	12	17	54	72	38	17th
1947–48	IIIS	42	11	12	19	43	73	34	22nd
1948–49	IIIS	42	15	18	9	55	55	48	6th
1949–50	IIIS	42	16	12	14	57	69	44	8th
1950–51	IIIS	46	13	17	16	71	79	43	13th
1951–52	IIIS	46	24	10	12	87	63	58	5th
1952–53	IIIS	46	19	12	15	81	75	50	7th
1953–54	IIIS	46	26	9	11	86	61	61	2nd
1954–55	IIIS	46	20	10	16	76	63	50	6th
1955–56	IIIS	46	29	7	10	112	50	65	2nd
1956–57	IIIS	46	19	14	13	86	65	52	6th
1957–58	IIIS	46	24	12	10	88	64	60	1st
1958–59	II	42	15	11	16	74	90	41	12th
1959–60	II	42	13	12	17	67	76	38	14th
1960–61	II	42	14	9	19	61	75	37	16th
1961–62	II	42	10	11	21	42	86	31	22nd
1962–63	III	46	12	12	22	58	84	36	22nd
1963–64	IV	46	19	12	15	71	52	50	8th
1964–65	IV	46	26	11	9	102	57	63	1st
1965–66	III	46	16	11	19	67	65	43	15th
1966–67	III	46	13	15	18	61	71	41	19th
1967–68	III	46	16	16	14	57	55	48	10th
1968–69	III	46	16	13	17	72	65	45	12th
1969–70	III	46	23	9	14	57	43	55	5th
1970–71	III	46	14	16	16	50	47	44	14th
1971–72	III	46	27	11	8	82	47	65	2nd
1972–73	II	42	8	13	21	46	83	29	22nd
1973–74	III	46	16	11	19	52	58	43	19th
1974–75	III	46	16	10	20	56	64	42	19th
1975–76	III	46	22	9	15	78	53	53	4th
1976–77	III	46	25	11	10	83	39	61	2nd
1977–78	II	42	22	12	8	63	38	56	4th
1978–79	II	42	23	10	9	72	39	56	2nd
1979–80	I	42	11	15	16	47	57	37	16th

Year	Div	P	W	D	L	F	A	Pts	Pos
1980–81	I	42	14	7	21	54	67	35	19th
1981–82	I	42	13	13	16	43	52	52	13th
1982–83	I	42	9	13	20	38	67	40	22nd
1983–84	II	42	17	9	16	69	60	60	9th
1984–85	II	42	20	12	10	58	34	72	6th
1985–86	II	42	16	8	18	64	64	56	11th
1986–87	II	42	9	12	21	37	54	39	22nd
1987–88	III	46	23	15	8	69	47	84	2nd
1988–89	II	46	14	9	23	57	66	51	19th
1989–90	II	46	15	9	22	56	72	54	18th
1990–91	II	46	21	7	18	63	69	70	6th
1991–92	II	46	12	11	23	56	77	47	23rd
1992–93	I	46	20	9	17	63	59	69	9th

In 1921–22 Irish international Jack Doran scored hat-tricks in successive Wednesdays for **Brighton & Hove Albion** against Exeter City. Away they won 3–0 and at home it was 3–1 for the club's first such trebles in the League.

BRISTOL CITY

Year	Div	P	W	D	L	F	A	Pts	Pos
1901–02	II	34	17	6	11	52	35	40	6th
1902–03	II	34	17	8	9	59	38	42	4th
1903–04	II	34	18	6	10	73	41	42	4th
1904–05	II	34	19	4	11	66	45	42	4th
1905–06	II	38	30	6	2	83	28	66	1st
1906–07	I	38	20	8	10	66	47	48	2nd
1907–08	I	38	12	12	14	58	61	36	10th
1908–09	I	38	13	12	13	45	58	38	8th
1909–10	I	38	12	8	18	45	60	32	16th
1910–11	I	38	11	5	22	43	66	27	19th
1911–12	II	38	14	6	18	41	60	34	13th
1912–13	II	38	9	15	14	46	72	33	16th
1913–14	II	38	16	9	13	52	50	41	8th
1914–15	II	38	15	7	16	62	56	37	13th
1915–19	Regional Leagues operating								
1919–20	II	42	13	17	12	46	43	43	8th
1920–21	II	42	19	13	10	49	29	51	3rd
1921–22	II	42	12	9	21	37	58	33	22nd
1922–23	IIIS	42	24	11	7	66	40	59	1st
1923–24	II	42	7	15	20	32	65	29	22nd
1924–25	IIIS	42	22	9	11	60	41	53	3rd
1925–26	IIIS	42	21	9	12	72	51	51	4th
1926–27	IIIS	42	27	8	7	104	54	62	1st
1927–28	II	42	15	9	18	76	79	39	12th
1928–29	II	42	13	10	19	58	72	36	20th
1929–30	II	42	13	9	20	61	83	35	20th
1930–31	II	42	15	8	19	54	82	38	16th
1931–32	II	42	6	11	25	39	78	23	22nd
1932–33	IIIS	42	12	13	17	83	90	37	15th
1933–34	IIIS	42	10	13	19	58	85	33	19th
1934–35	IIIS	42	15	9	18	52	68	39	15th
1935–36	IIIS	42	15	10	17	48	59	40	13th
1936–37	IIIS	42	15	6	21	58	70	36	16th

Year	Div	P	W	D	L	F	A	Pts	Pos
1937–38	IIIS	42	21	13	8	68	40	55	2nd
1938–39	IIIS	42	16	12	14	61	63	44	8th
1939–46	Regional Leagues operating								
1946–47	IIIS	42	20	11	11	94	56	51	3rd
1947–48	IIIS	42	18	7	17	77	65	43	7th
1948–49	IIIS	42	11	14	17	44	62	36	16th
1949–50	IIIS	42	15	10	17	60	61	40	15th
1950–51	IIIS	46	20	11	15	64	59	51	10th
1951–52	IIIS	46	15	12	19	58	69	42	15th
1952–53	IIIS	46	22	15	9	95	61	59	5th
1953–54	IIIS	46	25	6	15	88	68	56	3rd
1954–55	IIIS	46	30	10	6	101	47	70	1st
1955–56	II	42	19	7	16	80	64	45	11th
1956–57	II	42	16	9	17	74	79	41	13th
1957–58	II	42	13	9	20	63	88	35	17th
1958–59	II	42	17	7	18	74	70	41	10th
1959–60	II	42	11	5	26	60	97	27	22nd
1960–61	III	46	17	10	19	70	68	44	14th
1961–62	III	46	23	8	15	94	72	54	6th
1962–63	III	46	16	13	17	100	92	45	14th
1963–64	III	46	20	15	11	84	64	55	5th
1964–65	III	46	24	11	11	92	55	59	2nd
1965–66	II	42	17	17	8	63	48	51	5th
1966–67	II	42	12	14	16	56	62	38	15th
1967–68	II	42	13	10	19	48	62	36	19th
1968–69	II	42	11	16	15	46	53	38	16th
1969–70	II	42	13	13	16	54	50	39	14th
1970–71	II	42	10	11	21	46	64	31	19th
1971–72	II	42	18	10	14	61	49	46	8th
1972–73	II	42	17	12	13	63	51	46	5th
1973–74	II	42	14	10	18	47	54	38	16th
1974–75	II	42	21	8	13	47	33	50	5th
1975–76	II	42	19	15	8	59	35	53	2nd
1976–77	I	42	11	13	18	38	48	35	18th
1977–78	I	42	11	13	18	49	53	35	17th
1978–79	I	42	15	10	17	47	51	40	13th
1979–80	I	42	9	13	20	37	66	31	20th
1980–81	II	42	7	16	19	29	51	30	21st
1981–82	III	46	11	13	22	40	65	46	23rd
1982–83	IV	46	13	17	16	59	70	56	14th
1983–84	IV	46	24	10	12	70	44	82	4th
1984–85	III	46	24	9	13	74	47	81	5th
1985–86	III	46	18	14	14	69	60	68	9th
1986–87	III	46	21	14	11	63	36	77	6th
1987–88	III	46	18	12	16	68	56	66	8th
1988–89	III	46	19	17	10	67	51	74	5th
1989–90	III	46	26	15	5	71	35	93	1st
1990–91	II	46	20	7	19	68	71	67	9th
1991–92	II	46	13	15	18	55	71	54	17th
1992–93	I	46	14	14	18	49	67	56	15th

Bristol City were relegated in three successive seasons. On 1 September 1979 they were as high as sixth in Division One. By 4 December 1982 they were 92nd in the League as bottom club in Division Four.

BRISTOL ROVERS

Year	Div	P	W	D	L	F	A	Pts	Pos
1920–21	III	42	18	7	17	68	57	43	10th
1921–22	IIIS	42	14	10	18	52	67	38	14th
1922–23	IIIS	42	13	16	13	35	36	42	13th
1923–24	IIIS	42	15	13	14	52	46	43	9th
1924–25	IIIS	42	12	13	17	42	49	37	17th
1925–26	IIIS	42	15	6	21	66	69	36	19th
1926–27	IIIS	42	16	9	17	78	80	41	10th
1927–28	IIIS	42	14	4	24	67	93	32	19th
1928–29	IIIS	42	13	7	22	60	79	33	19th
1929–30	IIIS	42	11	8	23	67	93	30	20th
1930–31	IIIS	42	16	8	18	75	92	40	15th
1931–32	IIIS	42	13	8	21	65	92	34	18th
1932–33	IIIS	42	15	14	13	61	56	44	9th
1933–34	IIIS	42	20	11	11	77	47	51	7th
1934–35	IIIS	42	17	10	15	73	77	44	8th
1935–36	IIIS	42	14	9	19	69	95	37	17th
1936–37	IIIS	42	16	4	22	71	80	36	15th
1937–38	IIIS	42	13	13	16	46	61	39	15th
1938–39	IIIS	42	10	13	19	55	61	33	22nd
1939–46	Regional Leagues operating								
1946–47	IIIS	42	16	8	18	59	69	40	14th
1947–48	IIIS	42	13	8	21	71	75	34	20th
1948–49	IIIS	42	19	10	13	61	51	48	5th
1949–50	IIIS	42	19	5	18	51	51	43	9th
1950–51	IIIS	46	20	15	11	64	42	55	6th
1951–52	IIIS	46	20	12	14	89	53	52	7th
1952–53	IIIS	46	26	12	8	92	46	64	1st
1953–54	II	42	14	16	12	64	58	44	9th
1954–55	II	42	19	7	16	75	70	45	9th
1955–56	II	42	21	6	15	84	70	48	6th
1956–57	II	42	18	9	15	81	67	45	9th
1957–58	II	42	17	8	17	85	80	42	10th
1958–59	II	42	18	12	12	80	64	48	6th
1959–60	II	42	18	11	13	72	78	47	9th
1960–61	II	42	15	7	20	73	92	37	17th
1961–62	II	42	13	7	22	53	81	33	21st
1962–63	III	46	15	11	20	70	88	41	19th
1963–64	III	46	19	8	19	91	79	46	12th
1964–65	III	46	20	15	11	82	58	55	6th
1965–66	III	46	14	14	18	64	64	42	16th
1966–67	III	46	20	13	13	76	67	53	4th
1967–68	III	46	17	9	20	72	78	43	17th
1968–69	III	46	16	11	19	63	71	43	16th
1969–70	III	46	20	16	10	80	59	56	3rd
1970–71	III	46	19	13	14	65	50	51	6th
1971–72	III	46	21	12	13	75	56	54	6th
1972–73	III	46	20	13	13	77	56	53	5th
1973–74	III	46	22	17	7	65	33	61	2nd
1974–75	II	42	12	11	19	42	64	35	19th
1975–76	III	42	11	16	15	38	50	38	18th
1976–77	III	42	12	13	17	53	68	37	15th
1977–78	III	42	13	12	17	61	77	38	18th
1978–79	III	42	14	10	18	48	60	38	16th
1979–80	III	42	11	13	18	50	64	35	19th
1980–81	III	42	5	13	24	34	65	23	22nd

Year	Div	P	W	D	L	F	A	Pts	Pos
1981–82	III	46	18	9	19	58	65	61	15th
1982–83	III	46	22	9	15	84	58	75	7th
1983–84	III	46	22	13	11	68	54	79	5th
1984–85	III	46	21	12	13	66	48	75	6th
1985–86	III	46	14	12	20	51	75	54	16th
1986–87	III	46	13	12	21	49	75	51	19th
1987–88	III	46	18	12	16	68	56	66	8th
1988–89	III	46	19	17	10	67	51	74	5th
1989–90	III	46	26	15	5	71	35	93	1st
1990–91	II	46	15	13	18	56	59	58	13th
1991–92	II	46	16	14	16	60	63	62	13th
1992–93	I	46	10	11	25	55	87	41	24th

On 15 October 1977 **Bristol Rovers** beat Blackburn Rovers 4–1, Bobby Gould scoring three goals on his debut. On 7 October 1978 the same fixture produced another 4–1 win for Bristol Rovers with Paul Randall scoring a hat-trick.

BURNLEY

Year	Div	P	W	D	L	F	A	Pts	Pos
1888–89	FL	22	7	3	12	42	62	17	9th
1889–90	FL	22	4	5	13	36	65	13	11th
1890–91	FL	22	9	3	10	52	63	21	8th
1891–92	FL	26	11	4	11	49	45	26	7th
1892–93	I	30	13	4	13	51	44	30	6th
1893–94	I	30	15	4	11	61	51	34	5th
1894–95	I	30	11	4	15	44	56	26	9th
1895–96	I	30	10	7	13	48	44	27	10th
1896–97	I	30	6	7	17	43	61	19	16th
1897–98	II	30	20	8	2	80	24	48	1st
1898–99	I	34	15	9	10	45	47	39	3rd
1899–1900	I	34	11	5	18	34	54	27	17th
1900–01	II	34	20	4	10	53	29	44	3rd
1901–02	II	34	10	10	14	41	45	30	9th
1902–03	II	34	6	8	20	30	77	20	18th
1903–04	II	34	15	9	10	50	55	39	5th
1904–05	II	34	12	6	16	43	52	30	11th
1905–06	II	38	15	8	15	42	53	38	9th
1906–07	II	38	17	6	15	62	47	40	7th
1907–08	II	38	20	6	12	67	50	46	7th
1908–09	II	38	13	7	18	51	58	33	14th
1909–10	II	38	14	6	18	62	61	34	14th
1910–11	II	38	13	15	10	45	45	41	8th
1911–12	II	38	22	8	8	77	41	52	3rd
1912–13	II	38	21	8	9	88	53	50	2nd
1913–14	I	38	12	12	14	61	53	36	12th
1914–15	I	38	18	7	13	61	47	43	4th
1915–19	Regional Leagues operating								
1919–20	I	42	21	9	12	65	59	51	2nd
1920–21	I	42	23	13	6	79	36	59	1st
1921–22	I	42	22	5	15	72	54	49	3rd
1922–23	I	42	16	6	20	58	59	38	15th
1923–24	I	42	12	12	18	55	60	36	17th
1924–25	I	42	11	12	19	46	75	34	19th
1925–26	I	42	13	10	19	85	108	36	20th
1926–27	I	42	19	9	14	91	80	47	5th
1927–28	I	42	16	7	19	82	98	39	19th
1928–29	I	42	15	8	19	81	103	38	19th
1929–30	I	42	14	8	20	79	97	36	21st
1930–31	II	42	17	11	14	81	77	45	8th
1931–32	II	42	13	9	20	59	87	35	19th
1932–33	II	42	11	14	17	67	79	36	19th
1933–34	II	42	18	6	18	60	72	42	13th
1934–35	II	42	16	9	17	63	73	41	12th
1935–36	II	42	12	13	17	50	59	37	15th
1936–37	II	42	16	10	16	57	61	42	13th
1937–38	II	42	17	10	15	54	54	44	6th
1938–39	II	42	15	9	18	50	56	39	14th
1939–46	Regional Leagues operating								
1946–47	II	42	22	14	6	65	29	58	2nd
1947–48	I	42	20	12	10	56	43	52	3rd
1948–49	I	42	12	14	16	43	50	38	15th
1949–50	I	42	16	13	13	40	40	45	10th
1950–51	I	42	14	14	14	48	43	42	10th
1951–52	I	42	15	10	17	56	63	40	14th
1952–53	I	42	18	12	12	67	52	48	6th
1953–54	I	42	21	4	17	78	67	46	7th
1954–55	I	42	17	9	16	51	48	43	10th
1955–56	I	42	18	8	16	64	54	44	7th
1956–57	I	42	18	10	14	56	50	46	7th
1957–58	I	42	21	5	16	80	74	47	6th
1958–59	I	42	19	10	13	81	70	48	7th
1959–60	I	42	24	7	11	85	61	55	1st
1960–61	I	42	22	7	13	102	77	51	4th
1961–62	I	42	21	11	10	101	67	53	2nd
1962–63	I	42	22	10	10	78	57	54	3rd
1963–64	I	42	17	10	15	71	64	44	9th
1964–65	I	42	16	10	16	70	70	42	12th

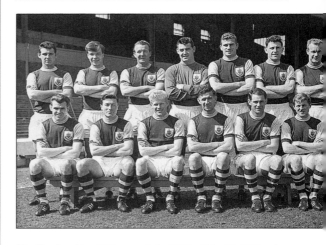

The Burnley side which reached the FA Cup Final in 1962 and finished runners-up in the League that season. This was a golden era which also saw the title come to Turf Moor for only the second time (Popperfoto)

Year	Div	P	W	D	L	F	A	Pts	Pos
1965–66	I	42	24	7	11	79	47	55	3rd
1966–67	I	42	15	9	18	66	76	39	14th
1967–68	I	42	14	10	18	64	71	38	14th
1968–69	I	42	15	9	18	55	82	39	14th
1969–70	I	42	12	15	15	56	61	39	14th
1970–71	I	42	7	13	22	29	63	27	21st
1971–72	II	42	20	6	16	70	55	46	7th
1972–73	II	42	24	14	4	72	35	62	1st
1973–74	I	42	16	14	12	56	53	46	6th
1974–75	I	42	17	11	14	68	67	45	10th
1975–76	I	42	9	10	23	43	66	28	21st
1976–77	II	42	11	14	17	46	64	36	16th
1977–78	II	42	15	10	17	56	64	40	11th
1978–79	II	42	14	12	16	51	62	40	13th
1979–80	II	42	6	15	21	39	73	27	21st
1980–81	III	46	18	14	14	60	48	50	8th
1981–82	III	46	21	17	8	66	45	80	1st
1982–83	II	42	12	8	22	56	66	44	21st
1983–84	III	46	16	14	16	76	61	62	12th
1984–85	III	46	11	13	22	60	73	46	21st
1985–86	IV	46	16	11	19	60	65	59	14th
1986–87	IV	46	12	13	21	53	74	49	22nd
1987–88	IV	46	20	7	19	57	62	67	10th
1988–89	IV	46	14	13	19	52	61	55	16th
1989–90	IV	46	14	14	18	45	55	56	16th
1990–91	IV	46	23	10	13	70	51	79	6th
1991–92	IV	42	25	8	9	79	43	83	1st
1992–93	II	46	15	16	15	57	59	61	13th

On the morning of their League Cup (Milk Cup) fifth round tie at Tottenham Hotspur on 19 January 1983, **Burnley** parted company with their manager Brian Miller. After a goalless first half they conceded a goal after 45 seconds of the second half, but then scored four times including two own-goals and won 4–1.

BURTON SWIFTS

Year	Div	P	W	D	L	F	A	Pts	Pos
1892–93	II	22	9	2	11	47	47	20	6th
1893–94	II	28	14	3	11	79	61	31	6th
1894–95	II	30	11	3	16	52	74	25	11th
1895–96	II	30	10	4	16	39	69	24	11th
1896–97	II	30	9	6	15	46	61	24	14th
1897–98	II	30	8	5	17	38	69	21	13th
1898–99	II	34	10	8	16	51	70	28	13th
1899–1900	II	34	9	6	19	43	84	24	15th
1900–01	II	34	8	4	22	34	66	20	18th

BURTON UNITED

Year	Div	P	W	D	L	F	A	Pts	Pos
1901–02	II	34	11	8	15	46	54	30	10th
1902–03	II	34	11	7	16	39	59	29	13th
1903–04	II	34	11	7	16	45	61	29	14th
1904–05	II	34	8	4	22	30	84	20	17th
1905–06	II	38	10	6	22	34	67	26	19th
1906–07	II	38	8	7	23	34	68	23	20th

One of the original members of the Football League Division Two in 1892, **Burton Swifts** subsequently changed their name to **Burton United**. They were involved in a match of 13 goals with Walsall on 24 February 1894, winning 8–5.

BURTON WANDERERS

Year	Div	P	W	D	L	F	A	Pts	Pos
1894–95	II	30	14	7	9	67	39	35	7th
1895–96	II	30	19	4	7	69	40	42	4th
1896–97	II	30	9	2	19	31	67	20	15th

The Capes brothers, Arthur and Adrian, each scored a hat-trick for **Burton Wanderers** in the 9–0 win over Newcastle United in Division Two on 15 April 1895. Adrian Capes actually scored four times.

BURY

Year	Div	P	W	D	L	F	A	Pts	Pos
1894–95	II	30	23	2	5	78	33	48	1st
1895–96	I	30	12	3	15	50	54	27	11th
1896–97	I	30	10	10	10	39	44	30	9th
1897–98	I	30	8	8	14	39	51	24	14th
1898–99	I	34	14	7	13	48	49	35	10th
1899–1900	I	34	13	6	15	40	44	32	12th
1900–01	I	34	16	7	11	53	37	39	5th
1901–02	I	34	13	8	13	44	38	34	7th
1902–03	I	34	16	3	15	54	43	35	8th
1903–04	I	34	7	15	12	40	53	29	12th
1904–05	I	34	10	4	20	47	67	24	17th
1905–06	I	38	11	10	17	57	74	32	17th
1906–07	I	38	13	6	19	58	68	32	16th
1907–08	I	38	14	11	13	58	61	39	7th
1908–09	I	38	14	8	16	63	77	36	17th
1909–10	I	38	12	9	17	62	66	33	13th
1910–11	I	38	9	11	18	43	71	29	18th
1911–12	I	38	6	9	23	32	59	21	20th
1912–13	II	38	15	8	15	53	57	38	11th
1913–14	II	38	15	10	13	39	40	40	10th
1914–15	II	38	15	8	15	61	56	38	11th
1915–19	Regional Leagues operating								
1919–20	II	42	20	8	14	60	44	48	5th
1920–21	II	42	15	10	17	45	49	40	11th
1921–22	II	42	15	10	17	54	55	40	11th
1922–23	II	42	18	11	13	55	46	47	6th
1923–24	II	42	21	9	12	63	35	51	2nd
1924–25	I	42	17	15	10	54	51	49	5th
1925–26	I	42	20	7	15	85	77	47	4th
1926–27	I	42	12	12	18	68	77	36	19th
1927–28	I	42	20	4	18	80	80	44	5th
1928–29	I	42	12	7	23	62	99	31	21st
1929–30	II	42	22	5	15	78	67	49	5th

Year	Div	P	W	D	L	F	A	Pts	Pos
1930–31	II	42	19	3	20	75	82	41	13th
1931–32	II	42	21	7	14	70	58	49	5th
1932–33	II	42	20	9	13	84	59	49	4th
1933–34	II	42	17	9	16	70	73	43	12th
1934–35	II	42	19	4	19	62	73	42	10th
1935–36	II	42	13	12	17	66	84	38	14th
1936–37	II	42	22	8	12	74	55	52	3rd
1937–38	II	42	18	5	19	63	60	41	10th
1938–39	II	42	12	13	17	65	74	37	16th
1939–46	Regional Leagues operating								
1946–47	II	42	12	12	18	80	78	36	17th
1947–48	II	42	9	16	17	58	68	34	20th
1948–49	II	42	17	6	19	67	76	40	12th
1949–50	II	42	14	9	19	60	65	37	18th
1950–51	II	42	12	8	22	60	86	32	20th
1951–52	II	42	15	7	20	57	69	37	17th
1952–53	II	42	13	9	20	53	81	35	20th
1953–54	II	42	11	14	17	54	72	36	17th
1954–55	II	42	15	11	16	77	72	41	13th
1955–56	II	42	16	8	18	86	90	40	15th
1956–57	II	42	8	9	25	60	96	25	21st
1957–58	IIIN	42	23	10	13	94	62	56	4th
1958–59	III	46	17	14	15	69	58	48	10th
1959–60	III	46	21	9	16	64	51	51	7th
1960–61	III	46	30	8	8	108	45	68	1st
1961–62	II	42	17	5	20	52	76	39	18th
1962–63	II	42	18	11	13	51	47	47	8th
1963–64	II	42	13	9	20	57	73	35	18th
1964–65	II	42	14	10	18	60	66	38	16th
1965–66	II	42	14	7	21	62	76	35	19th
1966–67	II	42	11	6	25	49	83	28	22nd
1967–68	III	46	24	8	14	91	65	56	2nd
1968–69	II	42	11	8	23	51	80	30	21st
1969–70	III	46	15	11	20	75	80	41	19th
1970–71	III	46	12	13	21	52	60	37	22nd
1971–72	IV	46	19	12	15	73	59	50	9th
1972–73	IV	46	14	18	14	58	51	46	12th
1973–74	IV	46	24	11	11	81	49	59	4th
1974–75	III	46	16	12	18	53	50	44	14th
1975–76	III	46	14	16	16	51	46	44	13th
1976–77	III	46	23	8	15	64	59	54	7th
1977–78	III	46	13	19	14	62	56	45	15th
1978–79	III	46	11	20	15	59	65	42	19th
1979–80	III	46	16	7	23	45	59	39	21st
1980–81	IV	46	17	11	18	70	62	45	12th
1981–82	IV	46	17	17	12	80	59	68	9th
1982–83	IV	46	23	12	11	74	46	81	5th
1983–84	IV	46	15	14	17	61	64	59	15th
1984–85	IV	46	24	12	10	76	50	84	4th
1985–86	III	46	12	13	21	63	67	49	20th
1986–87	III	46	14	13	19	54	60	55	16th
1987–88	III	46	15	14	17	58	57	59	14th
1988–89	III	46	16	13	17	55	67	61	13th
1989–90	III	46	21	11	14	70	49	74	5th
1990–91	III	46	20	13	13	67	56	73	7th
1991–92	III	46	13	12	21	55	74	51	21st
1992–93	III	42	18	9	15	63	55	63	7th

When **Bury** won the FA Cup in 1900 and again in 1903, they played a total of 13 cup-ties, including replays. They scored 27 goals and conceded just five. In fact only Sheffield United and Nottingham Forest managed to score against them.

CAMBRIDGE UNITED

Year	Div	P	W	D	L	F	A	Pts	Pos
1970–71	IV	46	15	13	18	51	66	43	20th
1971–72	IV	46	17	14	15	62	60	48	10th
1972–73	IV	46	20	17	9	67	57	57	3rd
1973–74	III	46	13	9	24	48	81	35	21st
1974–75	IV	46	20	14	12	62	44	54	6th
1975–76	IV	46	14	15	17	58	62	43	13th
1976–77	IV	46	26	13	7	87	40	65	1st
1977–78	III	46	23	12	11	72	51	58	2nd
1978–79	II	42	12	16	14	44	52	40	12th
1979–80	II	42	14	16	12	61	53	44	8th
1980–81	II	42	17	6	17	53	65	40	13th
1981–82	II	42	13	9	20	48	53	48	14th
1982–83	II	42	13	12	17	42	60	51	12th
1983–84	II	42	4	12	26	28	77	24	22nd
1984–85	III	46	4	9	33	37	95	21	24th
1985–86	IV	46	15	9	22	65	80	54	22nd
1986–87	IV	46	17	11	18	60	62	62	11th
1987–88	IV	46	16	13	17	50	52	61	15th
1988–89	IV	46	18	14	14	71	62	68	8th
1989–90	IV	46	21	10	15	76	66	73	6th
1990–91	III	46	25	11	10	75	45	86	1st
1991–92	II	46	19	17	10	65	47	74	5th
1992–93	I	46	11	16	19	48	69	49	23rd

On 12 December 1953 **Cambridge United** were beaten 2–1 by Bradford Park Avenue in an FA Cup second round match at Newmarket Road in front of a crowd of 10,000. At the Annual General Meeting of the Football League in 1970, Cambridge received 31 votes to 17 for Bradford, who thus lost their League status.

CARDIFF CITY

Year	Div	P	W	D	L	F	A	Pts	Pos
1920–21	II	42	24	10	8	59	32	58	2nd
1921–22	I	42	19	10	13	61	53	48	4th
1922–23	I	42	18	7	17	73	59	43	9th
1923–24	I	42	22	13	7	61	34	57	2nd
1924–25	I	42	16	11	15	56	51	43	11th
1925–26	I	42	16	7	19	61	76	39	16th
1926–27	I	42	16	9	17	55	65	41	14th
1927–28	I	42	17	10	15	70	80	44	6th
1928–29	I	42	8	13	21	43	59	29	22nd
1929–30	II	42	18	8	16	61	59	44	8th
1930–31	II	42	8	9	25	47	87	25	22nd

Year	Div	P	W	D	L	F	A	Pts	Pos
1931–32	IIIS	42	19	8	15	87	73	46	9th
1932–33	IIIS	42	12	7	23	69	99	31	19th
1933–34	IIIS	42	9	6	27	57	105	24	22nd
1934–35	IIIS	42	13	9	20	62	82	34	19th
1935–36	IIIS	42	13	10	19	60	73	36	20th
1936–37	IIIS	42	14	7	21	54	87	35	18th
1937–38	IIIS	42	15	12	15	67	54	42	10th
1938–39	IIIS	42	15	11	16	61	65	41	13th
1939–46	Regional Leagues operating								
1946–47	IIIS	42	30	6	6	93	30	66	1st
1947–48	II	42	18	11	13	61	58	47	5th
1948–49	II	42	19	13	10	62	47	51	4th
1949–50	II	42	16	10	16	41	44	42	10th
1950–51	II	42	17	16	9	53	45	50	3rd
1951–52	II	42	20	11	11	72	54	51	2nd
1952–53	I	42	14	12	16	54	46	40	12th
1953–54	I	42	18	8	16	51	71	44	10th
1954–55	I	42	13	11	18	62	76	37	20th
1955–56	I	42	15	9	18	55	69	39	17th
1956–57	I	42	10	9	23	53	88	29	21st
1957–58	II	42	14	9	19	63	77	37	15th
1958–59	II	42	18	7	17	65	65	43	9th
1959–60	II	42	23	12	7	90	62	58	2nd
1960–61	I	42	13	11	18	60	85	37	15th
1961–62	I	42	9	14	19	50	81	32	21st
1962–63	II	42	18	7	17	83	73	43	10th
1963–64	II	42	14	10	18	56	81	38	15th
1964–65	II	42	13	14	15	64	57	40	13th
1965–66	II	42	12	10	20	71	91	34	20th
1966–67	II	42	12	9	21	61	87	33	20th
1967–68	II	42	13	12	17	60	66	38	13th
1968–69	II	42	20	7	15	67	54	47	5th
1969–70	II	42	18	13	11	61	41	49	7th
1970–71	II	42	20	13	9	64	41	53	3rd
1971–72	II	42	10	14	18	56	69	34	19th
1972–73	II	42	11	11	20	43	58	33	20th
1973–74	II	42	10	16	16	49	62	36	17th
1974–75	II	42	9	14	19	36	62	32	21st
1975–76	III	46	22	13	11	69	48	57	2nd
1976–77	II	42	12	10	20	56	67	34	18th
1977–78	II	42	13	12	17	46	71	38	19th
1978–79	II	42	16	10	16	56	70	42	9th
1979–80	II	42	16	8	18	41	48	40	15th
1980–81	II	42	12	12	18	44	60	36	19th
1981–82	III	42	12	8	22	45	61	44	20th
1982–83	III	46	25	11	10	76	50	86	2nd
1983–84	II	42	15	6	21	53	66	51	15th
1984–85	II	42	9	8	25	47	79	35	21st
1985–86	III	46	12	9	25	53	82	45	22nd
1986–87	IV	46	15	16	15	48	50	61	13th
1987–88	IV	46	24	13	9	66	41	85	2nd
1988–89	III	46	14	15	17	44	56	57	16th
1989–90	III	46	12	14	20	51	70	50	21st
1990–91	IV	46	15	15	16	43	54	60	13th
1991–92	IV	42	17	15	10	66	53	66	9th
1992–93	III	42	25	8	9	77	47	83	1st

Right-back Jimmy Nelson was born in Scotland, brought up in Ireland, made his first representative appearance against England and played most of his senior football in Wales. He played for Belfast Crusaders and captained the Irish Alliance v England. He joined **Cardiff City** in 1922–23 and was later with Newcastle United and Southend United. He was capped four times by Scotland, the first occasion being the first time he kicked a ball in his native country.

CARLISLE UNITED

Year	Div	P	W	D	L	F	A	Pts	Pos
1928–29	IIIN	42	10	8	15	86	77	46	8th
1929–30	IIIN	42	16	7	19	90	101	39	15th
1930–31	IIIN	42	20	5	17	98	81	45	8th
1931–32	IIIN	40	11	11	18	64	79	33	18th
1932–33	IIIN	42	13	7	22	51	75	33	19th
1933–34	IIIN	42	15	8	19	66	81	38	13th
1934–35	IIIN	42	8	7	27	51	102	23	22nd
1935–36	IIIN	42	14	12	16	56	62	40	13th
1936–37	IIIN	42	18	8	16	65	68	44	10th
1937–38	IIIN	42	15	9	18	57	67	39	12th
1938–39	IIIN	42	13	7	22	66	111	33	19th
1939–46	Regional Leagues operating								
1946–47	IIIN	42	14	9	19	70	93	37	16th
1947–48	IIIN	42	18	7	17	88	77	43	9th
1948–49	IIIN	42	14	11	17	60	77	39	15th
1949–50	IIIN	42	16	15	11	68	51	47	9th
1950–51	IIIN	46	25	12	9	79	50	62	3rd
1951–52	IIIN	46	19	13	14	62	57	51	7th
1952–53	IIIN	46	18	13	15	82	68	49	9th
1953–54	IIIN	46	14	15	17	83	71	43	13th
1954–55	IIIN	46	15	6	25	78	89	36	20th
1955–56	IIIN	46	15	8	23	71	95	38	21st
1956–57	IIIN	46	16	13	17	76	85	45	15th
1957–58	IIIN	46	19	6	21	80	78	44	16th
1958–59	IV	46	19	12	15	62	65	50	10th
1959–60	IV	46	15	11	20	51	66	41	19th
1960–61	IV	46	13	13	20	61	79	39	19th
1961–62	IV	44	22	8	14	64	63	52	4th
1962–63	III	46	13	9	24	61	89	35	23rd
1963–64	IV	36	25	10	11	113	58	60	2nd
1964–65	III	46	25	10	11	76	53	60	1st
1965–66	II	42	17	5	20	60	63	39	14th
1966–67	II	42	23	6	13	71	54	52	3rd
1967–68	II	42	14	13	13	58	52	41	10th
1968–69	II	42	16	10	16	46	49	42	12th
1969–70	II	42	14	13	15	58	56	41	12th
1970–71	II	42	20	13	9	65	43	53	4th
1971–72	II	42	17	9	16	61	57	43	10th
1972–73	II	42	11	12	19	50	52	34	18th
1973–74	II	42	20	9	13	61	48	49	3rd
1974–75	I	42	12	5	25	43	59	29	22nd
1975–76	II	42	12	13	17	45	59	37	19th

Year	Div	P	W	D	L	F	A	Pts	Pos
1976–77	II	42	11	12	19	49	75	34	20th
1977–78	III	46	14	19	13	59	59	47	13th
1978–79	III	46	15	22	9	53	42	52	6th
1979–80	III	46	18	12	16	66	56	48	6th
1980–81	III	46	14	13	19	56	70	41	19th
1981–82	III	46	23	11	12	65	50	80	2nd
1982–83	II	42	12	12	18	68	70	48	14th
1983–84	II	42	16	16	10	48	41	64	7th
1984–85	II	42	13	8	21	50	67	47	16th
1985–86	II	42	13	7	22	47	71	46	20th
1986–87	III	46	10	8	28	39	78	38	23rd
1987–88	IV	46	12	8	26	57	86	44	23rd
1988–89	IV	46	15	15	16	53	52	60	12th
1989–90	IV	46	21	8	17	61	60	71	8th
1990–91	IV	46	13	9	24	47	89	48	20th
1991–92	IV	42	7	13	22	41	67	34	22nd
1992–93	III	42	11	11	20	51	65	44	18th

Jimmy McConnell, who still holds two **Carlisle United** goalscoring records, with most League goals in a season and in total aggregate, scored four hat-tricks in his first season with the club, 1928–29. He achieved 15 such trebles including four 4's before moving to Crewe Alexandra in 1932. In 1928–29 McConnell scored 42 League goals and finished with 126 at Carlisle.

CHARLTON ATHLETIC

Year	Div	P	W	D	L	F	A	Pts	Pos
1921–22	IIIS	42	13	11	18	43	56	37	16th
1922–23	IIIS	42	14	14	14	55	51	42	12th
1923–24	IIIS	42	11	15	16	38	45	37	14th
1924–25	IIIS	42	13	12	17	46	48	38	15th
1925–26	IIIS	42	11	13	18	48	68	35	21st
1926–27	IIIS	42	16	8	18	60	61	40	13th
1927–28	IIIS	42	15	13	14	60	70	43	11th
1928–29	IIIS	42	23	8	11	86	60	54	1st
1929–30	II	42	14	11	17	59	63	39	13th
1930–31	II	42	15	9	18	59	87	39	15th
1931–32	II	42	17	9	16	61	66	43	10th
1932–33	II	42	12	7	23	60	91	31	22nd
1933–34	IIIS	42	22	8	12	83	56	52	5th
1934–35	IIIS	42	27	7	8	103	52	61	1st
1935–36	II	42	22	11	9	85	58	55	2nd
1936–37	I	42	21	12	9	58	49	54	2nd
1937–38	I	42	16	14	12	65	51	46	4th
1938–39	I	42	22	6	14	75	59	50	3rd
1939–46	Regional Leagues operating								
1946–47	I	42	11	12	19	57	71	34	19th
1947–48	I	42	17	6	19	57	66	40	13th
1948–49	I	42	15	12	15	63	67	42	9th
1949–50	I	42	13	6	23	53	65	32	20th
1950–51	I	42	14	9	19	63	80	37	17th
1951–52	I	42	17	10	15	68	63	44	10th
1952–53	I	42	19	11	12	77	63	49	5th
1953–54	I	42	19	6	17	75	77	44	9th

Year	Div	P	W	D	L	F	A	Pts	Pos
1954–55	I	42	15	10	17	76	75	40	15th
1955–56	I	42	17	6	19	75	81	40	14th
1956–57	I	42	9	4	29	62	120	22	22nd
1957–58	II	42	24	7	11	107	69	55	3rd
1958–59	II	42	18	7	17	92	90	43	8th
1959–60	II	42	17	13	12	90	87	47	7th
1960–61	II	42	16	11	15	97	91	43	10th
1961–62	II	42	15	9	18	69	75	39	15th
1962–63	II	42	13	5	24	62	94	31	20th
1963–64	II	42	19	10	13	76	70	48	4th
1964–65	II	42	13	9	20	64	75	35	18th
1965–66	II	42	12	14	16	61	70	38	16th
1966–67	II	42	13	9	20	49	53	35	19th
1967–68	II	42	12	13	17	63	68	37	15th
1968–69	II	42	18	14	10	61	52	50	3rd
1969–70	II	42	7	17	18	35	76	31	20th
1970–71	II	42	8	14	20	41	65	30	20th
1971–72	II	42	12	9	21	55	77	33	21st
1972–73	III	46	17	11	18	69	67	45	11th
1973–74	III	46	19	8	19	66	73	46	14th
1974–75	III	46	22	11	13	76	61	55	3rd
1975–76	II	42	15	12	15	61	72	42	9th
1976–77	II	42	16	16	10	71	58	48	7th
1977–78	II	42	13	12	17	55	68	38	17th
1978–79	II	42	11	13	18	60	69	35	19th
1979–80	II	42	6	10	26	39	78	22	22nd
1980–81	III	46	25	9	12	63	44	59	3rd
1981–82	II	42	13	12	17	50	65	51	13th
1982–83	II	42	13	9	20	63	86	48	17th
1983–84	II	42	16	9	17	53	64	57	13th
1984–85	II	42	11	12	19	51	63	45	17th
1985–86	II	42	22	11	9	78	45	77	2nd
1986–87	I	38	11	11	20	45	55	44	19th
1987–88	I	40	9	15	16	38	52	42	17th
1988–89	I	38	10	12	16	44	58	42	14th
1989–90	I	38	7	9	22	31	57	30	19th
1990–91	II	46	13	17	16	57	61	56	16th
1991–92	II	46	20	11	15	54	48	71	7th
1992–93	I	46	16	13	17	49	46	61	12th

Charlton Athletic played the French national team in Paris on 11 April 1937 and beat them 5–2. They were late replacements for the Italians. The previous day Charlton had beaten Huddersfield Town 4–0 at The Valley. Charlton's scorers in Paris were: Don Welsh 2, George Tadman 2 and Harold Hobbis.

CHELSEA

Year	Div	P	W	D	L	F	A	Pts	Pos
1905–06	II	38	22	9	7	90	37	53	3rd
1906–07	II	38	26	5	7	80	34	57	2nd
1907–08	I	38	14	8	16	53	62	36	13th
1908–09	I	38	14	9	15	56	61	37	11th
1909–10	I	38	11	7	20	47	70	29	19th
1910–11	II	38	20	9	9	71	35	49	3rd

1911–12	II	38	24	6	8	64	34	54	2nd
1912–13	I	38	11	6	21	51	73	28	18th
1913–14	I	38	16	7	15	46	55	39	8th
1914–15	I	38	8	13	17	51	65	29	19th
1915–19	Regional Leagues operating								
1919–20	I	42	22	5	15	56	51	49	3rd
1920–21	I	42	13	13	16	48	58	39	18th
1921–22	I	42	17	12	13	40	43	46	9th
1922–23	I	42	9	18	15	45	53	36	19th
1923–24	I	42	9	14	19	31	53	32	21st
1924–25	II	42	16	15	11	51	37	47	5th
1925–26	II	42	19	14	9	76	49	52	3rd
1926–27	II	42	20	12	10	62	52	52	4th
1927–28	II	42	23	8	11	75	45	54	3rd
1928–29	II	42	17	10	15	64	65	44	9th
1929–30	II	42	22	11	9	74	46	55	2nd
1930–31	I	42	15	10	17	64	67	40	12th
1931–32	I	42	16	8	18	69	73	40	12th
1932–33	I	42	14	7	21	63	73	35	18th
1933–34	I	42	14	8	20	67	69	36	19th
1934–35	I	42	16	9	17	73	82	41	12th
1935–36	I	42	15	13	14	65	72	43	8th
1936–37	I	42	14	13	15	52	55	41	13th
1937–38	I	42	14	13	15	65	65	41	10th
1938–39	I	42	12	9	21	64	80	33	20th
1939–46	Regional Leagues operating								
1946–47	I	42	16	7	19	69	84	39	15th
1947–48	I	42	14	9	19	53	71	37	18th
1948–49	I	42	12	14	16	69	68	38	13th
1949–50	I	42	12	16	14	58	65	40	13th
1950–51	I	42	12	8	22	53	65	32	20th
1951–52	I	42	14	8	20	52	72	36	19th
1952–53	I	42	12	11	19	56	66	35	19th
1953–54	I	42	16	12	14	74	68	44	8th
1954–55	I	42	20	12	10	81	57	52	1st
1955–56	I	42	14	11	17	64	77	39	16th
1956–57	I	42	13	13	16	73	73	39	12th
1957–58	I	42	15	12	15	83	79	42	11th
1958–59	I	42	18	4	20	77	98	40	14th
1959–60	I	42	14	9	19	76	91	37	18th
1960–61	I	42	15	7	20	98	100	37	12th
1961–62	I	42	9	10	23	63	94	28	22nd
1962–63	II	42	24	4	14	81	42	52	2nd
1963–64	I	42	20	10	12	72	56	50	5th
1964–65	I	42	24	8	10	89	54	56	3rd
1965–66	I	42	22	7	13	65	53	51	5th
1966–67	I	42	15	14	13	67	62	44	9th
1967–68	I	42	18	12	12	62	68	48	6th
1968–69	I	42	20	10	12	73	53	50	5th
1969–70	I	42	21	13	8	70	50	55	3rd
1970–71	I	42	18	15	9	52	42	51	6th
1971–72	I	42	18	12	12	58	49	48	7th
1972–73	I	42	13	14	15	49	51	40	12th
1973–74	I	42	12	13	17	56	60	37	17th
1974–75	I	42	9	15	18	42	72	33	21st
1975–76	II	42	12	16	14	53	54	40	11th
1976–77	II	42	21	13	8	73	53	55	2nd

Chelsea's first game back in Division 1 after five seasons, at Highbury in 1984. Pat Nevin (left) celebrates the equalising goal scored by Kerry Dixon (9) in the 1–1 draw (Popperfoto)

1977–78	I	42	11	14	17	46	69	36	16th
1978–79	I	42	5	10	27	44	92	20	22nd
1979–80	II	42	23	7	12	66	52	53	4th
1980–81	II	42	14	12	16	46	41	40	12th
1981–82	II	42	15	12	15	60	60	57	12th
1982–83	II	42	11	14	17	51	61	47	18th
1983–84	II	42	25	13	4	90	40	89	1st
1984–85	I	42	18	12	12	63	48	66	6th
1985–86	I	42	20	11	11	57	56	71	6th
1986–87	I	42	13	13	16	53	64	52	14th
1987–88	I	40	9	15	16	50	68	42	18th
1988–89	II	46	29	12	5	96	50	99	1st
1989–90	I	38	16	12	10	58	50	60	5th
1990–91	I	38	13	10	15	58	69	49	11th
1991–92	I	42	13	14	15	50	60	53	14th
1992–93	PL	42	14	14	14	51	54	56	11th

By beating Orient 7–3 away on 10 November 1979, **Chelsea** reached their 1000th win in Football League games. At the time it was their highest score in an away fixture.

CHESTER CITY

(Chester until 1983)

Year	Div	P	W	D	L	F	A	Pts	Pos
1931–32	IIIN	40	21	8	11	78	60	50	3rd
1932–33	IIIN	42	22	8	12	94	66	52	4th
1933–34	IIIN	42	17	6	19	89	86	40	10th
1934–35	IIIN	42	20	14	8	91	58	54	3rd
1935–36	IIIN	42	22	11	9	100	45	55	2nd
1936–37	IIIN	42	22	9	11	87	57	53	3rd
1937–38	IIIN	42	16	12	14	77	72	44	9th
1938–39	IIIN	42	20	9	13	88	70	49	6th

Year	Div	P	W	D	L	F	A	Pts	Pos
1939–46	Regional Leagues operating								
1946–47	IIIN	42	25	6	11	95	51	56	3rd
1947–48	IIIN	42	13	9	20	64	67	35	20th
1948–49	IIIN	42	11	13	18	57	56	35	18th
1949–50	IIIN	42	17	6	19	70	79	40	12th
1950–51	IIIN	46	17	9	20	62	64	43	13th
1951–52	IIIN	46	15	9	22	72	85	39	19th
1952–53	IIIN	46	11	15	20	64	85	37	20th
1953–54	IIIN	46	11	10	25	48	67	32	24th
1954–55	IIIN	46	12	9	25	44	77	33	24th
1955–56	IIIN	46	13	14	19	52	82	40	17th
1956–57	IIIN	46	10	13	23	55	84	33	21st
1957–58	IIIN	46	13	13	20	73	81	39	21st
1958–59	IV	46	16	12	18	72	84	44	13th
1959–60	IV	46	14	12	20	59	77	40	20th
1960–61	IV	46	11	9	26	61	104	31	24th
1961–62	IV	44	7	12	25	54	96	26	23rd
1962–63	IV	46	15	9	22	51	66	39	21st
1963–64	IV	46	19	8	19	65	60	46	12th
1964–65	IV	46	25	6	15	119	81	56	8th
1965–66	IV	46	20	12	14	79	70	52	7th
1966–67	IV	46	15	10	21	54	78	40	19th
1967–68	IV	46	9	14	23	57	78	32	22nd
1968–69	IV	46	16	13	17	76	66	45	14th
1969–70	IV	46	21	6	19	58	66	48	11th
1970–71	IV	46	24	7	15	69	55	55	5th
1971–72	IV	46	10	18	18	47	56	38	20th
1972–73	IV	46	14	15	17	61	52	43	15th
1973–74	IV	46	17	15	14	54	55	49	7th
1974–75	IV	46	23	11	12	64	38	57	4th
1975–76	III	46	15	12	19	43	62	42	17th
1976–77	III	46	18	8	20	48	58	44	13th
1977–78	III	46	16	22	8	59	56	54	5th
1978–79	III	46	14	16	16	57	61	44	16th
1979–80	III	46	17	13	16	49	57	47	9th
1980–81	III	46	15	11	20	41	48	41	18th
1981–82	III	46	7	11	28	36	78	32	24th
1982–83	IV	46	15	11	20	55	60	56	13th
1983–84	IV	46	7	13	26	45	82	34	24th
1984–85	IV	46	15	9	22	60	72	54	16th
1985–86	IV	46	23	15	8	83	50	84	2nd
1986–87	III	46	13	17	16	61	59	56	15th
1987–88	III	46	14	16	16	51	62	58	15th
1988–89	III	46	19	11	16	64	61	68	8th
1989–90	III	46	13	15	18	43	55	54	16th
1990–91	IIII	46	14	9	23	46	58	51	19th
1991–92	III	46	14	14	18	56	59	56	18th
1992–93	II	46	8	5	33	49	102	29	24th

Before the start of the 1992–93 season, the individual record for goalscoring at **Chester City** was held by Gary Talbot with 83, achieved in two spells with the club. Stuart Rimmer was also in his second period at Chester having been signed originally from Everton and returned via Watford, Notts County, Walsall and Barnsley. His began the season on 80 goals and overtook Talbot's total on 15 September 1992 against Mansfield Town.

CHESTERFIELD

Year	Div	P	W	D	L	F	A	Pts	Pos
1899–1900	II	34	16	6	12	65	60	38	7th
1900–01	II	34	9	10	15	46	58	28	14th
1901–02	II	34	11	6	17	47	68	28	16th
1902–03	II	34	14	9	11	67	40	37	6th
1903–04	II	34	11	8	15	37	45	30	11th
1904–05	II	34	14	11	9	44	35	39	5th
1905–06	II	38	10	8	20	40	72	28	18th
1906–07	II	38	11	7	20	50	66	29	18th
1907–08	II	38	6	11	21	46	92	23	19th
1908–09	II	38	11	8	19	37	67	30	19th
Failed re-election									
1921–22	IIIN	38	16	3	19	48	67	35	13th
1922–23	IIIN	38	19	7	12	68	52	45	4th
1923–24	IIIN	42	22	10	10	70	39	54	3rd
1924–25	IIIN	42	17	11	14	60	44	45	7th
1925–26	IIIN	42	25	5	12	100	54	55	4th
1926–27	IIIN	42	21	5	16	92	68	47	7th
1927–28	IIIN	42	13	10	19	71	78	36	16th
1928–29	IIIN	42	18	5	19	71	77	41	11th
1929–30	IIIN	42	22	6	14	76	56	50	4th
1930–31	IIIN	42	26	6	10	102	57	58	1st
1931–32	II	42	13	11	18	64	86	37	17th
1932–33	II	42	12	10	20	61	84	34	21st
1933–34	IIIN	42	27	7	8	86	43	61	2nd
1934–35	IIIN	42	17	10	15	71	52	44	10th
1935–36	IIIN	42	24	12	6	92	39	60	1st
1936–37	II	42	16	8	18	84	89	40	15th
1937–38	II	42	16	9	17	63	63	41	11th
1938–39	II	42	20	9	13	69	52	49	6th
1939–46	Regional Leagues operating								
1946–47	II	42	18	14	10	58	44	50	4th
1947–48	II	42	16	7	19	54	55	39	16th
1948–49	II	42	15	17	10	51	45	47	6th
1949–50	II	42	15	9	18	43	47	39	14th
1950–51	II	42	9	12	21	44	69	30	21st
1951–52	IIIN	46	17	11	18	65	66	45	13th
1952–53	IIIN	46	18	11	17	65	63	47	12th
1953–54	IIIN	46	19	14	13	76	64	52	6th
1954–55	IIIN	46	24	6	16	81	70	54	6th
1955–56	IIIN	46	25	4	17	94	66	54	6th
1956–57	IIIN	46	22	9	15	96	79	53	6th
1957–58	IIIN	46	18	15	13	71	69	51	8th
1958–59	III	46	17	10	19	67	64	44	16th
1959–60	III	46	18	7	21	71	84	43	18th
1960–61	III	46	10	12	24	67	87	32	24th
1961–62	IV	44	14	9	21	70	87	37	19th
1962–63	IV	46	13	16	17	70	64	42	15th
1963–64	IV	46	15	12	19	57	71	42	16th
1964–65	IV	46	20	8	18	58	70	48	12th
1965–66	IV	46	13	13	20	62	78	39	20th
1966–67	IV	46	17	8	21	60	63	42	15th
1967–68	IV	46	21	11	14	71	50	53	7th
1968–69	IV	46	13	15	18	43	50	41	20th
1969–70	IV	46	27	10	9	77	32	64	1st

Year	Div	P	W	D	L	F	A	Pts	Pos
1970–71	III	46	17	17	12	66	38	51	5th
1971–72	III	46	18	8	20	57	57	44	13th
1972–73	III	46	17	9	20	57	61	43	16th
1973–74	III	46	21	14	11	55	42	56	5th
1974–75	III	46	16	12	18	62	66	44	15th
1975–76	III	46	17	9	20	69	69	43	14th
1976–77	III	46	14	10	22	56	64	38	18th
1977–78	III	46	17	14	15	58	49	48	9th
1978–79	III	46	13	14	19	51	65	40	20th
1979–80	III	46	23	11	12	71	46	57	4th
1980–81	III	46	23	10	13	72	48	56	5th
1981–82	III	46	18	10	18	57	58	64	11th
1982–83	III	46	8	13	25	43	68	37	24th
1983–84	IV	46	15	15	16	59	61	60	13th
1984–85	IV	46	26	13	7	64	35	91	1st
1985–86	III	46	13	14	19	61	64	53	17th
1986–87	III	46	13	15	18	56	69	54	17th
1987–88	III	46	15	10	21	41	70	55	18th
1988–89	III	46	14	7	25	51	86	49	22nd
1989–90	IV	46	19	14	13	63	50	71	7th
1990–91	IV	46	13	14	19	47	62	53	18th
1991–92	IV	46	14	11	17	49	61	53	13th
1992–93	III	42	15	11	16	59	63	56	12th

Jimmy Cookson was signed by **Chesterfield** from Manchester City as a full-back. But after three defeats he was switched to centre-forward against Tranmere Rovers on 3 October 1925, scored a hat-trick in a 4–0 away win and went on to register 44 League goals that season.

COLCHESTER UNITED

Year	Div	P	W	D	L	F	A	Pts	Pos
1950–51	IIIS	46	14	12	20	63	76	40	16th
1951–52	IIIS	46	17	12	17	56	77	46	10th
1952–53	IIIS	46	12	14	20	59	76	38	22nd
1953–54	IIIS	46	10	10	26	50	78	30	23rd
1954–55	IIIS	46	9	13	24	53	91	31	24th
1955–56	IIIS	46	18	11	17	76	81	47	12th
1956–57	IIIS	46	22	14	10	84	56	58	3rd
1957–58	IIIS	46	17	13	16	77	79	47	12th
1958–59	III	46	21	10	15	71	67	52	5th
1959–60	III	46	18	11	17	83	74	47	9th
1960–61	III	46	11	11	24	68	101	33	23rd
1961–62	IV	44	23	9	12	104	71	55	2nd
1962–63	III	46	18	11	17	73	93	47	12th
1963–64	III	46	12	19	15	70	68	43	17th
1964–65	III	46	10	10	26	50	89	30	23rd
1965–66	IV	46	23	10	13	70	47	56	4th
1966–67	III	46	17	10	19	76	73	44	13th
1967–68	III	46	9	15	22	50	87	33	23rd
1968–69	IV	46	20	12	14	57	53	52	6th
1969–70	IV	46	17	14	15	64	63	48	10th
1970–71	IV	46	21	12	13	70	54	54	6th
1971–72	IV	46	19	10	17	70	69	48	11th
1972–73	IV	46	10	11	25	48	76	31	22nd
1973–74	IV	46	24	12	10	73	36	60	3rd
1974–75	III	46	17	13	16	70	63	47	11th
1975–76	III	46	12	14	16	41	65	38	22nd
1976–77	IV	46	25	9	12	77	43	59	3rd
1977–78	III	46	15	18	13	55	44	48	8th
1978–79	III	46	17	17	12	60	55	51	7th
1979–80	III	46	20	12	14	64	56	52	5th
1980–81	III	46	14	11	21	45	65	39	22nd
1981–82	IV	46	20	12	14	82	57	72	6th
1982–83	IV	46	24	9	13	75	55	81	6th
1983–84	IV	46	17	16	13	69	53	67	8th
1984–85	IV	46	20	14	12	86	65	74	7th
1985–86	IV	46	19	13	14	88	63	70	6th
1986–87	IV	46	21	7	18	64	56	70	5th
1987–88	IV	46	19	10	17	47	51	67	9th
1988–89	IV	46	12	14	20	60	78	50	22nd
1989–90	IV	46	11	10	25	48	75	43	24th
1990–92	GM Vauxhall Conference								
1992–93	III	42	18	5	19	67	76	59	10th

In 1991–92 **Colchester United** became the first club to be eliminated from the FA Cup without conceding a goal in actual play. In their first round tie with Exeter City they played 210 minutes without a goal being scored by either side and then lost 4–2 on penalties.

COVENTRY CITY

Year	Div	P	W	D	L	F	A	Pts	Pos
1919–20	II	42	9	11	22	35	73	29	20th
1920–21	II	42	12	11	19	39	70	35	21st
1921–22	II	42	12	10	20	51	60	34	20th
1922–23	II	42	15	7	20	46	63	37	18th
1923–24	II	42	11	13	18	52	68	35	19th
1924–25	II	42	11	9	22	45	84	31	22nd
1925–26	IIIN	42	16	6	20	73	82	38	16th
1926–27	IIIS	42	15	7	20	71	86	37	15th
1927–28	IIIS	42	11	9	22	67	96	31	20th
1928–29	IIIS	42	14	14	14	62	57	42	11th
1929–30	IIIS	42	19	9	14	88	73	47	6th
1930–31	IIIS	42	16	9	17	75	65	41	14th
1931–32	IIIS	42	18	8	16	108	97	44	12th
1932–33	IIIS	42	19	6	17	106	77	44	6th
1933–34	IIIS	42	21	12	9	100	54	54	2nd
1934–35	IIIS	42	21	9	12	86	50	51	3rd
1935–36	IIIS	42	24	9	9	102	45	57	1st
1936–37	II	42	17	11	14	66	54	45	8th
1937–38	II	42	20	12	10	66	45	52	4th
1938–39	II	42	21	8	13	62	45	50	4th
1939–46	Regional Leagues operating								
1946–47	II	42	16	13	13	66	59	45	8th
1947–48	II	42	14	13	15	59	52	41	10th
1948–49	II	42	15	7	20	55	64	37	16th
1949–50	II	42	13	13	16	55	55	39	12th
1950–51	II	42	19	7	16	75	59	45	7th
1951–52	II	42	14	6	22	59	82	34	21st

1952–53	IIIS	46	19	12	15	77	62	50	6th
1953–54	IIIS	46	18	9	19	61	56	45	14th
1954–55	IIIS	46	18	11	17	67	59	47	9th
1955–56	IIIS	46	20	9	17	73	60	49	8th
1956–57	IIIS	46	16	12	18	74	84	44	16th
1957–58	IIIS	46	13	13	20	61	81	39	19th
1958–59	IV	46	24	12	10	84	47	60	2nd
1959–60	III	46	21	10	15	78	63	52	5th
1960–61	III	46	16	12	18	80	83	44	15th
1961–62	III	46	16	11	19	64	71	43	14th
1962–63	III	46	18	17	11	83	69	53	4th
1963–64	III	46	22	16	8	98	61	60	1st
1964–65	II	42	17	9	16	72	70	43	10th
1965–66	II	42	20	13	9	73	53	53	3rd
1966–67	II	42	23	13	6	74	43	59	1st
1967–68	I	42	9	15	18	51	71	33	20th
1968–69	I	42	10	11	21	46	64	31	20th
1969–70	I	42	19	11	12	58	48	49	6th
1970–71	I	42	16	10	16	37	38	42	10th
1971–72	I	42	9	15	18	44	67	33	18th
1972–73	I	42	13	9	20	40	55	35	19th
1973–74	I	42	14	10	18	43	54	38	16th
1974–75	I	42	12	15	15	51	62	39	14th
1975–76	I	42	13	14	15	47	57	40	14th
1976–77	I	42	10	15	17	48	59	35	19th
1977–78	I	42	18	12	12	75	62	48	7th
1978–79	I	42	14	16	12	58	68	44	10th
1979–80	I	42	16	7	19	56	66	39	15th
1980–81	I	42	13	10	19	48	68	36	16th
1981–82	I	42	13	11	18	56	62	50	14th
1982–83	I	42	13	9	20	48	59	48	19th
1983–84	I	42	13	11	18	57	77	50	19th
1984–85	I	42	15	5	22	47	64	50	18th
1985–86	I	42	11	10	21	48	71	43	17th
1986–87	I	42	17	12	13	50	45	63	10th
1987–88	I	40	13	14	13	46	53	53	10th
1988–89	I	38	14	13	11	47	42	55	7th
1989–90	I	38	14	7	17	39	59	49	12th
1990–91	I	38	11	11	16	42	49	44	16th
1991–92	I	42	11	11	20	35	44	44	19th
1992–93	PL	42	13	13	16	52	57	52	15th

On 6 April 1932 **Coventry City** made their first trip abroad playing a Dutch XI at Sparta's ground in Rotterdam. Coventry won 3–0 with goals from Cull, Jock Lauderdale and Clarrie Bourton.

CREWE ALEXANDRA

Year	Div	P	W	D	L	F	A	Pts	Pos
1892–93	II	22	6	3	13	42	69	15	10th
1893–94	II	28	6	7	15	42	73	19	12th
1894–95	II	30	3	4	23	26	103	10	16th
1895–96	II	30	5	3	22	30	95	13	16th
Failed re-election									
1921–22	IIIN	38	18	5	15	60	56	41	6th

1922–23	IIIN	38	17	9	12	48	38	43	6th
1923–24	IIIN	42	7	13	22	32	58	27	20th
1924–25	IIIN	42	13	13	16	53	78	39	15th
1925–26	IIIN	42	17	9	16	63	61	43	11th
1926–27	IIIN	42	14	9	19	71	81	37	15th
1927–28	IIIN	42	12	10	20	77	86	34	17th
1928–29	IIIN	42	18	8	16	80	68	44	9th
1929–30	IIIN	42	17	8	17	82	71	42	11th
1930–31	IIIN	42	14	6	22	66	93	34	18th
1931–32	IIIN	40	21	6	13	95	66	48	6th
1932–33	IIIN	42	20	3	19	80	84	43	10th
1933–34	IIIN	42	15	6	21	81	97	36	14th
1934–35	IIIN	42	14	11	17	66	86	39	13th
1935–36	IIIN	42	19	9	14	80	76	47	6th
1936–37	IIIN	42	10	12	20	55	83	32	20th
1937–38	IIIN	42	18	9	15	71	53	45	8th
1938–39	IIIN	42	19	6	17	82	70	44	8th
1939–46	Regional Leagues operating								
1946–47	IIIN	42	17	9	16	70	74	43	8th
1947–48	IIIN	42	18	7	17	61	63	43	10th
1948–49	IIIN	42	16	9	17	52	74	41	12th
1949–50	IIIN	42	17	14	11	68	55	48	7th
1950–51	IIIN	46	19	10	17	61	60	48	9th
1951–52	IIIN	46	17	8	21	63	82	42	16th
1952–53	IIIN	46	20	8	18	70	68	48	10th
1953–54	IIIN	46	14	13	19	49	67	41	16th
1954–55	IIIN	46	10	14	22	68	91	34	22nd
1955–56	IIIN	46	9	10	27	50	105	28	24th
1956–57	IIIN	46	6	9	31	43	110	21	24th
1957–58	IIIN	46	8	7	31	47	93	23	24th
1958–59	IV	46	15	10	21	70	82	40	18th
1959–60	IV	46	18	9	19	79	88	45	14th
1960–61	IV	46	20	9	17	61	67	49	9th
1961–62	IV	46	20	6	18	79	70	46	10th
1962–63	IV	46	24	11	11	86	58	59	3rd
1963–64	III	46	11	12	23	50	77	34	22nd
1964–65	IV	46	18	13	15	90	81	49	10th
1965–66	IV	46	16	9	21	61	63	41	14th
1966–67	IV	46	21	12	13	70	55	54	5th
1967–68	IV	46	20	18	8	74	49	58	4th
1968–69	III	46	13	9	24	52	76	35	23rd
1969–70	IV	46	16	12	18	51	51	44	15th
1970–71	IV	46	18	8	20	75	76	44	15th
1971–72	IV	46	10	9	27	43	69	29	24th
1972–73	IV	46	9	18	19	38	61	36	21st
1973–74	IV	46	14	10	22	43	71	38	21st
1974–75	IV	46	11	18	17	34	47	40	18th
1975–76	IV	46	13	15	18	58	57	41	16th
1976–77	IV	46	19	11	16	47	60	49	12th
1977–78	IV	46	15	14	17	50	69	44	15th
1978–79	IV	46	6	14	26	43	90	26	24th
1979–80	IV	46	11	13	22	35	68	35	23rd
1980–81	IV	46	13	14	19	48	61	40	18th
1981–82	IV	46	6	9	31	29	84	27	24th
1982–83	IV	46	11	8	27	53	71	41	23rd
1983–84	IV	46	16	11	19	56	67	59	16th
1984–85	IV	46	18	12	16	65	69	66	10th

1985–86	IV	46	18	9	19	54	61	63	12th
1986–87	IV	46	13	14	19	70	72	53	17th
1987–88	IV	46	13	19	14	57	53	58	17th
1988–89	IV	46	21	15	10	67	48	78	3rd
1989–90	III	46	15	17	14	56	53	62	12th
1990–91	III	46	11	11	24	62	80	44	22nd
1991–92	IV	42	20	10	12	66	51	70	6th
1992–93	III	42	21	7	14	75	56	70	6th

On 26 November 1892 **Crewe Alexandra** beat Port Vale 5–0, Jack Jones scoring three goals on his debut which was made during a downpour. Port Vale protested in vain about the conditions. Crewe's next League hat-trick was scored by Albert Winterburn in a 3–2 win at Lincoln City on 26 November 1921.

CRYSTAL PALACE

Year	Div	P	W	D	L	F	A	Pts	Pos
1920–21	III	42	24	11	7	70	34	59	1st
1921–22	II	42	13	13	16	45	51	39	14th
1922–23	II	42	13	11	18	54	62	37	16th
1923–24	II	42	13	13	16	53	65	39	15th
1924–25	II	42	12	10	20	38	54	34	21st
1925–26	IIIS	42	19	3	20	75	79	41	13th
1926–27	IIIS	42	18	9	15	84	81	45	6th
1927–28	IIIS	42	18	12	12	79	72	48	5th
1928–29	IIIS	42	23	8	11	81	67	54	2nd
1929–30	IIIS	42	17	12	13	81	74	46	9th
1930–31	IIIS	42	22	7	13	107	71	51	2nd
1931–32	IIIS	42	20	11	11	74	63	51	4th
1932–33	IIIS	42	19	8	15	78	64	46	5th
1933–34	IIIS	42	16	9	17	71	67	41	12th
1934–35	IIIS	42	19	10	13	86	64	48	5th
1935–36	IIIS	42	22	5	15	96	74	49	6th
1936–37	IIIS	42	13	12	17	62	61	38	14th
1937–38	IIIS	42	18	12	12	67	47	48th	7th
1938–39	IIIS	42	20	12	10	71	52	52	2nd
1939–46	Regional Leagues operating								
1946–47	IIIS	42	13	11	18	49	62	37	18th
1947–48	IIIS	42	13	13	16	49	49	39	13th
1948–49	IIIS	42	8	11	23	38	76	27	22nd
1949–50	IIIS	42	15	14	13	55	54	44	7th
1950–51	IIIS	46	8	11	27	33	84	27	24th
1951–52	IIIS	46	15	9	22	61	80	39	19th
1952–53	IIIS	46	15	13	18	66	82	43	13th
1953–54	IIIS	46	14	12	20	60	86	40	22nd
1954–55	IIIS	46	11	16	19	52	80	38	20th
1955–56	IIIS	46	12	10	24	54	83	34	23rd
1956–57	IIIS	46	11	18	17	62	75	40	20th
1957–58	IIIS	46	15	13	18	70	72	43	14th
1958–59	IV	46	20	12	14	90	71	52	7th
1959–60	IV	46	19	12	15	84	64	50	8th
1960–61	IV	46	29	6	11	110	69	64	2nd
1961–62	III	46	14	14	18	83	80	42	15th
1962–63	III	46	17	13	16	68	58	47	11th
1963–64	III	46	23	14	9	73	51	60	2nd
1964–65	II	42	16	13	13	55	51	45	7th
1965–66	II	42	14	13	15	47	52	41	11th
1966–67	II	42	19	10	13	61	55	48	7th
1967–68	II	42	14	11	17	56	56	39	11th
1968–69	II	42	22	12	8	70	47	56	2nd
1969–70	I	42	6	15	21	34	68	27	20th
1970–71	I	42	12	11	19	39	57	35	18th
1971–72	I	42	8	13	21	39	65	29	20th
1972–73	I	42	9	12	21	41	58	30	21st
1973–74	II	42	11	12	19	43	56	34	20th
1974–75	III	46	18	15	13	66	57	51	5th
1975–76	III	46	18	17	11	61	46	53	5th
1976–77	III	46	23	13	10	68	40	59	3rd
1977–78	II	42	13	15	14	50	47	41	9th
1978–79	II	42	19	19	4	51	24	57	1st
1979–80	I	42	12	16	14	41	50	40	13th
1980–81	I	42	6	7	29	47	83	19	22nd
1981–82	II	42	13	9	20	34	45	48	15th
1982–83	II	42	12	12	18	43	52	48	15th
1983–84	II	42	12	11	19	42	52	47	18th
1984–85	II	42	12	12	18	46	65	48	15th
1985–86	II	42	19	9	14	57	52	66	5th
1986–87	II	42	19	5	18	51	53	62	6th
1987–88	II	44	22	9	13	86	59	75	6th
1988–89	II	46	23	12	11	71	49	81	3rd
1989–90	I	38	13	9	16	42	66	48	15th
1990–91	I	38	20	9	9	50	41	69	3rd
1991–92	I	42	14	15	13	53	61	57	10th
1992–93	PL	42	11	16	15	48	61	49	20th

Edinburgh born Peter Simpson played for St Bernards before coming to England with Kettering Town. In an FA Cup tie against **Crystal Palace** on 24 November 1928, he impressed in a 2–0 defeat and was signed by Palace in 1929. Simpson scored all three goals on his debut against Norwich City, one via a defender. He still holds two goalscoring records for Palace, most League goals in a season, 46 in 1930–31, and 154 in aggregate. He later played for West Ham United, Reading and Aldershot.

DARLINGTON

Year	Div	P	W	D	L	F	A	Pts	Pos
1921–22	IIIN	38	22	6	10	81	37	50	2nd
1922–23	IIIN	38	15	10	13	59	46	40	9th
1923–24	IIIN	42	20	8	14	70	53	48	6th
1924–25	IIIN	42	24	10	8	78	33	58	1st
1925–26	II	42	14	10	18	72	77	38	15th
1926–27	II	42	12	6	24	79	98	30	21st
1927–28	IIIN	42	21	5	16	89	74	47	7th
1928–29	IIIN	42	13	7	22	64	88	33	19th
1929–30	IIIN	42	22	6	14	108	73	50	3rd
1930–31	IIIN	42	16	10	16	71	59	42	11th
1931–32	IIIN	40	17	4	19	66	69	38	11th
1932–33	IIIN	42	10	8	24	66	109	28	22nd

Year	Div	P	W	D	L	F	A	Pts	Pos
1933–34	IIIN	42	13	9	20	70	101	35	16th
1934–35	IIIN	42	21	9	12	80	59	51	5th
1935–36	IIIN	42	17	6	19	74	79	40	12th
1936–37	IIIN	42	8	14	20	66	96	30	22nd
1937–38	IIIN	42	11	10	21	54	79	32	19th
1938–39	IIIN	42	13	7	22	62	92	33	18th
1939–46	Regional Leagues operating								
1946–47	IIIN	42	15	6	21	68	80	36	17th
1947–48	IIIN	42	13	13	16	54	70	39	16th
1948–49	IIIN	42	20	6	16	83	74	46	4th
1949–50	IIIN	42	11	13	18	56	69	35	17th
1950–51	IIIN	46	13	13	20	59	77	39	18th
1951–52	IIIN	46	11	9	26	64	103	31	23rd
1952–53	IIIN	46	14	6	26	58	96	34	21st
1953–54	IIIN	46	12	14	20	50	71	38	21st
1954–55	IIIN	46	14	14	18	62	73	42	15th
1955–56	IIIN	46	16	9	21	60	73	41	15th
1956–57	IIIN	46	17	8	21	82	95	42	18th
1957–58	IIIN	46	17	7	22	78	89	41	20th
1958–59	IV	46	13	16	17	66	68	42	16th
1959–60	IV	46	17	9	20	63	73	43	15th
1960–61	IV	46	18	13	15	78	70	49	7th
1961–62	IV	44	18	9	17	61	73	45	13th
1962–63	IV	46	19	6	21	72	87	44	12th
1963–64	IV	46	14	12	20	66	93	40	19th
1964–65	IV	46	18	6	22	84	87	42	17th
1965–66	IV	46	25	9	12	72	53	59	2nd
1966–67	III	46	13	11	22	47	81	37	22nd
1967–68	IV	46	12	17	17	47	53	41	16th
1968–69	IV	46	17	18	11	62	45	52	5th
1969–70	IV	46	13	10	23	53	73	36	22nd
1970–71	IV	46	17	11	18	58	57	45	12th
1971–72	IV	46	14	11	21	64	82	39	19th
1972–73	IV	46	7	15	24	42	85	29	24th
1973–74	IV	46	13	13	20	40	62	39	20th
1974–75	IV	46	13	10	23	54	67	36	21st
1975–76	IV	46	14	10	22	48	57	38	20th
1976–77	IV	46	18	13	15	59	64	49	11th
1977–78	IV	46	14	13	19	52	59	41	19th
1978–79	IV	46	11	15	20	49	66	37	21st
1979–80	IV	46	9	17	20	50	74	35	22nd
1980–81	IV	46	19	11	16	65	59	49	8th
1981–82	IV	46	15	13	18	61	62	58	13th
1982–83	IV	46	13	13	20	61	71	52	17th
1983–84	IV	46	17	8	21	49	50	59	14th
1984–85	IV	46	24	13	9	66	49	85	3rd
1985–86	III	46	15	13	18	61	78	58	13th
1986–87	III	46	7	16	23	45	77	37	23rd
1987–88	IV	46	18	11	17	71	69	65	13th
1988–89	IV	46	8	18	20	53	76	42	24th
1989–90	GM Vauxhall Conference								
1990–91	IV	46	22	17	7	68	38	83	1st
1991–92	III	46	10	7	29	56	90	37	24th
1992–93	III	42	12	14	16	48	53	50	15th

Darlington were taken over at the end of the 1914–18 war by Darlington Forge Albion, a local works team.

DARWEN

Year	Div	P	W	D	L	F	A	Pts	Pos
1891–92	FL	26	4	3	19	38	112	11	14th
1892–93	II	22	14	2	6	60	36	30	3rd
1893–94	I	30	7	5	18	37	83	19	15th
1894–95	II	30	16	4	10	74	43	36	6th
1895–96	II	30	12	6	12	72	67	30	9th
1896–97	II	30	14	0	16	67	61	28	11th
1897–98	II	30	6	2	22	31	76	14	15th
1898–99	II	34	2	5	27	22	141	9	18th

Darwen are the only Football League club to have suffered as many as three defeats of ten or more goals in one season. In 1898–99 they were beaten 10–0 by Manchester City, Walsall and Loughborough Town in Division Two.

DERBY COUNTY

Year	Div	P	W	D	L	F	A	Pts	Pos
1888–89	FL	22	7	2	13	41	61	16	10th
1889–90	FL	22	9	3	10	43	55	21	7th
1890–91	FL	22	7	1	14	47	81	15	11th
1891–92	FL	26	10	4	12	46	52	24	10th
1892–93	I	30	9	9	12	52	64	27	13th
1893–94	I	30	16	4	10	73	62	36	3rd
1894–95	I	30	7	9	14	45	68	23	15th
1895–96	I	30	17	7	6	68	35	41	2nd
1896–97	I	30	16	4	10	70	50	36	3rd
1897–98	I	30	11	6	13	57	61	28	10th
1898–99	I	34	12	11	11	62	57	35	9th
1899–1900	I	34	14	8	12	45	43	36	6th
1900–01	I	34	12	7	15	55	42	31	12th
1901–02	I	34	13	9	12	39	41	35	6th
1902–03	I	34	16	3	15	50	47	35	9th
1903–04	I	34	9	10	15	58	60	28	14th
1904–05	I	34	12	8	14	37	48	32	11th
1905–06	I	38	14	7	17	39	58	35	15th
1906–07	I	38	9	9	20	41	59	27	19th
1907–08	II	38	21	4	13	77	45	46	6th
1908–09	II	38	16	11	11	55	41	43	5th
1909–10	II	38	22	9	7	72	47	53	4th
1910–11	II	38	17	8	13	73	52	42	6th
1911–12	II	38	23	8	7	74	28	54	1st
1912–13	I	38	17	8	13	69	66	42	7th
1913–14	I	38	8	11	19	55	71	27	20th
1914–15	II	38	23	7	8	71	33	53	1st
1915–19	Regional Leagues operating								
1919–20	I	42	13	12	17	47	57	38	18th
1920–21	I	42	5	16	21	32	58	26	21st
1921–22	II	42	15	9	18	60	64	39	12th
1922–23	II	42	14	11	17	46	50	39	14th
1923–24	II	42	21	9	12	75	42	51	3rd
1924–25	II	42	22	11	9	71	36	55	3rd
1925–26	II	42	25	7	10	77	42	57	2nd

1926–27	I	42	17	7	18	86	73	41	12th
1927–28	I	42	17	10	15	96	83	44	4th
1928–29	I	42	18	10	14	86	71	46	6th
1929–30	I	42	21	8	13	90	82	50	2nd
1930–31	I	42	18	10	14	94	79	46	6th
1931–32	I	42	14	10	18	71	75	38	15th
1932–33	I	42	15	14	13	76	69	44	7th
1933–34	I	42	17	11	14	68	54	45	4th
1934–35	I	42	18	9	15	81	66	45	6th
1935–36	I	42	18	12	12	61	52	48	2nd
1936–37	I	42	21	7	14	96	90	49	4th
1937–38	I	42	15	10	17	66	87	40	13th
1938–39	I	42	19	8	15	66	55	46	6th
1939–46	Regional Leagues operating								
1946–47	I	42	18	5	19	73	79	41	14th
1947–48	I	42	19	12	11	77	57	50	4th
1948–49	I	42	22	9	11	74	55	53	3rd
1949–50	I	42	17	10	15	69	61	44	11th
1950–51	I	42	16	8	18	81	75	40	11th
1951–52	I	42	15	7	20	63	80	37	17th
1952–53	I	42	11	10	21	59	74	32	22nd
1953–54	II	42	12	11	19	64	82	35	18th
1954–55	II	42	7	9	26	53	82	23	22nd
1955–56	IIIN	46	28	7	11	110	55	63	2nd
1956–57	IIIN	46	26	11	9	111	53	63	1st
1957–58	II	42	14	8	20	60	81	36	16th
1958–59	II	42	20	8	14	74	71	48	7th
1959–60	II	42	14	7	21	61	77	35	18th
1960–61	II	42	15	10	17	80	80	40	12th
1961–62	II	42	14	11	17	68	75	39	16th
1962–63	II	42	12	12	18	61	72	36	18th
1963–64	II	42	14	11	17	56	67	39	13th
1964–65	II	42	16	11	15	84	79	43	9th
1965–66	II	42	16	11	15	71	68	43	8th
1966–67	II	42	12	12	18	68	72	36	17th
1967–68	II	42	13	10	19	71	78	36	18th
1968–69	II	42	26	11	5	65	32	63	1st
1969–70	I	42	22	9	11	64	37	53	4th
1970–71	I	42	16	10	16	56	54	42	9th
1971–72	I	42	24	10	8	69	33	58	1st
1972–73	I	42	19	8	15	56	54	46	7th
1973–74	I	42	17	14	11	52	42	48	3rd
1974–75	I	42	21	11	10	67	49	53	1st
1975–76	I	42	21	11	10	75	58	53	4th
1976–77	I	42	9	19	14	50	55	37	15th
1977–78	I	42	14	13	15	54	59	41	12th
1978–79	I	42	10	11	21	38	71	31	19th
1979–80	I	42	11	8	23	47	67	30	21st
1980–81	II	42	15	15	12	57	52	45	6th
1981–82	II	42	12	12	18	53	68	48	16th
1982–83	II	42	10	19	13	49	58	49	13th
1983–84	II	42	11	9	22	36	72	42	20th
1984–85	III	46	19	13	14	65	54	70	7th
1985–86	III	46	23	15	8	80	41	84	3rd
1986–87	II	42	25	9	8	64	38	84	1st
1987–88	I	40	10	13	17	35	45	43	15th
1988–89	I	38	17	7	14	40	38	58	5th

Derby County players parade the Championship trophy at the Baseball Ground in 1972, watched by the famous management team of Brian Clough and Peter Taylor (Popperfoto)

1989–90	I	38	13	7	28	43	40	46	16th
1990–91	I	38	5	9	24	37	75	24	20th
1991–92	II	46	23	9	14	69	51	78	3rd
1992–93	I	46	19	9	18	68	57	66	8th

At the end of the 1909–10 season **Derby County** submitted a proposal to the Football League to increase promotion and relegation to four-up and four-down. Derby had finished fourth in Division Two with 53 points and an inferior goal average to Hull City and Oldham Athletic as well as a point behind Manchester City. The proposal was not accepted.

DONCASTER ROVERS

Year	Div	P	W	D	L	F	A	Pts	Pos
1901–02	II	34	13	8	13	49	58	34	7th
1902–03	II	34	9	7	18	35	72	25	16th
Failed re-election									
1904–05	II	34	3	2	29	23	81	8	18th
Failed re-election									

1923–24	IIIN	42	15	12	15	59	53	42	9th
1924–25	IIIN	42	14	10	18	54	65	38	18th
1925–26	IIIN	42	16	11	15	80	72	43	10th
1926–27	IIIN	42	18	11	13	81	65	47	8th
1927–28	IIIN	42	23	7	12	80	44	53	4th
1928–29	IIIN	42	20	10	12	76	66	50	5th
1929–30	IIIN	42	15	9	18	62	69	39	14th
1930–31	IIIN	42	13	11	18	65	65	37	15th
1931–32	IIIN	40	16	4	20	59	80	36	15th
1932–33	IIIN	42	17	14	11	77	79	48	6th
1933–34	IIIN	42	22	9	11	83	61	53	5th
1934–35	IIIN	42	26	5	11	87	44	57	1st
1935–36	II	42	14	9	19	51	71	37	18th
1936–37	II	42	7	10	25	30	84	24	22nd
1937–38	IIIN	42	21	12	9	74	49	54	2nd
1938–39	IIIN	42	21	14	7	87	47	56	2nd
1939–46	Regional Leagues operating								
1946–47	IIIN	42	33	6	3	123	40	72	1st
1947–48	II	42	9	11	22	40	66	29	21st
1948–49	IIIN	42	20	10	12	53	40	50	3rd
1949–50	IIIN	42	19	17	6	66	38	55	1st
1950–51	II	42	15	13	14	64	68	43	11th
1951–52	II	42	13	12	17	55	60	38	16th
1952–53	II	42	12	16	14	58	64	40	13th
1953–54	II	42	16	9	17	59	63	41	12th
1954–55	II	42	14	7	21	58	95	35	18th
1955–56	II	42	12	11	19	69	96	35	17th
1956–57	II	42	15	10	17	77	77	40	14th
1957–58	II	42	8	11	23	56	88	27	22nd
1958–59	III	46	14	5	27	50	90	33	22nd
1959–60	IV	46	16	10	20	69	76	42	17th
1960–61	IV	46	19	7	20	76	78	45	11th
1961–62	IV	44	11	7	26	60	85	29	21st
1962–63	IV	46	14	14	18	64	77	42	16th
1963–64	IV	46	15	12	19	70	75	42	14th
1964–65	IV	46	20	11	15	84	72	51	9th
1965–66	IV	46	24	11	11	85	54	59	1st
1966–67	III	46	12	8	26	58	117	32	23rd
1967–68	IV	46	18	15	13	66	56	51	10th
1968–69	IV	46	21	17	8	65	38	59	1st
1969–70	III	46	17	12	17	52	54	46	11th
1970–71	III	46	13	9	24	45	66	35	23rd
1971–72	IV	46	16	14	16	56	63	46	12th
1972–73	IV	46	15	12	19	49	58	42	17th
1973–74	IV	46	12	11	23	47	80	35	22nd
1974–75	IV	46	14	12	20	65	79	40	17th
1975–76	IV	46	19	11	16	75	69	49	10th
1976–77	IV	46	21	9	16	61	65	51	8th
1977–78	IV	46	14	17	15	52	65	45	12th
1978–79	IV	46	13	11	22	50	73	37	22nd
1979–80	IV	46	15	14	17	62	63	44	12th
1980–81	IV	46	22	12	12	59	49	56	3rd
1981–82	III	46	13	17	16	55	68	56	19th
1982–83	III	46	9	11	26	57	97	38	23rd
1983–84	IV	46	24	13	9	82	54	85	2nd
1984–85	III	46	17	8	21	72	74	59	14th
1985–86	III	46	16	16	14	45	52	64	11th

1986–87	III	46	14	15	17	56	62	57	13th
1987–88	III	46	8	9	29	40	84	33	24th
1988–89	IV	46	13	10	23	49	78	49	23rd
1989–90	IV	46	14	9	23	53	60	51	20th
1990–91	IV	46	17	14	15	56	46	65	11th
1991–92	IV	42	9	8	25	40	65	35	21st
1992–93	III	42	11	14	17	42	57	47	16th

Between December 1931 and September 1933, **Doncaster Rovers** were unbeaten at home in a run of 33 League games. The sequence was comprised of 23 wins and ten draws.

DURHAM

Year	Div	P	W	D	L	F	A	Pts	Pos
1921–22	IIIN	38	17	3	18	68	67	37	11th
1922–23	IIIN	38	9	10	19	43	59	28	20th
1923–24	IIIN	42	15	9	18	59	60	39	15th
1924–25	IIIN	42	13	13	16	50	68	39	13th
1925–26	IIIN	42	18	6	18	63	70	42	13th
1926–27	IIIN	42	12	6	24	58	105	30	20th
1927–28	IIIN	42	11	7	24	53	100	29	21st

On 6 December 1934 **Durham City** beat Grimsby Town 6–1 in a Division Three (North) match. Billy Bertram scored four goals.

EVERTON

Year	Div	P	W	D	L	F	A	Pts	Pos
1888–89	FL	22	9	2	11	35	46	20	8th
1889–90	FL	22	14	3	5	65	40	31	2nd
1890–91	FL	22	14	1	7	63	29	29	1st
1891–92	FL	26	12	4	10	49	49	28	5th
1892–93	FL	30	16	4	10	74	51	36	3rd
1893–94	I	30	15	3	12	90	57	33	6th
1894–95	I	30	18	6	6	82	50	42	2nd
1896–97	I	30	14	3	13	62	57	31	7th
1897–98	I	30	13	9	8	48	39	35	4th
1898–99	I	34	15	8	11	48	41	38	4th
1899–1900	I	34	13	7	14	47	49	33	11th
1900–01	I	34	16	5	13	55	42	37	7th
1901–02	I	34	17	7	10	53	35	41	2nd
1902–03	I	34	13	6	15	45	47	32	12th
1903–04	I	34	19	5	10	59	32	43	3rd
1904–05	I	34	21	5	8	63	36	47	2nd
1905–06	I	38	15	7	16	70	66	37	11th
1906–07	I	38	20	5	13	70	46	45	3rd
1907–08	I	38	15	6	17	58	64	36	11th
1908–09	I	38	18	10	10	82	57	46	2nd
1909–10	I	38	16	8	14	51	56	40	10th
1910–11	I	38	19	7	12	50	36	45	4th
1911–12	I	38	20	6	12	46	42	46	2nd

1912–13	I	38	15	7	16	48	54	37	11th
1913–14	I	38	12	11	15	46	55	35	15th
1914–15	I	38	19	8	11	76	47	46	1st
1915–19	Regional Leagues operating								
1919–20	I	42	12	14	16	69	68	38	16th
1920–21	I	42	17	13	12	66	55	47	7th
1921–22	I	42	12	12	18	57	55	36	20th
1922–23	I	42	20	7	15	63	59	47	5th
1923–24	I	42	18	13	11	62	53	49	7th
1924–25	I	42	12	11	19	40	60	35	17th
1925–26	I	42	12	18	12	72	70	42	11th
1926–27	I	42	12	10	20	64	90	34	20th
1927–28	I	42	20	13	9	106	66	53	1st
1928–29	I	42	17	4	21	63	75	38	18th
1929–30	I	42	12	11	19	80	92	35	22nd
1930–31	II	42	28	5	9	121	66	61	1st
1931–32	I	42	26	4	12	116	64	56	1st
1932–33	I	42	16	9	17	81	74	41	11th
1933–34	I	42	12	16	14	62	63	40	14th
1934–35	I	42	16	12	14	89	88	44	8th
1935–36	I	42	13	13	16	89	89	39	16th
1936–37	I	42	14	9	19	81	78	37	17th
1937–38	I	42	16	7	19	79	75	39	14th
1938–39	I	42	27	5	10	88	52	59	1st
1939–46	Regional Leagues operating								
1946–47	I	42	17	9	16	62	67	43	10th
1947–48	I	42	17	6	19	52	66	40	14th
1948–49	I	42	13	11	18	41	63	37	18th
1949–50	I	42	10	14	18	42	66	34	18th
1950–51	I	42	12	8	22	48	86	32	22nd
1951–52	II	42	17	10	15	64	58	44	7th
1952–53	II	42	12	14	16	71	75	38	16th
1953–54	II	42	20	16	6	92	58	56	2nd
1954–55	I	42	16	10	16	62	68	42	11th
1955–56	I	42	15	10	17	55	69	40	15th
1956–57	I	42	13	11	18	65	75	37	16th
1958–59	I	42	17	4	21	71	87	38	16th
1959–60	I	42	13	11	18	73	78	37	15th
1960–61	I	42	22	6	14	87	69	50	5th
1961–62	I	42	20	11	11	88	54	51	4th
1962–63	I	42	25	11	6	84	42	61	1st
1963–64	I	42	21	10	11	84	64	52	3rd
1964–65	I	42	17	15	10	69	60	49	4th
1965–66	I	42	15	11	16	56	62	41	11th
1966–67	I	42	19	10	13	65	46	48	6th
1967–68	I	42	23	6	13	67	40	52	5th
1968–69	I	42	21	15	6	77	36	57	3rd
1969–70	I	42	29	8	5	72	34	66	1st
1970–71	I	42	12	13	17	54	60	37	14th
1971–72	I	42	9	18	15	37	48	36	15th
1972–73	I	42	13	11	18	41	49	37	17th
1973–74	I	42	16	12	14	50	48	44	7th
1974–75	I	42	16	18	8	56	42	50	4th
1975–76	I	42	15	12	15	60	66	42	11th
1976–77	I	42	14	14	14	62	64	42	9th
1977–78	I	42	22	11	9	76	45	55	3rd
1978–79	I	42	17	17	8	52	40	51	3rd

1979–80	I	42	9	17	16	43	51	35	19th
1980–81	I	42	13	10	19	55	58	36	15th
1981–82	I	42	17	13	12	56	50	64	8th
1982–83	I	42	18	10	14	66	48	64	7th
1983–84	I	42	16	14	12	44	42	62	7th
1984–85	I	42	28	6	8	88	43	90	1st
1985–86	I	42	26	8	8	87	41	86	2nd
1986–87	I	42	26	8	8	76	31	86	1st
1987–88	I	40	19	13	8	53	27	70	4th
1988–89	I	38	14	12	12	50	45	54	8th
1989–90	I	38	17	8	13	57	46	59	6th
1990–91	I	38	13	12	13	50	46	51	9th
1991–92	I	42	13	14	15	52	51	53	12th
1992–93	PL	42	15	8	19	53	55	53	13th

A television play centred around the **Everton** club in the 1960s was inspired by Alex Young, signed in November 1960 from Hearts, who made 271 League and Cup appearances for the Goodison Park club and scored 87 goals before leaving for Glentoran and then Stockport County. The play was entitled The Golden Vision.

EXETER CITY

Year	Div	P	W	D	L	F	A	Pts	Pos
1920–21	IIIS	42	10	15	17	39	54	35	19th
1921–22	IIIS	42	11	12	19	38	59	34	21st
1922–23	IIIS	42	13	7	22	47	84	33	20th
1923–24	IIIS	42	15	7	20	37	52	37	16th
1924–25	IIIS	42	19	9	14	59	48	47	7th
1925–26	IIIS	42	15	5	22	72	70	35	20th
1926–27	IIIS	42	15	10	17	76	73	40	12th
1927–28	IIIS	42	17	12	13	70	60	46	8th
1928–29	IIIS	42	9	11	22	67	88	29	21st
1929–30	IIIS	42	12	11	19	67	73	35	16th
1930–31	IIIS	42	18	8	17	84	90	42	13th
1931–32	IIIS	42	20	7	15	77	62	47	7th
1932–33	IIIS	42	24	10	8	88	48	58	2nd
1933–34	IIIS	42	16	11	15	68	57	43	9th
1934–35	IIIS	42	16	9	17	70	75	41	11th
1935–36	IIIS	42	8	11	23	59	93	27	22nd
1936–37	IIIS	42	10	12	20	59	88	32	21st
1937–38	IIIS	42	13	12	17	57	70	38	17th
1938–39	IIIS	42	13	14	15	65	82	40	14th
1939–46	Regional Leagues operating								
1946–47	IIIS	42	15	9	18	60	69	39	15th
1947–48	IIIS	42	15	11	16	55	63	41	11th
1948–49	IIIS	42	15	10	17	63	76	40	12th
1949–50	IIIS	42	14	11	17	63	75	39	16th
1950–51	IIIS	46	18	6	22	62	85	42	14th
1951–52	IIIS	46	13	9	24	65	86	35	23rd
1952–53	IIIS	46	13	14	19	61	71	40	17th
1953–54	IIIS	46	20	8	18	68	58	48	9th
1954–55	IIIS	46	11	15	20	47	73	37	22nd
1955–56	IIIS	46	15	10	21	58	77	40	16th
1956–57	IIIS	46	12	13	21	61	79	37	21st

Year	Div	P	W	D	L	F	A	Pts	Pos
1957–58	IIIS	46	11	9	26	57	99	31	24th
1958–59	IV	46	23	11	12	87	61	57	5th
1959–60	IV	46	19	11	16	80	70	49	9th
1960–61	IV	46	14	10	22	66	94	38	21st
1961–62	IV	44	13	11	20	62	77	37	18th
1962–63	IV	46	16	10	20	57	77	42	17th
1963–64	IV	46	20	18	8	62	37	58	4th
1964–65	III	46	12	17	17	51	52	41	17th
1965–66	III	46	12	11	23	53	79	35	22nd
1966–67	IV	46	14	15	17	50	60	43	14th
1967–68	IV	46	11	16	19	45	65	38	20th
1968–69	IV	46	16	11	19	66	65	43	17th
1969–70	IV	46	14	11	21	57	59	39	18th
1970–71	IV	46	17	14	15	67	68	48	9th
1971–72	IV	46	16	11	19	61	68	43	15th
1972–73	IV	46	18	14	14	57	51	50	8th
1973–74	IV	*45	18	8	19	58	55	44	10th

*Scunthorpe United v Exeter City not played

Year	Div	P	W	D	L	F	A	Pts	Pos
1974–75	IV	46	19	11	16	60	63	49	9th
1975–76	IV	46	18	14	14	56	47	50	7th
1976–77	IV	46	25	12	9	70	46	62	2nd
1977–78	III	46	15	14	17	49	59	44	17th
1978–79	III	46	17	15	14	61	56	49	9th
1979–80	III	46	19	10	17	60	68	48	8th
1980–81	III	46	16	13	17	62	66	45	11th
1981–82	III	46	16	9	21	71	84	57	18th
1982–83	III	46	14	12	20	81	104	54	19th
1983–84	III	46	6	15	25	50	84	33	24th
1984–85	IV	46	13	14	19	57	79	53	18th
1985–86	IV	46	13	15	18	47	59	54	21st
1986–87	IV	46	11	23	12	53	49	56	14th
1987–88	IV	46	11	13	22	53	68	46	22nd
1988–89	IV	46	18	6	22	65	68	60	13th
1989–90	IV	46	28	5	13	83	48	89	1st
1990–91	III	46	16	9	21	58	52	57	16th
1991–92	III	46	14	11	21	57	80	53	20th
1992–93	II	46	11	17	18	54	69	50	19th

The first FA Cup tie in which **Exeter City** were involved produced their highest score. In the first qualifying round against Weymouth on 3 October 1908 they won 14–0, with Jim 'Daisy' Bell scoring six goals.

FULHAM

Year	Div	P	W	D	L	F	A	Pts	Pos
1907–08	II	38	22	5	11	82	49	49	4th
1908–09	II	38	13	11	14	58	48	37	10th
1909–10	II	38	14	13	11	51	43	41	7th
1910–11	II	38	15	7	16	52	48	37	10th
1911–12	II	38	16	7	15	66	58	39	8th
1912–13	II	38	17	5	16	65	55	39	9th
1913–14	II	38	16	6	16	46	43	38	11th
1914–15	II	38	15	7	16	53	47	37	12th
1915–19	Regional Leagues operating								
1919–20	II	42	19	9	14	61	50	47	6th

Year	Div	P	W	D	L	F	A	Pts	Pos
1920–21	II	42	16	10	16	43	47	42	9th
1921–22	II	42	18	9	15	57	38	45	7th
1922–23	II	42	16	12	14	43	32	44	10th
1923–24	II	42	10	14	18	45	56	34	20th
1924–25	II	42	15	10	17	41	56	40	12th
1925–26	II	42	11	12	19	46	77	34	19th
1926–27	II	42	13	8	21	58	92	34	18th
1927–28	II	42	13	7	22	68	89	33	21st
1928–29	IIIS	42	21	10	11	101	71	52	5th
1929–30	IIIS	42	18	11	13	87	83	47	7th
1930–31	IIIS	42	18	7	17	77	75	43	9th
1931–32	IIIS	42	24	9	9	111	62	57	1st
1932–33	II	42	20	10	12	78	65	50	3rd
1933–34	II	42	15	7	20	48	67	37	16th
1934–35	II	42	17	12	13	76	56	46	7th
1935–36	II	42	15	14	13	76	52	44	9th
1936–37	II	42	15	13	14	71	61	43	11th
1937–38	II	42	16	11	15	61	57	43	8th
1938–39	II	42	17	10	15	61	55	44	12th
1939–46	Regional Leagues operating								
1946–47	II	42	15	9	18	63	74	39	15th
1947–48	II	42	15	10	17	47	46	40	11th
1948–49	II	42	24	9	9	77	37	57	1st
1949–50	I	42	10	14	18	41	54	34	17th
1950–51	I	42	13	11	18	52	68	37	18th
1951–52	I	42	8	11	23	58	77	27	22nd
1952–53	II	42	17	10	15	81	71	44	8th
1953–54	II	42	17	10	15	98	85	44	8th
1954–55	II	42	14	11	17	76	79	39	14th
1955–56	II	42	20	6	16	89	79	46	9th
1956–57	II	42	19	4	19	84	76	42	11th
1957–58	II	42	20	12	10	97	59	52	5th
1958–59	II	42	27	6	9	96	61	60	2nd
1959–60	I	42	17	10	15	73	80	44	10th
1960–61	I	42	14	8	20	72	95	36	17th
1961–62	I	42	13	7	22	66	74	33	20th
1962–63	I	42	14	10	18	50	71	38	16th
1963–64	I	42	13	13	16	58	65	39	15th
1964–65	I	42	11	12	19	60	78	34	20th
1965–66	I	42	14	7	21	67	85	35	20th
1966–67	I	42	11	12	19	71	83	34	18th
1967–68	I	42	10	7	25	56	98	27	22nd
1968–69	II	42	7	11	24	40	81	25	22nd
1969–70	III	46	20	15	11	81	55	55	4th
1970–71	III	46	24	12	10	68	41	60	2nd
1971–72	II	42	12	10	20	45	68	34	20th
1972–73	II	42	16	12	14	58	49	44	9th
1973–74	II	42	16	10	16	39	43	42	13th
1974–75	II	42	13	16	13	44	39	42	9th
1975–76	II	42	13	14	15	45	47	40	12th
1976–77	II	42	11	13	18	44	61	35	17th
1977–78	II	42	14	13	15	49	49	41	10th
1978–79	II	42	13	15	14	50	47	41	10th
1979–80	II	42	11	7	24	42	74	29	20th
1980–81	III	46	15	13	18	57	64	43	13th
1981–82	III	46	21	15	10	77	51	78	3rd
1982–83	II	42	20	9	13	64	47	69	4th

1983–84	II	42	15	12	15	60	53	57	11th
1984–85	II	42	19	8	15	68	64	65	9th
1985–86	II	42	10	6	26	45	69	36	22nd
1986–87	III	46	12	17	17	59	77	53	18th
1987–88	III	46	19	9	18	69	60	66	9th
1988–89	III	46	22	9	15	69	67	75	4th
1989–90	III	46	12	15	19	55	66	51	20th
1990–91	III	46	10	16	20	41	56	46	21st
1991–92	III	46	19	13	14	57	53	70	9th
1992–93	II	46	16	17	13	57	55	65	12th

Fulham goalkeeper Arthur Reynolds had six consecutive clean sheets in successive seasons 1921–22 and 1922–23. He was the first player with the club to reach 300 League games and completed more than 400 in League and Cup. But for the war years he would have added handsomely to his total.

GAINSBOROUGH TRINITY

1896–97	II	30	12	7	11	50	47	31	7th
1897–98	II	30	12	6	12	50	54	30	9th
1898–99	II	34	10	5	19	56	72	25	14th
1899–1900	II	34	9	7	18	47	75	25	13th
1900–01	II	34	10	10	14	45	60	30	13th
1901–02	II	34	4	11	19	30	80	19	18th
1902–03	II	34	11	7	16	41	59	29	12th
1903–04	II	34	14	3	17	53	60	31	9th
1904–05	II	34	14	8	12	61	58	36	6th
1905–06	II	38	12	4	22	44	57	28	15th
1906–07	II	38	14	5	19	45	72	33	14th
1907–08	II	38	14	7	17	47	71	35	11th
1908–09	II	38	15	8	15	49	70	38	9th
1909–10	II	38	10	6	22	33	75	26	18th
1910–11	II	38	9	11	18	37	55	29	18th
1911–12	II	38	5	13	20	30	64	23	20th

In the first season after **Gainsborough Trinity** were elected to the Football League in 1896 they beat Arsenal 4–1 on 26 December. They repeated this success on 26 March 1898 when they won 1–0 and made a third victory over the Gunners on 29 December 1900, also by a single goal.

GATESHEAD

(South Shields until 1930)

Year	Div	P	W	D	L	F	A	Pts	Pos
1919–20	II	42	15	12	15	58	48	42	9th
1920–21	II	42	17	10	15	61	46	44	8th
1921–22	II	42	17	12	13	43	38	46	6th
1922–23	II	42	15	10	17	35	44	40	13th
1923–24	II	42	17	10	15	49	50	44	9th
1924–25	II	42	12	17	13	42	38	41	9th

1925–26	II	42	18	8	16	74	65	44	10th
1926–27	II	42	11	11	20	71	96	33	19th
1927–28	II	42	7	9	26	56	111	23	22nd
1928–29	IIIN	42	18	8	16	83	74	44	10th
1929–30	IIIN	42	18	10	14	77	74	46	7th
1930–31	IIIN	42	16	13	13	71	73	45	9th
1931–32	IIIN	40	25	7	8	94	48	57	2nd
1932–33	IIIN	42	19	9	14	78	67	47	7th
1933–34	IIIN	42	12	9	21	76	110	33	19th
1934–35	IIIN	42	13	8	21	58	96	34	19th
1935–36	IIIN	42	13	14	15	56	76	40	14th
1936–37	IIIN	42	11	10	21	63	98	32	21st
1937–38	IIIN	42	20	11	11	84	59	51	5th
1938–39	IIIN	42	14	14	14	74	67	42	10th
1939–46	Regional Leagues operating								
1946–47	IIIN	42	16	6	20	62	72	38	14th
1947–48	IIIN	42	19	11	12	75	57	49	4th
1948–49	IIIN	42	16	13	13	69	58	45	5th
1949–50	IIIN	42	23	7	12	87	54	53	2nd
1950–51	IIIN	46	21	8	17	84	62	50	8th
1951–52	IIIN	46	21	11	14	66	49	53	5th
1952–53	IIIN	46	17	15	14	76	60	49	8th
1953–54	IIIN	46	21	13	12	74	55	55	4th
1954–55	IIIN	46	20	12	14	65	69	52	7th
1955–56	IIIN	46	17	11	18	77	84	45	13th
1956–57	IIIN	46	17	10	19	72	90	44	17th
1957–58	IIIN	46	15	15	16	68	76	45	14th
1958–59	IV	46	16	8	22	56	85	40	20th
1959–60	IV	46	12	9	25	58	86	33	22nd

Top goalscorer in one Football League season for **Gateshead** was Jack Wesley with 25 goals in 1933–34.

GILLINGHAM

Year	Div	P	W	D	L	F	A	Pts	Pos
1920–21	III	42	8	12	22	34	74	28	22nd
1921–22	IIIS	42	14	8	20	47	60	36	18th
1922–23	IIIS	42	15	7	20	51	59	37	16th
1923–24	IIIS	42	12	13	17	43	58	37	15th
1924–25	IIIS	42	13	14	15	35	44	40	13th
1925–26	IIIS	42	17	8	17	53	49	42	10th
1926–27	IIIS	42	11	10	21	54	72	32	20th
1927–28	IIIS	42	13	11	18	62	81	37	16th
1928–29	IIIS	42	10	9	23	43	83	29	22nd
1929–30	IIIS	42	11	8	23	51	80	30	21st
1930–31	IIIS	42	14	10	18	61	76	38	16th
1931–32	IIIS	42	10	8	24	40	82	28	21st
1932–33	IIIS	42	18	8	16	72	61	44	7th
1933–34	IIIS	42	11	11	20	75	96	33	17th
1934–35	IIIS	42	11	13	18	55	75	35	20th
1935–36	IIIS	42	14	9	19	66	77	37	16th
1936–37	IIIS	42	18	8	16	52	66	44	11th
1937–38	IIIS	42	10	6	26	36	77	26	22nd
Failed re-election									
1950–51	IIIS	46	13	9	24	69	101	35	22nd

1951–52	IIIS	46	11	13	22	71	81	35	22nd
1952–53	IIIS	46	12	15	19	55	74	39	21st
1953–54	IIIS	46	19	10	17	61	66	48	10th
1954–55	IIIS	46	20	15	11	77	66	55	4th
1955–56	IIIS	46	19	10	17	69	71	48	10th
1956–57	IIIS	46	12	13	21	54	85	37	22nd
1957–58	IIIS	46	13	9	24	52	81	35	22nd
1958–59	IV	46	20	9	17	82	77	49	11th
1959–60	IV	46	21	10	15	74	69	52	7th
1960–61	IV	46	15	13	18	64	66	43	15th
1961–62	IV	44	13	11	20	73	94	37	20th
1962–63	IV	46	22	13	11	71	49	57	5th
1963–64	IV	46	23	14	9	59	30	60	1st
1964–65	III	46	23	9	14	70	50	55	7th
1965–66	III	46	22	8	16	62	54	52	6th
1966–67	III	46	15	16	15	58	62	46	11th
1967–68	III	46	18	12	16	59	63	48	11th
1968–69	III	46	13	15	18	54	63	41	20th
1969–70	III	46	13	13	20	52	64	39	20th
1970–71	III	46	10	13	23	42	67	33	24th
1971–72	IV	46	16	13	17	61	67	45	13th
1972–73	IV	46	19	11	16	63	58	49	9th
1973–74	IV	46	25	12	9	90	49	62	2nd
1974–75	III	46	17	14	15	65	60	48	10th
1975–76	III	46	12	19	15	58	68	43	15th
1976–77	III	46	14	12	18	55	64	44	12th
1977–78	III	46	15	20	11	67	60	50	7th
1978–79	III	46	21	17	8	65	42	59	4th
1979–80	III	46	14	14	18	49	51	42	16th
1980–81	III	46	12	18	16	48	58	42	15th
1981–82	III	46	20	11	15	64	56	71	6th
1982–83	III	46	16	13	17	58	59	61	13th
1983–84	III	46	20	10	16	74	69	70	8th
1984–85	III	46	25	8	13	80	62	83	4th
1985–86	III	46	22	13	11	81	54	79	5th
1986–87	III	46	23	9	14	65	48	78	5th
1987–88	III	46	14	17	15	77	61	59	13th
1988–89	III	46	12	4	30	47	81	40	23rd
1989–90	IV	46	17	11	18	46	48	62	14th
1990–91	IV	46	12	18	16	57	60	54	15th
1991–92	IV	44	15	12	15	63	53	57	11th
1992–93	III	42	9	13	20	48	64	40	21st

Jim Watson scored four hat-tricks in two seasons for **Gillingham**, one in 1935–36 v Aldershot, three the following term against Bristol City, Notts County and Swindon Town.

GLOSSOP NORTH END

Year	Div	P	W	D	L	F	A	Pts	Pos
1898–99	II	34	20	6	8	76	38	46	2nd
1899–1900	I	34	4	10	20	31	74	18	18th
1900–01	II	34	15	8	11	51	33	38	5th
1901–02	II	34	10	12	12	36	40	32	8th
1902–03	II	34	11	7	16	43	58	29	11th
1903–04	II	34	10	6	18	57	64	26	17th
1904–05	II	34	10	10	14	37	46	30	12th
1905–06	II	38	10	8	20	49	71	28	16th
1906–07	II	38	13	6	19	53	79	32	15th
1907–08	II	38	11	8	19	54	74	30	17th
1908–09	II	38	15	8	15	57	53	38	8th
1909–10	II	38	18	7	13	64	57	43	6th
1910–11	II	38	13	8	17	48	62	34	14th
1911–12	II	38	8	12	18	42	56	28	18th
1912–13	II	38	12	8	18	49	68	32	18th
1913–14	II	38	11	6	21	51	67	28	17th
1914–15	II	38	6	6	26	31	87	18	20th

Failed re-election

Glossop North End owed their relatively high status to the generosity of millionaire Samuel Hill-Wood. At one time he was paying as much as £35 a week on wages.

GRIMSBY TOWN

Year	Div	P	W	D	L	F	A	Pts	Pos
1892–93	II	22	11	1	10	42	41	23	4th
1893–94	II	28	15	2	11	71	58	32	5th
1894–95	II	30	18	1	11	79	52	37	9th
1895–96	II	30	20	2	8	82	38	42	3rd
1896–97	II	30	17	4	9	66	45	38	3rd
1897–98	II	30	10	4	16	52	62	24	12th
1898–99	II	34	15	5	14	71	60	35	10th
1899–1900	II	34	17	6	11	67	46	40	6th
1900–01	II	34	20	9	5	60	33	49	1st
1901–02	I	34	13	6	15	44	60	32	15th
1902–03	I	34	8	9	23	43	62	25	17th
1903–04	II	34	14	8	12	50	49	36	6th
1904–05	II	34	11	8	15	33	46	30	13th
1905–06	II	38	15	10	13	46	46	40	8th
1906–07	II	38	16	3	19	57	62	35	15th
1907–08	II	38	11	8	19	43	71	30	18th
1908–09	II	38	14	7	17	41	54	35	13th
1909–10	II	38	9	6	23	50	77	24	19th
Failed re-election									
1911–12	II	38	15	9	14	48	55	39	9th
1912–13	II	38	15	10	13	51	50	40	7th
1913–14	II	38	13	8	17	42	58	34	15th
1914–15	II	38	11	9	18	48	76	31	17th
1915–19	Regional Leagues operating								
1919–20	II	42	10	5	27	34	75	25	22nd
1920–21	III	42	15	9	18	49	59	39	13th
1921–22	IIIN	38	21	8	9	72	47	50	3rd
1922–23	IIIN	38	14	5	19	55	52	33	14th
1923–24	IIIN	42	14	13	15	49	47	41	11th
1924–25	IIIN	42	15	9	18	60	60	39	12th
1925–26	IIIN	42	26	9	7	91	40	61	1st
1926–27	II	42	11	12	19	75	91	34	17th
1927–28	II	42	14	12	16	69	83	40	11th
1928–29	II	42	24	5	13	82	61	53	2nd
1929–30	I	42	15	7	20	73	89	37	18th

Year	Div	P	W	D	L	F	A	Pts	Pos
1930–31	I	42	17	5	20	82	87	39	13th
1931–32	I	42	13	6	23	67	98	32	21st
1932–33	II	42	14	13	15	79	84	41	13th
1933–34	II	42	27	5	10	103	59	59	1st
1934–35	I	42	17	11	14	78	60	45	5th
1935–36	I	42	17	5	20	65	73	39	17th
1936–37	I	42	17	7	18	65	73	39	17th
1937–38	I	42	13	12	17	51	68	38	20th
1938–39	I	42	16	11	15	61	69	43	16th
1939–46	Regional Leagues operating								
1946–47	I	42	13	12	17	61	82	38	16th
1947–48	I	42	8	6	28	45	111	22	22nd
1948–49	II	42	15	10	17	72	76	40	11th
1949–50	II	42	16	8	18	74	73	40	11th
1950–51	II	42	8	12	22	61	95	28	22nd
1951–52	IIIN	46	29	8	9	96	45	66	2nd
1952–53	IIIN	46	21	10	15	75	59	52	5th
1953–54	IIIN	46	16	9	21	51	77	41	17th
1954–55	IIIN	46	13	8	25	47	78	34	23rd
1955–56	IIIN	46	31	6	9	76	29	68	1st
1956–57	II	42	17	5	20	61	62	39	16th
1957–58	II	42	17	6	19	86	83	40	13th
1958–59	II	42	9	10	23	62	90	28	21st
1959–60	III	46	18	16	12	87	70	52	4th
1960–61	III	46	20	10	16	77	69	50	6th
1961–62	III	46	28	6	12	80	56	62	2nd
1962–63	II	42	11	13	18	55	66	35	19th
1963–64	II	42	9	14	19	47	75	32	21st
1964–65	III	46	16	17	13	68	67	49	10th
1965–66	III	46	17	13	16	68	62	47	11th
1966–67	III	46	17	9	20	61	68	43	17th
1967–68	III	46	14	9	23	52	69	37	22nd
1968–69	IV	46	9	15	22	47	69	33	23rd
1969–70	IV	46	14	15	17	54	58	43	16th
1970–71	IV	46	18	7	21	57	71	43	19th
1971–72	IV	46	28	7	11	88	56	63	1st
1972–73	III	46	20	8	18	67	61	48	9th
1973–74	III	46	18	15	13	67	50	51	6th
1974–75	III	46	15	13	18	55	64	43	16th
1975–76	III	46	15	10	21	62	74	40	18th
1976–77	III	46	12	9	25	45	69	33	23rd
1977–78	IV	46	21	11	14	57	51	53	6th
1978–79	IV	46	26	9	11	82	49	61	2nd
1979–80	III	46	26	10	10	73	42	62	1st
1980–81	II	42	15	15	12	44	42	45	7th
1981–82	II	42	11	13	18	53	65	46	17th
1982–83	II	42	12	11	19	45	70	47	19th
1983–84	II	42	19	13	10	60	47	70	5th
1984–85	II	42	18	8	16	72	64	62	10th
1985–86	II	42	14	10	18	58	52	52	15th
1986–87	II	42	10	14	18	39	59	44	21st
1987–88	III	46	12	14	20	48	59	50	22nd
1988–89	IV	46	17	15	14	65	59	66	9th
1989–90	IV	46	22	13	11	70	47	79	2nd
1990–91	III	46	24	11	11	66	34	83	3rd
1991–92	II	46	14	11	21	47	62	53	19th
1992–93	I	46	19	7	20	58	57	64	9th

As a protest against having to play in the qualifying rounds of the FA Cup in 1890–91, **Grimsby Town**, then members of the Football Alliance, sent their reserve team to play Ecclesfield on 11 October 1890 in a first qualifying round. They lost 8–2.

HALIFAX TOWN

Year	Div	P	W	D	L	F	A	Pts	Pos
1921–22	IIIN	38	10	9	19	56	76	29	19th
1922–23	IIIN	38	17	7	14	53	46	41	7th
1923–24	IIIN	42	15	10	17	42	59	40	14th
1924–25	IIIN	42	16	11	15	56	52	43	9th
1925–26	IIIN	42	17	11	14	53	50	45	5th
1926–27	IIIN	42	21	11	10	70	53	53	4th
1927–28	IIIN	42	13	15	14	73	71	41	12th
1928–29	IIIN	42	13	13	16	63	62	39	13th
1929–30	IIIN	42	10	8	24	44	79	28	21st
1930–31	IIIN	42	13	9	20	55	89	35	17th
1931–32	IIIN	40	13	8	19	61	87	34	17th
1932–33	IIIN	42	15	8	19	71	90	38	15th
1933–34	IIIN	42	20	4	18	80	91	44	9th
1934–35	IIIN	42	25	5	12	76	67	55	2nd
1935–36	IIIN	42	15	7	20	57	61	37	17th
1936–37	IIIN	42	18	9	15	68	63	45	7th
1937–38	IIIN	42	12	12	18	44	66	36	18th
1938–39	IIIN	42	13	16	13	52	54	42	12th
1939–46	Regional Leagues operating								
1946–47	IIIN	42	8	6	28	43	92	22	22nd
1947–48	IIIN	42	7	13	22	43	76	27	21st
1948–49	IIIN	42	12	11	19	45	62	35	19th
1949–50	IIIN	42	12	8	22	38	85	32	21st
1950–51	IIIN	46	11	12	23	50	69	34	22nd
1951–52	IIIN	46	14	7	25	61	97	35	20th
1952–53	IIIN	46	16	15	15	68	68	47	14th
1953–54	IIIN	46	12	10	24	44	73	34	23rd
1954–55	IIIN	46	15	13	18	63	67	43	14th
1955–56	IIIN	46	14	11	21	66	76	39	19th
1956–57	IIIN	46	21	7	18	65	70	49	11th
1957–58	IIIN	46	20	11	15	83	69	51	7th
1958–59	III	46	21	8	17	80	77	50	9th
1959–60	III	46	18	10	18	70	72	46	15th
1960–61	III	46	16	17	13	71	78	49	9th
1961–62	III	46	15	10	21	62	84	40	18th
1962–63	III	46	9	12	25	64	106	30	24th
1963–64	IV	46	17	14	15	77	77	48	10th
1964–65	IV	46	11	6	29	54	103	28	23rd
1965–66	IV	46	15	11	20	67	75	41	15th
1966–67	IV	46	15	14	17	59	68	44	12th
1967–68	IV	46	15	16	15	52	49	46	11th
1968–69	IV	46	20	17	9	53	37	57	2nd
1969–70	III	46	14	15	17	47	63	43	18th
1970–71	III	46	22	12	12	74	55	56	3rd
1971–72	III	46	13	12	21	48	61	38	17th
1972–73	III	46	13	15	18	43	53	41	20th

Year	Div	P	W	D	L	F	A	Pts	Pos
1973–74	III	46	14	21	11	48	51	49	9th
1974–75	III	46	13	17	16	49	65	43	17th
1975–76	III	46	11	13	22	41	61	35	24th
1976–77	IV	46	11	14	21	47	58	36	21st
1977–78	IV	46	10	21	15	52	62	41	20th
1978–79	IV	46	9	8	29	39	72	26	23rd
1979–80	IV	46	13	13	20	46	72	39	18th
1980–81	IV	46	11	12	23	44	71	34	23rd
1981–82	IV	46	9	22	15	51	72	49	19th
1982–83	IV	46	16	12	18	59	66	60	11th
1983–84	IV	46	12	12	22	55	89	48	21st
1984–85	IV	46	14	5	26	42	69	50	21st
1985–86	IV	46	14	12	20	60	71	54	20th
1986–87	IV	46	15	10	21	59	74	55	15th
1987–88	IV	46	14	14	18	54	59	55	18th
1988–89	IV	46	13	11	22	69	75	50	21st
1989–90	IV	46	12	13	21	57	65	49	23rd
1990–91	IV	46	12	10	24	59	79	46	22nd
1991–92	IV	42	10	8	24	34	75	38	20th
1992–93	III	42	9	9	24	45	68	36	22nd

Relegated to GM-Vauxhall Conference

Halifax Town's most prolific marksman Ernest Dixon, who scored a club record 129 League goals between 1922 and 1929, was leading scorer in seven consecutive seasons before moving to Huddersfield Town in September 1929.

HARTLEPOOL UNITED

(Hartlepools United until 1968, Hartlepool until 1977)

Year	Div	P	W	D	L	F	A	Pts	Pos
1921–22	IIIN	38	17	8	13	52	39	42	4th
1922–23	IIIN	38	10	12	16	48	54	32	15th
1923–24	IIIN	42	7	11	24	33	70	25	21st
1924–25	IIIN	42	12	11	19	45	63	35	20th
1925–26	IIIN	42	18	8	16	82	73	44	6th
1926–27	IIIN	42	14	6	22	66	81	34	17th
1927–28	IIIN	42	16	6	20	69	81	38	15th
1928–29	IIIN	42	10	6	26	59	112	26	21st
1929–30	IIIN	42	17	11	14	81	74	45	8th
1930–31	IIIN	42	12	6	24	67	86	30	20th
1931–32	IIIN	40	16	5	19	78	100	37	13th
1932–33	IIIN	42	16	7	19	87	116	39	14th
1933–34	IIIN	42	16	7	19	89	93	39	11th
1934–35	IIIN	42	17	7	18	80	78	41	12th
1935–36	IIIN	42	15	12	15	57	61	42	8th
1936–37	IIIN	42	19	7	16	75	69	45	6th
1937–38	IIIN	42	10	12	20	53	80	32	20th
1938–39	IIIN	42	12	7	23	55	94	31	21st
1939–46	Regional Leagues operating								
1946–47	IIIN	42	15	9	18	64	73	39	13th
1947–48	IIIN	42	14	8	20	53	73	36	19th
1948–49	IIIN	42	14	10	18	45	58	38	16th
1949–50	IIIN	42	14	5	23	52	79	33	18th
1950–51	IIIN	46	16	7	23	64	66	39	16th
1951–52	IIIN	46	21	8	17	71	65	50	9th
1952–53	IIIN	46	16	14	16	57	61	46	17th
1953–54	IIIN	46	13	14	19	59	65	40	18th
1954–55	IIIN	46	25	5	16	64	49	55	5th
1955–56	IIIN	46	26	5	15	81	60	57	4th
1956–57	IIIN	46	25	9	12	90	63	59	2nd
1957–58	IIIN	46	16	12	18	73	76	44	17th
1958–59	IV	46	15	10	21	74	88	40	19th
1959–60	IV	46	10	7	29	59	109	27	24th
1960–61	IV	46	12	8	26	71	83	32	23rd
1961–62	IV	44	8	11	25	52	101	27	22nd
1962–63	IV	46	7	11	28	56	104	25	24th
1963–64	IV	46	12	9	25	54	93	33	23rd
1964–65	IV	46	15	13	18	61	85	43	15th
1965–66	IV	46	16	8	22	63	75	40	18th
1966–67	IV	46	22	7	17	66	64	51	8th
1967–68	IV	46	25	10	11	60	46	60	3rd
1968–69	III	46	10	19	17	40	66	39	22nd
1969–70	IV	46	10	10	26	42	82	30	23rd
1970–71	IV	46	8	12	26	34	74	28	23rd
1971–72	IV	46	17	6	23	58	69	40	18th
1972–73	IV	46	12	17	17	34	49	41	20th
1973–74	IV	46	16	12	18	48	47	44	11th
1974–75	IV	46	16	11	19	52	62	43	13th
1975–76	IV	46	16	10	20	62	78	42	14th
1976–77	IV	46	10	12	24	47	73	32	22nd
1977–78	IV	46	15	7	24	51	84	37	21st
1978–79	IV	46	13	18	15	57	66	44	13th
1979–80	IV	46	14	10	22	59	66	38	19th
1980–81	IV	46	20	9	17	64	61	49	9th
1981–82	IV	46	13	16	17	73	84	55	14th
1982–83	IV	46	13	9	24	46	76	48	22nd
1983–84	IV	46	10	10	26	47	85	40	23rd
1984–85	IV	46	14	10	22	54	67	52	18th
1985–86	IV	46	20	10	16	68	67	70	6th
1986–87	IV	46	11	18	17	44	65	51	18th
1987–88	IV	46	15	14	17	50	57	59	16th
1988–89	IV	46	14	10	22	50	78	52	19th
1989–90	IV	46	15	10	21	66	88	55	19th
1990–91	IV	46	24	10	12	67	48	82	3rd
1991–92	III	46	18	11	17	57	57	65	11th
1992–93	II	46	14	12	20	42	60	54	16th

After Andy Saville scored an 82nd minute penalty for **Hartlepool United** against Crystal Palace in an FA Cup third round tie on 2 January 1993, the team completed 1,227 minutes of League and Cup football without scoring another goal.

Their goal famine ended on 6 March at Blackpool, when Saville scored in the 51st minute. Saville could have avoided a League record by scoring from a penalty at Chester City on 20 February, but his effort was saved by Billy Stewart. Coventry City had completed 11 League games without a goal in 1919–20 and Hartlepool equalled this record.

HEREFORD UNITED

Year	Div	P	W	D	L	F	A	Pts	Pos
1972–73	IV	46	23	12	11	56	38	58	2nd
1973–74	III	46	14	15	17	53	57	43	18th
1974–75	III	46	16	14	16	64	66	46	12th
1975–76	III	46	26	11	9	86	55	63	1st
1976–77	II	42	8	15	19	57	78	31	22nd
1977–78	III	42	9	14	23	34	60	32	23rd
1978–79	IV	46	15	13	18	53	53	43	14th
1979–80	IV	46	11	14	21	38	52	36	21st
1980–81	IV	46	11	13	22	38	62	35	22nd
1981–82	IV	46	16	19	11	64	58	67	10th
1982–83	IV	46	11	8	27	42	79	41	24th
1983–84	IV	46	16	15	15	54	53	63	11th
1984–85	IV	46	22	11	13	65	47	77	5th
1985–86	IV	46	18	10	18	74	73	64	10th
1986–87	IV	46	14	11	21	60	61	53	16th
1987–88	IV	46	14	12	20	41	59	54	19th
1988–89	IV	46	14	16	16	66	72	58	15th
1989–90	IV	46	15	10	21	56	62	55	17th
1990–91	IV	46	13	14	19	53	58	53	17th
1991–92	IV	42	12	8	22	44	57	44	17th
1992–93	III	42	10	15	17	47	60	45	17th

On 6 September 1992, **Hereford United** had four players sent off at Northampton Town but still managed to draw 1–1 in a Division Three match. It was the first time four players from the same team had been dismissed in a Football League game.

HUDDERSFIELD TOWN

Year	Div	P	W	D	L	F	A	Pts	Pos
1910–11	II	38	13	8	17	57	58	34	13th
1911–12	II	38	13	6	19	50	64	32	17th
1912–13	II	38	17	9	12	66	40	43	5th
1913–14	II	38	13	8	17	47	53	34	13th
1914–15	II	38	17	8	13	61	42	42	8th
1915–19	Regional Leagues operating								
1919–20	II	42	28	8	6	97	38	64	2nd
1920–21	I	42	15	9	18	42	49	39	17th
1921–22	I	42	15	9	18	53	54	39	14th
1922–23	I	42	21	11	10	60	32	53	3rd
1923–24	I	42	23	11	8	60	33	57	1st
1924–25	I	42	21	16	5	69	28	58	1st
1925–26	I	42	23	11	8	92	60	57	1st
1926–27	I	42	17	17	8	76	60	51	2nd
1927–28	I	42	22	7	13	91	68	51	2nd
1928–29	I	42	14	11	17	70	61	39	16th
1929–30	I	42	17	9	16	63	69	43	10th
1930–31	I	42	18	12	12	81	65	48	5th
1931–32	I	42	19	10	13	80	63	48	4th
1932–33	I	42	18	11	13	66	53	47	6th
1933–34	I	42	23	10	9	90	61	56	2nd
1934–35	I	42	14	10	18	76	71	38	16th
1935–36	I	42	18	12	12	59	56	48	3rd

Year	Div	P	W	D	L	F	A	Pts	Pos
1936–37	I	42	12	15	15	62	64	39	15th
1937–38	I	42	17	5	20	55	68	39	15th
1938–39	I	42	12	11	19	58	64	35	19th
1939–46	Regional Leagues operating								
1946–47	I	42	13	7	22	53	79	33	20th
1947–48	I	42	12	12	18	51	60	36	19th
1948–49	I	42	12	10	20	40	69	34	20th
1949–50	I	42	14	9	19	52	73	37	15th
1950–51	I	42	15	6	21	64	92	36	19th
1951–52	I	42	10	8	24	49	82	28	21st
1952–53	II	42	24	10	8	84	33	58	2nd
1953–54	I	42	20	11	11	78	61	51	3rd
1954–55	I	42	14	13	15	63	68	41	12th
1955–56	I	42	14	7	21	54	83	35	21st
1956–57	II	42	18	6	18	68	74	42	12th
1957–58	II	42	14	16	12	63	66	44	9th
1958–59	II	42	16	8	18	62	55	40	14th
1959–60	II	42	19	9	14	73	52	47	6th
1960–61	II	42	13	9	20	62	71	35	20th
1961–62	II	42	16	12	14	67	59	44	7th
1962–63	II	42	17	14	11	63	50	48	6th
1963–64	II	42	15	10	17	57	64	40	12th
1964–65	II	42	17	10	15	53	51	44	8th
1965–66	II	42	19	13	10	62	36	51	4th
1966–67	II	42	20	9	13	58	46	49	6th
1967–68	II	42	13	12	17	46	61	38	14th
1968–69	II	42	17	12	13	53	46	46	6th
1969–70	II	42	24	12	6	68	37	60	1st
1970–71	I	42	11	14	17	40	49	36	15th
1971–72	I	42	6	13	23	27	59	25	22nd
1972–73	II	42	8	17	17	36	56	33	21st
1973–74	III	46	17	13	16	56	55	47	10th
1974–75	III	46	11	10	25	47	76	32	24th
1975–76	IV	46	21	14	11	56	41	56	5th
1976–77	IV	46	19	12	15	60	49	50	9th
1977–78	IV	46	15	15	16	63	55	45	11th
1978–79	IV	46	18	11	17	57	53	47	9th
1979–80	IV	46	27	12	7	101	48	66	1st
1980–81	III	46	21	14	11	71	40	56	4th
1981–82	III	46	15	12	19	64	59	57	17th
1982–83	III	46	23	13	10	84	49	82	3rd
1983–84	II	42	14	15	13	56	49	57	12th
1984–85	II	42	15	10	17	52	64	55	13th
1985–86	II	42	14	10	18	51	67	52	16th
1986–87	II	42	13	12	17	54	61	51	17th
1987–88	II	44	6	10	28	41	100	28	23rd
1988–89	III	46	17	9	20	63	73	60	14th
1989–90	III	46	17	14	15	61	62	65	8th
1990–91	III	46	18	13	15	57	51	67	11th
1991–92	III	46	22	12	12	59	38	78	3rd
1992–93	II	46	17	9	20	54	61	60	15th

In the 1923–24 season, when most League teams played the same opponents on successive Saturdays, Charlie Wilson scored a hat-trick for **Huddersfield Town** against Arsenal in a 3–1 win at Highbury on 15 December and followed this feat with another treble in a 6–1 victory over the Gunners at Huddersfield on 22 December.

HULL CITY

Year	Div	P	W	D	L	F	A	Pts	Pos
1905–06	II	38	19	6	13	67	54	44	5th
1906–07	II	38	15	7	16	65	57	37	9th
1907–08	II	38	21	4	13	73	62	46	8th
1908–09	II	38	19	6	13	63	39	44	4th
1909–10	II	38	23	7	8	80	46	53	3rd
1910–11	II	38	14	16	8	55	39	44	5th
1911–12	II	38	17	8	13	54	51	42	7th
1912–13	II	38	15	6	17	60	56	36	12th
1913–14	II	38	16	9	13	53	37	41	7th
1914–15	II	38	19	5	14	65	54	43	7th
1915–19	Regional Leagues operating								
1919–20	II	42	18	6	18	78	72	42	11th
1920–21	II	42	10	20	12	43	53	40	13th
1921–22	II	42	19	10	13	51	41	48	5th
1922–23	II	42	14	14	14	43	45	42	12th
1923–24	II	42	10	17	15	46	51	37	17th
1924–25	II	42	15	11	16	50	49	41	10th
1925–26	II	42	16	9	17	63	61	41	13th
1926–27	II	42	20	7	15	63	52	47	7th
1927–28	II	42	12	15	15	41	54	39	14th
1928–29	II	42	13	14	15	58	63	40	12th
1929–30	II	42	14	7	21	51	78	35	21st
1930–31	IIIN	42	20	10	12	99	55	50	6th
1931–32	IIIN	40	20	5	15	82	53	45	8th
1932–33	IIIN	42	26	7	9	100	45	59	1st
1933–34	II	42	13	12	17	52	68	38	15th
1934–35	II	42	16	8	18	63	74	40	13th
1935–36	II	42	5	10	27	47	111	20	22nd
1936–37	IIIN	42	17	12	13	68	69	46	5th
1937–38	IIIN	42	20	13	9	80	43	53	3rd
1938–39	IIIN	42	18	10	14	83	74	46	7th
1939–46	Regional Leagues operating								
1946–47	IIIN	42	16	8	18	49	53	40	11th
1947–48	IIIN	42	18	11	13	59	48	47	5th
1948–49	IIIN	42	27	11	4	93	28	65	1st
1949–50	II	42	17	11	14	64	72	45	7th
1950–51	II	42	16	11	15	74	70	43	10th
1951–52	II	42	13	11	18	60	70	37	18th
1952–53	II	42	14	8	20	57	69	36	18th
1953–54	II	42	16	6	20	64	66	38	15th
1954–55	II	42	12	10	20	44	69	34	19th
1955–56	II	42	10	6	26	53	97	26	22nd
1956–57	IIIN	46	21	10	15	84	69	52	8th
1957–58	IIIN	46	19	15	12	78	67	53	5th
1958–59	III	46	26	9	11	90	55	61	2nd
1959–60	II	42	10	10	22	48	76	30	21st
1960–61	III	46	17	12	17	73	73	46	11th
1961–62	III	46	20	8	18	67	54	48	10th
1962–63	III	46	19	10	17	74	69	48	10th
1963–64	III	46	16	17	13	73	68	49	8th
1964–65	III	46	23	12	11	91	57	58	4th
1965–66	III	46	31	7	8	109	62	69	1st
1966–67	II	42	16	7	19	77	72	39	12th
1967–68	II	42	12	13	17	58	73	37	17th
1968–69	II	42	13	16	13	59	52	42	11th
1969–70	II	42	15	11	16	72	70	41	13th
1970–71	II	42	19	13	10	54	41	51	5th
1971–72	II	42	14	10	18	49	53	38	12th
1972–73	II	42	14	12	16	64	59	40	13th
1973–74	II	42	13	17	12	46	47	43	9th
1974–75	II	42	15	14	13	40	53	44	8th
1975–76	II	42	14	11	17	45	49	39	14th
1976–77	II	42	10	17	15	45	53	37	14th
1977–78	II	42	8	12	22	34	52	28	22nd
1978–79	III	46	19	11	16	66	61	49	8th
1979–80	III	46	12	16	18	51	69	40	20th
1980–81	III	46	8	16	22	40	71	32	24th
1981–82	IV	46	19	12	15	70	61	69	8th
1982–83	IV	46	25	15	6	75	34	90	2nd
1983–84	III	46	23	14	9	71	38	53	4th
1984–85	III	46	25	12	9	88	49	87	3rd
1985–86	II	42	17	13	12	65	55	64	6th
1986–87	II	42	13	14	15	41	55	53	14th
1987–88	II	44	14	15	15	54	60	57	15th
1988–89	II	46	11	14	21	52	68	47	21st
1989–90	II	46	14	16	16	58	65	58	14th
1990–91	II	46	10	15	21	57	85	45	24th
1991–92	III	46	16	11	19	54	54	59	14th
1992–93	II	46	13	11	22	46	69	50	20th

On Easter Monday 1947, **Hull City** beat Carlisle United 2–0 in a Division Three (North) match. Ten of that team then had to turn out for the reserves in the evening of the same day. Their second team had travelled to Scunthorpe in the afternoon for a Midland League game and were due back to play Filey Town in the East Riding Cup. They were delayed on the way back, so all first team players except Ron Brown had to play. His replacement Denis Thompson scored five times in an 8–2 win.

IPSWICH TOWN

Year	Div	P	W	D	L	F	A	Pts	Pos
1938–39	IIIS	42	16	12	14	62	52	44	7th
1939–46	Regional Leagues operating								
1946–47	IIIS	42	16	14	12	61	53	46	6th
1947–48	IIIS	42	23	3	16	67	61	49	4th
1948–49	IIIS	42	18	9	15	78	77	45	7th
1949–50	IIIS	42	12	11	19	57	86	35	17th
1950–51	IIIS	46	23	6	17	69	58	52	8th
1951–52	IIIS	46	16	9	21	53	74	41	17th
1952–53	IIIS	46	13	15	18	60	69	41	16th
1953–54	IIIS	46	27	10	9	82	51	64	1st
1954–55	II	42	11	6	25	57	92	28	21st
1955–56	IIIS	46	25	14	7	106	60	64	3rd
1956–57	IIIS	46	25	9	12	101	54	59	1st
1957–58	II	42	16	12	14	68	69	44	8th
1958–59	II	42	17	6	19	62	77	40	16th
1959–60	II	42	19	6	17	78	68	44	11th
1960–61	II	42	26	7	9	100	55	59	1st
1961–62	I	42	24	8	10	93	67	56	1st

Ipswich Town players celebrate promotion to the new Premier League as champions of Division Two in 1992. Chris Kiwomya holds the trophy (Allsport/Ben Radford)

Year	Div	P	W	D	L	F	A	Pts	Pos
1962–63	I	42	12	11	19	59	78	35	17th
1963–64	I	42	9	7	26	56	121	25	22nd
1964–65	II	42	15	17	10	74	67	47	5th
1965–66	II	42	15	9	18	58	66	39	15th
1966–67	II	42	17	16	9	70	54	50	5th
1967–68	II	42	22	15	5	79	44	59	1st
1968–69	I	42	15	11	16	59	60	41	12th
1969–70	I	42	10	11	21	40	63	31	18th
1970–71	I	42	12	10	20	42	48	34	19th
1971–72	I	42	11	16	15	39	53	38	13th
1972–73	I	42	17	14	11	55	45	48	4th
1973–74	I	42	18	11	13	67	58	47	4th
1974–75	I	42	23	5	14	66	44	51	3rd
1975–76	I	42	16	14	12	54	48	46	6th
1976–77	I	42	22	8	12	66	39	56	3rd
1977–78	I	42	11	13	18	47	61	35	18th
1978–79	I	42	20	9	13	63	49	49	6th
1979–80	I	42	22	9	11	68	39	53	3rd
1980–81	I	42	23	10	9	77	43	56	2nd
1981–82	I	42	26	5	11	75	53	83	2nd
1982–83	I	42	15	13	14	64	50	58	9th
1983–84	I	42	15	8	19	55	57	53	12th
1984–85	I	42	13	11	18	46	57	50	17th
1985–86	I	42	11	8	23	32	55	41	20th
1986–87	II	42	17	13	12	59	43	64	5th
1987–88	II	44	19	9	16	61	73	66	8th
1988–89	II	46	22	7	17	71	61	73	8th
1989–90	II	46	19	12	15	67	66	69	9th
1990–91	II	46	13	18	15	60	68	57	14th
1991–92	II	46	24	12	10	70	50	84	1st
1992–93	PL	42	12	16	14	50	55	52	16th

Ipswich Town were the first Football League club to employ two Dutch players in Arnold Muhren and Frans Thijssen and one from the Soviet Union in Sergei Baltacha. They also marked their first season in the Premier League by signing the first Bulgar, Bontcho Guentchev.

LEEDS UNITED

Year	Div	P	W	D	L	F	A	Pts	Pos
1920–21	II	42	14	10	18	40	45	38	14th
1921–22	II	42	16	13	16	58	38	45	8th
1922–23	II	42	18	11	13	43	36	47	7th
1923–24	II	42	21	12	9	61	35	54	1st
1924–25	I	42	11	12	19	46	59	34	18th
1925–26	I	42	14	8	20	64	76	36	19th
1926–27	I	42	11	8	23	69	88	30	21st
1927–28	II	42	25	7	10	98	49	57	2nd
1928–29	I	42	16	9	17	71	84	41	13th
1929–30	I	42	20	6	16	79	63	46	5th
1930–31	I	42	12	7	23	68	81	31	21st
1931–32	II	42	22	10	10	78	54	54	2nd
1932–33	I	42	15	14	13	59	62	44	8th
1933–34	I	42	17	8	17	75	66	42	9th
1934–35	I	42	13	12	17	75	92	38	18th
1935–36	I	42	15	11	16	66	64	41	11th
1936–37	I	42	15	4	23	60	80	34	19th
1937–38	I	42	14	15	13	64	69	43	9th
1938–39	I	42	16	9	17	59	67	41	13th
1939–46	Regional Leagues operating								
1946–47	I	42	6	6	30	45	90	18	22nd
1947–48	II	42	14	8	20	62	72	36	18th
1948–49	II	42	12	13	17	55	63	37	15th
1949–50	II	42	17	13	7	54	45	47	5th
1950–51	II	42	20	8	14	63	55	48	5th
1951–52	II	42	18	11	13	59	57	47	6th
1952–53	II	42	14	15	13	71	63	43	10th
1953–54	II	42	15	13	14	89	81	43	10th
1954–55	II	42	23	7	12	70	53	53	4th
1955–56	II	42	23	6	13	80	60	52	2nd
1956–57	I	42	15	14	13	72	63	44	8th
1957–58	I	42	14	9	19	51	63	37	17th
1958–59	I	42	15	9	18	57	74	39	15th
1959–60	I	42	12	10	20	65	92	34	21st
1960–61	II	42	14	10	18	75	73	38	14th
1961–62	II	42	12	12	18	50	61	36	19th
1962–63	II	42	19	10	13	79	53	48	5th
1963–64	II	42	24	15	3	71	34	63	1st
1964–65	I	42	26	9	7	83	52	61	2nd
1965–66	I	42	23	9	10	79	38	55	2nd
1966–67	I	42	22	11	9	62	42	55	4th
1967–68	I	42	22	9	11	71	41	53	4th
1968–69	I	42	27	13	2	66	26	67	1st
1969–70	I	42	21	15	6	84	49	57	2nd
1970–71	I	42	27	10	5	72	30	64	2nd
1971–72	I	42	24	9	9	73	31	57	2nd
1972–73	I	42	21	11	10	71	45	53	3rd
1973–74	I	42	24	14	4	66	31	62	1st
1974–75	I	42	16	13	10	57	49	45	9th
1975–76	I	42	21	9	12	65	46	51	5th
1976–77	I	42	15	12	15	48	51	42	10th
1977–78	I	42	18	10	14	63	53	46	9th
1978–79	I	42	18	14	10	70	52	50	5th
1979–80	I	42	13	14	15	46	50	40	11th
1980–81	I	42	17	10	15	39	47	44	9th

Don Revie's great Leeds side, pictured at the start of their first Championship season, 1968–69. Their points total of 67 that season stood as a record for the next ten years (Popperfoto)

1981–82	I	42	10	12	20	39	61	42	20th
1982–83	II	42	13	21	8	51	46	60	8th
1983–84	II	42	16	12	14	55	56	60	10th
1984–85	II	42	19	12	11	66	43	69	7th
1985–86	II	42	15	8	19	56	72	53	14th
1986–87	II	42	19	11	12	58	44	68	4th
1987–88	II	44	19	12	13	61	51	69	7th
1988–89	II	46	17	16	13	59	50	67	10th
1989–90	II	46	23	13	8	79	52	85	1st
1990–91	I	38	19	7	12	65	47	64	4th
1991–92	I	42	22	16	4	74	37	82	1st
1992–93	PL	42	12	15	15	57	62	51	17th

In 1926–27, Tom Jennings scored three successive hat-tricks for **Leeds United** in a sequence of 3 4 4 2 1 1 1. This Scottish born centre-forward – Thomas Hamilton Oliver by name – scored 112 goals in 167 League appearances for the club.

LEICESTER CITY

(Leicester Fosse until 1919)

Year	Div	P	W	D	L	F	A	Pts	Pos
1894–95	II	30	15	8	7	72	53	38	4th
1895–96	II	30	14	4	12	57	44	32	8th
1896–97	II	30	13	4	13	59	57	30	9th
1897–98	II	30	13	7	10	46	35	33	7th
1898–99	II	34	18	9	7	64	42	45	3rd
1899–1900	II	34	17	9	8	53	36	43	5th
1900–01	II	34	11	10	13	39	37	32	11th
1901–02	II	34	12	5	17	38	56	29	14th
1902–03	II	34	10	8	16	41	65	28	15th
1903–04	II	34	6	10	18	42	82	22	18th
1904–05	II	34	11	7	17	40	55	29	14th
1905–06	II	38	15	12	11	53	48	42	7th

1906–07	II	38	20	8	10	62	39	48	3rd
1907–08	II	38	21	10	7	72	47	52	2nd
1908–09	I	38	8	9	21	54	102	25	20th
1909–10	II	38	20	4	14	79	58	44	5th
1910–11	II	38	14	5	19	52	62	33	15th
1911–12	II	38	15	7	16	49	66	37	10th
1912–13	II	38	13	7	18	49	65	33	15th
1913–14	II	38	11	4	23	62	54	26	18th
1914–15	II	38	10	4	24	47	88	24	19th
1915–19	Regional Leagues operating								
1919–20	II	42	15	10	17	41	61	40	14th
1920–21	II	42	12	16	14	39	46	40	12th
1921–22	II	42	14	17	11	39	34	45	9th
1922–23	II	42	21	9	12	65	44	51	3rd
1923–24	II	42	17	8	17	64	54	42	12th
1924–25	II	42	24	11	7	90	32	59	1st
1925–26	I	42	14	10	18	70	80	38	17th
1926–27	I	42	17	12	13	85	70	46	7th
1927–28	I	42	18	12	12	96	72	48	3rd
1928–29	I	42	21	9	12	96	67	51	2nd
1929–30	I	42	17	9	16	86	90	43	8th
1930–31	I	42	16	6	20	80	95	38	16th
1931–32	I	42	15	7	20	74	94	37	19th
1932–33	I	42	11	13	18	75	89	35	19th
1933–34	I	42	14	11	17	59	74	39	17th
1934–35	I	42	12	9	21	61	86	33	21st
1935–36	II	42	19	10	13	79	57	48	6th
1936–37	II	42	24	8	10	89	57	56	1st
1937–38	I	42	14	11	17	54	75	39	16th
1938–39	I	42	9	11	22	48	82	29	22nd
1939–46	Regional Leagues operating								
1946–47	II	42	18	7	17	69	64	43	9th
1947–48	II	42	16	11	15	60	57	43	9th
1948–49	II	42	10	16	16	62	79	36	19th
1949–50	II	42	12	15	15	55	65	39	15th
1950–51	II	42	15	11	16	68	58	41	14th
1951–52	II	42	19	9	14	78	64	47	5th
1952–53	II	42	18	12	12	89	74	48	5th
1953–54	II	42	23	10	9	97	60	56	1st
1954–55	I	42	12	11	19	74	86	35	21st
1955–56	II	42	21	6	15	94	78	48	5th
1956–57	II	42	25	11	6	109	67	61	1st
1957–58	I	42	14	5	23	91	112	33	18th
1958–59	I	42	11	10	21	67	98	32	19th
1959–60	I	42	13	13	16	66	75	39	12th
1960–61	I	42	18	9	15	87	70	45	6th
1961–62	I	42	17	6	19	72	71	40	14th
1962–63	I	42	20	12	10	79	53	52	4th
1963–64	I	42	16	11	15	61	58	43	11th
1964–65	I	42	11	13	18	69	85	35	18th
1965–66	I	42	21	7	14	80	65	49	7th
1966–67	I	42	18	8	16	78	71	44	8th
1967–68	I	42	13	12	17	64	69	38	13th
1968–69	I	42	9	12	21	39	68	30	21st
1969–70	II	42	19	13	10	64	50	51	3rd
1970–71	II	42	23	13	6	57	30	59	1st
1971–72	I	42	13	13	16	41	46	39	12th

1972–73	I	42	10	17	15	40	46	37	16th
1973–74	I	42	13	16	13	51	41	42	9th
1974–75	I	42	12	12	18	46	60	36	18th
1975–76	I	42	13	19	10	48	51	45	7th
1976–77	I	42	12	18	12	47	60	42	11th
1977–78	I	42	5	12	25	26	70	22	22nd
1978–79	II	42	10	17	15	43	52	37	17th
1979–80	II	42	21	13	8	58	38	55	1st
1980–81	I	42	13	6	23	40	67	32	21st
1981–82	II	42	18	12	12	56	48	66	8th
1982–83	II	42	20	10	12	72	44	70	3rd
1983–84	I	42	13	12	17	65	68	51	15th
1984–85	I	42	15	6	21	65	73	51	15th
1985–86	I	42	10	12	20	54	76	42	19th
1986–87	I	42	11	9	22	54	76	42	20th
1987–88	II	42	16	11	17	62	61	59	13th
1988–89	II	46	13	16	17	56	63	55	15th
1989–90	II	46	15	14	17	67	79	59	13th
1990–91	II	46	14	8	24	60	83	50	22nd
1991–92	II	46	23	8	15	62	55	77	4th
1992–93	I	46	22	10	14	71	64	76	6th

Though it was thought for many years that Arthur Chandler had created a record for scoring in 16 consecutive Football League matches in 1924–25 for **Leicester City** in Division Two, there may have been confusion over the truth which was that in the 1929 tour of South Africa he played in 16 of 17 FA XI tour games and scored in every one, totalling 33 goals.

LEYTON ORIENT

(Clapton Orient until 1946, Leyton Orient until 1966, Orient until 1987)

Year	Div	P	W	D	L	F	A	Pts	Pos
1905–06	II	38	7	7	24	35	78	21	20th
1906–07	II	38	11	8	19	45	67	30	17th
1907–08	II	38	11	10	17	40	65	32	14th
1908–09	II	38	12	9	17	37	49	33	15th
1909–10	II	38	12	6	20	37	60	30	16th
1910–11	II	38	19	7	12	44	35	45	4th
1911–12	II	38	21	3	14	61	44	45	4th
1912–13	II	38	10	14	14	34	47	34	14th
1913–14	II	38	16	11	11	47	35	43	6th
1914–15	II	38	16	9	13	50	48	41	9th
1915–19	Regional Leagues operating								
1919–20	II	42	16	6	20	51	59	38	16th
1920–21	II	42	16	13	13	43	42	45	7th
1921–22	II	42	15	9	18	43	50	39	15th
1922–23	II	42	12	12	18	40	50	36	19th
1923–24	II	42	14	15	13	40	36	43	10th
1924–25	II	42	14	12	16	42	42	40	11th
1925–26	II	42	12	9	21	50	65	33	20th
1926–27	II	42	12	7	23	60	96	31	20th
1927–28	II	42	11	12	19	55	85	34	20th

1928–29	II	42	12	8	22	45	72	32	22nd
1929–30	IIIS	42	14	13	15	55	62	41	12th
1930–31	IIIS	42	14	7	21	63	91	35	19th
1931–32	IIIS	42	12	11	19	77	90	35	16th
1932–33	IIIS	42	8	13	21	59	93	29	20th
1933–34	IIIS	42	16	10	16	75	69	42	11th
1934–35	IIIS	42	15	10	17	65	65	40	14th
1935–36	IIIS	42	16	6	20	55	61	38	14th
1936–37	IIIS	42	14	15	13	52	52	43	12th
1937–38	IIIS	42	13	7	22	42	61	33	19th
1938–39	IIIS	42	11	13	18	53	55	35	20th
1939–46	Regional Leagues operating								
1946–47	IIIS	42	12	8	22	54	75	32	19th
1947–48	IIIS	42	13	10	19	51	73	36	17th
1948–49	IIIS	42	11	12	19	58	80	34	19th
1949–50	IIIS	42	12	11	19	53	85	35	18th
1950–51	IIIS	46	15	8	23	53	75	38	19th
1951–52	IIIS	46	16	9	21	55	68	41	18th
1952–53	IIIS	46	16	10	20	68	73	42	14th
1953–54	IIIS	46	18	11	17	79	73	47	11th
1954–55	IIIS	46	26	9	11	89	47	61	2nd
1955–56	IIIS	46	29	8	9	106	49	66	1st
1956–57	II	42	15	10	17	66	84	40	15th
1957–58	II	42	18	5	19	77	79	41	12th
1958–59	II	42	14	8	20	71	78	36	17th
1959–60	II	42	15	14	13	76	61	44	10th
1960–61	II	42	14	8	20	55	78	36	19th
1961–62	II	42	22	10	10	69	40	54	2nd
1962–63	I	42	6	9	27	37	81	21	22nd
1963–64	II	42	13	10	19	54	72	36	16th
1964–65	II	42	12	11	19	50	72	35	19th
1965–66	II	42	5	13	24	38	80	23	22nd
1966–67	III	46	13	18	15	58	68	44	14th
1967–68	III	46	12	17	17	46	62	41	18th
1968–69	III	46	14	14	18	51	58	42	18th
1969–70	III	46	25	12	9	67	36	62	1st
1970–71	II	42	9	16	17	29	51	34	17th
1971–72	II	42	14	9	19	50	61	37	17th
1972–73	II	42	12	12	18	49	53	36	15th
1973–74	II	42	15	18	9	55	42	48	4th
1974–75	II	42	11	20	11	28	39	42	12th
1975–76	II	42	13	14	15	37	39	40	13th
1976–77	II	42	9	16	17	37	55	34	19th
1977–78	II	42	10	18	14	43	49	38	14th
1978–79	II	42	15	10	17	51	51	40	11th
1979–80	III	42	12	17	13	48	54	41	14th
1980–81	III	42	13	12	17	52	56	38	17th
1981–82	III	42	10	9	23	39	61	39	22nd
1982–83	III	46	15	9	22	64	88	54	20th
1983–84	III	46	18	9	19	71	81	63	11th
1984–85	III	46	11	13	22	51	76	46	22nd
1985–86	IV	46	20	12	14	79	64	72	5th
1986–87	IV	46	20	9	17	64	61	69	7th
1987–88	IV	46	19	12	15	85	63	69	8th
1988–89	IV	46	21	12	13	86	50	75	6th
1989–90	III	46	16	10	20	52	56	58	14th
1990–91	III	46	18	10	18	55	58	64	13th

Year	Div	P	W	D	L	F	A	Pts	Pos
1991–92	III	46	18	11	17	62	52	65	10th
1992–93	II	46	21	9	16	69	53	72	7th

Tom Johnston is the only **Leyton Orient** player to have scored a hat-trick in successive League matches. He did so on 21 December 1957 with three goals at home against Grimsby Town and four on Christmas Day again at Brisbane Road against Rotherham United in Division Two. These goals came in a consecutive sequence of 2 1 2 1 3 4 1 1 3. He scored 35 League goals in 30 games before being transferred to Blackburn Rovers for £15,000 in March 1958.

LINCOLN CITY

Year	Div	P	W	D	L	F	A	Pts	Pos
1892–93	II	22	7	3	12	45	51	17	9th
1893–94	II	28	11	6	11	59	58	28	8th
1894–95	II	30	10	0	20	52	92	20	13th
1895–96	II	30	9	4	17	53	75	22	13th
1896–97	II	30	5	2	23	27	85	12	16th
1897–98	II	30	6	5	19	43	83	17	14th
1898–99	II	34	12	7	15	51	56	31	12th
1899–1900	II	34	14	8	12	46	43	36	9th
1900–01	II	34	13	7	14	43	39	33	8th
1901–02	II	34	14	13	7	45	35	41	5th
1902–03	II	34	12	6	16	46	53	30	10th
1903–04	II	34	11	8	15	41	58	30	12th
1904–05	II	34	12	7	15	42	40	31	9th
1905–06	II	38	12	6	20	69	72	30	13th
1906–07	II	38	12	4	22	46	73	28	19th
1907–08	II	38	9	3	26	46	83	21	20th
Failed re-election									
1909–10	II	38	10	11	17	42	69	31	15th
1910–11	II	38	7	10	21	28	72	24	20th
Failed re-election									
1912–13	II	38	15	10	13	50	52	40	8th
1913–14	II	38	10	6	22	36	66	26	19th
1914–15	II	38	11	9	18	46	65	31	16th
1915–19	Regional Leagues operating								
1919–20	II	42	9	9	24	44	101	27	21st
Failed re-election									
1921–22	IIIN	38	14	6	18	48	59	34	14th
1922–23	IIIN	38	13	10	15	39	55	36	13th
1923–24	IIIN	42	10	12	20	48	59	32	19th
1924–25	IIIN	42	18	8	16	53	58	44	8th
1925–26	IIIN	42	17	5	20	66	82	39	15th
1926–27	IIIN	42	15	12	15	90	78	42	11th
1927–28	IIIN	42	24	7	11	91	64	55	2nd
1928–29	IIIN	42	21	6	15	91	67	48	6th
1929–30	IIIN	42	17	14	11	83	61	48	5th
1930–31	IIIN	42	25	7	10	102	59	57	2nd
1931–32	IIIN	40	26	5	9	106	47	57	1st
1932–33	II	42	12	13	17	72	87	37	18th
1933–34	II	42	9	8	25	44	75	26	22nd
1934–35	IIIN	42	22	7	13	87	58	51	4th
1935–36	IIIN	42	22	9	11	91	51	53	4th
1936–37	IIIN	42	25	7	10	103	57	57	2nd
1937–38	IIIN	42	19	8	15	66	50	46	7th
1938–39	IIIN	42	21	9	21	66	92	33	17th
1939–46	Regional Leagues operating								
1946–47	IIIN	42	17	5	20	86	87	39	12th
1947–48	IIIN	42	26	8	8	81	40	60	1st
1948–49	II	42	8	12	22	53	91	28	22nd
1949–50	IIIN	42	21	9	12	60	39	51	4th
1950–51	IIIN	46	25	8	13	89	58	58	5th
1951–52	IIIN	46	30	9	7	121	52	69	1st
1952–53	II	42	11	17	14	64	71	39	15th
1953–54	II	42	14	9	19	65	83	37	16th
1954–55	II	42	13	10	19	68	79	36	16th
1955–56	II	42	18	10	14	79	65	46	8th
1956–57	II	42	14	6	22	54	80	34	18th
1957–58	II	42	11	9	22	55	82	31	20th
1958–59	II	42	11	7	24	63	93	29	19th
1959–60	II	42	16	7	19	75	78	39	13th
1960–61	II	42	8	8	26	48	95	24	22nd
1961–62	III	46	9	17	20	57	87	35	22nd
1962–63	IV	46	13	9	24	68	89	35	22nd
1963–64	IV	46	19	9	18	67	75	47	11th
1964–65	IV	46	11	6	29	58	99	28	22nd
1965–66	IV	46	13	11	22	57	82	37	22nd
1966–67	IV	46	9	13	24	58	82	31	24th
1967–68	IV	46	17	9	20	71	68	43	13th
1968–69	IV	46	17	17	12	54	52	51	8th
1969–70	IV	46	17	16	13	66	52	50	8th
1970–71	IV	46	13	13	20	70	71	39	21st
1971–72	IV	46	21	14	11	77	59	56	5th
1972–73	IV	46	16	16	14	64	57	48	10th
1973–74	IV	46	16	12	18	63	67	44	12th
1974–75	IV	46	21	15	10	79	48	57	5th
1975–76	IV	46	32	10	4	111	39	74	1st
1976–77	III	46	19	14	13	77	70	52	9th
1977–78	III	46	15	15	16	53	61	45	16th
1978–79	III	46	7	11	28	41	88	25	24th
1979–80	IV	46	18	17	11	64	42	53	7th
1980–81	IV	46	25	15	6	66	25	65	2nd
1981–82	III	46	21	14	11	66	40	77	4th
1982–83	III	46	23	7	16	77	51	76	6th
1983–84	III	46	17	10	19	59	62	61	14th
1984–85	III	46	11	18	17	50	51	51	19th
1985–86	III	46	10	16	20	55	77	46	21st
1986–87	IV	46	12	12	22	45	65	48	24th
1987–88	GM Vauxhall Conference								
1988–89	IV	46	18	10	18	64	60	64	10th
1989–90	IV	46	18	14	14	48	48	68	10th
1990–91	IV	46	14	17	15	50	61	59	14th
1991–92	IV	42	17	11	14	50	44	62	10th
1992–93	III	42	18	9	15	57	53	63	8th

When **Lincoln City** won the championship of Division Three (North) in 1947–48, Jimmy Hutchinson scored 32 goals, over three times more goals than any other player. Geoff Marlow was second highest scorer with ten.

LIVERPOOL

Year	Div	P	W	D	L	F	A	Pts	Pos
1893–94	II	28	22	6	0	77	18	50	1st
1894–95	I	30	7	8	15	51	70	22	16th
1895–96	II	30	22	2	6	106	32	46	1st
1896–97	I	30	12	9	9	46	38	33	5th
1897–98	I	30	11	6	13	48	45	28	9th
1898–99	I	34	19	5	10	49	33	43	2nd
1899–1900	I	34	14	5	15	49	45	33	10th
1900–01	I	34	19	7	8	59	35	45	1st
1901–02	I	34	10	12	12	42	38	32	11th
1902–03	I	34	17	4	13	68	49	38	5th
1903–04	I	34	9	8	17	49	62	26	17th
1904–05	I	34	27	4	3	93	25	58	1st
1905–06	I	38	23	5	10	79	46	51	1st
1906–07	I	38	13	7	18	64	65	33	15th
1907–08	I	38	16	6	16	68	61	38	8th
1908–09	I	38	15	6	17	57	65	36	16th
1909–10	I	38	21	6	11	78	57	48	2nd
1910–11	I	38	15	7	16	53	53	37	13th
1911–12	I	38	12	10	16	49	55	34	17th
1912–13	I	38	16	5	17	61	71	37	12th
1913–14	I	38	14	7	17	46	62	35	16th
1914–15	I	38	14	9	15	65	75	37	14th
1915–19	Regional Leagues operating								
1919–20	I	42	19	10	13	59	44	48	4th
1920–21	I	42	18	15	9	63	35	51	4th
1921–22	I	42	22	13	7	63	36	57	1st
1922–23	I	42	26	8	8	70	31	60	1st
1923–24	I	42	15	11	16	49	48	41	12th
1924–25	I	42	20	10	12	63	55	50	4th
1925–26	I	42	14	16	12	70	63	44	7th
1926–27	I	42	18	7	17	69	61	43	9th
1927–28	I	42	13	13	16	84	87	39	16th
1928–29	I	42	17	12	13	90	64	46	5th
1929–30	I	42	16	9	17	63	79	41	12th
1930–31	I	42	15	12	15	86	85	42	9th
1931–32	I	42	19	6	17	81	93	44	10th
1932–33	I	42	14	11	17	79	84	39	14th
1933–34	I	42	14	10	18	79	87	38	18th
1934–35	I	42	19	7	16	85	88	45	7th
1935–36	I	42	13	12	17	60	64	38	19th
1936–37	I	42	12	11	19	62	84	35	18th
1937–38	I	42	15	11	16	65	71	41	11th
1938–39	I	42	14	14	14	62	63	42	11th
1939–46	Regional Leagues operating								
1946–47	I	42	25	7	10	84	52	57	1st
1947–48	I	42	16	10	16	65	61	42	11th
1948–49	I	42	13	14	15	53	43	40	12th
1949–50	I	42	17	14	11	64	54	48	8th
1950–51	I	42	16	11	15	53	59	43	9th
1951–52	I	42	12	19	11	57	61	43	11th
1952–53	I	42	14	8	20	61	82	36	17th
1953–54	I	42	9	10	23	68	97	28	22nd
1954–55	II	42	16	10	16	92	96	42	11th
1955–56	II	42	21	6	15	85	63	48	3rd
1956–57	II	42	21	11	10	82	54	53	3rd
1957–58	II	42	22	10	10	79	54	54	4th
1958–59	II	42	24	5	13	87	62	53	4th
1959–60	II	42	20	10	12	90	66	50	3rd
1960–61	II	42	21	10	11	87	58	52	3rd
1961–62	II	42	27	8	7	99	43	62	1st
1962–63	I	42	17	10	15	71	59	44	8th
1963–64	I	42	26	5	11	92	45	57	1st
1964–65	I	42	17	10	15	67	73	44	7th
1965–66	I	42	26	9	7	79	34	61	1st
1966–67	I	42	19	13	10	64	47	51	5th
1967–68	I	42	22	11	9	71	40	55	3rd
1968–69	I	42	25	11	6	63	24	61	2nd
1969–70	I	42	20	11	11	65	42	51	5th
1970–71	I	42	17	17	8	42	24	51	5th
1971–72	I	42	24	9	9	64	30	57	3rd
1972–73	I	42	25	10	7	72	42	60	1st
1973–74	I	42	22	13	7	52	31	57	2nd
1974–75	I	42	20	11	11	60	39	51	2nd
1975–76	I	42	23	14	5	66	31	60	1st
1976–77	I	42	23	11	8	62	33	57	1st
1977–78	I	42	24	9	9	65	34	57	2nd
1978–79	I	42	30	8	4	85	16	68	1st
1979–80	I	42	25	10	7	81	30	60	1st
1980–81	I	42	17	17	8	62	42	51	5th
1981–82	I	42	26	9	7	80	32	87	1st
1982–83	I	42	24	10	8	87	37	82	1st
1983–84	I	42	22	14	6	73	32	80	1st
1984–85	I	42	22	11	9	68	35	77	2nd
1985–86	I	42	26	10	6	89	37	88	1st
1986–87	I	42	23	8	11	72	42	77	2nd
1987–88	I	40	26	12	2	87	24	90	1st
1988–89	I	38	22	10	6	65	28	76	2nd
1989–90	I	38	23	10	5	78	37	79	1st
1990–91	I	38	23	7	8	77	40	76	2nd
1991–92	I	42	16	16	10	47	40	64	6th
1992–93	PL	42	16	11	15	62	55	59	6th

In the 1967–68 season **Liverpool** fielded an unchanged team for their first 12 League games and made only one

Liverpool parade the League Championship trophy in 1988, a season in which the destination of the title was, even by their standards, never in doubt (Allsport/David Cannon)

change in the first 17. The original team was: Lawrence, Lawler, Byrne, Smith, Yeats, Hughes, Callaghan, Hunt, Hateley, St John, Thompson. Liverpool used only 18 players that season and made only four substitutions.

LOUGHBOROUGH TOWN

Year	Div	P	W	D	L	F	A	Pts	Pos
1895–96	II	30	9	5	16	40	67	23	12th
1896–97	II	30	12	1	17	50	64	25	13th
1897–98	II	30	6	2	22	24	87	14	16th
1898–99	II	34	6	6	22	38	92	18	17th
1899–1900	II	34	1	6	27	18	100	8	18th

On 1 April 1899, **Loughborough Town** beat Darwen 10–0 in a Division Two match. At the end of the season Loughborough finished second from bottom but with twice as many points as Darwen.

LUTON TOWN

Year	Div	P	W	D	L	F	A	Pts	Pos
1897–98	II	30	13	4	13	68	50	30	8th
1898–99	II	34	10	3	21	51	95	23	15th
1899–1900	II	34	5	8	21	40	75	18	17th
Failed re-election
1920–21	III	42	16	12	14	61	56	44	9th
1921–22	IIIS	42	22	8	12	64	35	52	4th
1922–23	IIIS	42	21	7	14	68	49	49	5th
1923–24	IIIS	42	16	14	12	50	44	46	7th
1924–25	IIIS	42	10	17	15	49	57	37	16th
1925–26	IIIS	42	18	7	17	80	75	43	7th
1926–27	IIIS	42	15	14	13	68	66	44	8th
1927–28	IIIS	42	16	7	19	94	87	39	13th
1928–29	IIIS	42	19	11	12	89	73	49	7th
1929–30	IIIS	42	14	12	16	64	78	40	13th
1930–31	IIIS	42	19	8	15	76	51	46	7th
1931–32	IIIS	42	20	7	15	95	70	47	6th
1932–33	IIIS	42	13	13	16	78	78	39	14th
1933–34	IIIS	42	21	10	11	83	61	52	6th
1934–35	IIIS	42	19	12	11	92	60	50	4th
1935–36	IIIS	42	22	12	8	81	45	56	2nd
1936–37	IIIS	42	27	4	11	103	53	58	1st
1937–38	II	42	15	10	17	89	86	40	12th
1938–39	II	42	22	5	15	82	66	49	7th
1939–46	Regional Leagues operating
1946–47	II	42	16	7	19	71	73	39	13th
1947–48	II	42	14	12	16	56	59	40	13th
1948–49	II	42	14	12	16	55	57	40	10th
1949–50	II	42	10	18	14	41	51	38	17th
1950–51	II	42	9	14	19	57	70	32	19th
1951–52	II	42	16	12	14	77	78	44	8th
1952–53	II	42	22	8	12	84	49	52	3rd
1953–54	II	42	18	12	12	64	59	48	6th
1954–55	II	42	23	8	11	88	53	54	2nd
1955–56	I	42	17	8	17	66	64	42	10th
1956–57	I	42	14	9	19	58	76	37	16th
1957–58	I	42	19	6	17	69	63	44	8th
1958–59	I	42	12	13	17	68	71	37	17th
1959–60	I	42	9	12	21	50	73	30	22nd
1960–61	II	42	15	9	18	71	79	39	13th
1961–62	II	42	17	5	20	69	71	39	13th
1962–63	II	42	11	7	24	61	84	29	22nd
1963–64	III	46	16	10	20	64	80	42	18th
1964–65	III	46	11	11	24	51	94	33	21st
1965–66	IV	46	24	8	14	90	70	56	6th
1966–67	IV	46	16	9	21	59	73	41	17th
1967–68	IV	46	27	12	7	87	44	66	1st
1968–69	III	46	25	11	10	74	38	61	3rd
1969–70	III	46	23	14	9	77	43	60	2nd
1970–71	II	42	18	13	11	62	43	49	6th
1971–72	II	42	10	18	14	43	48	38	13th
1972–73	II	42	15	11	16	44	53	41	12th
1973–74	II	42	19	12	11	64	51	50	2nd
1974–75	II	42	11	11	20	47	65	33	20th
1975–76	II	42	19	10	13	61	51	48	7th
1976–77	II	42	23	6	15	67	48	48	6th
1977–78	II	42	14	10	18	54	52	38	13th
1978–79	II	42	13	10	19	60	57	36	18th
1979–80	II	42	16	17	9	66	45	49	6th
1980–81	II	42	18	12	12	61	46	48	5th
1981–82	II	42	25	13	4	86	46	88	1st
1982–83	I	42	12	13	17	65	84	49	18th
1983–84	I	42	14	9	19	53	66	51	16th
1984–85	I	42	15	9	18	57	61	54	13th
1985–86	I	42	18	12	12	61	44	66	9th
1986–87	I	42	18	12	12	47	45	66	7th
1987–88	I	40	14	11	15	57	58	53	9th
1988–89	I	38	10	11	17	42	52	41	16th
1989–90	I	38	10	13	15	43	57	43	17th
1990–91	I	38	10	7	21	42	61	37	18th
1991–92	I	42	10	12	20	38	71	42	20th
1992–93	I	46	10	21	15	48	62	51	20th

In 1923, **Luton Town** completed a club record 12 League matches without defeat after losing 2–1 at Exeter City on 6 October. They had seven games without conceding a goal and another five unbeaten until losing 4–0 at Brighton & Hove Albion on Boxing Day. During this period they conceded only four goals, two each in games with Bournemouth.

MAIDSTONE UNITED

Year	Div	P	W	D	L	F	A	Pts	Pos
1989–90	IV	46	22	7	17	77	61	73	5th
1990–91	IV	46	13	12	21	66	71	51	19th
1991–92	IV	42	8	18	16	45	56	42	18th
Withdrew from League

As a non-league club, **Maidstone United** reached the third round of the FA Cup five times in the post-war period. At the time of their demise only two other teams, Altrincham and Yeovil, had bettered this record.

MANCHESTER CITY

(Ardwick until 1894)

Year	Div	P	W	D	L	F	A	Pts	Pos
1892–93	II	22	9	3	10	45	40	21	5th
1893–94	II	28	8	2	18	47	71	18	13th
1894–95	II	30	14	3	13	82	72	31	9th
1895–96	II	30	21	4	5	63	38	46	2nd
1896–97	II	30	12	8	10	58	50	32	6th
1897–98	II	30	15	9	6	66	36	39	3rd
1898–99	II	34	23	6	5	92	35	52	1st
1899–1900	I	34	13	8	13	50	44	34	7th
1900–01	I	34	13	6	15	48	58	32	11th
1901–02	I	34	11	6	17	42	58	28	18th
1902–03	II	34	25	4	5	95	29	54	1st
1903–04	I	34	19	6	9	71	45	44	2nd
1904–05	I	34	20	6	8	66	37	46	3rd
1905–06	I	38	19	5	14	73	54	43	5th
1906–07	I	38	10	12	16	53	77	32	17th
1907–08	I	38	16	11	11	62	54	43	3rd
1908–09	I	38	15	4	19	67	69	34	19th
1909–10	II	38	23	8	7	81	40	54	1st
1910–11	I	38	9	13	16	43	58	31	17th
1911–12	I	38	13	9	16	56	58	35	15th
1912–13	I	38	18	8	12	53	37	44	6th
1913–14	I	38	14	8	16	51	53	36	13th
1914–15	I	38	15	13	10	49	39	43	5th
1915–19	Regional Leagues operating								
1919–20	I	42	18	9	15	71	62	45	7th
1920–21	I	42	24	6	12	70	50	54	2nd
1921–22	I	42	18	9	15	65	70	45	10th
1922–23	I	42	17	11	14	50	49	45	8th
1923–24	I	42	15	12	15	54	71	42	11th
1924–25	I	42	17	9	16	76	68	43	10th
1925–26	I	42	12	11	19	89	100	35	21st
1926–27	II	42	22	10	10	108	61	54	3rd
1927–28	II	42	25	9	8	100	59	59	1st
1928–29	I	42	18	9	15	95	86	45	8th
1929–30	I	42	19	9	14	91	81	47	3rd
1930–31	I	42	18	10	14	75	70	46	8th
1931–32	I	42	13	12	17	83	73	38	14th
1932–33	I	42	16	5	21	68	71	37	16th
1933–34	I	42	17	11	14	65	72	45	5th
1934–35	I	42	20	8	14	82	67	48	4th
1935–36	I	42	17	8	17	68	60	42	9th
1936–37	I	42	22	13	7	107	61	57	1st
1937–38	I	42	14	8	20	80	77	36	21st
1938–39	II	42	21	7	14	96	72	49	5th
1939–46	Regional Leagues operating								
1946–47	II	42	26	10	6	78	35	62	1st
1947–48	I	42	15	12	15	52	47	42	10th
1948–49	I	42	15	15	12	47	51	45	7th
1949–50	I	42	8	13	21	36	68	29	21st
1950–51	II	42	19	14	9	89	61	52	2nd
1951–52	I	42	13	13	16	58	61	39	15th
1952–53	I	42	14	7	21	72	87	35	20th
1953–54	I	42	14	9	19	62	77	37	17th
1954–55	I	42	18	10	14	76	69	46	7th
1955–56	I	42	18	10	14	82	69	46	4th
1956–57	I	42	13	9	20	78	88	35	18th
1957–58	I	42	22	5	15	104	100	49	5th
1958–59	I	42	11	9	22	64	95	31	20th
1959–60	I	42	17	3	22	78	84	37	15th
1960–61	I	42	13	11	18	79	90	37	13th
1961–62	I	42	17	7	18	78	81	41	12th
1962–63	I	42	10	11	21	58	102	31	21st
1963–64	II	42	18	10	14	84	66	46	6th
1964–65	II	42	16	9	17	63	62	41	11th
1965–66	II	42	22	15	5	76	44	59	1st
1966–67	I	42	12	15	15	43	52	39	15th
1967–68	I	42	26	6	10	86	43	58	1st
1968–69	I	42	15	10	17	64	55	40	13th
1969–70	I	42	16	11	15	55	48	43	10th
1970–71	I	42	12	17	22	47	42	41	11th
1971–72	I	42	23	11	8	77	45	57	4th
1972–73	I	42	15	11	16	57	60	41	11th
1973–74	I	42	14	12	16	39	46	40	14th
1974–75	I	42	18	10	14	54	54	46	8th
1975–76	I	42	16	11	15	64	46	43	8th
1976–77	I	42	21	14	7	60	34	56	2nd
1977–78	I	42	20	12	10	74	51	52	4th
1978–79	I	42	13	13	16	58	56	39	15th
1979–80	I	42	12	13	17	43	66	37	17th
1980–81	I	42	14	11	17	66	59	39	12th
1981–82	I	42	15	13	14	52	50	58	10th
1982–83	I	42	13	8	21	47	70	47	20th

The great Manchester City side of the late 1960s which under Joe Mercer and Malcolm Allison accumulated five different domestic and European trophies in just five seasons (Popperfoto)

Year	Div	P	W	D	L	F	A	Pts	Pos
1983–84	II	42	20	10	12	66	48	70	4th
1984–85	II	42	21	11	10	66	40	74	3rd
1985–86	I	42	11	12	19	43	57	45	15th
1986–87	I	42	8	15	19	36	57	39	21st
1987–88	II	42	19	8	17	80	60	65	9th
1988–89	II	42	23	13	10	77	53	82	2nd
1989–90	I	38	12	12	14	43	52	48	14th
1990–91	I	38	17	11	10	64	53	62	5th
1991–92	I	42	20	10	12	61	48	70	5th
1992–93	PL	42	15	12	15	56	51	57	9th

Tom Holford scored hat-tricks for **Manchester City** in three out of four consecutive matches at Hyde Road in January 1909: v Bradford City, Division One, 9 January; v Tottenham, FA Cup first round, 16 January; and v Everton, Division One, 30 January.

MANCHESTER UNITED

(Newton Heath until 1902)

Year	Div	P	W	D	L	F	A	Pts	Pos
1892–93	I	30	6	6	18	50	85	18	16th
1893–94	I	30	6	2	22	36	72	14	16th
1894–95	II	30	15	8	7	78	44	38	3rd
1895–96	II	30	15	3	12	66	57	33	6th
1896–97	II	30	17	5	8	56	34	39	2nd
1897–98	II	30	16	6	8	64	35	38	4th
1898–99	II	34	19	5	10	67	43	43	4th
1899–1900	II	34	20	4	10	63	27	44	4th
1900–01	II	34	14	4	16	42	38	32	10th
1901–02	II	34	11	6	17	38	53	28	16th
1902–03	II	34	15	8	11	53	38	38	5th
1903–04	II	34	20	8	6	63	33	48	3rd
1904–05	II	34	24	5	5	81	30	53	3rd
1905–06	II	38	28	6	4	90	28	62	2nd
1906–07	I	38	17	8	13	53	56	42	8th
1907–08	I	38	23	6	9	81	48	52	1st
1908–09	I	38	15	7	16	58	68	37	13th
1909–10	I	38	19	7	12	69	61	45	5th
1910–11	I	38	22	8	8	72	40	52	1st
1911–12	I	38	13	11	14	45	60	37	13th
1912–13	I	38	19	8	11	69	43	46	4th
1913–14	I	38	15	6	17	52	62	36	14th
1914–15	I	38	9	12	17	46	62	30	18th
1915–19	Regional Leagues operating								
1919–20	I	42	13	14	15	54	50	40	12th
1920–21	I	42	15	10	17	64	68	40	13th
1921–22	I	42	8	12	22	41	73	28	22nd
1922–23	II	42	17	14	11	51	36	48	4th
1923–24	II	42	13	14	15	52	44	40	14th
1924–25	II	42	23	11	8	57	23	57	2nd
1925–26	I	42	19	6	17	66	73	44	9th
1926–27	I	42	13	14	15	52	64	40	15th
1927–28	I	42	16	7	19	72	80	39	18th
1928–29	I	42	14	13	15	66	76	41	13th
1929–30	I	42	15	8	19	67	88	38	17th
1930–31	I	42	7	8	27	53	115	22	22nd
1931–32	II	42	17	8	17	71	72	42	12th
1932–33	II	42	15	13	14	71	68	43	6th
1933–34	II	42	14	6	22	59	85	34	20th
1934–35	II	42	23	4	15	76	55	50	5th
1935–36	II	42	22	12	8	85	43	56	1st
1936–37	I	42	10	12	20	55	78	32	21st
1937–38	II	42	22	9	11	82	50	53	2nd
1938–39	I	42	11	16	15	57	65	38	14th
1939–46	Regional Leagues operating								
1946–47	I	42	22	12	8	95	54	56	2nd
1947–48	I	42	19	14	9	81	48	52	2nd
1948–49	I	42	21	11	10	77	44	53	2nd
1949–50	I	42	18	14	10	69	44	50	4th
1950–51	I	42	24	8	10	74	40	56	2nd
1951–52	I	42	23	11	8	95	52	57	1st
1952–53	I	42	18	10	14	69	72	46	8th
1953–54	I	42	18	12	12	73	58	48	4th
1954–55	I	42	20	7	15	84	74	47	5th
1955–56	I	42	25	10	7	83	51	60	1st
1956–57	I	42	28	8	6	103	54	64	1st
1957–58	I	42	16	11	15	85	75	43	9th
1958–59	I	42	24	7	11	103	66	55	2nd
1959–60	I	42	19	7	16	102	80	45	7th
1960–61	I	42	18	9	15	88	76	45	7th
1961–62	I	42	15	9	18	72	75	39	15th
1962–63	I	42	12	10	20	67	81	34	19th
1963–64	I	42	23	7	12	90	62	53	2nd
1964–65	I	42	26	9	7	89	39	61	1st
1965–66	I	42	18	15	9	84	59	51	4th
1966–67	I	42	24	12	6	84	45	60	1st
1967–68	I	42	24	8	10	89	55	56	2nd
1968–69	I	42	15	12	15	57	53	42	11th
1969–70	I	42	14	17	11	66	61	45	8th
1970–71	I	42	16	11	15	65	66	43	8th
1971–72	I	42	19	10	13	69	61	48	8th
1972–73	I	42	12	13	17	44	60	37	18th
1973–74	I	42	10	12	20	38	48	32	21st
1974–75	II	42	26	9	7	66	30	61	1st
1975–76	I	42	23	10	10	68	42	56	3rd
1976–77	I	42	18	11	13	71	62	47	6th
1977–78	I	42	16	10	16	67	63	42	10th
1978–79	I	42	15	15	12	60	63	45	9th
1979–80	I	42	24	10	8	65	35	58	2nd
1980–81	I	42	15	18	9	51	36	48	8th
1981–82	I	42	22	12	8	59	29	78	3rd
1982–83	I	42	19	13	8	56	38	70	3rd
1983–84	I	42	20	14	8	71	41	74	4th
1984–85	I	42	22	10	10	77	47	76	4th
1985–86	I	42	22	10	10	70	36	76	4th
1986–87	I	42	14	14	14	52	45	56	11th
1987–88	I	40	23	12	5	71	38	81	2nd
1988–89	I	38	13	12	13	45	35	51	11th
1989–90	I	38	13	9	16	46	47	48	13th
1990–91	I	38	16	12	10	58	45	59	6th
1991–92	I	42	21	15	6	63	33	78	2nd

Manchester United finally laid the ghosts of the previous 26 seasons to rest in 1993 by clinching the new Premier League title in exciting fashion (Bob Thomas)

| 1992–93 | PL | 42 | 24 | 12 | 6 | 67 | 31 | 84 | 1st |

On 12 April 1992 **Manchester United** beat Nottingham Forest 1–0 in the Rumbelows Cup Final. Brian McClair scored his 100th goal for the club. It provided United with their third major trophy in successive years after the FA Cup in 1990 and the Cup-Winners' Cup in 1991.

MANSFIELD TOWN

Year	Div	P	W	D	L	F	A	Pts	Pos
1931–32	IIIS	42	11	10	21	75	108	32	20th
1932–33	IIIN	42	14	7	21	84	100	35	16th
1933–34	IIIN	42	11	12	19	81	88	34	17th
1934–35	IIIN	42	19	9	14	75	62	47	8th
1935–36	IIIN	42	14	9	19	80	91	37	19th
1936–37	IIIN	42	18	8	16	91	76	44	9th
1937–38	IIIS	42	15	9	18	62	67	39	14th
1938–39	IIIS	42	12	15	15	44	62	39	16th
1939–46	Regional Leagues operating								
1946–47	IIIS	42	9	10	23	48	96	28	22nd
1947–48	IIIN	42	17	11	14	57	51	45	8th
1948–49	IIIN	42	14	14	14	52	48	42	10th
1949–50	IIIN	42	18	12	12	66	54	48	8th
1950–51	IIIN	46	26	12	8	78	48	64	2nd
1951–52	IIIN	46	22	8	16	73	60	52	6th
1952–53	IIIN	46	16	14	16	55	62	46	18th
1953–54	IIIN	46	20	11	15	88	67	51	7th
1954–55	IIIN	46	18	9	19	65	71	45	13th
1955–56	IIIN	46	14	11	21	84	81	39	18th
1956–57	IIIN	46	17	10	19	91	90	44	16th
1957–58	IIIN	46	22	8	16	100	92	52	6th
1958–59	III	46	14	13	19	73	98	41	20th
1959–60	III	46	15	6	25	81	112	36	22nd
1960–61	IV	46	16	6	24	71	78	38	20th
1961–62	IV	44	19	6	19	77	66	44	14th
1962–63	IV	46	24	9	13	108	69	57	4th
1963–64	III	46	20	11	15	76	62	51	7th
1964–65	III	46	24	11	11	95	61	59	3rd
1965–66	III	46	15	8	23	59	89	38	19th
1966–67	III	46	20	9	17	84	79	49	9th
1967–68	III	46	12	13	21	51	67	37	20th
1968–69	III	46	16	11	19	58	62	43	15th
1969–70	III	46	21	11	14	70	49	53	6th
1970–71	III	46	18	15	13	64	62	51	7th
1971–72	III	46	8	20	18	41	63	36	21st
1972–73	IV	46	20	14	12	78	51	54	6th
1973–74	IV	46	13	17	16	62	69	43	17th
1974–75	IV	46	28	12	6	90	40	68	1st
1975–76	III	46	16	15	15	58	52	47	11th
1976–77	III	46	28	8	10	78	33	64	1st
1977–78	II	42	10	11	21	49	69	31	21st
1978–79	II	46	12	19	15	51	52	43	18th
1979–80	III	46	10	16	20	47	58	36	23rd
1980–81	IV	46	20	9	17	58	44	49	7th
1981–82	IV	46	13	10	23	63	81	47	20th
1982–83	IV	46	16	13	17	61	70	61	10th
1983–84	IV	46	13	13	20	66	70	52	19th
1984–85	IV	46	13	18	15	41	38	57	14th
1985–86	IV	46	23	12	11	74	47	81	3rd
1986–87	III	46	15	16	15	52	55	61	10th
1987–88	III	46	14	12	20	48	59	54	19th
1988–89	III	46	14	17	15	48	52	59	15th
1989–90	III	46	16	7	23	50	65	55	15th
1990–91	III	46	8	14	24	42	63	38	24th
1991–92	IV	42	23	8	11	75	53	77	3rd
1992–93	II	46	11	11	24	52	80	44	22nd

Mansfield Town recorded their first win over a Division One team when they beat West Ham United 3–0 in an FA Cup, fifth round tie at Field Mill on 26 February 1969. West Ham included Bobby Moore, Martin Peters, Geoff Hurst and Trevor Brooking in their team.

MERTHYR TOWN

Year	Div	P	W	D	L	F	A	Pts	Pos
1920–21	III	42	15	15	12	60	49	45	8th
1921–22	IIIS	42	17	6	19	45	56	40	11th
1922–23	IIIS	42	11	14	17	39	48	36	17th
1923–24	IIIS	42	11	16	15	45	65	38	13th
1924–25	IIIS	42	8	5	29	35	77	21	22nd
1925–26	IIIS	42	14	11	17	69	75	39	14th
1926–27	IIIS	42	13	9	20	63	80	35	17th
1927–28	IIIS	42	9	13	20	53	91	31	21st
1928–29	IIIS	42	11	8	23	55	103	30	20th
1929–30	IIIS	42	6	9	27	60	135	21	22nd

Merthyr Town had two Welsh international players, Moses Russell capped before the First World War and Rhys Williams shortly afterwards.

MIDDLESBROUGH

Year	Div	P	W	D	L	F	A	Pts	Pos
1899–1900	II	34	8	8	18	39	69	24	14th
1900–01	II	34	15	7	12	50	40	37	6th
1901–02	II	34	23	5	6	90	24	51	2nd
1902–03	I	34	14	4	16	41	50	32	13th
1903–04	I	34	9	12	13	46	47	30	10th
1904–05	I	34	9	8	17	36	56	26	15th
1905–06	I	38	10	11	17	56	71	31	18th
1906–07	I	38	15	6	17	56	63	36	11th
1907–08	I	38	17	7	14	54	45	41	6th
1908–09	I	38	14	9	15	59	53	37	9th
1909–10	I	38	11	9	18	56	73	31	17th
1910–11	I	38	11	10	17	49	63	32	16th
1911–12	I	38	16	8	14	56	45	40	7th
1912–13	I	38	11	10	17	55	69	32	16th
1913–14	I	38	19	5	14	77	60	43	3rd
1914–15	I	38	13	12	13	62	74	38	12th
1915–19	Regional Leagues operating								
1919–20	I	42	15	10	17	61	65	40	13th
1920–21	I	42	17	12	13	53	53	46	8th
1921–22	I	42	16	14	12	79	69	46	8th
1922–23	I	42	13	10	19	57	63	36	18th
1923–24	I	42	7	8	27	37	60	22	22nd
1924–25	II	42	10	19	13	36	44	39	13th
1925–26	II	42	21	2	19	77	68	44	9th
1926–27	II	42	27	8	7	122	60	62	1st
1927–28	I	42	11	15	16	81	88	37	22nd
1928–29	II	42	22	11	9	92	57	55	1st
1929–30	I	42	16	6	20	82	84	38	16th
1930–31	I	42	19	8	15	98	90	46	7th
1931–32	I	42	15	8	19	64	89	38	18th
1932–33	I	42	14	9	19	63	73	37	17th
1933–34	I	42	16	7	19	68	80	39	16th
1934–35	I	42	10	14	18	70	90	34	20th
1935–36	I	42	15	10	17	84	70	40	14th
1936–37	I	42	19	8	15	74	71	46	7th
1937–38	I	42	19	8	15	72	65	46	5th
1938–39	I	42	20	9	13	93	74	49	4th
1939–46	Regional Leagues operating								
1946–47	I	42	17	8	17	73	68	42	11th
1947–48	I	42	14	9	19	71	73	37	16th
1948–49	I	42	11	12	19	46	57	34	19th
1949–50	I	42	20	7	15	59	48	47	9th
1950–51	I	42	18	11	13	76	65	47	6th
1951–52	I	42	15	6	21	64	88	36	18th
1952–53	I	42	14	11	17	70	77	39	13th
1953–54	I	42	10	10	22	60	91	30	21st
1954–55	II	42	18	6	18	73	82	42	12th
1955–56	II	42	16	8	18	76	78	40	14th
1956–57	II	42	19	10	13	84	60	48	6th
1957–58	II	42	19	7	16	83	74	45	7th
1958–59	II	42	15	10	17	87	71	40	13th
1959–60	II	42	19	10	13	90	64	48	5th
1960–61	II	42	18	12	12	83	74	48	5th
1961–62	II	42	16	7	19	76	72	39	12th
1962–63	II	42	20	9	13	86	85	49	4th
1963–64	II	42	15	11	16	67	52	41	10th
1964–65	II	42	13	9	20	70	76	35	17th
1965–66	II	42	10	13	19	58	86	33	21st
1966–67	III	46	23	9	14	87	64	55	2nd
1967–68	II	42	17	12	13	60	54	46	6th
1968–69	II	42	19	11	12	58	49	49	4th
1969–70	II	42	20	10	12	55	45	50	4th
1970–71	II	42	17	14	11	60	43	48	7th
1971–72	II	42	19	8	15	50	48	46	9th
1972–73	II	42	17	13	12	46	43	47	4th
1973–74	II	42	27	11	4	77	30	65	1st
1974–75	I	42	18	12	12	54	40	48	7th
1975–76	I	42	15	10	17	46	45	40	13th
1976–77	I	42	14	13	15	40	45	41	12th
1977–78	I	42	12	15	15	42	54	39	14th
1978–79	I	42	15	10	17	57	50	40	12th
1979–80	I	42	16	12	14	50	44	44	9th
1980–81	I	42	16	5	21	53	61	37	14th
1981–82	I	42	8	15	19	34	52	39	22nd
1982–83	II	42	11	15	16	46	67	48	16th
1983–84	II	42	12	13	17	41	47	49	17th
1984–85	II	42	10	10	22	41	57	40	19th
1985–86	II	42	12	9	21	44	53	45	21st
1986–87	III	46	28	10	8	67	30	94	2nd
1987–88	II	44	22	12	10	63	36	78	3rd
1988–89	I	38	9	12	17	44	61	39	18th
1989–90	II	46	13	11	22	52	63	50	21st
1990–91	II	46	20	9	17	66	47	69	7th
1991–92	II	46	23	11	12	58	41	80	2nd
1992–93	PL	42	11	11	20	54	75	44	21st

George Camsell was top scorer for **Middlesbrough** in ten successive seasons from 1926 to 1936. His most prolific spell produced 29 goals in 12 consecutive League games during 1926–27 when he hit a club record 59.

MIDDLESBROUGH IRONOPOLIS

Year	Div	P	W	D	L	F	A	Pts	Pos
1893–94	II	28	8	4	16	37	72	20	11th

Middlesbrough Ironopolis had some success in the FA Cup, reaching the quarter-finals in 1893 and the last 16 during the following season.

MILLWALL

Year	Div	P	W	D	L	F	A	Pts	Pos
1920–21	III	42	18	11	13	42	30	47	7th
1921–22	IIIS	42	10	18	14	38	42	38	12th
1922–23	IIIS	42	14	18	10	45	40	46	6th
1923–24	IIIS	42	22	10	10	64	38	54	3rd
1924–25	IIIS	42	18	13	11	58	38	49	5th
1925–26	IIIS	42	21	11	10	73	39	53	3rd

Year	Div	P	W	D	L	F	A	Pts	Pos
1926–27	IIIS	42	23	10	9	89	51	56	3rd
1927–28	IIIS	42	30	5	7	127	50	65	1st
1928–29	II	42	16	7	19	71	86	39	14th
1929–30	II	42	12	15	15	57	73	39	14th
1930–31	II	42	16	7	19	71	80	39	14th
1931–32	II	42	17	9	16	61	61	43	9th
1932–33	II	42	16	11	15	59	57	43	7th
1933–34	II	42	11	11	20	39	68	33	21st
1934–35	IIIS	42	17	7	18	57	62	41	12th
1935–36	IIIS	42	14	12	16	58	71	40	12th
1936–37	IIIS	42	18	10	14	64	54	46	8th
1937–38	IIIS	42	23	10	9	83	37	56	1st
1938–39	II	42	14	14	14	64	53	42	13th
1939–46	Regional Leagues operating								
1946–47	II	42	14	8	20	56	79	36	18th
1947–48	II	42	9	11	22	44	74	29	22nd
1948–49	IIIS	42	17	11	14	63	64	45	8th
1950–51	IIIS	46	23	10	13	80	57	56	5th
1951–52	IIIS	46	23	12	11	74	53	58	4th
1952–53	IIIS	46	24	14	8	82	44	62	2nd
1953–54	IIIS	46	19	9	18	74	77	47	12th
1954–55	IIIS	46	20	11	15	72	68	51	5th
1955–56	IIIS	46	15	6	25	83	100	36	22nd
1956–57	IIIS	46	16	12	18	64	84	44	17th
1957–58	IIIS	46	11	9	26	63	91	31	23rd
1958–59	IV	46	20	10	16	76	69	50	9th
1959–60	IV	46	18	17	11	84	61	53	5th
1960–61	IV	46	21	8	17	97	86	50	6th
1961–62	IV	44	23	10	11	87	62	56	1st
1962–63	III	46	15	13	18	82	87	43	16th
1963–64	III	46	14	10	22	53	67	38	21st
1964–65	IV	46	23	16	7	78	45	62	2nd
1965–66	III	46	27	11	8	76	43	65	2nd
1966–67	II	42	18	9	15	49	58	45	8th
1967–68	II	42	14	17	11	62	50	45	7th
1968–69	II	42	17	9	16	57	49	43	10th
1969–70	II	42	15	14	13	56	56	44	10th
1970–71	II	42	19	9	14	59	42	47	8th
1971–72	II	42	19	17	6	64	46	55	3rd
1972–73	II	42	16	10	16	55	47	42	11th
1973–74	II	42	14	14	14	51	51	42	12th
1974–75	II	42	10	12	20	44	56	32	20th
1975–76	II	42	20	16	10	54	43	56	3rd
1976–77	II	42	17	13	14	57	53	43	10th
1977–78	III	42	12	14	16	49	57	38	16th
1978–79	II	42	11	10	21	42	61	32	21st
1979–80	III	46	16	13	17	65	59	45	14th
1980–81	III	46	14	14	18	43	60	42	16th
1981–82	III	46	18	13	15	62	62	67	9th
1982–83	III	46	14	13	19	64	78	55	17th
1983–84	III	46	18	13	15	71	65	67	9th
1984–85	III	46	26	12	8	83	42	90	2nd
1985–86	II	42	17	8	17	64	65	59	9th
1986–87	II	42	14	9	19	39	45	51	16th
1987–88	II	44	25	7	12	72	52	81	1st
1988–89	I	38	14	11	13	47	52	53	10th
1989–90	I	38	5	11	22	39	65	26	20th

Millwall briefly made it back to the top flight in the late 1980s, winning the Second Division title under John Docherty (right) and Frank McLintock (Allsport)

Year	Div	P	W	D	L	F	A	Pts	Pos
1990–91	II	46	20	13	13	70	51	73	5th
1991–92	II	46	17	10	19	64	71	61	15th
1992–93	I	46	18	16	12	65	53	70	7th

Millwall were founded in Docklands in 1885 as Millwall Rovers and originally known as the Dockers. They won the East End Cup three years in a row from 1887–1889.

NELSON

Year	Div	P	W	D	L	F	A	Pts	Pos
1921–22	IIIN	38	13	7	18	48	66	33	16th
1922–23	IIIN	38	24	3	11	61	41	51	1st
1923–24	II	42	10	13	19	40	74	33	21st
1924–25	IIIN	42	23	7	12	79	50	53	2nd
1925–26	IIIN	42	16	11	15	89	71	43	8th
1926–27	IIIN	42	22	7	13	104	75	51	5th
1927–28	IIIN	42	10	6	26	76	136	26	22nd
1928–29	IIIN	42	17	5	20	77	90	39	15th
1929–30	IIIN	42	13	7	22	51	80	33	19th
1930–31	IIIN	42	6	7	29	43	113	19	22nd

Joe Eddleston was the highest individual scorer for **Nelson** in a season. In 1924–25 his 26 goals topped the club's scoring lists. He subsequently played for Swindon Town.

NEW BRIGHTON TOWER

Year	Div	P	W	D	L	F	A	Pts	Pos
1898–99	II	34	18	7	9	71	52	43	5th
1899–1900	II	34	13	9	12	66	58	35	10th
1900–01	II	34	17	8	9	57	38	42	4th
Resigned									

NEW BRIGHTON

Year	Div	P	W	D	L	F	A	Pts	Pos
1923–24	IIIN	42	11	13	18	40	53	35	18th
1924–25	IIIN	42	23	7	12	75	50	53	3rd
1925–26	IIIN	42	17	8	17	69	67	42	12th
1926–27	IIIN	42	18	10	14	79	67	46	10th
1927–28	IIIN	42	14	14	14	72	62	42	10th
1928–29	IIIN	42	15	9	18	64	71	39	14th
1929–30	IIIN	42	16	8	18	69	79	40	13th
1930–31	IIIN	42	13	7	22	49	76	33	19th
1931–32	IIIN	40	8	8	24	38	76	24	20th
1932–33	IIIN	42	11	10	21	63	88	32	21st
1933–34	IIIN	42	14	8	20	62	87	36	15th
1934–35	IIIN	42	14	8	20	59	76	36	16th
1935–36	IIIN	42	9	6	27	43	102	24	22nd
1936–37	IIIN	42	13	11	18	55	70	37	15th
1937–38	IIIN	42	15	8	19	60	61	38	13th
1938–39	IIIN	42	15	9	18	68	73	39	16th
1939–46	Regional Leagues operating								
1946–47	IIIN	42	14	8	20	57	77	36	18th
1947–48	IIIN	42	8	9	25	38	81	25	22nd
1948–49	IIIN	42	14	8	20	46	58	36	17th
1949–50	IIIN	42	14	10	18	45	63	38	14th
1950–51	IIIN	46	11	8	27	40	90	30	24th

Failed re-election

New Brighton Tower played their last fixture on 27 April 1901 against Woolwich Arsenal. The only goal came when Arsenal's Jimmy Jackson put through his own goal.

For a year from January 1924, **New Brighton** had two goalkeeping brothers on the books, John and Bert Mehaffy. Both had a reputation for taking penalties on occasions, John scoring for the reserves and Bert in a Division Three (North) match against Ashington on Boxing Day 1923.

NEWCASTLE UNITED

Year	Div	P	W	D	L	F	A	Pts	Pos
1893–94	II	28	15	6	7	66	39	36	4th
1894–95	II	30	12	3	15	72	84	27	10th
1895–96	II	30	16	2	12	73	40	34	5th
1896–97	II	30	17	1	12	56	52	35	5th
1897–98	II	30	21	3	6	64	32	45	2nd
1898–99	I	34	11	8	15	49	48	30	13th
1899–1900	I	34	13	10	11	53	43	36	5th
1900–01	I	34	14	10	10	42	37	38	6th
1901–02	I	34	14	9	11	48	34	37	3rd
1902–03	I	34	14	4	16	41	51	32	14th
1903–04	I	34	18	6	10	58	45	42	4th
1904–05	I	34	23	2	9	72	33	48	1st
1905–06	I	38	18	7	13	74	48	43	4th
1906–07	I	38	22	7	9	74	46	51	1st
1907–08	I	38	15	12	11	65	54	42	4th
1908–09	I	38	24	5	9	65	41	53	1st
1909–10	I	38	19	7	12	70	56	45	4th
1910–11	I	38	15	10	13	61	43	40	8th
1911–12	I	38	18	8	12	64	50	44	3rd
1912–13	I	38	13	8	17	47	47	34	14th
1913–14	I	38	13	11	14	39	48	37	11th
1914–15	I	38	11	10	17	46	48	32	15th
1915–19	Regional Leagues operating								
1919–20	I	42	17	9	16	44	39	43	8th
1920–21	I	42	20	10	12	66	45	50	5th
1921–22	I	42	18	10	14	59	45	46	7th
1922–23	I	42	18	12	12	45	37	48	4th
1923–24	I	42	17	10	15	60	54	44	9th
1924–25	I	42	16	16	10	61	42	48	6th
1925–26	I	42	16	10	16	84	75	42	10th
1926–27	I	42	25	6	11	96	58	56	1st
1927–28	I	42	15	13	14	79	81	43	9th
1928–29	I	42	19	6	17	70	72	44	10th
1929–30	I	42	15	7	20	71	92	37	19th
1930–31	I	42	15	6	21	78	87	36	17th
1931–32	I	42	18	6	18	80	87	42	11th
1932–33	I	42	22	5	15	71	63	49	5th
1933–34	I	42	10	14	18	68	77	34	21st
1934–35	II	42	22	4	16	89	68	48	6th
1935–36	II	42	20	6	16	88	79	46	8th
1936–37	II	42	22	5	15	80	56	49	4th
1937–38	II	42	14	8	20	51	58	36	19th
1938–39	II	42	18	10	14	61	48	46	9th
1939–46	Regional Leagues operating								
1946–47	II	42	19	10	13	95	62	48	5th
1947–48	II	42	24	8	10	72	41	56	2nd
1948–49	I	42	20	12	10	70	56	52	4th
1949–50	I	42	19	12	11	77	55	50	5th
1950–51	I	42	18	13	11	62	53	49	4th
1951–52	I	42	18	9	15	98	73	45	8th
1952–53	I	42	14	9	19	59	70	37	16th
1953–54	I	42	14	10	18	72	77	38	15th
1954–55	I	42	17	9	16	89	77	43	8th
1955–56	I	42	17	7	18	85	70	41	11th
1956–57	I	42	14	8	20	67	87	36	17th
1957–58	I	42	12	8	22	73	81	32	19th
1958–59	I	42	17	7	18	80	80	41	11th
1959–60	I	42	18	8	16	82	78	44	8th
1960–61	I	42	11	10	21	86	109	32	21st
1961–62	II	42	15	9	18	64	58	39	11th
1962–63	II	42	18	11	13	79	59	47	7th
1963–64	II	42	20	5	17	74	69	45	8th
1964–65	II	42	24	9	9	81	45	57	1st
1965–66	I	42	14	9	19	50	63	37	15th
1966–67	I	42	12	9	21	39	81	33	20th
1967–68	I	42	13	15	14	54	67	41	10th
1968–69	I	42	15	14	13	61	55	44	9th
1969–70	I	42	17	13	12	57	35	47	7th
1970–71	I	42	14	13	15	44	46	41	12th
1971–72	I	42	15	11	16	49	52	41	11th
1972–73	I	42	16	13	13	60	51	45	9th
1973–74	I	42	13	12	17	49	48	38	15th
1974–75	I	42	15	9	18	59	72	39	15th
1975–76	I	42	15	9	18	71	62	39	15th
1976–77	I	42	18	13	11	64	49	49	5th

A marvellous season for Newcastle United in 1992–93 saw them promoted back to the top flight under Kevin Keegan (Bob Thomas)

1977–78	I	42	6	10	26	42	78	22	21st
1978–79	II	42	17	8	17	51	55	42	8th
1979–80	II	42	15	14	13	53	49	44	9th
1980–81	II	42	14	14	14	30	45	42	11th
1981–82	II	42	18	8	16	52	50	62	9th
1982–83	II	42	18	13	11	75	53	67	5th
1983–84	II	42	24	8	10	85	53	80	3rd
1984–85	I	42	13	13	16	55	70	52	14th
1985–86	I	42	17	12	13	67	72	63	11th
1986–87	I	42	12	11	19	47	65	47	17th
1987–88	I	40	14	14	12	55	53	56	8th
1988–89	I	38	7	10	21	32	63	31	20th
1989–90	II	46	22	14	10	80	55	80	3rd
1990–91	II	46	14	17	15	49	56	59	11th
1991–92	II	46	13	13	20	66	84	52	20th
1992–93	I	46	29	9	8	92	38	96	1st

On 5 September 1992, **Newcastle United** equalled their best start to a season, five victories, when they won 2–1 at Bristol Rovers. In 1908–09 they had gone on to win the Division One title. On 12 September they recorded six wins and a club record eight consecutively. They went on to win 11 in a row, 13 overall.

NEWPORT COUNTY

Year	Div	P	W	D	L	F	A	Pts	Pos
1920–21	III	42	14	9	19	43	64	37	15th
1921–22	IIIS	42	11	12	19	44	61	34	20th
1922–23	IIIS	42	8	11	23	40	70	27	22nd
1923–24	IIIS	42	17	9	16	56	64	43	10th
1924–25	IIIS	42	20	9	13	62	42	49	6th
1925–26	IIIS	42	12	13	17	42	49	37	17th
1926–27	IIIS	42	19	6	17	57	71	44	9th
1927–28	IIIS	42	18	9	15	81	84	45	9th
1928–29	IIIS	42	13	9	20	69	86	35	16th
1929–30	IIIS	42	12	10	20	74	85	34	18th

1930–31	IIIS	42	11	6	25	69	111	28	21st
1931–32	Suspended by Football League								
1932–33	IIIS	42	11	7	24	61	105	29	21st
1933–34	IIIS	42	8	17	17	49	70	33	18th
1934–35	IIIS	42	10	5	27	54	112	25	22nd
1935–36	IIIS	42	11	9	22	60	111	31	21st
1936–37	IIIS	42	12	10	20	67	98	34	19th
1937–38	IIIS	42	11	16	15	43	52	38	16th
1938–39	IIIS	42	22	11	9	58	45	55	1st
1939–46	Regional Leagues operating								
1946–47	II	42	10	3	29	61	133	23	22nd
1947–48	IIIS	42	14	13	15	61	73	41	12th
1948–49	IIIS	42	14	9	19	68	92	37	15th
1949–50	IIIS	42	13	8	21	67	98	34	21st
1950–51	IIIS	46	19	9	18	77	70	47	11th
1951–52	IIIS	46	21	12	13	77	76	54	6th
1952–53	IIIS	46	16	10	20	70	82	42	15th
1953–54	IIIS	46	19	6	21	61	81	44	15th
1954–55	IIIS	46	11	16	19	60	73	38	19th
1955–56	IIIS	46	15	9	22	58	79	39	19th
1956–57	IIIS	46	16	13	17	65	62	45	12th
1957–58	IIIS	46	17	14	15	73	67	48	11th
1958–59	III	46	17	9	20	69	68	43	17th
1959–60	III	46	20	6	20	80	79	46	13th
1960–61	III	46	17	11	18	81	90	45	13th
1961–62	III	46	7	8	31	46	102	22	24th
1962–63	IV	46	14	11	21	76	90	39	20th
1963–64	IV	46	17	8	21	64	73	42	15th
1964–65	IV	46	17	8	21	85	81	42	16th
1965–66	IV	46	18	12	16	75	75	48	9th
1966–67	IV	46	12	16	18	56	63	40	18th
1967–68	IV	46	16	13	17	58	63	45	12th
1968–69	IV	46	11	14	21	49	74	36	22nd
1969–70	IV	46	13	11	22	53	74	37	21st
1970–71	IV	46	10	8	28	55	85	28	22nd
1971–72	IV	46	18	8	20	60	72	44	14th
1972–73	IV	46	22	12	12	64	44	56	5th
1973–74	IV	46	16	14	16	56	65	45	9th
1974–75	IV	46	19	9	18	68	75	47	12th
1975–76	IV	46	13	9	24	57	90	35	22nd
1976–77	IV	46	14	10	22	42	58	38	19th
1977–78	IV	46	16	11	19	65	73	43	16th
1978–79	IV	46	21	10	15	66	55	52	8th
1979–80	IV	46	27	7	12	83	50	61	3rd
1980–81	III	46	15	13	18	64	61	43	12th
1981–82	III	46	14	16	16	54	54	58	16th
1982–83	III	46	23	9	14	76	54	78	4th
1983–84	III	46	16	14	16	58	75	62	13th
1984–85	III	46	13	13	20	55	67	52	18th
1985–86	III	46	11	18	17	52	65	51	19th
1986–87	III	46	8	13	25	49	86	37	24th
1987–88	III	46	6	7	33	35	105	25	24th

On 10 April 1930 Tudor 'Ted' Martin scored five of the goals by which **Newport County** beat Merthyr Town 10–0. A Welsh amateur international he later played in Ipswich Town's first League match.

NORTHAMPTON TOWN

Year	Div	P	W	D	L	F	A	Pts	Pos
1920–21	III	42	15	8	19	59	75	38	14th
1921–22	IIIS	42	13	11	18	47	71	37	17th
1922–23	IIIS	42	17	11	14	54	44	45	8th
1923–24	IIIS	42	17	11	14	64	47	45	8th
1924–25	IIIS	42	20	6	16	51	44	46	9th
1925–26	IIIS	42	17	7	18	82	80	41	12th
1926–27	IIIS	42	15	5	22	59	87	35	18th
1927–28	IIIS	42	23	9	10	102	64	55	2nd
1928–29	IIIS	42	20	12	10	96	57	52	3rd
1929–30	IIIS	42	21	8	13	82	58	50	4th
1930–31	IIIS	42	18	12	12	77	59	48	6th
1931–32	IIIS	42	16	7	19	69	69	39	14th
1932–33	IIIS	42	18	8	16	76	66	44	8th
1933–34	IIIS	42	14	12	16	71	78	40	13th
1934–35	IIIS	42	19	8	15	65	67	46	7th
1935–36	IIIS	42	15	8	19	62	90	38	15th
1936–37	IIIS	42	20	6	16	85	68	46	7th
1937–38	IIIS	42	17	9	16	51	57	43	9th
1938–39	IIIS	42	15	8	19	51	58	38	17th
1939–46	Regional Leagues operating								
1946–47	IIIS	42	15	10	17	72	75	40	13th
1947–48	IIIS	42	14	11	17	58	72	39	14th
1948–49	IIIS	42	12	9	21	51	62	33	20th
1949–50	IIIS	42	20	11	11	72	50	51	2nd
1950–51	IIIS	46	10	16	20	55	67	36	21st
1951–52	IIIS	46	22	5	19	93	74	49	8th
1952–53	IIIS	46	26	10	10	109	70	62	3rd
1953–54	IIIS	46	20	11	15	82	55	51	5th
1954–55	IIIS	46	19	8	19	73	81	46	13th
1955–56	IIIS	46	20	7	19	67	71	47	11th
1956–57	IIIS	46	18	9	19	66	73	45	14th
1957–58	IIIS	46	19	6	21	87	79	44	13th
1958–59	IV	46	21	9	16	85	78	51	8th
1959–60	IV	46	22	9	15	85	63	53	6th
1960–61	IV	46	25	10	11	90	62	60	3rd
1961–62	III	46	20	11	15	85	57	51	8th
1962–63	III	46	26	10	10	109	60	62	1st
1963–64	II	42	16	9	17	58	60	41	11th
1964–65	II	42	20	16	6	66	50	56	2nd
1965–66	I	42	10	13	19	55	92	33	21st
1966–67	II	42	12	6	24	47	84	30	21st
1967–68	III	46	14	13	19	58	72	41	17th
1968–69	III	46	14	12	20	54	61	40	21st
1969–70	IV	46	16	12	18	64	55	44	14th
1970–71	IV	46	19	13	14	63	59	51	7th
1971–72	IV	46	12	13	21	66	79	37	21st
1972–73	IV	46	10	11	25	40	73	31	23rd
1973–74	IV	46	20	13	13	63	48	53	5th
1974–75	IV	46	15	11	20	67	73	41	16th
1975–76	IV	46	29	10	7	87	40	68	2nd
1976–77	III	46	13	8	25	60	75	34	22nd
1977–78	IV	46	17	13	16	63	68	47	10th
1978–79	IV	46	15	9	22	64	76	39	19th
1979–80	IV	46	16	12	18	51	66	44	13th
1980–81	IV	46	18	13	15	65	67	49	10th
1981–82	IV	46	11	9	26	57	84	42	22nd
1982–83	IV	46	14	12	20	67	75	54	15th
1983–84	IV	46	13	14	19	53	78	53	18th
1984–85	IV	46	14	5	27	53	74	47	23rd
1985–86	IV	46	18	10	18	79	58	64	8th
1986–87	IV	46	30	9	7	103	53	99	1st
1987–88	III	46	18	19	9	70	51	73	6th
1988–89	III	46	16	6	24	66	76	54	20th
1989–90	III	46	11	14	21	51	68	47	22nd
1990–91	IV	46	18	13	15	57	58	67	10th
1991–92	IV	42	11	13	18	46	57	46	16th
1992–93	III	42	11	8	23	48	74	41	20th

Although Ted Bowen broke the then **Northampton Town** scoring record in 1928–29 with 34 League goals, one other player had notable success in front of goal that season. Ralph Hoten scored five goals in an 8–1 win over Crystal Palace on 27 October and four in a 6–1 victory against Torquay United two weeks later.

NORTHWICH VICTORIA

Year	Div	P	W	D	L	F	A	Pts	Pos
1892–93	II	22	9	2	11	42	58	20	7th
1893–94	II	28	3	3	22	30	98	9	15th

Drill Field has been the home of **Northwich Victoria** since 1875 and possibly even earlier, making it the oldest football ground in the world. The club was formed around 1874 and began as a hare and hounds club whose members also played soccer and rugby. It was decided to concentrate on soccer and Northwich Victoria came into existence.

NORWICH CITY

Year	Div	P	W	D	L	F	A	Pts	Pos
1920–21	III	42	10	16	16	44	53	36	16th
1921–22	IIIS	42	12	13	17	50	62	37	15th
1922–23	IIIS	42	13	10	19	51	71	36	18th
1923–24	IIIS	42	16	8	17	60	59	40	11th
1924–25	IIIS	42	14	13	15	53	51	41	12th
1925–26	IIIS	42	15	9	18	58	73	39	16th
1926–27	IIIS	42	12	11	19	59	71	35	16th
1927–28	IIIS	42	10	16	16	66	70	36	17th
1928–29	IIIS	42	14	6	22	69	81	34	17th
1929–30	IIIS	42	18	10	14	88	77	46	8th
1930–31	IIIS	42	10	8	24	47	76	28	22nd
1931–32	IIIS	42	17	12	13	76	67	46	10th
1932–33	IIIS	42	22	13	7	88	55	57	3rd
1933–34	IIIS	42	25	11	6	88	49	61	1st
1934–35	II	42	14	11	17	71	61	39	14th
1935–36	II	42	17	9	16	72	88	43	11th
1936–37	II	42	14	8	20	63	71	36	17th
1937–38	II	42	14	11	17	56	85	39	14th

Year	Div	P	W	D	L	F	A	Pts	Pos
1938–39	II	42	13	5	24	50	91	31	21st
1939–46	Regional Leagues operating								
1946–47	IIIS	42	10	8	24	64	100	28	21st
1947–48	IIIS	42	13	8	21	61	76	34	21st
1948–49	IIIS	42	16	12	14	67	49	44	10th
1949–50	IIIS	42	16	10	16	65	63	42	11th
1950–51	IIIS	46	25	14	7	82	45	64	2nd
1951–52	IIIS	46	26	9	11	89	50	61	3rd
1952–53	IIIS	46	25	10	11	99	55	60	4th
1953–54	IIIS	46	20	11	15	73	66	51	7th
1954–55	IIIS	46	18	10	18	60	60	46	11th
1955–56	IIIS	46	19	13	14	86	82	51	7th
1956–57	IIIS	46	8	15	23	61	94	31	24th
1957–58	IIIS	46	19	15	12	75	70	53	8th
1958–59	III	46	22	13	11	89	62	57	4th
1959–60	III	46	24	11	11	82	54	59	2nd
1960–61	II	42	20	9	13	70	53	49	4th
1961–62	II	42	14	11	17	61	70	39	17th
1962–63	II	42	17	8	17	80	79	42	13th
1963–64	II	42	11	13	18	64	80	35	17th
1964–65	II	42	20	7	15	61	57	47	6th
1965–66	II	42	12	15	15	52	52	39	13th
1966–67	II	42	13	14	15	49	55	40	11th
1967–68	II	42	16	11	15	60	65	43	9th
1968–69	II	42	15	10	17	53	66	40	13th
1969–70	II	42	16	11	15	69	57	43	11th
1970–71	II	42	15	14	13	54	52	44	10th
1971–72	II	42	21	15	6	60	36	57	1st
1972–73	I	42	11	10	21	36	63	32	20th
1973–74	I	42	7	15	20	37	62	29	22nd
1974–75	II	42	20	13	9	58	37	53	3rd
1975–76	I	42	16	10	16	58	58	42	10th
1976–77	I	42	14	9	19	47	64	37	16th
1977–78	I	42	11	18	13	52	66	40	13th
1978–79	I	42	7	23	12	51	57	37	16th
1979–80	I	42	13	14	15	58	66	40	12th
1980–81	I	42	13	7	22	49	73	33	20th
1981–82	II	42	22	5	15	64	50	71	3rd
1982–83	I	42	14	12	16	52	58	54	14th
1983–84	I	42	12	15	15	48	49	51	14th
1984–85	I	42	13	10	19	46	64	49	20th
1985–86	II	42	25	9	8	84	37	84	1st
1986–87	I	42	17	17	8	53	51	68	5th
1987–88	I	40	12	9	19	40	52	45	14th
1988–89	I	38	17	11	10	48	45	62	4th
1989–90	I	38	13	14	11	44	42	53	10th
1990–91	I	38	13	6	19	41	64	45	15th
1991–92	I	42	11	12	19	47	63	45	18th
1992–93	PL	42	21	9	12	61	65	72	3rd

Roy Hollis made his debut for **Norwich City** on 21 April 1948 and scored a hat-trick in the first 20 minutes against Queens Park Rangers during a 5–2 win. He went on to score 59 goals in 107 senior appearances and 54 in 88 reserve team games. He later played for Tottenham Hotspur and while with Southend United scored a hat-trick at Carrow Road on 27 December 1954.

NOTTINGHAM FOREST

Year	Div	P	W	D	L	F	A	Pts	Pos
1892–93	I	30	10	8	12	48	52	28	10th
1893–94	I	30	14	4	12	57	48	32	7th
1894–95	I	30	13	5	12	50	56	31	7th
1895–96	I	30	11	3	16	42	57	25	13th
1896–97	I	30	9	8	13	44	49	26	11th
1897–98	I	30	11	9	10	47	49	31	8th
1898–99	I	34	11	11	12	42	42	33	11th
1899–1900	I	34	13	8	13	56	55	34	8th
1900–01	I	34	16	7	11	53	36	39	4th
1901–02	I	34	13	9	12	43	43	35	5th
1902–03	I	34	14	7	13	49	47	35	10th
1903–04	I	34	11	9	14	57	57	31	9th
1904–05	I	34	9	7	18	40	61	25	16th
1905–06	I	38	13	5	20	58	79	31	19th
1906–07	II	38	28	4	6	74	36	60	1st
1907–08	I	38	13	11	14	59	62	37	9th
1908–09	I	38	14	8	16	66	57	36	14th
1909–10	I	38	11	11	16	54	72	33	14th
1910–11	I	38	9	7	22	55	75	25	20th
1911–12	II	38	13	7	18	46	48	33	15th
1912–13	II	38	12	8	18	58	59	32	17th
1913–14	II	38	7	9	22	37	76	23	20th
1914–15	II	38	10	9	19	43	77	29	18th
1915–19	Regional Leagues operating								
1919–20	II	42	11	9	22	43	73	31	18th
1920–21	II	42	12	12	18	48	55	36	18th
1921–22	II	42	22	12	8	51	30	56	1st
1922–23	I	42	13	8	21	41	70	34	20th
1923–24	I	42	10	12	20	42	64	32	20th
1924–25	I	42	6	12	24	29	65	24	22nd
1925–26	II	42	14	8	20	51	73	36	17th
1926–27	II	42	18	14	10	80	55	50	5th
1927–28	II	42	15	10	17	83	84	40	10th
1928–29	II	42	15	12	15	71	70	42	11th
1929–30	II	42	13	15	14	55	69	41	10th
1930–31	II	42	14	9	19	80	85	37	17th
1931–32	II	42	16	10	16	77	72	42	11th
1932–33	II	42	17	15	10	67	59	49	5th
1933–34	II	42	13	9	20	73	74	35	17th
1934–35	II	42	17	8	17	76	70	42	9th
1935–36	II	42	12	11	19	69	76	35	19th
1936–37	II	42	12	10	20	68	90	34	18th
1937–38	II	42	14	8	20	47	60	36	20th
1938–39	II	42	10	11	21	49	82	31	19th
1939–46	Regional Leagues operating								
1946–47	II	42	15	10	17	69	74	40	11th
1947–48	II	42	12	11	19	54	60	35	19th
1948–49	II	42	14	7	21	50	54	35	21st
1949–50	IIIS	42	20	9	13	67	39	49	4th
1950–51	IIIS	46	30	10	6	110	40	70	1st
1951–52	II	42	18	13	11	77	62	49	4th
1952–53	II	42	18	8	16	77	67	44	7th
1953–54	II	42	20	12	10	86	59	52	4th
1954–55	II	42	16	7	19	58	62	39	15th
1955–56	II	42	19	9	14	68	63	47	7th

Year	Div	P	W	D	L	F	A	Pts	Pos
1956–57	II	42	22	10	10	94	55	54	2nd
1957–58	I	42	16	10	16	69	63	42	10th
1958–59	I	42	17	6	19	71	74	40	13th
1959–60	I	42	13	9	20	50	74	35	20th
1960–61	I	42	14	9	19	62	78	37	13th
1961–62	I	42	13	10	19	63	79	36	19th
1962–63	I	42	17	10	15	67	69	44	9th
1963–64	I	42	16	9	17	64	68	41	13th
1964–65	I	42	17	13	12	71	67	47	5th
1965–66	I	42	14	8	20	56	72	36	18th
1966–67	I	42	23	10	9	64	41	56	2nd
1967–68	I	42	14	11	17	52	64	39	11th
1968–69	I	42	10	13	19	45	57	33	18th
1969–70	I	42	10	18	14	50	71	38	15th
1970–71	I	42	14	8	20	42	61	36	16th
1971–72	I	42	8	9	25	47	81	25	21st
1972–73	II	42	14	12	16	47	52	40	14th
1973–74	II	42	15	15	12	57	43	45	7th
1974–75	II	42	12	14	16	43	55	38	16th
1975–76	II	42	17	12	13	55	40	46	8th
1976–77	II	42	21	10	11	77	43	52	3rd
1977–78	I	42	25	14	3	69	24	64	1st
1978–79	I	42	21	18	3	61	26	60	2nd
1979–80	I	42	20	8	14	63	43	48	5th
1980–81	I	42	19	12	11	62	44	50	7th
1981–82	I	42	15	12	15	42	48	57	12th
1982–83	I	42	20	9	13	62	50	69	5th
1983–84	I	42	22	8	12	76	45	74	3rd
1984–85	I	42	19	7	16	56	48	64	9th
1985–86	I	42	19	11	12	69	53	68	8th
1986–87	I	42	18	11	13	64	51	65	8th
1987–88	I	40	20	13	7	67	39	73	3rd
1988–89	I	38	17	13	8	64	43	64	3rd
1989–90	I	38	15	9	14	55	47	54	9th
1990–91	I	38	14	12	12	65	50	54	8th
1991–92	I	42	16	11	15	60	58	59	8th
1992–93	PL	42	10	10	22	41	62	40	22nd

When **Nottingham Forest** beat Clapton 14–0 in the FA Cup, first round on 17 January 1891, they scored three goals within the first five minutes on their opponents' ground.

NOTTS COUNTY

Year	Div	P	W	D	L	F	A	Pts	Pos
1888–89	FL	22	5	2	15	40	73	12	11th
1889–90	FL	22	6	5	11	43	51	17	10th
1890–91	FL	22	11	4	7	52	35	26	3rd
1891–92	FL	26	11	4	11	55	51	26	8th
1892–93	I	30	10	4	16	53	61	24	14th
1893–94	II	28	18	3	7	70	31	39	3rd
1894–95	II	30	17	5	8	75	45	39	2nd
1895–96	II	30	12	2	16	57	54	26	10th
1896–97	II	30	19	4	7	92	43	42	1st
1897–98	I	30	8	8	14	36	46	24	13th
1898–99	I	34	12	13	9	47	51	37	5th
1899–1900	I	34	9	11	14	46	60	29	15th
1900–01	I	34	18	4	12	54	46	40	3rd
1901–02	I	34	14	4	16	51	57	32	13th
1902–03	I	34	12	7	15	41	49	31	15th
1903–04	I	34	12	5	17	37	61	29	13th
1904–05	I	34	5	8	21	36	69	18	18th
1905–06	I	38	11	12	15	55	71	34	16th
1906–07	I	38	8	15	15	46	50	31	18th
1907–08	I	38	13	8	17	39	51	34	18th
1908–09	I	38	14	8	16	51	48	36	15th
1909–10	I	38	15	10	13	67	59	40	9th
1910–11	I	38	14	10	14	37	45	38	11th
1911–12	I	38	14	7	17	46	63	35	16th
1912–13	I	38	7	9	22	28	56	23	19th
1913–14	II	38	23	7	8	77	36	53	1st
1914–15	I	38	9	13	16	41	57	31	16th
1915–19	Regional Leagues operating								
1919–20	I	42	12	12	18	56	74	36	21st
1920–21	II	42	18	11	13	55	40	47	6th
1921–22	II	42	12	15	15	47	51	39	13th
1922–23	I	42	23	7	12	46	34	53	1st
1923–24	I	42	14	14	14	44	49	42	10th
1924–25	I	42	16	13	13	42	31	45	9th
1925–26	I	42	13	7	22	54	74	33	22nd
1926–27	II	42	15	5	22	70	96	35	16th
1927–28	II	42	13	12	17	68	74	38	15th
1928–29	II	42	19	9	14	78	65	47	5th
1929–30	II	42	9	15	18	54	70	33	22nd
1930–31	IIIS	42	24	11	7	97	46	59	1st
1931–32	II	42	13	12	17	75	75	38	16th
1932–33	II	42	15	10	17	67	78	40	15th
1933–34	II	42	12	11	19	53	62	35	18th
1934–35	II	42	9	7	26	46	97	25	22nd
1935–36	IIIS	42	15	12	15	60	57	42	9th
1936–37	IIIS	42	23	10	9	74	52	56	2nd
1937–38	IIIS	42	16	9	17	50	50	41	11th
1938–39	IIIS	42	17	9	16	59	54	43	11th
1939–46	Regional Leagues operating								
1946–47	IIIS	42	15	10	17	63	63	40	12th
1947–48	IIIS	42	19	8	15	68	59	46	6th
1948–49	IIIS	42	19	5	18	102	68	43	11th
1949–50	IIIS	42	25	8	9	95	50	58	1st
1950–51	II	42	13	13	16	61	60	39	17th
1951–52	II	42	16	7	19	71	68	39	15th
1952–53	II	42	14	8	20	60	88	36	19th
1953–54	II	42	13	13	16	54	74	39	14th
1954–55	II	42	21	6	15	74	71	48	7th
1955–56	II	42	11	9	22	55	82	31	20th
1956–57	II	42	9	12	21	58	86	30	20th
1957–58	II	42	12	6	24	44	80	30	21st
1958–59	III	46	8	13	25	55	96	29	23rd
1959–60	IV	46	26	8	12	107	69	60	2nd
1960–61	III	46	21	9	16	82	77	51	5th
1961–62	III	46	17	9	20	67	74	43	13th
1962–63	III	46	19	13	14	73	74	51	7th
1963–64	III	46	9	9	28	45	92	27	24th

Year	Div	P	W	D	L	F	A	Pts	Pos
1964–65	IV	46	15	14	17	61	73	44	13th
1965–66	IV	46	19	12	15	61	53	50	8th
1966–67	IV	46	13	11	22	53	72	37	20th
1967–68	IV	46	15	11	20	53	79	41	17th
1968–69	IV	46	12	18	16	48	57	42	19th
1969–70	IV	46	22	8	16	73	62	52	7th
1970–71	IV	46	30	9	7	89	36	69	1st
1971–72	III	46	25	12	9	74	44	62	4th
1972–73	III	46	23	11	12	67	47	57	2nd
1973–74	II	42	15	13	14	55	60	43	10th
1974–75	II	42	12	16	14	49	59	40	14th
1975–76	II	42	19	11	12	60	41	49	5th
1976–77	II	42	19	10	13	65	60	48	8th
1977–78	II	42	11	16	15	54	62	38	15th
1978–79	II	42	14	16	12	48	60	44	6th
1979–80	II	42	11	15	16	51	52	37	17th
1980–81	II	42	18	17	7	49	38	53	2nd
1981–82	II	42	13	8	21	61	69	47	15th
1982–83	II	42	15	7	20	55	71	52	15th
1983–84	I	42	10	11	21	50	72	41	21st
1984–85	II	42	10	7	25	45	73	37	20th
1985–86	III	46	19	14	13	71	60	71	8th
1986–87	III	46	21	13	12	77	56	76	7th
1987–88	III	46	23	12	11	82	49	81	4th
1988–89	III	46	18	13	15	64	54	67	9th
1989–90	III	46	25	12	9	73	53	87	3rd
1990–91	II	46	23	11	12	76	55	80	4th
1991–92	I	42	10	10	22	40	62	40	21st
1992–93	I	46	12	16	18	55	70	52	17th

By 1881 **Notts County** were known as the team of brothers. At least two each from the following families had played for the club: Greenhalgh, Cursham, Ashwell, Morse, Dobson, Shelton, Jessop and Oswald.

OLDHAM ATHLETIC

Year	Div	P	W	D	L	F	A	Pts	Pos
1907–08	II	38	22	6	10	76	42	50	3rd
1908–09	II	38	17	6	15	55	43	40	6th
1909–10	II	38	23	7	8	79	39	53	2nd
1910–11	I	38	16	9	13	44	41	41	7th
1911–12	I	38	12	10	16	46	54	34	18th
1912–13	I	38	14	14	10	50	55	42	9th
1913–14	I	38	17	9	12	55	45	43	4th
1914–15	I	38	17	11	10	70	56	45	2nd
1915–19	Regional Leagues operating								
1919–20	I	45	15	8	19	49	52	38	17th
1920–21	I	42	9	15	18	49	86	33	19th
1921–22	I	42	13	11	18	38	50	37	19th
1922–23	I	42	10	10	22	35	65	30	22nd
1923–24	II	42	14	17	11	45	52	45	7th
1924–25	II	42	13	11	18	35	51	37	18th
1925–26	II	42	18	8	16	74	62	44	7th
1926–27	II	42	19	6	17	74	84	44	10th
1927–28	II	42	19	8	15	75	51	46	7th
1928–29	II	42	16	5	21	54	75	37	18th
1929–30	II	42	21	11	10	90	51	53	3rd
1930–31	II	42	16	10	16	61	72	42	12th
1931–32	II	42	13	10	19	62	84	36	18th
1932–33	II	42	15	8	19	67	80	38	16th
1933–34	II	42	17	10	15	72	60	44	9th
1934–35	II	42	10	6	26	56	95	26	21st
1935–36	IIIN	42	18	9	15	86	73	45	7th
1936–37	IIIN	42	20	11	11	77	59	51	4th
1937–38	IIIN	42	19	13	10	67	46	51	4th
1938–39	IIIN	42	22	5	15	76	59	49	5th
1939–46	Regional Leagues operating								
1946–47	IIIN	42	12	8	22	55	80	32	19th
1947–48	IIIN	42	14	13	15	63	64	41	11th
1948–49	IIIN	42	18	9	15	75	67	45	6th
1949–50	IIIN	42	16	11	15	58	63	43	11th
1950–51	IIIN	46	16	8	22	73	73	40	15th
1951–52	IIIN	46	24	9	13	90	61	57	4th
1952–53	IIIN	46	22	15	9	77	45	59	1st
1953–54	II	42	8	9	25	40	89	25	22nd
1954–55	IIIN	46	19	10	17	74	68	48	10th
1955–56	IIIN	46	10	18	18	76	86	38	20th
1956–57	IIIN	46	12	15	19	66	74	39	19th
1957–58	IIIN	46	14	17	15	72	84	45	15th
1958–59	IV	46	16	4	26	59	84	36	21st
1959–60	IV	46	8	12	26	41	83	28	23rd
1960–61	IV	46	19	7	20	79	88	45	12th
1961–62	IV	44	17	12	15	77	70	46	11th
1962–63	IV	46	24	11	11	95	60	59	2nd
1963–64	III	46	20	8	18	73	70	48	9th
1964–65	III	46	13	10	23	61	83	36	20th
1965–66	III	46	12	13	21	55	81	37	20th
1966–67	III	46	19	10	17	80	63	48	10th
1967–68	III	46	18	7	21	60	65	43	16th
1968–69	III	46	13	9	24	50	83	35	24th
1969–70	IV	46	13	13	20	60	65	39	19th
1970–71	IV	46	24	11	11	88	63	59	3rd
1971–72	III	46	17	11	18	59	63	45	11th
1972–73	III	49	19	16	11	72	54	54	4th
1973–74	III	46	25	12	9	83	47	62	1st
1974–75	II	42	10	15	17	40	48	35	18th
1975–76	II	42	13	12	17	57	68	38	17th
1976–77	II	42	14	10	18	52	64	38	13th
1977–78	II	42	13	16	13	54	58	42	8th
1978–79	II	42	13	13	16	52	61	39	14th
1979–80	II	42	16	11	15	49	53	43	11th
1980–81	II	42	12	15	15	39	48	39	15th
1981–82	II	42	15	14	13	50	51	59	11th
1982–83	II	42	14	19	9	64	47	61	7th
1983–84	II	42	13	8	21	47	73	47	19th
1984–85	II	42	15	8	19	49	67	53	14th
1985–86	II	42	17	9	16	62	61	60	8th
1986–87	II	42	22	9	11	65	44	75	3rd
1987–88	II	44	18	11	15	72	64	65	10th
1988–89	II	46	11	21	14	75	72	54	16th
1989–90	II	46	19	14	13	70	57	71	8th
1990–91	II	46	25	13	8	83	53	88	1st

Oldham celebrate making it to Division One for the first time in their history, after clinching the 1991 Second Division title at Boundary Park on the last day of the season (Allsport/Dan Smith)

| 1991–92 | I | 42 | 14 | 9 | 19 | 63 | 67 | 51 | 17th |
| 1992–93 | PL | 42 | 13 | 10 | 19 | 63 | 74 | 49 | 19th |

Eric Gemmell scored seven goals for **Oldham Athletic** in an 11–2 win over Chester on 19 January 1952 in Division Three (North). Six of his goals were in succession.

OXFORD UNITED

Year	Div	P	W	D	L	F	A	Pts	Pos
1962–63	IV	46	13	15	18	70	71	41	18th
1963–64	IV	46	14	13	19	59	63	41	18th
1964–65	IV	46	23	15	8	87	44	61	4th
1965–66	III	46	19	8	19	70	74	46	14th
1966–67	III	46	15	13	18	61	66	43	15th
1967–68	III	46	22	13	11	69	47	57	1st
1968–69	II	42	12	9	21	34	55	33	20th
1969–70	II	42	12	15	15	35	42	39	15th
1970–71	II	42	14	14	14	41	48	42	14th
1971–72	II	42	12	14	16	43	55	38	15th
1972–73	II	42	19	7	16	52	43	45	8th
1973–74	II	42	10	16	16	35	46	36	18th
1974–75	II	42	15	12	15	41	51	42	11th
1975–76	II	42	11	11	20	39	59	33	20th
1976–77	III	46	12	15	19	55	65	39	17th
1977–78	III	46	13	14	19	64	67	40	18th
1978–79	III	46	14	18	14	44	50	46	11th
1979–80	III	46	14	13	19	57	52	41	17th
1980–81	III	46	13	17	16	39	47	43	14th
1981–82	III	46	19	14	13	63	49	71	5th
1982–83	III	46	22	12	12	71	53	78	5th
1983–84	III	46	28	11	7	91	50	95	1st
1984–85	II	42	25	9	8	84	36	84	1st
1985–86	I	42	10	12	20	62	80	42	18th
1986–87	I	42	11	13	18	44	69	46	18th
1987–88	I	40	6	13	21	44	80	31	21st

1988–89	II	46	14	12	20	62	70	54	17th
1989–90	II	46	15	9	22	57	66	54	17th
1990–91	II	46	14	19	13	69	66	61	10th
1991–92	II	46	13	11	22	66	73	50	21st
1992–93	I	46	14	14	18	53	56	56	14th

Geoff Denial was the senior professional with **Oxford United** when they entered the Football League in 1960. Signed from Sheffield United primarily as a defender, he had also figured in part of the 1959–60 season as a forward and was top scorer with 28 goals in 40 Southern League matches.

PETERBOROUGH UNITED

Year	Div	P	W	D	L	F	A	Pts	Pos
1960–61	IV	46	28	10	8	134	65	66	1st
1961–62	III	46	26	6	14	107	82	58	5th
1962–63	III	46	20	11	15	93	75	51	6th
1963–64	III	46	18	11	17	75	70	47	10th
1964–65	III	46	22	7	17	85	74	51	8th
1965–66	III	46	17	12	17	80	66	46	13th
1966–67	III	46	14	15	17	66	71	43	15th
1967–68	III	46	20	10	16	79	67	31	24th
1968–69	IV	46	13	16	17	60	57	42	18th
1969–70	IV	46	17	14	15	77	69	48	9th
1970–71	IV	46	18	7	21	70	71	43	16th
1971–72	IV	46	17	16	13	82	64	50	8th
1972–73	IV	46	14	13	19	71	76	41	19th
1973–74	IV	46	27	11	8	75	38	65	1st
1974–75	III	46	19	12	15	47	53	50	7th
1975–76	III	46	15	18	13	63	63	48	10th
1976–77	III	46	13	15	18	55	65	41	16th
1977–78	III	46	20	16	10	47	33	56	4th
1978–79	III	46	11	14	21	44	63	36	21st
1979–80	IV	46	21	10	15	58	47	52	8th
1980–81	IV	46	17	18	11	68	54	52	5th
1981–82	IV	46	24	10	12	71	57	82	5th
1982–83	IV	46	17	13	16	58	52	64	9th
1983–84	IV	46	18	14	14	72	48	68	7th
1984–85	IV	46	16	14	16	54	53	62	11th
1985–86	IV	46	13	17	16	52	64	56	17th
1986–87	IV	46	17	14	15	57	50	65	10th
1987–88	IV	46	20	10	16	52	53	70	7th
1988–89	IV	46	14	12	20	52	74	54	17th
1989–90	IV	46	17	17	12	59	46	68	9th
1990–91	IV	46	21	17	8	67	45	80	4th
1991–92	III	46	20	14	12	65	58	74	6th
1992–93	I	46	16	14	16	55	63	62	10th

When **Peterborough United** defeated Derby County 1–0 on 15 August 1992 in a Division One match, it was the 16th consecutive season without defeat in their opening game.

PLYMOUTH ARGYLE

Year	Div	P	W	D	L	F	A	Pts	Pos
1920–21	III	42	11	21	10	35	34	43	11th
1921–22	IIIS	42	25	11	6	63	24	61	2nd
1922–23	IIIS	42	23	7	12	61	29	53	2nd
1923–24	IIIS	42	23	9	10	70	34	55	2nd
1924–25	IIIS	42	23	10	9	77	38	56	2nd
1925–26	IIIS	42	24	8	10	107	67	56	2nd
1926–27	IIIS	42	25	10	7	95	61	60	2nd
1927–28	IIIS	42	23	7	12	85	54	53	3rd
1928–29	IIIS	42	20	12	10	83	51	52	4th
1929–30	IIIS	42	30	8	4	98	38	68	1st
1930–31	II	42	14	8	20	76	84	36	18th
1931–32	II	42	20	9	13	100	66	49	4th
1932–33	II	42	16	9	17	63	67	41	14th
1933–34	II	42	15	13	14	69	70	43	10th
1934–35	II	42	19	8	15	75	64	46	8th
1935–36	II	42	20	8	14	71	57	48	7th
1936–37	II	42	18	13	11	71	53	49	5th
1937–38	II	42	14	12	16	57	65	40	13th
1938–39	II	42	15	8	19	49	55	38	15th
1939–46	Regional Leagues operating								
1946–47	II	42	14	5	23	79	96	33	19th
1947–48	II	42	9	20	13	40	58	38	17th
1948–49	II	42	12	12	18	49	64	36	20th
1949–50	II	42	8	16	18	44	65	32	21st
1950–51	IIIS	46	24	9	13	85	55	57	4th
1951–52	IIIS	46	29	8	9	107	53	66	1st
1952–53	II	42	20	9	13	66	60	49	4th
1953–54	II	42	9	16	17	65	82	34	19th
1954–55	II	42	12	7	23	57	82	31	20th
1955–56	II	42	10	8	24	54	87	28	21st
1956–57	IIIS	46	16	11	19	68	73	43	18th
1957–58	IIIS	46	25	8	13	67	48	58	3rd
1958–59	III	46	23	16	7	89	59	62	1st
1959–60	II	42	13	9	20	61	89	53	19th
1960–61	II	42	17	8	17	81	82	42	11th
1961–62	II	42	19	8	15	75	75	46	5th
1962–63	II	42	15	12	15	76	73	42	12th
1963–64	II	42	8	16	18	45	67	32	20th
1964–65	II	42	16	8	18	63	79	40	15th
1965–66	II	42	12	13	17	54	63	37	18th
1966–67	II	42	14	9	19	59	58	37	16th
1967–68	II	42	9	9	24	38	72	27	22nd
1968–69	III	46	17	15	14	53	49	49	5th
1969–70	III	46	16	11	19	56	64	43	17th
1970–71	III	46	12	19	15	63	63	43	15th
1971–72	III	46	20	10	16	74	64	50	8th
1972–73	III	46	20	10	16	74	66	50	8th
1973–74	III	46	17	10	19	59	54	44	17th
1974–75	III	46	24	11	11	79	58	59	2nd
1975–76	II	42	13	12	17	48	54	38	16th
1976–77	II	42	8	16	18	46	65	32	21st
1977–78	III	46	11	17	18	61	68	39	19th
1978–79	III	46	15	14	17	67	68	44	15th
1979–80	III	46	16	12	18	59	55	44	15th
1980–81	III	46	19	14	13	56	44	52	7th
1981–82	III	46	18	11	17	64	56	65	10th
1982–83	III	46	19	8	19	61	66	65	8th
1983–84	III	46	13	12	21	56	62	51	19th
1984–85	III	46	15	14	17	62	65	59	15th
1985–86	III	46	26	9	11	88	53	87	2nd
1986–87	II	42	16	13	13	62	57	61	7th
1987–88	II	44	16	8	20	65	67	56	16th
1988–89	II	46	14	12	20	55	66	54	18th
1989–90	II	46	14	13	19	58	63	55	16th
1990–91	II	46	12	17	17	54	68	53	18th
1991–92	II	46	13	9	24	42	64	48	22nd
1992–93	II	46	16	12	18	59	64	60	14th

On 26 December 1960 **Plymouth Argyle** were beaten 6–4 away to Charlton Athletic. The following day they reversed the score against Charlton with Wilf Carter becoming the first Argyle player to score as many as five goals in a League game.

PORTSMOUTH

Year	Div	P	W	D	L	F	A	Pts	Pos
1920–21	III	42	12	15	15	46	48	39	12th
1921–22	III	42	18	17	7	62	39	53	3rd
1922–23	III	42	19	8	15	58	52	46	7th
1923–24	III	42	24	11	7	87	30	59	1st
1924–25	II	42	15	18	9	58	50	48	4th
1925–26	II	42	17	10	15	79	74	44	11th
1926–27	II	42	23	8	11	87	49	54	2nd
1927–28	I	42	16	7	19	66	90	39	20th
1928–29	I	42	15	6	21	56	80	36	20th
1929–30	I	42	15	10	17	66	62	40	13th
1930–31	I	42	18	13	11	84	67	49	4th
1931–32	I	42	19	7	16	62	62	45	8th
1932–33	I	42	18	7	17	74	76	43	9th
1933–34	I	42	15	12	15	52	55	42	10th

The first post-war team to win consecutive League Championships, delighted Pompey players celebrate their achievement with the rest of the town (Popperfoto)

Year	Div	P	W	D	L	F	A	Pts	Pos
1934–35	I	42	15	10	17	71	72	40	14th
1935–36	I	42	17	8	17	54	67	42	10th
1936–37	I	42	17	10	15	62	66	44	9th
1937–38	I	42	13	12	17	62	68	38	19th
1938–39	I	42	12	13	17	47	70	37	17th
1939–46	Regional Leagues operating								
1946–47	I	42	16	9	17	66	60	41	12th
1947–48	I	42	19	7	16	68	50	45	8th
1948–49	I	42	25	8	9	84	42	58	1st
1949–50	I	42	22	9	11	74	38	53	1st
1950–51	I	42	16	15	11	71	68	47	7th
1951–52	I	42	20	8	14	68	58	48	4th
1952–53	I	42	14	10	18	74	83	38	15th
1953–54	I	42	14	11	17	81	89	39	14th
1954–55	I	42	18	12	12	74	62	48	3rd
1955–56	I	42	16	9	17	78	85	41	12th
1956–57	I	42	10	13	19	62	92	33	19th
1957–58	I	42	12	8	22	73	88	32	20th
1958–59	I	42	6	9	27	64	112	21	22nd
1959–60	II	42	10	12	20	59	77	32	20th
1960–61	II	42	11	11	20	64	91	33	21st
1961–62	III	46	27	11	8	87	47	65	1st
1962–63	II	42	13	11	18	63	79	37	16th
1963–64	II	42	16	11	15	79	70	43	9th
1964–65	II	42	12	10	20	56	77	34	20th
1965–66	II	42	16	8	18	74	78	40	12th
1966–67	II	42	13	13	16	59	70	39	14th
1967–68	II	42	18	13	11	68	55	49	5th
1968–69	II	42	12	14	16	58	58	38	15th
1969–70	II	42	13	9	20	66	80	35	17th
1970–71	II	42	10	14	18	46	61	34	16th
1971–72	II	42	12	13	17	59	68	37	16th
1972–73	II	42	12	11	19	42	59	35	17th
1973–74	II	42	14	12	16	45	62	40	15th
1974–75	II	42	12	13	17	44	54	37	17th
1975–76	II	42	9	7	26	32	61	25	22nd
1976–77	III	46	11	14	21	53	70	36	20th
1977–78	III	46	7	17	22	41	75	31	24th
1978–79	IV	46	20	12	14	62	48	52	7th
1979–80	IV	46	24	12	10	91	49	60	4th
1980–81	III	46	22	9	15	55	42	53	6th
1981–82	III	46	14	19	13	56	51	61	13th
1982–83	III	46	27	10	9	74	41	91	1st
1983–84	II	42	14	7	21	73	64	49	16th
1984–85	II	42	20	14	8	69	50	74	4th
1985–86	II	42	22	7	13	69	41	73	4th
1986–87	II	42	23	9	10	53	28	78	2nd
1987–88	I	40	7	14	19	36	66	35	19th
1988–89	II	46	13	12	21	53	62	51	20th
1989–90	II	46	15	16	15	62	65	61	12th
1990–91	II	46	14	11	21	58	70	53	17th
1991–92	II	46	19	12	15	65	51	69	9th
1992–93	I	46	26	10	10	80	46	88	3rd

Portsmouth included eight internationals in five of their Southern League games in 1902–03: Albert Houlker, Daniel Cunliffe, Steve Smith, Fred Wheldon and Arthur Chadwick (England); Matt Reilly (Ireland); Bob Marshall and Sandy Brown (Scotland).

PORT VALE

(Burslem Port Vale until 1913)

Year	Div	P	W	D	L	F	A	Pts	Pos
1919–20	II	42	16	8	18	59	62	40	13th
1920–21	II	42	11	14	17	43	49	36	17th
1921–22	II	42	14	8	20	43	57	36	18th
1922–23	II	42	14	9	19	39	51	37	17th
1923–24	II	42	13	12	17	50	66	38	16th
1924–25	II	42	17	8	17	48	56	42	8th
1925–26	II	42	18	8	16	68	57	44	8th
1926–27	II	42	16	13	13	88	78	45	8th
1927–28	II	42	18	8	16	68	57	44	9th
1928–29	II	42	15	4	23	71	86	34	21st
1929–30	IIIN	42	30	7	5	103	37	67	1st
1930–31	II	42	21	5	16	67	61	47	5th
1931–32	II	42	13	7	22	58	89	33	20th
1932–33	II	42	14	10	18	66	79	38	17th
1933–34	II	42	19	7	16	60	55	45	8th
1934–35	II	42	11	12	19	55	74	34	18th
1935–36	II	42	12	8	22	56	106	32	21st
1936–37	IIIN	42	17	10	15	58	64	44	11th
1937–38	IIIN	42	12	14	16	65	73	38	15th
1938–39	IIIS	42	14	9	19	52	58	37	18th
1939–46	Regional Leagues operating								
1946–47	IIIS	42	17	9	16	68	63	43	10th
1947–48	IIIS	42	16	11	15	63	54	43	8th
1948–49	IIIS	42	14	11	17	51	54	39	13th
1949–50	IIIS	42	15	11	16	47	42	41	13th
1950–51	IIIS	46	16	13	17	60	65	45	12th
1951–52	IIIS	46	14	15	17	50	66	43	13th
1952–53	IIIN	46	20	18	8	67	35	58	2nd
1953–54	IIIN	46	26	17	3	74	21	69	1st
1954–55	II	42	12	11	19	48	71	35	17th
1955–56	II	42	16	13	13	60	58	45	12th
1956–57	II	42	8	6	28	57	101	22	22nd
1957–58	IIIS	46	16	10	20	67	58	42	15th
1958–59	IV	46	26	12	8	101	58	64	1st
1959–60	III	46	20	6	20	80	79	46	13th
1960–61	III	46	17	15	14	96	79	49	7th
1961–62	III	46	17	11	18	65	58	45	12th
1962–63	III	46	23	8	15	72	58	54	3rd
1963–64	III	46	16	14	16	53	49	46	13th
1964–65	III	46	9	14	23	41	76	32	22nd
1965–66	IV	46	15	9	22	48	59	39	19th
1966–67	IV	46	14	15	17	55	58	43	13th
1967–68	IV	46	12	15	19	61	72	39	18th
1968–69	IV	46	16	14	16	46	46	46	13th
1969–70	IV	46	20	19	7	61	33	59	4th
1970–71	III	46	15	12	19	52	59	42	17th
1971–72	III	46	13	15	18	43	59	41	15th
1972–73	III	46	21	11	14	56	69	53	6th

Year	Div	P	W	D	L	F	A	Pts	Pos
1973–74	III	46	14	14	18	52	58	42	20th
1974–75	III	46	18	15	13	61	54	51	6th
1975–76	III	46	15	16	15	55	54	46	12th
1976–77	III	46	11	16	19	47	71	38	19th
1977–78	III	46	8	20	18	46	67	36	21st
1978–79	IV	46	14	14	18	57	70	42	16th
1979–80	IV	46	12	12	22	56	70	36	20th
1980–81	IV	46	12	15	19	57	68	39	19th
1981–82	IV	46	18	16	12	56	49	70	7th
1982–83	IV	46	26	10	10	67	34	88	3rd
1983–84	III	46	11	10	25	51	83	43	23rd
1984–85	IV	46	14	18	14	61	59	60	12th
1985–86	IV	46	21	16	9	67	37	79	4th
1986–87	III	46	15	12	19	76	70	57	12th
1987–88	III	46	18	11	17	58	56	65	11th
1988–89	III	46	24	12	10	78	48	84	3rd
1989–90	II	46	15	16	15	62	57	61	11th
1990–91	II	46	15	12	19	56	64	57	15th
1991–92	II	46	10	15	21	42	59	45	24th
1992–93	II	46	26	11	9	79	44	89	3rd

In 1978 this advertisement appeared in a Stoke newspaper: 'Required one part-time sweeper, two mornings per week. Suitable for OAP, apply Secretary **Port Vale** Football Club.'

PRESTON NORTH END

Year	Div	P	W	D	L	F	A	Pts	Pos
1888–89	FL	22	18	4	0	74	15	40	1st
1889–90	FL	22	15	3	4	71	30	33	1st
1890–91	FL	22	12	3	7	44	23	27	2nd
1891–92	FL	26	18	1	7	61	31	37	2nd
1892–93	I	30	18	3	10	57	39	37	2nd
1893–94	I	30	10	3	17	44	56	23	14th
1894–95	I	30	15	5	10	62	46	35	4th
1895–96	I	30	11	6	13	44	48	28	9th
1896–97	I	30	11	12	7	55	40	34	4th
1897–98	I	30	8	8	14	35	43	24	12th
1898–99	I	34	10	9	15	44	47	29	14th
1899–1900	I	34	12	4	18	38	48	28	16th
1900–01	I	34	9	7	18	49	75	25	17th
1901–02	II	34	18	6	10	71	32	42	3rd
1902–03	II	34	13	10	11	56	40	36	7th
1903–04	II	34	20	10	4	62	24	50	1st
1904–05	I	34	13	10	11	42	37	36	8th
1905–06	I	38	17	13	8	54	39	47	2nd
1906–07	I	38	14	7	17	44	57	35	14th
1907–08	I	38	12	12	14	47	53	36	12th
1908–09	I	38	13	11	14	48	44	37	10th
1909–10	I	38	15	5	18	52	58	35	12th
1910–11	I	38	12	11	15	40	49	35	14th
1911–12	I	38	13	7	18	40	57	33	19th
1912–13	II	38	19	15	4	56	33	53	1st
1913–14	I	38	12	6	20	52	69	30	19th
1914–15	II	38	20	10	8	61	42	50	2nd

Year	Div	P	W	D	L	F	A	Pts	Pos
1915–19	Regional Leagues operating								
1919–20	I	42	14	10	18	57	73	38	19th
1920–21	I	42	15	9	18	61	65	39	16th
1921–22	I	42	13	12	17	42	65	38	16th
1922–23	I	42	13	11	18	60	64	37	16th
1923–24	I	42	12	10	20	52	67	34	18th
1924–25	I	42	10	6	26	37	74	26	21st
1925–26	II	42	18	7	17	71	84	43	12th
1926–27	II	42	20	9	13	74	72	49	6th
1927–28	II	42	22	9	11	100	66	53	4th
1928–29	II	42	15	9	18	78	79	39	13th
1929–30	II	42	13	11	18	65	80	37	16th
1930–31	II	42	17	11	14	83	64	45	7th
1931–32	II	42	16	10	16	75	77	42	13th
1932–33	II	42	16	10	16	74	70	42	9th
1933–34	II	42	23	6	13	71	52	52	2nd
1934–35	I	42	15	12	15	62	67	42	11th
1935–36	I	42	18	8	16	67	64	44	7th
1936–37	I	42	14	13	15	56	67	41	14th
1937–38	I	42	16	17	9	64	44	49	3rd
1938–39	I	42	16	12	14	63	59	44	9th
1939–46	Regional Leagues operating								
1946–47	I	42	18	11	13	76	74	47	7th
1947–48	I	42	20	7	15	67	68	47	7th
1948–49	I	42	11	11	20	62	75	34	21st
1949–50	II	42	18	9	15	60	49	45	6th
1950–51	II	42	26	5	11	91	49	57	1st
1951–52	I	42	17	12	13	74	54	46	7th
1952–53	I	42	21	12	9	85	60	54	2nd
1953–54	I	42	19	5	18	87	58	43	11th
1954–55	I	42	16	8	18	83	64	40	14th
1955–56	I	42	14	8	20	73	72	36	19th
1956–57	I	42	23	10	9	84	56	56	3rd
1957–58	I	42	26	7	9	100	51	59	2nd
1958–59	I	42	17	7	18	70	77	41	12th
1959–60	I	42	16	12	14	79	76	44	9th
1960–61	I	42	10	10	22	43	71	30	22nd
1961–62	II	42	15	10	17	55	57	40	10th
1962–63	II	42	13	11	18	59	74	37	17th
1963–64	II	42	23	10	9	79	54	56	3rd
1964–65	II	42	14	13	15	76	81	41	12th
1965–66	II	42	11	15	16	62	70	37	17th
1966–67	II	42	16	7	19	65	67	39	13th
1967–68	II	42	12	11	19	43	65	35	20th
1968–69	II	42	12	15	15	38	44	39	14th
1969–70	II	42	8	12	22	43	63	28	22nd
1970–71	III	46	22	17	7	63	39	61	1st
1971–72	II	42	12	12	18	52	58	36	18th
1972–73	II	42	11	12	19	37	64	34	19th
1973–74	II	42	9	14	19	40	62	31	21st
1974–75	III	46	19	11	16	63	56	49	9th
1975–76	III	46	19	10	17	62	57	48	8th
1976–77	III	46	21	12	13	64	43	54	6th
1977–78	III	46	20	16	10	63	38	56	3rd
1978–79	II	42	12	18	12	59	57	42	7th
1979–80	II	42	12	19	11	56	52	43	10th
1980–81	II	42	11	14	17	41	62	36	20th

Year	Div	P	W	D	L	F	A	Pts	Pos
1981–82	III	46	16	13	17	50	56	61	14th
1982–83	III	46	15	13	18	60	69	58	16th
1983–84	III	46	15	11	20	66	66	56	16th
1984–85	III	46	13	7	26	51	100	46	23rd
1985–86	IV	46	11	10	25	54	89	43	23rd
1986–87	IV	46	26	12	8	72	47	90	2nd
1987–88	III	46	15	13	18	48	59	58	16th
1988–89	III	46	19	15	12	79	60	72	6th
1989–90	III	46	14	10	22	65	79	52	19th
1990–91	III	46	15	11	20	54	67	56	17th
1991–92	III	46	15	12	19	61	72	57	17th
1992–93	II	46	13	8	25	65	94	47	21st

Johnny Goodall was the first player to score hat-tricks in successive Football League games, helping **Preston North End** to beat Wolverhampton Wanderers 5–2 and Notts County 7–0 in October–November 1888.

QUEENS PARK RANGERS

Year	Div	P	W	D	L	F	A	Pts	Pos
1920–21	III	42	22	9	11	61	32	53	3rd
1921–22	IIIS	42	18	13	11	53	44	49	5th
1922–23	IIIS	42	16	10	16	54	49	42	11th
1923–24	IIIS	42	11	9	22	37	77	31	22nd
1924–25	IIIS	42	14	8	20	42	63	36	19th
1925–26	IIIS	42	6	9	27	37	84	21	22nd
1926–27	IIIS	42	15	9	18	65	71	39	14th
1927–28	IIIS	42	17	9	16	72	71	43	10th
1928–29	IIIS	42	19	14	9	82	61	52	6th
1929–30	IIIS	42	21	9	12	80	68	51	3rd
1930–31	IIIS	42	20	3	19	82	75	43	8th
1931–32	IIIS	42	15	12	15	79	73	42	13th
1932–33	IIIS	42	13	11	18	72	87	37	16th
1933–34	IIIS	42	24	6	12	70	51	54	4th
1934–35	IIIS	42	16	9	17	63	72	41	13th
1935–36	IIIS	42	22	9	11	84	53	53	4th
1936–37	IIIS	42	18	9	15	73	52	45	9th
1937–38	IIIS	42	22	9	11	80	47	53	3rd
1938–39	IIIS	42	15	14	13	68	49	44	6th
1939–46	Regional Leagues operating								
1946–47	IIIS	42	23	11	8	74	40	57	2nd
1947–48	IIIS	42	26	9	7	74	37	61	1st
1948–49	II	42	14	11	17	44	62	39	13th
1949–50	II	42	11	12	19	40	37	34	20th
1950–51	II	42	15	10	17	71	82	40	16th
1951–52	II	42	11	12	19	52	81	34	22nd
1952–53	IIIS	46	12	15	19	61	82	39	20th
1953–54	IIIS	46	16	10	20	60	68	42	18th
1954–55	IIIS	46	15	14	17	69	75	44	15th
1955–56	IIIS	46	14	11	21	64	86	39	18th
1956–57	IIIS	46	18	11	17	61	60	47	10th
1957–58	IIIS	46	18	14	14	64	65	50	10th
1958–59	III	46	19	8	19	74	77	46	13th
1959–60	III	46	18	13	15	73	54	49	8th
1960–61	III	46	25	10	11	93	60	60	3rd
1961–62	III	46	24	11	11	111	73	59	4th
1962–63	III	46	17	11	18	85	76	45	13th
1963–64	III	46	18	9	19	76	78	45	15th
1964–65	III	46	17	12	17	72	80	46	14th
1965–66	III	46	24	9	13	95	65	57	3rd
1966–67	III	46	26	15	5	103	38	67	1st
1967–68	II	42	25	8	9	67	36	58	2nd
1968–69	I	42	4	10	28	39	95	18	22nd
1969–70	II	42	17	11	14	66	57	45	9th
1970–71	II	42	16	11	15	58	53	43	11th
1971–72	II	42	20	14	8	57	28	54	4th
1972–73	II	42	14	13	5	81	37	61	2nd
1973–74	I	42	13	17	12	56	52	43	8th
1974–75	I	42	16	10	16	54	54	42	11th
1975–76	I	42	24	11	7	67	33	59	2nd
1976–77	I	42	13	12	17	47	42	38	14th
1977–78	I	42	9	15	18	47	64	33	19th
1978–79	I	42	6	13	23	45	73	25	20th
1979–80	II	42	18	13	11	75	53	49	4th
1980–81	II	42	15	13	14	56	46	43	8th
1981–82	II	42	21	6	15	65	43	69	4th
1982–83	II	42	26	7	9	77	36	85	1st
1983–84	I	42	22	7	13	67	37	73	5th

Gerry Francis skippered QPR to their highest League position ever in 1976 and returned to Loftus Road in 1992 as manager, his first season producing a top-five finish (Allsport)

1984–85	I	42	13	11	18	53	72	50	19th
1985–86	I	42	15	7	20	53	64	52	13th
1986–87	I	42	13	11	18	48	64	50	16th
1987–88	I	40	19	10	11	48	38	67	5th
1988–89	I	38	14	11	13	43	37	53	9th
1989–90	I	38	13	11	14	45	44	50	11th
1990–91	I	38	12	10	16	44	53	46	12th
1991–92	I	42	12	18	15	48	47	54	11th
1992–93	PL	42	17	12	13	63	55	63	5th

On 23 January 1993, **Queens Park Rangers** lost 2–1 to Manchester City in an FA Cup fourth round tie. It was their first home defeat in the competition since losing 2–1 to Watford in the third round in January 1980. In between, Rangers played 16 games at Loftus Road with 10 wins and six draws.

READING

Year	Div	P	W	D	L	F	A	Pts	Pos
1920–21	III	42	12	7	23	42	59	31	20th
1921–22	IIIS	42	14	10	18	40	47	38	13th
1922–23	IIIS	42	10	14	18	36	55	34	19th
1923–24	IIIS	42	13	9	20	51	57	35	18th
1924–25	IIIS	42	14	10	18	37	38	38	14th
1925–26	IIIS	42	23	11	8	77	52	57	1st
1926–27	II	42	16	8	18	64	72	40	14th
1927–28	II	42	11	13	18	53	75	35	18th
1928–29	II	42	15	9	18	63	86	39	15th
1929–30	II	42	12	11	19	54	67	35	19th
1930–31	II	42	12	6	24	72	96	30	21st
1931–32	IIIS	42	23	9	10	97	67	55	2nd
1932–33	IIIS	42	19	13	10	103	71	51	4th
1933–34	IIIS	42	21	12	9	82	50	54	3rd
1934–35	IIIS	42	21	11	10	89	65	53	2nd
1935–36	IIIS	42	26	2	14	87	62	54	3rd
1936–37	IIIS	42	19	11	12	76	60	49	5th
1937–38	IIIS	42	20	11	11	71	63	51	6th
1938–39	IIIS	42	16	14	12	69	59	46	5th
1939–46	Regional Leagues operating								
1946–47	IIIS	42	16	11	15	83	74	43	9th
1947–48	IIIS	42	15	11	16	56	58	41	10th
1948–49	IIIS	42	25	5	12	77	50	55	2nd
1949–50	IIIS	42	17	8	17	70	64	42	10th
1950–51	IIIS	46	21	15	10	88	53	57	3rd
1951–52	IIIS	46	29	3	14	112	60	61	2nd
1952–53	IIIS	46	19	8	19	69	64	46	11th
1953–54	IIIS	46	20	9	17	86	73	49	8th
1954–55	IIIS	46	13	15	18	65	73	41	18th
1955–56	IIIS	46	15	9	22	70	79	39	17th
1956–57	IIIS	46	18	9	19	80	81	45	13th
1957–58	IIIS	46	21	13	12	79	51	55	5th
1958–59	III	46	21	8	17	78	63	50	6th
1959–60	III	46	18	10	18	84	77	46	11th
1960–61	III	46	14	12	20	72	83	40	18th
1961–62	III	46	22	9	15	77	66	53	7th

1962–63	III	46	16	8	22	74	78	40	20th
1963–64	III	46	21	10	15	79	62	52	6th
1964–65	III	46	16	14	16	70	70	46	13th
1965–66	III	46	19	13	14	70	63	51	8th
1966–67	III	46	22	9	15	76	57	53	4th
1967–68	III	46	21	9	16	70	60	51	5th
1968–69	III	46	15	13	18	67	66	43	14th
1969–70	III	46	21	11	14	87	77	53	8th
1970–71	III	46	14	11	21	48	85	39	21st
1971–72	IV	46	17	8	21	56	76	42	16th
1972–73	IV	46	17	18	11	51	38	52	7th
1973–74	IV	46	16	19	11	58	37	51	6th
1974–75	IV	46	21	10	15	63	47	52	7th
1975–76	IV	46	24	12	10	70	51	60	3rd
1976–77	III	46	13	9	24	49	73	35	21st
1977–78	IV	46	18	14	14	55	52	50	8th
1978–79	IV	46	26	13	7	76	35	65	1st
1979–80	III	46	16	16	14	66	65	48	7th
1980–81	III	46	18	10	18	62	62	46	10th
1981–82	III	46	17	11	18	67	75	62	12th
1982–83	III	46	12	17	17	63	80	53	21st
1983–84	IV	46	22	16	8	84	56	82	3rd
1984–85	III	46	19	12	15	68	62	69	9th
1985–86	III	46	29	7	10	67	50	94	1st
1986–87	II	42	14	11	17	52	59	53	13th
1987–88	II	44	10	12	22	44	70	42	22nd
1988–89	III	46	15	11	20	68	72	56	18th
1989–90	III	46	15	19	12	57	53	64	10th
1990–91	III	46	17	8	21	53	66	59	15th
1991–92	III	46	16	13	17	59	62	61	12th
1992–93	II	46	18	15	13	66	51	69	8th

Steve Hetzke wore every shirt except the No. 7 during his 11 years with **Reading** from 1971 to 1982. He was also nominated as the emergency goalkeeper in 1974–75, but was not called upon to deputise during a game.

ROCHDALE

Year	Div	P	W	D	L	F	A	Pts	Pos
1921–22	IIIN	38	11	4	23	52	77	26	20th
1922–23	IIIN	38	13	10	15	42	53	36	12th
1923–24	IIIN	42	25	12	5	60	26	62	2nd
1924–25	IIIN	42	21	7	14	75	53	49	6th
1925–26	IIIN	42	27	5	10	104	58	59	3rd
1926–27	IIIN	42	26	6	10	105	65	58	2nd
1927–28	IIIN	42	17	7	18	74	77	41	13th
1928–29	IIIN	42	13	10	19	79	96	36	17th
1929–30	IIIN	42	18	7	17	89	91	43	10th
1930–31	IIIN	42	12	6	24	62	107	30	21st
1931–32	IIIN	40	4	3	33	48	135	11	21st
1932–33	IIIN	42	13	7	22	58	80	33	18th
1933–34	IIIN	42	9	6	27	53	103	24	22nd
1934–35	IIIN	42	11	11	20	53	71	33	20th
1935–36	IIIN	42	10	13	19	58	88	33	20th
1936–37	IIIN	42	13	9	20	69	86	35	18th

Year	Div	P	W	D	L	F	A	Pts	Pos
1937–38	IIIN	42	13	11	18	67	78	37	17th
1938–39	IIIN	42	15	9	18	92	82	39	15th
1939–46	Regional Leagues operating								
1946–47	IIIN	42	19	10	13	80	64	48	6th
1947–48	IIIN	42	15	11	16	48	72	41	12th
1948–49	IIIN	42	18	9	15	55	53	45	7th
1949–50	IIIN	42	21	9	12	68	41	51	3rd
1950–51	IIIN	46	17	11	18	69	92	45	11th
1951–52	IIIN	46	11	13	22	47	79	35	21st
1952–53	IIIN	46	14	5	27	62	83	33	22nd
1953–54	IIIN	46	15	10	21	59	77	40	18th
1954–55	IIIN	46	17	14	15	69	66	48	12th
1955–56	IIIN	46	17	13	16	66	84	47	12th
1956–57	IIIN	46	18	12	16	65	65	48	13th
1957–58	IIIN	46	19	8	19	79	67	46	10th
1958–59	III	46	8	12	26	37	79	28	24th
1959–60	IV	46	18	10	18	65	60	46	12th
1960–61	IV	46	17	8	21	60	66	42	17th
1961–62	IV	44	19	7	18	71	71	45	12th
1962–63	IV	46	20	11	15	67	59	51	7th
1963–64	IV	46	12	15	19	56	59	39	20th
1964–65	IV	46	22	14	10	74	53	58	6th
1965–66	IV	46	16	5	25	71	87	37	21st
1966–67	IV	46	13	11	22	53	75	37	21st
1967–68	IV	46	12	14	20	51	72	38	19th
1968–69	IV	46	18	20	8	68	35	56	3rd
1969–70	III	46	18	10	18	69	60	46	9th
1970–71	III	46	14	15	17	61	68	43	16th
1971–72	III	46	12	13	21	57	83	37	18th
1972–73	III	46	14	17	15	48	54	45	13th
1973–74	III	46	2	17	27	38	94	21	24th
1974–75	IV	46	13	13	20	59	75	39	19th
1975–76	IV	46	12	18	16	40	54	42	15th
1976–77	IV	46	13	12	21	50	59	38	18th
1977–78	IV	46	8	8	30	43	85	24	24th
1978–79	IV	46	15	9	22	47	64	39	20th
1979–80	IV	46	7	13	26	33	79	27	24th
1980–81	IV	46	14	15	17	60	70	43	15th
1981–82	IV	46	10	16	20	50	62	46	21st
1982–83	IV	46	11	16	19	55	73	49	20th
1983–84	IV	46	11	13	22	52	80	46	22nd
1984–85	IV	46	13	14	19	55	69	53	17th
1985–86	IV	46	14	13	19	57	77	55	18th
1986–87	IV	46	11	17	18	54	73	50	21st
1987–88	IV	46	11	15	20	47	76	48	21st
1988–89	IV	46	13	14	19	56	82	53	18th
1989–90	IV	46	20	6	20	52	55	66	12th
1990–91	IV	46	15	17	14	50	53	62	12th
1991–92	IV	42	18	13	11	57	53	67	8th
1992–93	III	42	16	10	16	70	70	58	11th

In 1937–38, **Rochdale** signed an outside-right Thomas McMurray from Glenavon. He was released towards the end of the same season to join Tunbridge Wells Rangers. At 5ft 2in he was one of the shortest players to play League football and one of few Irishmen to play county cricket for Surrey.

ROTHERHAM TOWN

(Rotherham County 1919, Rotherham United 1925)

Year	Div	P	W	D	L	F	A	Pts	Pos
1893–94	II	28	6	3	19	44	91	15	14th
1894–95	II	30	11	2	17	55	62	24	12th
1895–96	II	30	7	3	20	34	97	17	15th
Failed re-election									

ROTHERHAM COUNTY

Year	Div	P	W	D	L	F	A	Pts	Pos
1919–20	II	42	13	8	21	51	83	34	17th
1920–21	II	42	12	12	18	37	53	36	19th
1921–22	II	42	14	11	17	32	43	39	16th
1922–23	II	42	13	9	20	44	63	35	21st
1923–24	IIIN	42	23	6	13	70	43	52	4th
1924–25	IIIN	42	7	7	28	42	88	21	22nd

ROTHERHAM UNITED

Year	Div	P	W	D	L	F	A	Pts	Pos
1925–26	IIIN	42	17	7	18	69	92	41	14th
1926–27	IIIN	42	10	12	20	70	92	32	19th
1927–28	IIIN	42	14	11	17	65	69	39	14th
1928–29	IIIN	42	15	9	18	60	77	39	16th
1929–30	IIIN	42	11	8	23	67	113	30	20th
1930–31	IIIN	42	13	12	17	81	83	38	14th
1931–32	IIIN	40	14	4	22	63	72	32	19th
1932–33	IIIN	42	14	6	22	60	84	34	17th
1933–34	IIIN	42	10	8	24	53	91	28	21st
1934–35	IIIN	42	19	7	16	86	73	45	9th
1935–36	IIIN	42	16	9	17	69	66	41	11th
1936–37	IIIN	42	14	7	21	78	91	35	17th
1937–38	IIIN	42	20	10	12	68	56	50	6th
1938–39	IIIN	42	17	8	17	64	64	42	11th
1939–46	Regional Leagues operating								
1946–47	IIIN	42	29	6	7	114	53	64	2nd
1947–48	IIIN	42	25	9	8	95	49	59	2nd
1948–49	IIIN	42	28	6	8	90	46	62	2nd
1949–50	IIIN	42	19	10	13	80	59	48	6th
1950–51	IIIN	46	31	9	6	103	41	71	1st
1951–52	II	42	17	8	17	73	71	42	9th
1952–53	II	42	16	9	17	75	74	41	12th
1953–54	II	42	21	7	14	80	67	49	5th
1954–55	II	42	25	4	13	94	64	54	3rd
1955–56	II	42	12	9	21	56	75	33	19th
1956–57	II	42	13	11	18	74	75	37	17th
1957–58	II	42	14	5	23	65	101	33	18th
1958–59	II	42	10	9	23	42	82	29	20th
1959–60	II	42	17	13	12	61	60	47	8th
1960–61	II	42	12	13	17	65	64	37	15th
1961–62	II	42	16	9	17	70	76	41	9th
1962–63	II	42	17	6	19	67	74	40	14th
1963–64	II	42	19	7	16	90	78	45	7th
1964–65	II	42	14	12	16	70	69	40	14th
1965–66	II	42	16	14	12	75	74	46	7th
1966–67	II	42	13	10	19	61	70	36	18th

Year	Div	P	W	D	L	F	A	Pts	Pos
1967–68	II	42	10	11	21	42	76	31	21st
1968–69	III	46	16	13	17	56	50	45	11th
1969–70	III	46	15	14	17	62	54	44	14th
1970–71	III	46	17	16	13	64	60	50	8th
1971–72	III	46	20	15	11	69	52	55	5th
1972–73	III	46	17	7	22	51	65	41	21st
1973–74	IV	46	15	13	18	56	58	43	15th
1974–75	IV	46	22	15	9	71	41	59	3rd
1975–76	III	46	15	12	19	54	65	42	16th
1976–77	III	46	22	15	9	69	44	59	4th
1977–78	III	46	13	13	20	51	68	39	20th
1978–79	III	46	17	10	19	49	55	44	17th
1979–80	III	46	18	10	18	58	66	46	13th
1980–81	III	46	24	13	9	62	32	61	1st
1981–82	II	42	20	7	15	66	54	67	7th
1982–83	II	42	10	15	17	45	68	45	20th
1983–84	III	46	15	9	22	57	64	54	18th
1984–85	III	46	18	11	17	55	55	65	12th
1985–86	III	46	15	12	19	61	59	57	14th
1986–87	III	46	15	12	19	48	57	57	14th
1987–88	III	46	12	16	18	50	66	52	21st
1988–89	IV	46	22	16	8	66	35	82	1st
1989–90	III	46	17	13	16	71	62	64	9th
1990–91	III	46	10	12	24	50	87	42	23rd
1991–92	IV	42	22	11	9	70	37	77	2nd
1992–93	II	46	17	14	15	60	60	65	11th

Rotherham United have been champions of the Third Division, Third Division (North) and Fourth Division since the war.

SCARBOROUGH

Year	Div	P	W	D	L	F	A	Pts	Pos
1987–88	IV	46	17	14	15	56	48	65	12th
1988–89	IV	46	21	14	11	67	52	77	5th
1989–90	IV	46	15	10	21	60	73	55	18th
1990–91	IV	46	19	12	15	59	56	69	9th
1991–92	IV	42	15	12	15	64	68	57	12th
1992–93	III	42	15	9	18	66	71	54	13th

When **Scarborough** beat Lincoln City 6–4 in an FA Cup, second round tie on 13 December 1930, it was the highest aggregate score for the competition in which a non-league side defeated a League club.

SCUNTHORPE UNITED

(Scunthorpe & Lindsey United until 1958)

Year	Div	P	W	D	L	F	A	Pts	Pos
1950–51	IIIN	46	13	18	15	58	57	44	12th
1951–52	IIIN	46	14	16	16	65	74	44	14th
1952–53	IIIN	46	16	14	16	62	56	46	15th
1953–54	IIIN	46	21	15	10	77	56	57	3rd
1954–55	IIIN	46	23	12	11	81	53	58	3rd
1955–56	IIIN	46	20	8	18	75	63	48	9th
1956–57	IIIN	46	15	15	16	71	69	45	14th
1957–58	IIIN	46	29	8	9	88	50	66	1st
1958–59	II	42	12	9	21	55	84	33	18th
1959–60	II	42	13	10	19	57	71	36	15th
1960–61	II	42	14	15	13	69	64	43	9th
1961–62	II	42	21	7	14	86	71	49	4th
1962–63	II	42	16	12	14	57	59	44	9th
1963–64	II	42	10	10	22	52	82	30	22nd
1964–65	III	46	14	12	20	65	72	40	18th
1965–66	III	46	21	11	14	80	67	53	4th
1966–67	III	46	17	8	21	58	73	42	18th
1967–68	III	46	10	12	24	56	87	32	23rd
1968–69	IV	46	18	8	20	61	60	44	16th
1969–70	IV	46	18	10	18	67	65	46	12th
1970–71	IV	46	15	13	18	56	61	43	17th
1971–72	IV	46	22	13	11	56	37	57	4th
1972–73	III	46	10	10	26	33	72	30	24th
1973–74	IV	*45	14	12	19	47	64	42	18th
* Scunthorpe v Exeter City not played									
1974–75	IV	46	7	15	24	41	78	29	24th
1975–76	IV	46	14	10	22	50	59	38	19th
1976–77	IV	46	13	11	22	49	73	37	20th
1977–78	IV	46	14	16	16	50	55	44	14th
1978–79	IV	46	17	11	18	54	60	45	12th
1979–80	IV	46	14	15	17	58	75	43	14th
1980–81	IV	46	11	20	15	60	69	42	16th
1981–82	IV	46	9	15	22	43	79	42	23rd
1982–83	IV	46	23	14	9	71	42	83	4th
1983–84	III	46	9	19	18	54	73	46	21st
1984–85	IV	46	19	14	13	83	62	71	9th
1985–86	IV	46	15	14	17	50	55	59	15th
1986–87	IV	46	18	12	16	73	57	66	8th
1987–88	IV	46	20	17	9	76	51	77	4th
1988–89	IV	46	21	14	11	77	57	77	4th
1989–90	IV	46	17	15	14	69	54	66	11th
1990–91	IV	46	20	11	15	71	62	71	8th
1991–92	IV	42	21	9	12	64	59	72	5th
1992–93	III	42	14	12	16	57	54	54	14th

It was **Scunthorpe United** who initiated the move to extend the size of the Football League by two clubs in each of the two Third Divisions in 1950, persuading Everton to propose and Sheffield Wednesday to second the motion.

SHEFFIELD UNITED

Year	Div	P	W	D	L	F	A	Pts	Pos
1892–93	II	22	16	3	3	62	19	35	2nd
1893–94	II	30	13	5	12	47	61	31	10th
1894–95	I	30	14	4	12	57	55	32	6th
1895–96	I	30	10	6	14	40	50	26	12th
1896–97	I	30	13	10	7	42	29	36	2nd
1897–98	I	30	17	8	5	56	31	42	1st
1898–99	I	34	9	11	14	45	51	29	16th
1899–1900	I	34	18	12	4	63	33	48	2nd

Year	Div	P	W	D	L	F	A	Pts	Pos
1900–01	I	34	12	7	15	35	52	31	14th
1901–02	I	34	13	7	14	53	48	33	10th
1902–03	I	34	17	5	12	58	44	39	4th
1903–04	I	34	15	8	11	62	57	38	7th
1904–05	I	34	19	2	13	64	56	40	6th
1905–06	I	38	15	6	17	57	62	36	13th
1906–07	I	38	17	11	10	57	55	45	4th
1907–08	I	38	12	11	15	52	58	35	17th
1908–09	I	38	14	9	15	51	59	37	12th
1909–10	I	38	16	10	12	62	41	42	6th
1910–11	I	38	15	8	15	49	43	38	9th
1911–12	I	38	13	10	15	63	56	36	14th
1912–13	I	38	14	6	18	56	70	34	15th
1913–14	I	38	16	5	17	63	60	37	10th
1914–15	I	38	15	13	10	49	41	43	6th
1915–19	Regional Leagues operating								
1919–20	I	42	16	8	18	59	69	40	14th
1920–21	I	42	6	18	18	42	68	30	20th
1921–22	I	42	15	10	17	59	54	40	11th
1922–23	I	42	16	10	16	68	64	42	10th
1923–24	I	42	19	12	11	69	49	50	5th
1924–25	I	42	13	13	16	55	63	39	14th
1925–26	I	42	19	8	15	102	82	46	5th
1926–27	I	42	17	10	15	74	86	44	8th
1927–28	I	42	15	10	17	79	86	40	13th
1928–29	I	42	15	11	16	86	85	41	11th
1929–30	I	42	15	6	21	91	96	36	20th
1930–31	I	42	14	10	18	78	84	38	15th
1931–32	I	42	20	6	16	80	75	46	7th
1932–33	I	42	17	9	16	74	80	43	10th
1933–34	I	42	12	7	23	58	101	31	22nd
1934–35	II	42	16	9	17	79	70	41	11th
1935–36	II	42	20	12	10	79	50	52	3rd
1936–37	II	42	18	10	14	66	54	46	7th
1937–38	II	42	22	9	11	73	56	53	3rd
1938–39	II	42	20	14	8	69	41	54	2nd
1939–46	Regional Leagues operating								
1946–47	I	42	21	7	14	89	75	49	6th
1947–48	I	42	16	10	16	65	70	42	12th
1948–49	I	42	11	11	20	57	78	33	22nd
1949–50	II	42	19	14	9	68	49	52	3rd
1950–51	II	42	16	12	14	72	62	44	8th
1951–52	II	42	18	5	19	90	76	41	11th
1952–53	II	42	25	10	7	97	55	60	1st
1953–54	I	42	11	11	20	69	90	33	20th
1954–55	I	42	17	7	18	70	86	41	13th
1955–56	I	42	12	9	21	63	77	33	22nd
1956–57	II	42	19	8	15	87	76	46	7th
1957–58	II	42	21	10	11	75	50	52	6th
1958–59	II	42	23	7	12	82	48	53	3rd
1959–60	II	42	19	12	11	68	51	50	4th
1960–61	II	42	26	6	10	81	51	58	2nd
1961–62	I	42	19	9	14	61	69	47	5th
1962–63	I	42	16	12	14	58	60	44	10th
1963–64	I	42	16	11	15	61	64	43	12th
1964–65	I	42	12	11	19	50	64	35	19th
1965–66	I	42	16	11	15	56	59	43	9th
1966–67	I	42	16	10	16	52	59	42	10th
1967–68	I	42	11	10	21	49	70	32	21st
1968–69	II	42	16	11	15	61	50	43	8th
1969–70	II	42	22	5	15	73	38	49	6th
1970–71	II	42	21	14	7	73	39	56	2nd
1971–72	I	42	17	12	13	61	60	46	10th
1972–73	I	42	15	10	17	51	59	40	14th
1973–74	I	42	14	12	16	44	49	40	13th
1974–75	I	42	18	13	11	58	51	49	6th
1975–76	I	42	6	10	26	33	82	22	22nd
1976–77	II	42	14	12	16	54	63	40	11th
1977–78	II	42	16	8	18	62	73	40	12th
1978–79	II	42	11	12	19	52	69	34	20th
1979–80	III	46	18	10	18	60	66	46	12th
1980–81	III	46	14	13	19	65	62	40	21st
1981–82	IV	46	27	15	4	94	41	96	1st
1982–83	III	46	19	7	20	62	64	64	11th
1983–84	III	46	24	11	11	86	53	83	3rd
1984–85	II	42	10	14	18	54	66	44	18th
1985–86	II	42	17	11	14	64	63	62	7th
1986–87	II	42	15	13	14	50	49	58	9th
1987–88	II	44	13	7	24	45	74	46	21st
1988–89	III	46	25	9	12	93	54	84	2nd
1989–90	II	46	24	13	9	62	41	85	2nd
1990–91	I	38	13	7	18	36	55	46	13th
1991–92	I	42	16	9	17	65	63	57	9th
1992–93	PL	42	14	10	18	54	53	52	14th

It took **Sheffield United** until midway through the 1892–93 season before they recorded their first away win. But at Burslem Port Vale on 10 December they were four goals ahead after only six minutes and went on to win 10–0.

SHEFFIELD WEDNESDAY

(Also known as The Wednesday until 1929)

Year	Div	P	W	D	L	F	A	Pts	Pos
1892–93	I	30	12	3	15	55	65	27	12th
1893–94	I	30	9	8	13	48	57	26	12th
1894–95	I	30	12	4	14	50	55	28	8th
1895–96	I	30	12	5	13	44	53	29	7th
1896–97	I	30	10	11	9	42	37	31	6th
1897–98	I	30	15	3	12	51	42	33	5th
1898–99	I	34	8	8	18	32	61	24	18th
1899–1900	II	34	25	4	5	84	22	54	1st
1900–01	I	34	13	10	11	52	42	36	8th
1901–02	I	34	13	8	13	48	52	34	9th
1902–03	I	34	19	4	11	54	36	42	1st
1903–04	I	34	20	7	7	48	28	47	1st
1904–05	I	34	14	5	15	61	57	33	9th
1905–06	I	38	18	8	12	63	52	44	3rd
1906–07	I	38	12	11	15	49	60	35	13th
1907–08	I	38	19	4	15	73	64	42	5th
1908–09	I	38	17	6	15	67	61	40	5th

1909–10	I	38	15	9	14	60	63	39	11th
1910–11	I	38	17	8	13	47	48	42	6th
1911–12	I	38	16	9	13	69	49	41	5th
1912–13	I	38	21	7	10	75	55	49	3rd
1913–14	I	38	13	8	17	53	70	34	18th
1914–15	I	38	15	13	10	61	54	43	7th
1915–1919	Regional Leagues operating								
1919–1920	I	42	7	9	26	28	64	23	22nd
1920–21	II	42	15	11	16	48	48	41	10th
1921–22	II	42	15	14	13	47	50	44	10th
1922–23	II	42	17	12	13	54	47	46	8th
1923–24	II	42	16	12	14	54	51	44	8th
1924–25	II	42	15	8	19	50	56	38	14th
1925–26	II	42	27	6	9	88	48	60	1st
1926–27	I	42	15	9	18	75	92	39	16th
1927–28	I	42	13	13	16	81	78	39	14th
1928–29	I	42	21	10	11	86	62	52	1st
1929–30	I	42	26	8	8	105	57	60	1st
1930–31	I	42	22	8	12	102	75	52	3rd
1931–32	I	42	22	6	14	96	82	50	3rd
1932–33	I	42	21	9	12	80	68	51	3rd
1933–34	I	42	16	9	17	62	67	41	11th
1934–35	I	42	18	13	11	70	64	49	3rd
1935–36	I	42	13	12	17	63	77	38	20th
1936–37	I	42	9	12	21	53	69	30	22nd
1937–38	II	42	14	10	18	49	56	38	17th
1938–39	II	42	21	11	10	88	59	53	3rd
1939–46	Regional Leagues operating								
1946–47	II	42	12	8	22	67	88	32	20th
1947–48	II	42	20	11	11	66	53	51	4th
1948–49	II	42	15	13	14	63	56	43	8th
1949–50	II	42	18	16	8	67	48	52	2nd
1950–51	I	42	12	8	22	64	83	32	21st
1951–52	II	42	21	11	10	100	66	53	1st
1952–53	I	42	12	11	19	62	72	35	18th
1953–54	I	42	15	6	21	70	91	36	19th
1954–55	I	42	8	10	24	63	100	26	22nd
1955–56	II	42	21	13	8	101	62	55	1st
1956–57	I	42	16	6	20	82	88	38	14th
1957–58	I	42	12	7	23	69	92	31	22nd
1958–59	II	42	28	6	8	106	48	62	1st
1959–60	I	42	19	11	12	80	59	49	5th
1960–61	I	42	23	12	7	78	47	58	2nd
1961–62	I	42	20	6	16	72	58	46	6th
1962–63	I	42	19	10	13	77	63	48	6th
1963–64	I	42	19	11	12	84	67	49	6th
1964–65	I	42	16	11	15	57	55	43	8th
1965–66	I	42	14	8	20	56	66	36	17th
1966–67	I	42	14	13	15	56	47	41	11th
1967–68	I	42	11	12	19	51	63	34	19th
1968–69	I	42	10	16	16	41	54	36	15th
1969–70	I	42	8	9	25	40	71	25	22nd
1970–71	II	42	12	12	18	51	69	36	15th
1971–72	II	42	13	12	17	51	58	38	14th
1972–73	II	42	17	10	15	59	55	44	10th
1973–74	II	42	12	11	19	51	63	35	19th
1974–75	II	42	5	11	26	29	64	21	22nd
1975–76	III	46	12	16	18	48	59	40	20th
1976–77	III	46	22	9	15	65	55	53	8th
1977–78	III	46	15	16	15	50	52	46	14th
1978–79	III	46	13	19	14	53	53	45	14th
1979–80	III	46	21	16	9	81	47	58	3rd
1980–81	II	42	17	8	17	53	51	42	10th
1981–82	II	42	20	10	12	55	51	70	4th
1982–83	II	42	16	15	11	60	47	63	6th
1983–84	II	42	26	10	6	72	34	88	2nd
1984–85	I	42	17	14	11	58	45	65	8th
1985–86	I	42	21	10	11	63	54	73	5th
1986–87	I	42	13	13	16	58	59	52	13th
1987–88	I	40	15	8	17	52	66	53	11th
1988–89	I	38	10	12	16	34	51	42	15th
1989–90	I	38	11	10	17	35	51	43	18th
1990–91	II	46	22	16	8	80	51	82	3rd
1991–92	I	42	21	12	9	62	49	75	3rd
1992–93	PL	42	15	14	13	55	51	59	7th

Sheffield Wednesday celebrated their 100th birthday on 5 September 1967. The following evening in a match against Fulham, they allowed half-price admission throughout the ground. Wednesday won 4–2 in front of a crowd of 26,551 which was much lower than the two previous home games.

SHREWSBURY TOWN

Year	Div	P	W	D	L	F	A	Pts	Pos
1950–51	IIIN	46	15	7	24	43	74	37	20th
1951–52	IIIS	46	13	10	23	62	86	36	20th
1952–53	IIIS	46	12	12	22	68	91	36	23rd
1953–54	IIIS	46	14	12	20	65	76	40	21st
1954–55	IIIS	46	16	10	20	70	78	42	16th
1955–56	IIIS	46	17	12	17	69	66	46	13th
1956–57	IIIS	46	15	18	13	72	79	48	9th
1957–58	IIIS	46	15	10	21	49	71	40	17th
1958–59	IV	46	24	10	12	101	63	58	4th
1959–60	III	46	18	16	12	97	75	52	3rd
1960–61	III	46	15	16	15	83	75	46	10th
1961–62	III	46	13	12	21	73	84	38	19th
1962–63	III	46	16	12	18	83	81	44	15th
1963–64	III	46	18	11	17	73	80	47	11th
1964–65	III	46	15	12	19	76	84	42	16th
1965–66	III	46	19	11	16	73	64	49	10th
1966–67	III	46	20	12	14	77	62	52	6th
1967–68	III	46	20	15	11	61	49	55	3rd
1968–69	III	46	16	11	19	51	67	43	17th
1969–70	III	46	13	18	15	62	63	44	15th
1970–71	III	46	16	13	17	58	62	45	13th
1971–72	III	46	17	10	19	73	65	44	12th
1972–73	III	46	15	14	17	46	54	44	15th
1973–74	III	46	10	11	25	41	62	31	22nd
1974–75	IV	46	26	10	10	80	49	62	2nd
1975–76	III	46	19	10	17	61	59	48	9th
1976–77	III	46	18	11	17	65	59	47	10th

Year	Div	P	W	D	L	F	A	Pts	Pos
1977–78	III	46	16	15	15	63	57	47	11th
1978–79	III	46	21	19	6	61	41	61	1st
1979–80	II	42	18	5	19	60	53	41	13th
1980–81	II	42	11	17	14	46	47	39	14th
1981–82	II	42	11	13	18	37	57	46	18th
1982–83	II	42	15	14	13	48	48	59	9th
1983–84	II	42	17	10	15	49	53	61	8th
1984–85	II	42	18	11	13	66	53	65	8th
1985–86	II	42	14	9	19	52	64	51	17th
1986–87	II	42	15	6	21	41	53	51	18th
1987–88	II	44	11	16	17	42	54	49	18th
1988–89	II	46	8	18	20	40	67	42	22nd
1989–90	III	46	16	15	15	59	54	63	11th
1990–91	III	46	14	10	22	61	68	52	18th
1991–92	III	46	12	11	23	53	68	47	22nd
1992–93	III	42	17	11	14	57	52	62	9th

Different players scored hat-tricks in three successive home matches for **Shrewsbury Town** in 1977–78: 8 October, Chic Bates in 3–0 v Port Vale; 22 October, Ian Atkins including two penalties in 6–1 v Portsmouth and 5 November, Sam Irvine in 3–0 v Hereford United including one penalty.

SOUTHAMPTON

Year	Div	P	W	D	L	F	A	Pts	Pos
1920–21	III	42	19	16	7	64	28	54	2nd
1921–22	IIIS	42	23	15	4	68	21	61	1st
1922–23	II	42	14	14	14	40	40	42	11th
1923–24	II	42	17	14	11	52	31	48	5th
1924–25	II	42	13	18	11	40	36	44	7th
1925–26	II	42	15	8	19	63	63	38	14th
1926–27	II	42	15	12	15	60	62	42	13th
1927–28	II	42	14	7	21	68	77	35	17th
1928–29	II	42	17	14	11	74	60	48	4th
1929–30	II	42	17	11	14	77	76	45	7th
1930–31	II	42	19	6	17	74	62	44	9th
1931–32	II	42	17	7	18	66	77	41	14th
1932–33	II	42	18	5	19	66	66	41	12th
1933–34	II	42	15	8	19	54	58	38	14th
1934–35	II	42	11	12	19	46	75	34	19th
1935–36	II	42	14	9	19	47	65	37	17th
1936–37	II	42	11	12	19	53	77	34	19th
1937–38	II	42	15	9	18	55	77	39	15th
1938–39	II	42	13	9	20	56	82	35	18th
1939–46	Regional Leagues operating								
1946–47	II	42	15	9	18	69	76	39	14th
1947–48	II	42	21	10	11	71	53	52	3rd
1948–49	II	42	23	9	10	69	36	55	3rd
1949–50	II	42	19	14	9	64	48	52	4th
1950–51	II	42	15	13	14	66	73	43	12th
1951–52	II	42	15	11	16	61	73	41	13th
1952–53	II	42	10	13	19	68	85	33	21st
1953–54	IIIS	46	22	7	17	76	63	51	6th
1954–55	IIIS	46	24	11	11	75	51	59	3rd

Year	Div	P	W	D	L	F	A	Pts	Pos
1955–56	IIIS	46	18	8	20	91	81	44	14th
1956–57	IIIS	46	22	10	14	76	52	54	4th
1957–58	IIIS	46	22	10	14	112	74	54	6th
1958–59	III	46	17	11	18	88	80	45	14th
1959–60	III	46	26	9	11	106	75	61	1st
1960–61	II	42	18	8	16	84	81	44	8th
1961–62	II	42	18	9	15	77	62	45	6th
1962–63	II	42	17	8	17	72	67	42	11th
1963–64	II	42	19	9	14	100	73	47	5th
1964–65	II	42	17	14	11	83	63	48	4th
1965–66	II	42	22	10	10	85	56	54	2nd
1966–67	I	42	14	6	22	74	92	34	19th
1967–68	I	42	13	11	18	66	83	37	16th
1968–69	I	42	16	13	13	57	48	45	7th
1969–70	I	42	6	17	19	46	67	29	19th
1970–71	I	42	17	12	13	56	44	46	7th
1971–72	I	42	12	7	23	52	80	31	19th
1972–73	I	42	11	18	13	47	52	40	13th
1973–74	I	42	11	14	17	47	68	36	20th
1974–75	II	42	15	11	16	53	54	41	13th
1975–76	II	42	21	7	14	66	50	49	6th
1976–77	II	42	17	10	15	72	67	44	9th
1977–78	II	42	22	13	7	70	39	57	2nd
1978–79	I	42	12	16	14	47	53	40	14th
1979–80	I	42	18	9	15	65	53	45	8th
1980–81	I	42	20	10	12	76	56	50	6th
1981–82	I	42	19	9	14	72	67	66	7th
1982–83	I	42	15	12	15	54	58	57	12th
1983–84	I	42	22	11	9	66	38	77	2nd
1984–85	I	42	19	11	12	56	47	68	5th
1985–86	I	42	12	10	20	51	62	46	14th
1986–87	I	42	14	10	18	69	68	52	12th
1987–88	I	40	12	14	14	49	53	50	12th
1988–89	I	38	10	15	13	52	66	45	13th
1989–90	I	38	15	10	13	71	63	55	7th
1990–91	I	38	12	9	17	58	69	45	14th
1991–92	I	42	14	10	18	39	55	52	16th
1992–93	PL	42	13	11	18	54	61	50	18th

Charles Burgess (C.B.) Fry played for England against Scotland on March 1901 at **Southampton**. He had two other Saints with him: goalkeeper Archie Turner, the first Hampshire player to be capped by England, and Jack Robinson. England won 3–0.

SOUTHEND UNITED

Year	Div	P	W	D	L	F	A	Pts	Pos
1920–21	III	42	14	8	20	44	61	36	17th
1921–22	IIIS	42	8	11	23	34	74	27	22nd
1922–23	IIIS	42	12	13	17	49	54	37	15th
1923–24	IIIS	42	12	10	20	53	84	34	19th
1924–25	IIIS	42	19	5	18	51	61	43	10th
1925–26	IIIS	42	19	4	19	78	73	42	11th
1926–27	IIIS	42	14	6	22	64	77	34	19th
1927–28	IIIS	42	20	6	16	80	64	46	7th

		P	W	D	L	F	A	Pts	Pos
1928–29	IIIS	42	15	11	16	80	75	41	12th
1929–30	IIIS	42	15	13	14	69	59	43	11th
1930–31	IIIS	42	22	5	15	76	60	49	5th
1931–32	IIIS	42	21	11	10	77	53	53	3rd
1932–33	IIIS	42	15	11	16	65	82	41	13th
1933–34	IIIS	42	12	10	20	51	74	34	16th
1934–35	IIIS	42	11	9	22	65	78	31	21st
1935–36	IIIS	42	13	10	19	61	62	36	18th
1936–37	IIIS	42	17	11	14	78	67	45	10th
1937–38	IIIS	42	15	10	17	70	68	40	12th
1938–39	IIIS	42	16	9	17	61	64	41	12th
1939–46	Regional Leagues operating								
1946–47	IIIS	42	17	10	15	71	60	44	8th
1947–48	IIIS	42	15	13	14	51	58	43	9th
1948–49	IIIS	42	9	16	17	41	46	34	18th
1949–50	IIIS	42	19	13	10	66	48	51	3rd
1950–51	IIIS	46	21	10	15	92	69	52	7th
1951–52	IIIS	46	19	10	17	75	66	48	9th
1952–53	IIIS	46	18	13	15	69	74	49	8th
1953–54	IIIS	46	18	7	21	69	71	43	16th
1954–55	IIIS	46	17	12	17	83	80	46	10th
1955–56	IIIS	46	21	11	14	88	80	53	4th
1956–57	IIIS	46	18	12	16	73	65	48	7th
1957–58	IIIS	46	21	12	13	90	58	54	7th
1958–59	III	46	21	8	17	85	80	50	8th
1959–60	III	46	19	8	19	76	74	46	12th
1960–61	III	46	14	11	21	60	76	39	20th
1961–62	III	46	13	16	17	57	69	42	16th
1962–63	III	46	19	12	15	75	77	50	8th
1963–64	III	46	15	15	16	77	78	45	14th
1964–65	III	46	19	8	19	78	71	46	12th
1965–66	III	46	16	4	26	54	83	36	21st
1966–67	IV	46	22	9	15	70	49	53	6th
1967–68	IV	46	20	14	12	77	58	54	6th
1968–69	IV	46	19	13	14	78	61	51	7th
1969–70	IV	46	15	10	21	59	85	40	17th
1970–71	IV	46	14	15	17	53	66	43	18th
1971–72	IV	46	24	12	10	81	55	60	2nd
1972–73	III	46	17	10	19	61	54	44	14th
1973–74	III	46	16	14	16	62	62	46	12th
1974–75	III	46	13	16	17	46	51	42	18th
1975–76	III	46	12	13	21	65	75	37	23rd
1976–77	IV	46	15	19	12	52	45	49	10th
1977–78	IV	46	25	10	11	66	39	60	2nd
1978–79	III	46	15	15	16	51	49	45	13th
1979–80	III	46	14	10	22	47	58	38	22nd
1980–81	IV	46	30	7	9	79	31	67	1st
1981–82	III	46	18	15	13	63	51	69	7th
1982–83	III	46	15	14	17	66	65	59	15th
1983–84	III	46	10	14	22	55	76	44	22nd
1984–85	IV	46	13	11	22	58	83	50	20th
1985–86	IV	46	18	10	18	69	67	64	9th
1986–87	IV	46	25	5	16	68	55	80	3rd
1987–88	III	46	14	13	19	65	83	55	17th
1988–89	III	46	13	15	18	56	75	54	21st
1989–90	IV	46	22	19	5	61	48	75	3rd
1990–91	III	46	26	7	13	67	51	85	2nd
1991–92	II	46	17	11	18	63	63	62	12th
1992–93	I	46	13	13	20	54	64	52	18th

Jim Shankly scored a club record seven League hat-tricks for **Southend United** between 1928 and 1931, including a best individual total of five goals in the 6–0 win over Merthyr Town on 1 March 1930.

SOUTHPORT

Year	Div	P	W	D	L	F	A	Pts	Pos
1921–22	IIIN	38	14	10	14	55	44	38	9th
1922–23	IIIN	38	12	7	19	32	46	31	17th
1923–24	IIIN	42	16	14	12	44	42	46	7th
1924–25	IIIN	42	22	7	13	59	37	51	4th
1925–26	IIIN	42	11	10	21	62	92	32	20th
1926–27	IIIN	42	15	9	18	80	85	39	12th
1927–28	IIIN	42	20	5	17	79	70	45	8th
1928–29	IIIN	42	16	8	18	75	85	40	12th
1929–30	IIIN	42	15	13	14	81	74	43	9th
1930–31	IIIN	42	22	9	11	88	56	53	5th
1931–32	IIIN	40	18	10	12	58	53	46	7th
1932–33	IIIN	42	17	7	18	70	67	41	12th
1933–34	IIIN	42	8	17	17	63	90	33	18th
1934–35	IIIN	42	10	12	20	55	85	32	21st
1935–36	IIIN	42	11	9	22	48	90	31	21st
1936–37	IIIN	42	12	13	17	73	87	37	14th
1937–38	IIIN	42	12	14	16	53	82	38	16th
1938–39	IIIN	42	20	10	12	75	54	50	4th
1939–46	Regional Leagues operating								
1946–47	IIIN	42	7	11	24	53	85	25	21st
1947–48	IIIN	42	14	11	17	60	63	39	15th
1948–49	IIIN	42	11	9	22	45	64	31	21st
1949–50	IIIN	42	12	13	17	51	71	37	16th
1950–51	IIIN	46	13	10	23	56	72	36	21st
1951–52	IIIN	46	15	11	20	53	71	41	17th
1952–53	IIIN	46	20	11	15	63	60	51	6th
1953–54	IIIN	46	17	12	17	63	60	46	11th
1954–55	IIIN	46	16	16	14	47	44	48	11th
1955–56	IIIN	46	23	11	12	66	53	57	5th
1956–57	IIIN	46	10	12	24	52	94	32	22nd
1957–58	IIIN	46	11	6	29	52	88	28	23rd
1958–59	IV	46	7	12	27	41	86	26	24th
1959–60	IV	46	10	14	22	48	92	34	21st
1960–61	IV	46	19	6	21	69	67	44	14th
1961–62	IV	44	17	9	18	61	71	43	17th
1962–63	IV	46	15	14	17	72	106	44	13th
1963–64	IV	46	15	9	22	63	88	39	21st
1964–65	IV	46	8	16	22	58	89	32	20th
1965–66	IV	46	18	12	16	68	69	48	10th
1966–67	IV	46	23	13	10	69	42	59	2nd
1967–68	III	46	17	12	17	65	65	46	14th
1968–69	III	46	17	13	16	71	64	47	8th
1969–70	III	46	14	10	22	48	66	38	22nd
1970–71	IV	46	21	6	19	63	57	48	8th
1971–72	IV	46	18	14	14	66	46	50	7th

Year	Div	P	W	D	L	F	A	Pts	Pos
1972–73	IV	46	26	10	10	71	48	62	1st
1973–74	III	46	6	16	24	35	82	28	23rd
1974–75	IV	46	15	17	14	56	56	47	11th
1975–76	IV	46	8	10	28	41	77	26	23rd
1976–77	IV	46	3	19	24	53	77	25	23rd
1977–78	IV	46	6	19	21	52	76	31	23rd

John Woolfall Rimmer was the first **Southport** player to win amateur international honours for England and the first to score a hat-trick in a League game.

STALYBRIDGE CELTIC

Year	Div	P	W	D	L	F	A	Pts	Pos
1921–22	IIIN	38	18	5	15	62	63	41	7th
1922–23	IIIN	38	15	6	17	42	47	36	11th

Stalybridge Celtic won their first League game beating Chesterfield 6–0 in a Division Three (North) fixture on 27 August 1921. Jim Thompson scored a hat-trick.

STOCKPORT COUNTY

Year	Div	P	W	D	L	F	A	Pts	Pos
1900–01	II	34	11	3	20	38	68	25	17th
1901–02	II	34	8	7	19	36	72	23	17th
1902–03	II	34	7	6	21	39	74	20	17th
1903–04	II	34	8	11	15	40	72	27	16th
Failed re-election									
1905–06	II	38	13	9	16	44	56	35	10th
1906–07	II	38	12	11	15	42	52	35	12th
1907–08	II	38	12	8	18	48	67	32	13th
1908–09	II	38	14	3	21	39	71	31	18th
1909–10	II	38	13	8	17	50	47	34	13th
1910–11	II	38	11	8	19	47	79	30	17th
1911–12	II	38	11	11	16	47	54	33	16th
1912–13	II	38	8	10	20	56	78	26	19th
1913–14	II	38	13	10	15	55	57	36	12th
1914–15	II	38	15	7	16	54	60	37	14th
1915–19	Regional Leagues operating								
1919–20	II	42	14	9	19	52	61	37	16th
1920–21	II	42	9	12	21	42	75	30	22nd
1921–22	IIIN	38	24	8	6	60	21	56	1st
1922–23	II	42	14	8	20	43	58	36	20th
1923–24	II	42	13	16	13	44	52	42	11th
1924–25	II	42	13	11	18	37	57	37	19th
1925–26	II	42	8	9	25	51	97	25	22nd
1926–27	IIIN	42	22	7	13	93	69	49	6th
1927–28	IIIN	42	23	8	11	89	51	54	3rd
1928–29	IIIN	42	28	6	8	111	58	62	2nd
1929–30	IIIN	42	28	7	7	106	44	63	2nd
1930–31	IIIN	42	20	9	13	77	61	49	7th
1931–32	IIIN	40	13	11	16	55	53	37	12th
1932–33	IIIN	42	21	12	9	99	58	54	3rd
1933–34	IIIN	42	24	11	7	115	52	59	3rd
1934–35	IIIN	42	22	3	17	90	72	47	7th
1935–36	IIIN	42	20	8	14	65	49	48	5th
1936–37	IIIN	42	23	14	5	84	39	60	1st
1937–38	II	42	11	9	22	43	70	31	22nd
1938–39	IIIN	42	17	9	16	91	77	43	9th
1939–46	Regional Leagues operating								
1946–47	IIIN	42	24	2	16	78	53	50	4th
1947–48	IIIN	42	13	12	17	63	67	38	17th
1948–49	IIIN	42	16	11	15	61	56	43	8th
1949–50	IIIN	42	19	7	16	55	52	45	10th
1950–51	IIIN	46	20	8	18	63	63	48	10th
1951–52	IIIN	46	23	13	10	74	40	59	3rd
1952–53	IIIN	46	17	13	16	82	69	47	11th
1953–54	IIIN	46	18	11	17	77	67	47	10th
1954–55	IIIN	46	18	12	16	84	70	48	9th
1955–56	IIIN	46	21	9	16	90	61	51	7th
1956–57	IIIN	46	23	8	15	91	75	54	5th
1957–58	IIIN	46	18	11	17	74	67	47	9th
1958–59	III	46	13	10	23	65	78	36	21st
1959–60	IV	46	19	11	16	58	54	49	10th
1960–61	IV	46	18	9	19	57	66	45	13th
1961–62	IV	44	17	9	18	70	69	43	16th
1962–63	IV	46	15	11	20	56	70	41	19th
1963–64	IV	46	15	12	19	50	68	42	17th
1964–65	IV	46	10	7	29	44	87	27	24th
1965–66	IV	46	18	6	22	71	70	42	13th
1966–67	IV	46	26	12	8	69	42	64	1st
1967–68	III	46	19	9	18	70	75	47	13th
1968–69	III	46	16	14	16	67	68	46	9th
1969–70	III	46	6	11	29	27	71	23	24th
1970–71	IV	46	16	14	16	49	65	46	11th
1971–72	IV	46	9	14	23	55	87	32	23rd
1972–73	IV	46	18	12	16	53	53	48	11th
1973–74	IV	46	7	20	19	44	69	34	24th
1974–75	IV	46	12	14	20	43	70	38	20th
1975–76	IV	46	13	12	21	43	76	38	21st
1976–77	IV	46	13	19	14	53	57	45	14th
1977–78	IV	46	16	10	20	56	56	42	18th
1978–79	IV	46	14	12	20	58	60	40	17th
1979–80	IV	46	14	12	20	48	72	40	16th
1980–81	IV	46	16	7	23	44	57	39	20th
1981–82	IV	46	12	13	21	48	67	49	18th
1982–83	IV	46	14	12	20	60	79	54	16th
1983–84	IV	46	17	11	18	60	64	62	12th
1984–85	IV	46	13	8	25	58	79	47	22nd
1985–86	IV	46	17	13	16	63	71	64	11th
1986–87	IV	46	13	12	21	40	69	51	19th
1987–88	IV	46	12	15	19	44	58	51	20th
1988–89	IV	46	10	21	15	54	52	51	20th
1989–90	IV	46	21	11	14	68	62	74	4th
1990–91	IV	46	23	13	10	84	47	82	2nd
1991–92	III	46	22	10	14	75	51	76	5th
1992–93	II	46	19	15	12	81	57	72	6th

Stockport County lost their League status in 1904, finishing 16th out of 18 clubs, five points ahead of bottom club Leicester City who were re-elected. In the three previous seasons Stockport had been 17th. In 1904–05 they won the Lancashire Combination and were successfully voted back into the Football League.

STOKE CITY

(Former club Stoke went bankrupt in 1908)

Year	Div	P	W	D	L	F	A	Pts	Pos
1888–89	FL	22	4	4	14	26	51	12	12th
1889–90	FL	22	3	4	15	27	69	10	12th
Failed re-election									
1891–92	FL	26	5	4	17	38	61	14	13th
1892–93	I	30	12	5	13	58	48	29	7th
1893–94	I	30	13	3	14	65	79	29	11th
1894–95	I	30	9	6	15	50	67	24	14th
1895–96	I	30	15	0	15	56	47	30	6th
1896–97	I	30	11	3	16	48	59	25	13th
1897–98	I	30	8	8	14	35	55	24	16th
1898–99	I	34	13	7	14	47	52	33	12th
1899–1900	I	34	13	8	13	37	45	34	9th
1900–01	I	34	11	5	18	46	57	27	16th
1901–02	I	34	11	9	14	45	55	31	16th
1902–03	I	34	15	7	12	46	38	37	6th
1903–04	I	34	10	7	17	54	57	27	16th
1904–05	I	34	13	4	17	40	58	30	12th
1905–06	I	38	16	7	15	54	55	39	10th
1906–07	I	38	8	10	20	41	64	26	20th
1907–08	II	38	16	5	17	57	52	37	10th
Resigned									
1919–20	II	42	18	6	18	60	54	42	10th
1920–21	II	42	12	11	19	46	56	35	20th
1921–22	II	42	18	16	8	60	44	52	2nd
1922–23	I	42	10	10	22	47	67	30	21st
1923–24	II	42	14	18	10	44	42	46	6th
1924–25	II	42	12	11	19	34	46	35	20th
1925–26	II	42	12	8	22	54	77	32	21st
1926–27	IIIN	42	27	9	6	92	40	63	1st
1927–28	II	42	22	8	12	78	59	52	5th
1928–29	II	42	17	12	13	74	51	46	6th
1929–30	II	42	16	8	18	74	72	40	11th
1930–31	II	42	17	10	15	64	71	44	11th
1931–32	II	42	19	14	9	69	48	52	3rd
1932–33	II	42	25	6	11	78	39	56	1st
1933–34	I	42	15	11	16	58	71	41	12th
1934–35	I	42	18	6	18	71	70	42	10th
1935–36	I	42	20	7	15	57	57	47	4th
1936–37	I	42	15	12	15	72	57	42	10th
1937–38	I	42	13	12	17	58	59	38	17th
1938–39	I	42	17	12	13	71	68	46	7th
1939–46	Regional Leagues operating								
1946–47	I	42	24	7	11	90	53	55	4th
1947–48	I	42	14	10	18	41	55	38	15th
1948–49	I	42	16	9	17	66	68	41	11th
1949–50	I	42	11	12	19	45	75	34	19th
1950–51	I	42	13	14	15	50	59	40	13th
1951–52	I	42	12	7	23	49	88	31	20th
1952–53	I	42	12	10	20	53	66	34	21st
1953–54	II	42	12	17	13	71	60	41	11th
1954–55	II	42	21	10	11	69	46	52	5th
1955–56	II	42	20	4	18	71	62	44	13th
1956–57	II	42	20	8	14	83	58	48	5th
1957–58	II	42	18	6	18	75	73	42	11th
1958–59	II	42	21	7	14	72	58	49	5th
1959–60	II	42	14	7	21	66	83	35	17th
1960–61	II	42	12	12	18	51	59	36	18th
1961–62	II	42	17	8	17	55	57	42	8th
1962–63	II	42	20	13	9	73	50	53	1st
1963–64	I	42	14	10	18	77	78	38	17th
1964–65	I	42	16	10	16	67	66	42	11th
1965–66	I	42	15	12	15	65	64	42	10th
1966–67	I	42	17	7	18	63	58	41	12th
1967–68	I	42	14	7	21	50	73	35	18th
1968–69	I	42	9	15	18	40	63	33	19th
1969–70	I	42	15	15	12	56	52	45	9th
1970–71	I	42	12	13	17	44	48	37	13th
1971–72	I	42	10	15	17	39	56	35	17th
1972–73	I	42	14	10	18	61	56	38	15th
1973–74	I	42	15	16	11	54	42	46	5th
1974–75	I	42	17	15	10	64	48	49	5th
1975–76	I	42	15	11	16	48	50	41	12th
1976–77	I	42	10	14	18	28	51	34	21st
1977–78	II	42	16	10	16	53	49	42	7th
1978–79	II	42	20	16	6	58	31	56	3rd
1979–80	I	42	13	10	19	44	58	36	18th
1980–81	I	42	12	18	12	51	60	42	11th
1981–82	I	42	12	8	22	44	63	44	18th
1982–83	I	42	16	9	17	53	64	57	13th
1983–84	I	42	13	11	18	44	63	50	18th
1984–85	I	42	3	8	31	24	91	17	22nd
1985–86	II	42	14	15	13	48	50	57	10th
1986–87	II	42	16	10	16	63	53	58	8th

Stoke City saw off neighbours Port Vale to take the new Second Division title in 1993 and brought the crowds flocking back to the Victoria Ground (Bob Thomas)

Year	Div	P	W	D	L	F	A	Pts	Pos
1987–88	II	44	17	11	16	50	57	62	11th
1988–89	II	46	15	14	17	57	72	59	13th
1989–90	II	46	6	19	21	35	63	37	24th
1990–91	III	46	16	12	18	55	59	60	14th
1991–92	III	46	21	14	11	69	49	77	4th
1992–93	II	46	27	12	7	73	34	93	1st

When **Stoke City** drew 0–0 at home with Bolton Wanderers on 5 September 1992, they began a sequence of 25 unbeaten matches in Division Two for a club record. They lost 1–0 to Leyton Orient on 27 February 1993. During the run they won 17 and drew eight games.

SUNDERLAND

Year	Div	P	W	D	L	F	A	Pts	Pos
1890–91	FL	22	10	5	7	51	31	23	7th
1891–92	FL	26	21	0	5	93	36	42	1st
1892–93	I	30	22	4	4	100	36	48	1st
1893–94	I	30	17	4	9	72	44	38	2nd
1894–95	I	30	21	5	4	80	37	47	1st
1895–96	I	30	15	7	8	52	41	37	5th
1896–97	I	30	7	9	14	34	47	23	15th
1897–98	I	30	16	5	9	43	30	37	2nd
1898–99	I	34	15	6	13	41	41	36	7th
1899–1900	I	34	19	3	12	50	35	41	3rd
1900–01	I	34	15	13	6	57	26	43	2nd
1901–02	I	34	19	6	9	50	35	44	1st
1902–03	I	34	16	9	9	51	36	41	3rd
1903–04	I	34	17	5	12	63	49	39	6th
1904–05	I	34	16	8	10	60	44	40	5th
1905–06	I	38	15	5	18	61	70	35	14th
1906–07	I	38	14	9	15	65	66	37	10th
1907–08	I	38	16	3	19	78	75	35	16th
1908–09	I	38	21	2	15	78	63	44	3rd
1909–10	I	38	18	5	15	66	51	41	8th
1910–11	I	38	15	15	8	67	48	45	3rd
1911–12	I	38	14	11	13	58	51	39	8th
1912–13	I	38	25	4	9	86	43	54	1st
1913–14	I	38	17	6	15	63	52	40	7th
1914–15	I	38	18	5	15	81	72	41	8th
1915–19	Regional Leagues operating								
1919–20	I	42	22	4	16	72	59	48	5th
1920–21	I	42	14	13	15	57	60	41	12th
1921–22	I	42	16	8	18	60	62	40	12th
1922–23	I	42	22	10	10	72	54	54	2nd
1923–24	I	42	22	9	11	71	54	53	3rd
1924–25	I	42	19	10	13	64	51	48	3rd
1925–26	I	42	21	6	15	96	80	48	3rd
1926–27	I	42	21	7	14	98	70	49	3rd
1927–28	I	42	15	9	18	74	76	39	15th
1928–29	I	42	20	7	15	93	75	47	4th
1929–30	I	42	18	7	17	76	80	43	9th
1930–31	I	42	16	9	17	89	85	41	11th
1931–32	I	42	15	10	17	67	73	40	13th
1932–33	I	42	15	10	17	63	80	40	12th
1933–34	I	42	16	12	14	81	56	44	6th
1934–35	I	42	19	16	7	90	51	54	2nd
1935–36	I	42	25	6	11	109	74	56	1st
1936–37	I	42	19	6	17	89	87	44	8th
1937–38	I	42	14	16	12	55	57	44	8th
1938–39	I	42	13	12	17	54	67	38	16th
1939–46	Regional Leagues operating								
1946–47	I	42	18	8	16	65	66	44	9th
1947–48	I	42	13	10	19	56	67	36	20th
1948–49	I	42	13	17	12	49	58	43	8th
1949–50	I	42	21	10	11	83	62	52	3rd
1950–51	I	42	12	16	14	63	73	40	12th
1951–52	I	42	15	12	15	70	61	42	12th
1952–53	I	42	15	13	14	68	82	43	9th
1953–54	I	42	14	8	20	81	89	36	18th
1954–55	I	42	15	18	9	64	54	48	4th
1955–56	I	42	17	9	16	80	95	43	9th
1956–57	I	42	12	8	22	67	88	32	20th
1957–58	I	42	10	12	20	54	97	32	21st
1958–59	II	42	16	8	18	64	75	40	15th
1959–60	II	42	12	12	18	52	65	36	16th
1960–61	II	42	17	13	12	75	60	47	6th
1961–62	II	42	22	9	11	85	50	53	3rd
1962–63	II	42	20	12	10	84	55	52	3rd
1963–64	II	42	25	11	6	81	37	61	2nd
1964–65	I	42	14	9	19	64	74	37	15th
1965–66	I	42	14	8	20	51	72	36	19th
1966–67	I	42	14	8	20	58	72	36	17th
1967–68	I	42	13	11	18	51	61	37	15th
1968–69	I	42	11	12	19	43	67	34	17th
1969–70	I	42	6	14	22	30	68	26	21st
1970–71	II	42	15	12	15	52	54	42	13th
1971–72	II	42	17	16	9	67	57	50	5th
1972–73	II	42	17	12	13	59	49	46	6th
1973–74	II	42	19	9	14	58	44	47	6th
1974–75	II	42	19	13	10	65	35	51	4th
1975–76	II	42	24	8	10	67	36	56	1st
1976–77	I	42	11	12	19	46	54	34	20th
1977–78	II	42	14	16	12	67	59	44	6th
1978–79	II	42	22	11	9	70	44	55	4th
1979–80	II	42	21	12	9	69	42	54	2nd
1980–81	I	42	14	7	21	52	53	35	17th
1981–82	I	42	11	11	20	38	58	44	19th
1982–83	I	42	12	14	16	48	61	50	16th
1983–84	I	42	13	13	16	42	53	52	13th
1984–85	I	42	10	10	22	40	62	40	21st
1985–86	II	42	13	11	18	47	61	50	18th
1986–87	II	42	12	12	18	49	59	48	20th
1987–88	III	46	27	12	7	92	48	93	1st
1988–89	II	46	16	15	15	60	60	63	11th
1989–90	II	46	20	14	12	70	64	74	6th
1990–91	I	38	8	10	20	38	60	34	19th
1991–92	II	46	14	11	21	61	65	53	18th
1992–93	I	46	13	11	22	50	64	50	21st

On 10 May 1933, **Sunderland** played their first game under floodlights, a 3–0 win against Racing Club in Paris.

SWANSEA CITY

(Swansea Town until 1970)

Year	Div	P	W	D	L	F	A	Pts	Pos
1920–21	III	42	18	15	9	56	45	51	5th
1921–22	IIIS	42	13	15	14	50	47	41	10th
1922–23	IIIS	42	22	9	11	78	45	53	3rd
1923–24	IIIS	42	22	8	12	60	48	52	4th
1924–25	IIIS	42	23	11	8	68	35	57	1st
1925–26	II	42	19	11	12	77	57	49	5th
1926–27	II	42	16	11	15	68	72	43	12th
1927–28	II	42	18	12	12	75	63	48	6th
1928–29	II	42	13	10	19	62	75	36	19th
1929–30	II	42	14	9	19	57	61	37	15th
1930–31	II	42	12	10	20	51	74	34	20th
1931–32	II	42	16	7	19	73	75	39	15th
1932–33	II	42	19	4	19	50	54	42	10th
1933–34	II	42	10	15	17	51	60	35	19th
1934–35	II	42	14	8	20	56	67	36	17th
1935–36	II	42	15	9	18	67	76	39	13th
1936–37	II	42	15	7	20	50	65	37	16th
1937–38	II	42	13	12	17	45	73	38	18th
1938–39	II	42	11	12	19	50	83	34	19th
1939–46	Regional Leagues operating								
1946–47	II	42	11	7	24	55	83	29	21st
1947–48	IIIS	42	18	12	12	70	52	48	5th
1948–49	IIIS	42	27	8	7	87	34	62	1st
1949–50	II	42	17	9	16	53	49	43	8th
1950–51	II	42	16	4	22	54	77	36	18th
1951–52	II	42	12	12	18	72	76	36	19th
1952–53	II	42	15	12	15	78	81	42	11th
1953–54	II	42	13	8	21	58	82	34	20th
1954–55	II	42	17	9	16	86	83	43	10th
1955–56	II	42	20	6	16	83	81	46	10th
1956–57	II	42	19	7	16	90	90	45	10th
1957–58	II	42	11	9	22	72	99	31	19th
1958–59	II	42	16	9	17	79	81	41	11th
1959–60	II	42	15	10	17	82	84	40	12th
1960–61	II	42	18	11	13	77	73	47	7th
1961–62	II	42	12	12	18	61	83	36	20th
1962–63	II	42	15	9	18	51	72	39	15th
1963–64	II	42	12	9	21	63	74	33	19th
1964–65	II	42	11	10	21	62	84	32	22nd
1965–66	III	46	15	11	20	81	96	41	17th
1966–67	III	46	12	15	19	85	89	39	21st
1967–68	IV	46	16	10	20	63	77	42	15th
1968–69	IV	46	19	11	16	58	54	49	10th
1969–70	IV	46	21	18	7	66	45	60	3rd
1970–71	III	46	15	16	15	59	56	46	11th
1971–72	III	46	17	10	19	46	59	44	14th
1972–73	III	46	14	9	23	51	73	37	23rd
1973–74	IV	46	16	11	19	45	46	43	14th
1974–75	IV	46	15	6	25	46	73	36	22nd
1975–76	IV	46	16	15	15	66	57	47	11th
1976–77	IV	46	25	8	13	92	68	58	5th
1977–78	IV	46	23	10	13	87	47	56	3rd
1978–79	III	46	24	12	10	83	61	60	3rd
1979–80	II	42	17	9	16	48	53	43	12th
1980–81	II	42	18	14	10	64	44	50	3rd
1981–82	I	42	21	6	15	58	51	69	6th
1982–83	I	42	10	11	21	51	69	41	21st
1983–84	II	42	7	8	27	36	85	29	21st
1984–85	III	46	12	11	23	53	80	47	20th
1985–86	III	46	11	10	25	43	87	43	24th
1986–87	IV	46	17	11	18	56	61	62	12th
1987–88	IV	46	20	10	16	62	56	70	6th
1988–89	III	46	15	16	15	51	53	61	12th
1989–90	III	46	14	12	20	45	63	54	17th
1990–91	III	46	13	9	24	49	72	48	20th
1991–92	III	46	14	14	18	55	65	56	19th
1992–93	II	46	20	13	13	65	47	73	5th

In the 1931–32 season **Swansea Town** had to play Wrexham in a Welsh Cup Final replay and chose the day before their final Division Two game against Bury. Nine of the same team appeared in both games which Swansea won by the same 2–0 score.

SWINDON TOWN

Year	Div	P	W	D	L	F	A	Pts	Pos
1920–21	III	42	21	10	11	73	49	52	4th
1921–22	IIIS	42	16	13	13	72	60	45	6th
1922–23	IIIS	42	17	11	14	62	56	45	9th
1923–24	IIIS	42	17	13	12	58	44	47	6th
1924–25	IIIS	42	20	11	11	66	38	51	4th
1925–26	IIIS	42	20	6	16	69	64	46	6th
1926–27	IIIS	42	21	9	12	100	85	51	5th
1927–28	IIIS	42	19	9	14	90	69	47	6th
1928–29	IIIS	42	15	13	14	75	72	43	10th
1929–30	IIIS	42	13	12	17	73	83	38	14th
1930–31	IIIS	42	18	6	18	89	94	42	12th
1931–32	IIIS	42	14	6	22	70	84	34	17th
1932–33	IIIS	42	9	11	22	60	105	29	22nd
1933–34	IIIS	42	17	11	14	64	68	45	8th
1934–35	IIIS	42	13	12	17	67	78	38	16th
1935–36	IIIS	42	14	8	20	64	73	36	19th
1936–37	IIIS	42	14	11	17	75	73	39	13th
1937–38	IIIS	42	17	10	15	49	49	44	8th
1938–39	IIIS	42	18	8	16	72	77	44	9th
1939–46	Regional Leagues operating								
1946–47	IIIS	42	19	11	12	84	73	49	4th
1947–48	IIIS	42	10	16	16	41	46	36	16th
1948–49	IIIS	42	18	15	9	64	56	51	4th
1949–50	IIIS	42	15	11	16	59	62	41	14th
1950–51	IIIS	46	18	4	24	55	67	40	17th
1951–52	IIIS	46	14	14	18	51	68	42	16th
1952–53	IIIS	46	14	12	20	64	79	40	18th
1953–54	IIIS	46	15	10	21	67	70	40	19th
1954–55	IIIS	46	11	15	20	46	64	37	21st
1955–56	IIIS	46	8	14	24	34	78	30	24th
1956–57	IIIS	46	15	6	25	66	96	36	23rd
1957–58	IIIS	46	21	15	10	79	50	57	4th

Year	Div	P	W	D	L	F	A	Pts	Pos
1958–59	III	46	16	13	17	59	57	45	15th
1959–60	III	46	19	8	19	69	78	46	16th
1960–61	III	46	14	15	17	62	55	43	16th
1961–62	III	46	17	15	14	78	71	49	9th
1962–63	III	46	22	14	10	87	56	58	2nd
1963–64	II	42	14	10	18	57	69	38	14th
1964–65	II	42	14	5	23	63	81	33	21st
1965–66	III	46	19	13	14	74	48	51	7th
1966–67	III	46	20	10	16	81	59	50	8th
1967–68	III	46	16	17	13	74	51	49	9th
1968–69	III	46	27	10	9	71	35	64	2nd
1969–70	II	42	17	16	9	57	47	50	5th
1970–71	II	42	15	12	15	61	51	42	12th
1971–72	II	42	15	12	15	47	47	42	11th
1972–73	II	42	10	16	16	46	60	36	16th
1973–74	II	42	7	11	24	36	72	25	22nd
1974–75	III	46	21	11	14	64	58	53	4th
1975–76	III	46	16	8	22	62	75	40	19th
1976–77	III	46	15	15	16	68	75	45	11th
1977–78	III	46	16	16	14	67	60	48	10th
1978–79	III	46	25	7	14	74	52	57	5th
1979–80	III	46	19	8	19	71	63	46	10th
1980–81	III	46	13	15	18	51	56	41	17th
1981–82	III	46	13	13	20	55	71	52	22nd
1982–83	IV	46	19	11	16	61	54	68	8th
1983–84	IV	46	15	13	18	58	56	58	17th
1984–85	IV	46	21	9	16	62	58	72	8th
1985–86	IV	46	32	6	8	82	43	102	1st
1986–87	III	46	25	12	9	77	47	87	3rd
1987–88	II	44	16	11	17	73	60	59	12th
1988–89	II	46	20	16	10	68	53	76	6th
1989–90	II	46	20	14	12	79	59	74	4th
1990–91	II	46	12	14	20	65	73	50	21st
1991–92	II	46	18	15	13	69	55	69	8th
1992–93	I	46	21	13	12	74	59	76	5th

On 2 January 1926, **Swindon Town** were entertaining Bournemouth in a Division Three (South) match when they found themselves 2–0 down in ten minutes. They went on to win 8–2 with Frank 'Swerver' Richardson claiming four goals.

THAMES

Year	Div	P	W	D	L	F	A	Pts	Pos
1930–31	IIIS	42	13	8	21	54	93	34	20th
1931–32	IIIS	42	7	9	26	53	109	23	22nd

On 5 September 1931 Jimmy Dimmock scored his 100th League goal in a Division Three (South) game for **Thames** against Gillingham. His previous 99 had been achieved for Tottenham Hotspur over a 12 year period.

TORQUAY UNITED

Year	Div	P	W	D	L	F	A	Pts	Pos
1927–28	IIIS	42	8	14	20	53	103	30	22nd
1928–29	IIIS	42	14	6	22	66	84	34	18th
1929–30	IIIS	42	10	11	21	64	94	31	19th
1930–31	IIIS	42	17	9	16	80	84	43	11th
1931–32	IIIS	42	12	9	21	72	106	33	19th
1932–33	IIIS	42	16	12	14	72	67	44	10th
1933–34	IIIS	42	13	7	22	53	93	33	20th
1934–35	IIIS	42	18	6	18	81	75	42	10th
1935–36	IIIS	42	16	9	17	62	62	41	10th
1936–37	IIIS	42	11	10	21	57	80	32	20th
1937–38	IIIS	42	9	12	21	38	73	30	20th
1938–39	IIIS	42	14	9	19	54	70	37	19th
1939–46	Regional Leagues operating								
1946–47	IIIS	42	15	12	15	52	61	42	11th
1947–48	IIIS	42	11	13	18	63	62	35	18th
1948–49	IIIS	42	17	11	14	65	70	45	9th
1949–50	IIIS	42	19	10	13	66	63	48	5th
1950–51	IIIS	46	14	9	23	64	81	37	20th
1951–52	IIIS	46	17	10	19	86	98	44	11th
1952–53	IIIS	46	18	9	19	87	88	45	12th
1953–54	IIIS	46	17	12	17	81	88	46	13th
1954–55	IIIS	46	18	12	16	82	82	48	8th
1955–56	IIIS	46	20	12	14	86	63	52	5th
1956–57	IIIS	46	24	11	11	89	64	59	2nd
1957–58	IIIS	46	11	13	22	49	74	35	21st
1958–59	IV	46	16	12	18	78	77	44	12th
1959–60	IV	46	26	8	12	84	58	60	3rd
1960–61	III	46	14	17	15	75	83	45	12th
1961–62	III	46	15	6	25	76	100	36	21st
1962–63	IV	46	20	16	10	75	56	56	6th
1963–64	IV	46	20	11	15	80	54	51	6th
1964–65	IV	46	21	7	18	70	70	49	11th
1965–66	IV	46	24	10	12	72	49	58	3rd
1966–67	III	46	21	9	16	73	54	51	7th

Wembley goalscorers (left to right) Paul Bodin, Craig Maskell, Glenn Hoddle and Shaun Taylor celebrate Swindon's 4–3 play-off win over Leicester in 1993 (Allsport/Mike Hewitt)

1967–68	III	46	21	11	14	60	56	53	4th
1968–69	III	46	18	12	16	54	46	48	6th
1969–70	III	46	14	17	15	62	59	45	13th
1970–71	III	46	19	11	16	54	57	49	10th
1971–72	III	46	10	12	24	41	69	32	23rd
1972–73	IV	46	12	17	17	44	47	41	18th
1973–74	IV	46	13	17	16	52	57	43	16th
1974–75	IV	46	14	14	18	46	61	42	14th
1975–76	IV	46	18	14	14	55	63	50	9th
1976–77	IV	46	17	9	20	59	67	43	16th
1977–78	IV	46	16	15	15	57	56	47	9th
1978–79	IV	46	19	8	19	58	65	46	11th
1979–80	IV	46	15	17	14	70	69	47	9th
1980–81	IV	46	18	5	23	55	63	41	17th
1981–82	IV	46	14	13	19	47	59	55	15th
1982–83	IV	46	17	7	22	56	65	58	12th
1983–84	IV	46	18	13	15	59	64	67	9th
1984–85	IV	46	9	14	23	38	63	41	24th
1985–86	IV	46	9	10	27	43	88	37	24th
1986–87	IV	46	10	18	18	56	72	48	23rd
1987–88	IV	46	21	14	11	66	41	77	5th
1988–89	IV	46	17	8	21	45	60	59	14th
1989–90	IV	46	15	12	19	53	66	57	15th
1990–91	IV	46	18	18	10	64	47	72	7th
1991–92	III	46	13	8	25	42	68	47	23rd
1992–93	III	42	12	7	23	45	67	43	19th

Torquay United celebrated their 50th anniversary League match on 27 August 1977. They drew 1–1 with Wimbledon, who were making their first appearance as a Football League team. On 27 August 1927, United had drawn 1–1 with Exeter City.

TOTTENHAM HOTSPUR

Year	Div	P	W	D	L	F	A	Pts	Pos
1908–09	II	38	20	11	7	67	32	51	2nd
1909–10	I	38	11	10	17	53	69	32	15th
1910–11	I	38	13	6	19	52	63	32	15th
1911–12	I	38	14	9	15	53	53	37	12th
1912–13	I	38	12	6	20	45	72	30	17th
1913–14	I	38	12	10	16	50	62	34	17th
1914–15	I	38	8	12	18	57	90	28	20th
1915–19	Regional Leagues operating								
1919–20	II	42	32	6	4	102	32	70	1st
1920–21	I	42	19	9	14	70	48	47	6th
1921–22	I	42	21	9	12	65	39	51	2nd
1922–23	I	42	17	7	18	50	50	41	12th
1923–24	I	42	12	14	16	50	56	38	15th
1924–25	I	42	15	12	15	52	43	42	12th
1925–26	I	42	15	9	18	66	79	39	15th
1926–27	I	42	16	9	17	76	78	41	13th
1927–28	I	42	15	8	19	74	86	38	21st
1928–29	II	42	17	9	16	75	81	43	10th
1929–30	II	42	15	9	18	59	61	39	12th
1930–31	II	42	22	7	13	88	55	51	3rd

1931–32	II	42	16	11	15	87	78	43	8th
1932–33	II	42	20	15	7	96	51	55	2nd
1933–34	I	42	21	7	14	79	56	49	3rd
1934–35	I	42	10	10	22	54	93	30	22nd
1935–36	II	42	18	13	11	91	55	49	5th
1936–37	II	42	17	9	16	88	66	43	10th
1937–38	II	42	19	6	17	76	54	44	5th
1938–39	II	42	19	9	14	67	62	47	8th
1939–46	Regional Leagues operating								
1946–47	II	42	17	14	11	65	53	48	6th
1947–48	II	42	15	14	13	56	43	44	8th
1948–49	II	42	17	16	9	72	44	50	5th
1949–50	II	42	27	7	8	81	35	61	1st
1950–51	I	42	25	10	7	82	44	60	1st
1951–52	I	42	22	9	11	76	51	53	2nd
1952–53	I	42	15	11	16	78	69	41	10th
1953–54	I	42	16	5	21	65	76	37	16th
1954–55	I	42	16	8	18	72	73	40	16th
1955–56	I	42	15	7	20	61	71	37	18th
1956–57	I	42	22	12	8	104	56	56	2nd
1957–58	I	42	21	9	12	93	77	51	3rd
1958–59	I	42	13	10	19	85	95	36	18th
1959–60	I	42	21	11	10	86	50	53	3rd
1960–61	I	42	31	4	7	115	55	66	1st
1961–62	I	42	21	10	11	88	69	52	3rd
1962–63	I	42	23	9	10	111	62	55	2nd
1963–64	I	42	22	7	13	97	81	51	4th
1964–65	I	42	19	7	16	87	71	45	6th
1965–66	I	42	16	12	14	75	66	44	8th
1966–67	I	42	24	8	10	71	48	56	3rd
1967–68	I	42	19	9	14	70	59	47	7th
1968–69	I	42	14	17	11	61	51	45	6th
1969–70	I	42	17	9	16	54	55	43	11th
1970–71	I	42	19	14	9	54	33	52	3rd
1971–72	I	42	19	13	10	63	42	51	6th
1972–73	I	42	16	13	13	58	48	45	8th

The greatest ever Spurs side, Double winners in 1961, pictured with the two trophies. They retained the FA Cup the following year (Popperfoto)

Year	Div	P	W	D	L	F	A	Pts	Pos
1973–74	I	42	14	14	14	45	50	42	11th
1974–75	I	42	13	8	21	52	63	34	19th
1975–76	I	42	14	15	13	63	63	43	9th
1976–77	I	42	12	9	21	48	72	33	22nd
1977–78	II	42	20	16	6	83	49	56	3rd
1978–79	I	42	13	15	14	48	61	41	11th
1979–80	I	42	15	10	17	52	62	40	14th
1980–81	I	42	14	15	13	70	68	43	10th
1981–82	I	42	20	11	11	67	48	71	4th
1982–83	I	42	20	9	13	65	50	69	4th
1983–84	I	42	17	10	15	64	65	61	8th
1984–85	I	42	23	8	11	78	51	77	3rd
1985–86	I	42	19	8	15	74	52	65	10th
1986–87	I	42	21	8	13	68	43	71	3rd
1987–88	I	40	12	11	17	38	48	47	13th
1988–89	I	38	15	12	11	60	46	57	6th
1989–90	I	38	19	6	13	59	47	63	3rd
1990–91	I	38	11	16	11	51	50	49	10th
1991–92	I	42	15	7	20	58	63	52	15th
1992–93	PL	42	16	11	15	60	66	59	8th

On 7 February 1993 **Tottenham Hotspur** were trailing 1–0 to Southampton in a Premier League match at White Hart Lane when they scored four goals in 4 minutes 44 seconds timed at: 54 mins, 45 secs; 56 mins, 17; 57 mins, 51; 59 mins, 29. Spurs won 4–2.

TRANMERE ROVERS

Year	Div	P	W	D	L	F	A	Pts	Pos
1921–22	IIIN	38	9	11	18	51	61	29	18th
1922–23	IIIN	38	12	8	18	49	59	32	16th
1923–24	IIIN	42	13	15	14	51	60	41	12th
1924–25	IIIN	42	14	4	24	59	78	32	21st
1925–26	IIIN	42	19	6	17	73	83	44	7th
1926–27	IIIN	42	19	8	15	85	67	46	9th
1927–28	IIIN	42	22	9	11	105	72	53	5th
1928–29	IIIN	42	22	3	17	79	77	47	7th
1929–30	IIIN	42	16	9	17	83	86	41	12th
1930–31	IIIN	42	24	6	12	111	74	54	4th
1931–32	IIIN	40	19	11	10	107	58	49	4th
1932–33	IIIN	42	17	8	17	70	66	42	11th
1933–34	IIIN	42	20	7	15	84	63	47	7th
1934–35	IIIN	42	20	11	11	74	55	51	6th
1935–36	IIIN	42	22	11	9	93	58	55	3rd
1936–37	IIIN	42	12	9	21	71	88	33	19th
1937–38	IIIN	42	23	10	9	81	41	56	1st
1938–39	II	42	6	5	31	39	99	17	22nd
1939–46	Regional Leagues operating								
1946–47	IIIN	42	17	7	18	66	77	41	10th
1947–48	IIIN	42	16	4	22	54	72	36	18th
1948–49	IIIN	42	13	15	14	46	57	41	11th
1949–50	IIIN	42	19	11	12	51	48	49	5th
1950–51	IIIN	46	24	11	11	83	62	59	4th
1951–52	IIIN	46	21	6	19	76	71	48	11th
1952–53	IIIN	46	21	5	20	65	63	47	12th
1953–54	IIIN	46	18	7	21	59	70	43	14th
1954–55	IIIN	46	13	11	22	55	70	37	19th
1955–56	IIIN	46	16	9	21	59	84	41	16th
1956–57	IIIN	46	7	13	26	51	91	27	23rd
1957–58	IIIN	46	18	10	18	82	76	46	11th
1958–59	III	46	21	8	17	82	67	50	7th
1959–60	III	46	14	13	19	72	75	41	20th
1960–61	III	46	15	8	23	79	115	38	21st
1961–62	IV	44	20	4	20	70	81	44	15th
1962–63	IV	46	20	10	16	81	67	50	8th
1963–64	IV	46	20	11	15	85	73	51	7th
1964–65	IV	46	27	6	13	99	56	60	5th
1965–66	IV	46	24	8	14	93	66	56	5th
1966–67	IV	46	22	14	10	66	43	58	4th
1967–68	III	46	14	12	20	62	74	40	19th
1968–69	III	46	19	10	17	70	68	48	7th
1969–70	III	46	14	16	16	56	72	44	16th
1970–71	III	46	10	22	14	45	55	42	18th
1971–72	III	46	10	16	20	50	71	36	20th
1972–73	III	46	15	16	15	56	52	46	10th
1973–74	III	46	15	16	15	50	44	45	16th
1974–75	III	46	14	9	23	55	57	37	22nd
1975–76	IV	46	24	10	12	89	55	58	4th
1976–77	III	46	13	17	16	51	53	43	14th
1977–78	III	46	16	15	15	57	52	47	12th
1978–79	III	46	6	16	24	45	78	28	23rd
1979–80	IV	46	14	13	19	50	56	41	15th
1980–81	IV	46	13	10	23	59	73	36	21st
1981–82	IV	46	14	18	14	51	56	60	11th
1982–83	IV	46	13	11	22	49	71	50	19th
1983–84	IV	46	17	15	14	53	53	66	10th
1984–85	IV	46	24	3	19	83	66	75	6th
1985–86	IV	46	15	9	22	74	73	54	19th
1986–87	IV	46	11	17	18	54	72	50	20th
1987–88	IV	46	19	9	18	61	53	64	14th
1988–89	IV	46	21	17	8	62	43	80	2nd
1989–90	III	46	23	11	12	86	49	80	4th
1990–91	III	46	23	9	14	64	46	78	5th
1991–92	II	46	14	19	13	56	56	61	14th
1992–93	I	46	23	10	13	72	56	79	4th

Disappointment that **Tranmere Rovers** lost their first FA Cup game, in the first qualifying round on 3 October 1891 when beaten 5–1 at home by Northwich Victoria before a crowd of 2,000, was relieved the following week when they beat Manchester Scottish 14–0 in a friendly. Jack McKinley from the penalty spot had been their first cup scorer.

WALSALL

(Walsall Town Swifts until 1895)

Year	Div	P	W	D	L	F	A	Pts	Pos
1892–93	II	22	5	3	14	37	75	13	12th
1893–94	II	28	10	3	15	51	61	23	10th
1894–95	II	30	10	0	20	47	92	20	14th

Failed re-election

Year	Div	P	W	D	L	F	A	Pts	Pos
1896–97	II	30	11	4	15	53	69	26	12th
1897–98	II	30	12	5	13	58	58	29	10th
1898–99	II	34	15	12	7	79	36	42	6th
1899–1900	II	34	12	8	14	50	55	32	12th
1900–01	II	34	7	13	14	40	56	27	16th

Failed re-election

Year	Div	P	W	D	L	F	A	Pts	Pos
1921–22	IIIN	38	18	3	17	66	65	39	8th
1922–23	IIIN	38	19	8	11	51	44	46	3rd
1923–24	IIIN	42	14	8	20	44	59	36	17th
1924–25	IIIN	42	13	11	18	44	53	37	19th
1925–26	IIIN	42	10	6	26	58	107	26	21st
1926–27	IIIN	42	14	10	18	68	81	38	14th
1927–28	IIIS	42	12	9	21	75	101	33	18th
1928–29	IIIS	42	13	12	17	73	79	38	14th
1929–30	IIIS	42	13	8	21	71	78	34	17th
1930–31	IIIS	42	14	9	19	78	95	37	17th
1931–32	IIIN	40	16	3	21	57	85	35	16th
1932–33	IIIN	42	19	10	13	75	58	48	5th
1933–34	IIIN	42	23	7	12	97	60	53	4th
1934–35	IIIN	42	13	10	19	81	72	36	14th
1935–36	IIIN	42	16	9	17	79	59	41	10th
1936–37	IIIS	42	13	10	19	62	84	36	17th
1937–38	IIIS	42	11	7	24	52	88	29	21st
1938–39	IIIS	42	11	11	20	68	69	33	21st
1939–46	Regional Leagues operating								
1946–47	IIIS	42	17	12	13	74	59	46	5th
1947–48	IIIS	42	21	9	12	70	40	51	3rd
1948–49	IIIS	42	15	8	19	56	64	38	14th
1949–50	IIIS	42	9	16	17	61	62	34	19th
1950–51	IIIS	46	15	10	21	52	62	40	15th
1951–52	IIIS	46	13	5	28	55	94	31	24th
1952–53	IIIS	46	7	10	29	56	118	24	24th
1953–54	IIIS	46	9	8	29	40	87	26	24th
1954–55	IIIS	46	10	14	22	75	86	34	23rd
1955–56	IIIS	46	15	8	23	68	84	38	20th
1956–57	IIIS	46	16	12	18	80	74	44	15th
1957–58	IIIS	46	14	9	23	61	75	37	20th
1958–59	IV	46	21	10	15	95	64	52	6th
1959–60	IV	46	28	9	9	102	60	65	1st
1960–61	III	46	28	6	12	98	60	62	2nd
1961–62	II	42	14	11	17	70	75	39	14th
1962–63	II	42	11	9	22	53	89	31	21st
1963–64	III	46	13	14	19	59	76	40	19th
1964–65	III	46	15	7	24	55	80	37	19th
1965–66	III	46	20	10	16	77	64	50	9th
1966–67	III	46	18	10	18	65	72	46	12th
1967–68	III	46	19	12	15	74	61	50	7th
1968–69	III	46	14	16	16	50	49	44	13th
1969–70	III	46	17	12	17	54	67	46	12th
1970–71	III	46	14	11	21	51	57	39	20th
1971–72	III	46	15	18	13	62	57	48	9th
1972–73	III	46	18	7	21	56	66	43	17th
1973–74	III	46	16	13	17	57	48	45	15th
1974–75	III	46	18	13	15	67	52	49	8th
1975–76	III	46	18	14	14	74	61	50	7th
1976–77	III	46	13	15	18	57	65	41	15th
1977–78	III	46	18	17	11	61	50	53	6th
1978–79	III	46	10	12	24	56	71	32	22nd
1979–80	IV	46	23	18	6	75	47	64	2nd
1980–81	III	46	13	15	18	59	74	41	20th
1981–82	III	46	13	14	19	51	55	53	20th
1982–83	III	46	17	13	16	64	63	64	10th
1983–84	III	46	22	9	15	68	61	75	6th
1984–85	III	46	18	13	15	58	52	67	11th
1985–86	III	46	22	9	15	90	64	75	6th
1986–87	III	46	22	9	15	80	67	75	8th
1987–88	III	46	23	13	10	68	50	82	3rd
1988–89	II	46	5	16	25	41	80	31	24th
1989–90	III	46	9	14	23	40	72	41	24th
1990–91	IV	46	12	17	17	48	51	53	16th
1991–92	IV	42	12	13	17	48	58	49	15th
1992–93	III	42	22	7	13	76	61	73	5th

The first game played by **Walsall Town Swifts** in April 1888 came after the amalgamation of Walsall Swifts and Walsall Town. It was the final of the Lord Mayor of Birmingham's Charity Cup against Aston Villa at Perry Barr. An estimated 500 supporters travelled from Walsall to see the new team composed of six ex-Swifts and five from the Town club. They forced a replay after extra time but the Birmingham FA refused to allow a replay at Walsall who withdrew from the competition.

WATFORD

Year	Div	P	W	D	L	F	A	Pts	Pos
1920–21	III	42	20	8	14	59	44	48	6th
1921–22	IIIS	42	13	18	11	54	48	44	7th
1922–23	IIIS	42	17	10	15	57	54	44	10th
1923–24	IIIS	42	9	15	18	45	54	33	20th
1924–25	IIIS	42	17	9	16	38	47	43	11th
1925–26	IIIS	42	15	9	18	73	89	39	15th
1926–27	IIIS	42	12	8	22	57	87	32	21st
1927–28	IIIS	42	14	10	18	68	78	38	15th
1928–29	IIIS	42	19	10	13	79	74	48	8th
1929–30	IIIS	42	15	8	19	60	73	38	15th
1930–31	IIIS	42	14	7	21	72	75	35	18th
1931–32	IIIS	42	19	8	15	81	79	46	11th
1932–33	IIIS	42	16	12	14	66	63	44	11th
1933–34	IIIS	42	15	7	20	71	63	37	15th
1934–35	IIIS	42	19	9	14	76	49	47	6th
1935–36	IIIS	42	20	9	13	80	54	49	5th
1936–37	IIIS	42	19	11	12	85	60	49	4th
1937–38	IIIS	42	21	11	10	73	43	53	4th
1938–39	IIIS	42	17	12	13	62	51	46	4th
1939–46	Regional Leagues operating								
1946–47	IIIS	42	17	5	20	61	76	39	16th
1947–48	IIIS	42	14	10	18	57	79	38	15th
1948–49	IIIS	42	10	15	17	41	54	35	17th
1949–50	IIIS	42	16	13	13	45	35	45	6th
1950–51	IIIS	46	9	11	26	54	88	29	23rd

1951–52	IIIS	46	13	10	23	57	81	36	21st
1952–53	IIIS	46	15	17	14	62	63	47	10th
1953–54	IIIS	46	21	10	15	85	69	52	4th
1954–55	IIIS	46	18	14	14	71	62	50	7th
1955–56	IIIS	46	13	11	22	52	85	37	21st
1956–57	IIIS	46	18	10	18	72	75	46	11th
1957–58	IIIS	46	13	16	17	59	77	42	16th
1958–59	IV	46	16	10	20	81	79	42	15th
1959–60	IV	46	24	9	13	92	67	57	4th
1960–61	III	46	20	12	14	85	72	52	4th
1961–62	III	46	14	13	19	63	74	41	17th
1962–63	III	46	17	8	21	82	85	42	17th
1963–64	III	46	23	12	11	79	59	58	3rd
1964–65	III	46	17	16	13	71	64	50	9th
1965–66	III	46	17	13	16	55	51	47	12th
1966–67	III	46	20	14	12	61	46	54	3rd
1967–68	III	46	21	8	17	74	50	50	6th
1968–69	III	46	27	10	9	74	34	64	1st
1969–70	II	42	9	13	20	44	57	31	19th
1970–71	II	42	10	13	19	38	60	33	18th
1971–72	II	42	5	9	28	24	75	19	22nd
1972–73	III	46	12	17	17	43	48	41	19th
1973–74	III	46	19	12	15	64	56	50	7th
1974–75	III	46	10	17	19	52	75	37	23rd
1975–76	IV	46	22	6	18	62	62	50	8th
1976–77	IV	46	18	15	13	67	55	51	7th
1977–78	IV	46	30	11	5	85	38	71	1st
1978–79	III	46	24	12	10	83	52	60	2nd
1979–80	II	42	12	13	17	39	46	37	18th
1980–81	II	42	16	11	15	50	45	43	9th
1981–82	II	42	23	11	8	76	42	80	2nd
1982–83	I	42	22	5	15	74	57	71	2nd
1983–84	I	42	16	9	17	68	77	57	11th
1984–85	I	42	14	13	15	81	71	55	11th
1985–86	I	42	16	11	15	69	62	59	12th
1986–87	I	42	18	9	15	67	54	63	9th
1987–88	I	40	7	11	22	27	51	32	20th
1988–89	II	46	22	12	12	74	48	78	4th
1989–90	II	46	14	15	17	58	60	57	15th
1990–91	II	46	12	15	19	45	59	51	20th
1991–92	II	46	18	11	17	51	48	65	10th
1992–93	I	46	14	13	19	57	71	55	16th

In the 1930s a hole, big enough to take a horse and cart, opened overnight at the Vicarage Road ground of **Watford**. It took all morning of the match that day to fill it in. In the 1960s one two feet deep and two feet wide appeared against Grimsby Town, whose full-back Brian Keeble fell into it. In the 1980s another hole appeared in the ground.

WEST BROMWICH ALBION

Year	Div	P	W	D	L	F	A	Pts	Pos
1888–89	I	22	10	2	10	40	46	22	6th
1889–90	I	22	11	3	8	47	50	25	5th
1890–91	I	22	5	2	15	34	57	12	12th
1891–92	I	26	6	6	14	51	58	18	12th
1892–93	I	30	12	5	13	58	69	29	8th
1893–94	I	30	14	4	12	66	59	32	8th
1894–95	I	30	10	4	16	51	66	24	13th
1895–96	I	30	6	7	17	30	59	19	16th
1896–97	I	30	10	6	14	33	56	26	12th
1897–98	I	30	11	10	9	44	45	32	7th
1898–99	I	34	12	6	16	42	57	30	14th
1899–1900	I	34	11	8	15	43	51	30	13th
1900–01	I	34	7	8	19	35	62	22	18th
1901–02	II	34	25	5	4	82	29	55	1st
1902–03	I	34	16	4	14	54	53	36	7th
1903–04	I	34	7	10	17	36	60	24	18th
1904–05	II	34	13	4	17	56	48	30	10th
1905–06	II	38	22	8	8	79	36	52	4th
1906–07	II	38	21	5	12	83	45	47	4th
1907–08	II	38	19	9	10	61	39	47	5th
1908–09	II	38	19	13	6	56	27	51	3rd
1909–10	II	38	16	5	17	58	56	37	11th
1910–11	II	38	22	9	7	67	41	53	1st
1911–12	I	38	15	9	14	43	47	39	9th
1912–13	I	38	13	12	13	57	50	38	10th
1913–14	I	38	15	13	10	46	42	43	5th
1914–15	I	38	15	10	13	49	43	40	11th
1915–19	Regional Leagues operating								
1919–20	I	42	28	4	10	104	47	60	1st
1920–21	I	42	13	14	15	54	58	40	14th
1921–22	I	42	15	10	17	51	63	40	13th
1922–23	I	42	17	11	14	58	49	45	7th
1923–24	I	42	12	14	16	51	62	38	16th
1924–25	I	42	23	10	9	58	34	56	2nd
1925–26	I	42	16	8	18	79	78	40	13th
1926–27	I	42	11	8	23	65	86	30	22nd
1927–28	II	42	17	12	13	90	70	46	8th
1928–29	II	42	19	8	15	80	79	46	7th
1929–30	II	42	21	5	16	105	73	47	6th
1930–31	II	42	22	10	10	83	49	54	2nd
1931–32	I	42	20	6	16	77	55	46	6th
1932–33	I	42	20	9	13	83	70	49	4th
1933–34	I	42	17	10	15	78	70	44	7th
1934–35	I	42	17	10	15	83	83	44	9th
1935–36	I	42	16	6	20	89	88	38	18th
1936–37	I	42	16	6	20	77	98	38	16th
1937–38	I	42	14	8	20	74	91	36	22nd
1938–39	II	42	18	9	15	89	72	45	10th
1939–46	Regional Leagues operating								
1946–47	II	42	20	8	14	88	75	48	7th
1947–48	II	42	18	9	15	63	58	45	7th
1948–49	II	42	24	8	10	69	39	56	2nd
1949–50	I	42	14	12	16	47	53	40	14th
1950–51	I	42	13	11	18	53	61	37	16th
1951–52	I	42	14	13	15	74	77	41	13th
1952–53	I	42	21	8	13	66	60	50	4th
1953–54	I	42	22	9	11	86	63	53	2nd
1954–55	I	42	16	8	18	76	96	40	17th
1955–56	I	42	18	5	19	58	70	41	13th

Year	Div	P	W	D	L	F	A	Pts	Pos
1956–57	I	42	14	14	14	59	61	42	11th
1957–58	I	42	18	14	10	92	70	50	4th
1958–59	I	42	18	13	11	88	68	49	5th
1959–60	I	42	19	11	12	83	57	49	4th
1960–61	I	42	18	5	19	67	71	41	10th
1961–62	I	42	15	13	14	83	67	43	9th
1962–63	I	42	16	7	19	71	79	39	14th
1963–64	I	42	16	11	15	70	61	43	10th
1964–65	I	42	13	13	16	70	65	39	14th
1965–66	I	42	19	12	11	91	69	50	6th
1966–67	I	42	16	7	19	77	73	39	13th
1967–68	I	42	17	12	13	75	62	46	8th
1968–69	I	42	16	11	15	64	67	43	10th
1969–70	I	42	14	9	19	58	66	37	16th
1970–71	I	42	10	15	17	58	75	35	17th
1971–72	I	42	12	11	19	42	54	35	16th
1972–73	I	42	9	10	23	38	62	28	22nd
1973–74	II	42	14	16	12	48	45	44	8th
1974–75	II	42	18	9	15	54	42	45	6th
1975–76	II	42	20	13	9	50	33	53	3rd
1976–77	I	42	16	13	13	62	56	45	7th
1977–78	I	42	18	14	10	62	53	50	6th
1978–79	I	42	24	11	7	72	35	59	3rd
1979–80	I	42	11	19	12	54	50	41	10th
1980–81	I	42	20	12	10	60	42	52	4th
1981–82	I	42	11	11	20	46	57	44	17th
1982–83	I	42	15	12	15	51	49	57	11th
1983–84	I	42	14	9	19	48	62	51	17th
1984–85	I	42	16	7	19	58	62	55	12th
1985–86	I	42	4	12	26	35	89	24	22nd
1986–87	II	42	13	12	17	51	49	51	15th
1987–88	II	44	12	11	21	50	69	47	20th
1988–89	II	46	18	18	10	65	41	72	9th
1989–90	II	46	12	15	19	67	71	51	20th
1990–91	II	46	10	18	18	52	61	48	23rd
1991–92	III	46	19	14	13	64	49	71	7th
1992–93	II	46	25	10	11	88	54	85	4th

Goalkeeper Joe Reader was the only **West Bromwich Albion** player to appear at the club's three major grounds: The Hawthorns, Stoney Lane and The Four Acres. His association with the Throstles lasted 66 years from 1885 to 1950, as he continued as a coach and then steward. He was an ever present for five seasons: 1890–91, 1892–93, 1894–95, 1897–98 and 1899–1900.

WEST HAM UNITED

Year	Div	P	W	D	L	F	A	Pts	Pos
1919–20	II	42	19	9	14	47	40	47	7th
1920–21	II	42	19	10	13	51	30	48	5th
1921–22	II	42	20	8	14	52	39	48	4th
1922–23	II	42	20	11	11	63	38	51	2nd
1923–24	I	42	13	15	14	40	43	41	13th
1924–25	I	42	15	12	15	62	60	42	13th
1925–26	I	42	15	7	20	63	76	37	18th
1926–27	I	42	19	8	15	86	70	46	6th
1927–28	I	42	14	11	17	81	88	39	17th
1928–29	I	42	15	9	18	86	96	39	17th
1929–30	I	42	19	5	18	86	79	43	7th
1930–31	I	42	14	8	20	79	94	36	18th
1931–32	I	42	12	7	23	62	107	31	22nd
1932–33	II	42	13	9	20	75	93	35	20th
1933–34	II	42	17	11	14	78	70	45	7th
1934–35	II	42	26	4	12	80	63	56	3rd
1935–36	II	42	22	8	12	90	68	52	4th
1936–37	II	42	19	11	12	73	55	49	6th
1937–38	II	42	14	14	14	53	52	42	9th
1938–39	II	42	17	10	15	70	52	44	11th
1939–46	Regional Leagues operating								
1946–47	II	42	16	8	18	70	76	40	12th
1947–48	II	42	16	14	12	55	53	46	6th
1948–49	II	42	18	10	14	56	58	46	7th
1949–50	II	42	12	12	18	53	61	36	19th
1950–51	II	42	16	10	16	68	69	42	13th
1951–52	II	42	15	11	16	67	77	41	12th
1952–53	II	42	13	13	16	58	60	39	14th
1953–54	II	42	15	9	18	67	69	39	13th
1954–55	II	42	18	10	14	74	70	46	8th
1955–56	II	42	14	11	17	74	69	39	16th
1956–57	II	42	19	8	15	59	63	46	8th
1957–58	II	42	23	11	8	101	54	57	1st
1958–59	I	42	21	6	15	85	70	48	6th
1959–60	I	42	16	6	20	75	91	38	14th
1960–61	I	42	13	10	19	77	88	36	16th
1961–62	I	42	17	10	15	76	82	44	8th
1962–63	I	42	14	12	16	73	69	40	12th
1963–64	I	42	14	12	16	69	74	40	14th
1964–65	I	42	19	4	19	82	71	42	9th
1965–66	I	42	15	9	18	70	83	39	12th
1966–67	I	42	14	8	20	80	84	36	16th
1967–68	I	42	14	10	18	73	69	38	12th
1968–69	I	42	13	18	11	66	50	44	8th
1969–70	I	42	12	12	18	51	60	36	17th
1970–71	I	42	10	14	18	47	60	34	20th
1971–72	I	42	12	12	18	47	51	36	14th
1972–73	I	42	17	12	13	67	53	46	6th
1973–74	I	42	11	15	16	55	60	37	18th
1974–75	I	42	13	13	16	58	59	39	13th
1975–76	I	42	13	10	19	48	71	36	18th
1976–77	I	42	11	14	17	46	65	36	17th
1977–78	I	42	12	8	22	52	69	32	20th
1978–79	II	42	18	14	10	70	39	50	5th
1979–80	II	42	20	7	15	54	43	47	7th
1980–81	II	42	28	10	4	79	29	66	1st
1981–82	I	42	14	16	12	66	57	58	9th
1982–83	I	42	20	4	18	68	62	64	8th
1983–84	I	42	17	9	16	60	55	60	9th
1984–85	I	42	13	12	17	51	68	51	16th
1985–86	I	42	26	6	10	74	40	84	3rd
1986–87	I	42	14	10	18	52	67	52	15th
1987–88	I	40	9	15	16	40	52	42	16th
1988–89	I	38	10	8	20	37	62	38	19th

Year	Div	P	W	D	L	F	A	Pts	Pos
1989–90	II	46	20	12	14	80	57	72	7th
1990–91	II	46	24	15	7	60	34	87	2nd
1991–92	I	42	9	11	22	37	59	38	22nd
1992–93	I	46	26	10	10	81	41	88	2nd

As a mark of respect to the late Bobby Moore, **West Ham United** 'retired' the No.6 shirt he wore when playing for the club, for the match with Wolverhampton Wanderers on 6 March 1993. Ian Bishop wore a No.12 shirt instead.

WIGAN ATHLETIC

Year	Div	P	W	D	L	F	A	Pts	Pos
1978–79	IV	46	21	13	12	63	48	55	6th
1979–80	IV	46	21	13	12	76	61	55	6th
1980–81	IV	46	18	11	17	51	55	47	11th
1981–82	IV	46	26	13	7	80	46	91	3rd
1982–83	III	46	15	9	22	60	72	54	18th
1983–84	III	46	16	13	17	46	56	61	15th
1984–85	III	46	15	14	17	60	64	59	16th
1985–86	III	46	23	14	9	82	48	83	4th
1986–87	III	46	25	10	11	83	60	85	4th
1987–88	III	46	20	12	14	70	61	72	7th
1988–89	III	46	14	14	18	55	53	56	17th
1989–90	III	46	13	14	19	48	64	53	18th
1990–91	III	46	20	9	17	71	54	69	10th
1991–92	III	46	15	14	17	58	64	59	15th
1992–93	II	46	10	11	25	43	72	41	23rd

In the 1934–35 season, **Wigan Athletic** became the first non-league club to register a 6–1 FA Cup win on the ground of a Football League club by winning at Carlisle United.

WIGAN BOROUGH

Year	Div	P	W	D	L	F	A	Pts	Pos
1921–22	IIIN	38	11	9	18	46	72	31	17th
1922–23	IIIN	38	18	8	12	64	39	44	5th
1923–24	IIIN	42	14	14	14	55	53	42	10th
1924–25	IIIN	42	15	11	16	62	65	41	11th
1925–26	IIIN	42	13	11	18	68	74	37	17th
1926–27	IIIN	42	11	10	21	66	83	32	18th
1927–28	IIIN	42	10	10	22	56	97	30	20th
1928–29	IIIN	42	21	9	12	82	49	51	4th
1929–30	IIIN	42	13	7	22	60	88	33	18th
1930–31	IIIN	42	19	5	18	76	86	43	10th
1931–32	Resigned 26.10.31								

John Jepson was the leading scorer for **Wigan Borough** in 1930–31 with 28 goals in 35 appearances. A centre-forward of many clubs, he assisted two other teams who lost League status, Accrington Stanley and Nelson.

WIMBLEDON

Year	Div	P	W	D	L	F	A	Pts	Pos
1977–78	IV	46	14	16	16	66	67	44	13th
1978–79	IV	46	25	11	10	78	46	61	3rd
1979–80	III	46	10	14	22	52	81	34	24th
1980–81	IV	46	23	9	14	64	46	55	4th
1981–82	III	46	14	11	21	61	75	53	21st
1982–83	IV	46	29	11	6	96	45	98	1st
1983–84	III	46	26	9	11	97	76	87	2nd
1984–85	II	42	16	10	16	71	75	58	12th
1985–86	II	42	21	13	8	58	37	76	3rd
1986–87	I	42	19	9	14	57	50	66	6th
1987–88	I	40	14	15	11	58	47	57	7th
1988–89	I	38	14	9	15	50	46	51	12th
1989–90	I	38	13	16	9	47	40	55	8th
1990–91	I	38	14	14	10	53	46	56	7th
1991–92	I	42	13	14	15	53	53	53	13th
1992–93	PL	42	14	12	16	56	55	54	12th

When **Wimbledon** beat Sutton United 4–2 in the FA Amateur Cup final at Wembley on 4 May 1963, centre-forward Eddie Reynolds headed all four goals.

WOLVERHAMPTON WANDERERS

Year	Div	P	W	D	L	F	A	Pts	Pos
1888–89	FL	22	12	4	6	51	37	28	3rd
1989–90	FL	22	10	5	7	51	38	25	4th
1890–91	FL	22	12	2	8	39	50	26	4th
1891–92	FL	26	11	4	11	59	46	26	6th
1892–93	FL	30	12	4	14	47	68	28	11th
1893–94	I	30	14	3	13	53	63	31	9th
1894–95	I	30	9	7	14	43	63	25	11th
1895–96	I	30	10	1	19	61	65	21	14th
1986–97	I	30	11	6	13	45	41	28	10th
1897–98	I	30	14	7	9	57	41	35	3rd
1898–99	I	34	14	7	13	54	48	35	8th
1899–1900	I	34	15	9	10	48	37	39	4th
1900–01	I	34	9	13	12	39	55	31	13th
1901–02	I	34	13	6	15	46	57	32	14th
1902–03	I	34	14	5	15	48	57	33	11th
1903–04	I	34	14	8	12	44	66	36	8th
1904–05	I	34	11	4	19	47	73	26	14th
1905–06	I	38	8	7	23	58	99	23	20th
1906–07	II	38	17	7	14	66	53	41	6th
1907–08	II	38	15	7	16	50	45	37	9th
1908–09	II	38	14	11	13	56	48	39	7th
1909–10	II	38	17	6	15	64	63	40	8th
1910–11	II	38	15	8	15	51	52	38	9th
1911–12	II	38	16	10	12	57	33	42	5th
1912–13	II	38	14	10	14	56	54	38	10th
1913–14	II	38	18	5	13	51	52	41	9th
1914–15	II	38	19	7	12	77	52	45	4th
1915–19	Regional Leagues operating								
1919–20	II	42	10	10	22	55	80	30	19th

Year	Div	P	W	D	L	F	A	Pts	Pos
1920–21	II	42	16	6	20	49	66	38	15th
1921–22	II	42	13	11	18	44	49	37	17th
1922–23	II	42	9	9	24	42	77	27	22nd
1923–24	IIIN	42	24	15	3	76	27	63	1st
1924–25	II	42	20	6	16	55	51	46	6th
1925–26	II	42	21	7	14	84	60	49	4th
1926–27	II	42	14	7	21	73	75	35	15th
1927–28	II	42	13	10	19	63	91	36	16th
1928–29	II	42	15	7	20	77	81	37	17th
1929–30	II	42	16	9	17	77	79	41	9th
1930–31	II	42	21	5	16	84	67	47	4th
1931–32	II	42	24	8	10	115	49	36	1st
1932–33	I	42	13	9	20	80	96	35	20th
1933–34	I	42	14	12	16	74	86	40	15th
1934–35	I	42	15	8	19	88	94	38	17th
1935–36	I	42	15	10	17	77	76	40	15th
1936–37	I	42	21	5	16	84	67	47	5th
1937–38	I	42	20	11	11	72	49	51	2nd
1938–39	I	42	22	11	9	88	39	55	2nd
1939–46	Regional Leagues operating								
1946–47	I	42	25	6	11	98	56	56	3rd
1947–48	I	42	19	9	14	83	70	47	5th
1948–49	I	42	17	12	13	79	66	46	6th
1949–50	I	42	20	13	9	76	41	53	2nd
1950–51	I	42	15	8	19	74	61	38	14th
1951–52	I	42	12	14	16	73	73	38	16th
1952–53	I	42	19	13	10	86	63	51	3rd
1953–54	I	42	25	7	10	96	56	57	1st
1954–55	I	42	19	10	13	89	70	48	2nd
1955–56	I	42	20	9	13	89	65	49	3rd
1956–57	I	42	20	8	14	94	70	48	6th
1957–58	I	42	28	8	6	103	47	64	1st
1958–59	I	42	28	5	9	110	49	61	1st
1959–60	I	42	24	6	12	106	67	54	2nd
1960–61	I	42	25	7	10	103	75	57	3rd
1961–62	I	42	13	10	19	73	86	36	18th
1962–63	I	42	20	10	12	93	65	50	5th
1963–64	I	42	12	15	15	70	80	39	16th
1964–65	I	42	13	4	25	59	89	30	21st
1965–66	II	42	20	10	12	87	61	50	6th
1966–67	II	42	25	8	9	88	48	58	2nd
1967–68	I	42	14	8	20	66	75	36	17th
1968–69	I	42	10	15	17	41	58	35	16th
1969–70	I	42	12	16	14	55	57	40	13th
1970–71	I	42	22	8	12	64	54	52	4th
1971–72	I	42	18	11	13	65	57	47	9th
1972–73	I	42	18	11	13	66	54	47	5th
1973–74	I	42	13	15	14	49	49	41	12th
1974–75	I	42	14	11	17	57	54	39	12th
1975–76	I	42	10	10	22	51	68	30	20th
1976–77	II	42	22	13	7	84	45	57	1st
1977–78	I	42	12	12	18	51	64	36	15th
1978–79	I	42	13	8	21	44	68	34	18th
1979–80	I	42	19	9	14	58	47	47	6th
1980–81	I	42	13	9	20	43	55	35	18th
1981–82	I	42	10	10	22	32	63	40	21st
1982–83	II	42	20	15	7	68	44	75	2nd
1983–84	I	42	6	11	25	27	80	29	22nd
1984–85	II	42	8	9	25	37	79	33	22nd
1985–86	III	46	11	10	25	57	98	43	23rd
1986–87	IV	46	24	7	15	69	50	79	4th
1987–88	IV	46	27	9	10	82	43	90	1st
1988–89	III	46	26	14	6	96	49	92	1st
1989–90	II	46	18	13	15	67	60	67	10th
1990–91	II	46	13	19	14	63	63	58	12th
1991–92	II	46	18	10	18	61	54	64	11th
1992–93	I	46	16	13	17	57	56	61	11th

Wolverhampton Wanderers are the only club to have won the championship of four divisions of the Football League plus the regional Division Three (North).

Stan Cullis' great Wolves side of the 1950s, champions again in 1958. After retaining the title in 1959 they won the FA Cup the following season to complete a memorable decade (Popperfoto)

WORKINGTON

Year	Div	P	W	D	L	F	A	Pts	Pos
1951–52	IIIN	46	11	7	28	50	91	29	24th
1952–53	IIIN	46	11	10	25	55	91	32	23rd
1953–54	IIIN	46	13	14	19	59	80	40	20th
1954–55	IIIN	46	18	14	14	68	55	50	8th
1955–56	IIIN	46	19	9	18	75	63	47	10th
1956–57	IIIN	46	24	10	12	93	63	58	4th
1957–58	IIIN	46	14	13	19	72	81	41	19th
1958–59	IV	46	12	17	17	63	78	41	17th
1959–60	IV	46	14	14	18	68	60	42	16th
1960–61	IV	46	21	7	18	74	76	49	8th
1961–62	IV	44	19	11	14	69	70	49	8th
1962–63	IV	46	17	13	16	76	68	47	10th
1963–64	IV	46	24	11	11	76	52	59	3rd
1964–65	III	46	17	12	17	58	69	46	15th
1965–66	III	46	19	14	13	67	57	52	5th
1966–67	III	46	12	7	27	55	89	31	24th

Year	Div	P	W	D	L	F	A	Pts	Pos
1967–68	IV	46	10	11	25	54	87	31	23rd
1968–69	IV	46	15	17	14	40	43	47	12th
1969–70	IV	46	12	14	20	46	64	38	20th
1970–71	IV	46	18	12	16	48	49	48	10th
1971–72	IV	46	16	19	11	50	34	51	6th
1972–73	IV	46	17	12	17	59	61	46	13th
1973–74	IV	46	11	13	22	43	74	35	23rd
1974–75	IV	46	10	11	25	36	66	31	23rd
1975–76	IV	46	7	7	32	30	87	27	24th
1976–77	IV	46	4	11	31	41	102	19	24th

Jim Dailey scored a club record 26 League goals in 1956–57 when **Workington** finished fourth in Division Three (North) with 58 points. Between 1953 and 1958 he also set an aggregate record of 84 League goals at Borough Park.

WREXHAM

Year	Div	P	W	D	L	F	A	Pts	Pos
1921–22	IIIN	38	14	9	15	51	56	37	12th
1922–23	IIIN	38	14	10	14	38	48	38	10th
1923–24	IIIN	42	10	18	14	37	44	38	16th
1924–25	IIIN	42	15	8	19	53	61	38	16th
1925–26	IIIN	42	11	10	21	63	92	32	19th
1926–27	IIIN	42	14	10	18	65	73	38	13th
1927–28	IIIN	42	18	6	18	64	67	42	11th
1928–29	IIIN	42	21	10	11	91	69	52	3rd
1929–30	IIIN	42	13	8	21	67	88	34	17th
1930–31	IIIN	42	21	12	9	94	62	54	3rd
1931–32	IIIN	40	18	7	15	64	69	43	10th
1932–33	IIIN	42	24	9	9	106	51	57	2nd
1933–34	IIIN	42	23	5	14	102	73	51	6th
1934–35	IIIN	42	16	11	15	76	69	43	11th
1935–36	IIIN	42	15	7	20	66	75	37	18th
1936–37	IIIN	42	16	12	14	71	57	44	8th
1937–38	IIIN	42	16	11	15	58	63	43	10th
1938–39	IIIN	42	17	7	18	66	79	41	14th
1939–46	Regional Leagues operating								
1946–47	IIIN	42	17	12	13	65	51	46	7th
1947–48	IIIN	42	21	8	13	74	54	50	3rd
1948–49	IIIN	42	17	9	16	56	62	43	9th
1949–50	IIIN	42	10	12	20	39	54	32	20th
1950–51	IIIN	46	15	12	19	55	71	42	14th
1951–52	IIIN	46	15	9	22	63	73	39	18th
1952–53	IIIN	46	24	8	14	86	66	56	3rd
1953–54	IIIN	46	21	9	16	81	68	51	8th
1954–55	IIIN	46	13	12	21	65	77	38	18th
1955–56	IIIN	46	16	10	20	66	73	42	14th
1956–57	IIIN	46	19	10	17	97	74	48	12th
1957–58	IIIN	46	17	12	17	61	63	46	12th
1958–59	III	46	14	14	18	63	77	42	18th
1959–60	III	46	14	8	24	68	101	36	23rd
1960–61	IV	46	17	8	21	62	56	42	16th
1961–62	IV	44	22	9	13	96	56	53	3rd
1962–63	III	46	20	9	17	84	83	49	9th
1963–64	III	46	13	6	27	75	107	32	23rd
1964–65	IV	46	17	9	20	84	92	43	14th
1965–66	IV	46	13	9	24	72	104	35	24th
1966–67	IV	46	16	20	10	76	62	52	7th
1967–68	IV	46	20	13	13	72	53	53	8th
1968–69	IV	46	18	14	14	61	52	50	9th
1969–70	IV	46	26	9	11	84	49	61	2nd
1970–71	III	46	18	13	15	72	65	49	9th
1971–72	III	46	16	8	22	59	63	40	16th
1972–73	III	46	14	17	15	55	54	45	12th
1973–74	III	46	22	12	12	63	43	56	4th
1974–75	III	46	15	15	16	65	55	45	13th
1975–76	III	46	20	12	14	66	55	52	6th
1976–77	III	46	24	10	12	80	54	58	5th
1977–78	III	46	23	15	8	78	45	61	1st
1978–79	II	42	12	14	16	45	42	38	15th
1979–80	II	42	16	6	20	40	49	38	16th
1980–81	II	42	12	14	16	43	45	38	16th
1981–82	II	42	11	11	20	40	56	44	21st
1982–83	III	46	12	15	19	57	76	51	22nd
1983–84	IV	46	11	15	20	59	74	48	20th
1984–85	IV	46	15	9	22	67	70	54	15th
1985–86	IV	46	17	9	20	68	80	60	13th
1986–87	IV	46	15	20	11	70	51	65	9th
1987–88	IV	46	20	6	20	69	58	66	11th
1988–89	IV	46	19	14	13	77	63	71	7th
1989–90	IV	46	13	12	21	51	67	51	21st
1990–91	IV	46	10	10	26	48	74	40	24th
1991–92	IV	42	14	9	19	52	73	51	14th
1992–93	III	42	23	11	8	75	52	80	2nd

Wrexham defender Wayne Cegielski picked up a useful tip while he was playing with Schalke 04 in Germany. To prevent snow clogging up boots, the soles were dabbed in methylated spirit. The ball was similarly treated. Wrexham tried it in an FA Cup third round tie on 1 February 1979 against Stockport County. Wrexham won 6–2 with Cegielski among the goalscorers.

YORK CITY

Year	Div	P	W	D	L	F	A	Pts	Pos
1929–30	IIIN	42	15	16	11	77	64	46	6th
1930–31	IIIN	42	18	6	18	85	82	42	12th
1931–32	IIIN	40	18	7	15	76	81	43	9th
1932–33	IIIN	42	13	6	23	72	92	32	20th
1933–34	IIIN	42	15	8	19	71	74	38	12th
1934–35	IIIN	42	15	6	21	76	82	36	15th
1935–36	IIIN	42	13	12	17	62	95	38	16th
1936–37	IIIN	42	16	11	15	79	70	43	12th
1937–38	IIIN	42	16	10	16	70	68	42	11th
1938–39	IIIN	42	12	8	22	66	92	32	20th
1939–46	Regional Leagues operating								
1946–47	IIIN	42	14	9	19	67	81	37	15th
1947–48	IIIN	42	13	14	15	65	60	40	13th
1948–49	IIIN	42	15	9	18	74	74	39	14th

1949–50	IIIN	42	9	13	20	52	70	31	22nd
1950–51	IIIN	46	12	15	19	66	77	39	17th
1951–52	IIIN	46	18	13	15	73	52	49	10th
1952–53	IIIN	46	20	13	13	60	45	53	4th
1953–54	IIIN	46	12	13	21	64	86	37	22nd
1954–55	IIIN	46	24	10	12	92	63	58	4th
1955–56	IIIN	46	19	9	18	85	72	47	11th
1956–57	IIIN	46	21	10	15	75	61	52	7th
1957–58	IIIN	46	17	12	17	68	76	46	13th
1958–59	IV	46	21	18	7	73	52	60	3rd
1959–60	III	46	13	12	21	57	73	38	21st
1960–61	IV	46	21	9	16	80	60	51	5th
1961–62	IV	44	20	10	14	84	53	50	6th
1962–63	IV	46	16	11	19	67	62	43	14th
1963–64	IV	46	14	7	25	52	66	35	22nd
1964–65	IV	46	28	6	12	91	56	62	3rd
1965–66	III	46	9	9	28	53	106	27	24th
1966–67	IV	46	12	11	23	65	79	35	22nd
1967–68	IV	46	11	14	21	65	68	36	21st
1968–69	IV	46	14	11	21	53	75	39	21st
1969–70	IV	46	16	14	16	55	62	46	13th
1970–71	IV	46	23	10	13	78	54	56	4th
1971–72	IV	46	12	12	22	57	66	36	19th
1972–73	III	46	13	15	18	42	46	41	18th
1973–74	III	46	21	19	6	67	38	61	3rd
1974–75	II	42	14	10	18	51	55	38	15th
1975–76	II	42	10	8	24	39	71	28	21st
1976–77	III	46	10	12	24	50	89	32	24th
1977–78	IV	46	12	12	22	50	69	36	22nd
1978–79	IV	46	18	11	17	51	55	47	10th
1979–80	IV	46	14	11	21	65	82	39	17th
1980–81	IV	46	12	9	25	47	66	33	24th
1981–82	IV	46	14	8	24	69	91	50	17th
1982–83	IV	46	22	13	11	88	58	79	7th
1983–84	IV	46	31	8	7	96	39	101	1st
1984–85	III	46	20	9	17	70	57	69	8th
1985–86	III	46	20	11	15	77	58	71	7th
1986–87	III	46	12	13	21	55	79	49	20th
1987–88	III	46	8	9	29	48	91	33	23rd
1988–89	IV	46	17	13	16	62	63	64	11th
1989–90	IV	46	16	16	14	55	53	64	13th
1990–91	IV	46	11	13	22	45	57	46	21st
1991–92	IV	42	8	16	18	42	58	40	19th
1992–93	III	42	21	12	9	72	45	75	4th

Sid Storey cost **York City** only £100 when they signed him in 1947 from Wombwell Athletic. He spent ten seasons as an inside-forward at Bootham Crescent and on being released was given an entry in the club's minute book: 'Outstanding service and loyalty'. He subsequently played for Barnsley, Accrington Stanley and Bradford Park Avenue. During the war he assisted Huddersfield Town.

LEAGUE FOOTBALL

LEAGUE CHAMPIONS

Season ending	Champions	Matches	Pts	Home						Away						Goal av	No. of players	Ever present	Winning margin (pts)
				W	D	L	F	A	Pts	W	D	L	F	A	Pts				
1889	Preston North End	22	40	10	1	0	39	7	21	8	3	0	35	8	19	3.36	18	2	11
1890	Preston North End	22	33	8	1	2	41	12	17	7	2	2	30	18	16	3.23	19	3	2
1891	Everton	22	29	9	0	2	39	12	18	5	1	5	24	17	11	2.86	21	3	2
1892	Sunderland	26	42	13	0	0	55	11	26	8	0	5	38	25	16	3.57	15	2	5
1893	Sunderland	30	48	13	2	0	58	17	28	9	2	4	42	19	20	3.33	15	3	11
1894	Aston Villa	30	44	12	2	1	49	13	26	7	4	4	35	29	18	2.80	24	1	6
1895	Sunderland	30	47	13	2	0	51	14	28	8	3	4	29	23	19	2.66	16	2	5
1896	Aston Villa	30	45	14	1	0	47	17	29	6	4	5	31	28	16	2.60	17	2	4
1897	Aston Villa	30	47	10	3	2	36	16	23	11	2	2	37	22	24	2.43	17	4	11
1898	Sheffield United	30	42	9	4	2	27	14	22	8	4	3	29	17	20	1.86	23	1	5
1899	Aston Villa	34	45	15	2	0	58	13	32	4	5	8	18	27	13	2.23	24	1	2
1900	Aston Villa	34	50	12	4	1	45	18	28	10	2	5	32	17	22	2.26	21	2	2
1901	Liverpool	34	45	12	2	3	36	13	26	7	5	5	23	22	19	1.73	18	3	2
1902	Sunderland	34	44	12	3	2	32	14	27	7	3	7	18	21	17	1.47	19	1	3
1903	Sheffield Weds.	34	42	12	3	2	31	7	27	7	1	9	23	29	15	1.58	23	3	1
1904	Sheffield Weds.	34	47	14	3	0	34	10	31	6	4	7	14	18	16	1.41	22	2	3
1905	Newcastle United	34	48	14	1	2	41	12	29	9	1	7	31	21	19	2.11	21	0	1

Season ending	Champions	Matches	Pts	Home						Away						Goal av	No. of players	Ever present	Winning margin (pts)
				W	D	L	F	A	Pts	W	D	L	F	A	Pts				
1906	Liverpool	38	51	14	3	2	49	15	31	9	2	8	30	31	20	2.07	21	1	4
1907	Newcastle United	38	51	18	1	0	51	12	37	4	6	9	23	34	14	1.94	27	0	3
1908	Manchester United	38	52	15	1	3	43	19	31	8	5	6	38	29	21	2.13	25	0	9
1909	Newcastle United	38	53	14	1	4	32	20	29	10	4	5	33	21	24	1.71	25	1	7
1910	Aston Villa	38	53	17	2	0	62	19	36	6	5	8	22	23	17	2.21	18	0	5
1911	Manchester United	38	52	14	4	1	47	18	32	8	4	7	25	22	20	1.89	26	0	1
1912	Blackburn Rovers	38	49	13	6	0	35	10	32	7	3	9	25	33	17	1.57	21	0	3
1913	Sunderland	38	54	14	2	3	47	17	30	11	2	6	39	26	24	2.26	22	1	4
1914	Blackburn Rovers	38	51	14	4	1	51	15	32	6	7	6	27	27	19	2.05	21	1	7
1915	Everton	38	46	8	5	6	44	29	21	11	3	5	32	18	25	2.00	24	0	1

No national competition 1916–1919; regional leagues in operation

Season ending	Champions	Matches	Pts	Home						Away						Goal av	No. of players	Ever present	Winning margin (pts)
				W	D	L	F	A	Pts	W	D	L	F	A	Pts				
1920	West Bromwich A.	42	60	17	1	3	65	21	35	11	3	7	39	26	25	2.47	18	1	9
1921	Burnley	42	59	17	3	1	56	16	37	6	10	5	23	20	22	1.88	23	1	5
1922	Liverpool	42	57	15	4	2	43	15	34	7	9	5	20	21	23	1.50	22	2	6
1923	Liverpool	42	60	17	3	1	50	13	37	9	5	7	20	18	23	1.66	19	3	6
1924	Huddersfield Town	42	57	15	5	1	35	9	35	8	6	7	25	24	22	1.42	22	1	gl av.
1925	Huddersfield Town	42	58	10	8	3	31	10	28	11	8	2	38	18	30	1.64	22	0	2
1926	Huddersfield Town	42	57	14	6	1	50	17	34	9	5	7	42	43	23	2.19	24	0	5
1927	Newcastle United	42	56	19	1	1	64	20	39	6	5	10	32	38	17	2.28	21	3	5
1928	Everton	42	53	11	8	2	60	28	30	9	5	7	42	38	23	2.42	24	2	2
1929	Sheffield Weds.	42	52	18	3	0	55	16	39	3	7	11	31	46	13	2.04	22	4	1
1930	Sheffield Weds.	42	60	15	4	2	56	20	34	11	4	6	49	37	26	2.50	22	1	10
1931	Arsenal	42	66	14	5	2	67	27	33	14	5	2	60	32	33	3.02	22	1	7
1932	Everton	42	56	18	0	3	84	30	36	8	4	9	32	34	20	2.76	20	0	2
1933	Arsenal	42	58	14	3	4	70	27	31	11	5	5	48	34	27	2.80	23	1	4
1934	Arsenal	42	59	15	4	2	45	19	34	10	5	6	30	28	25	1.78	23	1	3
1935	Arsenal	42	58	15	4	2	74	17	34	8	8	5	41	29	24	2.73	25	0	4
1936	Sunderland	42	56	17	2	2	71	33	36	8	4	9	38	41	20	2.59	23	2	8
1937	Manchester City	42	57	15	5	1	56	22	35	7	8	6	51	39	22	2.54	22	4	3
1938	Arsenal	42	52	15	4	2	52	16	34	6	6	9	25	28	18	1.83	29	0	1
1939	Everton	42	59	17	3	1	60	18	37	10	2	9	28	34	22	2.09	22	1	4

No national competition 1940–1946; regional leagues were in operation

Season ending	Champions	Matches	Pts	Home						Away						Goal av	No. of players	Ever present	Winning margin (pts)
				W	D	L	F	A	Pts	W	D	L	F	A	Pts				
1947	Liverpool	42	57	13	3	5	42	24	29	12	4	5	42	28	28	2.00	26	0	1
1948	Arsenal	42	52	15	3	3	56	15	33	8	10	3	25	17	26	1.92	19	2	7
1949	Portsmouth	42	58	18	3	0	52	12	39	7	5	9	32	30	19	2.00	18	2	5
1950	Portsmouth	42	56	12	7	2	44	15	31	10	2	9	30	23	22	1.76	25	2	gl av.
1951	Tottenham H.	42	60	17	2	2	54	21	36	8	8	5	28	23	24	1.95	19	2	4
1952	Manchester United	42	57	15	3	3	55	21	33	8	8	5	40	31	24	2.26	24	1	4
1953	Arsenal	42	54	15	3	3	60	30	33	6	9	6	37	34	21	2.30	21	0	gl av.
1954	Wolverhampton W.	42	57	16	1	4	61	25	33	9	6	6	35	31	24	2.28	22	1	4
1955	Chelsea	42	52	11	5	5	43	29	27	9	7	5	38	28	25	1.92	20	2	4
1956	Manchester United	42	60	18	3	0	51	20	39	7	7	7	32	31	21	1.97	24	1	11
1957	Manchester United	42	64	14	4	3	55	25	32	14	4	3	48	29	22	2.45	24	0	8
1958	Wolverhampton W.	42	64	17	3	1	60	21	37	11	5	5	43	26	27	2.45	21	0	5
1959	Wolverhampton W.	42	61	15	3	3	68	19	33	13	2	6	42	30	28	2.61	22	0	6
1960	Burnley	42	55	15	2	4	52	28	32	9	5	7	33	33	23	2.02	18	3	1
1961	Tottenham H.	42	66	15	3	3	65	28	33	16	1	4	50	27	33	2.73	17	4	8
1962	Ipswich Town	42	56	17	2	2	58	28	36	7	6	8	35	39	20	2.21	16	3	3
1963	Everton	42	61	14	7	0	48	17	35	11	4	6	36	25	26	2.00	20	2	6
1964	Liverpool	42	57	16	0	5	60	18	32	10	5	6	32	27	25	2.19	17	3	4
1965	Manchester United	42	61	16	4	1	52	13	36	10	5	6	37	26	25	2.11	18	4	gl av.

Season ending	Champions	Matches	Pts	Home						Away						Goal av	No. of players	Ever present	Winning margin (pts)
				W	D	L	F	A	Pts	W	D	L	F	A	Pts				
1966	Liverpool	42	61	17	2	2	52	15	36	9	7	5	27	19	25	1.88	14	5	6
1967	Manchester United	42	60	17	4	0	51	13	38	7	8	6	33	32	22	2.00	20	2	4
1968	Manchester City	42	58	17	2	2	52	16	36	9	4	8	34	27	22	2.04	21	1	2
1969	Leeds United	42	67	18	3	0	41	9	39	9	10	2	25	17	28	1.57	17	4	6
1970	Everton	42	66	17	3	1	46	19	37	12	5	4	26	15	29	1.71	17	4	9
1971	Arsenal	42	65	18	3	0	41	6	39	11	4	6	30	23	26	1.69	16	3	1
1972	Derby County	42	58	16	4	1	43	10	36	8	6	7	26	23	22	1.64	16	2	1
1973	Liverpool	42	60	17	3	1	45	19	37	8	7	6	27	23	23	1.71	16	3	3
1974	Leeds United	42	62	12	8	1	38	18	32	12	6	3	28	13	30	1.57	20	2	5
1975	Derby County	42	53	14	4	3	41	18	32	7	7	7	26	31	21	1.59	16	2	2
1976	Liverpool	42	60	14	5	2	41	21	33	9	9	3	25	10	27	1.57	19	2	1
1977	Liverpool	42	57	18	3	0	47	11	39	5	8	8	15	22	18	1.47	17	3	1
1978	Nottingham Forest	42	64	15	6	0	37	8	36	10	8	3	32	16	28	1.64	16	1	7
1979	Liverpool	42	68	19	2	0	51	4	40	11	6	4	34	12	28	2.02	15	4	8
1980	Liverpool	42	60	15	6	0	46	8	36	8	10	4	35	22	24	1.92	17	3	2
1981	Aston Villa	42	60	16	3	2	40	13	35	10	5	6	32	27	25	1.71	14	7	4
1982	Liverpool	42	87	14	3	4	39	14	45	12	6	3	41	18	42	1.90	16	3	4
1983	Liverpool	42	82	16	4	1	55	16	52	8	6	7	32	21	30	2.07	16	4	11
1984	Liverpool	42	80	14	5	2	50	12	47	8	9	4	23	20	33	1.73	15	5	3
1985	Everton	42	90	16	3	2	58	17	51	12	3	6	30	26	42	2.09	25	1	13
1986	Liverpool	42	88	16	4	1	58	14	52	10	6	5	31	23	36	2.11	18	1	3
1987	Everton	42	86	16	4	1	49	11	52	10	4	7	27	20	34	1.80	23	1	9
1988	Liverpool	40	90	15	5	0	49	9	50	11	7	2	38	15	40	2.17	22	2	9
1989	Arsenal	38	76	10	6	3	35	19	36	12	4	3	38	17	40	1.92	17	3	gls
1990	Liverpool	38	79	13	5	1	38	15	44	10	5	4	40	22	35	2.05	21	2	9
1991	Arsenal	38	*83	15	4	0	51	10	49	9	9	1	23	8	*34	1.94	19	4	7
1992	Leeds United	42	82	13	8	0	38	13	47	9	8	4	36	24	35	1.76	23	2	4
1993	Manchester United	42	84	14	5	2	39	14	47	10	7	4	28	17	37	1.60	20	4	10

*Two points deducted; disciplinary decision by FA following incident in match with Manchester United.

PREMIER LEAGUE

The idea of a super league had gained ground among leading clubs in the Football League at various times during the 1980s. With the proliferation of fixtures it was argued that a smaller domestic competition was essential for the well-being of players who were being asked to extend themselves beyond reasonable limits as the game's tempo increased. Moreover the England team was suffering as the demands on top players escalated.

This was a worthy enough concept, but hid what was more likely to be the thinking behind it: the bigger clubs wanted a larger slice of the income being generated by the game.

There were several threats to go it alone, but the Football League had succeeded in keeping their 92-club, four divisions intact until the Football Association introduced its Blueprint for the Future of Football towards the end of the 1990–91 season.

This document gave the opportunity for those

The new Premier League had worthy champions in Manchester United and a wealthy new force to be reckoned with in Blackburn Rovers. Mark Hughes goes for goal at Old Trafford (Bob Thomas)

keen to breakaway from the constraints of the Football League, with the knowledge that there would be not only official approval, but the real promise of vast sums of money being attracted into club coffers through sponsorship and television finance. All this was presented in a package designed with the intention of proposing changes for the benefit of the England team, whose players would have fewer matches with which to contend.

As far as the top division was concerned the principle plan was for an 18-team set-up to be established, giving ample time for the England team manager to prepare his elite for international matches. The proposal was flawed in one respect: to design a League purposely for the sole benefit of a national team requiring at most 12 games a year was misguided.

There had already been a move to reduce the number of teams in the First Division to 20, but the clubs were unhappy with this and there had been a reversion to 22. Yet here was a scheme to cut out four clubs from the top division.

However, since the revolution was not one to be started by the clubs themselves, but by the establishment of the game itself, it was left to the Football League to attempt a rearguard action at best to save what they could of their 100-year-old structure.

That the initiative by the Football Association was divisive was not in question and assurances for the whole of what was to remain of the Football League did not provide much comfort at Lytham St Annes, the headquarters of the oldest domestic league in the world.

There were obvious arguments on the side of change: progress had to be made, otherwise clubs would only have tradition to hold them back.

Holding back the progressive clubs for the sake of the entire League was another persuasive argument in advocating such a venture as the FA Premier League. Clearly the FA did not want to mount a takeover bid for the entire Football League, just the most commercially viable portion of it.

But there was a rebellion inside the revolution. The wider conflict might have been between the Football Association and the Football League; the more localised friction involved the big clubs wanting to distance themselves financially from the rest.

There was a weakness in the administration of the Football League, not in the efficient manner in which the day to day running of the four divisions was concerned, but in the fact that there was a distinct lack of leadership. The Football Association cleverly exploited this area of susceptibility.

In order to realise excellence and quality it was of paramount importance that huge resources of money would have to be ploughed into the Premier League. They came through the massive £304 million injection from BskyB and the BBC.

On 20 February 1992, the FA Council gave its approval to the 22-club Premier League, to commence on 15 August. With the original idea of an 18-club league rejected, the three up and three down principle with the new Football League would stay until the end of the 1994–95 season when four Premier clubs would be relegated and only two promoted in their place.

The Professional Footballers Association disputed TV money with the Premier League and the First Division's 587 players were asked to back strike action. The problem was resolved on 27 April when the PFA accepted an increased offer of £1.5 million for the 1992–93 season.

Referees in Premier League matches would wear a green strip with black as second choice, the half-time interval was extended to 15 minutes and each team would have three substitutes, one of which had to be a goalkeeper, though only two players could be replaced. It was also agreed that there would be no loan transfers between Premier clubs.

This then was the background to the launch of the new competition in August 1992. Outwardly there seemed little change, other than the member clubs having withdrawn from the Football League. They were operating in surroundings much as they had been the season before, though with ground alterations continuing in line with the Taylor Report in the wake of the Hillsborough disaster in 1989.

But there were fewer people watching Premier matches compared with the old First Division. This was for a variety of reasons, including the continuing recession, increased admission prices and the fact that armchair fans had lost the outlet of ITV and fewer were inclined to avail themselves of a satellite dish to watch Sky.

Then in February 1993, after months of wrangling between a clique of Premier clubs known as the Platinum Eight who wanted to develop their own sponsorship deals, the Premier League announced it had secured a four-year £12 million deal with Bass and from August 1993 the competition was to be known as the FA Carling Premiership.

LEAGUE FACTS & FEATS

Twenty-three different teams have won the Football League championship. Liverpool have been the most successful with 18 titles followed by Arsenal with ten. Everton have had nine, Manchester United eight and Aston Villa seven.

The 12 original members of the Football League in 1888 were: Preston North End, Aston Villa, Wolverhampton Wanderers, Blackburn Rovers, Bolton Wanderers, West Bromwich Albion, Accrington, Everton, Burnley, Derby County, Notts County and Stoke, finishing the 1888–89 season in that order.

Notts County and Blackburn Rovers were the last two clubs to open their League programme in 1888. While the other ten began on 8 September, Notts and Rovers started a week later. Notts played at Everton, Blackburn at home to Accrington. The first goal was scored by Jack Gordon (Preston North End), the first own goal by George Cox (Aston Villa).

Results and attendances from the first day of the Football League were: Bolton 3, Derby 6 (4,000); Everton 2, Accrington 1 (12,000); Preston 5, Burnley 2 (6,000); Stoke 0, West Bromwich 2 (4,524); Wolves 1, Aston Villa 1 (2,500).

Despite their late start to League football, Notts County became the first club to reach 3,000 League matches. They achieved this milestone in a Division Two game against Nottingham Forest on 25 March 1975 which ended in a 2–2 draw. Yet as one of four clubs who were forced to seek re-election to the League after its inaugural season, they had received seven votes, just two more than Birmingham St George's.

Aston Villa were the first to score 6,000 goals in the Football League. They reached this milestone in a 1–1 draw against Bournemouth at Villa Park on 17 October 1987.

Everton hold the record for the largest championship-winning points margin in Division One, following the

The Everton side which carried all before them in 1984–85. Champions by a record margin, they clinched the title with five games still remaining (Bob Thomas)

introduction of three points for a win. In 1984–85 they had a 13-point lead over the runners-up Liverpool. Under the previous two-points system, 11 points was the record, held jointly by Preston North End (1888–89), Sunderland (1892–93), Aston Villa (1896–97) and Manchester United (1955–56).

Goal average was used to determine the League champions in 1923–24, 1949–50, 1952–53 and 1964–65. Goal difference had to be used in 1988–89, but as this was identical for both teams, Arsenal won the title by scoring more goals than Liverpool.

In 1992–93, the Football League scrapped goal difference for its three-division competition in favour of most goals scored when teams were level on points, followed by the fewest conceded if this did not separate them. Failing this second option, a play-off would place them.

Accrington became the first permanent casualty among the initial members of the Football League in 1888. After being relegated to Division Two in 1893 they left the League before the next season. Manchester United had actually finished five points below them at the bottom of the table.

Stoke had not been re-elected in 1890, but came back the following year only to be relegated again in 1907. After one season in Division Two, they resigned from the League for financial reasons, but were re-elected in 1919.

The highest-scoring championship winners in the post-war period were Tottenham Hotspur in 1960–61 with 115 goals at an average of 2.73 per game. Spurs were also the last team in Division One to score a century of goals, which they did in 1962–63 with 111 goals as runners-up.

Between the wars, the highest-scoring winners were Arsenal in 1930–31 with 127 goals for an average of 3.02 per game. But the overall record is held by Sunderland, who in 1891–92 won the title with 93 goals at an average of 3.57 goals per game. In 1930–31 the top three finished with a century of goals: Arsenal (127), Aston Villa (128), Sheffield Wednesday (102).

On 30 August 1986 only 12 goals were scored in 11 Division Two matches. No team scored more than once. On 1 October 1983 there were 53 goals scored in 11 Division Two matches. The scores included a 7, two 5's, three 4's and three 3's.

On 26 December 1963 there were 66 goals scored in the ten Division One matches played.

On 1 February 1936 there were 209 goals scored in 44 League matches, equalling the record of 2 January 1932 when one match fewer had been played due to Wigan Borough's resignation in October 1931. On 1 February 1936 the goals were divided as follows: Division One 46; Division Two 46; Division Three (South) 49; Division Three (North) 68. On 2 January 1932 it was: Division One 56; Division Two 53; Division Three (South) 57; Division Three (North) 43.

On 6 September 1986 the Division One programme did not produce one home win. There were eight away wins and three draws. Similarly in Division Two there were seven away wins and four draws on 26 December 1987.

On 13 February 1926 all Division One clubs at home won their matches and it happened again on 10 December 1955. All 12 Division Two games were won by home teams on 26 November 1988.

Nine of 11 Division One games on 18 September 1948 were drawn.

Of the 12 Division Three matches played on 18/19 October 1968, all produced home wins.

On 28 April 1923, there were no away goals scored in Division One and only three drawn games. Only ten goals were scored on the day.

On 2 November 1991, only 89 goals were scored in 44 League matches. Only nine were scored in the 11 Division One matches.

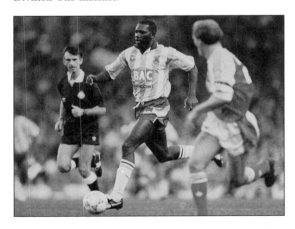

It was a day of few goals in Division One on 2 November 1991 but Mike Small was on target for West Ham in their 1–0 win over champions Arsenal at Highbury (Allsport)

Extensions to the League: 1891 (14 clubs); 1892 with addition of Division Two (28); 1893 (31); 1894 (32); 1898 (36); 1905 (40); 1919 (44); 1920 with addition of Division Three (66); 1921 with addition of more clubs

and formation of two regional sections of Division Three (86); 1923 (88); 1950 (92); 1991 (93); 1992 (92). In 1958 the two regional Division Three's were replaced with a Division Three and Division Four. In 1992, the FA Premier League replaced the Football League's Division One, the League re-numbering their three divisions 1, 2 and 3.

Three up and three down promotion and relegation was introduced for the 1973–74 season in the top three divisions. There were still four relegated from Division Three and four promoted from Division Four. It was the first change from two up and two down for the top two divisions in 81 years.

A series of Test Matches had operated between Divisions One and Two for six seasons from 1893 to 1898 to determine promotion and relegation. In 1987 play-offs were introduced as part of the promotion and relegation issue and for the first time the club finishing bottom of Division Four was relegated to the GM Vauxhall Conference.

Clubs who have left the Football League during a season have been: Leeds City (expelled October 1919), Wigan Borough (withdrew October 1931), Accrington Stanley (withdrew March 1962) and Aldershot (expelled March 1992).

Preston North End as the first League champions in 1889 were undefeated in their 22 matches. In 1991 Arsenal became the first champions of the century to lose just once in winning the title.

In 1907–08, Blackburn Rovers and Arsenal finished equal 14th in Division One with identical records: played 38, won 12, drew 12, lost 14, goals for 51, goals against 63, points 36.

In 1992–93 Coventry City became the first club to play in seven different first-class divisions in England when they became founder members of the Premier League. They had previously played in Divisions One, Two, Three and Four as well as both regional sections of Division Three.

Liverpool used only 14 players including five who were ever-present, when they won the League Championship in 1965–66. Aston Villa used 14 during their title-winning season 1980–81, with seven ever-present players.

Northampton Town with 103 goals in 1986–87 as Division Four champions were the last first-class club in England to score a century of goals since Huddersfield Town scored 101 goals in 1979–80 also as Division Four champions.

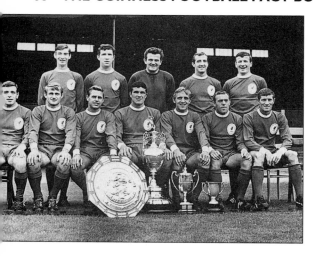

The Liverpool side which won the League title in 1966. Given manager Bill Shankly's famous mistrust of injured players, it was as well he had a record five ever-presents that season (Popperfoto)

Most wins in a season

Tottenham Hotspur won 31 of their 42 Division One matches in 1960–61. They finished eight points ahead of Sheffield Wednesday to win the championship with 66 points. Of their 115 goals, all but 24 were contributed by their most regular five forwards: Bobby Smith scored 28 goals, Les Allen 23, Cliff Jones 15, John White 13 and Terry Dyson 12. Only four other teams have scored more goals in Division One. Spurs achieved the League and Cup double that season, the third side to accomplish the feat at the time.

Tottenham Hotspur also won 32 of their 42 Division Two matches in 1919–20. Nineteen of these came from home wins but it was a 3–1 victory at Stoke on 10 April that clinched the championship. Up to then, they had failed to score just once in the League. Bert Bliss with 31 goals was their leading scorer.

Millwall won 30 of their 42 Division Three (South) matches in 1927–28. Nineteen of these came from wins at home where only two points were dropped in drawn matches.

Plymouth Argyle won 30 of their 42 Division Three (South) matches in 1929–30. They had finished as runners-up six times in succession during the previous eight seasons. They were undefeated until the 19th match and their total of 68 points was a club record.

Cardiff City won 30 of their 42 Division Three (South) matches in 1946–47. Eighteen of these came from wins at Ninian Park, where they dropped just three points in drawn games and conceded only 11 goals.

Nottingham Forest won 30 of their 46 Division Three (South) matches in 1950–51. Sixteen of these came from home wins. Only six matches were lost overall and ten drawn. The club also achieved a record 70 points and a record total of 110 goals. Thirty-two points were gained from away matches.

Bristol City won 30 of their 46 Division Three (South) matches in 1954–55. Thirteen came from away wins. The club also achieved a record 70 points.

Doncaster Rovers won 33 of their 42 Division Three (North) matches in 1946–47. They won 18 away games, taking 37 points, lost only three times overall and finished with a record 72 points.

Aston Villa won 32 of their 46 Division Three matches in 1971–72. Twenty matches were won at home, including 11 consecutively between October and March.

Lincoln City won 32 of their 46 Division Four matches in 1975–76. Twenty-one of these came from home wins. Only two points were dropped in drawn games on their own ground. The club also set records for the most wins, most points and fewest defeats in a season in the division.

Swindon Town won 32 of their 46 Division Four matches in 1985–86. Twenty of these came from home wins and only one game was lost at the County Ground. Yet overall they had won just two of their first eight games and were fourth from bottom on 28 September. However, they were undefeated in their last 21 matches.

Fewest wins in a season

Stoke achieved only three wins in 22 Division One matches in 1889–90. They finished bottom with 10 points, only two fewer than the previous season when they had won just four games. They failed to gain re-election but subsequently returned to the League in 1891 when it was extended to 14 clubs.

Woolwich Arsenal managed only three wins in 38 Division One matches in 1912–13. They amassed just 18 points, scoring 26 goals, finished bottom and were relegated to the Second Division.

Stoke City also achieved just three wins in 42 Division One matches in 1984–85. Their 17 points included just five from drawn games and ensured relegation. The club also set records for most defeats, fewest goals scored and fewest points in a season in the division.

Loughborough Town won only one match out of 34 Division Two games in 1899–1900. They drew six games but finished bottom, ten points behind their nearest rivals Luton Town. They scored 18 goals but conceded 100 and failed to gain re-election.

Queens Park Rangers achieved six wins in 42 Division Three (South) matches in 1925–26. They won one away game and drew nine overall but finished bottom, 14 points behind Charlton Athletic.

Merthyr Town also achieved six wins in 42 Division Three (South) matches in 1929–30. They too won one away game, drew nine overall, and finished bottom, nine points behind Gillingham.

Rochdale managed only four wins in 40 Division Three (North) matches in 1931–32. They suffered 33 defeats, including 17 in succession, as well as a record 13 consecutive home defeats.

Rochdale achieved just two wins in 46 Division Three matches in 1973–74. They completed their last 22 fixtures without a win and took only nine points from them in drawn games.

Southport achieved only three wins in 46 matches in Division Four in 1976–77. They failed to win away from home, but drew seven times. At home they drew another 12 and succeeded in finishing six points above the bottom club Workington, who failed to gain re-election.

Most drawn games in a season

Norwich City drew 23 of their 42 Division One matches in 1978–79. They finished 16th, drawing 10 times at home and 13 away in gaining 37 points under the two points for a win system.

Exeter City drew 23 of their 46 Division Four matches in 1986–87. They finished 14th, also drawing 10 times at home and 13 away in gaining 56 points under the three points for a win system.

In 1978–79 Carlisle United in Division Three equalled the record of 22 drawn games which had been held by three clubs: Tranmere Rovers in Division Three in 1970–71; Aldershot in Division Four in 1971–72 and Chester in Division Three in 1977–78. Carlisle finished sixth, with Tranmere 18th, Aldershot 17th and Chester fifth.

Most defeats in a season

Stoke City suffered 31 defeats in 42 Division One matches in 1984–85. Fifteen came from home matches and 16 away. They scored in just 17 games.

Tranmere Rovers suffered 31 defeats in 42 Division Two matches in 1938–39. They finished 14 points adrift and took just one point from away games.

Chester City suffered 33 defeats in 46 Division Two matches in 1992–93, the first season of the new 3-division Football League.

Cambridge United suffered 33 defeats in 46 Division Three matches in 1984–85. Eighteen came from home matches and 15 away. Four matches were won, two at home and two away. They finished 25 points adrift.

Merthyr Town suffered 29 defeats in 42 Division Three (South) matches in 1924–25. Their 21 points was a record low for the division. They achieved only two points from away games, both of which were drawn.

Walsall suffered 29 defeats in 46 Division Three (South) matches in 1952–53. They won five times at home, twice away and achieved 24 points. They finished bottom, 12 points behind their nearest rivals.

Walsall also suffered 29 defeats in 46 Division Three (South) matches during the following 1953–54 season. They won eight times at home, once away and achieved 26 points. They finished bottom again.

Rochdale suffered 33 defeats in 40 Division Three (North) matches in 1931–32. Only 11 points were taken, including just one away from home. A total of 135 goals were conceded.

Newport County suffered 33 defeats in 46 Division Four matches in 1987–88. Four matches were won at home, two away. Fourteen defeats were inflicted at home and 19 away. Their total of 25 points was 19 fewer than their nearest rivals. They were relegated to the GM Vauxhall Conference.

Fewest defeats in a season

Preston North End went through 22 Division One matches in the inaugural 1888–89 season without defeat. Only four points were dropped, including just one at home, to Aston Villa on 10 November. Their opponents that day finished runners-up, 11 points behind them.

Arsenal were beaten only once in 38 matches in Division One when they were champions in 1990–91. They lost 2–1 at Chelsea on 2 February.

Leeds United suffered only two defeats in 42 Division One matches in 1968–69. These were on 28 September at Manchester City's Maine Road ground when they lost 3–1, and at Burnley's Turf Moor on 19 October where they were beaten 5–1. After this reverse, Leeds had a run of 28 undefeated matches until season's end.

Liverpool completed 28 Division Two matches without defeat in 1893–94. They won 22 and drew six. Liverpool then won their Test match for promotion and drew the first two games of the following season to establish a run of 31 consecutive matches without defeat.

Burnley suffered only two defeats in 30 Division Two matches in 1897–98. They won 20 and drew eight of their games. The 80 goals they scored included nine at home to Loughborough Town, and their heaviest defeat was 2–0 at Luton Town.

Bristol City suffered only two defeats in 38 Division Two matches in 1905–06. They won 30 and drew six of their games. Thirty-one of their points came from away fixtures which produced 13 wins and five draws. They also won 14 consecutive League matches.

Leeds United suffered only three defeats in 42 Division Two matches in 1963–64. They won 24 games, which was one fewer than the runners-up, Sunderland, who finished two points below them.

Queens Park Rangers suffered five defeats in 46 Division Three matches in 1966–67. They won 26 and drew 15 of their games. They finished 12 points ahead of runners-up Middlesbrough and scored 103 goals, conceding only 38. That same season they won the League Cup.

It was a memorable year for Rodney Marsh (above, white shirt) and QPR in 1966–67, with the Third Division title being won at a canter and top-flight opposition defeated in the final of the League Cup at Wembley (Popperfoto)

Southampton suffered only four defeats in 42 Division Three (South) matches in 1921–22. They conceded just 21 goals, a record for the division. Their 61 points was also a club record. They won 23 matches, two fewer than Plymouth Argyle who finished as runners-up on goal average behind them.

Plymouth Argyle suffered only four defeats in 42 Division Three (South) matches in 1929–30. Their 68

points was a club record. They conceded only 38 goals and won 30 of their matches.

Port Vale suffered only three defeats in 46 Division Three (North) matches in 1953–54. They won 26 games and drew 17. Both figures were better than those of any of their rivals and they finished 11 points ahead of Barnsley, the runners-up.

Doncaster Rovers suffered only three defeats in 42 Division Three (North) matches in 1946–47. Of their record 33 wins, 18 came away from home and they established a record points total of 72.

Wolverhampton Wanderers suffered only three defeats in 42 Division Three (North) matches in 1923–24. Twenty-four matches were won, one fewer than runners-up Rochdale, who finished a point behind. Fifteen games were drawn by Wolves and only 27 goals conceded, one more than by Rochdale.

Lincoln City suffered only four defeats in 46 Division Four matches in 1975–76. They won 32 games, achieved a record 74 points and scored 111 goals.

Bournemouth suffered only four defeats in 46 Division Four matches in 1981–82. They won only 23 games but drew 19 in finishing fourth and achieving promotion. After staying unbeaten in their opening nine matches, they lost twice in succession, but after their fourth defeat in February they remained unbeaten in the last 17 games.

Sheffield United also suffered only four defeats in 46 Division Four matches in 1981–82. They won 27 games and remained unbeaten at home, where they dropped eight points in draws. They finished with 96 points.

Winning sequences

Tottenham Hotspur won 11 successive Division One matches from the start of the 1960–61 season. They also achieved eight consecutive away wins and a total of 16 throughout the season, compared with 15 at home.

Newcastle United won 11 successive Division One matches from the start of the 1992–93 season, in which they finished as champions and won promotion to the Premier League.

Manchester United won 14 successive Division Two matches in the 1904–05 season, an achievement which was equalled by Bristol City in 1905–06 and Preston North End in 1950–51.

Everton won the last four Division One matches of 1893–94 and the first eight of 1894–95 for a winning sequence of 12 games.

Unbeaten sequences

Nottingham Forest completed 42 Division One matches without defeat after losing 1–0 to Leeds United on 19 November 1977. The run ended in a 2–0 defeat against Liverpool on 9 December 1978. The sequence consisted of 21 wins and 21 draws. On 30 September 1978 their 2–1 win at Aston Villa had equalled Leeds United's record of 34 consecutive matches without defeat, established in the 1968–69 and 1969–70 seasons.

Burnley went 30 Division One matches without defeat after losing 2–0 to Bradford Park Avenue on 4 September 1920. The run ended in a 3–0 defeat against Manchester City on 26 March 1921.

Leeds United were undefeated in the first 29 matches of the 1973–74 season, before losing 3–2 at Stoke City on 23 February 1974. Liverpool equalled this performance in 1987–88. Their run of 29 games ended with a 1–0 defeat at Everton on 20 March 1988.

Sequences without a win

Cambridge United completed 31 Division Two matches in 1983–84 without a win. After defeating Oldham Athletic 2–1 on 1 October 1983 they did not achieve another victory until 28 April 1984 when they beat Newcastle United 1–0. Cambridge finished bottom and were relegated.

Sheffield United failed to win any of their first 16 matches in Division One during 1990–91. During this period they drew only four times and scored just seven goals. Yet they improved in the second half of the season and had a spell of seven successive wins, finishing in 13th place.

Losing sequences

Rochdale lost 17 successive Division Three (North) matches in 1931–32. After defeating New Brighton 3–2 on 7 November 1931 they did not add to their points total until drawing 1–1 with the same opposition on 9 March 1932. Rochdale finished bottom with only eleven points from 40 matches, as Wigan Borough had resigned and had their record expunged.

Manchester United lost their first 12 matches in Division One during the 1930–31 season. Their first win was 2–0 against Birmingham at Old Trafford on 1 November 1930. They did not recover from this disastrous start and finished bottom with 22 points, nine adrift.

Nelson completed 24 away matches in Division Three (North) without gaining a point. Their 1–1 draw with

Halifax Town on 29 March 1930 was in fact the last time they managed a league point away from home, because they failed to gain re-election at the end of the 1930–31 season.

Merthyr Town played 61 away matches in Division Three (South) without a win between September 1922 and September 1925. In the 1922–23 season they still finished 17th; they were 13th the following season, 1923–24, but in 1924–25 they finished bottom with 21 points.

Most goals in a season

Aston Villa scored 128 goals in 42 Division One matches during 1930–31. They scored in every home match and failed in only three away games. Eighty-six goals came at home and in 20 games four goals or more were recorded. At Villa Park, Middlesbrough were beaten 8–1, Manchester United 7–0, Huddersfield Town 6–1 and Arsenal 5–1. Villa also won 6–1 at Huddersfield and 4–0 at Birmingham. Top scorer was Pongo Waring with 49 goals while Eric Houghton had 30. Yet Villa could only finish as runners-up, seven points behind Arsenal.

Middlesbrough scored 122 goals in 42 Division Two matches during 1926–27. On three occasions they scored seven goals: against Portsmouth and Swansea Town at home and also at Grimsby, while they managed six on two other occasions. Portsmouth actually finished eight points behind them and were also promoted. Yet Middlesbrough had managed just one point and scored only one goal in their first four League matches. In the fourth they brought in George Camsell, who ended the season as their top scorer with 59 goals. His total included eight hat-tricks.

Millwall scored 127 goals in 42 Division Three (South) matches in 1927–28. Unbeaten at home where they dropped only two points, Millwall also won 11 times away and finished ten points ahead of second-placed Northampton Town. Millwall achieved 9–1 wins against Torquay United and Coventry City as well as scoring seven goals once and six on four occasions, including once away. However, they themselves also lost heavily, 5–0 and 6–1 at Bournemouth and Brentford respectively.

Bradford City scored 128 goals in 42 Division Three (North) matches in 1928–29. They managed double figures in their opening League game at home to Rotherham United, whom they defeated 11–1, the club's record victory. But promotion was not clinched until the last match of the season, a 3–1 home win over South Shields. Top scorer Albert Whitehurst, signed from Liverpool in February 1929, was their leading marksman with 24 goals in 15 matches, including seven in succession against Tranmere Rovers on 6 March in an 8–0 win. Bradford City were unbeaten during this run after Whitehurst's appearance.

Queens Park Rangers scored 111 goals in 46 Division Three matches in 1961–62. On three occasions they scored six goals, but also lost 6–3 at home to Reading. They could finish no higher than fourth and Bournemouth, who were third, edged them out on goal average, despite scoring 42 fewer goals than Rangers.

Peterborough United scored 134 goals in 46 Division Four matches in 1960–61. Seven goals were scored against Aldershot and Exeter City, and six on four occasions including once away at Stockport, who were ironically the only team to prevent Peterborough from scoring at home during the season. Terry Bly was top scorer with 52, a record for the division. The second best supported team in the division at home with an average attendance of 14,222, Peterborough also drew the crowds away from home with 12,182 on average in their first season in the Football League.

Most goals conceded in a season

Blackpool conceded 125 goals in 42 Division One matches during 1930–31. Their heaviest defeat, a club record 10–1, was suffered against Huddersfield Town on 13 December 1930. Seven goals were conceded on three occasions, including at home to Leeds United in a 7–3 defeat. But Blackpool escaped relegation by one point, finishing above Leeds. The previous season they had won promotion as Division Two champions with record points and goals.

Darwen conceded 141 goals in 34 Division Two matches during 1898–99. It proved to be the last of the club's eventful eight seasons in the League. They suffered three 10–0 reverses, away to Loughborough Town, Manchester City and Walsall, as well as losing 9–0 at Manchester United and 9–2 at Grimsby Town. They contrived just nine points, just one of them away in a 2–2 draw at Gainsborough Trinity. At the end of the season they were not re-elected.

Merthyr Town conceded 135 goals in 42 Division Three (South) matches in 1929–30. They finished bottom, nine points behind their nearest rivals Gillingham. Merthyr were not re-elected in what was their third application for re-admission. However, apart from losing 10–0 away to Newport County and 8–2 at home to Brighton & Hove Albion, Merthyr had not conceded more than six goals in any other game.

Nelson conceded 136 goals in 42 Division Three (North) matches in 1927–28. Their heaviest defeats were 9–1 at Bradford City, 8–0 at Stockport County and 7–1 at Accrington Stanley. Although they finished bottom, it was Durham City, who were three points above them, who failed to gain re-election.

Accrington Stanley conceded 123 goals in 46 Division Three matches in 1959–60. However, only twice did they let in as many as six goals, losing 6–1 at Southend United and Tranmere Rovers. They also had a 5–4 win of their own at Bradford City and took 14 points from seven away wins, more than they achieved at home. They were bottom with 27 points.

Hartlepools United conceded 109 goals in 46 Division Four matches in 1959–60. They lost 7–2 at Watford, but apart from a 6–2 defeat at Bradford Park Avenue and another at home to Doncaster Rovers, they did not let in more than five in any other games. They finished bottom, one point behind their nearest rivals Oldham Athletic.

Fewest goals scored in a season

Stoke City scored just 24 goals in 42 Division One matches in 1984–85. They did not score more than two goals in any one game and failed to score at all in 25. With 17 points they were 23 behind their nearest rivals Sunderland, and were relegated in last place.

Watford scored only 24 goals in 42 Division Two matches in 1971–72. They too failed to score more than two goals in any one match, and did not score at all in 23. In the second half of the season they scored only six goals in 21 matches.

Crystal Palace scored 33 goals in 42 Division Three (South) matches in 1950–51. Though they beat Gillingham 4–3 at home and Newport County 4–2 away, they failed to score at all in 24 games. They finished bottom with 27 points, two behind their nearest rivals Watford.

Stockport County scored only 27 goals in 46 Division Three matches in 1969–70. A 3–1 win over Doncaster Rovers at home was their best win and they failed to score at all in 25 games. They finished bottom, seven points adrift of their nearest rivals Barrow.

Crewe Alexandra scored only 32 goals in 42 Division Three (North) matches in 1923–24. They also failed to score more than two goals in any one game and did not score at all in 18. Although they managed just 27 points, it was two more than Hartlepools United and Barrow, and Crewe did not have to apply for re-election.

In 1981–82, Crewe Alexandra scored only 29 goals in Division Four. They beat Scunthorpe United 3–0 but failed to score more than two goals in any other game. In 23 matches they did not score at all. They finished bottom, 15 points behind their nearest rivals Scunthorpe.

Fewest goals conceded in a season

Liverpool conceded only 16 goals in 42 Division One matches in 1978–79. Goalkeeper Ray Clemence, who played in every match, was beaten three times on one occasion, away to Aston Villa on 16 April 1979 in a 3–1 defeat, but did not let more than one goal past him in any other game. On 28 occasions he kept a clean sheet, including 17 times at home where just four goals were conceded. Liverpool were champions eight points ahead of Nottingham Forest. Liverpool's 85 goals were the highest by the League champions since 1967–68. They conceded only seven goals in the last 21 games.

Manchester United conceded only 23 goals in 42 Division Two matches in 1924–25. Yet only a late revival, in which they took as many points in the last six matches as they had achieved in the previous eleven, enabled them to gain promotion in second place. Significantly they drew their last match at Barnsley 0–0.

Southampton conceded 21 goals in 42 Division Three (South) matches in 1921–22. They were champions and were promoted, though with two matches remaining Plymouth Argyle had led them by four points. However, while Southampton won twice, Plymouth lost their last two games and were edged out on goal average.

Port Vale conceded 21 goals in 46 Division Three (North) matches in 1953–54. The three games they lost also established a record for fewest defeats. Five goals were conceded at home, over four matches. Port Vale kept a clean sheet in 30 games overall, and in winning the championship they had an 11-point lead over runners-up Barnsley.

Middlesbrough conceded only 30 goals in 46 Division Three matches in 1986–87. Three times they let in three goals, but on 27 occasions the defence did not concede. They were unbeaten in their last 13 games and finished second to achieve promotion.

Lincoln City conceded 25 goals in 46 Division Four matches in 1980–81. They were runners-up two points behind the champions Southend United, who conceded only 31 goals themselves. Two goals were the most City let in during any one match and this occurred just four times in the season. They kept their goal intact on 25 occasions. From December to mid-March they also completed 14 games without defeat.

BEST STARTERS

Teams with the longest unbeaten runs in League matches from the start of each season:

Season	Team (Division)	Unbeaten in first	Season	Team (Division)	Unbeaten in first
1888–89	Preston North End (1)	all 22	1903–04	Preston North End (2)	13
1889–90	Accrington Stanley (1)	3	1904–05	Liverpool (2)	13
	Aston Villa (1)	3	1905–06	Sheffield Wednesday (1)	7
1890–91	Everton (1)	7		Manchester United (2)	7
1891–92	Aston Villa (1)	4	1906–07	Bolton Wanderers (1)	7
	Bolton Wanderers (1)	4		Hull City (2)	7
1892–93	Sunderland (1)	8	1907–08	Everton (1)	6
1893–94	Liverpool (2)	all 28*	1908–09	Birmingham City (2)	8
1894–95	Everton (1)	8	1909–10	Sheffield United (1)	9
1895–96	Liverpool (2)	5	1910–11	Sunderland (1)	14
	Newton Heath (2)	5	1911–12	Clapton Orient (2)	7
1896–97	Sheffield United (1)	8	1912–13	Hull City (2)	8
1897–98	Sheffield United (1)	14	1913–14	Blackburn Rovers (1)	10
1898–99	Sheffield United (1)	11	1914–15	Manchester City (1)	11
1899–1900	Sheffield United (1)	22	1919–20	Tottenham Hotspur (2)	12
1900–01	Small Heath (2)	14	1920–21	South Shields (2)	7
1901–02	Lincoln City (2)	7	1921–22	Portsmouth (3S)	10
1902–03	Blackpool (2)	6	1922–23	Portsmouth (3S)	8
			1923–24	Cardiff City (1)	11
			1924–25	Huddersfield Town (1)	10
			1925–26	Chelsea (2)	14

* Liverpool also won one Test match and then began the next season with two games undefeated.

Season	Team (Division)	Unbeaten in first	Season	Team (Division)	Unbeaten in first
1926–27	Stoke City (3N)	9	1964–65	Bradford Park Avenue (4)	12
1927–28	Charlton Athletic (3S)	12	1965–66	Bristol City (2)	7
1928–29	Luton Town (3S)	10	1966–67	Chelsea (1)	10
	Wrexham (3N)	10	1967–68	Torquay United (3)	10
1929–30	Plymouth Argyle (3S)	18	1968–69	Darlington (4)	14
1930–31	Notts County (3S)	18	1969–70	Port Vale (4)	18
1931–32	Southend United (3S)	15	1970–71	Notts County (4)	9
1932–33	Brentford (3S)	14	1971–72	Norwich City (2)	13
1933–34	Aldershot (3S)	8	1972–73	Burnley (2)	16
1934–35	Tranmere Rovers (3N)	8	1973–74	Leeds United (1)	29
1935–36	Huddersfield Town (1)	9	1974–75	Manchester United (2)	9
	Chesterfield (3N)	9	1975–76	Bury (3)	10
1935–36	Tranmere Rovers (3N)	9	1976–77	Leicester City (1)	6
1936–37	Chester (3N)	9		Manchester City (1)	6
	Hull City (3N)	9		Wolverhampton Wanderers (2)	6
1937–38	Coventry City (2)	15		Stockport County (4)	6
1938–39	Southport (3N)	9	1977–78	Manchester City (1)	8
1946–47	Barnsley (2)	10		Brighton & Hove Albion (2)	8
1947–48	Arsenal (1)	17		Tottenham Hotspur (2)	8
1948–49	Derby County (1)	16		Southend United (4)	8
1949–50	Liverpool (1)	19	1978–79	Everton (1)	19
1950–51	Newcastle United (1)	11	1979–80	Walsall (4)	13
1951–52	Oldham Athletic (3N)	9	1980–81	Ipswich Town (1)	14
1952–53	Oldham Athletic (3N)	13	1981–82	Oldham Athletic (2)	9
1953–54	Norwich City (3S)	12	1982–83	Wimbledon (4)	11
1954–55	Bristol City (3S)	13	1983–84	Sheffield Wednesday (2)	15
1955–56	Blackpool (1)	8	1984–85	Portsmouth (2)	10
1956–57	Manchester United (1)	12	1985–86	Reading (3)	14
1957–58	Scunthorpe United (3N)	8	1986–87	Exeter City (4)	13
1958–59	Fulham (2)	12	1987–88	Liverpool (1)	29
1959–60	Millwall (4)	19	1988–89	Millwall (1)	8
1960–61	Tottenham Hotspur (1)	16	1989–90	Blackburn Rovers (2)	10
1961–62	Bournemouth (3)	14	1990–91	Arsenal (1)	23
1962–63	Huddersfield Town (2)	13	1991–92	Manchester United (1)	12
1963–64	Gillingham (4)	13	1992–93	Wolverhampton Wanderers (1)	12

FA CUP

WANDERERS

Year	Date	Score	Runners-up	Venue	Att.
1872	16 March	1–0	Royal Engineers	Oval	2,000
1873	29 March	2–0	Oxford University	Lillie Bridge	3,000
1876	11 March	1–1*	Old Etonians	Oval	3,000
Replay	18 March	3–0	Old Etonians	Oval	3,500
1877	24 March	2–1*	Oxford University	Oval	3,000
1878	23 March	3–1	Royal Engineers	Oval	4,500

* after extra time

Formed in 1860 as Forest FC by ex-public school and university players. First FA Cup final goal scored by M.P. Betts, an Old Harrovian, who played under the assumed name of A.H. Chequer because he had once played for Harrow Chequers. Wanderers gained a bye to the 1873 final, since it was the 'Challenge' Cup and chose their own venue as Lillie Bridge. The rule was then dropped. They won three further trophies but chose not to retain the actual trophy. They gave it back to the FA on the condition that it was not to be won outright by any other club. C.H.R. (Charles) Wollaston appeared in all five of their finals.

OXFORD UNIVERSITY

Year	Date	Score	Runners-up	Venue	Att.
1874	14 March	2–0	Royal Engineers	Oval	2,000

Cambridge might have written the rules at one time, but Oxford became the only University side to win the cup. One of the strongest teams at the time, they included four England internationals.

ROYAL ENGINEERS

Year	Date	Score	Runners-up	Venue	Att.
1875	13 March	1–1*	Old Etonians	Oval	3,000
Replay	16 March	2–0	Old Etonians	Oval	3,000

The only service team to win the cup and involved in the first drawn final. The team was composed of commissioned officers and included Scottish international Capt. Renny-Tailyour, capped at both soccer and rugby.

OLD ETONIANS

Year	Date	Score	Runners-up	Venue	Att.
1879	29 March	1–0	Clapham Rovers	Oval	5,000
1882	25 March	1–0	Blackburn Rovers	Oval	6,500

They included the red-bearded Hon. A.F. Kinnaird, already a veteran cup finalist on six occasions and later to become Lord Kinnaird, FA President. He had won five winners' medals in nine finals. At the end of the game in 1882, he jumped for joy and stood on his head. In 1911 he was presented with the cup itself.

CLAPHAM ROVERS

Year	Date	Score	Runners-up	Venue	Att.
1880	10 April	1–0	Oxford University	Oval	6,000

Formed in 1869 as a rugby and soccer club, they retained dual sporting interests. Their team was built around half-back N.C. (Norman) Bailey, who won 21 caps for England and R.H. (Reginald) Birkett, who also played for his country at rugby. The Old Boys' stamina lasted well despite a marathon quarter-final against Darwen.

OLD CARTHUSIANS

Year	Date	Score	Runners-up	Venue	Att.
1881	9 April	3–0	Old Etonians	Oval	4,500

The former pupils of Charterhouse enjoyed their finest

hour and they were the first team to show any real teamwork in equalling the record score in a final at the time.

BLACKBURN OLYMPIC

Year	Date	Score	Runners-up	Venue	Att.
1883	31 March	2–1*	Old Etonians	Oval	8,000

The cup went north for the first time. The winning team was driven on a wagonette by six horses accompanied by a brass band through cheering crowds in Blackburn. They were the first team to train for the match, going away to Blackpool.

BLACKBURN ROVERS

Year	Date	Score	Runners-up	Venue	Att.
1884	29 March	2–1	Queen's Park	Oval	4,000
1885	4 April	2–0	Queen's Park	Oval	12,500
1886	3 April	0–0	West Bromwich A	Oval	15,000
Replay	10 April	2–0	West Bromwich A	Racec'se Gd	12,000
1890	29 March	6–1	Sheffield Wed	Oval	20,000
1891	25 March	3–1	Notts County	Oval	23,000

The cup stayed in Blackburn for another three years. Scotland's Queen's Park had two goals disallowed because they were used to a different 'offside' interpretation. Their second appearance produced the first five-figure attendance. Blackburn fans travelled 'Oop for t'Coop' and the phrase stuck. They released flights of pigeons and set a pattern for such invasions of the south – contemporarily described as a 'northern horde of uncouth garb and strange oaths'. Rovers received a silver shield for their third victory, but having watched the Boat Race in freezing conditions they were in poor shape for the afternoon's game and drew. For the first time the final went out of London at Derby, where captain and centre-forward James Brown clinched the game with a dribble half the length of the field. Blackburn went close to another threesome in the 1890s, James Forrest collecting two more medals to make a total of five in teams which put six past Sheffield Wednesday – William Townley getting three – and three past Notts County. Their last success was as underdogs, but they scored after 30 seconds.

ASTON VILLA

Year	Date	Score	Runners-up	Venue	Att.
1887	2 April	2–0	West Bromwich A	Oval	15,500

1895	20 April	1–0	West Bromwich A	Crystal Pal	42,560
1897	10 April	3–2	Everton	Crystal Pal	65,891
1905	15 April	2–0	Newcastle United	Crystal Pal	101,117
1913	19 April	1–0	Sunderland	Crystal Pal	120,081
1920	24 April	1–0*	Huddersfield Town	Stam. Br'ge	50,018
1957	4 May	2–1	Manchester United	Wembley	100,000

First winners from the midlands after a disputed offside goal and first final to be decided between teams from the same city. Villa repeated their success over Albion in 1895 in the first final at Crystal Palace. Many of the crowd missed the only goal scored after 40 seconds by John Devey. The club put the cup on show in a Birmingham shop and it was stolen, never recovered and the club were fined £25. The 1897 triumph was the completion of their League and Cup double, all five final goals coming in 25 minutes of the first half with the lead changing hands three times. In 1905 Harry Hampton scored both goals. Eight years later they met Sunderland. Villa were second to their opponents in the League. It was the first time that the two top League teams had met in the final. The 120,081 crowd was a world record. Clem Stephenson told Sunderland's Charlie Buchan early on that 'I dreamt we should win 1–0 with a goal headed by Barber'. They did. With ten internationals on duty they won again in 1920, though the only goal luckily rebounded off the back of Kirton's neck. Villa's seventh win in 1957 was marred by a controversial collision between Peter McParland and Manchester United's goalkeeper Ray Wood, who was carried off on a stretcher.

WEST BROMWICH ALBION

Year	Date	Score	Runners-up	Venue	Att.
1888	24 March	2–1	Preston North End	Oval	19,000
1892	19 March	3–0	Aston Villa	Oval	25,000
1931	25 April	2–1	Birmingham	Wembley	92,406
1954	1 May	3–2	Preston North End	Wembley	100,000
1968	18 May	1–0*	Everton	Wembley	100,000

Third time lucky for Albion in their third successive final. They achieved it with an all-English eleven, the first time the winners had been drawn from one country. Their wage bill was £10 a week yet they beat proud Preston North End, the team who had beaten Hyde United 26–0 on the way to the final. The gates were closed at The Oval for the first time ever at a football match with 17,000 inside. Sixty-six years later, Albion beat Preston in the last minute. Albion gained revenge on Villa in 1892, the last final at The Oval and one graced with a crossbar and goalnets for the first time. In 1931 Albion coupled victory with promotion to

West Bromwich Albion celebrate the defeat of neighbours Birmingham in 1931, Albion's third Cup win. The Baggies were in fact a Second Division side at the time and had also clinched promotion that season (Popperfoto)

Division One. Their last success came from a single goal scored by Jeff Astle in the third minute of extra time.

PRESTON NORTH END

Year	Date	Score	Runners-up	Venue	Att.
1889	30 March	3–0	Wolverhampton W	Oval	22,000
1938	30 April	1–0*	Huddersfield Town	Wembley	93,497

They won the League championship without losing a match and the Cup without conceding a goal. But their second success came when George Mutch converted the first Wembley penalty in off the bar 60 seconds from the end of extra time to avenge a similar defeat against Huddersfield Town 16 years earlier.

WOLVERHAMPTON WANDERERS

Year	Date	Score	Runners-up	Venue	Att.
1893	26 March	1–0	Everton	Fallowfield	45,000
1908	25 April	3–1	Newcastle United	Crystal Pal	74,967
1949	30 April	3–1	Leicester City	Wembley	99,000
1960	7 May	3–0	Blackburn Rovers	Wembley	100,000

Out of London for the first time and played at Fallowfield, Manchester, the final was watched by a crowd of 45,000. The gates were shut and thousands locked out. Those inside spilled on to the pitch and from the experience of this game, enclosures and crash barriers emerged. In 1908, despite Newcastle having 90 per cent of the play, Wolves, then in Division Two, won with the Rev. Kenneth Hunt, the last amateur to gain an FA Cup winners' medal, opening the scoring after half-an-hour. In 1949 they had four internationals in

attack, Billy Wright in the half-back line and
England's goalkeeper Bert Williams. In 1960 Wolves
beat a Blackburn side who lost Dave Whelan with a
broken leg.

NOTTS COUNTY

Year	Date	Score	Runners-up	Venue	Att.
1894	31 March	4–1	Bolton Wanderers	Goodison	37,000

Notts County became the first Division Two team to win
the Cup – a one-sided affair in which James Logan
scored a hat-trick for the winners and it was the only
final ever held originally (excluding replays) at Everton.

SHEFFIELD WEDNESDAY

Year	Date	Score	Runners-up	Venue	Att.
1896	18 April	2–1	Wolverhampton W	Crystal Pal	48,836
1907	20 April	2–1	Everton	Crystal Pal	84,584
1935	27 April	4–2	West Bromwich A	Wembley	93,204

A new trophy was available and went to Yorkshire for
the first time with two opportunist goals from outside-
left Fred Spiksley, one of which went in and out so fast
that the Wolves goalkeeper thought it still in play. They
won again in 1907 by the odd goal in three – a Battle of
the Roses against Everton, the winner a 'soft' header
coming four minutes from time. Two goals in the last
five minutes by Ellis Rimmer gave Wednesday their
third cup. Rimmer had been given a lucky horseshoe at
half-time.

NOTTINGHAM FOREST

Year	Date	Score	Runners-up	Venue	Att.
1898	16 April	3–1	Derby County	Crystal Pal	62,017
1959	2 May	2–1	Luton Town	Wembley	100,000

Midland rivals Derby County were beaten in their first
final despite the presence of Steve Bloomer in their
team. Forest had lost 5–0 at Derby a week before. Forest
overcame an even greater handicap during their next
success, when they lost Roy Dwight with a broken leg.
Dwight watched the second half on TV from a hospital
bed. Forest manager Billy Walker had been in charge of
Sheffield Wednesday's 1935 team and captained Aston
Villa in 1920.

* after extra time

SHEFFIELD UNITED

Year	Date	Score	Runners-up	Venue	Att.
1899	15 April	4–1	Derby County	Crystal Pal	73,833
1902	19 April	1–1	Southampton	Crystal Pal	76,914
Replay	26 April	2–1	Southampton	Crystal Pal	33,068
1915	24 April	3–0	Chelsea	Old Trafford	49,557
1925	25 April	1–0	Cardiff City	Wembley	91,763

'Nudger' Needham securely shackled Bloomer and Harry
Thickett played with broken ribs and a ruptured side in
50 yards of bandages to bring the trophy back to
Sheffield after three years. In 1902 they won after a
replay when the goal area, penalty area and penalty spot
were relatively new. With World War One in progress
the 1915 final held at Old Trafford was known as the
Khaki Cup final, as the crowd was packed with
servicemen. Ten years later United took advantage of
one Cardiff error and Thomas Doyle and Harold
Johnson won medals as their fathers had done
respectively in 1899 and 1902.

BURY

Year	Date	Score	Runners-up	Venue	Att.
1900	21 April	4–0	Southampton	Crystal Pal	68,945
1903	18 April	6–0	Derby County	Crystal Pal	63,102

Aptly named the Shakers, they beat Southampton by
four clear goals in 1900 and the ill-fated Derby for a
final record score of 6–0 in 1903. Their run was
achieved without having a goal scored against them.

MANCHESTER CITY

Year	Date	Score	Runners-up	Venue	Att.
1904	23 April	1–0	Bolton Wanderers	Crystal Pal	61,374
1934	28 April	2–1	Portsmouth	Wembley	93,258
1956	5 May	3–1	Birmingham City	Wembley	100,000
1969	26 April	1–0	Leicester City	Wembley	100,000

A goal by Welshman Billy Meredith was enough to win
the first all-Lancashire final. The attacking centre-half,
wing-halves playing wide, individual dribbling and ball
control were the vogue. Losing 1–0 to Portsmouth 17
minutes from the end of the 1934 final, City were
grateful for Fred Tilson's half-time comment that 'he
would get two'. He did just that. In goal teenage Frank
Swift fainted at the end. The 'Revie Plan' was
instrumental in City taking the Cup in 1956 with
Revie's deep-lying scheming. Bert Trautmann bravely
played out the dying minutes with a broken neck. One
goal by Neil Young was sufficient to beat Leicester in

1969 in the 'Cabbage Patch' final, so called because of the state the Wembley pitch was in that day following the earlier Horse of the Year show.

EVERTON

Year	Date	Score	Runners-up	Venue	Att.
1906	21 April	1–0	Newcastle United	Crystal Pal	75,609
1933	29 April	3–0	Manchester City	Wembley	92,950
1966	14 May	3–2	Sheffield Wed	Wembley	100,000
1984	19 May	2–0	Watford	Wembley	100,000

In 1906, the outstanding right-winger John Sharp crossed for Alec Young to score 15 minutes from time. Dixie Dean had the No. 9 shirt for Everton in 1933, but his opposite number wore 14 as the players were numbered for the first time but unusually from 1–22. After being two goals down in 1966, they won 3–2 with Mike Trebilcock scoring twice. But Wednesday became the first beaten side to do a lap of honour at Wembley. Graeme Sharp in-off-a-post and Andy Gray with a controversial header out of goalkeeper Steve Sherwood's hands provided the goals in 1984.

MANCHESTER UNITED

Year	Date	Score	Runners-up	Venue	Att.
1909	26 April	1–0	Bristol City	Crystal Pal	71,401
1948	24 April	4–2	Blackpool	Wembley	99,000
1963	25 May	3–1	Leicester City	Wembley	100,000
1977	21 May	2–1	Liverpool	Wembley	100,000
1983	21 May	2–2*	Brighton & Hove A	Wembley	100,000
Replay	26 May	4–0	Brighton & Hove A	Wembley	100,000
1985	18 May	1–0*	Everton	Wembley	100,000
1990	12 May	3–3*	Crystal Palace	Wembley	80,000
Replay	17 May	1–0	Crystal Palace	Wembley	80,000

Billy Meredith was now a United stalwart and United supporters brought stone jars of strong ale and inch-thick sandwiches. The only goal came after they hit the crossbar. Their 1948 victory by 4–2 was arguably the finest ever final at Wembley. Their pedigree had shown in beating six Division One teams on the way. The front line of Jimmy Delaney, Johnny Morris, Jack Rowley, Stan Pearson and Charlie Mitten was in superb form and Johnny Carey steadied them with his 'keep playing football' speech. In 1963 Pat Crerand and Albert Quixall probed the openings and David Herd and Denis Law supplied the goals, when a winter of postponements had put the final back to May 25 for the first time. Their fourth success against Liverpool in a meeting of the country's two best-supported teams prevented what their opponents were hoping would be a treble of League, FA

Cup and European Cup achievements. In 1983 Brighton & Hove Albion nearly snatched a late win, but United overran their victims in the replay when Norman Whiteside became the youngest final scorer at 18 years, 18 days. Kevin Moran became the first player sent off in a final in 1985, but Whiteside drove in the only goal for United. In 1990, six goals enlivened an ordinary game; United's goalkeeper Les Sealey became the first on-loan finalist in the replay.

NEWCASTLE UNITED

Year	Date	Score	Runners-up	Venue	Att.
1910	23 April	1–1	Barnsley	Crystal Pal	77,747
Replay	28 April	2–0	Barnsley	Goodison	69,000
1924	26 April	2–0	Aston Villa	Wembley	91,695
1932	23 April	2–1	Arsenal	Wembley	92,298
1951	28 April	2–0	Blackpool	Wembley	100,000
1952	3 May	1–0	Arsenal	Wembley	100,000
1955	7 May	3–1	Manchester City	Wembley	100,000

For the fourth time in six seasons they appeared in the final – this time to succeed over Barnsley but only after a last-minute header by Jock Rutherford forced a replay during which the crowd broke on to the field at Everton. The quality of United's football with players like Peter McWilliam, Colin Veitch and Bill McCracken had always deserted them in the finals down south, but not here. In 1924 they had to bring into the side an inexperienced goalkeeper Bradley who 'played a blinder'. Controversy in 1932 with the 'over-the-goal-line' equaliser against Arsenal when Jimmy Richardson crossed for Jack Allen to level the scores and put United on the way to winning. A Jackie Milburn duo finished Blackpool in 1951, one of them a solo effort after a 40 yard run. But it took them 84 minutes to score the next year against a ten-man Arsenal who had lost Walley Barnes after 15 minutes. Then George Robledo, United's Chilean-born centre-forward, headed a goal. Three years later injury to another back, Jimmy Meadows of Manchester City, helped to put the cup on Tyneside for the sixth time, though a Jackie Milburn goal in 45 seconds contributed. Milburn, Bobby Cowell and Bobby Mitchell won their third winners' medals and Newcastle made it five wins – a record then at Wembley.

BRADFORD CITY

Year	Date	Score	Runners-up	Venue	Att.
1911	22 April	0–0	Newcastle United	Crystal Pal	69,098
Replay	26 April	1–0	Newcastle United	Old Trafford	58,000

With no copyright existing at the time, replicas of the cup made it necessary for a change of design. With this third FA Cup trophy made in Bradford, it was appropriately won by a team from that city – but it has never returned. City fielded a team with a record number of eight Scots.

BARNSLEY

Year	Date	Score	Runners-up	Venue	Att.
1912	20 April	0–0	West Bromwich A	Crystal Pal	54,556
Replay	24 April	1–0*	West Bromwich A	Bramall L'e	38,555

A Division Two club, they reached the final after a marathon 12-match run including replays. Extra time was needed in the replay before they won through. Typical of their spirit was the defender who took a boot off for attention to his foot but raced back without it to clear a dangerous attack. After that match, extra time was enforced during the final. Tufnell scored in the dying seconds of the replay.

TOTTENHAM HOTSPUR

Year	Date	Score	Runners-up	Venue	Att.
1901	20 April	2–2	Sheffield United	Crystal Pal	110,820
Replay	27 April	3–1	Sheffield United	Burnden Pk	20,470
1921	23 April	1–0	Wolverhampton W	Stam'd Br.	72,805
1961	6 May	2–0	Leicester City	Wembley	100,000
1962	5 May	3–1	Burnley	Wembley	100,000
1967	20 May	2–1	Chelsea	Wembley	100,000
1981	9 May	1–1*	Manchester City	Wembley	100,000
Replay	14 May	3–2	Manchester City	Wembley	100,000
1982	22 May	1–1*	Queen's Park R	Wembley	100,000
Replay	27 May	1–0	Queen's Park R	Wembley	100,000
1991	18 May	2–1*	Nottingham Forest	Wembley	80,000

They were members of the Southern League in 1901 and the last non-league team to win the cup. A world-record crowd of 110,820 basked in the sun and some climbed trees for a better vantage point. But it took a replay before Spurs won, with Alex Brown scoring a record 15 goals overall in the competition. In 1921 a classical team contained Arthur Grimsdell, Fanny Walden and Jimmy Dimmock and they made light of the cloudburst during the game which turned the pitch into a quagmire. Forty years on another year ending in '1' produced the first double of the century. The following year they kept the trophy when Danny Blanchflower made it safe with the fourth penalty awarded at Wembley nine minutes from the end. In the first all-London final, Spurs made it five out of five, with Dave Mackay winning his third cup winners' medal. It was six in the 100th final after Wembley's first final replay and a memorable dribble by Ricky Villa provided the highlight. Seven out of seven the

following year, Glenn Hoddle scoring in the first game and clinching it with a replay penalty. Spurs kept their tradition of the first year in the decade in 1991, despite losing a goal and Paul Gascoigne early on with a self-inflicted injury.

HUDDERSFIELD TOWN

Year	Date	Score	Runners-up	Venue	Att.
1922	29 April	1–0	Preston North End	Stam'd Br.	53,000

The first time that a Cup Final was decided by a penalty kick. Preston players complained bitterly that the infringement had occurred outside the area. But Billy Smith, who had been brought down, took the kick and scored despite the antics of the goalkeeper who was still allowed to move before the kick was taken in those days. It was the last final at Stamford Bridge.

BURNLEY

Year	Date	Score	Runners-up	Venue	Att.
1914	25 April	1–0	Liverpool	Crystal Pal	72,778

Defences were on top in this second all-Lancashire final with Liverpool and it fell to Burnley's captain Tommy Boyle to become the first man to receive the FA Cup from a reigning monarch as the match was attended by King George V.

BOLTON WANDERERS

Year	Date	Score	Runners-up	Venue	Att.
1923	28 April	2–0	West Ham United	Wembley	126,047
1926	24 April	1–0	Manchester City	Wembley	91,447
1929	27 April	2–0	Portsmouth	Wembley	92,576
1958	3 May	2–0	Manchester United	Wembley	100,000

Wembley's first final had an official attendance of 126,047 but between 160,000 and 200,000 probably gained admission and swarmed all over the pitch. Owing to the man on the white horse – PC Scorey and 'Billy' – and the good sense of the crowd, a disaster was averted. The game was eventually played with the pitch ringed with spectators. David Jack was the first to score at Wembley. Since then finals have been all-ticket. Bolton won again in 1926 and 1929. Five Bolton players won their third winners' medals. In 1958 the sympathy of the country was with Manchester United after Munich, but Wanderers won again, Nat Lofthouse bundling goalkeeper Harry Gregg over the line for one goal.

* after extra time

CARDIFF CITY

Year	Date	Score	Runners-up	Venue	Att.
1927	23 April	1–0	Arsenal	Wembley	91,206

The only team to take the FA Cup out of England. Cardiff won it through a tragic error by the Arsenal goalkeeper Dan Lewis – a Welsh international. Cardiff had one Englishman, four Irishmen, three Scots and three Welshmen. It was the first Cup Final to be broadcast.

ARSENAL

Year	Date	Score	Runners-up	Venue	Att.
1930	26 April	2–0	Huddersfield Town	Wembley	92,488
1936	25 April	1–0	Sheffield United	Wembley	93,384
1950	29 April	2–0	Liverpool	Wembley	100,000
1971	8 May	2–1*	Liverpool	Wembley	100,000
1979	12 May	3–2	Manchester United	Wembley	100,000
1993	16 May	1–1*	Sheffield Wed	Wembley	79,347
Replay	20 May	2–1*	Sheffield Wed	Wembley	62,267

Masterminded by manager Herbert Chapman in 1930 and with a deep-lying inside-forward in Alex James, a short-legged artist in long shorts, Bob John at wing-half and Cliff Bastin on the wing, Arsenal won in style. Above, the Graf Zeppelin flew. 'Policeman' Herbie Roberts at centre-half, 'Iron Man' Wilf Copping at wing-half and flying winger Joe Hulme appearing in his fourth final, featured in 1936 though the real hero was marksman Ted Drake, who played with an injured knee heavily bandaged. Two goals by Reg Lewis were enough in 1950 while in 1971 it was the great 'double' year for the Gunners who beat Liverpool as they had 21 years

Arsenal won the FA Cup for the sixth time in 1993 with Ian Wright scoring in both the final (above) and the replay. He had scored twice for Crystal Palace in 1990 (Allsport/Simon Bruty)

before; substitute Eddie Kelly scored the equaliser which turned the game Arsenal's way, five days after clinching the championship. In 1979 Arsenal's two-goal lead vanished as Manchester United scored twice to level in 86 and 88 minutes, only for Alan Sunderland to seal it 60 seconds later. The replayed win over Sheffield Wednesday was clinched in injury time after extra time by a headed goal from Andy Linighan, playing with a broken nose.

SUNDERLAND

Year	Date	Score	Runners-up	Venue	Att.
1937	1 May	3–1	Preston North End	Wembley	93,495
1973	5 May	1–0	Leeds United	Wembley	100,000

The TV cameras were at the final for the first time and inspired by local lad Raich Carter, Sunderland gradually pulled around after conceding a goal to win 3–1. The cup went to Wearside for the second time on Wembley's 50th anniversary when as a Division Two side they overcame Leeds United after goalkeeper Jimmy Montgomery produced a crucial 70th minute double save.

PORTSMOUTH

Year	Date	Score	Runners-up	Venue	Att.
1939	29 April	4–1	Wolverhampton W	Wembley	99,370

When the Wolves autograph book came into the Pompey dressing-room before the game, the signatures were alleged to have been shaky and unrecognisable. It gave Portsmouth confidence and with Jack Tinn's 'lucky spats' and the Pompey Chimes ringing out, Wolves were beaten, one of the Portsmouth scorers being Bert Barlow, signed from Wolves that season.

DERBY COUNTY

Year	Date	Score	Runners-up	Venue	Att.
1946	27 April	4–1*	Charlton Athletic	Wembley	98,000

Derby's Cup luck changed at last. Before the final, Derby captain Jack Nicholas went to a gypsy encampment where a curse put on them in 1895 was ceremoniously removed. Carter, of previous Sunderland fame, combined with Peter Doherty to defeat Charlton whose Bert Turner scored for both sides. And the ball burst during the game.

*after extra time

CHARLTON ATHLETIC

Year	Date	Score	Runners-up	Venue	Att.
1947	26 April	1–0*	Burnley	Wembley	99,000

The ball burst again. And with only six minutes remaining, Burnley's formidable defence was holding out until Chris Duffy volleyed a goal. After scoring he raced the length of the field before being caught by his delighted colleagues.

BLACKPOOL

Year	Date	Score	Runners-up	Venue	Att.
1953	2 May	4–3	Bolton Wanderers	Wembley	100,000

It was Stanley Matthews' final, but only after an injury-hit Bolton crashed in the last 20 minutes after leading 3–1. Stan Mortensen scored a hat-trick – the equaliser from a free-kick at which his colleague Ernie Taylor said: 'Bet you sixpence you don't score'. Then a jinking Matthews run and cross to Bill Perry sealed it.

WEST HAM UNITED

Year	Date	Score	Runners-up	Venue	Att.
1964	2 May	3–2	Preston North End	Wembley	100,000
1975	3 May	2–0	Fulham	Wembley	100,000
1980	10 May	1–0	Arsenal	Wembley	100,000

John Sissons, then the youngest cup final scorer at 18, walked off with a sympathetic arm round Preston's Howard Kendall, at 17 years 345 days the youngest Wembley finalist at the time. Geoff Hurst scored a goal on the ground where he was to make World Cup history two years later. Two goals by Alan Taylor who had been playing for Fourth Division Rochdale six months before, gave them their second win during a match in which neither trainer had to be called upon. The Hammers then won the first Cockney Cup Final and Paul Allen at 17 years 256 days became the youngest Wembley finalist.

LIVERPOOL

Year	Date	Score	Runners-up	Venue	Att.
1965	1 May	2–1*	Leeds United	Wembley	100,000
1974	4 May	3–0	Newcastle United	Wembley	100,000
1986	10 May	3–1	Everton	Wembley	98,000
1989	20 May	3–2*	Everton	Wembley	82,800
1992	9 May	2–0	Sunderland	Wembley	79,544

Bill Shankly led his team to success. He had been a player in the 1937 and 1938 finals. Liverpool were handicapped by a shoulder injury to Gerry Byrne but it was a defence-dominated final which went to extra time. Three second-half goals gave them victory in 1974 which paid little heed to Newcastle's Wembley tradition. Ian Rush scored twice in the first all-Merseyside final after Gary Lineker had opened for Everton. Liverpool thus clinched the fifth League and Cup double. The second all-Merseyside affair saw substitutes Ian Rush and Stuart McCall make history by each scoring twice for their respective teams. In 1992 Liverpool's captain Mark Wright became the first to receive the new FA Cup, the fourth in the history of the competition, in Liverpool's centenary year. When Rush scored he became the highest scorer of FA Cup final goals with five.

CHELSEA

Year	Date	Score	Runners-up	Venue	Att.
1970	11 April	2–2*	Leeds United	Wembley	100,000
Replay	29 April	2–1*	Leeds United	Old Trafford	62,078

For the first time the game was not settled at Wembley. It needed a replay at Old Trafford. Twice Chelsea were behind yet equalised and in the replay were behind again before finally getting the winner from David Webb, who had been turned almost inside out in the original game at Wembley by Eddie Gray of Leeds.

LEEDS UNITED

Year	Date	Score	Runners-up	Venue	Att.
1972	6 May	1–0	Arsenal	Wembley	100,000

The Centenary Year final and Leeds beat the League and Cup holders of 1971 with a goal made for Allan Clarke by Mick Jones who dislocated his elbow.

SOUTHAMPTON

Year	Date	Score	Runners-up	Venue	Att.
1976	1 May	1–0	Manchester United	Wembley	100,000

Third time lucky for Southampton, the sixth Second Division side to succeed, and for whom Bobby Stokes scored seven minutes from the end.

IPSWICH TOWN

Year	Date	Score	Runners-up	Venue	Att.
1978	6 May	1–0	Arsenal	Wembley	100,000

The 40th different team to win the trophy, the only goal coming from Roger Osborne in the 76th minute. It was his last kick in the match because he had to be substituted through exhaustion.

COVENTRY CITY

Year	Date	Score	Runners-up	Venue	Att.
1987	16 May	3–2*	Tottenham H	Wembley	98,000

Spurs' invincibility ended as Coventry took their first major trophy in 104 years after extra time. Tottenham's Gary Mabbutt scored for both teams.

WIMBLEDON

Year	Date	Score	Runners-up	Venue	Att.
1988	14 May	1–0	Liverpool	Wembley	98,000

Dave Beasant became the first goalkeeper to save a penalty in a Wembley FA Cup Final, when he stopped John Aldridge's shot. The Dons with just 11 years as a Football League club overturned the hot favourites.

after extra time

FA CUP FACTS & FEATS

For more than 100 years it was wrongly reported that Wanderers had beaten Oxford University 2–0 in the 1877 FA Cup final at the Oval. But the Football Calendar 1877 clearly stated that the Wanderers goalkeeper Kinnaird, after stopping the ball from one of his defenders, stepped back with the ball in his hands between his posts and a goal was rightly given to the University. Thus after 90 minutes the score was 1–1 and extra time necessary. It appears that after the game Kinnaird pleaded that the ball did not cross the line and thus it was recorded as 2–0. In fact the Football Association still have it thus in their official records.

Derby County hold the record for the highest number of wins in one season for the FA Cup proper. In 1945–46 they recorded nine, because for the only time in the history of the competition, ties were decided on a home and away basis. Derby also scored 37 goals and Raich Carter was their top scorer with 12. But he was not the leading marksman in the competition that season. Harry Brooks (Aldershot) scored 13 including five on two occasions. In the 1945–46 series, Charlton Athletic managed to reach the final despite losing a match on the way, in the two-legged ties which operated. They were beaten 2–1 at Fulham.

The 1886 final was the first to be staged between professional teams: Blackburn Rovers and West Bromwich Albion.

In nine consecutive FA Cup competitions, from 1934–35 to 1948–49, the team who defeated Preston North End either won the Cup or at least reached the final.

The oldest known FA Cup final eleven of all time was the Arsenal team which defeated Liverpool in 1950. Its average age was slightly over 31.

Right-back Tom Smart made the quickest-ever rise from minor soccer to an FA Cup-winning team. Signed from Halesowen on 17 January 1920, he was in Aston Villa's team which defeated Huddersfield Town on 24 April.

Notts County won a Division One away match against Blackburn Rovers by 7–1 on 14 March 1891. On 25 March, Rovers beat them 3–1 in the Cup final.

J. Tibbotson, living in Derby, was the appointed referee for the Newcastle United v Barnsley final in 1910. It transpired he had been born at Dodworth, just outside Barnsley. The South Yorkshire team vainly protested against his appointment, fearing that he might concentrate on avoiding 'favouritism', and would actually penalise Barnsley. Newcastle won after a replay.

Until 1985 no player had been sent off in a final, but in 1913 there was such a stormy row between Aston Villa centre-forward Harry Hampton and Sunderland centre-half Charlie Thomson that both were suspended for a month.

Only three pairs of brothers have appeared in the same FA Cup winning teams in this century: Denis and Leslie Compton (Arsenal, 1950); Ted and George Robledo (Newcastle United, 1952); and Brian and Jimmy Greenhoff (Manchester United, 1977).

Only eight players have scored in all six rounds of the FA Cup (from the third round) in one season: Ellis Rimmer (Sheffield Wednesday, 1935); Frank O'Donnell (Preston North End, 1937); Stan Mortensen (Blackpool, 1948); Jackie Milburn (Newcastle United, 1951); Nat Lofthouse (Bolton Wanderers, 1935); Charlie Wayman (Preston North End, 1954); Jeff Astle (West Bromwich Albion, 1968) and Peter Osgood (Chelsea, 1970).

On 20 July 1912, the FA decided that extra time must be played in the final if scores were level at full time. This was after three consecutive replayed games. The next match to require extra time was Aston Villa v Huddersfield Town at Stamford Bridge on 24 April 1920. After 90 minutes the players shook hands and left the field, thinking the game was over.

Jackie Milburn's second goal for Newcastle United at Wembley in 1951. Milburn is one of only six players to score in every round of the FA Cup in one season (Popperfoto)

FA President Francis Marindin played in the 1872 and 1874 finals and refereed a further eight up to the 1890 match.

Between 1909 and 1927 there were 15 consecutive finals in which the beaten team failed to score. Three goals is the highest by a defeated team, Bolton Wanderers losing 4–3 to Blackpool in 1953. Manchester United and Crystal Palace drew 3–3 in the 1990 final.

The first match to be screened in colour on television was the FA Cup Final between Everton and West Bromwich Albion in 1968.

The 1969 final was played on 26 April between Manchester City and Leicester City. There had been no earlier final played since Aston Villa and Newcastle United on 18 April 1905.

At the celebration dinner in 1901, Tottenham Hotspur tied blue and white ribbons on the handles of the trophy, a custom which has since become a tradition.

Peter Goring is the only player to have appeared in an FA Cup winning team and finish as his club's leading scorer in his first season as a Football League player. In 1949–50 he was Arsenal's leading marksman with 21 League goals, though he did not score in the cup.

After playing his first League game for Sheffield Wednesday on 9 April 1966 Graham Pugh was in their final team against Everton on 14 May.

Jim Issac, inside-right for Huddersfield Town in the 1938 final, was playing in his first cup-tie for the club on that day. He had been signed from Bedlington United in November 1934.

There has been only one final with two pairs of brothers on the field. In 1876 when Wanderers beat Old Etonians 3–0 in a replay the winning team included the brothers Frank and Hubert Heron, while the Old Boys had the brothers the Hon. Edward and Hon. Alfred Lyttelton.

Aston Villa scored 40 goals in the FA Cup in 1886–87 from ten matches, a record for a team reaching the final. They were also given a bye in the fourth round that season.

LEAGUE CUP

Milk Cup 1982–86 Littlewoods Cup 1987–90 Rumbelows Cup 1991–92 Coca Cola Cup 1993–

ASTON VILLA

Year	Score	Runners-up	Venue	Att.
1961	3–2†	Rotherham United (1)	Millmoor	12,226
		Rotherham United (2)	Villa Park	31,202
1975	1–0	Norwich City	Wembley	100,000
1977	0–0	Everton	Wembley	100,000
	1–1*	Everton	Hillsborough	55,000
	3–2*	Everton	Old Trafford	54,749

NORWICH CITY

1962	4–0†	Rochdale (1)	Spotland	11,123
		Rochdale (2)	Carrow Road	19,708
1985	1–0	Sunderland	Wembley	100,000

BIRMINGHAM CITY

1963	3–1†	Aston Villa (1)	St Andrew's	31,850
		Aston Villa (2)	Villa Park	37,920

LEICESTER CITY

1964	4–3†	Stoke City (1)	Victoria Ground	22,309
		Stoke City (2)	Filbert Street	25,372

CHELSEA

1965	3–2†	Leicester City (1)	Stamford Bridge	20,690
		Leicester City (2)	Filbert Street	26,958

* after extra time   † on aggregate

WEST BROMWICH ALBION

Year	Score	Runners-up	Venue	Att.
1966	5–3†	West Ham United (1)	Upton Park	28,341
		West Ham United (2)	The Hawthoms	31,925

QUEEN'S PARK RANGERS

Year	Score	Runners-up	Venue	Att.
1967	3–2	West Bromwich Albion	Wembley	97,952

LEEDS UNITED

Year	Score	Runners-up	Venue	Att.
1968	1–0	Arsenal	Wembley	97,887

SWINDON TOWN

Year	Score	Runners-up	Venue	Att.
1969	3–1*	Arsenal	Wembley	98,189

MANCHESTER CITY

Year	Score	Runners-up	Venue	Att.
1970	2–1	West Bromwich Albion	Wembley	97,963
1976	2–1	Newcastle United	Wembley	100,000

TOTTENHAM HOTSPUR

Year	Score	Runners-up	Venue	Att.
1971	2–0	Aston Villa	Wembley	100,000
1973	1–0	Norwich City	Wembley	100,000

STOKE CITY

Year	Score	Runners-up	Venue	Att.
1972	2–1	Chelsea	Wembley	100,000

WOLVERHAMPTON WANDERERS

Year	Score	Runners-up	Venue	Att.
1974	2–1	Manchester City	Wembley	100,000
1980	1–0	Nottingham Forest	Wembley	100,000

* after extra time   † on aggregate

NOTTINGHAM FOREST

Year	Score	Runners-up	Venue	Att.
1978	0–0*	Liverpool	Wembley	100,000
	1–0	Liverpool	Old Trafford	54,375
1979	3–2	Southampton	Wembley	100,000
1989	3–1	Luton Town	Wembley	76,130
1990	1–0	Oldham Athletic	Wembley	74,343

LIVERPOOL

Year	Score	Runners-up	Venue	Att.
1981	1–1*	West Ham United	Wembley	100,000
	2–1	West Ham United	Villa Park	36,693
1982	3–1*	Tottenham Hotspur	Wembley	100,000
1983	2–1*	Manchester United	Wembley	100,000
1984	0–0*	Everton	Wembley	100,000
	1–0	Everton	Maine Road	52,089

OXFORD UNITED

Year	Score	Runners-up	Venue	Att.
1986	3–0	Queen's Park Rangers	Wembley	90,396

ARSENAL

Year	Score	Runners-up	Venue	Att.
1987	2–1	Liverpool	Wembley	96,000
1993	2–1	Sheffield Wednesday	Wembley	74,007

LUTON TOWN

Year	Score	Runners-up	Venue	Att.
1988	3–2	Arsenal	Wembley	95,732

SHEFFIELD WEDNESDAY

Year	Score	Runners-up	Venue	Att.
1991	1–0	Manchester United	Wembley	80,000

MANCHESTER UNITED

Year	Score	Runners-up	Venue	Att.
1992	1–0	Nottingham Forest	Wembley	76,810

Nottingham Forest went a record 25 League Cup matches without defeat in reaching three consecutive finals. Here they celebrate victory over Southampton in 1979 (Popperfoto)

LEAGUE CUP FACTS & FEATS

When Norwich City won the League Cup in 1961–62, they figured in only six rounds, though the competition comprised seven: one to five inclusive, semi-final and final. In the fourth round they drew a bye. The top clubs did not enter the competition that season.

John Boyle (Chelsea in 1965), Danny Campbell (West Bromwich Albion 1966), Jimmy Neighbour (Tottenham Hotspur 1971) and Geoff Palmer (Wolverhampton Wanderers 1974) all figured in League Cup-winning teams in the seasons of their Football League debuts.

Rochdale's Spotland is destined to remain as the only Division Four club ground on which a League Cup final has been played. The first leg of the 1962 final was played there, when they lost to Norwich City, watched by a crowd of 11,123.

Two weeks before the League Cup final on 13 March 1982, the National Dairy Council concluded a sponsorship deal with the Football League for the League Cup which was then renamed the Milk Cup. Liverpool won and took two trophies back to Anfield after the final.

Since then the League Cup has been sponsored by Littlewoods 1987–1990, Rumbelows 1991–1992 and Coca Cola from 1993.

Liverpool have won the League Cup four times and in successive years from 1981 to 1984, being involved in extra time on each occasion and two replays.

When Barry Venison captained Sunderland against Norwich City in the 1985 final, he was 20 years, 7 months and eight days, the youngest ever Wembley captain.

Norman Whiteside was only 17 years, 324 days old when scoring for Manchester United against Liverpool in the 1983 final.

Liverpool set the most successful cup sequence by a Football League club in 25 successive rounds in the League Cup. They won every tie after the semi-final in 1980 until the third round in 1984.

There have been three failures from the penalty spot in finals: Ray Graydon (Aston Villa) in 1975, Clive Walker (Sunderland) in 1985 and Nigel Winterburn (Arsenal) in 1988. But Graydon managed to follow up and score after Kevin Keelan had saved his kick.

OTHER DOMESTIC CUPS

Full Members Cup (1986–87) Simod Cup (1988–89) Zenith Data Systems Cup (1990–92)

CHELSEA

Year	Score	Runners-up	Attendance
1986	5–4	Manchester City	68,000
1990	1–0	Middlesbrough	76,369

BLACKBURN ROVERS

1987	1–0	Charlton Athletic	40,000

Chelsea were the first winners of the Full Members Cup in 1986 and had one of the most consistent records in the seven seasons of the competition (Allsport/Simon Bruty)

READING

1988	4–1	Luton Town	61,740

NOTTINGHAM FOREST

1989	4–3	Everton	46,606
1992	3–2	Southampton	67,688

CRYSTAL PALACE

1991	4–1	Everton	52,460

Associate Members Cup (1984) Freight Rover Trophy (1985–86) Sherpa Van Trophy (1986–89) Leyland-DAF Cup (1990–91) Autoglass Trophy (1992–93)

BOURNEMOUTH

Year	Score	Runners-up	Attendance
1984	2–1	Hull City	6,514

WIGAN ATHLETIC

1985	3–1	Brentford	34,932

BRISTOL CITY

1986	3–0	Bolton Wanderers	55,330

MANSFIELD TOWN

Year	Score	Runners-up	Attendance
1987	1–1	Bristol City	60,050
		(Mansfield Town won 5–4 on penalties)	

WOLVERHAMPTON WANDERERS

1988	2–0	Burnley	80,841

BOLTON WANDERERS

1989	4–1	Torquay United	46,513

TRANMERE ROVERS

1990	2–1	Bristol Rovers	48,402

BIRMINGHAM CITY

1991	3–2	Tranmere Rovers	58,756

STOKE CITY

1992	1–0	Stockport County	48,339

PORT VALE

1993	2–1	Stockport County	35,885

Anglo-Italian Cup

CREMONESE

Year	Score	Runners-up	Venue	Attendance
1993	3–1	Derby County	Wembley	37,024

FA Charity Shield 1974–92 (at Wembley)

Year	Champions		Cup winners	Attendance
1974	Leeds United	1–1	Liverpool	67,000
	(Liverpool won 6–5 on penalties)			
1975	Derby County	2–0	West Ham United	59,000
1976	Liverpool	1–0	Southampton	76,500
1977	Liverpool	0–0	Manchester United	82,000
1978	Nottingham Forest	5–0	Ipswich Town	68,000
1979	Liverpool	3–1	Arsenal	92,000
1980	Liverpool	1–0	West Ham United	90,000
1981	Aston Villa	2–2	Tottenham Hotspur	92,500
1982	Liverpool	1–0	Tottenham Hotspur	82,000
1983	Liverpool	0–2	Manchester United	92,000
1984	Liverpool	0–1	Everton	100,000
1985	Everton	2–0	Manchester United	82,000
1986	Liverpool	1–1	Everton	88,000
1987	Everton	1–0	Coventry City	88,000
1988	Liverpool	2–1	Wimbledon	54,000
1989	Arsenal	0–1	Liverpool	64,000
1990	Liverpool	1–1	Manchester United	66,558
1991	Arsenal	0–0	Tottenham Hotspur	65,483
1992	Leeds United	4–3	Liverpool	61,291

A–Z SCOTTISH CLUBS

Season by season League record

ABERCORN

Year	Div	P	W	D	L	F	A	Pts	Pos
1890–91	SL	18	5	2	11	36	47	12	7th
1891–92	SL	22	6	5	11	47	59	17	9th
1892–93	SL	18	5	1	12	35	52	11	9th
1893–94	II	18	5	2	11	42	60	12	7th
1894–95	II	18	7	3	8	48	65	17	8th
1895–96	II	18	12	3	3	55	31	27	1st
1896–97	I	18	1	1	16	21	88	3	10th
1897–98	II	18	6	4	8	33	41	16	7th
1898–99	II	18	4	1	13	41	65	9	10th
1899–1900	II	18	7	2	9	46	39	16	6th
1900–01	II	18	9	3	6	37	33	21	3rd
1901–02	II	22	4	5	13	27	57	13	11th
1902–03	II	22	5	2	15	35	58	12	10th

1903–04	II	22	6	4	12	38	55	16	10th
1904–05	II	22	8	1	13	31	45	17	11th
1905–06	II	22	6	5	11	29	45	17	10th
1906–07	II	22	5	7	10	29	47	17	9th
1907–08	II	22	9	5	8	33	30	23	4th
1908–09	II	22	13	5	4	40	18	31	1st
1909–10	II	22	7	8	7	38	40	22	5th
1910–11	II	22	9	1	12	39	50	19	11th
1911–12	II	22	13	4	5	43	22	30	2nd
1912–13	II	26	12	7	7	33	31	31	4th
1913–14	II	22	10	3	9	32	32	23	6th
1914–15	II	26	5	7	14	35	65	17	12th

Abercorn managed only three points in Division One during 1896–97. They had a solitary victory 3–2 against St Mirren and a 2–2 draw with Hibernian.

ABERDEEN

Year	Div	P	W	D	L	F	A	Pts	Pos
1904–05	II	22	7	7	8	36	26	21	7th
1905–06	I	30	8	8	14	37	49	24	12th
1906–07	I	34	10	10	14	48	55	30	12th
1907–08	I	34	13	9	12	45	44	35	8th
1908–09	I	34	15	6	13	61	53	36	7th
1909–10	I	34	16	8	10	44	29	40	4th
1910–11	I	34	19	10	5	53	28	48	2nd
1911–12	I	34	14	7	13	44	44	35	8th
1912–13	I	34	14	9	11	47	40	37	8th
1913–14	I	38	10	10	18	38	55	30	13th
1914–15	I	38	11	11	16	39	52	33	14th
1915–16	SL	38	11	12	15	51	64	34	11th
1916–17	SL	38	7	7	24	36	68	21	20th
1917–19	Did not compete								
1919–20	SL	42	11	13	18	46	64	35	17th
1920–21	SL	42	14	14	14	53	54	42	11th
1921–22	I	42	13	9	20	48	54	35	15th
1922–23	I	38	15	12	11	46	34	42	5th
1923–24	I	38	13	10	15	37	41	36	12th
1924–25	I	38	11	10	17	46	56	32	15th
1925–26	I	38	13	10	15	49	54	36	11th
1926–27	I	38	13	14	11	73	72	40	8th
1927–28	I	38	19	5	14	71	61	43	7th
1928–29	I	38	16	8	14	81	68	40	7th
1929–30	I	38	23	7	8	85	61	53	3rd
1930–31	I	38	17	7	14	79	63	41	6th
1931–32	I	38	16	9	13	57	49	41	7th
1932–33	I	38	18	6	14	85	58	42	6th
1933–34	I	38	18	8	12	90	57	44	5th
1934–35	I	38	17	10	11	68	54	44	6th
1935–36	I	38	26	9	3	96	50	61	3rd
1936–37	I	38	23	8	7	89	44	54	2nd
1937–38	I	38	15	9	14	74	59	39	6th
1938–39	I	38	20	6	12	91	61	46	3rd
1939–46	Regional Leagues operating								
1946–47	A	30	16	7	7	58	41	39	3rd
1947–48	A	30	10	7	13	45	45	27	10th
1948–49	A	30	7	11	12	39	48	25	13th
1949–50	A	30	11	4	15	48	56	26	8th
1950–51	A	30	15	5	10	61	50	35	5th
1951–52	A	30	10	7	13	65	58	27	11th
1952–53	A	30	11	5	14	64	68	27	10th
1953–54	A	30	15	3	12	66	51	33	9th
1954–55	A	30	24	1	5	73	26	49	1st
1955–56	A	34	18	10	6	87	50	46	2nd
1956–57	I	34	18	2	14	79	59	38	5th
1957–58	I	34	14	2	18	68	76	30	12th
1958–59	I	34	12	5	17	63	66	29	13th
1959–60	I	34	11	6	17	54	72	28	15th
1960–61	I	34	14	8	12	72	72	36	6th
1961–62	I	34	10	9	15	60	73	29	12th
1962–63	I	34	17	7	10	70	47	41	6th
1963–64	I	34	12	8	14	53	53	32	9th
1964–65	I	34	12	8	14	59	75	32	12th
1965–66	I	34	15	6	13	61	54	36	8th
1966–67	I	34	17	8	9	72	38	42	4th
1967–68	I	34	16	5	13	63	48	37	5th
1968–69	I	34	9	8	17	50	59	26	15th
1969–70	I	34	14	7	13	55	45	35	8th
1970–71	I	34	24	6	4	68	18	54	2nd
1971–72	I	34	21	8	5	80	26	50	2nd
1972–73	I	34	16	11	7	61	34	43	4th
1973–74	I	34	13	16	5	46	26	42	4th
1974–75	I	34	16	9	9	66	43	41	5th
1975–76	Pr	36	11	10	15	49	50	32	7th
1976–77	Pr	36	16	11	9	56	42	43	3rd
1977–78	Pr	36	22	9	5	68	29	53	2nd
1978–79	Pr	36	13	14	9	59	36	40	4th
1979–80	Pr	36	19	10	7	68	36	48	1st
1980–81	Pr	36	19	11	6	61	26	49	2nd
1981–82	Pr	36	23	7	6	71	29	53	2nd
1982–83	Pr	36	25	5	6	76	24	55	3rd
1983–84	Pr	36	25	7	4	78	21	57	1st
1984–85	Pr	36	27	5	4	89	26	59	1st
1985–86	Pr	36	16	12	8	62	31	44	4th
1986–87	Pr	44	21	16	7	63	29	58	4th
1987–88	Pr	44	21	17	6	56	25	59	4th
1988–89	Pr	36	18	14	4	51	25	50	2nd
1989–90	Pr	36	17	10	9	56	33	44	2nd
1990–91	Pr	36	22	9	5	62	27	53	2nd
1991–92	Pr	44	17	14	13	55	42	48	6th
1992–93	Pr	44	27	10	7	87	36	64	2nd

On 10 April 1954, **Aberdeen** beat Rangers 6–0 in a Scottish Cup semi-final. Joe O'Neil scored a hat-trick after being surprisingly selected less than three weeks after fracturing his skull in a League game. It was Rangers' heaviest defeat in the competition.

The Aberdeen side which broke the hegemony of the Old Firm in 1980 by taking the League title. Gordon Strachan (front row, second from left) also won a Championship medal in England with Leeds United (Popperfoto)

AIRDRIEONIANS

Year	Div	P	W	D	L	F	A	Pts	Pos
1894–95	II	18	8	2	8	68	45	18	6th
1895–96	II	18	7	4	7	48	44	18	5th
1896–97	II	18	10	1	7	48	39	21	4th
1897–98	II	18	6	2	10	44	56	14	8th
1898–99	II	18	6	3	9	35	46	15	6th
1899–1900	II	18	4	3	11	27	49	11	9th
1900–01	II	18	11	1	6	46	35	23	2nd
1901–02	II	22	10	5	7	40	32	25	4th
1902–03	II	22	15	5	2	43	19	35	1st
1903–04	I	26	7	4	15	32	62	18	12th
1904–05	I	26	11	5	10	38	45	27	4th
1905–06	I	30	15	8	7	53	31	38	3rd
1906–07	I	34	18	6	10	59	44	42	4th
1907–08	I	34	18	5	11	58	41	41	6th
1908–09	I	34	16	9	9	67	46	41	5th
1909–10	I	34	12	9	13	46	57	33	9th
1910–11	I	34	12	9	13	49	53	33	11th
1911–12	I	34	12	8	14	40	41	32	10th
1912–13	I	34	15	11	8	64	46	41	4th
1913–14	I	38	18	12	8	72	43	48	6th
1914–15	I	38	14	7	17	54	60	35	10th
1915–16	SL	38	11	8	19	44	71	30	15th
1916–17	SL	38	21	8	9	71	38	50	4th
1917–18	SL	34	10	6	18	46	58	26	15th
1918–19	SL	34	9	11	14	45	54	29	13th
1919–20	SL	42	17	10	15	57	43	44	7th
1920–21	SL	42	17	9	16	71	64	43	10th
1921–22	I	42	12	11	19	46	56	35	16th
1922–23	I	38	20	10	8	58	38	50	2nd
1923–24	I	38	20	10	8	72	46	50	2nd
1924–25	I	38	25	7	6	85	31	57	2nd
1925–26	I	38	23	4	11	95	54	50	2nd
1926–27	I	38	18	9	11	97	64	45	4th
1927–28	I	38	12	11	15	59	69	35	13th
1928–29	I	38	12	7	19	56	65	31	15th
1929–30	I	38	16	4	18	60	66	36	12th
1930–31	I	38	17	5	16	59	66	39	9th
1931–32	I	38	13	6	19	74	81	32	14th
1932–33	I	38	10	3	25	55	102	23	18th
1933–34	I	38	10	6	22	59	103	26	18th
1934–35	I	38	13	7	18	64	72	33	14th
1935–36	I	38	9	9	20	68	91	27	19th
1936–37	II	34	18	8	8	85	60	44	4th
1937–38	II	34	21	5	8	100	53	47	3rd
1938–39	II	34	21	5	8	85	57	47	4th
1939–46	Regional Leagues operating								
1946–47	B	26	19	4	3	78	48	32	2nd
1947–48	A	30	7	7	16	39	78	21	15th
1948–49	B	30	16	9	5	76	42	41	3rd
1949–50	B	30	19	6	5	79	40	44	2nd
1950–51	A	30	10	4	16	52	67	24	14th
1951–52	A	30	11	4	15	54	69	26	13th
1952–53	A	30	10	6	14	53	75	26	14th
1953–54	A	30	5	5	20	41	92	15	15th
1954–55	B	30	18	10	2	103	61	46	1st
1955–56	A	34	14	8	12	85	96	36	7th
1956–57	I	34	13	4	17	77	89	30	11th
1957–58	I	34	13	2	19	71	92	28	16th
1958–59	I	34	15	7	12	64	62	37	5th
1959–60	I	34	11	6	17	56	80	28	16th
1960–61	I	34	10	10	14	61	71	30	13th
1961–62	I	34	9	7	18	57	78	25	15th
1962–63	I	34	14	2	18	52	76	30	11th
1963–64	I	34	11	4	19	52	97	26	15th
1964–65	I	34	5	4	25	48	110	14	17th
1965–66	II	36	22	6	8	107	56	50	2nd
1966–67	I	34	11	6	17	41	53	28	13th
1967–68	I	34	10	9	15	45	58	29	13th
1968–69	I	34	13	11	10	46	44	37	7th
1969–70	I	34	12	8	14	59	64	32	12th
1970–71	I	34	13	8	13	60	65	34	9th
1971–72	I	34	7	12	15	44	76	26	15th
1972–73	I	34	4	8	22	34	75	16	18th
1973–74	II	36	28	4	4	102	25	60	1st
1974–75	I	34	11	9	14	43	55	31	11th
1975–76	I	26	7	11	8	44	41	25	7th
1976–77	I	39	13	12	14	63	58	38	6th
1977–78	I	39	12	10	17	50	64	34	10th
1978–79	I	39	16	8	15	72	61	40	6th
1979–80	I	39	21	9	9	78	47	51	2nd
1980–81	Pr	36	10	9	17	36	55	29	7th
1981–82	Pr	36	5	8	23	31	76	18	10th
1982–83	I	39	16	7	16	62	46	39	5th
1983–84	I	39	13	10	16	45	53	36	10th
1984–85	I	39	17	8	14	70	59	42	5th
1985–86	I	39	12	11	16	51	50	35	9th
1986–87	I	44	20	11	13	58	46	51	5th
1987–88	I	44	16	13	15	65	68	45	6th
1988–89	I	39	17	13	9	66	44	47	4th
1989–90	I	39	23	8	8	77	45	54	2nd
1990–91	I	39	21	11	7	69	43	53	2nd
1991–92	Pr	44	13	10	21	50	70	36	7th
1992–93	Pr	44	6	17	21	35	70	29	12th

In 1958–59, **Airdrie** scored 64 League goals and only seven different players contributed to them plus one from an opponent. Five players scored 57 between them.

ALBION ROVERS

Year	Div	P	W	D	L	F	A	Pts	Pos
1903–04	II	22	8	5	9	47	37	19	9th
1904–05	II	22	8	4	10	38	53	20	8th
1905–06	II	22	12	3	7	48	29	27	3rd
1906–07	II	22	10	3	9	43	36	23	6th
1907–08	II	22	7	5	10	36	48	19	9th
1908–09	II	22	9	2	11	37	48	20	10th
1909–10	II	22	7	5	10	34	39	19	9th
1910–11	II	22	10	5	7	27	21	25	3rd
1911–12	II	22	6	1	15	26	50	13	12th
1912–13	II	26	10	3	13	38	40	23	9th

Year	Div	P	W	D	L	F	A	Pts	Pos
1913–14	II	22	10	7	5	38	33	27	2nd
1914–15	II	26	9	7	10	37	42	25	9th
1915–19	Regional Leagues operating								
1919–20	SL	42	10	7	25	42	77	27	22nd
1920–21	SL	42	11	12	19	57	68	34	17th
1921–22	I	42	17	10	15	55	51	44	11th
1922–23	I	38	8	10	20	38	64	26	19th
1923–24	II	38	15	12	11	67	53	42	5th
1924–25	II	38	15	5	18	46	61	35	15th
1925–26	II	38	16	6	16	78	71	38	9th
1926–27	II	38	11	11	16	74	87	33	16th
1927–28	II	38	17	4	17	79	69	38	8th
1928–29	II	36	18	8	10	95	67	44	4th
1929–30	II	38	24	6	8	101	60	54	3rd
1930–31	II	38	14	11	13	80	83	39	9th
1931–32	II	38	13	2	23	81	104	28	16th
1932–33	II	34	19	2	13	82	57	40	5th
1933–34	II	34	20	5	9	74	47	45	1st
1934–35	I	38	10	9	19	62	77	29	16th
1935–36	I	38	13	4	21	69	92	30	16th
1936–37	I	38	5	6	27	53	116	16	20th
1937–38	II	34	20	8	6	97	50	48	2nd
1938–39	I	38	12	6	20	65	90	30	16th
1939–46	Regional Leagues operating								
1946–47	B	26	10	7	9	50	54	27	4th
1947–48	B	30	19	4	7	58	49	42	2nd
1948–49	A	30	3	2	25	30	105	8	16th
1949–50	B	30	10	7	13	49	61	27	11th
1950–51	B	30	14	4	12	56	51	32	8th
1951–52	B	30	6	10	14	39	57	22	14th
1952–53	B	30	5	4	21	44	77	14	16th
1953–54	B	30	12	7	11	55	63	31	7th
1954–55	B	30	8	10	12	50	69	26	11th
1955–56	B	36	8	11	17	58	82	27	17th
1956–57	II	36	18	6	12	98	80	42	5th
1957–58	II	36	12	5	19	53	79	29	17th
1958–59	II	36	14	7	15	84	79	35	10th
1959–60	II	36	14	8	14	71	78	36	10th
1960–61	II	36	9	6	21	60	89	24	17th
1961–62	II	36	10	5	21	42	74	25	18th
1962–63	II	36	18	2	16	72	79	38	7th
1963–64	II	36	12	12	12	67	71	36	9th
1964–65	II	36	14	5	17	56	60	33	11th
1965–66	II	36	18	7	11	58	54	43	7th
1966–67	II	38	17	6	15	66	62	40	8th
1967–68	II	36	14	9	13	62	55	37	8th
1968–69	II	36	19	5	12	60	56	43	7th
1969–70	SL	36	14	5	17	53	64	33	11th
1970–71	II	36	15	9	12	53	52	39	7th
1971–72	II	36	7	6	23	36	61	20	18th
1972–73	II	36	5	8	23	35	83	18	18th
1973–74	II	36	7	6	23	38	72	20	17th
1974–75	II	38	16	7	15	72	64	39	12th
1975–76	II	26	7	10	9	35	38	24	9th
1976–77	II	39	15	12	12	74	61	42	6th
1977–78	II	39	16	8	15	68	68	40	8th
1978–79	II	39	15	10	14	57	56	40	7th
1979–80	II	39	16	12	11	73	56	44	4th
1980–81	II	39	13	9	17	59	72	34	12th
1981–82	II	39	13	5	21	52	74	31	11th
1982–83	II	39	14	6	19	55	66	34	10th
1983–84	II	39	8	11	20	46	76	27	14th
1984–85	II	39	13	8	18	49	72	34	9th
1985–86	II	39	8	8	23	38	86	24	13th
1986–87	II	39	15	9	15	48	51	39	8th
1987–88	II	39	10	11	18	45	75	31	12th
1988–89	II	39	21	8	10	65	48	50	1st
1989–90	I	39	8	11	20	50	78	27	13th
1990–91	II	39	11	13	15	48	63	35	11th
1991–92	II	39	5	10	24	42	81	20	14th
1992–93	II	39	6	10	23	36	76	22	14th

Of all first-class clubs in the English and Scottish Leagues operating in 1992–93, **Albion Rovers** had the smallest capacity with 1238. This included 538 seated spectators.

ALLOA

Year	Div	P	W	D	L	F	A	Pts	Pos
1921–22	II	38	26	8	4	81	32	60	1st
1922–23	I	38	6	11	21	27	52	23	20th
1923–24	II	38	14	6	18	44	53	34	16th
1924–25	II	38	17	11	10	57	33	45	4th
1925–26	II	38	11	8	19	54	63	30	16th
1926–27	II	38	11	11	16	70	78	33	15th
1927–28	II	38	12	11	15	72	76	35	15th
1928–29	II	36	12	7	17	64	77	31	13th
1929–30	II	38	9	6	23	55	104	24	19th
1931–31	II	38	15	5	18	65	87	35	13th
1931–32	II	38	14	7	17	73	74	35	13th
1932–33	II	34	14	5	15	60	58	33	11th
1933–34	II	34	11	9	14	55	68	31	15th
1934–35	II	34	12	10	12	68	61	34	10th
1935–36	II	34	19	6	9	65	51	44	4th
1936–37	II	34	13	7	14	64	65	33	9th
1937–38	II	34	11	4	19	78	106	26	11th
1938–39	II	34	22	4	8	91	46	48	2nd
1939–46	Regional Leagues operating								
1946–47	B	26	11	5	10	51	57	27	5th
1947–48	B	30	10	6	14	53	77	24	12th
1948–49	B	30	10	3	17	42	85	23	14th
1949–50	B	30	5	3	22	47	96	13	16th
1950–51	B	30	7	4	19	58	98	18	16th
1951–52	B	30	13	6	11	55	49	32	7th
1952–53	B	30	12	5	13	63	68	29	9th
1953–54	B	30	7	10	13	50	72	24	11th
1954–55	B	30	7	6	17	51	75	20	15th
1955–56	B	36	12	7	17	67	73	31	13th
1956–57	II	36	11	5	20	66	99	27	15th
1957–58	II	36	15	9	12	88	78	39	8th
1958–59	II	36	12	7	17	76	81	31	13th
1959–60	II	36	13	5	18	70	85	31	13th
1960–61	II	36	13	7	15	78	68	33	11th

Year	Div	P	W	D	L	F	A	Pts	Pos
1961–62	II	36	17	8	11	92	78	42	4th
1962–63	II	36	15	6	15	57	56	36	9th
1963–64	II	36	11	5	20	64	92	27	16th
1964–65	II	36	14	8	14	71	81	36	10th
1965–66	II	36	14	10	12	65	65	38	8th
1966–67	II	38	15	4	19	55	74	34	13th
1967–68	II	36	11	6	19	42	69	28	17th
1968–69	II	36	7	7	22	45	79	21	18th
1969–70	II	36	19	5	12	62	41	43	6th
1970–71	II	36	9	11	16	56	86	29	16th
1971–72	II	36	9	4	23	41	75	22	16th
1972–73	II	36	11	11	14	45	49	33	12th
1973–74	II	36	15	4	17	47	58	34	12th
1974–75	II	38	11	11	16	49	56	33	15th
1975–76	II	26	14	7	5	44	28	35	3rd
1976–77	II	39	19	13	7	73	45	51	2nd
1977–78	I	39	8	8	23	44	84	24	13th
1978–79	II	39	16	9	14	57	62	41	6th
1979–80	II	39	11	7	21	44	64	29	14th
1980–81	II	39	15	12	12	61	54	42	6th
1981–82	II	39	19	12	8	66	42	50	2nd
1982–83	I	39	14	11	14	52	52	39	6th
1983–84	I	39	8	10	21	41	64	26	14th
1984–85	II	39	20	10	9	58	40	50	2nd
1985–86	I	39	6	14	19	49	74	26	14th
1986–87	II	39	17	7	15	48	50	41	6th
1987–88	II	39	16	8	15	50	46	40	7th
1988–89	II	39	17	11	11	66	48	45	2nd
1989–90	I	39	6	13	20	41	70	25	14th
1990–91	II	39	13	11	15	51	46	37	9th
1991–92	II	39	20	10	9	58	38	50	3rd
1992–93	II	39	16	12	11	63	54	44	5th

Alloa scored five goals in ten minutes against Armadale in a Division Two match on 26 March 1927. Alloa won 6–2.

ARBROATH

Year	Div	P	W	D	L	F	A	Pts	Pos
1921–22	II	38	11	11	16	45	56	33	16th
1922–23	II	38	8	12	18	45	69	28	20th
1923–24	II	38	12	8	18	49	51	32	17th
1924–25	II	38	16	10	12	47	46	42	5th
1925–26	II	38	17	4	17	80	73	38	10th
1926–27	II	38	13	6	19	64	82	32	19th
1927–28	II	38	16	4	18	84	86	36	10th
1928–29	II	38	19	9	8	90	60	47	3rd
1929–30	II	38	16	7	15	83	87	39	9th
1930–31	II	38	15	4	19	83	94	34	15th
1931–32	II	38	17	5	16	82	78	39	11th
1932–33	II	34	14	5	15	65	62	33	10th
1933–34	II	34	20	4	10	83	53	44	3rd
1934–35	II	34	23	4	7	78	42	50	2nd
1935–36	I	38	11	11	16	46	69	33	12th
1936–37	I	38	13	5	20	57	84	31	14th
1937–38	I	38	11	13	14	58	79	35	11th
1938–39	I	38	11	8	19	54	75	30	17th
1939–46	Regional Leagues operating								
1946–47	B	26	7	6	13	42	63	20	12th
1947–48	B	30	10	3	17	55	62	23	13th
1948–49	B	30	12	8	10	62	56	32	7th
1949–50	B	30	5	9	16	47	69	19	14th
1950–51	B	30	8	5	17	46	78	21	13th
1951–52	B	30	6	4	20	40	83	16	16th
1952–53	B	30	13	7	10	52	57	33	7th
1953–54	B	30	8	7	15	53	67	23	14th
1954–55	B	30	8	8	14	55	72	24	12th
1955–56	B	36	10	6	20	47	67	26	18th
1956–57	II	36	17	4	15	79	57	38	10th
1957–58	II	36	21	5	10	89	72	47	3rd
1958–59	II	36	23	5	8	86	59	51	2nd
1959–60	I	34	4	7	23	38	106	15	18th
1960–61	II	36	13	7	16	56	76	33	12th
1961–62	II	36	17	7	12	66	59	41	6th
1962–63	II	36	18	4	14	74	51	40	6th
1963–64	II	36	20	6	10	79	46	46	3rd
1964–65	II	36	13	13	10	56	51	39	7th
1965–66	II	36	15	13	8	72	52	43	6th
1966–67	II	38	25	7	6	75	32	57	3rd
1967–68	II	36	24	5	7	87	34	53	2nd
1968–69	I	34	5	6	23	41	82	16	18th
1969–70	II	36	20	4	12	76	39	44	5th
1970–71	II	36	19	8	9	80	52	46	3rd
1971–72	II	36	22	8	6	71	41	52	2nd
1972–73	I	34	9	8	17	39	63	26	15th
1973–74	I	34	10	7	17	52	69	27	13th
1974–75	I	34	5	7	22	34	66	17	18th
1975–76	I	26	11	4	11	41	39	26	5th
1976–77	I	39	17	3	19	46	62	37	8th
1977–78	I	39	11	13	15	42	55	35	10th
1978–79	I	39	11	11	17	50	61	33	10th
1979–80	I	39	9	10	20	50	79	28	13th
1980–81	II	39	13	12	14	58	54	38	9th
1981–82	II	39	20	10	9	62	50	50	3rd
1982–83	II	39	21	7	11	78	51	49	3rd
1983–84	II	39	18	6	15	51	46	42	5th
1984–85	II	39	9	7	23	35	66	25	14th
1985–86	II	39	15	9	15	55	50	39	8th
1986–87	II	39	11	7	21	46	66	29	11th
1987–88	II	39	10	14	15	54	66	34	9th
1988–89	II	39	11	15	13	56	63	37	10th
1989–90	II	39	12	10	17	47	61	34	12th
1990–91	II	39	8	11	10	41	59	27	14th
1991–92	II	39	12	14	13	49	48	38	7th
1992–93	II	39	18	8	13	59	50	44	6th

On 2 February 1974, **Arbroath** beat Rangers 3–2 for the first time at Ibrox. Rangers were awarded two penalties in the match, Sandy Jardine shooting wide from the first and Derek Parlane hitting a second in off a post with another effort.

ARMADALE

Year	Div	P	W	D	L	F	A	Pts	Pos
1921–22	II	38	20	5	13	64	49	45	3rd
1922–23	II	38	15	11	12	63	52	41	6th
1923–24	II	38	16	6	16	56	63	38	11th
1924–25	II	38	15	5	18	55	62	35	15th
1925–26	II	38	14	5	19	82	101	33	15th
1926–27	II	38	12	10	16	69	78	34	14th
1927–28	II	38	8	8	22	53	112	24	20th
1928–29	II	36	8	7	21	47	99	23	19th
1929–30	II	38	13	5	20	56	91	31	15th
1930–31	II	38	13	2	23	74	99	28	18th
1931–32	II	38	10	5	23	68	102	25	18th
1932–33	Fixtures uncompleted; expelled								

Armadale finished sixth in Division Two during 1922–23 but remained unbeaten that season until losing 3–2 at home to King's Park on 13 December.

ARTHURLIE

Year	Div	P	W	D	L	F	A	Pts	Pos
1901–02	II	22	6	5	11	32	42	17	10th
1902–03	II	22	6	8	8	34	46	20	9th
1903–04	II	22	5	5	12	37	50	15	11th
1904–05	II	22	9	5	8	37	42	23	6th
1905–06	II	22	10	2	10	42	43	22	6th
1906–07	II	22	12	3	7	50	39	27	3rd
1907–08	II	22	6	5	11	33	45	17	11th
1908–09	II	22	5	1	16	29	55	11	12th
1909–10	II	22	6	5	11	34	47	17	10th
1910–11	II	22	7	5	10	26	33	19	10th
1911–12	II	22	7	5	10	26	30	19	8th
1912–13	II	26	7	5	14	37	49	19	13th
1913–14	II	22	8	4	10	35	37	20	9th
1914–15	II	26	6	4	16	36	66	16	13th
Regional Leagues operating									
1924–25	II	38	14	8	16	56	60	36	12th
1925–26	II	38	17	5	16	81	75	39	7th
1926–27	II	38	18	5	15	90	83	41	7th
1927–28	II	38	18	4	16	84	90	40	7th
1928–29	II	32	9	7	16	51	73	25	17th
Resigned with four games to play									

Arthurlie beat Armadale 10–0 on 1 October 1927 and Owen McNally scored eight goals. At the time he was on loan from Celtic, whom he had joined from his local club Denny Hibs. He subsequently played for Hamilton Academicals, Bray Unknowns, Cardiff City, Lausanne, Sligo Rovers, Distillery, Leicester City, and Racing Club de Paris. He was also given representative honours for the Irish League v Football League.

AYR PARKHOUSE

Year	Div	P	W	D	L	F	A	Pts	Pos
1906–07	II	22	5	2	15	32	64	12	12th
1907–08	II	22	11	0	11	38	38	22	6th
1908–09	II	22	8	5	9	29	31	21	7th
1909–10	II	22	4	3	15	27	43	11	12th
Failed re-election									

Ayr Parkhouse amalgamated with Ayr Football Club in 1910 to form Ayr United. Ayr Parkhouse were famous for playing an entire season without drawing a League game.

AYR UNITED

Year	Div	P	W	D	L	F	A	Pts	Pos
1897–98	II	18	7	2	9	36	42	16	6th
1898–99	II	18	5	3	10	35	51	13	8th
1899–1900	II	18	6	2	10	39	48	14	8th
1900–01	II	18	9	0	9	32	34	18	6th
1901–02	II	22	8	5	9	27	33	21	8th
1902–03	II	22	12	3	7	34	24	27	3rd
1903–04	II	22	11	6	5	33	30	28	3rd
1904–05	II	22	11	1	10	46	37	23	5th
1905–06	II	22	9	3	10	43	51	21	7th
1906–07	II	22	7	6	9	34	38	20	8th
1907–08	II	22	11	5	6	40	33	27	3rd
1908–09	II	22	10	3	9	43	36	23	5th
1909–10	II	22	9	3	10	37	40	21	7th
1910–11	II	22	12	3	7	52	36	27	2nd
1911–12	II	22	16	3	3	54	24	35	1st
1912–13	II	26	13	8	5	45	19	34	1st
1913–14	I	38	13	7	18	58	74	33	10th
1914–15	I	38	20	8	10	55	40	48	5th
1915–16	SL	38	20	8	10	72	45	48	4th
1916–17	SL	38	12	7	19	46	59	31	15th
1917–18	SL	34	5	9	20	32	61	19	18th
1918–19	SL	34	14	9	11	57	53	37	7th
1919–20	SL	42	15	10	17	72	69	40	10th
1920–21	SL	42	14	12	16	62	69	40	14th
1921–22	I	42	13	12	17	55	63	38	14th
1922–23	I	38	13	12	13	43	44	38	10th
1923–24	I	38	12	10	16	38	60	34	14th
1924–25	I	38	11	8	19	43	65	30	19th
1925–26	II	38	20	12	6	7	39	52	3rd
1926–27	II	38	13	15	10	67	68	41	8th
1927–28	II	38	24	6	8	117	60	54	1st
1928–29	I	38	12	7	19	65	84	31	16th
1929–30	I	38	16	6	16	70	92	38	9th
1930–31	I	38	8	11	19	53	92	27	18th
1931–32	I	38	11	7	20	70	90	29	17th
1932–33	I	38	13	4	21	62	96	30	16th
1933–34	I	38	16	10	12	87	92	42	8th
1934–35	I	38	12	5	21	61	112	29	18th
1935–36	I	38	11	3	24	53	98	25	20th
1936–37	II	34	25	4	5	122	49	54	1st

Year	Div	P	W	D	L	F	A	Pts	Pos
1937–38	I	38	9	15	14	66	85	33	17th
1938–39	I	38	13	9	16	76	83	35	14th
1939–46	Regional Leagues operating								
1946–47	B	26	9	2	15	56	73	20	11th
1947–48	B	30	9	9	12	59	61	27	10th
1948–49	B	30	10	7	13	51	70	27	9th
1949–50	B	30	8	6	16	53	80	22	13th
1950–51	B	30	15	6	9	64	40	36	3rd
1951–52	B	30	17	5	8	55	45	39	3rd
1952–53	B	30	17	2	11	76	56	36	5th
1953–54	B	30	11	8	11	50	56	30	9th
1954–55	B	30	14	4	12	61	73	32	8th
1955–56	B	36	24	3	9	103	55	51	2nd
1956–57	I	34	7	5	22	48	89	19	18th
1957–58	II	36	18	6	12	98	81	42	5th
1958–59	II	36	28	4	4	115	48	60	1st
1959–60	I	34	14	6	14	65	73	34	8th
1960–61	I	34	5	12	17	51	81	22	18th
1961–62	II	36	15	8	13	71	63	38	9th
1962–63	II	36	13	8	15	68	77	34	13th
1963–64	II	36	12	5	19	58	83	29	14th
1964–65	II	36	9	6	21	49	67	24	18th
1965–66	II	36	22	9	5	78	37	53	1st
1966–67	I	34	1	7	26	20	86	9	18th
1967–68	II	36	18	6	12	69	48	42	5th
1968–69	II	36	23	7	6	82	31	53	2nd
1969–70	I	34	12	6	16	37	52	30	14th
1970–71	I	34	9	8	17	37	54	26	14th
1971–72	I	34	9	10	15	40	58	28	12th
1972–73	I	34	16	8	10	50	51	40	6th
1973–74	I	34	15	8	11	44	40	38	7th
1974–75	I	34	14	8	12	50	61	36	7th
1975–76	Pr	36	14	5	17	46	59	33	6th
1976–77	Pr	36	11	8	17	44	68	30	8th
1977–78	Pr	36	9	6	21	36	68	24	9th
1978–79	I	39	21	5	13	71	52	47	4th
1979–80	I	39	16	12	11	64	51	44	3rd
1980–81	I	39	17	11	11	59	42	45	6th
1981–82	I	39	15	12	12	56	50	42	6th
1982–83	I	39	12	8	19	45	61	32	12th
1983–84	I	39	10	12	17	56	70	32	12th
1984–85	I	39	15	9	15	57	52	39	7th
1985–86	I	39	10	11	18	41	60	31	13th
1986–87	II	39	22	8	9	70	49	52	4th
1987–88	II	39	27	7	5	95	31	61	1st
1988–89	I	39	13	9	17	56	72	35	11th
1989–90	I	39	11	13	15	41	62	35	10th
1990–91	I	39	10	12	17	47	59	32	12th
1991–92	I	44	18	11	15	63	55	47	6th
1992–93	I	44	14	18	12	49	44	46	7th

In 1966–67 **Ayr United** did not win a match until their 32nd when they beat St Johnstone on 8 April 1967. They had played 29 League games, drawn with Rangers in the League Cup and lost to Elgin City in the Scottish Cup.

BATHGATE

Year	Div	P	W	D	L	F	A	Pts	Pos
1921–22	II	38	16	11	11	56	41	43	5th
1922–23	II	38	16	9	13	57	55	41	5th
1923–24	II	38	16	12	10	58	49	44	3rd
1924–25	II	38	12	10	16	58	74	34	16th
1925–26	II	38	7	6	25	60	105	20	19th
1926–27	II	38	13	7	18	76	98	33	17th
1927–28	II	38	10	11	17	62	81	31	19th
1928–29	Resigned during season								

Three special trains took 2,500 **Bathgate** supporters to Hampden Park for a Scottish Cup second round tie against Queen's Park in 1922–23. A crowd of 50,000 including the Duke of York who kicked-off saw a 1–1 draw. Bathgate lost the replay 2–0 in front of 6,000.

BERWICK RANGERS

Year	Div	P	W	D	L	F	A	Pts	Pos
1955–56	B	36	11	9	16	52	77	31	14th
1956–57	II	36	7	6	23	58	114	20	18th
1957–58	II	36	5	5	26	37	109	15	19th
1958–59	II	36	16	6	14	63	66	38	9th
1959–60	II	36	16	5	15	62	55	37	9th
1960–61	II	36	14	9	13	62	69	37	9th
1961–62	II	36	16	6	14	83	70	38	8th
1962–63	II	36	11	7	18	57	77	29	17th
1963–64	II	36	10	10	16	68	84	30	12th
1964–65	II	36	15	9	12	73	70	39	8th
1965–66	II	36	12	11	13	69	58	35	11th
1966–67	II	38	16	6	16	63	55	38	10th
1967–68	II	36	13	4	19	34	54	30	14th
1968–69	II	36	7	9	20	42	70	23	16th
1969–70	II	36	15	5	16	67	55	35	9th
1970–71	II	36	10	10	16	42	60	30	14th
1971–72	II	36	14	4	18	53	50	32	13th
1972–73	II	36	16	5	15	45	54	37	9th
1973–74	II	36	16	13	7	53	35	45	6th
1974–75	II	38	17	6	15	53	49	40	10th
1975–76	II	26	7	5	14	32	44	19	11th
1976–77	II	39	13	10	16	37	51	36	8th
1977–78	II	39	16	16	7	68	51	48	4th
1978–79	II	39	22	10	7	82	44	54	1st
1979–80	I	39	8	15	16	57	64	31	12th
1980–81	I	39	5	12	22	31	82	22	14th
1981–82	II	39	20	8	11	66	38	48	4th
1982–83	II	39	13	10	16	47	60	36	9th
1983–84	II	39	16	11	12	60	38	43	3rd
1984–85	II	39	8	12	19	36	49	28	13th
1985–86	II	39	7	11	21	45	80	25	12th
1986–87	II	39	8	7	24	40	69	23	14th
1987–88	II	39	6	4	29	32	77	16	13th
1988–89	II	39	10	13	16	50	59	33	13th
1989–90	II	39	18	5	16	66	57	41	5th

1990–91	II	39	15	10	14	51	57	40	8th
1991–92	II	39	10	11	18	50	65	31	12th
1992–93	II	39	16	7	16	56	64	39	8th

On 4 October 1952 **Berwick Rangers** beat Stirling Albion Reserves 9–1 in a Division C, North-East Section match. They were a goal down in five minutes and later missed a penalty.

BO'NESS

Year	Div	P	W	D	L	F	A	Pts	Pos
1921–22	II	38	16	7	15	57	49	39	6th
1922–23	II	38	12	17	9	48	46	41	7th
1923–24	II	38	13	11	14	45	52	37	13th
1924–25	II	38	16	9	13	71	48	41	6th
1925–26	II	38	17	5	16	65	70	39	8th
1926–27	II	38	23	10	6	86	41	56	1st
1927–28	I	38	9	8	21	48	86	26	19th
1928–29	II	35	15	5	15	62	62	35	10th
1929–30	II	38	15	4	19	67	95	34	13th
1930–31	II	38	9	4	25	54	100	22	20th
1931–32	II	38	15	4	19	70	103	34	14th
1932–33	Expelled November 1932								

Bo'ness were expelled from the Scottish League Division Two in November 1932 when they were unable to meet their £50 match guarantee.

BRECHIN CITY

Year	Div	P	W	D	L	F	A	Pts	Pos
1929–30	II	38	7	4	27	57	125	18	20th
1930–31	II	38	13	7	18	52	84	33	16th
1931–32	II	38	9	7	22	52	97	25	19th
1932–33	II	34	11	4	19	65	95	26	15th
1933–34	II	34	13	5	16	60	70	31	14th
1934–35	II	34	10	6	18	51	98	26	15th
1935–36	II	34	8	6	20	57	96	22	16th
1936–37	II	34	8	9	17	64	98	25	16th
1937–38	II	34	5	2	27	53	139	12	18th
1938–39	II	34	11	9	14	82	106	31	10th
1939–46	Regional Leagues operating								
1946–54	C Division								
1954–55	B	30	8	3	19	53	89	19	16th
1955–56	B	36	18	6	12	60	56	42	6th
1956–57	II	36	15	10	11	72	68	40	6th
1957–58	II	36	16	8	12	80	81	40	7th
1958–59	II	36	16	10	10	79	65	42	5th
1959–60	II	36	14	6	16	66	66	34	12th
1960–61	II	36	9	9	18	60	78	27	14th
1961–62	II	36	5	2	29	44	123	12	19th
1962–63	II	36	3	3	30	39	113	9	19th
1963–64	II	36	10	8	18	61	98	28	15th
1964–65	II	36	6	7	23	53	102	19	19th

1965–66	II	36	10	7	19	52	92	27	16th
1966–67	II	38	8	7	23	58	93	23	20th
1967–68	II	36	8	12	16	45	62	28	16th
1968–69	II	36	8	6	22	40	78	22	17th
1969–70	II	36	11	6	19	47	74	28	14th
1970–71	II	36	6	7	23	30	73	19	19th
1971–72	II	36	8	7	21	41	79	23	15th
1972–73	II	36	5	4	27	46	99	14	19th
1973–74	II	36	5	4	27	33	99	14	19th
1974–75	II	38	9	7	22	44	85	25	17th
1975–76	II	26	6	5	15	28	52	17	13th
1976–77	II	39	7	12	20	51	77	26	13th
1977–78	II	39	7	6	26	45	73	20	14th
1978–79	II	39	9	14	16	49	65	32	11th
1979–80	II	39	15	10	14	61	59	40	7th
1980–81	II	39	15	14	10	52	46	44	4th
1981–82	II	39	18	10	11	61	43	46	5th
1982–83	II	39	21	13	5	77	38	55	1st
1983–84	II	39	14	14	11	56	58	42	5th
1984–85	I	39	14	9	16	49	57	37	9th
1985–86	I	39	13	9	17	58	64	35	10th
1986–87	I	44	11	10	23	44	72	32	11th
1987–88	II	39	20	8	11	56	40	48	4th
1988–89	II	39	15	13	11	58	49	43	3rd
1989–90	II	39	19	11	9	59	44	49	1st
1990–91	I	39	7	10	22	44	80	24	14th
1991–92	II	39	13	12	14	54	55	38	8th
1992–93	II	39	23	7	9	62	32	53	2nd

Brechin City suffered three 10–0 defeats inside three months during 1937–38: v Cowdenbeath 20 November, v Albion Rovers 15 January and v Airdrie 12 February.

BROXBURN UNITED

Year	Div	P	W	D	L	F	A	Pts	Pos
1921–22	II	38	14	11	13	43	43	39	6th
1922–23	II	38	14	12	12	42	45	40	8th
1923–24	II	38	7	8	18	48	58	32	19th
1924–25	II	38	12	10	16	58	74	34	18th
1925–26	II	38	7	6	25	60	105	20	20th

Broxburn United achieved their record attendance in the Scottish Cup. For a third round tie against Falkirk they had 9,000 in 1924–25. They won 2–1.

CAMBUSLANG

Year	Div	P	W	D	L	F	A	Pts	Pos
1890–91	SL	18	8	4	6	47	42	20	4th
1891–92	SL	22	2	6	14	22	53	10	11th

In the 1887–88 Scottish Cup semi-final **Cambuslang** and Abercorn drew 1–1, but Cambuslang won the replay 10–1.

CELTIC

Year	Div	P	W	D	L	F	A	Pts	Pos
1890–91	SL	18	11	3	4	48	21	21	3rd
1891–92	SL	22	16	3	3	62	22	35	2nd
1892–93	SL	18	14	1	3	54	25	29	1st
1893–94	I	18	14	1	3	53	32	29	1st
1894–95	I	18	11	4	3	52	31	26	2nd
1895–96	I	18	15	0	3	64	25	30	1st
1896–97	I	18	10	4	4	42	18	24	4th
1897–98	I	18	15	3	0	56	13	33	1st
1898–99	I	18	11	2	5	51	33	24	3rd
1899–1900	I	18	9	7	2	46	27	25	2nd
1900–01	I	20	13	3	4	49	28	29	2nd
1901–02	I	18	11	4	3	38	28	26	2nd
1902–03	I	22	8	10	4	36	30	26	5th
1903–04	I	26	18	2	6	68	27	38	3rd
1904–05	I	26	19	3	4	68	31	41	1st
1905–06	I	30	24	1	5	76	19	49	1st
1906–07	I	34	23	9	2	80	30	55	1st
1907–08	I	34	24	7	3	86	27	55	1st
1908–09	I	34	23	5	6	71	24	51	1st
1909–10	I	34	24	6	4	63	22	54	1st
1910–11	I	34	15	11	8	48	18	41	5th
1911–12	I	34	17	11	6	58	33	45	2nd
1912–13	I	34	22	5	7	53	28	49	2nd
1913–14	I	38	30	5	3	81	14	65	1st
1914–15	I	38	30	5	3	91	25	65	1st
1915–16	SL	38	32	33	3	116	23	67	1st
1916–17	SL	38	27	10	1	77	17	64	1st
1917–18	SL	34	24	7	3	66	26	55	2nd
1918–19	SL	34	26	6	2	70	22	58	1st
1919–20	SL	42	29	10	3	89	31	68	2nd
1920–21	SL	42	30	6	6	86	35	66	2nd
1921–22	I	42	27	13	2	83	20	67	1st
1922–23	I	38	19	8	11	52	39	46	3rd
1923–24	I	38	17	12	9	56	33	46	3rd
1924–25	I	38	18	8	12	76	43	44	4th
1925–26	I	38	25	8	5	97	40	58	1st
1926–27	I	38	21	7	10	101	55	49	3rd
1927–28	I	38	23	9	6	93	39	55	2nd
1928–29	I	38	22	7	9	67	44	51	2nd
1929–30	I	38	22	5	11	88	46	49	4th
1930–31	I	38	24	10	4	101	34	58	2nd
1931–32	I	38	20	8	10	94	50	48	3rd
1932–33	I	38	20	8	10	75	44	48	4th
1933–34	I	38	18	11	9	78	53	47	3rd
1934–35	I	38	24	4	10	92	45	52	2nd
1935–36	I	38	32	2	4	115	33	66	1st
1936–37	I	38	22	8	8	89	58	52	3rd
1937–38	I	38	27	7	4	114	42	61	1st
1938–39	I	38	20	8	10	99	53	48	2nd
1939–46	Regional Leagues operating								
1946–47	A	30	13	6	11	53	55	32	7th
1947–48	A	30	10	5	15	41	56	25	12th
1948–49	A	30	12	7	11	48	40	31	6th
1949–50	A	30	14	7	9	51	50	35	5th
1950–51	A	30	12	5	13	48	46	29	7th
1951–52	A	30	10	8	12	52	55	28	9th
1952–53	A	30	11	7	12	51	54	29	8th
1953–54	A	30	20	3	7	72	29	43	1st
1954–55	A	30	19	8	3	76	37	46	2nd
1955–56	A	34	16	9	9	55	39	41	5th
1956–57	I	34	15	8	11	58	43	38	5th
1957–58	I	34	19	8	7	84	47	46	3rd
1958–59	I	34	14	8	12	70	53	36	6th
1959–60	I	34	12	9	13	73	59	33	9th
1960–61	I	34	15	9	10	64	46	39	4th
1961–62	I	34	19	8	7	81	37	46	3rd
1962–63	I	34	19	6	9	76	44	44	4th
1963–64	I	34	19	9	6	89	34	47	3rd
1964–65	I	34	16	5	13	76	57	37	8th
1965–66	I	34	27	3	4	106	30	57	1st
1966–67	I	34	26	6	2	111	33	58	1st
1967–68	I	34	30	3	1	106	24	63	1st
1968–69	I	34	23	8	3	89	32	54	1st
1969–70	I	34	27	3	4	96	33	57	1st
1970–71	I	34	25	6	3	89	23	56	1st
1971–72	I	34	28	4	2	96	28	60	1st
1972–73	I	34	26	5	3	93	28	57	1st
1973–74	I	34	23	7	4	82	27	53	1st
1974–75	I	34	20	5	9	81	41	45	3rd
1975–76	Pr	36	21	6	9	71	42	48	2nd
1976–77	Pr	36	23	9	4	79	39	55	1st
1977–78	Pr	36	15	6	15	63	54	36	5th
1978–79	Pr	36	21	6	9	61	37	48	1st
1979–80	Pr	36	18	11	7	61	38	47	2nd
1980–81	Pr	36	26	4	6	84	37	56	1st
1981–82	Pr	36	24	7	5	79	33	55	1st
1982–83	Pr	36	25	5	6	90	36	55	2nd
1983–84	Pr	36	21	8	7	80	41	50	2nd
1984–85	Pr	36	22	8	6	77	30	52	2nd
1985–86	Pr	36	20	10	6	67	38	50	1st
1986–87	Pr	44	27	9	8	90	41	63	2nd
1987–88	Pr	44	31	10	3	79	23	72	1st

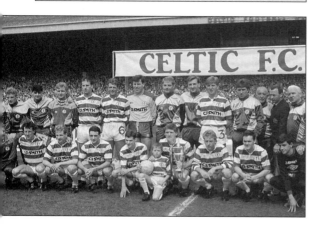

In 1988 Celtic celebrated their Centenary Year in the best possible fashion by doing the Double. Here the team shows off the Premier League Championship trophy at Parkhead (Bob Thomas)

		P	W	D	L	F	A	Pts	Pos
1988–89	Pr	36	21	4	11	66	44	46	3rd
1989–90	Pr	36	10	14	12	37	37	34	5th
1990–91	Pr	36	17	7	12	52	38	41	3rd
1991–92	Pr	44	26	10	8	88	42	62	3rd
1992–93	Pr	44	24	12	8	68	41	60	3rd

Bobby Lennox scored 20 goals for **Celtic** in 12 consecutive Scottish League matches from 2 March 1968 to 30 April as follows: 1 3 1 1 1 4 2 1 1 2 1 2.

CLACKMANNAN

Year	Div	P	W	D	L	F	A	Pts	Pos
1921–22	II	38	10	7	21	41	75	27	20th

Clackmannan were beaten 8–1 away by Armadale on 4 April 1921 to suffer their heaviest defeat. This despite the fact that the half-time score was only 1–1.

CLYDE

Year	Div	P	W	D	L	F	A	Pts	Pos
1891–92	SL	22	8	4	10	63	62	20	7th
1892–93	SL	18	2	2	14	25	55	6	10th
1893–94	II	18	11	2	5	51	36	24	3rd
1894–95	I	18	8	0	10	40	49	16	7th
1895–96	I	18	4	3	11	39	59	11	9th
1896–97	I	18	4	0	14	27	65	8	9th
1897–98	I	18	1	3	14	20	84	5	10th
1898–99	I	18	4	4	10	23	48	12	8th
1899–1900	I	18	2	0	16	25	70	4	10th
1900–01	II	18	9	2	7	43	35	20	4th
1901–02	II	22	5	3	14	22	50	13	12th
1902–03	II	22	2	7	13	22	40	11	12th
1903–04	II	22	12	5	5	51	36	29	2nd
1904–05	II	22	13	6	3	38	22	32	1st
1905–06	II	22	11	9	2	37	21	31	2nd
1906–07	I	34	15	6	13	47	52	36	8th
1907–08	I	34	5	8	21	36	75	18	17th
1908–09	I	34	21	6	7	61	37	48	3rd
1909–10	I	34	14	9	11	47	40	37	5th
1910–11	I	34	14	11	9	45	36	39	7th
1911–12	I	34	19	4	11	56	32	42	3rd
1912–13	I	34	13	9	12	41	44	35	9th
1913–14	I	38	11	11	16	46	46	33	9th
1914–15	I	38	12	6	20	44	59	30	17th
1915–16	SL	38	11	7	20	49	71	29	16th
1916–17	SL	38	10	14	14	41	51	34	13th
1917–18	SL	34	9	2	23	37	72	20	17th
1918–19	SL	34	7	6	21	45	75	20	17th
1919–20	SL	42	14	9	19	64	71	37	15th
1920–21	SL	42	21	3	18	63	62	45	7th
1921–22	I	42	16	12	14	60	51	44	10th
1922–23	I	38	12	9	17	36	44	33	16th
1923–24	I	38	10	9	19	40	70	29	19th
1924–25	II	38	20	7	11	72	39	47	3rd
1925–26	II	38	24	5	9	87	51	53	2nd
1926–27	I	38	10	9	19	54	85	29	17th
1927–28	I	38	10	11	17	46	72	31	15th
1928–29	I	38	12	6	20	47	71	30	17th
1929–30	I	38	13	11	14	64	69	37	11th
1930–31	I	38	15	4	19	60	87	34	12th
1931–32	I	38	13	9	16	58	70	35	13th
1932–33	I	38	15	5	18	69	75	35	12th
1933–34	I	38	10	11	17	56	70	31	14th
1934–35	I	38	14	10	14	71	69	38	10th
1935–36	I	38	10	8	20	63	84	28	18th
1936–37	I	38	16	6	16	59	70	38	10th
1937–38	I	38	10	13	15	68	78	33	15th
1938–39	I	38	17	5	16	78	70	39	9th
1939–46	Regional Leagues operating								
1946–47	A	30	9	9	12	55	65	27	10th
1947–48	A	30	12	7	11	52	57	31	6th
1948–49	A	30	9	6	15	50	67	24	14th
1949–50	A	30	10	4	16	56	73	24	13th
1950–51	A	30	8	7	15	37	57	23	15th
1951–52	B	30	19	6	5	100	45	44	1st
1952–53	A	30	13	4	13	78	78	30	5th
1953–54	A	30	15	4	11	64	67	34	8th
1954–55	A	30	11	9	10	59	50	31	7th
1955–56	A	34	8	6	20	50	74	22	17th
1956–57	II	36	29	6	1	122	39	64	1st
1957–58	I	34	18	6	10	84	61	42	4th
1958–59	I	34	12	4	18	62	66	28	15th
1959–60	I	34	15	9	10	77	69	39	6th
1960–61	I	34	6	11	17	55	77	23	17th
1960–61	I	34	6	11	17	55	77	23	17th
1961–62	II	36	15	4	7	108	47	54	1st
1962–63	I	34	9	5	20	49	83	23	17th
1963–64	II	36	22	9	5	81	44	53	2nd
1964–65	I	34	17	6	11	64	58	40	7th
1965–66	I	34	13	4	17	62	64	30	11th
1966–67	I	34	20	6	8	64	48	46	3rd
1967–68	I	34	15	4	15	55	55	34	8th
1968–69	I	34	9	13	12	35	50	31	13th
1969–70	I	34	9	7	18	34	56	25	16th
1970–71	I	34	8	10	16	33	59	26	15th
1971–72	I	34	7	10	17	33	66	24	17th
1972–73	II	36	23	10	3	68	28	56	1st
1973–74	I	34	8	9	17	29	65	25	15th
1974–75	I	34	6	10	18	40	63	22	16th
1975–76	I	26	5	4	17	34	52	14	14th
1976–77	II	39	15	11	13	68	64	41	7th
1977–78	II	39	21	11	7	71	32	53	1st
1978–79	I	39	13	8	18	54	65	34	9th
1979–80	I	39	6	13	20	43	69	25	14th
1980–81	II	39	14	12	13	68	63	40	8th
1981–82	II	39	24	11	4	79	38	59	1st
1982–83	I	39	12	13	14	53	50	37	10th
1983–84	I	39	12	13	14	53	50	37	8th
1984–85	I	39	14	11	14	47	48	39	8th

1985–86	I	39	9	17	13	49	59	35	11th
1986–87	I	44	11	16	17	48	56	38	9th
1987–88	I	44	17	6	21	73	75	40	9th
1988–89	I	39	9	16	14	40	52	34	12th
1989–90	I	39	10	15	14	39	46	35	9th
1990–91	I	39	9	9	21	41	61	27	13th
1991–92	II	39	18	7	14	61	43	43	5th
1992–93	II	39	22	10	7	77	42	54	1st

Immediately after the First World War, **Clyde** played in khaki shirts. The club had secured a deal with Army surplus stores, but the innovation proved unpopular with supporters and was soon dropped.

CLYDEBANK

Year	Div	P	W	D	L	F	A	Pts	Pos
1914–15	II	26	13	4	9	68	37	30	5th
Regional Leagues operating									
1917–18	SL	34	14	5	15	55	56	33	9th
1918–19	SL	34	12	8	14	52	65	32	10th
1919–20	SL	42	20	8	14	78	54	48	5th
1920–21	SL	42	7	14	21	47	72	28	20th
1921–22	I	42	6	8	28	34	103	20	22nd
1922–23	II	38	21	10	7	69	29	52	2nd
1923–24	I	38	10	5	23	42	71	25	20th
1924–25	II	38	20	8	10	65	42	48	2nd
1925–26	I	38	7	8	23	55	92	22	20th
1926–27	II	38	18	9	11	94	75	45	3rd
1927–28	II	38	16	3	19	78	80	35	14th
1928–29	II	36	11	5	20	70	86	27	16th
1929–30	II	38	7	10	21	66	92	24	18th
1930–31	II	38	10	2	26	61	108	22	19th
Disbanded									

Although the former **Clydebank** club had one of the most consistent goalscorers ever produced in first-class football when Jimmy McGrory played on loan to them in 1923–24, they were relegated. During the period between 1921 and 1926 they were either promoted or went down for five consecutive seasons.

CLYDEBANK

Year	Div	P	W	D	L	F	A	Pts	Pos
1966–67	II	38	8	8	22	59	92	24	18th
1967–68	II	36	13	8	15	62	73	34	9th
1968–69	II	36	6	15	15	52	67	27	13th
1969–70	II	36	10	10	16	47	65	30	13th
1970–71	II	36	17	8	11	57	43	42	5th
1971–72	II	36	14	11	11	60	52	39	9th
1972–73	II	36	9	6	21	48	72	21	17th
1973–74	II	36	13	8	15	47	48	34	10th
1974–75	II	38	18	8	12	50	40	44	7th
1975–76	II	26	17	6	3	44	13	40	1st

1976–77	I	39	24	10	5	89	38	58	2nd
1977–78	Pr	36	6	7	23	23	64	19	10th
1978–79	I	39	24	6	9	78	50	54	3rd
1979–80	I	39	14	8	17	58	57	36	9th
1980–81	I	39	10	13	16	48	59	33	10th
1981–82	I	39	19	8	12	61	53	46	4th
1982–83	I	39	20	10	9	72	49	50	3rd
1983–84	I	39	16	13	10	62	50	45	4th
1984–85	I	39	17	14	8	57	37	48	2nd
1985–86	Pr	36	6	8	22	29	77	20	10th
1986–87	Pr	44	6	12	26	35	93	24	11th
1987–88	I	44	21	7	16	59	61	49	3rd
1988–89	I	39	18	12	9	80	55	48	3rd
1989–90	I	39	17	10	12	75	64	44	3rd
1990–91	I	39	13	10	16	65	70	36	8th
1991–92	I	44	12	12	20	59	77	36	9th
1992–93	I	44	16	13	15	71	66	45	8th

Clydebank took over ailing Clydebank Juniors and after a year in the Combined Reserve League became a senior club in June 1965.

COWDENBEATH

Year	Div	P	W	D	L	F	A	Pts	Pos
1905–06	II	22	7	3	12	27	39	17	9th
1906–07	II	22	10	5	7	36	39	23	7th
1907–08	II	22	5	4	13	26	35	14	12th
1908–09	II	22	4	4	14	19	42	12	11th
1909–10	II	22	7	3	12	22	34	17	11th
1910–11	II	22	9	5	8	31	27	23	5th
1911–12	II	22	12	2	8	39	31	26	4th
1912–13	II	26	12	6	8	36	27	30	5th
1913–14	II	22	13	5	4	34	17	31	1st
1914–15	II	26	16	5	5	49	17	37	1st
1915–21	Regional Leagues								
1921–22	II	38	19	9	10	56	30	47	2nd
1922–23	II	38	16	6	16	56	52	36	11th
1923–24	II	38	23	9	6	78	33	55	2nd
1924–25	I	38	16	10	12	76	65	42	5th
1925–26	I	38	18	6	14	87	68	42	7th
1926–27	I	38	18	6	14	74	60	42	7th
1927–28	I	38	16	7	15	66	68	39	9th
1928–29	I	38	14	5	19	55	69	33	13th
1929–30	I	38	13	7	18	64	74	33	16th
1930–31	I	38	17	7	14	58	65	41	7th
1931–32	I	38	15	8	15	66	78	38	12th
1932–33	I	38	10	5	23	65	111	25	17th
1933–34	I	38	5	5	28	58	118	15	20th
1934–35	II	34	13	6	15	84	75	32	12th
1935–36	II	34	13	5	16	76	77	31	10th
1936–37	II	34	14	10	10	75	59	38	6th
1937–38	II	34	17	9	8	115	71	43	6th
1938–39	II	34	28	4	2	120	45	60	1st
1939–46	Regional Leagues operating								
1946–47	B	26	6	6	14	44	77	18	14th

Year	Div	P	W	D	L	F	A	Pts	Pos
1947–48	B	30	12	8	10	56	53	32	5th
1948–49	B	30	9	5	16	53	58	23	13th
1949–50	B	30	16	3	11	63	56	35	5th
1950–51	B	30	12	3	15	61	57	27	11th
1951–52	B	30	12	8	10	66	67	32	8th
1952–53	B	30	8	7	15	37	54	23	13th
1953–54	B	30	9	5	16	67	81	23	13th
1954–55	B	30	8	5	17	55	72	21	14th
1955–56	B	36	16	7	13	80	85	39	7th
1956–57	II	36	20	5	11	87	65	45	3rd
1957–58	II	36	17	8	11	100	85	42	6th
1958–59	II	36	13	5	18	67	79	31	14th
1959–60	II	36	6	2	28	42	124	14	19th
1960–61	II	36	17	6	13	71	65	40	8th
1961–62	II	36	11	9	16	65	77	31	14th
1962–63	II	36	15	7	14	72	61	37	8th
1963–64	II	36	7	11	18	46	72	25	17th
1964–65	II	36	11	10	15	55	62	32	12th
1965–66	II	36	15	7	14	69	68	37	10th
1966–67	II	38	16	8	14	70	55	40	6th
1967–68	II	36	12	8	16	57	62	32	12th
1968–69	II	36	12	5	19	54	67	29	12th
1969–70	II	36	24	7	5	81	35	55	2nd
1970–71	I	34	7	3	24	33	77	17	18th
1971–72	II	36	19	10	7	69	28	48	5th
1972–73	II	36	14	10	12	57	53	38	7th
1973–74	II	36	11	9	16	59	85	31	13th
1974–75	II	38	5	12	22	39	76	21	19th
1975–76	II	26	11	7	8	44	43	29	5th
1976–77	II	39	13	5	21	46	64	31	12th
1977–78	II	39	13	8	18	75	78	34	10th
1978–79	II	39	16	10	13	63	58	42	5th
1979–80	II	39	14	12	13	54	52	40	8th
1980–81	II	39	18	9	12	63	48	45	3rd
1981–82	II	39	11	13	15	51	57	33	9th
1982–83	II	39	13	12	14	54	53	38	8th
1983–84	II	39	10	9	20	44	58	29	13th
1984–85	II	39	18	11	10	68	39	47	4th
1985–86	II	39	14	9	16	52	53	37	10th
1986–87	II	39	16	8	15	59	55	40	7th
1987–88	II	39	10	13	16	51	66	33	11th
1988–89	II	39	13	14	12	48	52	38	8th
1989–90	II	39	13	13	13	58	54	39	7th
1990–91	II	39	18	9	12	64	50	45	3rd
1991–92	II	39	22	7	10	74	52	51	2nd
1992–93	I	44	3	7	34	33	109	13	12th

Cowdenbeath goalkeeper Ray Allan made his 400th League appearance on 21 January 1989 in a 2–2 draw at home with Queen's Park.

COWLAIRS

Year	Div	P	W	D	L	F	A	Pts	Pos
1890–91	SL	18	3	4	11	24	50	6	10th

Failed re-election

| 1893–94 | II | 18 | 13 | 1 | 4 | 75 | 32 | 27 | 2nd |
| 1894–95 | II | 18 | 2 | 3 | 13 | 37 | 77 | 7 | 10th |

Cowlairs were involved in a 7–5 win over Abercorn on 28 February 1891, but suffered their heaviest defeat when losing 8–1 to Partick Thistle on 11 November 1893.

DUMBARTON

Year	Div	P	W	D	L	F	A	Pts	Pos
1890–91	SL	18	13	3	2	61	21	29	1st
1891–92	SL	22	18	1	3	79	28	37	1st
1892–93	SL	18	8	1	9	35	35	17	7th
1893–94	I	18	7	5	6	32	35	19	5th
1894–95	I	18	3	1	14	27	58	7	10th
1895–96	I	18	4	0	14	36	74	8	10th
1896–97	II	18	2	2	14	27	64	6	10th
Failed re-election									
1906–07	II	22	11	3	8	52	35	25	4th
1907–08	II	22	12	5	5	49	32	27	2nd
1908–09	II	22	10	5	7	34	34	25	4th
1909–10	II	22	9	5	8	44	38	23	4th
1910–11	II	22	15	1	6	55	31	31	1st
1911–12	II	22	13	1	8	47	31	27	3rd
1912–13	II	26	12	5	9	39	30	29	6th
1913–14	I	38	10	7	21	45	87	27	19th
1914–15	I	38	13	8	17	51	66	34	13th
1915–16	SL	38	13	11	14	53	64	37	9th
1916–17	SL	38	12	11	15	56	73	35	10th
1917–18	SL	34	13	8	13	48	49	34	8th
1918–19	SL	34	7	8	19	31	57	22	15th
1919–20	SL	42	13	13	16	57	65	39	11th
1920–21	SL	42	10	4	28	41	89	24	21st
1921–22	I	42	10	10	22	46	81	30	20th
1922–23	II	38	17	8	13	61	40	42	4th
1923–24	II	38	17	5	16	55	58	39	10th
1924–25	II	38	15	10	13	45	44	40	8th
1925–26	II	38	14	10	14	54	78	38	11th
1926–27	II	38	13	6	19	69	84	32	18th
1927–28	II	38	16	4	18	66	72	36	11th
1928–29	II	36	11	9	16	59	78	31	14th
1929–30	II	38	14	2	22	77	95	30	16th
1930–31	II	38	15	8	15	73	72	38	10th
1931–32	II	38	14	10	14	70	68	38	12th
1932–33	II	34	14	6	14	69	67	34	9th
1933–34	II	34	17	3	14	67	68	37	6th
1934–35	II	34	9	4	21	60	105	22	16th
1935–36	II	34	5	6	23	52	121	16	18th
1936–37	II	34	11	5	18	57	83	27	15th
1937–38	II	34	17	5	12	85	66	39	7th
1938–39	II	34	9	12	13	68	76	30	11th
1939–46	Regional Leagues operating								
1946–47	B	26	7	4	15	41	54	18	13th
1947–48	B	30	9	7	14	66	79	25	11th
1948–49	B	30	8	6	16	52	79	22	15th
1949–50	B	30	6	4	20	39	62	16	15th

Year	Div	P	W	D	L	F	A	Pts	Pos
1950–51	B	30	12	5	13	52	53	29	9th
1951–52	B	30	10	8	12	51	57	28	10th
1952–53	B	30	11	6	13	58	67	28	10th
1953–54	B	30	7	8	15	51	92	22	16th
Relegated to Division C									
1955–56	B	36	21	5	10	83	62	47	4th
1956–57	II	36	17	4	15	101	70	38	9th
1957–58	II	36	20	4	12	92	57	44	4th
1958–59	II	36	19	7	10	94	61	45	4th
1959–60	II	36	18	7	11	67	53	43	6th
1960–61	II	36	15	5	16	78	82	35	10th
1961–62	II	36	9	10	17	49	66	28	17th
1962–63	II	36	15	4	17	64	64	34	12th
1963–64	II	36	16	6	14	67	59	38	6th
1964–65	II	36	13	6	17	55	67	32	14th
1965–66	II	36	14	7	15	63	61	35	12th
1966–67	II	38	12	9	17	56	64	33	14th
1967–68	II	36	11	11	14	63	74	33	10th
1968–69	II	36	11	5	20	46	69	27	14th
1969–70	II	36	17	6	11	55	46	40	7th
1970–71	II	36	19	6	11	87	46	44	4th
1971–72	II	36	24	4	8	89	51	52	1st
1972–73	I	34	6	11	17	43	72	23	16th
1973–74	I	34	11	7	16	43	58	29	10th
1974–75	I	34	7	10	17	44	55	24	14th
1975–76	I	26	12	4	10	35	46	28	4th
1976–77	I	39	14	9	16	63	68	37	7th
1977–78	I	39	16	17	6	65	48	49	4th
1978–79	I	39	14	11	14	58	49	39	7th
1979–80	I	39	19	6	14	59	51	44	4th
1980–81	I	39	13	11	15	49	50	37	8th
1981–82	I	39	13	9	17	49	61	35	11th
1982–83	I	39	13	10	16	50	59	36	8th
1983–84	I	39	20	11	8	66	44	51	2nd
1984–85	Pr	36	6	7	23	29	64	19	9th
1985–86	I	39	16	11	12	59	52	43	6th
1986–87	I	44	23	7	14	67	52	53	3rd
1987–88	I	44	12	12	20	51	70	36	12th
1988–89	II	39	12	10	17	45	55	34	12th
1989–90	II	39	15	10	14	70	73	40	6th
1990–91	II	39	15	10	14	49	49	40	7th
1991–92	II	39	20	12	7	65	37	52	1st
1992–93	I	44	15	7	22	56	71	37	9th

The highest score in a Scottish Cup semi-final was achieved in 1882 when **Dumbarton** beat Cartvale 11–2.

DUNDEE

Year	Div	P	W	D	L	F	A	Pts	Pos
1893–94	I	18	6	3	9	43	58	15	8th
1894–95	I	18	6	2	10	28	33	14	8th
1895–96	I	18	7	2	9	33	42	16	5th
1896–97	I	18	10	2	6	38	30	22	5th
1897–98	I	18	5	3	10	29	36	13	7th
1898–99	I	18	1	2	15	23	65	4	10th
1899–1900	I	18	4	7	7	36	39	15	6th

Year	Div	P	W	D	L	F	A	Pts	Pos
1900–01	I	20	6	5	9	36	35	17	7th
1901–02	I	18	4	5	9	16	31	13	9th
1902–03	I	22	13	5	4	31	12	31	2nd
1903–04	I	26	13	2	11	54	45	28	5th
1904–05	I	26	10	5	11	38	32	25	7th
1905–06	I	30	11	12	7	40	33	34	7th
1906–07	I	34	18	12	4	53	26	48	2nd
1907–08	I	34	20	8	6	70	27	48	4th
1908–09	I	34	22	6	6	70	32	50	2nd
1909–10	I	34	14	8	12	52	44	36	6th
1910–11	I	34	18	5	11	54	42	41	6th
1911–12	I	34	13	9	12	52	41	35	8th
1912–13	I	34	8	13	13	33	46	29	14th
1913–14	I	38	19	5	14	64	53	43	7th
1914–15	I	38	12	9	17	43	61	33	15th
1915–16	SL	38	18	4	16	57	49	40	8th
1916–17	SL	38	13	4	21	58	71	30	16th
Withdrew from competition									
1919–20	SL	42	22	6	14	79	65	50	4th
1920–21	SL	42	19	11	12	54	48	49	4th
1921–22	I	42	19	11	12	57	40	49	4th
1922–23	I	38	17	7	14	51	45	41	7th
1923–24	I	38	15	13	10	70	57	43	5th
1924–25	I	38	14	8	16	48	55	36	8th
1925–26	I	38	14	9	15	47	59	37	10th
1926–27	I	38	17	9	12	77	51	43	5th
1927–28	I	38	14	7	17	65	80	35	14th
1928–29	I	38	9	11	18	58	68	29	18th
1929–30	I	38	14	6	18	51	58	34	14th
1930–31	I	38	17	5	16	65	63	39	8th
1931–32	I	38	14	10	14	61	72	38	11th
1932–33	I	38	12	9	17	58	74	33	15th
1933–34	I	38	15	6	17	68	64	36	12th
1934–35	I	38	16	8	14	63	63	40	8th
1935–36	I	38	11	10	17	67	80	32	13th
1936–37	I	38	12	15	11	58	69	39	9th
1937–38	I	38	13	6	19	70	74	32	19th
1938–39	II	34	15	7	12	99	63	37	6th
1939–46	Regional Leagues operating								
1946–47	B	26	21	3	2	113	30	45	1st
1947–48	A	30	15	3	12	67	51	33	4th
1948–49	A	30	20	5	5	71	48	45	2nd
1949–50	A	30	12	7	11	49	46	31	6th
1950–51	A	30	15	8	7	47	30	38	3rd
1951–52	A	30	11	6	13	53	52	28	8th
1952–53	A	30	9	11	8	44	37	29	7th
1953–54	A	30	14	6	10	46	47	34	7th
1954–55	A	30	13	4	13	48	48	30	8th
1955–56	A	34	12	6	16	56	65	30	13th
1956–57	I	34	13	6	15	55	61	32	10th
1957–58	I	34	13	5	16	49	65	31	11th
1958–59	I	34	16	9	9	61	51	41	4th
1959–60	I	34	16	10	8	70	49	42	4th
1960–61	I	34	13	6	15	61	53	32	10th
1961–62	I	34	25	4	5	80	46	54	1st
1962–63	I	34	12	9	13	60	49	33	9th
1963–64	I	34	20	5	9	94	50	45	6th

Year	Div	P	W	D	L	F	A	Pts	Pos
1964–65	I	34	15	10	9	86	63	40	6th
1965–66	I	34	14	6	14	61	61	34	9th
1966–67	I	34	16	9	9	74	51	41	6th
1967–68	I	34	13	7	14	62	59	33	9th
1968–69	I	34	10	12	12	47	48	32	9th
1969–70	I	34	15	6	13	49	44	36	6th
1970–71	I	34	14	10	10	53	45	38	5th
1971–72	I	34	14	13	7	59	38	41	5th
1972–73	I	34	17	9	8	68	43	43	5th
1973–74	I	34	16	7	11	67	48	39	5th
1974–75	I	34	16	6	12	48	42	38	6th
1975–76	Pr	36	11	10	15	49	62	32	9th
1976–77	I	39	21	9	9	90	55	51	3rd
1977–78	I	39	25	7	7	91	44	57	3rd
1978–79	I	39	24	7	8	68	36	55	1st
1979–80	Pr	36	10	6	20	47	73	26	9th
1980–81	I	39	22	8	9	64	40	52	2nd
1981–82	Pr	36	11	4	21	46	72	26	8th
1982–83	Pr	36	9	11	16	42	53	29	6th
1983–84	Pr	36	11	5	20	50	74	27	8th
1984–85	Pr	36	15	7	14	48	50	37	6th
1985–86	Pr	36	14	7	15	45	51	35	6th
1986–87	Pr	44	18	12	14	74	57	48	6th
1987–88	Pr	44	17	7	20	70	64	41	7th
1988–89	Pr	36	9	10	17	34	48	28	8th
1989–90	Pr	36	5	14	17	41	65	24	10th
1990–91	I	39	22	8	9	59	33	52	3rd
1991–92	I	44	23	12	9	80	48	58	1st
1992–93	Pr	44	11	12	21	48	68	34	10th

Dundee were fated to meet Celtic in the Scottish Cup during the 1970s with disastrous results. They lost seven times out of seven including five semi-finals: 1970 2–1 sf; 1972 4–0 qf; 1973 3–0 sf; 1974 1–0 sf; 1975 1–0 sf; 1977 2–0 sf; 1979 7–1 3rd round.

DUNDEE HIBERNIANS

Year	Div	P	W	D	L	F	A	Pts	Pos
1910–11	II	22	7	5	10	29	36	19	9th
1911–12	II	22	5	5	12	21	41	15	10th
1912–13	II	26	6	10	10	34	43	22	10th
1913–14	II	22	11	4	7	36	31	26	4th
1914–15	II	26	8	3	15	48	61	19	11th
1915–21	Regional Leagues								
1921–22	II	38	10	8	20	47	65	28	19th

DUNDEE UNITED

Year	Div	P	W	D	L	F	A	Pts	Pos
1923–24	II	38	12	15	11	41	41	39	9th
1924–25	II	38	20	10	8	58	44	50	1st
1925–26	I	38	11	6	21	52	74	28	17th
1926–27	I	38	13	9	16	55	69	35	14th
1927–28	I	38	14	8	16	66	67	36	11th
1928–29	I	38	14	10	14	57	70	38	9th
1929–30	I	38	6	7	25	48	96	19	20th

Year	Div	P	W	D	L	F	A	Pts	Pos
1930–31	II	38	18	6	14	76	64	42	6th
1931–32	II	38	6	7	25	40	118	19	19th
1932–33	II	34	14	4	16	65	67	32	13th
1933–34	II	34	10	4	20	81	88	24	17th
1934–35	II	34	18	6	10	105	65	42	4th
1935–36	II	34	16	5	13	108	81	37	7th
1936–37	II	34	9	9	16	72	97	27	14th
1937–38	II	34	9	5	20	69	104	23	14th
1938–39	II	34	15	3	16	78	69	33	9th
1939–46	Regional Leagues operating								
1946–47	B	26	9	4	13	53	60	22	10th
1947–48	B	30	10	2	18	58	88	22	15th
1948–49	B	30	10	7	13	60	67	27	8th
1949–50	B	30	14	5	11	74	56	33	7th
1950–51	B	30	16	4	10	78	58	36	4th
1951–52	B	30	16	5	9	75	60	37	4th
1952–53	B	30	12	5	13	52	56	29	8th
1953–54	B	30	8	6	16	54	79	22	15th
1954–55	B	30	8	6	16	55	70	22	13th
1955–56	B	36	12	14	10	78	65	38	8th
1956–57	II	36	14	6	16	75	80	34	13th
1957–58	II	36	12	9	15	81	77	33	9th
1958–59	II	36	9	7	20	62	86	25	17th
1959–60	II	36	22	6	8	90	45	50	2nd
1960–61	I	34	13	7	14	60	58	33	9th
1961–62	I	34	13	6	15	70	71	32	10th
1962–63	I	34	15	11	8	67	52	41	7th
1963–64	I	34	13	8	13	65	49	34	8th
1964–65	I	34	15	6	13	59	51	36	9th
1965–66	I	34	19	5	10	79	51	43	5th
1966–67	I	34	14	9	11	68	62	37	9th
1967–68	I	34	10	11	13	53	72	31	11th
1968–69	I	34	17	9	8	61	49	43	5th
1969–70	I	34	16	6	12	62	64	38	5th
1970–71	I	34	14	8	12	53	54	36	6th
1971–72	I	34	12	7	15	55	70	31	9th
1972–73	I	34	17	5	12	56	51	39	7th
1973–74	I	34	15	7	12	55	51	37	8th
1974–75	I	34	19	7	8	72	43	45	4th
1975–76	Pr	36	12	8	16	46	48	32	8th
1976–77	Pr	36	16	9	11	54	45	41	4th
1977–78	Pr	36	16	8	12	42	32	40	3rd
1978–79	Pr	36	18	8	10	56	37	44	3rd
1979–80	Pr	36	12	13	11	43	30	37	4th
1980–81	Pr	36	17	9	10	66	42	43	5th
1981–82	Pr	36	15	10	11	61	38	40	4th
1982–83	Pr	36	24	8	4	90	35	56	1st
1983–84	Pr	36	18	11	7	67	39	47	3rd
1984–85	Pr	36	20	7	9	67	33	47	3rd
1985–86	Pr	36	18	11	7	59	31	47	3rd
1986–87	Pr	44	24	12	8	66	36	60	3rd
1987–88	Pr	44	16	15	13	54	47	47	5th
1988–89	Pr	36	16	12	8	44	26	44	4th
1989–90	Pr	36	11	13	12	36	39	35	4th
1990–91	Pr	36	17	7	12	41	29	41	4th
1991–92	Pr	44	19	13	12	66	50	51	4th
1992–93	Pr	44	19	9	16	56	49	47	4th

Dundee United scored 42 goals in six consecutive matches during the period between 7 March and 13 April 1936: Edinburgh City 6–3, Cowdenbeath 6–1, Stenhousemuir 6–1, Leith Athletic 8–2, Forfar Athletic 4–3 and East Stirling 12–1.

DUNDEE WANDERERS

Year	Div	P	W	D	L	F	A	Pts	Pos
1894–95	II	17	3	1	13	44	86	9	9th

The brief sojourn in the Scottish League enjoyed by **Dundee Wanderers** was full of goalscoring both for and against. But their heaviest defeat was sustained on 1 December 1894 when they lost 15–1 to Airdrie.

DUNFERMLINE ATHLETIC

Year	Div	P	W	D	L	F	A	Pts	Pos
1912–13	II	26	13	7	6	45	27	33	2nd
1913–14	II	22	11	4	7	46	28	26	3rd
1914–15	II	26	13	2	11	45	39	28	6th
1915–21	Regional Leagues								
1921–22	II	38	14	10	14	56	42	38	8th
1922–23	II	38	11	11	16	47	44	33	13th
1923–24	II	38	14	11	13	52	45	39	7th
1924–25	II	38	14	7	17	62	57	35	13th
1925–26	II	38	26	7	5	109	43	59	1st
1926–27	I	38	10	8	20	53	85	28	18th
1927–28	I	38	4	4	30	41	126	12	20th
1928–29	II	36	13	7	16	66	72	33	11th
1929–30	II	38	16	6	16	99	85	38	10th
1930–31	II	38	20	7	11	83	50	47	3rd
1931–32	II	38	17	6	15	78	73	40	10th
1932–33	II	34	20	7	7	89	44	47	3rd
1933–34	II	34	20	4	10	90	52	44	2nd
1934–35	I	38	13	5	20	56	96	31	15th
1935–36	I	38	13	8	7	73	92	34	10th
1936–37	I	38	5	11	22	65	98	21	19th
1937–38	II	34	17	5	12	82	76	39	9th
1938–39	II	34	18	5	11	99	78	41	5th
1939–46	Regional Leagues operating								
1946–47	B	26	10	3	13	50	72	23	8th
1947–48	B	30	13	3	14	72	71	29	7th
1948–49	B	30	16	9	5	80	58	41	4th
1949–50	B	30	16	4	10	71	57	36	3rd
1950–51	B	30	12	4	14	58	73	28	10th
1951–52	B	30	15	2	13	74	65	32	6th
1952–53	B	30	9	9	12	51	58	27	11th
1953–54	B	30	11	9	10	48	57	31	8th
1954–55	B	30	19	4	7	72	40	42	2nd
1955–56	A	34	10	6	18	42	82	26	16th
1956–57	I	34	9	6	19	54	74	24	17th
1957–58	II	36	24	5	7	120	42	53	2nd
1958–59	I	34	10	8	16	68	87	28	16th
1959–60	I	34	10	9	15	72	80	29	13th
1960–61	I	34	12	7	15	65	81	31	12th
1961–62	I	34	19	5	10	77	46	43	4th
1962–63	I	34	13	8	13	50	47	34	8th
1963–64	I	34	18	9	7	64	33	45	5th
1964–65	I	34	22	5	7	83	36	49	3rd
1965–66	I	34	19	6	9	94	55	44	4th
1966–67	I	34	14	10	10	72	52	38	8th
1967–68	I	34	17	5	12	64	41	39	4th
1968–69	I	34	19	7	8	63	45	45	3rd
1969–70	I	34	15	5	14	45	45	35	9th
1970–71	I	34	6	11	17	44	56	23	16th
1971–72	I	34	7	9	18	31	50	23	18th
1972–73	II	36	23	6	7	95	32	52	2nd
1973–74	I	34	8	8	18	43	65	24	16th
1974–75	I	34	7	9	18	46	66	23	15th
1975–76	I	26	5	10	11	30	51	20	13th
1976–77	II	39	20	10	9	52	36	50	3rd
1977–78	II	39	18	12	9	64	41	48	3rd
1978–79	II	39	19	14	6	66	40	52	2nd
1979–80	I	39	11	13	15	39	57	35	10th
1980–81	I	39	10	7	22	41	58	27	12th
1981–82	I	39	11	14	14	46	56	36	10th
1982–83	I	39	7	17	15	39	69	31	13th
1983–84	II	39	13	10	16	44	45	36	9th
1984–85	II	39	17	15	7	61	36	49	3rd
1985–86	II	39	23	11	5	91	47	57	1st
1986–87	I	44	23	10	11	61	41	56	2nd
1987–88	Pr	44	8	10	26	41	84	26	11th
1988–89	I	39	22	10	7	60	36	54	1st
1989–90	Pr	36	11	8	17	37	50	30	8th
1990–91	Pr	36	8	11	17	38	61	27	8th
1991–92	Pr	44	4	10	30	22	80	18	12th
1992–93	I	44	22	8	14	64	47	52	3rd

In 1925–26, **Dunfermline Athletic** scored 109 goals in the Scottish Division Two, beating the previous total of Falkirk's by four goals.

EAST FIFE

Year	Div	P	W	D	L	F	A	Pts	Pos
1921–22	II	38	15	7	16	55	54	37	12th
1922–23	II	38	16	7	15	48	42	39	9th
1923–24	II	38	14	9	15	54	47	37	12th
1924–25	II	38	17	5	16	66	58	39	9th
1925–26	II	38	20	9	9	98	73	49	4th
1926–27	II	38	19	4	15	103	91	42	6th
1927–28	II	38	18	7	13	87	73	43	4th
1928–29	II	35	15	6	14	88	77	36	8th
1929–30	II	38	26	5	7	114	58	57	2nd
1930–31	I	38	8	4	26	45	113	20	20th
1931–32	II	38	18	5	15	107	77	41	8th
1932–33	II	34	15	4	15	85	71	34	7th
1933–34	II	34	12	8	14	71	76	32	13th

Year	Div	P	W	D	L	F	A	Pts	Pos
1934–35	II	34	16	3	15	79	73	35	9th
1935–36	II	34	16	6	12	86	79	38	6th
1936–37	II	34	15	8	11	76	51	38	5th
1937–38	II	34	19	5	10	104	61	43	5th
1938–39	II	34	21	6	7	99	61	48	3rd
1939–46	Regional Leagues operating								
1946–47	B	26	12	7	7	58	39	31	3rd
1947–48	B	30	25	3	2	103	36	53	1st
1948–49	A	30	16	3	11	64	46	35	4th
1949–50	A	30	15	7	8	58	43	37	4th
1950–51	A	30	10	8	12	48	66	28	10th
1951–52	A	30	17	3	10	71	49	37	3rd
1952–53	A	30	16	7	7	72	48	39	3rd
1953–54	A	30	13	8	9	55	45	34	6th
1954–55	A	30	9	6	15	51	62	24	11th
1955–56	A	34	13	5	16	61	69	31	12th
1956–57	I	34	10	6	18	59	82	26	15th
1957–58	I	34	10	3	21	45	88	23	17th
1958–59	II	36	15	8	13	83	81	38	8th
1959–60	II	36	7	6	23	50	87	20	18th
1960–61	II	36	14	4	18	70	80	32	13th
1961–62	II	36	15	7	14	60	59	37	10th
1962–63	II	36	15	6	15	60	69	36	11th
1963–64	II	36	16	13	7	92	57	45	4th
1964–65	II	36	15	7	14	78	77	37	9th
1965–66	II	36	20	4	12	72	55	44	4th
1966–67	II	38	19	4	15	70	63	42	5th
1967–68	II	36	21	7	8	71	47	49	3rd
1968–69	II	36	21	6	9	82	45	48	3rd
1969–70	II	36	15	4	17	59	63	34	10th
1970–71	II	36	22	7	7	86	44	51	2nd
1971–72	I	34	5	15	14	34	61	25	16th
1972–73	I	34	11	8	15	46	54	30	9th
1973–74	I	34	9	6	19	26	51	24	17th
1974–75	II	38	20	7	11	57	42	47	5th
1975–76	I	26	8	7	11	39	53	23	12th
1976–77	I	39	8	13	18	40	71	29	12th
1977–78	I	39	4	11	24	39	74	19	14th
1978–79	II	39	17	9	13	64	53	43	4th
1979–80	II	39	12	9	18	45	57	33	10th
1980–81	II	39	10	15	14	44	53	35	11th
1981–82	II	39	14	9	16	48	51	37	7th
1982–83	II	39	16	11	12	68	43	43	6th
1983–84	II	39	20	7	12	57	42	47	2nd
1984–85	I	39	12	12	15	55	56	36	10th
1985–86	I	39	14	15	10	54	46	43	5th
1986–87	I	44	15	21	8	68	55	51	4th
1987–88	I	44	13	10	21	61	76	36	11th
1988–89	II	39	14	13	12	56	55	41	5th
1989–90	II	39	12	12	15	60	63	36	9th
1990–91	II	39	14	9	16	57	65	37	10th
1991–92	II	39	19	11	9	72	57	49	4th
1992–93	II	39	14	10	15	70	64	38	9th

On 7 January 1991, **East Fife** beat Inverness Thistle 1–0 in a replayed Scottish Cup second round tie after a 1–1 draw. It was the first time they had failed to beat a non-league team at the first time of asking in the competition.

EAST STIRLINGSHIRE

Year	Div	P	W	D	L	F	A	Pts	Pos
1900–01	II	18	7	4	7	35	39	18	7th
1901–02	II	22	8	3	11	36	46	19	9th
1902–03	II	22	9	3	10	46	41	21	8th
1903–04	II	22	8	5	9	35	40	21	6th
1904–05	II	22	7	5	10	38	38	19	9th
1905–06	II	22	1	10	11	26	47	12	12th
1906–07	II	22	6	4	12	37	48	16	11th
1907–08	II	22	9	5	8	30	32	23	5th
1908–09	II	22	9	3	10	28	34	21	9th
1909–10	II	22	9	2	11	38	43	20	8th
1910–11	II	22	7	6	9	28	35	20	7th
1911–12	II	22	7	3	12	21	31	17	9th
1912–13	II	26	12	8	6	43	27	32	3rd
1913–14	II	22	7	8	7	40	36	22	8th
1914–15	II	26	13	5	8	53	46	31	4th
1915–21	Regional Leagues								
1921–22	II	38	12	10	16	43	60	34	15th
1922–23	II	38	10	8	20	48	69	28	19th
1923–24	Did not compete								
1924–25	II	38	11	8	19	58	72	30	18th
1925–26	II	38	10	7	21	59	89	27	18th
1926–27	II	38	18	8	12	93	75	44	5th
1927–28	II	38	14	10	14	84	76	38	9th
1928–29	II	36	14	4	18	71	75	32	12th
1929–30	II	38	16	4	18	83	75	36	12th
1930–31	II	38	17	7	14	85	74	41	7th
1931–32	II	38	26	3	9	111	55	55	1st
1932–33	I	38	7	3	28	55	115	17	20th
1933–34	II	34	14	7	13	65	74	35	9th
1934–35	II	34	11	7	16	57	76	29	14th
1935–36	II	34	13	8	13	70	75	34	8th
1936–37	II	34	18	2	14	81	78	38	7th
1937–38	II	34	9	7	18	55	95	25	13th
1938–39	II	34	9	4	21	89	130	22	17th
1939–46	Regional Leagues operating								
1946–48	C Division								
1948–49	B	30	6	6	18	38	67	18	16th
1949–55	C Division								
1955–56	B	36	9	10	17	66	94	28	16th
1956–57	II	36	5	7	24	56	121	17	19th
1957–58	II	36	12	5	19	55	79	29	15th
1958–59	II	36	10	8	18	50	77	28	15th
1959–60	II	36	10	8	18	68	82	28	15th
1960–61	II	36	9	7	20	59	100	25	16th
1961–62	II	36	15	4	17	70	81	34	11th
1962–63	II	36	20	9	7	80	50	49	2nd
1963–64	I	34	5	2	27	37	91	12	18th
1964–65*	II	36	15	10	11	64	50	40	5th
1965–66	II	36	9	5	22	59	91	23	17th
1966–67	II	38	7	10	21	44	87	24	19th
1967–68	II	36	9	10	17	61	74	28	15th
1968–69	II	36	17	5	14	70	62	39	9th
1969–70	II	36	14	5	17	58	75	33	12th
1970–71	II	36	9	9	18	57	86	27	17th
1971–72	II	36	17	7	12	60	58	41	8th

Year	Div	P	W	D	L	F	A	Pts	Pos
1972–73	II	36	12	8	16	52	69	32	13th
1973–74	II	36	9	5	22	47	73	23	16th
1974–75	II	38	16	8	14	56	52	40	9th
1975–76	II	26	8	8	10	33	33	24	8th
1976–77	II	39	12	8	19	47	63	32	10th
1977–78	II	39	15	8	16	55	65	38	9th
1978–79	II	39	12	8	19	61	87	32	12th
1979–80	II	39	21	7	11	55	40	49	2nd
1980–81	I	39	6	17	16	41	56	29	11th
1981–82	I	39	7	10	22	38	77	24	13th
1982–83	II	39	7	9	23	41	79	23	13th
1983–84	II	39	10	11	18	51	66	31	11th
1984–85	II	39	8	15	16	38	53	31	12th
1985–86	II	39	11	6	22	49	69	28	11th
1986–87	II	39	6	11	22	33	56	23	13th
1987–88	II	39	15	13	11	51	47	43	6th
1988–89	II	39	13	11	15	54	58	37	9th
1989–90	II	39	8	10	21	34	66	26	14th
1990–91	II	39	9	11	19	36	71	29	13th
1991–92	II	39	15	11	13	61	70	41	6th
1992–93	II	39	8	9	22	50	85	25	13th

East Stirling won the C Division of the Scottish League in 1947–48 losing just one game in dropping five points. They were promoted to Division B.

EDINBURGH CITY

Year	Div	P	W	D	L	F	A	Pts	Pos
1931–32	II	38	5	7	26	78	146	17	20th
1932–33	II	34	4	4	26	39	133	12	18th
1933–34	II	34	4	6	24	37	111	14	18th
1934–35	II	34	3	2	29	45	134	8	18th
1935–36	II	34	8	9	17	57	83	25	15th
1936–37	II	34	2	3	29	42	120	7	18th
1937–38	II	34	7	3	24	77	135	17	17th
1938–39	II	34	6	4	24	58	119	16	18th
1939–46	Regional Leagues operating								
1946–49	C Division								

When **Edinburgh City** drew 4–4 with Forfar Athletic on 28 August 1937 in a Division Two match the crowd of 500 included the Earl of Strathmore.

FALKIRK

Year	Div	P	W	D	L	F	A	Pts	Pos
1902–03	II	22	8	7	7	39	37	23	7th
1903–04	II	22	11	4	7	50	34	26	4th
1904–05	II	22	12	4	6	31	25	28	2nd
1905–06	I	30	9	5	16	52	68	23	13th
1906–07	I	34	17	7	10	73	58	41	5th
1907–08	I	34	22	7	5	102	40	51	2nd
1908–09	I	34	13	7	14	58	56	33	9th
1909–10	I	34	22	8	4	71	28	52	2nd
1910–11	I	34	17	10	7	65	42	44	3rd
1911–12	I	34	15	6	13	46	43	36	7th
1912–13	I	34	14	12	8	56	38	40	6th
1913–14	I	38	20	9	9	69	51	49	5th
1914–15	I	38	16	7	15	48	48	39	6th
1915–16	SL	38	12	9	17	45	61	33	12th
1916–17	SL	38	12	10	16	57	57	34	12th
1917–18	SL	34	9	9	16	38	58	27	14th
1918–19	SL	34	6	8	20	46	72	20	16th
1919–20	SL	42	10	11	21	45	74	31	20th
1920–21	SL	42	11	12	19	54	72	34	18th
1921–22	I	42	16	17	9	48	38	49	5th
1922–23	I	38	14	17	7	44	32	45	4th
1923–24	I	38	13	6	19	46	53	32	15th
1924–25	I	38	12	8	18	44	54	32	16th
1925–26	I	38	14	14	10	61	57	42	8th
1926–27	I	38	16	10	12	77	60	42	6th
1927–28	I	38	16	5	17	76	69	37	10th
1928–29	I	38	14	8	16	68	86	36	11th
1929–30	I	38	16	9	13	62	64	41	7th
1930–31	I	38	14	4	20	77	87	32	14th
1931–32	I	38	11	5	22	70	76	27	18th
1932–33	I	38	15	6	17	70	70	36	11th
1933–34	I	38	16	6	16	73	68	38	10th
1934–35	I	38	9	6	23	58	82	24	20th
1935–36	II	34	28	3	3	132	34	59	1st
1936–37	I	38	19	6	13	98	66	44	7th
1937–38	I	38	19	9	10	82	52	47	4th
1938–39	I	38	19	7	12	73	63	45	5th
1939–46	Regional Leagues operating								
1946–47	A	30	8	10	12	62	61	26	11th
1947–48	A	30	10	10	10	55	48	30	7th
1948–49	A	30	12	8	10	70	54	32	5th
1949–50	A	30	7	10	13	48	72	24	14th
1950–51	A	30	7	4	19	35	81	18	16th
1951–52	B	30	18	7	5	80	34	43	2nd
1952–53	A	30	11	4	15	53	63	26	13th
1953–54	A	30	9	7	14	47	61	25	13th
1954–55	A	30	8	8	14	42	54	24	12th
1955–56	A	34	11	6	17	58	75	28	14th
1956–57	I	34	10	8	16	51	70	28	14th
1957–58	I	34	11	9	14	64	82	31	10th
1958–59	I	34	10	7	17	58	79	27	17th
1959–60	II	36	15	9	12	77	43	39	8th
1960–61	II	36	24	6	6	100	40	54	2nd
1961–62	I	34	11	4	19	45	68	26	14th
1962–63	I	34	12	3	19	54	69	27	13th
1963–64	I	34	11	6	17	54	84	28	14th
1964–65	I	34	7	7	20	43	85	21	16th
1965–66	I	34	15	1	18	48	72	31	10th
1966–67	I	34	11	4	19	33	70	26	14th
1967–68	I	34	7	12	15	36	50	26	15th
1968–69	I	34	5	8	21	33	69	18	17th
1969–70	II	36	25	6	5	94	34	56	1st
1970–71	I	34	13	9	12	46	53	35	7th
1971–72	I	34	10	7	17	44	60	27	14th
1972–73	I	34	7	12	15	38	56	26	14th

Year	Div	P	W	D	L	F	A	Pts	Pos
1973–74	I	34	4	14	16	33	58	22	18th
1974–75	II	38	26	2	10	76	29	54	1st
1975–76	I	26	10	5	11	38	35	25	8th
1976–77	I	39	6	8	25	36	85	20	14th
1977–78	II	39	15	14	10	51	46	44	5th
1978–79	II	39	19	12	8	66	37	50	3rd
1979–80	II	39	19	12	8	65	35	50	1st
1980–81	I	39	13	8	18	39	52	34	9th
1981–82	I	39	11	14	14	49	52	36	9th
1982–83	I	39	15	6	18	45	55	36	8th
1983–84	I	39	16	6	17	46	54	38	7th
1984–85	I	39	19	7	13	65	54	45	3rd
1985–86	I	39	17	11	11	57	39	45	2nd
1986–87	Pr	44	8	10	26	31	70	26	10th
1987–88	Pr	44	10	11	23	41	75	31	10th
1988–89	I	39	22	8	9	71	37	52	2nd
1989–90	I	39	14	15	10	59	46	43	4th
1990–91	I	39	21	12	6	70	35	54	1st
1991–92	Pr	44	12	11	21	54	73	35	9th
1992–93	Pr	44	11	7	26	60	86	29	11th

Despite being born in Lancashire, Jocky Simpson was brought up in Scotland and played for Laurieston Juniors and Scotland Boys. He joined **Falkirk** in 1904–05 and was capped eight times by England while with Blackburn Rovers as an outside-right.

FORFAR ATHLETIC

Year	Div	P	W	D	L	F	A	Pts	Pos
1921–22	II	38	11	12	15	44	53	34	14th
1922–23	II	38	13	7	18	51	73	33	15th
1923–24	II	38	14	7	17	43	68	35	14th
1924–25	II	38	10	7	21	46	67	27	20th
1925–26	Did not compete								
1926–27	II	38	15	7	16	66	79	37	9th
1927–28	II	38	18	7	13	83	73	43	5th
1928–29	II	35	14	10	11	69	75	38	7th
1929–30	II	38	18	5	15	98	95	41	8th
1930–31	II	38	15	6	17	78	83	36	12th
1931–32	II	38	19	7	12	90	79	45	6th
1932–33	II	34	12	4	18	68	87	28	14th
1933–34	II	34	13	7	14	77	71	33	11th
1934–35	II	34	13	8	13	77	73	34	11th
1935–36	II	34	10	7	17	60	81	27	13th
1936–37	II	34	11	8	15	73	89	30	12th
1937–38	II	34	8	6	20	67	100	22	15th
1938–39	II	34	11	3	20	74	18	25	15th
1939–46	Regional Leagues operating								
1946–49	C Division								
1949–50	B	30	11	8	11	53	56	30	10th
1950–51	B	30	9	3	18	43	76	21	14th
1951–52	B	30	10	4	16	59	97	24	12th
1952–53	B	30	8	4	18	54	88	20	15th
1953–54	B	30	10	4	16	38	69	24	12th
1954–55	B	30	11	6	13	63	80	28	10th
1955–56	B	36	10	9	17	62	79	25	15th
1956–57	II	36	9	5	22	75	100	23	16th
1957–58	II	36	13	6	17	70	71	32	12th
1958–59	II	36	12	9	15	73	87	33	12th
1959–60	II	36	10	8	18	53	84	28	16th
1960–61	II	36	10	4	22	65	98	24	18th
1961–62	II	36	11	8	17	68	76	30	16th
1962–63	II	36	9	5	22	73	99	23	18th
1963–64	II	36	8	22	57	104	20	18th
1964–65	II	36	9	7	20	63	89	25	17th
1965–66	II	36	7	3	26	61	120	17	19th
1966–67	II	38	12	3	23	74	106	27	16th
1967–68	II	36	14	10	12	57	63	38	7th
1968–69	II	36	18	7	11	71	56	47	6th
1969–70	II	36	11	1	24	55	83	23	18th
1970–71	II	36	9	11	16	63	75	29	15th
1971–72	II	36	6	9	21	32	84	21	17th
1972–73	II	36	10	9	17	38	66	29	16th
1973–74	II	36	5	6	25	42	94	16	18th
1974–75	II	38	1	7	30	27	102	9	20th
1975–76	II	26	4	10	12	28	48	18	12th
1976–77	II	39	7	10	22	43	68	24	14th
1977–78	II	39	17	8	14	61	55	42	6th
1978–79	II	39	13	12	14	55	52	38	8th
1979–80	II	39	19	8	12	63	51	46	3rd
1980–81	II	39	17	9	13	63	57	43	5th
1981–82	II	39	15	15	9	59	35	45	6th
1982–83	II	39	18	12	9	58	38	48	4th
1983–84	II	39	27	9	3	73	31	63	1st
1984–85	I	39	14	13	12	54	49	41	6th
1985–86	I	39	17	10	12	51	43	44	4th
1986–87	I	44	14	15	15	61	63	43	7th
1987–88	I	44	16	16	12	67	58	48	4th
1988–89	I	39	10	16	13	52	56	36	9th
1989–90	I	39	8	15	16	51	65	29	12th
1990–91	I	39	9	15	15	50	57	33	10th
1991–92	I	44	5	12	27	36	85	22	12th
1992–93	II	39	18	10	11	74	54	46	4th

In 1988–89 **Forfar Athletic** goalkeeper Stewart Kennedy was chosen as Player of the Year by the club's supporters. He was in his 40th year.

HAMILTON ACADEMICAL

Year	Div	P	W	D	L	F	A	Pts	Pos
1897–98	II	18	5	2	11	28	51	12	9th
1898–99	II	18	7	1	10	48	58	15	5th
1899–1900	II	18	7	1	10	33	46	15	7th
1900–01	II	18	4	4	10	44	51	12	9th
1901–02	II	22	11	3	8	45	40	25	5th
1902–03	II	22	11	1	10	44	35	23	6th
1903–04	II	22	16	5	1	56	19	37	1st
1904–05	II	22	12	3	7	40	22	27	3rd
1905–06	II	22	12	2	8	45	34	26	4th
1906–07	I	34	8	5	21	40	64	21	16th

Year	Div	P	W	D	L	F	A	Pts	Pos
1907–08	I	34	10	8	16	54	65	28	11th
1908–09	I	34	6	12	16	42	72	24	16th
1909–10	I	34	11	6	17	50	67	28	15th
1910–11	I	34	8	5	21	31	60	21	16th
1911–12	I	34	11	8	15	32	44	30	12th
1912–13	I	34	12	8	14	44	47	32	10th
1913–14	I	38	11	6	21	46	65	28	18th
1914–15	I	38	16	6	16	60	55	38	7th
1915–16	SL	38	19	3	16	68	76	41	7th
1916–17	SL	38	13	9	16	54	73	35	11th
1917–18	SL	34	11	6	17	52	63	28	12th
1918–19	SL	34	11	5	18	49	75	27	14th
1919–20	SL	42	11	7	24	56	86	29	21st
1920–21	SL	42	14	12	16	44	57	40	15th
1921–22	I	42	9	16	17	51	62	34	18th
1922–23	I	38	11	7	20	43	59	29	18th
1923–24	I	38	15	6	17	52	57	36	12th
1924–25	I	38	15	3	20	50	63	33	13th
1925–26	I	38	13	9	16	68	79	35	12th
1926–27	I	38	13	9	16	60	85	35	15th
1927–28	I	38	11	6	21	67	86	28	18th
1928–29	I	38	13	9	16	58	83	35	12th
1929–30	I	38	14	7	17	76	81	35	13th
1930–31	I	38	16	5	17	59	57	37	10th
1931–32	I	38	16	6	16	84	65	38	10th
1932–33	I	38	18	6	14	92	78	42	8th
1933–34	I	38	15	8	15	65	79	38	11th
1934–35	I	38	19	10	9	87	67	48	4th
1935–36	I	38	15	7	16	77	74	37	6th
1936–37	I	38	18	5	15	91	96	41	8th
1937–38	I	38	13	7	18	81	76	33	13th
1938–39	I	38	18	5	15	67	71	41	7th
1939–46	Regional Leagues operating								
1946–47	A	30	2	7	21	38	85	11	16th
1947–48	B	30	17	6	7	75	45	40	3rd
1948–49	B	30	9	8	13	48	57	26	10th
1949–50	B	30	14	6	10	57	44	34	6th
1950–51	B	30	12	8	10	65	49	32	7th
1951–52	B	30	12	6	12	47	51	30	9th
1952–53	B	30	20	3	7	72	40	43	2nd
1953–54	A	30	4	3	23	29	94	11	16th
1954–55	B	30	17	5	8	74	51	39	3rd
1955–56	B	36	13	7	16	86	84	33	11th
1956–57	II	36	14	8	14	69	68	36	11th
1957–58	II	36	12	9	15	70	79	33	10th
1958–59	II	36	15	8	13	76	62	38	7th
1959–60	II	36	21	6	9	91	62	48	4th
1960–61	II	36	17	7	12	84	80	41	6th
1961–62	II	36	14	5	17	78	79	33	13th
1962–63	II	36	18	8	10	69	56	44	4th
1963–64	II	36	12	6	18	65	81	30	13th
1964–65	II	36	21	8	7	86	53	50	2nd
1965–66	I	34	3	2	29	27	117	8	18th
1966–67	II	38	18	8	12	74	60	44	4th
1967–68	II	36	13	7	16	49	58	33	11th
1968–69	II	36	8	8	20	37	72	24	15th
1969–70	II	36	8	4	24	42	92	20	19th
1970–71	II	36	8	7	21	50	79	23	18th
1971–72	II	36	4	8	24	31	93	16	19th
1972–73	II	36	16	6	14	67	63	38	8th
1973–74	II	36	24	7	5	68	38	55	3rd
1974–75	II	38	21	7	10	69	30	49	4th
1975–76	I	26	7	10	9	37	37	24	9th
1976–77	I	39	11	10	18	44	59	32	10th
1977–78	I	39	12	12	15	54	56	36	7th
1978–79	I	39	17	9	13	62	60	43	5th
1979–80	I	30	15	10	14	60	59	40	7th
1980–81	I	39	15	7	17	61	57	37	7th
1981–82	I	39	16	8	15	52	49	40	7th
1982–83	I	39	11	12	16	54	66	34	11th
1983–84	I	39	11	14	14	43	46	36	9th
1984–85	I	39	16	11	12	48	49	43	4th
1985–86	I	39	24	8	7	77	44	56	1st
1986–87	Pr	44	6	9	29	39	93	21	12th
1987–88	I	44	22	12	10	67	39	56	1st
1988–89	Pr	36	6	2	28	19	76	14	10th
1989–90	I	39	14	13	12	52	53	41	6th
1990–91	I	39	16	10	13	50	41	42	6th
1991–92	I	44	22	13	9	72	48	57	3rd
1992–93	I	44	19	12	13	65	45	50	5th

During the big freeze of 1963, **Hamilton Academical** played six home games during January and February while most other clubs were idle. In 1979 during similar wintry conditions they managed three at Douglas Park, which is situated in a hollow.

HEART OF MIDLOTHIAN

Year	Div	P	W	D	L	F	A	Pts	Pos
1890–91	SL	18	6	2	10	31	37	14	6th
1891–92	SL	22	15	4	3	65	35	34	3rd
1892–93	SL	18	8	2	8	39	42	18	5th
1893–94	I	18	11	4	3	46	32	26	2nd
1894–95	I	18	15	1	2	50	18	31	1st
1895–96	I	18	11	0	7	68	36	22	4th
1896–97	I	18	13	2	3	47	22	28	1st
1897–98	I	18	8	4	6	54	33	20	4th
1898–99	I	18	12	2	4	56	30	26	2nd
1899–1900	I	18	10	3	5	41	24	23	4th
1900–01	I	20	5	4	11	22	30	14	10th
1901–02	I	18	10	2	6	32	21	22	3rd
1902–03	I	22	11	6	5	46	27	28	4th
1903–04	I	26	18	3	5	62	34	39	2nd
1904–05	I	26	11	3	12	46	44	25	8th
1905–06	I	30	18	7	5	64	27	43	2nd
1906–07	I	34	11	13	10	47	43	35	9th
1907–08	I	34	11	6	17	50	62	28	12th
1908–09	I	34	12	8	14	54	49	32	12th
1909–10	I	34	12	7	15	59	50	31	12th
1910–11	I	34	8	8	18	42	59	24	14th
1911–12	I	34	16	8	10	54	40	40	4th
1912–13	I	34	17	7	10	71	43	41	3rd

1913–14	I	38	23	8	7	70	29	54	3rd
1914–15	I	38	27	7	4	83	32	61	2nd
1915–16	SL	37	20	6	11	66	45	46	6th
1916–17	SL	38	14	4	20	44	59	32	14th
1917–18	SL	34	14	4	16	41	58	32	10th
1918–19	SL	34	14	9	11	59	52	37	6th
1919–20	SL	42	14	9	19	57	72	37	16th
1920–21	SL	42	20	10	12	74	49	50	3rd
1921–22	I	42	11	10	21	50	60	32	19th
1922–23	I	38	11	15	12	51	50	37	12th
1923–24	I	38	14	10	14	61	50	38	9th
1924–25	I	38	12	11	15	65	69	35	10th
1925–26	I	38	21	8	9	87	56	50	3rd
1926–27	I	38	12	11	15	65	64	35	13th
1927–28	I	38	20	7	11	89	50	47	4th
1928–29	I	38	19	9	10	91	57	47	4th
1929–30	I	38	14	9	15	69	69	37	10th
1930–31	I	38	19	6	13	90	63	44	5th
1931–32	I	38	17	5	16	63	61	39	8th
1932–33	I	38	21	8	9	84	51	50	3rd
1933–34	I	38	17	10	11	86	59	44	6th
1934–35	I	38	20	10	8	87	51	50	3rd
1935–36	I	38	20	7	11	88	55	47	5th
1936–37	I	38	24	3	11	99	60	51	5th
1937–38	I	38	26	6	6	90	50	58	2nd
1938–39	I	38	20	5	13	98	70	45	4th
1939–46	Regional Leagues operating								
1946–47	A	30	16	6	8	52	43	38	4th
1947–48	A	30	10	8	12	37	42	28	9th
1948–49	A	30	12	6	12	64	54	30	8th
1949–50	A	30	20	3	7	86	40	43	3rd
1950–51	A	30	16	5	9	72	45	37	4th
1951–52	A	30	14	7	9	69	53	35	4th
1952–53	A	30	12	6	12	59	50	30	4th
1953–54	A	30	16	6	8	70	45	38	2nd
1954–55	A	30	16	7	7	74	45	39	4th
1955–56	A	34	19	7	8	99	47	45	3rd
1956–57	I	34	24	5	5	81	48	53	2nd
1957–58	I	34	29	4	1	132	29	62	1st
1958–59	I	34	21	6	7	92	51	48	2nd
1959–60	I	34	23	8	3	102	51	54	1st
1960–61	I	34	13	8	13	51	53	34	7th
1961–62	I	34	16	6	12	54	49	38	6th
1962–63	I	34	17	9	8	85	59	43	5th
1963–64	I	34	19	9	6	74	40	47	4th
1964–65	I	34	22	6	6	90	49	50	2nd
1965–66	I	34	13	12	9	56	48	38	7th
1966–67	I	34	11	8	15	39	48	30	11th
1967–68	I	34	13	4	17	56	61	30	12th
1968–69	I	34	14	8	12	52	54	36	8th
1969–70	I	34	13	12	9	50	36	38	4th
1970–71	I	34	13	7	14	41	40	33	11th
1971–72	I	34	13	13	8	53	49	39	6th
1972–73	I	34	12	6	16	39	50	30	10th
1973–74	I	34	14	10	10	54	43	38	6th
1974–75	I	34	11	13	10	47	52	35	8th
1975–76	Pr	36	13	9	14	39	45	35	5th
1976–77	Pr	36	7	13	16	49	66	27	9th
1977–78	I	39	24	10	5	77	42	58	2nd
1978–79	Pr	36	8	7	21	49	71	23	9th
1979–80	I	39	20	13	6	58	39	53	1st
1980–81	Pr	36	6	6	24	27	71	18	10th
1981–82	I	39	21	8	10	65	37	50	3rd
1982–83	I	39	22	10	7	79	38	54	2nd
1983–84	Pr	36	10	16	10	38	47	36	5th
1984–85	Pr	36	13	5	18	47	64	31	7th
1985–86	Pr	36	20	10	6	59	33	50	2nd
1986–87	Pr	44	21	14	9	64	43	56	5th
1987–88	Pr	44	23	16	5	74	32	62	2nd
1988–89	Pr	36	9	13	14	35	42	31	6th
1989–90	Pr	36	16	12	8	54	35	44	3rd
1990–91	Pr	36	14	7	15	48	55	35	5th
1991–92	Pr	44	27	9	8	60	37	63	2nd
1992–93	Pr	44	15	14	15	46	51	44	5th

In 1957–58, **Hearts** had the greatest goal difference achieved by any first-class club in either England or Scotland, finishing their League programme by scoring 132 goals and conceding just 29.

HIBERNIAN

Year	Div	P	W	D	L	F	A	Pts	Pos
1893–94	II	18	13	3	2	83	29	29	1st
1894–95	II	18	14	2	2	92	27	30	1st
1895–96	I	18	11	2	5	58	39	24	3rd
1896–97	I	18	12	2	4	50	20	26	2nd
1897–98	I	18	10	2	6	48	28	22	3rd
1898–99	I	18	10	3	5	42	43	23	4th
1899–1900	I	18	9	6	3	43	24	24	3rd
1900–01	I	20	9	7	4	29	22	25	3rd
1901–02	I	18	6	4	8	36	24	16	6th
1902–03	I	22	16	5	1	48	18	37	1st
1903–04	I	26	7	5	14	29	40	19	10th
1904–05	I	26	9	8	9	39	39	26	5th
1905–06	I	30	10	5	15	35	40	25	11th
1906–07	I	34	10	10	14	40	49	30	12th
1907–08	I	34	17	8	9	55	42	42	5th
1908–09	I	34	16	7	11	40	32	39	6th
1909–10	I	34	14	6	14	33	40	34	8th
1910–11	I	34	15	6	13	44	48	36	9th
1911–12	I	34	12	5	17	44	47	29	13th
1912–13	I	34	16	5	13	63	54	37	6th
1913–14	I	38	12	6	20	58	75	30	13th
1914–15	I	38	12	11	15	59	66	35	11th
1915–16	SL	38	9	7	22	44	70	25	19th
1916–17	SL	38	10	10	18	57	72	30	17th
1917–18	SL	34	8	9	17	42	57	25	16th
1918–19	SL	34	5	4	25	28	87	14	18th
1919–20	SL	42	13	7	22	60	79	33	18th
1920–21	SL	42	16	9	17	58	57	41	13th
1921–22	I	42	16	14	12	55	44	46	7th
1922–23	I	38	17	7	14	45	40	41	8th

Year	Div	P	W	D	L	F	A	Pts	Pos
1923–24	I	38	15	11	12	66	52	41	7th
1924–25	I	38	22	8	8	78	43	52	3rd
1925–26	I	38	12	6	20	72	77	30	16th
1926–27	I	38	16	7	15	62	71	39	9th
1927–28	I	38	13	9	16	73	75	35	12th
1928–29	I	38	13	6	19	54	62	32	14th
1929–30	I	38	9	11	18	45	62	29	17th
1930–31	I	38	9	7	22	49	81	25	19th
1931–32	II	38	18	8	12	73	52	44	7th
1932–33	II	34	25	4	5	80	29	54	1st
1933–34	I	38	12	3	23	51	69	27	16th
1934–35	I	38	14	8	16	59	70	36	11th
1935–36	I	38	11	7	20	56	82	29	17th
1936–37	I	38	6	13	19	54	83	25	17th
1937–38	I	38	11	13	14	57	65	35	10th
1938–39	I	38	14	7	17	68	69	35	13th
1939–46	Regional Leagues operating								
1946–47	A	30	19	6	5	69	33	44	2nd
1947–48	A	30	22	4	4	86	27	48	1st
1948–49	A	30	17	5	8	75	52	39	3rd
1949–50	A	30	22	5	3	86	34	49	2nd
1950–51	A	30	22	4	4	78	26	48	1st
1951–52	A	30	20	5	5	92	36	45	1st
1952–53	A	30	19	5	6	93	51	43	2nd
1953–54	A	30	15	4	11	72	51	34	5th
1954–55	A	30	15	4	11	64	54	34	5th
1955–56	A	34	19	7	8	86	50	45	4th
1956–57	I	34	12	9	13	69	56	33	9th
1957–58	I	34	13	5	16	59	60	31	9th
1958–59	I	34	13	6	15	68	70	32	10th
1959–60	I	34	14	7	13	106	85	35	7th
1960–61	I	34	15	4	15	66	69	34	8th
1961–62	I	34	14	5	15	58	72	33	8th
1962–63	I	34	8	9	17	47	67	25	16th
1963–64	I	34	12	6	16	59	66	30	10th
1964–65	I	34	21	4	9	75	47	46	4th
1965–66	I	34	16	6	12	81	55	38	6th
1966–67	I	34	19	4	11	72	49	42	5th
1967–68	I	34	20	5	9	67	49	45	3rd
1968–69	I	34	12	7	15	60	59	31	12th
1969–70	I	34	19	6	9	65	40	44	3rd
1970–71	I	34	10	10	14	47	53	30	12th
1971–72	I	34	19	6	9	62	34	44	4th
1972–73	I	34	19	7	8	74	33	45	3rd
1973–74	I	34	20	9	5	75	42	49	2nd
1974–75	I	34	20	9	5	69	37	49	2nd
1975–76	Pr	36	18	7	11	55	43	43	3rd
1976–77	Pr	36	8	18	10	34	35	34	6th
1977–78	Pr	36	15	7	14	51	43	37	4th
1978–79	Pr	36	12	13	11	44	48	37	5th
1979–80	Pr	36	6	6	24	29	67	18	10th
1980–81	I	39	24	9	6	67	24	57	1st
1981–82	Pr	36	11	14	11	38	40	36	6th
1982–83	Pr	36	7	15	14	35	51	29	7th
1983–84	Pr	36	12	7	17	45	55	31	7th
1984–85	Pr	36	10	7	19	38	61	27	8th
1985–86	Pr	36	11	6	19	49	63	28	8th
1986–87	Pr	44	10	13	21	44	70	33	9th
1987–88	Pr	44	12	19	13	41	42	43	6th
1988–89	Pr	36	13	9	14	37	36	35	5th
1989–90	Pr	36	12	10	14	34	41	34	7th
1990–91	Pr	36	6	13	17	24	51	25	9th
1991–92	Pr	44	16	17	11	53	45	49	5th
1992–93	Pr	44	12	13	19	54	64	37	7th

Hibernian won 11–1 away at Airdrieonians in Division One on 24 October 1959 and 10–2 away to Partick Thistle on 19 December 1959.

JOHNSTONE

Year	Div	P	W	D	L	F	A	Pts	Pos
1911–12	II	22	10	4	8	29	27	24	5th
1912–13	II	26	9	6	11	31	43	24	8th
1913–14	II	22	4	4	14	20	55	12	12th
1914–15	II	26	11	5	10	41	52	27	8th
1915–21	Regional Leagues operating								
1921–22	II	38	14	10	14	46	59	38	11th
1922–23	II	38	13	6	19	41	62	32	16th
1923–24	II	38	16	7	15	60	56	39	8th
1924–25	II	38	12	4	22	53	85	28	19th

Johnstone beat Greenock Abstainers 20–0 in the Scottish Cup first round on 5 September 1891.

KILMARNOCK

Year	Div	P	W	D	L	F	A	Pts	Pos
1895–96	II	18	10	1	7	45	45	21	4th
1896–97	II	18	10	1	7	44	33	21	3rd
1897–98	II	18	14	1	3	64	29	29	1st
1898–99	II	18	14	4	0	73	24	32	1st
1899–1900	I	18	6	6	6	30	37	18	5th
1900–01	I	20	7	4	9	35	47	18	5th
1901–02	I	18	5	6	7	21	25	16	7th
1902–03	I	22	6	4	12	24	43	16	9th
1903–04	I	26	4	5	17	24	63	13	14th
1904–05	I	26	9	5	12	29	45	23	9th
1905–06	I	30	8	4	18	46	68	20	15th
1906–07	I	34	8	5	21	40	72	21	17th
1907–08	I	34	6	13	15	38	61	25	14th
1908–09	I	34	13	7	14	47	61	33	10th
1909–10	I	34	12	8	14	53	60	32	11th
1910–11	I	34	12	10	12	43	45	34	10th
1911–12	I	34	11	4	19	38	60	26	16th
1912–13	I	34	10	11	13	37	54	31	11th
1913–14	I	38	11	9	18	48	68	31	12th
1914–15	I	38	15	4	19	55	59	34	12th
1915–16	SL	38	12	11	15	46	49	35	10th
1916–17	SL	38	18	7	13	69	45	43	6th
1917–18	SL	34	19	5	10	69	41	43	3rd

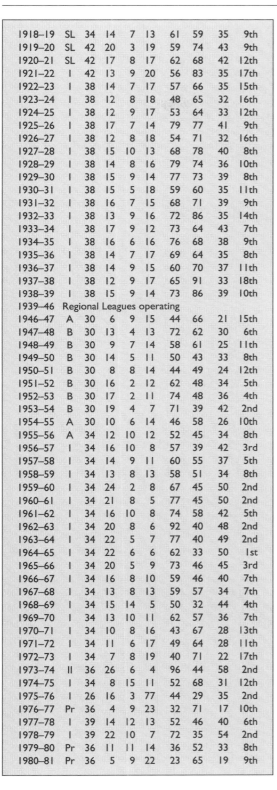

1918–19	SL	34	14	7	13	61	59	35	9th
1919–20	SL	42	20	3	19	59	74	43	9th
1920–21	SL	42	17	8	17	62	68	42	12th
1921–22	I	42	13	9	20	56	83	35	17th
1922–23	I	38	14	7	17	57	66	35	15th
1923–24	I	38	12	8	18	48	65	32	16th
1924–25	I	38	12	9	17	53	64	33	12th
1925–26	I	38	17	7	14	79	77	41	9th
1926–27	I	38	12	8	18	54	71	32	16th
1927–28	I	38	15	10	13	68	78	40	8th
1928–29	I	38	14	8	16	79	74	36	10th
1929–30	I	38	15	9	14	77	73	39	8th
1930–31	I	38	15	5	18	59	60	35	11th
1931–32	I	38	16	7	15	68	71	39	9th
1932–33	I	38	13	9	16	72	86	35	14th
1933–34	I	38	17	9	12	73	64	43	7th
1934–35	I	38	16	6	16	76	68	38	9th
1935–36	I	38	14	7	17	69	64	35	8th
1936–37	I	38	14	9	15	60	70	37	11th
1937–38	I	38	12	9	17	65	91	33	18th
1938–39	I	38	15	9	14	73	86	39	10th
1939–46	Regional Leagues operating								
1946–47	A	30	6	9	15	44	66	21	15th
1947–48	B	30	13	4	13	72	62	30	6th
1948–49	B	30	9	7	14	58	61	25	11th
1949–50	B	30	14	5	11	50	43	33	8th
1950–51	B	30	8	8	14	44	49	24	12th
1951–52	B	30	16	2	12	62	48	34	5th
1952–53	B	30	17	2	11	74	48	36	4th
1953–54	B	30	19	4	7	71	39	42	2nd
1954–55	A	30	10	6	14	46	58	26	10th
1955–56	A	34	12	10	12	52	45	34	8th
1956–57	I	34	16	10	8	57	39	42	3rd
1957–58	I	34	14	9	11	60	55	37	5th
1958–59	I	34	13	8	13	58	51	34	8th
1959–60	I	34	24	2	8	67	45	50	2nd
1960–61	I	34	21	8	5	77	45	50	2nd
1961–62	I	34	16	10	8	74	58	42	5th
1962–63	I	34	20	8	6	92	40	48	2nd
1963–64	I	34	22	5	7	77	40	49	2nd
1964–65	I	34	22	6	6	62	33	50	1st
1965–66	I	34	20	5	9	73	46	45	3rd
1966–67	I	34	16	8	10	59	46	40	7th
1967–68	I	34	13	8	13	59	57	34	7th
1968–69	I	34	15	14	5	50	32	44	4th
1969–70	I	34	13	10	11	62	57	36	7th
1970–71	I	34	10	8	16	43	67	28	13th
1971–72	I	34	11	6	17	49	64	28	11th
1972–73	I	34	7	8	19	40	71	22	17th
1973–74	II	36	26	6	4	96	44	58	2nd
1974–75	I	34	8	15	11	52	68	31	12th
1975–76	I	26	16	3	77	44	29	35	2nd
1976–77	Pr	36	4	9	23	32	71	17	10th
1977–78	I	39	14	12	13	52	46	40	6th
1978–79	I	39	22	10	7	72	35	54	2nd
1979–80	Pr	36	11	11	14	36	52	33	8th
1980–81	Pr	36	5	9	22	23	65	19	9th

Kilmarnock in 1965 were the last team to win the Scottish League title before the Old Firm took over for the next fourteen seasons. It was the only time the title came to Rugby Park (Popperfoto)

1981–82	I	39	17	17	5	60	29	51	2nd
1982–83	Pr	36	3	11	22	28	91	17	10th
1983–84	I	39	16	6	17	57	53	38	6th
1984–85	I	39	12	10	17	42	61	34	12th
1985–86	I	39	18	8	13	62	49	44	3rd
1986–87	I	44	17	11	16	62	53	45	6th
1987–88	I	44	13	11	20	55	60	37	10th
1988–89	I	39	10	14	15	47	60	34	13th
1989–90	II	39	22	4	12	67	39	48	2nd
1990–91	I	39	15	13	11	58	48	43	5th
1991–92	I	44	21	12	11	59	37	54	4th
1992–93	I	44	21	12	11	67	40	54	2nd

In 1964–65 **Kilmarnock** entered Europe for the first time in the Fairs Cup. In the first round they were paired with Eintracht Frankfurt and lost the first leg 3–0 away on 2 September. Twenty days later at home they were trailing 1–0 before scoring five times and going through on a 5–4 aggregate.

KING'S PARK

Year	Div	P	W	D	L	F	A	Pts	Pos
1921–22	II	38	10	12	16	47	65	32	17th
1922–23	II	38	14	6	18	46	60	34	12th
1923–24	II	38	15	8	15	54	46	38	10th
1924–25	II	38	15	8	15	54	46	38	10th
1925–26	II	38	14	9	15	67	73	37	13th
1926–27	II	38	13	9	16	76	75	35	12th
1927–28	II	38	16	12	10	84	68	44	3rd
1928–29	II	38	8	13	15	60	84	29	15th
1929–30	II	38	17	8	13	109	80	42	6th
1930–31	II	38	14	6	18	78	70	34	14th

1931–32	II	38	14	5	19	97	93	33	15th
1932–33	II	34	13	8	13	85	80	34	8th
1933–34	II	34	14	8	12	78	70	36	7th
1934–35	II	34	18	2	14	86	71	38	7th
1935–36	II	34	11	5	18	55	109	27	14th
1936–37	II	34	11	3	20	61	106	25	17th
1937–38	II	34	11	4	19	64	96	26	12th
1938–39	II	34	12	2	20	87	92	26	13th

Alex Haddow of **King's Park** scored a hat-trick in five consecutive Division Two matches in 1932: v Armadale 23 January (four goals), Stenhousemuir 6 February (five), Edinburgh City 13 February (three), Montrose 20 February (three) and Brechin 27 February (three).

LEITH ATHLETIC

Year	Div	P	W	D	L	F	A	Pts	Pos
1891–92	I	22	12	1	9	51	40	25	4th
1892–93	I	18	8	1	9	43	31	17	8th
1893–94	I	18	4	2	16	36	46	10	9th
1894–95	I	18	3	1	14	32	64	7	9th
1895–96	II	18	11	1	6	55	31	23	2nd
1896–97	II	18	13	1	4	55	27	27	2nd
1897–98	II	18	9	2	7	40	39	20	4th
1898–99	II	18	12	3	3	63	38	27	2nd
1899–1900	II	18	9	1	8	32	37	19	5th
1900–01	II	18	5	2	11	22	32	12	8th
1901–02	II	22	9	3	10	34	38	21	7th
1902–03	II	22	11	5	6	43	42	27	4th
1903–04	II	22	8	4	10	42	40	20	7th
1904–05	II	22	10	4	8	36	26	24	4th
1905–06	II	22	15	4	3	46	22	34	1st
1906–07	II	22	10	4	8	40	35	24	5th
1907–08	II	22	8	5	9	41	40	21	7th
1908–09	II	22	10	3	9	37	33	23	6th
1909–10	II	22	13	7	2	44	19	33	1st
1910–11	II	22	9	6	7	42	43	24	4th
1911–12	II	22	9	4	9	31	34	22	7th
1912–13	II	26	5	8	13	26	47	18	14th
1913–14	II	22	5	9	8	31	37	19	10th
1914–15	II	26	15	7	4	54	31	37	2nd

Reverted to Regional Leagues
1924–26 C Division, then Regional Leagues

1927–28	II	38	13	9	16	67	71	35	13th
1928–29	II	36	18	7	11	78	56	43	5th
1929–30	II	38	23	11	4	92	42	57	1st
1930–31	I	38	8	11	19	51	85	27	17th
1931–32	I	38	6	4	28	46	137	16	20th
1932–33	II	34	10	5	19	43	81	25	16th
1933–34	II	34	12	8	14	63	60	32	12th
1934–35	II	34	16	5	13	53	56	37	8th
1935–36	II	34	15	3	16	67	77	33	9th
1936–37	II	34	13	5	16	62	65	31	11th
1937–38	II	34	10	5	13	71	56	37	10th
1938–39	II	34	10	4	20	57	83	24	16th

1939–46 Regional Leagues operating
1946–47 C Division

1947–48	II	30	6	7	17	45	84	19	18th

C Division

Leith Athletic were drawn away to Fraserburgh in the Scottish Cup second round on 31 January 1954, after receiving a bye in the first round. They had not completed any competitive fixtures, just a couple of friendlies. But they gathered a team and were only beaten 5–4 in front of a crowd of 2,181.

LINTHOUSE

Year	Div	P	W	D	L	F	A	Pts	Pos
1895–96	II	18	5	1	12	25	48	11	10th
1896–97	II	18	8	2	8	44	52	14*	7th
1897–98	II	18	6	4	8	37	39	16	5th
1898–99	II	18	5	1	12	29	62	11	9th
1899–1900	II	18	2	5	11	28	68	9	10th

* The four points that **Linthouse** had deducted in 1896–97 for fielding an ineligible player cost them two places in the table. They would have finished fifth.

LOCHGELLY

Year	Div	P	W	D	L	F	A	Pts	Pos
1914–15	II	26	9	3	14	44	60	21	10th

Regional Leagues operating

1921–22	II	38	11	9	18	46	56	31	18th
1922–23	II	38	16	5	17	41	64	37	10th
1923–24	II	38	4	4	30	20	86	12	20th

On 16 February 1924 **Lochgelly** were beaten 8–3 at home by King's Park. The 11 goals scored in this match were exactly a third of the total involved in Lochgelly's home games.

MEADOWBANK THISTLE

Year	Div	P	W	D	L	F	A	Pts	Pos
1974–75	II	38	9	5	24	26	87	23	18th
1975–76	II	26	5	6	15	24	53	16	14th
1976–77	II	39	8	16	15	41	57	32	11th
1977–78	II	39	6	10	23	43	89	22	13th
1978–79	II	39	8	8	23	37	74	24	14th
1979–80	II	39	12	8	19	42	70	32	12th
1980–81	II	39	11	7	21	42	64	29	13th
1981–82	II	39	10	10	19	49	62	30	12th
1982–83	II	39	23	8	8	64	45	54	2nd
1983–84	I	39	12	10	17	49	69	34	11th
1984–85	I	39	11	10	18	50	66	32	13th

1985–86	II	39	19	11	9	68	45	49	3rd
1986–87	II	39	23	9	7	69	38	55	1st
1987–88	I	44	20	12	12	70	51	52	2nd
1988–89	I	39	13	10	16	45	50	36	10th
1989–90	I	39	13	13	13	41	46	39	7th
1990–91	I	39	10	13	16	56	68	33	11th
1991–92	I	44	7	16	21	37	59	30	10th
1992–93	I	44	11	10	23	51	80	32	11th

On 9 November 1985 **Meadowbank Thistle** beat Raith Rovers 6–0 in a Division Two match. All the goals came in the second half and were shared by five players.

1983–84	II	39	12	7	20	36	59	31	12th
1984–85	II	39	22	9	8	57	40	53	1st
1985–86	I	39	10	14	15	43	54	34	12th
1986–87	I	44	9	11	24	37	74	29	12th
1987–88	II	39	12	11	16	45	51	35	8th
1988–89	II	39	15	11	13	54	55	41	6th
1989–90	II	39	10	12	17	53	63	32	13th
1990–91	II	39	20	6	13	54	34	46	2nd
1991–92	I	44	5	17	22	45	85	27	11th
1992–93	II	39	10	7	22	46	71	27	12th

Charlie Burgess was only 15 years of age when he made his debut at left-back for **Montrose** in the years before the turn of the century. He subsequently played for Millwall, Newcastle United and Portsmouth.

MONTROSE

Year	Div	P	W	D	L	F	A	Pts	Pos
1929–30	II	38	14	10	14	79	87	38	11th
1930–31	II	38	19	3	16	75	90	41	8th
1931–32	II	38	11	6	21	60	96	28	17th
1932–33	II	34	8	5	21	63	89	21	17th
1933–34	II	34	11	4	19	53	81	26	16th
1934–35	II	34	7	6	21	58	105	20	17th
1935–36	II	34	13	3	18	58	82	29	12th
1936–37	II	34	11	6	17	65	100	28	13th
1937–38	II	34	7	8	19	56	88	22	16th
1938–39	II	34	10	5	19	82	96	25	14th
1939–46	Regional Leagues operating								
1946–55	C Division								
1955–56	B	36	4	3	29	44	133	11	19th
1956–57	II	36	7	7	22	54	124	21	17th
1957–58	II	36	13	6	17	55	72	32	14th
1958–59	II	36	6	6	24	49	96	18	19th
1959–60	II	36	19	5	12	60	52	43	7th
1960–61	II	36	19	2	15	75	65	40	7th
1961–62	II	36	15	11	10	63	50	41	5th
1962–63	II	36	13	5	18	57	70	31	15th
1963–64	II	36	19	6	11	79	57	44	5th
1964–65	II	36	10	9	17	80	91	29	16th
1965–66	II	36	15	7	14	67	63	37	9th
1966–67	II	38	13	8	17	63	77	34	12th
1967–68	II	36	10	11	15	54	64	31	13th
1968–69	II	36	15	4	17	59	71	34	10th
1969–70	II	36	15	7	14	57	55	37	8th
1970–71	II	36	17	7	12	78	64	41	6th
1971–72	II	36	15	6	15	73	54	36	10th
1972–73	II	36	18	8	10	82	58	44	6th
1973–74	II	36	15	7	14	71	64	37	8th
1974–75	II	38	23	7	8	70	37	53	3rd
1975–76	I	26	12	6	8	53	43	30	3rd
1976–77	I	39	16	9	14	61	62	41	5th
1977–78	I	39	10	9	20	55	71	29	11th
1978–79	I	39	8	9	22	55	92	25	13th
1979–80	II	39	14	10	15	60	63	38	9th
1980–81	II	39	16	8	15	66	55	40	7th
1981–82	II	39	12	8	19	49	74	32	10th
1982–83	II	39	8	6	25	37	86	22	14th

MORTON

Year	Div	P	W	D	L	F	A	Pts	Pos
1893–94	II	18	4	1	13	36	62	9	8th
1894–95	II	18	9	1	8	59	63	19	5th
1895–96	II	18	4	4	10	32	40	12	9th
1896–97	II	18	7	2	9	38	40	16	5th
1897–98	II	18	9	4	5	47	38	22	3rd
1898–99	II	18	6	1	11	36	41	13	7th
1899–1900	II	18	14	0	4	66	25	28	2nd
1900–01	I	20	9	3	8	40	40	21	4th
1901–02	I	18	1	5	12	18	40	7	10th
1902–03	I	22	2	5	15	22	55	9	12th
1903–04	I	26	7	4	15	32	53	18	11th
1904–05	I	26	7	4	15	27	50	18	13th
1905–06	I	30	10	6	14	35	54	26	10th
1906–07	I	34	11	6	17	41	50	28	13th
1907–08	I	34	9	9	16	43	66	27	13th
1908–09	I	34	8	7	19	39	90	23	17th
1909–10	I	34	11	3	20	38	60	25	17th
1910–11	I	34	9	11	14	49	51	29	13th
1911–12	I	34	14	9	11	44	44	37	6th
1912–13	I	34	11	7	16	50	59	29	13th
1913–14	I	38	26	2	10	76	51	54	4th
1914–15	I	38	18	12	8	74	48	48	4th
1915–16	SL	37	22	7	8	83	35	51	3rd
1916–17	SL	38	24	6	8	72	39	54	2nd
1917–18	SL	34	17	9	8	53	42	43	4th
1918–19	SL	34	18	11	5	76	38	47	3rd
1919–20	SL	42	16	13	13	71	48	45	6th
1920–21	SL	42	15	14	13	66	58	44	9th
1921–22	I	42	16	10	16	58	57	42	12th
1922–23	I	38	12	11	15	44	47	35	14th
1923–24	I	38	16	5	17	48	54	37	11th
1924–25	I	38	12	9	17	46	69	33	14th
1925–26	I	38	12	7	19	57	84	31	15th
1926–27	I	38	12	4	22	56	101	28	19th
1927–28	II	38	13	8	17	65	82	34	18th
1928–29	II	36	21	8	7	85	49	50	2nd
1929–30	I	38	10	7	21	67	95	27	18th

Year	Div	P	W	D	L	F	A	Pts	Pos
1930–31	I	38	11	7	20	58	83	29	16th
1931–32	I	38	12	7	19	78	87	31	15th
1932–33	I	38	6	9	23	49	97	21	19th
1933–34	II	34	17	5	12	67	64	39	5th
1934–35	II	34	17	4	13	88	64	38	6th
1935–36	II	34	21	6	7	117	60	48	3rd
1936–37	II	34	23	5	6	110	42	51	2nd
1937–38	I	38	6	3	29	64	127	15	20th
1938–39	II	34	11	6	17	74	88	28	12th
1939–46	Regional Leagues operating								
1946–47	A	30	12	10	8	58	45	34	6th
1947–48	A	30	9	6	15	47	43	24	14th
1948–49	A	30	7	8	15	39	51	22	15th
1949–50	B	30	20	7	3	77	33	47	1st
1950–51	A	30	10	4	16	47	59	24	12th
1951–52	A	30	9	6	15	49	56	24	15th
1952–53	B	30	15	3	12	79	57	33	6th
1953–54	B	30	15	3	12	85	65	33	5th
1954–55	B	30	12	5	13	58	69	29	9th
1955–56	B	36	15	6	15	71	69	36	9th
1956–57	II	36	18	7	11	81	70	43	4th
1957–58	II	36	12	8	16	77	83	32	13th
1958–59	II	36	13	8	15	68	85	34	11th
1959–60	II	36	10	8	18	67	79	28	14th
1960–61	II	36	5	11	20	56	93	21	19th
1961–62	II	36	19	6	11	78	64	44	3rd
1962–63	II	36	23	2	11	100	49	48	3rd
1963–64	II	36	32	3	1	135	37	67	1st
1964–65	I	34	13	7	14	54	54	33	10th
1965–66	I	34	8	5	21	42	84	21	17th
1966–67	II	38	33	3	2	113	20	69	1st
1967–68	I	34	15	6	13	57	53	36	6th
1968–69	I	34	12	8	14	58	68	32	10th
1969–70	I	34	13	9	12	52	52	35	9th
1970–71	I	34	13	8	13	44	44	34	8th
1971–72	I	34	10	7	17	46	52	27	13th
1972–73	I	34	10	8	16	47	53	28	12th
1973–74	I	34	8	10	16	37	49	26	14th
1974–75	I	34	6	10	18	31	62	22	17th
1975–76	I	26	7	9	10	31	40	23	11th
1976–77	I	39	20	10	9	77	52	50	4th
1977–78	I	39	25	8	6	85	42	58	1st
1978–79	Pr	36	12	12	12	52	53	36	7th
1979–80	Pr	36	14	8	14	51	46	36	6th
1980–81	Pr	36	10	8	18	36	58	28	8th
1981–82	Pr	36	9	12	15	31	54	30	7th
1982–83	Pr	36	6	8	22	30	74	20	9th
1983–84	I	39	21	12	6	75	46	54	1st
1984–85	Pr	36	5	2	29	29	100	12	10th
1985–86	I	39	14	11	14	57	63	39	7th
1986–87	I	44	24	9	11	88	56	57	1st
1987–88	Pr	44	3	10	31	27	100	16	12th
1988–89	I	39	16	9	14	46	46	41	5th
1989–90	I	39	9	16	14	38	46	34	11th
1990–91	I	39	11	13	15	48	55	35	9th
1991–92	I	44	17	12	15	66	59	46	7th
1992–93	I	44	19	10	15	65	56	48	6th

In June 1947 Derby County paid **Morton** £15,500, then a record transfer fee, for inside-left Billy Steel, whose handful of post-war appearances had included three caps for Scotland and an appearance for Great Britain against the Rest of Europe.

MOTHERWELL

Year	Div	P	W	D	L	F	A	Pts	Pos
1894–95	II	18	10	2	6	56	39	22	2nd
1895–96	II	18	5	3	10	31	47	13	8th
1896–97	II	18	6	1	11	40	55	13	9th
1897–98	II	18	3	4	11	31	56	10	10th
1898–99	II	18	7	6	5	41	40	20	4th
1899–1900	II	18	9	1	8	38	36	19	4th
1900–01	II	18	4	3	11	26	42	11	10th
1901–02	II	22	12	2	8	50	44	26	3rd
1902–03	II	22	12	4	6	44	35	28	2nd
1903–04	I	26	6	3	17	26	61	15	13th
1904–05	I	26	6	2	18	28	53	14	14th
1905–06	I	30	9	8	13	50	62	26	9th
1906–07	I	34	12	9	13	45	49	33	10th
1907–08	I	34	12	7	15	61	53	31	10th
1908–09	I	34	11	6	17	47	73	28	14th
1909–10	I	34	12	8	14	59	60	32	10th
1910–11	I	34	8	4	22	37	66	20	17th
1911–12	I	34	11	5	18	34	44	27	14th
1912–13	I	34	12	13	9	47	39	37	7th
1913–14	I	38	11	6	21	49	66	28	17th
1914–15	I	38	10	10	18	49	66	30	18th
1915–16	SL	38	11	8	19	55	81	30	14th
1916–17	SL	38	16	6	16	57	58	38	8th
1917–18	SL	34	16	9	9	70	51	41	5th
1918–19	SL	34	14	10	10	51	40	38	5th
1919–20	SL	42	23	11	8	73	53	57	3rd
1920–21	SL	42	19	10	13	75	51	48	5th
1921–22	I	42	16	7	19	63	58	39	13th
1922–23	I	38	13	10	15	59	60	36	13th
1923–24	I	38	15	7	16	58	63	37	10th
1924–25	I	38	10	10	18	55	64	30	18th
1925–26	I	38	19	8	11	67	46	46	5th
1926–27	I	38	23	5	10	81	52	51	2nd
1927–28	I	38	23	9	6	92	46	55	3rd
1928–29	I	38	20	10	8	85	66	50	3rd
1929–30	I	38	25	5	8	104	48	55	2nd
1930–31	I	38	24	8	6	102	42	56	3rd
1931–32	I	38	30	6	2	119	31	66	1st
1932–33	I	38	27	5	6	114	53	59	2nd
1933–34	I	38	29	4	5	97	45	62	2nd
1934–35	I	38	15	10	13	83	64	40	7th
1935–36	I	38	18	12	8	77	58	48	4th
1936–37	I	38	22	7	9	96	54	51	4th
1937–38	I	38	17	10	11	78	69	44	5th
1938–39	I	38	16	5	17	82	86	37	12th
1939–46	Regional Leagues operating								

Year	Div	P	W	D	L	F	A	Pts	Pos
1946–47	A	30	12	5	13	58	54	29	8th
1947–48	A	30	13	3	14	45	47	29	8th
1948–49	A	30	10	5	15	44	49	25	12th
1949–50	A	30	10	5	15	53	58	25	10th
1950–51	A	30	11	6	13	58	65	28	9th
1951–52	A	30	12	7	11	51	57	31	7th
1952–53	A	30	10	5	15	57	80	25	15th
1953–54	B	30	21	3	6	109	43	45	1st
1954–55	A	30	9	4	17	42	62	22	15th
1955–56	A	34	11	11	12	53	59	33	10th
1956–57	I	34	16	5	13	72	66	37	7th
1957–58	I	34	12	8	14	68	67	32	8th
1958–59	I	34	18	8	8	83	50	44	3rd
1959–60	I	34	16	8	10	71	61	40	5th
1960–61	I	34	15	8	11	70	57	38	5th
1961–62	I	34	13	6	15	65	62	32	9th
1962–63	I	34	10	11	13	60	63	31	10th
1963–64	I	34	9	11	14	51	62	29	11th
1964–65	I	34	10	8	16	45	54	28	14th
1965–66	I	34	12	4	18	52	69	28	13th
1966–67	I	34	10	11	13	59	60	31	10th
1967–68	I	34	6	7	21	40	66	19	17th
1968–69	II	36	30	4	2	112	23	64	1st
1969–70	I	34	11	10	13	49	51	32	11th
1970–71	I	34	13	8	13	43	47	34	10th
1971–72	I	34	11	7	16	49	69	29	10th
1972–73	I	34	11	9	14	38	48	31	8th
1973–74	I	34	14	7	13	45	40	35	9th
1974–75	I	34	14	5	15	52	57	33	10th
1975–76	Pr	36	16	8	12	56	48	40	4th
1976–77	Pr	36	10	12	14	57	60	32	7th
1977–78	Pr	36	13	7	16	45	52	33	6th
1978–79	Pr	36	5	7	24	33	86	17	10th
1979–80	I	39	16	11	12	59	48	43	6th
1980–81	I	39	19	11	9	65	51	49	5th
1981–82	I	39	26	9	4	92	36	61	1st
1982–83	Pr	36	11	5	20	39	73	27	8th
1983–84	Pr	36	4	7	25	31	75	15	10th
1984–85	I	39	21	8	10	62	36	50	1st
1985–86	Pr	36	7	6	23	33	66	20	9th
1986–87	Pr	44	11	12	21	43	64	34	8th
1987–88	Pr	44	13	10	21	37	56	36	8th
1988–89	Pr	36	7	13	16	35	44	27	9th
1989–90	Pr	36	11	12	13	43	47	34	6th
1990–91	Pr	36	12	9	15	51	50	33	6th
1991–92	Pr	44	10	14	20	43	61	34	10th
1992–93	Pr	44	11	13	20	46	62	35	9th

In a Scottish League Cup match on 11 August 1962, **Motherwell** were leading Falkirk 9–0 at half-time, but only won 9–1. Their total came from just two players: Bobby Russell with five goals and Pat Quinn with four.

NITHSDALE WANDERERS

Year	Div	P	W	D	L	F	A	Pts	Pos
1925–26	II	38	15	7	16	78	102	37	12th
1926–27	II	38	7	9	22	59	100	23	20th

Nithsdale Wanderers were involved in a 6–6 draw away to Arthurlie on 13 February 1926, during their short career as a Scottish League club.

NORTHERN

Year	Div	P	W	D	L	F	A	Pts	Pos
1893–94	II	18	3	3	12	29	66	9	9th

The highest win and heaviest defeat sustained by **Northern** involved seven goals. On 10 March 1894 they beat Abercorn 5–2, but had lost 7–0 away to Cowlairs on 9 September 1893.

PARTICK THISTLE

Year	Div	P	W	D	L	F	A	Pts	Pos
1893–94	II	18	10	0	8	56	58	20	5th
1894–95	II	18	8	2	8	50	60	18	7th
1895–96	II	18	8	2	8	44	54	18	6th
1896–97	II	18	14	3	1	61	28	31	1st
1897–98	I	18	6	1	11	34	64	13	8th
1898–99	I	18	2	2	14	19	58	6	9th
1899–1900	II	18	14	1	3	56	26	29	1st
1900–01	I	20	4	2	14	28	49	10	11th
1901–02	II	22	14	3	5	55	26	31	2nd
1902–03	I	22	6	7	9	34	50	19	8th
1903–04	I	26	10	7	9	46	41	27	7th
1904–05	I	26	12	2	12	36	56	26	6th
1905–06	I	30	15	6	9	44	40	36	5th
1906–07	I	34	9	8	17	40	60	26	14th
1907–08	I	34	8	9	17	43	69	25	15th
1908–09	I	34	2	4	28	38	102	8	18th
1909–10	I	34	8	10	16	47	59	26	16th
1910–11	I	34	17	8	9	50	41	42	4th
1911–12	I	34	16	8	10	47	40	40	5th
1912–13	I	34	10	4	20	40	55	24	17th
1913–14	I	38	10	9	19	37	51	29	15th
1914–15	I	38	15	8	15	56	58	38	8th
1915–16	SL	38	19	8	11	65	41	46	5th
1916–17	SL	38	14	7	17	44	43	35	9th
1917–18	SL	34	14	12	8	51	37	40	6th
1918–19	SL	34	17	7	10	62	43	41	4th
1919–20	SL	42	13	12	17	51	62	38	13th
1920–21	SL	42	17	12	13	53	39	46	6th
1921–22	I	42	20	8	14	57	53	48	6th
1922–23	I	38	14	9	15	51	48	37	11th
1923–24	I	38	15	9	14	58	55	39	8th
1924–25	I	38	14	10	14	60	61	38	7th

Year	Div	P	W	D	L	F	A	Pts	Pos
1925–26	I	38	10	13	15	64	73	33	14th
1926–27	I	38	15	6	17	89	74	36	11th
1927–28	I	38	18	7	13	85	67	43	6th
1928–29	I	38	17	7	14	91	70	41	6th
1929–30	I	38	16	9	13	72	61	41	6th
1930–31	I	38	24	5	9	76	44	53	4th
1931–32	I	38	19	4	15	58	59	42	6th
1932–33	I	38	17	6	15	75	55	40	10th
1933–34	I	38	14	5	19	73	78	33	13th
1934–35	I	38	15	5	18	61	68	35	13th
1935–36	I	38	12	10	16	64	72	34	9th
1936–37	I	38	11	12	15	73	68	34	13th
1937–38	I	38	15	9	14	68	70	39	7th
1938–39	I	38	17	4	17	74	87	38	11th
1939–46	Regional Leagues operating								
1946–47	A	30	16	3	11	74	59	35	5th
1947–48	A	30	16	4	10	61	42	36	3rd
1948–49	A	30	9	9	12	50	63	27	11th
1949–50	A	30	13	3	14	55	45	29	7th
1950–51	A	30	13	7	10	57	48	33	6th
1951–52	A	30	12	7	11	48	51	31	6th
1952–53	A	30	10	9	11	55	63	29	9th
1953–54	A	30	17	1	12	76	54	35	3rd
1954–55	A	30	11	7	12	49	61	29	9th
1955–56	A	34	13	7	14	62	60	33	9th
1956–57	I	34	13	8	13	53	51	34	8th
1957–58	I	34	17	3	14	69	71	37	6th
1958–59	I	34	14	6	14	59	66	34	9th
1959–60	I	34	14	4	16	54	78	32	10th
1960–61	I	34	13	6	15	59	69	32	11th
1961–62	I	34	16	3	15	60	55	35	7th
1962–63	I	34	20	6	8	66	44	46	3rd
1963–64	I	34	15	5	14	55	54	35	7th
1964–65	I	34	11	10	13	57	58	32	11th
1965–66	I	34	10	10	14	55	64	30	12th
1966–67	I	34	9	12	13	49	68	30	12th
1967–68	I	34	12	7	15	51	67	31	10th
1968–69	I	34	9	10	15	39	53	28	14th
1969–70	I	34	5	7	22	41	82	17	18th
1970–71	II	36	23	10	3	78	26	56	1st
1971–72	I	34	12	10	12	53	54	34	7th
1972–73	I	34	10	8	16	40	53	28	13th
1973–74	I	34	9	10	15	33	46	28	11th
1974–75	I	34	10	10	14	48	62	30	13th
1975–76	I	26	17	7	2	47	19	41	1st
1976–77	Pr	36	11	13	12	40	44	35	5th
1977–78	Pr	36	14	5	17	52	64	33	7th
1978–79	Pr	36	13	8	15	42	39	34	8th
1979–80	Pr	36	11	14	11	43	47	36	7th
1980–81	Pr	36	10	10	16	32	48	30	6th
1981–82	Pr	36	6	10	20	35	59	22	9th
1982–83	I	39	20	9	10	66	45	49	4th
1983–84	I	39	19	8	12	67	50	46	3rd
1984–85	I	39	13	9	17	50	55	35	11th
1985–86	I	39	10	16	13	53	64	36	8th
1986–87	I	44	12	15	17	49	54	39	8th
1987–88	I	44	16	9	19	60	64	41	8th
1988–89	I	39	13	11	15	57	58	37	8th
1989–90	I	39	12	14	13	62	53	38	8th
1990–91	I	39	16	13	10	56	53	45	4th
1991–92	I	44	23	11	10	52	36	57	2nd
1992–93	Pr	44	12	12	20	50	71	36	8th

From 17 October 1987 and for the next seven consecutive games **Partick Thistle** used seven different goalkeepers for a variety of reasons.

PORT GLASGOW ATHLETIC

Year	Div	P	W	D	L	F	A	Pts	Pos
1893–94	II	18	9	2	7	52	53	13*	6th
1894–95	II	18	8	4	6	62	56	20	3rd
1895–96	II	18	6	4	8	40	41	16	7th
1896–97	II	18	4	5	9	39	50	13	8th
1897–98	II	18	12	1	5	66	35	25	2nd
1898–99	II	18	12	1	5	75	51	25	3rd
1899–1900	II	18	10	0	8	50	41	20	3rd
1900–01	II	18	9	1	8	45	44	19	5th
1901–02	II	22	14	4	4	71	31	32	1st
1902–03	I	22	3	5	14	26	49	11	11th
1903–04	I	26	8	4	14	32	49	20	9th
1904–05	I	26	8	5	13	30	51	21	11th
1905–06	I	30	6	8	16	38	68	20	14th
1906–07	I	34	7	7	20	30	67	21	18th
1907–08	I	34	5	7	22	39	98	17	18th
1908–09	I	34	10	8	16	39	52	28	13th
1909–10	I	34	3	5	26	25	95	11	18th
1910–11	II	22	8	3	11	27	32	19	8th

* **Port Glasgow Athletic** were involved in the only instance of a team registering negative points in a season. In 1893–94 they had only six points in Division Two when the three they had achieved by beating Northern and drawing with Clyde were deducted for fielding an unregistered player. They were also fined four points which left them temporarily at least with minus one point.

QUEEN OF THE SOUTH

Year	Div	P	W	D	L	F	A	Pts	Pos
1925–26	II	38	10	8	20	64	88	28	17th
1926–27	II	38	16	4	18	72	80	36	11th
1927–28	II	38	15	6	17	92	106	36	12th
1928–29	II	36	16	4	16	86	79	36	9th
1929–30	II	38	18	6	14	65	63	42	7th
1930–31	II	38	18	6	14	83	66	47	5th
1931–32	II	38	18	5	15	99	91	41	9th
1932–33	II	34	20	9	5	93	59	49	2nd
1933–34	I	38	21	3	14	75	78	45	4th
1934–35	I	38	11	7	20	52	72	29	17th
1935–36	I	38	11	9	18	54	72	31	15th
1936–37	I	38	8	8	22	49	95	24	18th

Year	Div	P	W	D	L	F	A	Pts	Pos
1937–38	I	38	11	11	16	58	71	33	16th
1938–39	I	38	17	9	12	69	64	43	6th
1939–46	Regional Leagues operating								
1946–47	A	30	9	8	13	44	69	26	12th
1947–48	A	30	10	5	15	49	74	25	13th
1948–49	A	30	11	8	11	47	53	30	10th
1949–50	A	30	5	6	19	31	63	16	15th
1950–51	B	30	21	3	6	69	35	45	1st
1951–52	A	30	10	8	12	50	60	28	10th
1952–53	A	30	10	8	12	43	61	28	10th
1953–54	A	30	14	4	12	72	53	32	10th
1954–55	A	30	9	6	15	38	56	24	13th
1955–56	A	34	16	5	13	69	73	37	6th
1956–57	I	34	10	5	19	54	96	25	16th
1957–58	I	34	12	5	17	61	72	29	15th
1958–59	I	34	6	6	22	38	101	18	18th
1959–60	II	36	21	7	8	94	52	49	3rd
1960–61	II	36	20	3	13	77	52	43	5th
1961–62	II	36	24	5	7	78	33	53	2nd
1962–63	I	34	10	6	18	36	75	26	15th
1963–64	I	34	5	6	23	40	92	16	17th
1964–65	II	36	16	13	7	84	50	45	3rd
1965–66	II	36	18	11	7	83	53	47	3rd
1966–67	II	38	15	9	14	84	76	39	9th
1967–68	II	36	16	6	14	73	57	38	6th
1968–69	II	36	20	7	9	75	41	47	5th
1969–70	II	36	22	6	8	72	49	50	3rd
1970–71	II	36	13	9	14	50	56	35	11th
1971–72	II	36	17	9	10	56	38	43	7th
1972–73	II	36	13	8	15	45	52	34	11th
1973–74	II	36	20	7	9	73	41	47	4th
1974–75	II	38	23	7	8	77	33	53	2nd
1975–76	I	26	9	6	11	41	47	24	10th
1976–77	I	39	11	13	15	58	65	35	9th
1977–78	I	39	8	13	18	44	68	29	12th
1978–79	I	39	8	8	23	43	93	24	14th
1979–80	II	39	11	9	19	51	69	31	13th
1980–81	II	39	16	14	9	66	53	46	2nd
1981–82	I	39	4	10	25	44	93	18	14th
1982–83	II	39	17	8	14	75	55	42	7th
1983–84	II	39	16	10	13	51	46	42	6th
1984–85	II	39	10	14	15	42	56	34	8th
1985–86	II	39	23	9	7	71	36	55	2nd
1986–87	I	44	11	12	21	50	71	34	10th
1987–88	I	44	14	15	15	56	67	43	7th
1988–89	I	39	2	8	29	38	99	10	14th
1989–90	II	39	11	14	14	58	69	36	10th
1990–91	II	39	9	12	18	46	62	30	12th
1991–92	II	39	14	5	20	71	86	33	11th
1992–93	II	39	12	9	18	57	72	33	10th

Jimmy Welsh scored three goals within six minutes of his debut for **Queen of the South** against Cowdenbeath on 16 November 1968. Queen of the South won 4–0.

QUEEN'S PARK

Year	Div	P	W	D	L	F	A	Pts	Pos
1900–01	I	20	7	3	10	33	37	17	8th
1901–02	I	18	5	4	9	21	32	14	8th
1902–03	I	22	5	5	12	33	48	15	10th
1903–04	I	26	6	9	11	28	47	21	8th
1904–05	I	26	6	8	12	28	45	20	12th
1905–06	I	30	5	4	21	39	87	14	16th
1906–07	I	34	9	6	19	51	66	24	15th
1907–08	I	34	7	8	19	54	84	22	16th
1908–09	I	34	6	13	15	42	65	25	15th
1909–10	I	34	12	6	16	54	74	30	14th
1910–11	I	34	5	4	25	28	80	14	18th
1911–12	I	34	8	9	17	29	53	25	17th
1912–13	I	34	5	3	26	34	88	13	18th
1913–14	I	38	10	9	19	52	84	29	16th
1914–15	I	38	4	5	29	27	90	13	20th
1915–16	SL	38	11	6	21	53	100	28	18th
1916–17	SL	38	11	7	20	56	81	29	18th
1917–18	SL	34	14	6	14	64	63	34	7th
1918–19	SL	34	15	5	14	59	57	35	8th
1919–20	SL	42	14	10	18	67	73	38	12th
1920–21	SL	42	11	11	20	45	80	33	19th
1921–22	I	42	9	10	23	38	82	28	21st
1922–23	II	38	24	9	5	73	31	57	1st
1923–24	I	38	11	9	18	43	60	31	17th
1924–25	I	38	12	8	18	50	71	32	17th
1925–26	I	38	15	4	19	70	81	34	13th
1926–27	I	38	15	6	17	74	84	36	12th
1927–28	I	38	12	6	20	69	80	30	16th
1928–29	I	38	18	7	13	100	69	43	5th
1929–30	I	38	15	4	19	67	80	34	15th
1930–31	I	38	13	7	18	71	72	33	13th
1931–32	I	38	13	5	20	59	79	31	16th
1932–33	I	38	17	7	14	78	79	41	9th
1933–34	I	38	13	5	20	65	85	31	15th
1934–35	I	38	13	10	15	61	80	36	12th
1935–36	I	38	11	10	17	58	75	32	14th
1936–37	I	38	9	12	17	51	77	30	15th
1937–38	I	38	11	12	15	59	74	34	12th
1938–39	I	38	11	5	22	57	83	27	19th
1939–46	Regional Leagues operating								
1946–47	A	30	8	6	16	47	60	22	13th
1947–48	A	30	9	2	19	45	75	20	16th
1948–49	B	30	14	7	9	66	49	35	5th
1949–50	B	30	12	7	11	63	59	31	9th
1950–51	B	30	13	7	10	56	53	33	6th
1951–52	B	30	8	4	18	40	62	20	15th
1952–53	B	30	15	7	8	70	46	37	3rd
1953–54	B	30	9	9	12	56	51	27	10th
1954–55	B	30	15	5	10	65	36	35	4th
1955–56	B	36	23	8	5	78	28	54	1st
1956–57	I	34	11	7	16	55	59	29	13th
1957–58	I	34	4	1	29	41	114	9	18th
1958–59	II	36	9	6	21	53	80	24	18th
1959–60	II	36	17	2	17	65	79	36	11th

1960–61	II	36	10	6	20	61	87	26	15th
1961–62	II	36	12	9	15	64	62	33	12th
1962–63	II	36	13	6	17	66	72	32	14th
1963–64	II	36	17	4	15	57	54	38	7th
1964–65	II	36	17	9	10	57	41	43	4th
1965–66	II	36	13	7	16	62	65	33	13th
1966–67	II	38	15	10	13	78	68	40	7th
1967–68	II	36	20	8	8	76	47	48	4th
1968–69	II	36	13	7	16	50	59	33	11th
1969–70	II	36	10	6	20	38	62	26	15th
1970–71	II	36	13	4	19	51	72	30	13th
1971–72	II	36	12	9	15	47	61	33	12th
1972–73	II	36	9	12	15	44	61	30	14th
1973–74	II	36	12	4	20	42	64	28	14th
1974–75	II	38	10	10	18	41	54	30	16th
1975–76	II	26	10	9	7	41	33	29	4th
1976–77	II	39	17	11	11	65	51	45	5th
1977–78	II	39	13	15	11	52	51	41	7th
1978–79	II	39	8	12	19	46	57	28	13th
1979–80	II	39	16	9	14	59	47	41	5th
1980–81	II	39	16	18	5	62	43	50	1st
1981–82	I	39	13	10	16	41	41	36	8th
1982–83	I	39	6	11	22	44	80	23	14th
1983–84	II	39	14	8	17	58	63	36	10th
1984–85	II	39	12	9	18	48	55	33	10th
1985–86	II	39	19	8	12	61	39	46	4th
1986–87	II	39	9	19	11	48	49	37	9th
1987–88	II	39	21	9	9	64	44	51	3rd
1988–89	II	39	10	18	11	50	49	38	7th
1989–90	II	39	13	10	16	40	51	36	11th
1990–91	II	39	17	8	14	48	42	42	5th
1991–92	II	39	14	7	18	59	63	35	9th
1992–93	II	39	8	12	19	51	73	28	11th

When **Queen's Park** played at Kilmarnock on 16 November 1935 they wore red, black and yellow hooped shirts.

RAITH ROVERS

Year	Div	P	W	D	L	F	A	Pts	Pos
1902–03	II	22	3	5	14	34	55	11	11th
1903–04	II	22	8	5	9	40	38	21	5th
1904–05	II	22	9	1	12	30	34	19	10th
1905–06	II	22	6	7	9	36	42	19	8th
1906–07	II	22	6	4	12	39	47	16	10th
1907–08	II	22	14	2	6	37	23	30	1st
1908–09	II	22	11	6	5	46	22	28	2nd
1909–10	II	22	14	5	3	36	21	33	1st
1910–11	I	34	7	10	17	36	56	24	15th
1911–12	I	34	9	9	16	39	59	27	15th
1912–13	I	34	8	10	16	46	60	26	16th
1913–14	I	38	13	6	19	56	57	32	11th
1914–15	I	38	9	10	19	53	68	28	19th
1915–16	SL	38	9	5	24	30	65	23	20th
1916–17	SL	38	8	7	23	42	91	23	19th

Regional Leagues

1919–20	SL	42	11	10	21	61	82	32	19th
1920–21	SL	42	16	5	21	54	58	37	16th
1921–22	I	42	19	13	10	66	43	51	3rd
1922–23	I	38	13	13	12	31	43	39	9th
1923–24	I	38	18	7	13	56	38	43	4th
1924–25	I	38	14	8	16	52	60	36	9th
1925–26	I	38	11	4	23	46	81	26	19th
1926–27	II	38	21	7	10	92	52	49	2nd
1927–28	I	38	11	7	20	60	89	29	17th
1928–29	I	38	9	6	23	52	105	24	20th
1929–30	II	38	18	8	12	94	67	44	5th
1930–31	II	38	20	6	12	93	72	46	4th
1931–32	II	38	20	6	12	83	65	46	3rd
1932–33	II	34	16	4	14	83	67	36	6th
1933–34	II	34	15	5	14	71	55	35	8th
1934–35	II	34	13	3	18	68	73	29	13th
1935–36	II	34	9	3	22	60	96	21	17th
1936–37	II	34	16	4	14	72	66	36	8th
1937–38	II	34	27	5	2	142	54	59	1st
1938–39	I	38	10	2	26	65	99	22	20th
1939–46	Regional Leagues operating								
1946–47	B	26	10	6	10	45	52	26	6th
1947–48	B	30	14	6	10	83	66	34	4th
1948–49	B	30	20	2	8	80	44	42	1st
1949–50	A	30	9	8	13	45	54	26	9th
1950–51	A	30	13	2	15	52	52	28	8th
1951–52	A	30	14	5	11	43	42	33	5th
1952–53	A	30	9	8	13	47	53	26	12th
1953–54	A	30	10	6	14	56	60	26	12th
1954–55	A	30	10	3	17	49	57	23	14th
1955–56	A	34	12	9	13	58	75	33	11th
1956–57	I	34	16	7	11	84	58	39	4th
1957–58	I	34	14	7	13	66	56	35	7th
1958–59	I	34	10	9	15	60	70	29	14th
1959–60	I	34	14	3	17	64	62	31	11th
1960–61	I	34	10	7	17	46	67	27	16th
1961–62	I	34	10	7	17	51	73	27	13th
1962–63	I	34	2	5	27	35	118	9	18th
1963–64	II	36	15	5	16	70	61	35	10th
1964–65	II	36	9	14	13	54	61	32	13th
1965–66	II	36	16	11	9	71	43	43	5th
1966–67	II	38	27	4	7	95	44	58	2nd
1967–68	I	34	9	7	18	58	86	25	16th
1968–69	I	34	8	5	21	45	67	21	16th
1969–70	I	34	5	11	18	32	67	21	17th
1970–71	II	36	15	9	12	62	62	39	8th
1971–72	II	36	13	8	15	56	65	34	11th
1972–73	II	36	19	9	8	73	42	47	3rd
1973–74	II	36	18	9	9	69	48	45	5th
1974–75	II	38	14	9	15	48	44	37	13th
1975–76	II	26	15	10	1	45	22	40	2nd
1976–77	I	39	8	11	20	45	68	27	13th
1977–78	II	39	19	15	5	63	34	53	2nd
1978–79	I	39	12	8	19	47	55	32	11th
1979–80	I	39	14	15	10	59	46	43	5th
1980–81	I	39	20	10	9	49	32	50	4th

Year	Div	P	W	D	L	F	A	Pts	Pos
1981–82	I	39	11	7	21	31	59	29	12th
1982–83	I	39	13	8	18	64	63	34	9th
1983–84	I	39	10	11	18	53	62	31	13th
1984–85	II	39	18	6	15	69	57	42	7th
1985–86	II	39	15	7	17	67	65	37	9th
1986–87	II	39	16	20	3	73	44	52	2nd
1987–88	I	44	19	7	18	81	76	45	5th
1988–89	I	39	15	10	14	50	52	40	7th
1989–90	I	39	15	12	12	57	50	42	5th
1990–91	I	39	14	9	16	54	64	37	7th
1991–92	I	44	21	11	12	59	42	53	5th
1992–93	I	44	25	15	4	85	41	65	1st

In 1975–76 **Raith Rovers** were unbeaten away in Division Two, winning nine and drawing four games. They finished the season on 40 points but in second place behind Clydebank on goal difference. They were promoted to Division One.

RANGERS

Year	Div	P	W	D	L	F	A	Pts	Pos
1890–91	SL	18	13	3	2	58	25	29	2nd
1891–92	SL	22	12	2	9	59	46	24	5th
1892–93	SL	18	12	4	2	41	27	28	2nd
1893–94	I	18	8	4	6	44	30	20	4th
1894–95	I	18	10	2	6	41	26	22	3rd
1895–96	I	18	11	4	3	57	39	26	2nd
1896–97	I	18	11	3	4	64	30	25	3rd
1897–98	I	18	13	3	2	71	15	29	2nd
1898–99	I	18	18	0	0	79	18	36	1st
1899–1900	I	18	15	2	1	69	27	32	1st
1900–01	I	20	17	1	2	60	25	35	1st
1901–02	I	18	13	2	3	43	29	28	1st
1902–03	I	22	12	5	5	56	30	29	3rd
1903–04	I	26	16	6	4	80	33	38	4th
1904–05	I	26	18	5	3	83	28	41	2nd
1905–06	I	30	15	7	8	58	48	37	4th
1906–07	I	34	19	7	8	69	33	45	3rd
1907–08	I	34	21	8	5	74	40	50	3rd
1908–09	I	34	19	7	8	91	38	45	4th
1909–10	I	34	20	6	8	70	35	46	3rd
1910–11	I	34	23	6	5	90	34	52	1st
1911–12	I	34	24	3	7	86	34	51	1st
1912–13	I	34	24	5	5	76	41	53	1st
1913–14	I	38	27	5	6	79	31	59	2nd
1914–15	I	38	23	4	11	74	47	50	3rd
1915–16	SL	38	25	6	7	87	39	56	2nd
1916–17	SL	38	24	5	9	68	32	53	3rd
1917–18	SL	34	25	6	3	66	24	56	1st
1918–19	SL	34	26	5	3	86	16	57	2nd
1919–20	SL	42	31	9	2	106	25	71	1st
1920–21	SL	42	35	6	1	91	24	76	1st
1921–22	I	42	28	10	4	83	26	66	2nd
1922–23	I	38	23	9	6	67	29	55	1st
1923–24	I	38	25	9	4	72	22	59	1st
1924–25	I	38	25	10	3	77	27	60	1st
1925–26	I	38	19	6	13	79	55	44	6th
1926–27	I	38	23	10	5	85	41	56	1st
1927–28	I	38	26	8	4	109	36	60	1st
1928–29	I	38	30	7	1	107	32	67	1st
1929–30	I	38	28	4	6	94	32	60	1st
1930–31	I	38	27	6	5	96	29	60	1st
1931–32	I	38	28	5	5	118	42	61	2nd
1932–33	I	38	26	10	2	113	43	62	1st
1933–34	I	38	30	6	2	118	41	66	1st
1934–35	I	38	25	5	8	96	46	55	1st
1935–36	I	38	27	7	4	110	43	61	2nd
1936–37	I	38	26	9	3	88	32	61	1st
1937–38	I	38	18	13	7	75	49	49	3rd
1938–39	I	38	25	9	4	112	55	59	1st
1939–46	Regional Leagues operating								
1946–47	A	30	21	4	5	76	26	46	1st
1947–48	A	30	21	4	5	64	28	46	2nd
1948–49	A	30	20	6	4	63	32	46	1st
1949–50	A	30	22	6	2	58	26	50	1st
1950–51	A	30	17	4	9	64	37	38	2nd
1951–52	A	30	16	9	5	61	31	41	2nd
1952–53	A	30	18	7	5	80	39	43	1st
1953–54	A	30	13	8	9	56	35	34	4th
1954–55	A	30	19	3	8	67	33	41	3rd
1955–56	A	34	22	8	4	85	27	52	1st
1956–57	I	34	26	3	5	96	48	55	1st
1957–58	I	34	22	5	7	89	49	49	2nd
1958–59	I	34	21	8	5	92	51	50	1st
1959–60	I	34	17	8	9	72	38	42	3rd
1960–61	I	34	23	5	6	88	46	51	1st
1961–62	I	34	22	7	5	84	31	51	2nd
1962–63	I	34	25	7	2	94	28	57	1st
1963–64	I	34	25	5	4	85	31	55	1st
1964–65	I	34	18	8	8	78	35	44	5th
1965–66	I	34	25	5	4	91	29	55	2nd
1966–67	I	34	24	7	3	92	31	55	2nd
1967–68	I	34	28	5	1	93	34	61	2nd
1968–69	I	34	21	7	6	81	32	49	2nd
1969–70	I	34	19	7	8	67	40	45	2nd
1970–71	I	34	16	9	9	58	34	41	4th
1971–72	I	34	21	2	11	71	38	44	3rd
1972–73	I	34	26	4	4	74	30	56	2nd
1973–74	I	34	21	6	7	67	34	48	3rd
1974–75	I	34	25	6	3	86	33	56	1st
1975–76	Pr	36	23	8	5	60	24	54	1st
1976–77	Pr	36	18	10	8	62	37	46	2nd
1977–78	Pr	36	24	7	5	76	39	55	1st
1978–79	Pr	36	18	9	9	52	35	45	2nd
1979–80	Pr	36	15	7	14	50	46	37	5th
1980–81	Pr	36	16	12	8	60	32	44	3rd
1981–82	Pr	36	16	11	9	57	45	43	3rd
1982–83	Pr	36	13	12	11	52	41	38	4th
1983–84	Pr	36	15	12	9	53	41	42	4th
1984–85	Pr	36	13	12	11	47	38	38	4th
1985–86	Pr	36	13	9	14	53	45	35	5th
1986–87	Pr	44	31	7	6	85	23	69	1st

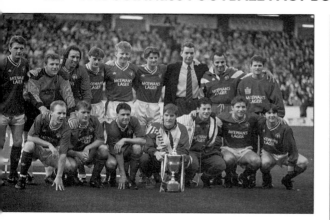

Rangers celebrate their 1992 League title, four in a row for the Ibrox men. A fifth title followed in 1993 and sights were firmly set on emulating Celtic's nine in a row (Allsport/Chris Cole)

1987–88	Pr	44	26	8	10	85	34	60	3rd
1988–89	Pr	36	26	4	6	62	26	56	1st
1989–90	Pr	36	20	11	5	48	19	51	1st
1990–91	Pr	36	24	7	5	62	23	55	1st
1991–92	Pr	44	33	6	5	101	31	72	1st
1992–93	Pr	44	33	7	4	97	35	73	1st

In 1898–99 when **Rangers** had a 100 per cent record, they came nearest to dropping a point against Hibernian at Edinburgh. They were 2–0 down 20 minutes from the start and only scored the winning goal in the last minute to win 4–3.

RENTON

Year	Div	P	W	D	L	F	A	Pts	Pos
1891–92	SL	22	8	4	10	38	44	20	8th
1892–93	SL	18	5	5	8	31	44	15	8th
1893–94	I	18	1	2	15	23	52	4	10th
1894–95	II	17	10	0	7	46	44	20	4th
(Failed to play Dundee Wanderers)									
1895–96	II	18	9	3	6	40	28	21	3rd
1896–97	II	18	6	2	10	34	40	14	6th
1897–98	Resigned after four matches								

Renton played West Bromwich Albion in 1888 when the respective winners of the Scottish and FA Cup met in the unofficial Championship of the World. Renton won 4–1.

ST BERNARDS

Year	Div	P	W	D	L	F	A	Pts	Pos
1893–94	I	18	11	1	6	53	39	23	3rd
1894–95	I	18	8	1	9	37	40	17	6th
1895–96	I	18	7	1	10	36	53	15	7th

1896–97	I	18	7	0	11	32	40	14	7th
1897–98	I	18	4	1	13	35	67	9	9th
1898–99	I	18	4	4	10	30	37	12	7th
1899–1900	I	18	4	4	10	29	47	12	9th
1900–01	II	18	11	5	3	42	26	27	1st
1901–02	II	22	10	2	10	30	31	22	6th
1902–03	II	22	12	2	8	45	42	26	5th
1903–04	II	22	9	2	11	31	43	20	8th
1904–05	II	22	3	5	14	23	53	11	12th
1905–06	II	22	9	4	9	42	44	22	5th
1906–07	II	22	14	4	4	41	24	32	1st
1907–08	II	22	8	5	9	31	32	21	8th
1908–09	II	22	9	3	10	34	37	21	8th
1909–10	II	22	12	3	7	43	31	27	3rd
1910–11	II	22	10	2	10	36	41	22	6th
1911–12	II	22	9	5	8	38	36	23	6th
1912–13	II	26	12	3	11	39	34	27	7th
1913–14	II	22	8	6	8	39	31	22	7th
1914–15	II	26	18	1	7	66	34	37	3rd
1915–21	Regional Leagues operating								
1921–22	II	38	15	8	15	50	49	38	9th
1922–23	II	38	8	15	15	39	50	29	18th
1923–24	II	38	11	10	17	49	54	32	18th
1924–25	II	38	14	4	20	52	70	32	17th
1925–26	II	38	15	5	18	86	82	35	14th
1926–27	II	38	14	6	18	70	77	34	13th
1927–28	II	38	15	5	18	75	103	35	17th
1928–29	II	38	16	9	11	77	55	41	6th
1929–30	II	38	13	6	19	65	65	32	14th
1930–31	II	38	14	9	15	85	66	37	11th
1931–32	II	38	19	7	12	81	62	45	5th
1932–33	II	34	13	6	15	67	64	32	12th
1933–34	II	34	15	4	15	75	56	34	10th
1934–35	II	34	20	7	7	103	47	47	3rd
1935–36	II	34	18	4	12	106	78	40	5th
1936–37	II	34	22	4	8	102	51	48	3rd
1937–38	II	34	20	5	9	75	49	45	4th
1938–39	II	34	15	6	13	79	79	36	7th
Regional Leagues									

On 18 February 1939 **St Bernards** beat Forfar Athletic 6–2. Late choice at centre-forward was Jimmy Johnston who scored all six goals.

ST JOHNSTONE

Year	Div	P	W	D	L	F	A	Pts	Pos
1912–13	II	26	7	7	12	29	38	21	11th
1913–14	II	22	9	5	8	48	38	23	5th
1914–15	II	26	10	6	10	56	53	26	8th
1915–21	Regional Leagues								
1921–22	II	38	12	11	15	41	52	35	13th
1922–23	II	38	19	12	7	60	39	48	3rd
1923–24	II	38	22	12	4	79	33	56	1st
1924–25	I	38	12	11	15	56	71	35	11th
1925–26	I	38	9	10	19	43	78	28	18th

Year	Div	P	W	D	L	F	A	Pts	Pos
1926–27	I	38	13	9	16	55	69	35	14th
1927–28	I	38	14	8	16	66	67	36	11th
1928–29	I	38	14	10	14	57	70	38	9th
1929–30	I	38	6	7	25	48	96	19	20th
1930–31	II	38	18	6	14	76	64	42	6th
1931–32	II	38	24	7	7	102	52	55	2nd
1932–33	I	38	17	10	11	70	57	44	5th
1933–34	I	38	17	6	15	74	53	40	9th
1934–35	I	38	18	10	10	66	46	46	5th
1935–36	I	38	15	7	16	70	81	37	7th
1936–37	I	38	14	8	16	74	68	36	12th
1937–38	I	38	16	7	15	78	81	39	8th
1938–39	I	38	17	6	15	85	82	40	8th
1939–46	Regional Leagues operating								
1946–47	B	26	9	4	13	45	47	22	9th
1947–48	B	30	11	5	14	69	63	27	9th
1948–49	B	30	14	4	12	58	51	32	6th
1949–50	B	30	15	6	9	64	56	36	4th
1950–51	B	30	14	5	11	68	53	33	5th
1951–52	B	30	9	7	14	62	68	25	11th
1952–53	B	30	8	6	16	41	63	22	14th
1953–54	B	30	14	3	13	80	71	31	6th
1954–55	B	30	15	2	13	60	51	32	7th
1955–56	B	36	21	7	8	86	45	49	3rd
1956–57	II	36	14	6	16	79	80	34	12th
1957–58	II	36	12	9	15	67	85	33	11th
1958–59	II	36	15	10	11	54	44	40	6th
1959–60	II	36	24	5	7	87	47	53	1st
1960–61	I	34	10	9	15	47	63	29	15th
1961–62	I	34	9	7	18	35	61	25	17th
1962–63	II	36	25	5	6	83	37	55	1st
1963–64	I	34	11	6	17	54	70	28	13th
1964–65	I	34	9	11	14	57	62	29	13th
1965–66	I	34	9	8	17	58	81	26	14th
1966–67	I	34	10	5	19	53	73	25	15th
1967–68	I	34	10	7	17	43	52	27	14th
1968–69	I	34	16	5	13	66	59	37	6th
1969–70	I	34	11	9	14	50	62	31	13th
1970–71	I	34	19	6	9	59	44	44	3rd
1971–72	I	34	12	8	14	52	58	32	8th
1972–73	I	34	10	9	15	52	67	29	11th
1973–74	I	34	9	10	15	41	60	28	12th
1974–75	I	34	11	12	11	41	44	34	9th
1975–76	Pr	36	3	5	28	29	79	11	10th
1976–77	I	39	8	13	18	42	64	29	11th
1977–78	I	39	15	6	18	52	64	36	8th
1978–79	I	39	10	11	18	57	66	31	12th
1979–80	I	39	12	10	17	57	74	34	11th
1980–81	I	39	20	11	8	64	45	51	3rd
1981–82	I	39	17	8	14	69	60	42	5th
1982–83	I	39	25	5	9	59	37	55	1st
1983–84	Pr	36	10	3	23	36	81	23	9th
1984–85	I	39	10	5	24	51	78	25	14th
1985–86	II	39	18	6	15	63	55	42	6th
1986–87	II	39	16	13	10	59	49	45	5th
1987–88	II	39	25	9	5	74	24	59	2nd
1988–89	I	39	14	12	13	51	42	40	6th
1989–90	I	39	25	8	6	81	39	58	1st
1990–91	Pr	36	11	9	16	41	54	31	7th
1991–92	Pr	44	13	10	21	52	73	36	8th
1992–93	Pr	44	10	20	14	52	66	40	6th

Willie Imrie was **St Johnstone**'s first Secretary-Treasurer in 1885. In 1929 an unrelated Willie Imrie became the only St Johnstone player to score a goal in a full international for Scotland v Norway, in one of his two appearances for his country.

ST MIRREN

Year	Div	P	W	D	L	F	A	Pts	Pos
1890–91	SL	18	5	1	12	39	62	11	8th
1891–92	SL	22	4	5	13	43	60	13	10th
1892–93	SL	18	9	2	7	40	39	20	3rd
1893–94	I	18	7	3	8	50	46	17	6th
1894–95	I	18	9	1	8	34	36	19	5th
1895–96	I	18	5	3	10	31	51	13	8th
1896–97	I	18	9	1	8	38	29	19	6th
1897–98	I	18	8	2	8	30	36	18	6th
1898–99	I	18	8	4	6	46	32	20	5th
1899–1900	I	18	3	6	9	30	46	12	8th
1900–01	I	20	5	6	9	33	43	16	9th
1901–02	I	18	8	3	7	29	28	19	5th
1902–03	I	22	7	8	7	39	40	22	6th
1903–04	I	26	11	5	10	45	38	27	6th
1904–05	I	26	9	4	13	33	36	22	10th
1905–06	I	30	13	5	12	41	37	31	8th
1906–07	I	34	12	13	9	50	44	37	7th
1907–08	I	34	13	10	11	50	59	36	7th
1908–09	I	34	15	6	13	53	45	36	7th
1909–10	I	34	13	5	16	49	58	31	13th
1910–11	I	34	12	7	15	46	57	31	12th
1911–12	I	34	7	10	17	39	52	24	18th
1912–13	I	34	10	10	14	50	60	30	12th
1913–14	I	38	8	6	24	38	73	22	20th
1914–15	I	38	14	8	16	56	65	36	9th
1915–16	SL	38	13	4	21	50	67	30	13th
1916–17	SL	38	15	10	13	49	43	40	7th
1917–18	SL	34	11	7	16	42	50	29	11th
1918–19	SL	34	10	12	12	43	55	32	11th
1919–20	SL	42	15	8	19	63	81	38	14th
1920–21	SL	42	7	4	31	43	92	18	22nd
1921–22	I	42	17	12	13	71	61	46	8th
1922–23	I	38	15	12	11	54	44	42	6th
1923–24	I	38	15	12	11	53	45	42	6th
1924–25	I	38	18	4	16	65	63	40	6th
1925–26	I	38	20	7	11	62	52	47	4th
1926–27	I	38	16	5	17	78	76	37	10th
1927–28	I	38	15	8	12	77	76	44	5th
1928–29	I	38	16	8	14	78	74	40	8th
1929–30	I	38	18	5	15	73	56	41	5th
1930–31	I	38	11	8	19	49	72	30	15th
1931–32	I	38	20	4	14	77	56	44	5th

Year	Div	P	W	D	L	F	A	Pts	Pos
1932–33	I	38	18	6	14	73	60	42	7th
1933–34	I	38	9	9	20	46	75	27	17th
1934–35	I	38	11	5	22	49	70	27	19th
1935–36	II	34	25	2	7	114	41	52	2nd
1936–37	I	38	11	7	20	68	81	29	16th
1937–38	I	38	14	5	19	58	66	33	14th
1938–39	I	38	11	7	20	57	80	29	18th
1939–46	Regional Leagues operating								
1946–47	A	30	9	4	17	47	65	22	14th
1947–48	A	30	13	5	12	54	58	31	5th
1948–49	A	30	13	4	13	51	47	30	9th
1949–50	A	30	8	9	13	42	49	25	11th
1950–51	A	30	9	7	14	35	51	25	11th
1951–52	A	30	10	5	15	43	58	25	14th
1952–53	A	30	11	8	11	52	58	30	6th
1953–54	A	30	12	4	14	44	54	28	11th
1954–55	A	30	12	8	10	55	54	32	6th
1955–56	A	34	10	7	17	57	70	27	15th
1956–57	I	34	12	6	16	58	72	30	12th
1957–58	I	34	11	8	15	59	66	30	13th
1958–59	I	34	14	7	13	71	74	35	7th
1959–60	I	34	11	6	17	78	86	28	14th
1960–61	I	34	11	7	16	53	58	29	14th
1961–62	I	34	10	5	19	52	80	25	16th
1962–63	I	34	10	8	16	52	72	28	12th
1963–64	I	34	12	5	17	44	74	29	12th
1964–65	I	34	9	6	19	38	70	24	15th
1965–66	I	34	9	4	21	44	82	22	16th
1966–67	I	34	4	7	23	25	81	15	17th
1967–68	II	36	27	8	1	100	23	62	1st
1968–69	I	34	11	10	13	40	54	32	11th
1969–70	I	34	8	9	17	39	54	25	15th
1970–71	I	34	7	9	18	38	56	23	17th
1971–72	II	36	24	2	10	84	47	50	4th
1972–73	II	36	19	7	10	79	50	45	5th
1973–74	II	36	12	10	14	62	66	34	11th
1974–75	II	38	19	8	11	74	52	46	6th
1975–76	I	26	9	8	9	37	37	26	6th
1976–77	I	39	25	12	2	91	38	62	1st
1977–78	Pr	36	11	8	17	52	63	30	8th
1978–79	Pr	36	15	6	15	45	41	36	6th
1979–80	Pr	36	15	12	9	56	49	42	3rd
1980–81	Pr	36	18	8	10	56	47	44	4th
1981–82	Pr	36	14	9	13	49	52	37	5th
1982–83	Pr	36	11	12	13	47	51	34	5th
1983–84	Pr	36	9	14	13	55	59	32	6th
1984–85	Pr	36	17	4	15	51	56	38	5th
1985–86	Pr	36	13	5	18	42	63	31	7th
1986–87	Pr	44	12	12	20	36	51	36	7th
1987–88	Pr	44	10	15	19	41	64	35	9th
1988–89	Pr	36	11	7	18	39	55	29	7th
1989–90	Pr	36	10	10	16	28	48	30	9th
1990–91	Pr	36	5	9	22	28	59	34	10th
1991–92	Pr	44	6	12	26	33	73	24	11th
1992–93	I	44	21	9	14	62	52	51	4th

St Mirren and Notts County were invited to Spain to mark the opening of a new £75,000 stadium by playing an exhibition match. St Mirren won 2–1.

STENHOUSEMUIR

Year	Div	P	W	D	L	F	A	Pts	Pos
1921–22	II	38	14	10	14	50	51	38	10th
1922–23	II	38	13	7	18	53	67	33	14th
1923–24	II	38	16	11	11	58	45	43	4th
1924–25	II	38	15	7	16	51	58	37	11th
1925–26	II	38	19	10	9	74	52	48	5th
1926–27	II	38	12	12	14	69	75	36	10th
1927–28	II	38	15	5	18	75	81	35	16th
1928–29	II	35	9	6	20	52	90	24	18th
1929–30	II	38	11	5	22	75	108	27	17th
1930–31	II	38	13	6	19	78	98	32	17th
1931–32	II	38	19	8	11	88	76	46	4th
1932–33	II	34	18	6	10	67	58	42	4th
1933–34	II	34	18	4	12	70	73	40	4th
1934–35	II	34	17	5	12	86	80	39	5th
1935–36	II	34	13	3	18	59	78	29	11th
1936–37	II	34	14	4	16	82	86	32	10th
1937–38	II	34	17	5	12	87	78	39	8th
1938–39	II	34	15	5	14	74	69	35	8th
1939–46	Regional Leagues operating								
1946–47	B	26	8	7	11	43	53	23	7th
1947–48	B	30	6	11	13	53	83	23	14th
1948–49	B	30	8	8	14	50	54	24	12th
1949–50	B	30	8	8	14	54	72	24	12th
1950–51	B	30	9	2	19	51	80	20	15th
1951–52	B	30	8	6	16	57	74	22	13th
1952–53	B	30	10	6	14	56	65	26	12th
1953–54	B	30	14	8	8	66	48	36	4th
1954–55	B	30	12	8	10	70	51	32	6th
1955–56	B	36	20	4	12	82	54	44	5th
1956–57	II	36	13	6	17	71	81	32	14th
1957–58	II	36	12	5	19	68	98	29	16th
1958–59	II	36	20	6	10	87	68	46	3rd
1959–60	II	36	20	4	12	86	67	44	5th
1960–61	II	36	24	2	10	99	69	50	3rd
1961–62	II	36	13	5	18	69	86	31	15th
1962–63	II	36	13	5	18	54	75	31	16th
1963–64	II	36	15	5	16	83	75	35	11th
1964–65	II	36	11	8	17	49	74	30	15th
1965–66	II	36	6	7	23	47	93	19	18th
1966–67	II	38	9	9	20	62	104	27	17th
1967–68	II	36	7	6	23	34	93	20	19th
1968–69	II	36	6	6	24	55	125	18	19th
1969–70	II	36	10	6	20	47	89	26	16th
1970–71	II	36	14	8	14	64	70	36	10th
1971–72	II	36	10	8	18	41	58	28	14th
1972–73	II	36	14	8	14	44	41	36	10th
1973–74	II	36	11	5	20	44	59	27	15th
1974–75	II	38	14	11	13	52	42	39	11th
1975–76	II	26	9	5	12	39	44	23	10th

Year	Div	P	W	D	L	F	A	Pts	Pos
1976–77	II	39	15	5	19	38	49	35	9th
1977–78	II	39	10	10	19	43	67	30	12th
1978–79	II	39	12	8	19	54	58	32	10th
1979–80	II	39	16	9	14	56	51	41	6th
1980–81	II	39	13	11	15	63	58	37	10th
1981–82	II	39	11	6	22	41	65	28	13th
1982–83	II	39	7	15	17	43	66	29	11th
1983–84	II	39	14	11	14	47	57	39	7th
1984–85	II	39	15	15	9	45	43	45	5th
1985–86	II	39	16	8	15	55	63	40	7th
1986–87	II	39	10	9	20	37	58	29	12th
1987–88	II	39	12	9	18	49	58	33	10th
1988–89	II	39	9	11	19	44	59	29	14th
1989–90	II	39	18	8	13	60	53	44	4th
1990–91	II	39	16	12	11	56	42	44	4th
1991–92	II	39	11	8	20	46	57	30	13th
1992–93	II	39	15	10	14	59	48	40	7th

On 15 April 1950 in a Division B match, **Stenhousemuir** beat Dunfermline Athletic 7–6 after leading 3–2 at half-time.

Year	Div	P	W	D	L	F	A	Pts	Pos
1978–79	I	39	13	9	17	43	55	35	8th
1979–80	I	39	13	13	13	40	40	39	8th
1980–81	I	39	6	11	22	18	48	23	13th
1981–82	II	39	12	11	16	39	44	35	8th
1982–83	II	39	18	10	11	57	41	46	5th
1983–84	II	39	14	14	11	51	42	42	4th
1984–85	II	39	15	13	11	62	47	43	6th
1985–86	II	39	18	8	13	57	43	44	5th
1986–87	II	39	20	12	7	55	33	52	3rd
1987–88	II	39	18	10	11	60	51	46	5th
1988–89	II	39	15	12	12	64	55	42	4th
1989–90	II	39	20	7	12	73	50	47	3rd
1990–91	II	39	20	14	5	62	24	54	1st
1991–92	I	44	14	13	17	50	57	41	8th
1992–93	I	44	11	13	20	44	61	35	10th

Joe Hughes was **Stirling Albion**'s leading scorer in 1969–70 with 27 League goals. His best individual performance in the season was scoring a hat-trick in a 6–0 win over Forfar Athletic on 8 November 1969.

STIRLING ALBION

Year	Div	P	W	D	L	F	A	Pts	Pos
1947–48	B	30	11	6	13	85	66	28	8th
1948–49	B	30	20	2	8	71	47	42	2nd
1949–50	A	30	6	3	21	38	77	15	16th
1950–51	B	30	21	3	6	78	44	45	2nd
1951–52	A	30	5	5	20	36	99	15	16th
1952–53	B	30	20	4	6	64	43	44	1st
1953–54	A	30	10	4	16	39	62	24	14th
1954–55	A	30	2	2	26	29	105	6	16th
1955–56	A	34	4	5	25	23	82	13	18th
1956–57	II	36	17	5	14	81	64	39	8th
1957–58	II	36	25	5	6	105	48	55	1st
1958–59	I	34	11	8	15	54	64	30	12th
1959–60	I	34	7	8	19	55	72	22	17th
1960–61	II	36	24	7	5	89	37	55	1st
1961–62	I	34	6	6	22	34	76	18	18th
1962–63	II	36	16	4	16	74	75	36	10th
1963–64	II	36	6	8	22	47	99	20	19th
1964–65	II	36	26	7	3	84	31	59	1st
1965–66	I	34	9	8	17	40	68	26	15th
1966–67	I	34	5	9	20	31	85	19	16th
1967–68	I	34	4	4	26	29	105	12	18th
1968–69	II	36	21	6	9	67	40	48	4th
1969–70	II	36	18	10	8	70	40	46	4th
1970–71	II	36	12	8	16	61	61	32	12th
1971–72	II	36	21	8	7	75	37	50	3rd
1972–73	II	36	19	9	8	70	39	47	4th
1973–74	II	36	17	6	13	76	50	40	7th
1974–75	II	38	17	9	12	67	55	43	8th
1975–76	II	26	9	7	12	41	33	25	6th
1976–77	II	39	22	11	6	59	29	55	1st
1977–78	I	39	15	12	12	60	52	42	5th

STRANRAER

Year	Div	P	W	D	L	F	A	Pts	Pos
1955–56	B	36	14	5	17	77	92	33	12th
1956–57	II	36	15	10	11	79	77	40	7th
1957–58	II	36	9	7	20	54	83	25	18th
1958–59	II	36	8	11	17	63	76	27	16th
1959–60	II	36	10	3	23	53	79	23	17th
1960–61	II	36	19	6	11	83	55	44	4th
1961–62	II	36	14	11	11	61	62	39	7th
1962–63	II	36	16	10	10	81	70	42	5th
1963–64	II	36	16	6	14	71	73	38	8th
1964–65	II	36	17	6	13	74	64	40	6th
1965–66	II	36	9	10	17	64	83	28	15th
1966–67	II	38	13	7	18	57	73	33	15th
1967–68	II	36	8	4	24	41	80	20	18th
1968–69	II	36	17	7	12	57	45	41	8th
1969–70	II	36	9	7	20	56	75	25	17th
1970–71	II	36	14	8	14	54	52	36	9th
1971–72	II	36	18	8	10	70	62	44	6th
1972–73	II	36	13	4	19	56	78	30	15th
1973–74	II	36	14	8	14	64	70	36	9th
1974–75	II	38	12	11	15	47	65	35	14th
1975–76	II	26	11	3	12	49	43	25	7th
1976–77	II	39	20	6	13	74	53	46	4th
1977–78	II	39	13	7	19	54	63	33	11th
1978–79	II	39	18	2	19	52	66	38	9th
1979–80	II	39	12	8	19	51	65	32	11th
1980–81	II	39	7	8	24	36	83	22	14th
1981–82	II	39	7	6	26	36	85	20	14th
1982–83	II	39	10	7	22	46	79	27	12th
1983–84	II	39	13	12	14	47	47	38	8th
1984–85	II	39	13	6	20	52	67	32	11th
1985–86	II	39	9	5	25	41	82	23	14th
1986–87	II	39	9	11	19	41	59	29	10th

1987–88	II	39	4	8	27	34	84	16	14th
1988–89	II	39	12	12	15	59	64	36	11th
1989–90	II	39	15	8	16	57	59	38	8th
1990–91	II	39	18	4	17	61	60	40	6th
1991–92	II	39	13	9	17	46	56	35	10th
1992–93	II	39	19	15	5	69	44	53	3rd

When **Stranraer** beat Bo'ness 5–3 in the final of the Scottish Qualifying Cup in 1937–38 at Somerset Park, Ayr their goalkeeper Andrew Loudon saved three penalties.

THIRD LANARK

Year	Div	P	W	D	L	F	A	Pts	Pos
1890–91	SL	18	8	3	7	38	39	15	5th
1891–92	SL	22	9	4	9	44	47	22	6th
1892–93	SL	18	9	1	8	54	40	19	4th
1893–94	I	18	7	3	8	37	45	17	7th
1894–95	I	18	10	1	7	51	39	21	4th
1895–96	I	18	7	1	10	47	51	15	6th
1896–97	I	18	5	1	12	29	46	11	8th
1897–98	I	18	8	2	8	37	38	18	5th
1898–99	I	18	7	3	8	33	38	17	6th
1899–1900	I	18	5	5	8	31	36	15	7th
1900–01	I	20	6	6	8	20	29	18	6th
1901–02	I	18	7	5	6	30	26	19	4th
1902–03	I	22	8	5	9	34	27	21	7th
1903–04	I	26	20	3	3	61	26	43	1st
1904–05	I	26	14	7	5	60	28	35	3rd
1905–06	I	30	16	2	12	62	39	34	6th
1906–07	I	34	15	9	10	57	48	39	6th
1907–08	I	34	13	7	14	45	50	33	9th
1908–09	I	34	11	10	13	56	49	32	11th
1909–10	I	34	13	8	13	62	44	34	7th
1910–11	I	34	16	7	11	59	53	39	8th
1911–12	I	34	12	7	15	40	57	31	11th
1912–13	I	34	8	12	14	31	41	28	15th
1913–14	I	38	13	10	15	42	51	36	8th
1914–15	I	38	10	12	16	51	57	32	16th
1915–16	SL	38	9	11	18	38	56	29	17th
1916–17	SL	38	19	11	8	53	47	49	5th
1917–18	SL	34	10	7	17	56	62	27	13th
1918–19	SL	34	11	9	14	60	60	31	12th
1919–20	SL	42	16	11	15	57	62	43	8th
1920–21	SL	42	19	6	17	74	61	44	8th
1921–22	I	42	17	12	13	58	52	46	9th
1922–23	I	38	11	8	19	40	59	30	17th
1923–24	I	38	11	8	19	54	78	30	18th
1924–25	I	38	11	8	19	53	84	30	20th
1925–26	II	38	19	8	11	72	47	46	6th
1926–27	II	38	17	10	11	67	48	44	4th
1927–28	II	38	18	9	11	99	66	45	2nd
1928–29	I	38	10	6	22	71	102	26	19th
1929–30	II	38	23	6	9	92	53	52	4th
1930–31	II	38	27	7	4	107	42	61	1st
1931–32	I	38	21	4	13	92	81	46	4th
1932–33	I	38	14	7	17	70	80	35	13th
1933–34	I	38	8	9	21	62	103	25	19th
1934–35	II	34	23	6	5	94	43	52	1st
1935–36	I	38	14	5	19	63	71	33	11th
1936–37	I	38	20	6	12	79	61	46	6th
1937–38	I	38	11	13	14	68	73	35	9th
1938–39	I	38	12	8	18	80	96	32	15th
1939–46	Regional Leagues operating								
1946–47	A	30	11	6	13	56	64	28	9th
1947–48	A	30	10	6	14	56	73	26	11th
1948–49	A	30	13	5	12	56	52	31	7th
1949–50	A	30	11	3	16	44	62	25	12th
1950–51	A	30	11	2	17	40	51	24	13th
1951–52	A	30	9	8	13	51	62	26	12th
1952–53	A	30	8	4	18	52	75	20	16th
1953–54	B	30	13	10	7	78	48	36	3rd
1954–55	B	30	13	7	10	63	49	33	5th
1955–56	B	36	16	3	17	80	64	35	10th
1956–57	II	36	24	3	9	105	51	51	2nd
1957–58	I	34	13	4	17	69	88	30	14th
1958–59	I	34	11	10	13	74	83	32	11th
1959–60	I	34	13	4	17	75	83	30	12th
1960–61	I	34	20	2	12	100	80	42	3rd
1961–62	I	34	13	5	16	59	60	31	11th
1962–63	I	34	9	8	17	56	68	26	14th
1963–64	I	34	9	7	18	47	74	25	16th
1964–65	I	34	3	1	30	22	99	7	18th
1965–66	II	36	12	8	16	55	65	32	14th
1966–67	II	38	13	8	17	67	78	34	11th
Resigned									

Third Lanark goalkeeper Jimmy Brownlie missed only one international for Scotland between 1909 and 1914 with injury and was capped 16 times.

THISTLE

Year	Div	P	W	D	L	F	A	Pts	Pos
1893–94	II	18	2	3	13	31	74	7	10th

Thistle suffered their heaviest defeat when losing 13–1 to Partick Thistle in Division Two on 10 March 1894.

VALE OF LEVEN

Year	Div	P	W	D	L	F	A	Pts	Pos
1890–91	SL	18	5	1	12	27	65	11	9th
1891–92	SL	22	0	5	17	24	100	5	12th
Regional Leagues									
1905–06	II	22	6	4	12	34	49	16	11th
1906–07	II	22	13	1	8	54	35	27	2nd
1907–08	II	22	5	8	9	25	31	18	10th
1908–09	II	22	12	4	6	39	25	28	3rd
1909–10	II	22	8	5	9	36	38	21	6th
1910–11	II	22	4	8	10	22	31	16	12th

1911–12	II	22	6	1	15	19	37	13	11th
1912–13	II	26	8	5	13	28	45	21	12th
1913–14	II	22	5	3	14	23	47	13	11th
1914–15	II	26	4	5	17	33	66	13	14th
Regional Leagues									
1921–22	II	38	17	10	11	56	43	44	4th

1922–23	II	38	11	8	19	50	59	30	17th
1923–24	II	38	11	9	18	41	67	31	19th

Vale Of Leven conceded ten goals on two occasions during 1891–92. They lost 10–0 at Leith Athletic on 19 September and 10–3 at Clyde on 15 April.

SCOTTISH LEAGUE

LEAGUE CHAMPIONS

Season	Champions	P	W	D	L	F	A	Pts	Margin
1890–91	Dumbarton	18	13	3	2	61	21	29	8
	Rangers	18	13	3	2	58	25	29	8
1891–92	Dumbarton	22	18	1	3	79	28	37	2
1892–93	Celtic	18	14	1	3	54	25	29	1
1893–94	Celtic	18	14	1	3	53	32	29	3
1894–95	Hearts	18	15	1	2	50	18	31	5
1895–96	Celtic	18	15	0	3	64	25	30	4
1896–97	Hearts	18	13	2	3	47	22	28	2
1897–98	Celtic	18	15	3	0	56	13	33	4
1898–99	Rangers	18	18	0	0	79	18	36	10
1899–1900	Rangers	18	15	2	1	69	27	32	7
1900–01	Rangers	20	17	1	2	60	25	35	6
1901–02	Rangers	18	13	2	3	43	29	28	2
1902–03	Hibernian	22	16	5	1	48	18	37	6
1903–04	Third Lanark	26	20	3	3	61	26	43	4
1904–05	Celtic	26	19	3	4	68	31	41	p-o
1905–06	Celtic	30	24	1	5	76	19	49	6
1906–07	Celtic	34	23	9	2	80	30	55	7
1907–08	Celtic	34	24	7	3	86	27	55	4
1908–09	Celtic	34	23	5	6	71	24	51	1
1909–10	Celtic	34	24	6	4	63	22	54	2
1910–11	Rangers	34	23	6	5	90	34	52	4
1911–12	Rangers	34	24	3	7	86	34	51	6
1912–13	Rangers	34	24	5	5	76	41	53	4
1913–14	Celtic	38	30	5	3	81	14	65	6
1914–15	Celtic	38	30	5	3	91	25	65	4
1915–16	Celtic	38	32	3	3	116	23	67	11
1916–17	Celtic	38	27	10	1	77	17	64	10
1917–18	Rangers	34	25	6	3	66	24	56	1
1918–19	Celtic	34	26	6	2	70	22	58	1
1919–20	Rangers	42	31	9	2	106	25	71	3
1920–21	Rangers	42	35	6	1	91	24	76	10
1921–22	Celtic	42	27	13	2	83	20	67	1
1922–23	Rangers	38	23	9	6	67	29	55	5
1923–24	Rangers	38	25	9	4	72	22	59	9
1924–25	Rangers	38	25	10	3	77	27	60	3
1925–26	Celtic	38	25	8	5	97	40	58	8
1926–27	Rangers	38	23	10	5	85	41	56	5
1927–28	Rangers	38	26	8	4	109	36	60	5
1928–29	Rangers	38	30	7	1	107	32	67	16
1929–30	Rangers	38	28	4	6	94	32	60	5
1930–31	Rangers	38	27	6	5	96	29	60	2
1931–32	Motherwell	38	30	6	2	119	31	66	5
1932–33	Rangers	38	26	10	2	113	43	62	3
1933–34	Rangers	38	30	6	2	118	41	66	4
1934–35	Rangers	38	25	5	8	96	46	55	3
1935–36	Celtic	38	32	2	4	115	33	66	5
1936–37	Rangers	38	26	9	3	88	32	61	7
1937–38	Celtic	38	27	7	4	114	42	61	3
1938–39	Rangers	38	25	9	4	112	55	59	11
1939–46 No National competition, regional leagues in operation									
1946–47	Rangers	30	21	4	5	76	26	46	2
1947–48	Hibernian	30	22	4	4	86	27	48	2
1948–49	Rangers	30	20	6	4	63	32	46	1
1949–50	Rangers	30	22	6	2	58	26	50	1
1950–51	Hibernian	30	22	4	4	78	26	48	10
1951–52	Hibernian	30	20	5	5	92	36	45	4
1952–53	Rangers	30	18	7	5	80	39	43	gl.av.
1953–54	Celtic	30	20	3	7	72	29	43	5
1954–55	Aberdeen	30	24	1	5	73	26	49	3
1955–56	Rangers	34	22	8	4	85	27	52	6
1956–57	Rangers	34	26	3	5	96	48	55	2
1957–58	Hearts	34	29	4	1	132	29	62	13
1958–59	Rangers	34	21	8	5	92	51	50	2
1959–60	Hearts	34	23	8	3	102	51	54	4
1960–61	Rangers	34	23	5	6	88	46	51	1
1961–62	Dundee	34	25	4	5	80	46	54	3
1962–63	Rangers	34	25	7	2	94	28	57	9
1963–64	Rangers	34	25	5	4	85	31	55	6
1964–65	Kilmarnock	34	22	6	6	62	33	50	gl.av.
1965–66	Celtic	34	27	3	4	106	30	57	2
1966–67	Celtic	34	26	6	2	111	33	58	3
1967–68	Celtic	34	30	3	1	106	24	63	2
1968–69	Celtic	34	23	8	3	89	32	54	5
1969–70	Celtic	34	27	3	4	96	33	57	12
1970–71	Celtic	34	25	6	3	89	23	56	2
1971–72	Celtic	34	28	4	2	96	28	60	10
1972–73	Celtic	34	26	5	3	93	28	57	1
1973–74	Celtic	34	23	7	4	82	27	53	4

Season	Champions	P	W	D	L	F	A	Pts	Margin
1974–75	Rangers	34	25	6	3	86	33	56	7
1975–76*	Rangers	36	23	8	5	60	24	54	6
1976–77	Celtic	36	23	9	4	79	39	55	9
1977–78	Rangers	36	24	7	5	76	39	55	2
1978–79	Celtic	36	21	6	9	61	37	48	3
1979–80	Aberdeen	36	19	10	7	68	36	48	1
1980–81	Celtic	36	26	4	6	84	37	56	7
1981–82	Celtic	36	24	7	5	79	33	55	2
1982–83	Dundee Utd	36	24	8	4	90	35	56	1
1983–84	Aberdeen	36	25	7	4	78	21	57	7
1984–85	Aberdeen	36	27	5	4	89	26	59	7
1985–86	Celtic	36	20	10	6	67	38	50	gl.dif.
1986–87	Rangers	44	31	7	6	85	23	69	6
1987–88	Celtic	44	31	10	3	79	23	72	10
1988–89	Rangers	36	26	4	6	62	26	56	6
1989–90	Rangers	36	20	11	5	48	19	51	7
1990–91	Rangers	36	24	7	5	62	23	55	2
1991–92	Rangers	44	33	6	5	101	31	72	9
1992–93	Rangers	44	33	7	4	97	35	73	9

* Premier Division introduced

SCOTTISH LEAGUE FACTS & FEATS

Most wins in a season

Aberdeen won 27 of their 36 Premier Division matches in 1984–85. They won one more game away than at home and retained their championship title. Their worst spell came in December–January when in four games, they picked up just two points from draws. Overall they lost just four times.

Rangers won 33 of their 44 Premier Division matches in 1991–92. They did not go to the top until 19 October and were in second place on several weeks before finally taking over again on 11 January. They were unbeaten in 16 games from 30 November to 1 January and began this sequence with seven successive wins. Rangers won 19 away matches, 14 at home.

Rangers also won 33 of their 44 Premier Division matches in 1992–93, winning 20 at home and 13 away. After losing 4–3 at Dundee on 15 August they did not lose again until 20 March, when they were defeated 2–1 at Celtic Park.

Rangers won 35 of their 42 Division One matches in 1920–21. They began with a 4–1 win over Airdrieonians and were undefeated in their first 23 games, dropping only two points (at Aberdeen and Ayr) before losing 2–0 at home to Celtic in their only defeat. From the end of

September until mid-December they had a winning run of 12 matches.

Morton won 33 of their 38 Division Two matches in 1966–67. They finished as champions, having lost only two matches and conceded only 20 goals, the fewest on record in the division. Their 69 points was another Division Two record.

Fewest wins in a season

St Johnstone achieved only three wins in 36 Premier Division matches in 1975–76. From early October to mid-April they completed 27 games without a win. They scored just 29 goals, failed to score in 17 matches, and were relegated.

Kilmarnock achieved only three wins in 36 Premier Division matches in 1982–83. Only twice did they manage to score more than two goals in a game in a total of 28, and their defence conceded 91 goals including an 8–1 and a 7–0 defeat.

Vale of Leven failed to win any of their 22 Division One matches in 1891–92. They achieved only five points and were not re-elected.

Ayr United achieved only one win in 34 Division One matches in 1966–67. That solitary success came courtesy of a penalty scored by centre-half Eddie Monan at home to St Johnstone on 8 April.

East Stirling won only one of their 22 Division Two matches in 1905–06. They did manage to draw 10 times but finished bottom. Their only victory was achieved on 11 November when they won 4–2 at Ayr.

Stuart McCall (right) of Rangers challenges Aberdeen's Roy Aitken in 1992–93. The Gers won a record 33 League matches for the second consecutive season (Allsport/Shaun Botterill)

Forfar Athletic achieved only one win in 38 Division Two matches in 1974–75. They finished 12 points behind their nearest rivals at the bottom of the table. Only one point came from their last 15 games.

Most defeats in a single season

Morton suffered 29 defeats in 36 Premier Division matches in 1984–85. Unusually, their number of wins (five) outnumbered the drawn games (two) but they suffered 13 consecutive defeats and also conceded a record 100 goals. They first hit the bottom on 29 September and remained there for the rest of the season.

St Mirren suffered 31 defeats in 42 Division One matches in 1920–21. They did win seven games and for much of the season kept just ahead of Dumbarton until a slump in their last 15 games produced 13 defeats and they finished six points behind their nearest rivals. Their goals against total of 92 was the worst in either the Scottish or Football League that season. Fourteen of their defeats were at home.

Cowdenbeath suffered 34 defeats in 44 First Division matches in 1992–93. They failed to win a single match at home but won three away.

Brechin City suffered 30 defeats in 36 Division Two matches in 1962–63. They finished bottom, 14 points behind their nearest rivals. Their nine points came from three wins and three draws and they lost 13 at home.

Lochgelly United suffered 30 defeats in 38 Division Two matches in 1923–24. They finished bottom, 20 points adrift of their nearest rivals. They won four and drew four other games but scored only 21 goals.

Fewest defeats in a season

Celtic suffered only three defeats in 44 Premier Division matches in 1987–88, and had a mid-season run of 26 games unbeaten. Their only defeats came at home to Dundee United and away at Dunfermline and Hearts.

Celtic went through 18 Division One matches in 1897–98 without a defeat. Only three points were dropped. In 1898–99 Rangers won all their Division One matches, while in the same season Kilmarnock were undefeated in Division Two, dropping only four points in 18 games.

Rangers suffered only one defeat in 42 Division One matches in 1920–21. Celtic beat them 2–0 on New Year's Day with inside-left Joe Cassidy scoring both goals. Heart of Midlothian suffered only one defeat in 34 Division One matches in 1957–58, as did both

Rangers and Celtic in 1967–68. That season Celtic were champions, two points ahead of Rangers.

Clyde suffered only one defeat in 36 Division Two matches in 1956–57. They were not beaten until 20 April, losing 4–1 away to Forfar Athletic who finished fourth from bottom. Clyde scored 122 goals and finished as champions with 64 points, 13 ahead of their nearest rivals.

Morton suffered only one defeat in 36 Division Two matches in 1962–63. They were not beaten until 1 February when they lost 3–1 away to East Fife. Morton scored 135 goals and achieved 67 points to finish champions by a margin of 14 points.

St Mirren suffered only one defeat in 36 Division Two matches in 1967–68. They were beaten on 4 November, losing 2–1 away to East Fife. St Mirren scored exactly 100 goals for their 62 points to finish champions, nine points ahead of their nearest rivals.

Most points in a season

Rangers achieved 73 points in 44 Premier Division matches in 1992–93. They finished nine points ahead of Aberdeen, the runners-up. They were unbeaten at home, winning 20 of their 22 games at Ibrox.

Rangers totalled 76 points in 42 Division One matches in 1920–21. They finished ten points ahead of Celtic, the runners-up, and 26 points in front of Hearts who were third. Rangers' only defeat was 2–0 at home to Celtic on New Year's Day when they were weakened by injuries. The previous season they had established a new record

Celtic at home to Dundee in April 1988, the climax to a Championship season which saw them lose only three times. They won this game 3–0 to clinch the title (Allsport/Simon Bruty)

with a total of 71 points. In these two seasons they lost only three of 84 League games played and enjoyed one spell of 56 consecutive games in which they were beaten only once, a 2–1 home defeat by Clydebank.

Morton achieved 69 points in 38 Division Two matches in 1966–67. They finished 11 points ahead of Raith Rovers, the runners-up. Morton suffered only two defeats and won 33 games, scoring 113 goals.

Most draws in a season

Hibernian drew 18 of their 36 Premier Division matches in 1976–77. They drew ten at home and eight away and had one run of eight games which produced seven draws. They scored 34 goals and conceded 35.

Sequences

After losing 2–0 at Tynecastle to Hearts on 13 November 1915, Celtic completed 62 Division One matches without defeat until losing 2–0 at home to Kilmarnock on 21 April 1917. They won 49 and drew 13 of their games. In 1915–16 they won the championship by a margin of 11 points and retained their title the following season by ten points.

Most goals scored in a season

Rangers scored 101 goals in 44 Premier Division matches in 1991–92. It was the first time a team had reached a century since the inception of the division. Their biggest win came in the first game on 10 August when they beat St Johnstone 6–0 at Ibrox. Ally McCoist with 34 was leading scorer and finished as Europe's Golden Boot winner, but he was not a regular choice until the tenth match. Mark Hateley provided further scoring support with 21 goals.

Dundee United scored 90 goals in 36 Premier Division matches in 1982–83, their total being equalled by Celtic in the same season and again in 1986–87. Dundee United were champions in 1982–83 with 56 points, one ahead of Celtic. They were most consistent, losing only four times, including two defeats in succession in January. They clinched the title with a 2–1 win away to Tayside rivals Dundee on 14 May in the last game of the season. But they had virtually made certain of a first ever Championship with a 3–2 win at Celtic Park on 20 April. Celtic lost their next game 1–0 at Aberdeen, among six defeats. In 1986–87 Celtic surrendered a seven point lead over Rangers at the turn of the year and had to be content with being runners-up to their great rivals.

Heart of Midlothian scored 132 goals in 34 Division One matches during 1957–58. They were League champions by a margin of 13 points over runners-up Rangers. They suffered only one defeat, 2–1 away to Clyde, and collected a club record 62 points. Hearts beat East Fife 9–0, Falkirk 9–1 and Queen's Park 8–0.

Raith Rovers scored 142 goals in 34 Division Two matches, during 1937–38. They never failed to score in any of their games and achieved five scores of six goals or more at home. They won 8–2 away at Brechin City, 8–1 at East Stirling and 8–3 at Alloa.

Most goals conceded in a season

Morton conceded 100 goals in 36 Premier Division matches in 1984–85 and the same total in 44 games in 1987–88. In 1984–85 they began well enough with two wins but won only three other matches and overall drew just twice. In one spell they were beaten on 13 consecutive occasions. They finished bottom and were relegated. In 1987–88 they won only three games and had a run of 28 without a win. They drew 10 times but finished bottom again.

Leith Athletic conceded 137 goals in 38 Division One matches during 1931–32. They were relegated having finished bottom, three points behind Dundee United. Leith won six and drew four of their matches.

Edinburgh City conceded 146 goals in 38 Division Two matches in 1931–32. They finished bottom, eight points below their nearest rivals. Though they scored as many as 78 goals themselves, they managed to keep their goal intact only twice. Their heaviest defeats were 8–2 away to Alloa and 8–4 at home to Queen of the South.

Fewest goals scored in a season

Hamilton Academical scored only 19 goals in 36 Premier Division matches in 1988–89. They won six games but failed to score in 22, and did not score more than twice in any game. Although they won two of their first six matches and finished the season with two consecutive wins, this did not prevent them from being relegated. Their defence conceded eight goals to Celtic at Parkhead.

Morton scored only 18 goals in 18 Division One matches in 1901–02. They achieved seven points, won only one game and finished bottom, six points behind their nearest rivals.

Stirling Albion scored only 18 goals in 39 Division One matches in 1980–81. They achieved 23 points including six wins, two of which were away. Their highest win was 4–2 at home to East Stirling but overall they failed to score in 27 games. They were relegated but finished one point above Berwick Rangers.

Lochgelly United scored only 20 goals in 38 Division Two matches in 1923–24. They finished bottom with 12 points from four wins and four draws and were 19 points away from their nearest rivals.

Albion Rovers scored only 19 goals in 22 Division Two matches in 1911–12 while Johnstone (not to be confused with St Johnstone) scored 20 from 22 games in the same division in 1913–14.

Fewest goals conceded in a season

Rangers conceded only 19 goals in 36 Premier Division matches in 1989–90. In as many as 20 of these they were able to prevent the opposition from scoring. No team scored more than two goals against them in any game. They finished as champions seven points ahead of their nearest rivals.

Celtic conceded only 14 goals in 38 Division One matches in 1913–14. They kept their goal intact in 26 games and only Hearts were able to score more than a single goal against them, winning 2–0 at Tynecastle. Fourteen goals represent the lowest total of goals conceded in any Scottish League season irrespective of the number of games played.

Morton conceded only 20 goals in 38 Division Two matches in 1966–67. They lost just twice and were champions with 69 points. In 21 games they prevented the opposition from scoring. No team scored more than two goals against them in a match.

SCOTTISH CUP

Tennents Cup 1992–

QUEEN'S PARK

Year	Score	Runners-up	Venue	Attendance
1874	2–0	Clydesdale	First Hampden	3,500
1875	3–0	Renton	First Hampden	7,000
1876	1–1	3rd Lanark Rifles	Hamilton Crescent	10,000
Replay	2–0	3rd Lanark Rifles	Hamilton Crescent	6,000
1880	3–0	Thornliebank	First Cathkin	4,000
1881	2–1	Dumbarton	First Cathkin	15,000
Replay	3–1	Dumbarton	First Cathkin	7,000
1882	2–2	Dumbarton	First Cathkin	12,500
Replay	4–1	Dumbarton	First Cathkin	14,000
1884	w. o	Vale of Leven		
1886	3–1	Renton	First Cathkin	7,000
1890	1–1	Vale of Leven	Ibrox	11,000
Replay	2–1	Vale of Leven	Ibrox	14,000
1893	0–0	Celtic	Ibrox	18,771
Replay	2–1	Celtic	Ibrox	13,239

VALE OF LEVEN

1877	1–1	Rangers	Hamilton Crescent	10,000
Replay	1–1	Rangers	Hamilton Crescent	15,000
2nd Replay	3–2	Rangers	First Hampden	12,000
1878	1–0	3rd Lanark Rifles	First Hampden	5,000
1879	1–1	Rangers	First Hampden	9,000

DUMBARTON

1883	2–2	Vale of Leven	First Hampden	9,000
Replay	2–1	Vale of Leven	First Hampden	12,000

RENTON

Year	Score	Runners-up	Venue	Attendance
1885	0–0	Vale of Leven	Second Hampden	2,500
Replay	3–1	Vale of Leven	Second Hampden	3,500
1888	6–1	Cambuslang	Second Hampden	11,000

HIBERNIAN

1887	2–1	Dumbarton	Second Hampden	12,000
1902	1–0	Celtic	Celtic Park	16,000

THIRD LANARK

1889	3–0	Celtic	Second Hampden	18,000
Replay	2–1	Celtic	Second Hampden	13,000
1905	0–0	Rangers	Hampden Park	54,000
Replay	3–1	Rangers	Hampden Park	55,000

HEART OF MIDLOTHIAN

1891	1–0	Dumbarton	Second Hampden	10,836
1896	3–1	Hibernian	Logie Green	17,034
1901	4–3	Celtic	Ibrox	12,000
1906	1–0	Third Lanark	Ibrox	25,000
1956	3–1	Celtic	Hampden Park	133,339

CELTIC

1892	1–0	Queen's Park	Ibrox	40,000
Replay	5–1	Queen's Park	Ibrox	26,000

Year	Score	Runners-up	Venue	Attendance
1899	2–0	Rangers	Second Hampden	25,000
1900	4–3	Queen's Park	Ibrox	15,000
1904	3–2	Rangers	Hampden Park	65,000
1907	3–0	Heart of Mid	Hampden Park	50,000
1908	5–1	St Mirren	Hampden Park	55,000
1909	2–2	Rangers	Hampden Park	70,000
Replay	1–1	Rangers	Hampden Park	61,000
1911	0–0	Hamilton Acad	Ibrox	45,000
Replay	2–0	Hamilton Acad	Ibrox	24,700
1912	2–0	Clyde	Ibrox	46,000
1914	0–0	Hibernian	Ibrox	56,000
Replay	4–1	Hibernian	Ibrox	40,000
1923	1–0	Hibernian	Hampden Park	80,100
1925	2–1	Dundee	Hampden Park	75,137
1927	3–1	East Fife	Hampden Park	80,070
1931	2–2	Motherwell	Hampden Park	105,000
Replay	4–2	Motherwell	Hampden Park	98,579
1933	1–0	Motherwell	Hampden Park	102,339
1937	2–1	Aberdeen	Hampden Park	147,365
1951	1–0	Motherwell	Hampden Park	131,943
1954	2–1	Aberdeen	Hampden Park	129,926
1965	3–2	Dunfermline Ath	Hampden Park	108,800
1967	2–0	Aberdeen	Hampden Park	127,117
1969	4–0	Rangers	Hampden Park	138,874
1971	1–1	Rangers	Hampden Park	120,092
Replay	2–1	Rangers	Hampden Park	103,332
1972	6–1	Hibernian	Hampden Park	106,102
1974	3–0	Dundee United	Hampden Park	75,959
1975	3–1	Airdrieonians	Hampden Park	75,457
1977	1–0	Rangers	Hampden Park	54,252
1980	1–0	Rangers	Hampden Park	70,303
1985	2–1	Dundee United	Hampden Park	60,346
1988	2–1	Dundee United	Hampden Park	74,000
1989	1–0	Rangers	Hampden Park	72,069

RANGERS

Year	Score	Runners-up	Venue	Attendance
1894	3–1	Celtic	Second Hampden	17,000
1897	5–1	Dumbarton	Second Hampden	14,000
1898	2–0	Kilmarnock	Second Hampden	13,000
1903	1–1	Heart of Mid	Celtic Park	40,000
Replay	0–0	Heart of Mid	Celtic Park	35,000
2nd Replay	2–0	Heart of Mid	Celtic Park	32,000
1928	4–0	Celtic	Hampden Park	118,115
1930	0–0	Partick Thistle	Hampden Park	107,475
Replay	2–1	Partick Thistle	Hampden Park	103,686
1932	1–1	Kilmarnock	Hampden Park	111,982
Replay	3–0	Kilmarnock	Hampden Park	104,965
1934	5–0	St. Mirren	Hampden Park	113,403
1935	2–1	Hamilton Acad	Hampden Park	87,286
1936	1–0	Third Lanark	Hampden Park	88,859
1948	1–1	Morton	Hampden Park	129,176
Replay	1–0	Morton	Hampden Park	133,570
1949	4–1	Clyde	Hampden Park	108,435
1950	3–0	East Fife	Hampden Park	118,262
1953	1–1	Aberdeen	Hampden Park	129,681

Year	Score	Runners-up	Venue	Attendance
Replay	1–0	Aberdeen	Hampden Park	112,619
1960	2–0	Kilmarnock	Hampden Park	108,017
1962	2–0	St Mirren	Hampden Park	126,930
1963	1–1	Celtic	Hampden Park	129,527
Replay	3–0	Celtic	Hampden Park	120,263
1964	3–1	Dundee	Hampden Park	120,982
1966	0–0	Celtic	Hampden Park	126,552
Replay	1–0	Celtic	Hampden Park	98,202
1973	3–2	Celtic	Hampden Park	122,714
1976	3–1	Heart of Mid	Hampden Park	85,354
1978	2–1	Aberdeen	Hampden Park	61,563
1979	0–0	Hibernian	Hampden Park	50,610
Replay	0–0	Hibernian	Hampden Park	33,506
2nd Replay	3–2	Hibernian	Hampden Park	30,602
1981	0–0	Dundee United	Hampden Park	55,000
Replay	4–1	Dundee United	Hampden Park	43,009
1992	2–1	Airdrieonians	Hampden Park	44,045
1993	2–1	Aberdeen	Celtic Park	50,715

DUNDEE

Year	Score	Runners-up	Venue	Attendance
1910	2–2	Clyde	Ibrox	62,300
Replay	0–0	Clyde	Ibrox	24,500
2nd replay	2–1	Clyde	Ibrox	25,400

FALKIRK

Year	Score	Runners-up	Venue	Attendance
1913	2–0	Raith Rovers	Celtic Park	45,000
1957	1–1	Kilmarnock	Hampden Park	83,000
Replay	2–1	Kilmarnock	Hampden Park	79,785

KILMARNOCK

Year	Score	Runners-up	Venue	Attendance
1920	3–2	Albion Rovers	Hampden Park	95,000
1929	2–0	Rangers	Hampden Park	114,708

EAST FIFE

Year	Score	Runners-up	Venue	Attendance
1938	1–1	Kilmarnock	Hampden Park	80,091
replay	4–2	Kilmarnock	Hampden Park	92,716

CLYDE

Year	Score	Runners-up	Venue	Attendance
1939	4–0	Motherwell	Hampden Park	94,799
1955	1–1	Celtic	Hampden Park	106,111
Replay	1–0	Celtic	Hampden Park	68,735
1958	1–0	Hibernian	Hampden Park	95,124

ABERDEEN

Year	Score	Runners-up	Venue	Attendance
1947	2–1	Hibernian	Hampden Park	82,140
1970	3–1	Celtic	Hampden Park	108,434
1982	4–1	Rangers	Hampden Park	53,788
1983	1–0	Rangers	Hampden Park	62,070
1984	2–1	Celtic	Hampden Park	58,900
1986	3–0	Heart of Mid	Hampden Park	62,841
1990	0–0	Celtic	Hampden Park	60,493
		won 9–8 on penalties		

PARTICK THISTLE

Year	Score	Runners-up	Venue	Attendance
1921	1–0	Rangers	Celtic Park	28,300

MORTON

1922	1–0	Rangers	Hampden Park	75,000

AIRDRIEONIANS

1924	2–0	Hibernian	Ibrox	59,218

ST MIRREN

1926	2–0	Celtic	Hampden Park	98,620
1959	3–1	Aberdeen	Hampden Park	108,591
1987	1–0	Dundee United	Hampden Park	51,782

MOTHERWELL

1952	4–0	Dundee	Hampden Park	136,274
1991	4–3	Dundee United	Hampden Park	57,319

DUNFERMLINE ATHLETIC

1961	0–0	Celtic	Hampden Park	113,618
Replay	2–0	Celtic	Hampden Park	87,866
1968	3–1	Heart of Mid	Hampden Park	56,366

An exciting final in 1991 saw underdogs Motherwell take the Scottish Cup 4–3 at the expense of perennial runners-up Dundee United, who suffered their fourth such defeat in seven years (Allsport/Ben Radford)

SCOTTISH CUP FACTS & FEATS

Celtic are the most successful team in the history of the Scottish Cup, but are only three wins ahead of their rivals Rangers. Charles Campbell with eight winners medals in 1874, 1875, 1876, 1880, 1881, 1882, 1884 and 1886 is the most successful individual. Jimmy

St Mirren's Iain Ferguson, who subsequently joined Rangers, celebrates after his goal in extra time had given the Paisley side a surprise win in 1987 (Allsport)

McMenemy won six of his seven winners medals with Celtic – the other with Partick Thistle – and Billy McNeill appeared in a record 12 finals all as captain and was on the winning side seven times. Celtic share the highest score in a final, having beaten Hibernian 6–1 in 1972. John 'Dixie' Deans scored three goals in this match, the second Celtic player to achieve a hat-trick in the final, Jimmy Quinn having scored all three goals against Rangers in 1904, the first final at the present Hampden Park. Bobby Lennox scored in three consecutive finals. Joe Kennaway was the first foreign born player to appear in a winning team when he was in goal for Celtic in 1933 and 1937. He was born in Montreal. In 1967 Celtic achieved the 'grand slam' of all possible trophies at domestic and European level.

Rangers are the Scottish Cup's second most consistent team. They achieved three in a row from 1934 to 1936, again from 1948 to 1950 and 1962 to 1964. Bob McPhail achieved six of his seven winning medals with Rangers, the other with Airdrie. In 1935 he even missed a penalty, but Rangers still beat Hamilton Academical 2–1. Alfie Conn, who played in Rangers' winning team against Celtic in 1973 was in Celtic's successful team four years later at Rangers' expense.

Kaj Johansen was the first foreign player to score in a final, the Dane scoring the only goal in the 1966 replayed final. Ralph Brand scored in three consecutive finals 1962 to 1964 and the 1963 replay.

Queen's Park, the only amateur team in senior football in Britain, won all ten of their finals before the turn of the century.

Aberdeen achieved three wins in a row from 1982 to 1984 and were involved in the first final which was decided by penalty kicks when they beat Celtic 9–8 after a goalless draw in 1990.

East Fife are the only club outside the top flight to have won the cup.

All three occasions in which a team has had a player sent off have resulted in the depleted side losing: Jock Buchanan (Rangers) 1928; Roy Aitken (Celtic) 1984 and Walter Kidd (Hearts) 1986.

SCOTTISH LEAGUE CUP

Bell's 1979–80, 1980–81; Skol Cup 1984–85 to date

RANGERS

Year	Date	Score	Runners-up	Attendance
1946–47	5 April	4–0	Aberdeen	82,584
1948–49	12 March	2–0	Raith Rovers	53,359
1960–61	29 October	2–0	Kilmarnock	82,063
1961–62	18 December	3–1*	Heart of Mid	47,552
1963–64	26 October	5–0	Morton	105,907
1964–65	24 October	2–1	Celtic	91,000
1970–71	24 October	1–0	Celtic	106,263
1975–76	25 October	1–0	Celtic	58,806
1977–78	18 March	2–1**	Celtic	60,168
1978–79	31 March	2–1	Aberdeen	54,000
1981–82	28 November	2–1	Dundee United	53,795
1983–84	25 March	3–2**	Celtic	66,369
1984–85	28 October	1–0	Dundee United	44,698
1986–87	26 October	2–1	Celtic	74,219
1987–88	25 October	3–3**(*)	Aberdeen	71,961
1988–89	23 October	3–2	Aberdeen	72,122
1990–91	28 October	2–1**	Celtic	62,817
1992–93	25 October	2–1**	Aberdeen	45,298

*After 1–1 draw **After extra time (*) Won 5–3 on penalties*

EAST FIFE

1947–48	1 November	4–1*	Falkirk	30,664
1949–50	29 October	3–0	Dunfermline Ath.	38,897
1953–54	24 October	3–2	Partick Thistle	38,529

After 0–0 (aet)

MOTHERWELL

1950–51	28 October	3–0	Hibernian	63,074

DUNDEE

1951–52	27 October	3–2	Rangers	91,075
1952–53	25 October	2–0	Kilmarnock	51,830
1973–74	15 December	1–0	Celtic	27,974

HEART OF MIDLOTHIAN

1954–55	23 October	4–2	Motherwell	55,640
1958–59	25 October	5–1	Partick Thistle	59,960
1959–60	24 October	2–1	Third Lanark	57,974
1962–63	27 October	1–0	Kilmarnock	51,280

ABERDEEN

1955–56	22 October	2–1	St Mirren	44,103
1976–77	6 November	2–1*	Celtic	69,268
1985–86	27 October	3–0	Hibernian	40,065
1989–90	22 October	2–1	Rangers	61,190

After extra time

CELTIC

1956–57	31 October	3–0*	Partick Thistle	31,126
1957–58	19 October	7–1	Rangers	82,293
1965–66	23 October	2–1	Rangers	107,609
1966–67	29 October	1–0	Rangers	94,532
1967–68	28 October	5–3	Dundee	66,660
1968–69	5 April	6–2	Hibernian	74,000
1969–70	25 October	1–0	St. Johnstone	73,067
1974–75	26 October	6–3	Hibernian	53,848
1982–83	4 December	2–1	Rangers	55,372

After 0–0 draw

One of the most famous League Cup Finals in 1957–58 saw Celtic's second win in the competition but is remembered most for the 7–1 scoreline they ran up against Rangers (Popperfoto)

PARTICK THISTLE

1971–72	23 October	4–1	Celtic	62,740

HIBERNIAN

1972–73	9 December	2–1	Celtic	71,696
1991–92	27 October	2–0	Dunfermline Athletic	40,377

DUNDEE UNITED

1979–80	12 December	3–0*	Aberdeen	28,984
1980–81	6 December	3–0	Dundee	24,466

*After 0–0 draw (aet)

SCOTTISH LEAGUE CUP FACTS & FEATS

Rangers have been the most successful club in the Scottish League Cup with twice as many wins as their nearest rivals. In the 1963–64 final, Jim Forrest established an individual record when he scored four of the five goals by which Rangers beat Morton. His goals came in the second half: 52 mins, 60, 87 and 89, scoring the first two and last two goals. Rangers won the first final to be decided on penalties when they beat Aberdeen 5–3 after a 3–3 draw in 1987–88. Celtic had five successive wins from 1965–66 to 1969–70 and hold the record for the highest win in a final, having beaten Rangers 7–1 in 1957–58.

WELSH FOOTBALL

Although the Football Association of Wales was formed in 1876 it was not until 1992 that a National League was started, sponsored by Konica, the film and camera concern.

The new League of Wales comprised ten clubs from the Abacus Welsh League, eight from the Cymru Alliance and two from the HFS Loans League. UEFA awarded a European Cup place to Cwmbran, the inaugural winners of the League of Wales, and controversially suggested and that Cup-Winners' Cup places for Welsh clubs might also be dependent on membership of the League of Wales.

The chief reason for the delay in implementing a nationwide competition was that for many years the four leading Welsh clubs – Cardiff City, Swansea City, Wrexham and Newport County – had been playing in the Football League.

Just as the Welsh Cup, which had been first contested in 1877–78, had provided access to the European Cup-Winners' Cup, the incentive for a place in the European Cup itself seemed an attraction which could no longer be ignored. But although Cardiff intimated that they might be prepared to forego their Football League status and join the new Konica League of Wales, there was no actual movement.

Indeed for around a dozen non-league clubs, the prospect of playing in a National League was of such disinterest that they preferred to remain in competitions outside the country. Pressure was put on them, but some like Newport AFC, the club which arose from the ashes of Newport County, decided to move headquarters to England rather than be forced into the League of Wales.

There had been a Welsh League founded in 1902, but it was divided regionally and included the reserve teams of clubs who were members of the Football League for many years.

The fact that four Welsh clubs were established in England meant that the Welsh Cup could not be played on a Saturday. In the early days of the competition it was open to clubs outside Wales, notably in Cheshire and Shropshire. Indeed the same concession has applied since then.

The first Welsh Cup final was won by Wrexham who defeated Druids 1–0. The match was a historic one for other reasons. Wrexham used three half-backs, the idea of their captain Charles Murless, one of the first clubs to add one player to its middle line.

Billy Meredith played in two Welsh Cup finals for Chirk and later became the first Welshman to win Welsh and FA Cup winners medals. England international centre-half Billy Wedlock was another who played in two Welsh finals for Aberdare.

Clubs in the north dominated the competition and Wrexham still share the record for most wins. It was not until 1911 that a southern team won it when Cardiff City were successful.

Cardiff also made history in 1927 when they achieved a unique treble taking the Welsh Cup, FA Cup and Charity Shield in the same year. In the Welsh Cup final they beat Rhyl 2–0.

In the years after the Second World War, Merthyr were one of the strongest teams in non-league football, playing in the Southern League. Twice they managed to beat both Cardiff and Swansea in Welsh Cup finals. They beat Swansea 2–0 in 1949 and Cardiff 3–2 after a 1–1 draw two years later.

The four League clubs were often unable or unwilling to field full first teams in the Welsh Cup, but

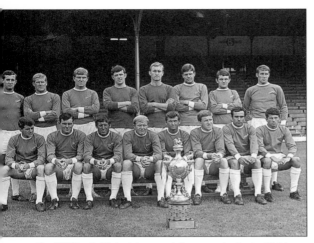

Cardiff City hold the joint record for most wins in the Welsh Cup. Here the Bluebirds show off the trophy in 1967 as they prepare for another season in Europe (Popperfoto)

occasionally a final involving two of them attracted more than average interest. In 1956 the midweek final involving Cardiff and Swansea drew nearly 40,000. Cardiff were 3–0 ahead at one time, but had already lost Harry Kirtley, their inside-forward, carried off with a broken leg. Swansea pulled two goals back but lost 3–2.

Entry to the Cup-Winners' Cup gave an extra impetus to clubs playing in the Welsh Cup. Cardiff City managed to reach the semi-final in 1967–68 when they accounted for Shamrock Rovers, NAC Breda (Holland) and Moscow Torpedo (USSR) before losing 3–2 at home to Hamburg (West Germany) after holding their opponents to a 1–1 draw away.

But the early seasons in Europe produced a couple of surprises when non-Football League teams qualified for the Cup-Winners' Cup. Bangor City made a sensational start in 1962–63 beating Napoli (Italy). They won 2–0 in the home leg and though beaten 3–1 away, forced a play-off which they narrowly lost 2–1 at Highbury.

The following season it was the turn of Borough United to try their luck. They actually came through the first round, beating Sliema Wanderers 2–0 at home after a 0–0 draw away. In the second round they were beaten by Slovan Bratislava (Czechoslovakia).

Bangor did better themselves on their second venture in Europe during 1985–86. They beat Fredrikstad (Norway) on the away goals rule after a 1–1 draw on aggregate, but lost 3–0 over two legs to Atletico Madrid (Spain).

Two seasons later Merthyr, now a member of the GM Vauxhall Conference, the leading competition under the Football League, also reached Europe. They took a 2–1 lead over Atalanta (Italy) on the home leg, but were beaten by two clear goals away.

The first Welsh Cup final in which there was no Welsh participation at all was in 1934 when Bristol City beat Tranmere Rovers 3–0 at Chester in a replay after a 1–1 draw, thus neither the finalists nor the ground had any Welsh connection.

The Welsh Cup can also claim the longest result known in a first class match. It was recorded in the third round in 1988–89 when Kidderminster Harriers beat Llanfairpwllgwyngyllgocerychwyrndro-bwllilantysiliogogogoch . . . . 3–0.

IRISH LEAGUE

The Irish FA was formed in 1880 and the first Irish Cup produced an entry of seven clubs. In the final, Mayola Park beat Cliftonville, Ireland's oldest club formed in 1879, 1–0. Thirteen teams competed the following season and 18 in the one after that. From 1884 to 1886, Distillery achieved a hat-trick of wins.

At the time around the turn of the century, regiments of the British Army were stationed all over Ireland and several entered the Irish Cup from time to time. In 1890 the Gordon Highlanders became the first such to win it, beating Cliftonville 3–1 in the final after a 2–2 draw. That same season, Ulster beat Milltown 16–0 in an early round, with left-winger McIlvenney scoring ten goals.

That same year, the Irish League began operating for the first time with eight teams: Cliftonville,

Clarence, Distillery, Glentoran, Linfield, Milford, Oldpark and Ulster. Milford lost all 14 games. After two seasons the membership was increased to ten, but there were problems and the complement was reduced to six. Linfield were winners of the first three Irish League championships. From 1907–09, Linfield had another treble of Irish League titles.

In 1893 the first Irish League representative match was played against Scotland and the following year, a fixture was arranged with the Football League.

In 1900, on the eve of the Irish Cup semi-final, the King's Own Scottish Borderers, stationed in Dublin, were ordered to Aldershot to equip for the Transvaal and the South African War. They were due to play Cliftonville who thus had a walkover into the final.

The other semi-final involved Bohemians and

Belfast Celtic. Bohemians won 2–1 and included in their team was half-back Dr. J. Whelan of the Royal Army Medical Corps. He travelled from London to play and immediately afterwards hurried to the Great Northern Station catching a train to Queenstown. The following day he sailed for South Africa as surgeon to the 11th Field Hospital. Cliftonville won the final 2–1.

Although Dublin clubs had reached the final of the Cup on several occasions, it was not until Shelbourne's 2–0 win over Belfast Celtic that one of them won it in 1906.

While the First World War caused a halt to the Irish League fixtures, clubs struggling on in reduced regional games, the Irish Cup continued to be played. Then in 1919–20 came a serious incident in the Irish Cup semi-final replay between Glentoran and Belfast Celtic when shots were fired into a crowd.

The game played on St. Patrick's Day at Cliftonville saw Celtic full-back Fred Barrett sent off for a foul, spectators invading the pitch and the players sent to the dressing-room. The 'Sinn Fein' flag was raised and rival supporters sang political songs.

Protests, writs and withdrawals followed, but the split between Dublin and Belfast widened and with the formation of the Irish Free State, two associations ruled football in Ireland. From 1921–22 no more teams entered from Dublin.

The first intermediate club to reach the Cup final were Willowfield, a Belfast team, in 1924. They were beaten 1–0 by Queen's Island. But in 1928 they reached the final again, this time beating Larne 1–0 in the final.

In 1929 Ballymena United won the cup at the first attempt in their first year as a senior club. The following year Joe Bambrick scored all four goals as Linfield beat Ballymena 4–3 in the final. Four months earlier Bambrick had scored six goals for Ireland in an international.

During the Second World War, the Cup again carried on while the Irish League was replaced by the Northern Ireland Regional League in which Belfast Celtic, Distillery, Linfield, Glentoran, Cliftonville, Glenavon, Portadown and Coleraine competed at varying times. There was also a North-South tournament which proved extremely popular despite the restrictions imposed by wartime.

The Cup also saw the return of service teams to the competition. And in 1942 matches were decided on a home-and-away principle and produced exactly 100 goals for the series.

In January 1941 Peter O'Connor, the Belfast Celtic centre-forward, scored 11 goals in the 13–0 win over Glenavon, a record individual score in the province.

Celtic, founded in 1891, had entered the Irish League in 1896, but withdrew from 1915 to 1917 and again in 1920 until 1924 during the early days of the break-up of Ireland into two countries. Then a Boxing Day game at Windsor Park in 1948 produced scenes which caused the club to withdraw once and for all from the game. During a riot, their centre-forward Jimmy Jones had his leg broken when he was attacked by the crowd.

Belfast Celtic went on tour to America at the end of the season beating the full Scottish National team 2–0 on 29 May in New York and never played again.

In 1955 on the 75th anniversary of the Irish FA and Irish Cup, Dundela, an intermediate club in the Irish Alliance, won the cup beating Glenavon 3–0 in the final.

Only two Irish clubs have survived the second round in one of the three major European competitions. In 1966–67 Linfield beat Aris Bonnevoie (Luxembourg) and Valerengen (Norway) before losing to CSKA Sofia in the quarter-final of the European Cup and in 1973–74 Glentoran beat Chimia Ramnicu (Romania) and Brann Bergen (Norway), before losing out to Borussia Moenchengladbach (West Germany) in the same stage of the Cup-Winners' Cup.

Derry City withdrew from the Irish League in October 1972 during the height of the troubles in the Province and have subsequently played in the League of Ireland.

Michael Hughes, formerly of Irish League side Carrick Rovers, now a regular for Northern Ireland and playing club football in France for Strasbourg (Allsport/Ben Radford)

LEAGUE OF IRELAND

The Football Association of Ireland came into being in 1921, but was not recognised by the Irish FA until the split which finally left the country in two halves. In 1923 the new body in the south was sanctioned and in 1924 the Republic of Ireland joined FIFA.

Of course, clubs in the south had played in the Irish League for many years, but the Leinster Football Association had been the first regional body in what is now the Republic, as far back as 1892 when five Dublin clubs formed its membership. The Leinster Senior Cup began in 1892–93 and in the early years had British Army regiments competing in it.

However, the earliest recording of a match in the south was on 7 November 1883 when Dublin University met a Dublin Association at College Park. Derry Celtic, Bohemians and Shelbourne joined the Irish League in 1900. Bohemians, founded in 1890, are the oldest club in the country.

Roy Keane was signed by Nottingham Forest from Cobh Ramblers in the League of Ireland. Three years on Keane was transferred to Manchester United for a record fee (Allsport)

In 1921–22 a League competition was started as the Football League of the Irish Free State when the Leinster FA clubs severed their connection with the Irish FA and decided on their own governing body.

Eight clubs formed the initial league: Bohemians, Dublin United, Frankfurt, Olympia, St James' Gate, Shelbourne, YMCA and W&R Jacobs. Twelve teams completed the following season including Athlone Town and Shamrock Rovers. Bray Unknowns and Fordsons (later Cork FC) were added in 1924–25 and Dundalk in 1926–27. Waterford entered in 1930–31 and Cork Bohemians in 1932–33.

A Cup competition was also instituted in 1921–22 and St James' Gate achieved a League and Cup double in that inaugural season.

Inter-League matches were also arranged, initially against Wales in February 1924 which resulted in a 3–3 draw. Shortly afterwards a visit from Glasgow Celtic aroused considerable interest and broke existing attendance records.

In 1926 came the first meeting with their rivals north of the border when the Irish League was met for the first time, the Republic winning 3–1.

However, development of the game in the Republic was held back by the attitude of the Gaelic Athletic Association which discouraged all other games. This hampered progress outside Dublin and Cork in particular.

Links with the north were maintained and in 1923 the FAI Cup was even won by Alton United, a Belfast junior club. An unofficial All-Ireland Championship in 1924–25 saw Shamrock Rovers beat Glentoran 2–0 in the final.

However in 1935 a Youth Cup was started, and the Scottish League was played for the first time four years later and beaten 2–1.

Although the Republic was neutral in the Second World War, there were inevitable restrictions in the country and the senior game at least was confined to Dublin, Cork, Dundalk and Limerick. Sligo and Waterford dropped out because of travelling problems.

Interest remained high, however, and the 1945 Cup Final between Shamrock Rovers and Bohemians packed Dalymount Park with 41,000, the highest crowd to watch a game in the Republic.

Shamrock have been the outstanding team overall in the country. They won four championships in succession from 1984 to 1987 and had a run of five consecutive cup wins from 1929–33 and another six between 1964 and 1969. They recorded the highest win in the League on 28 October 1928 when they beat Bray Unknowns 11–0 at Milltown.

Dan McCaffery twice scored five goals in a League game in 1960–61. Playing for Drumcondra he hit five against Bohemians in November and five against his former club Sligo Rovers in January.

A second division was added to the championship in 1985 and that same year Derry City were admitted to the competition, though based in Northern Ireland. In 1988–89 Derry won three titles in a season: the League, Cup and League Cup.

In Europe, Republic teams have never managed to move past the second round, but among several fine performances, the only venture made by University College, Dublin saw them hold Everton to a goalless draw at home and restrict their English First Division opponents to just one goal at Goodison Park.

At present there are 12 teams in the Premier League, each team playing the others three times, while the ten teams in the First Division are similarly employed throughout the season.

Since the Gaelic Association withdrew its objections to soccer and other sports, rapid strides have been made in Ireland. The flow to England of players of first-class ability has never diminished and with a lessening of the qualification to play for the Republic, international performances have been considerably enhanced during the past ten years.

The competitive nature of the present set-up has been evident from the fact that not since the mid-1980s when Shamrock Rovers held sway, has one team dominated proceedings.

In 1991–92 Shelbourne were champions, their first such success for 30 years. But all three representatives in Europe were eliminated in the first round for the ninth consecutive year.

GOALSCORING

Jimmy McGrory is the only player to have achieved more than one goal per game during a substantial career in British football. He scored 410 in 408 Scottish League games for Celtic and Clydebank, where he was on loan. Born 26 April 1904 he played for St Roch's and scored in their 1922 Scottish Junior Cup final win over Kilwinning Rangers. He joined Celtic the following season and made his debut at Third Lanark on 20 January in a 1–0 defeat. He had to wait until his third game before scoring his first goal.

In 1923–24 he was loaned to Clydebank for most of the season before returning to assist Celtic in the Glasgow Charity Cup. His other records with Celtic were scoring eight goals against Dunfermline Athletic on 14 January 1928 in a 9–0 win and a three-minute hat-trick against Motherwell on 14 March 1936 in a 5–0 win.

His League goals record: *1922–23* 1; *1923–24* 13 (Clydebank); *1924–25* 17; *1925–26* 35; *1926–27* 49; *1927–28* 47; *1928–29* 20; *1930–31* 37; *1931–32* 28; *1932–33* 22; *1933–34* 17; *1934–35* 18; *1935–36* 50; *1936–37* 19; *1937–38* 5. He retired in October 1937. His last game was on 16 October and he scored in a 4–3 win over Queen's Park. His overall total of League and cup goals was 550.

The highest number of League goals scored in a season in Scotland was achieved by Jimmy Smith of Ayr United in 1927–28 when he scored 66 goals. These included two 5's, three 4's, and six hat-tricks. His overall total for the season was 84, from two in the Scottish Cup, one in the Ayr Charity Cup and 15 in friendly and tour games.

Ian Rush passed a personal milestone of 300 goals in all competitions for Liverpool on the last day of the 1992–93 season (Allsport/Anton Want)

In the Football League the overall record number of League goals was achieved by George Arthur Rowley with 434 goals. His total might well have been considerably more, but for his debut during the wartime regional football and being unable to establish himself in the early post-war season.

His League goals record: *1946–47* West Bromwich Albion 0; *1947–48* 4; *1948–49* 0; *1948–49* Fulham 19; *1949–50* 8; *1950–51* Leicester City 28; *1951–52* 38; *1952–53* 39; *1953–54* 30; *1954–55* 23; *1955–56* 29; *1956–57* 44; *1957–58* 20; *1958–59* Shrewsbury Town 38; *1959–60* 32; *1960–61* 28; *1961–62* 23; *1962–63* 24; *1963–64* 5; *1964–65* 2.

William Ralph 'Dixie' Dean scored 60 League goals in 39 games for Everton in 1927–28. Dean hit one 5, one 4, five hat-tricks. His overall total for the season was 82, from three in the FA Cup, six in Inter-League games, eight in International trials and five in international matches for England. Dean scored 379 League goals in his career.

His League goals record: *1923–24* Tranmere Rovers 0; *1924–25* 27; *1924–25* Everton 2; *1925–26* 32; *1926–27* 21; *1927–28* 60; *1928–29* 26; *1929–30* 23; *1930–31* 39; *1931–32* 45; *1932–33* 24; *1933–34* 9; *1934–35* 26; *1935–36* 17; *1936–37* 24; *1937–38* 1; *1937–38* Notts County 0; *1938–39* 3.

Dean then joined Sligo Rovers and added 11 goals for them. During the war he played only briefly in England.

The season before Dean's 60 goals, George Camsell had scored 59 in Division Two for Middlesbrough during 1926–27. He missed the first four matches. His contribution included one 5, three 4's and five hat-tricks, a record for scoring at least three times on nine occasions. He began with Durham City and with Middlesbrough scored 325 goals in 418 appearances. At Durham he scored 20 in 21 games.

Camsell was the first player to score a century of League and Cup goals over two consecutive seasons. In 1926–27 he added five FA Cup goals to his 59 in the League and in 1927–28 he scored 33 League and four FA Cup goals.

Steve Bull scored 34 League and 18 Cup goals in 1987–88 for Wolverhampton Wanderers, followed by 37 League and 13 Cup goals in 1988–89. Bull's 1987–88 Cup goals consisted of 12 in the Sherpa Van Trophy, three Littlewoods Cup and three FA Cup; in 1988–89 there were 11 Sherpa Van Trophy and two Littlewoods Cup goals.

However, the highest number of goals scored in one season of first-class football in the British Isles is 96. This was achieved by Fred Roberts, of Glentoran, in 1930–31. His total came from 55 Irish League, 4 Irish Cup, 28 City Cup, 7 Antrim Shield and 2 Belfast Charity Cup.

Joe Bambrick of Linfield scored 94 in 1929–30: 50 Irish League, 7 Irish Cup 10 City Cup, 5 Antrim Shield, 9 Belfast Charity Cup, 5 Inter-League, 1 Gold Cup, 1 Condor Cup, 6 internationals.

Hughie Gallacher scored 387 League goals in 543 matches between 1921 and 1939. He is the highest goalscorer among players who have played in both English and Scottish football. He was with Airdrieonians Newcastle United, Chelsea, Derby County, Notts County, Grimsby Town and Gateshead.

Jimmy Greaves scored five Division One goals for Chelsea on three occasions: against Wolverhampton Wanderers in August 1958, Preston in December 1959 and West Bromwich Albion in December 1960. No other player since the war has scored five or more, more than once, in matches in any division. Greaves also became the youngest-ever player to score five times in a Division One match. He claimed six Division One hat-tricks for Chelsea in 1960–61 and four hat-tricks for Tottenham Hotspur in both 1962–63 and 1963–64. Again no other player can claim more than four such feats in Division One for any post-war season.

Kenny Dalglish achieved a century of League goals on both sides of the border. He scored 112 for Celtic and 118 for Liverpool.

Guy Whittingham was top scorer in the English domestic leagues in 1992–93 with 42 Division One goals for Portsmouth (Allsport/ Anton Want)

MANAGERS

Bob Paisley was manager of Liverpool between 1974 and 1983. During this period they won 13 major honours: the League Championship six times, European Cup three times, League Cup three times and the UEFA Cup once. He served 53 years with the club as player, assistant-manager, manager and finally director before resigning in February 1992.

Jim McLean was appointed manager of Dundee United on 24 November 1971 and announced his intention to resign in February 1993 as soon as a replacement could be found. On 20 December 1988, after two years as a club director, he was also elected chairman.

Sir Matt Busby was the longest serving manager with one club. He was in charge of Manchester United from October 1945 to June 1971, his last two years as General manager and team manager.

In 1992–93 Brian Clough retired after 27 years in football management, starting with Hartlepool United in October 1965 and guiding Derby County, Brighton & Hove Albion and, briefly, Leeds United before taking control of Nottingham Forest in January 1975.

West Ham United have had only seven managers throughout their history: Syd King, Charlie Paynter, Ted Fenton, Ron Greenwood, John Lyall, Lou Macari and Billy Bonds.

Shortest reign as a Football League club manager was the three days in which Bill Lambton took charge of Scunthorpe United in April 1959. But in May 1984 Dave Bassett had been named as Crystal Palace manager, only to change his mind four days later without signing a contract.

Steve Murray was appointed manager of Forfar Athletic on 18 August 1980 and informed the club's board of directors that he was resigning on 21 August, though the news was withheld from the playing staff until 23 August.

Clough is one of only two managers to have won the League Championship with different clubs. Herbert Chapman achieved the feat with Huddersfield Town in 1923–24 and 1924–25, Arsenal in 1930–31 and 1932–33; Clough with Derby County 1971–72 and Nottingham Forest 1977–78.

Clough completed 1000 matches as a manager when Forest won 3–2 at Tottenham Hotspur on 30 December 1989.

The most extensive family in football management was the Maley dynasty. Tom Maley, born in Scotland, managed Manchester City and Bradford Park Avenue; Willie, his brother, born in Ireland, managed Celtic; and Alec, born in England, managed Hibernian. Charlie Maley, son of Tom, was secretary of both Bradford clubs City and Park Avenue and also of Leicester City.

Charles Foweraker was the only man to manage the same Football League club for 20 years between the wars when he was in charge of Bolton Wanderers.

Eric Taylor was with Sheffield Wednesday from August 1929 to June 1974, graduating on the administrative staff from junior to assistant secretary and secretary before the war. He became manager in 1942, secretary-manager in 1945 and general manager and secretary from September 1958.

Eddie Davison had served Sheffield Wednesday as a goalkeeper from 1908 to 1926 after joining them from Gateshead Town. He made one appearance for England. Before taking over as Sheffield United manager in June 1932 he had been in charge of Chesterfield where he returned after leaving United in the summer of 1952.

Billy Walker was appointed manager of Sheffield Wednesday in December 1933 and took up a similar position with Nottingham Forest in March 1939 after being in charge of Chelmsford for a short time. He remained at Forest for 21 years until 1960 when he retired to be appointed a manager member of the Club Committee.

Joe Smith became manager of Blackpool in 1935 after four seasons in charge of Reading. Over the next 23 years the club won promotion to Division One in 1937, were FA Cup runners-up in 1948 and 1951, winners in 1953 and Division One runners-up in 1955–56.

Jimmy Seed had just over 23 years in charge of Charlton Athletic from May 1933 to September 1956. Under his guidance, Charlton won promotion in successive seasons from Division Three (South) to Division One and in 1936–37, their first season in that division, they were runners-up. They also won the FA Cup in 1947 after finishing runners-up the previous season.

Helmut Schoen, who retired as West Germany's team manager after the 1978 World Cup finals, was the most successful international coach. In 1966 his team finished runners-up in the World Cup, were third in 1970 and became European Championship winners in 1972. They won the World Cup in 1974 and were runners-up in the European Championship in 1976. Schoen had been in charge for 14 years.

George Raynor was in charge of Sweden when they won the Olympic Games gold medal in 1948, third place in the 1950 World Cup and 1952 Olympics, then to the runners-up spot in the 1958 World Cup.

Ernst Happel won 19 domestic titles with eight clubs in five different countries and he was Austria's team manager when he died in November 1992.

Since the Second World War, three players have appeared in and later managed both FA Cup and League Championship-winning teams. Joe Mercer played for Arsenal in their 1948 and 1953 League successes and 1950 FA Cup and later managed Manchester City when they won the championship in 1968 and the FA Cup the following year. Kenny Dalglish played for Liverpool in the 1979, 1980, 1982, 1983 and 1984 Championship successes and as player-manager, guided them to the League and FA Cup double in 1986. Since then, as a manager, Dalglish has won the League title twice, in 1988 and 1990, and the FA Cup in 1989. George Graham was in the Arsenal side which won the League and FA Cup double in 1971. He took over as manager at Highbury in 1986 and has won League titles in 1989 and 1991 and the FA Cup in 1993.

George Graham, who completed the set of all three domestic trophies as manager of Arsenal when the Gunners won the FA Cup in 1993, rolling back the years in 1991 (Allsport/Steve Morton)

BRITISH ISLES IN INTERNATIONALS

ENGLAND

	P	W	D	L	F	A
Albania	2	2	0	0	7	0
Argentina	10	4	4	2	15	11
Australia	5	3	2	0	5	2
Austria	15	8	3	4	54	25
Belgium	18	13	4	1	67	24
Bohemia	1	1	0	0	4	0
Brazil	17	3	7	7	15	22
Bulgaria	5	3	2	0	7	1
Cameroon	2	2	0	0	5	2
Canada	1	1	0	0	1	0
Chile	4	2	2	0	4	1
CIS	1	0	1	0	2	2
Colombia	2	1	1	0	5	1
Cyprus	2	2	0	0	6	0
Czechoslovakia	12	7	3	2	25	17
Denmark	13	8	4	1	26	11
Ecuador	1	1	0	0	2	0
Egypt	2	2	0	0	5	0
FIFA (Rest of the World)	3	2	1	0	9	5
Finland	9	8	1	0	34	6

	P	W	D	L	F	A
France	22	15	3	4	62	27
Germany	5	2	1	2	13	9
East Germany	4	3	1	0	7	3
West Germany	16	7	3	6	24	19
Greece	5	4	1	0	10	1
Holland	11	4	5	2	18	12
Hungary	18	12	1	5	47	27
Iceland	1	0	1	0	1	1
Northern Ireland	96	74	6	16	319	80
Republic of Ireland	13	5	6	2	19	12
Israel	2	1	1	0	2	1
Italy	17	6	5	6	25	22
Kuwait	1	1	0	0	1	0
Luxembourg	7	7	0	0	38	3
Malaysia	1	1	0	0	4	2
Malta	2	2	0	0	6	0
Mexico	6	3	1	2	14	3
Morocco	1	0	1	0	0	0
New Zealand	2	2	0	0	3	0
Norway	8	5	1	2	26	7
Paraguay	1	1	0	0	3	0

	P	W	D	L	F	A
Peru	2	1	0	1	5	4
Poland	10	4	5	1	13	6
Portugal	15	8	5	2	35	17
Romania	8	2	5	1	6	4
San Marino	1	1	0	0	6	0
Saudi Arabia	1	0	1	0	1	1
Scotland	107	43	24	40	188	168
Spain	17	10	2	5	35	20
Sweden	14	6	4	4	24	16
Switzerland	15	10	2	3	37	12
Tunisia	1	0	1	0	1	1
Turkey	8	7	1	0	29	0
USA	6	4	0	2	29	7
Uruguay	8	2	2	4	8	11
USSR	11	5	3	3	19	13
Wales	97	62	21	14	239	90
Yugoslavia	14	5	5	4	23	20

	P	W	D	L	F	A
New Zealand	1	1	0	0	5	2
Norway	11	7	3	1	30	14
Paraguay	1	0	0	1	2	3
Peru	3	1	1	1	4	4
Poland	6	1	2	3	7	9
Portugal	13	4	3	6	13	16
Romania	5	2	2	1	7	4
San Marino	2	2	0	0	6	0
Saudi Arabia	1	0	1	0	2	2
Spain	10	3	3	4	16	16
Sweden	7	4	1	2	11	8
Switzerland	12	6	2	4	20	19
Turkey	1	0	0	1	2	4
Uruguay	4	1	1	2	4	10
USA	2	2	0	0	7	0
USSR	4	0	1	3	2	6
Wales	101	60	23	18	238	111
Yugoslavia	8	2	5	1	16	11
Zaire	1	1	0	0	2	0

SCOTLAND

	P	W	D	L	F	A
Argentina	3	1	1	1	3	4
Austria	14	3	4	7	18	28
Australia	2	1	1	0	2	0
Belgium	12	4	1	7	17	20
Brazil	8	0	2	6	2	12
Bulgaria	5	2	3	0	5	3
Canada	4	4	0	0	10	1
Chile	2	2	0	0	6	2
CIS	1	1	0	0	3	0
Colombia	1	0	1	0	0	0
Costa Rica	1	0	0	1	0	1
Cyprus	4	4	0	0	18	3
Czechoslovakia	10	5	1	4	18	16
Denmark	10	8	0	2	17	6
Egypt	1	0	0	1	1	3
England	107	40	24	43	168	188
Estonia	2	2	0	0	6	1
Finland	5	4	1	0	14	4
France	10	6	0	4	12	11
Germany	4	1	1	2	3	4
East Germany	6	2	1	3	6	4
West Germany	8	2	3	3	14	14
Holland	10	5	2	3	13	11
Hungary	7	2	2	3	13	15
Iceland	2	2	0	0	4	0
Iran	1	0	1	0	1	1
Northern Ireland	92	61	16	15	254	81
Republic of Ireland	6	2	2	2	8	4
Israel	3	3	0	0	5	1
Italy	5	1	1	3	1	8
Luxembourg	3	2	1	0	9	0
Malta	3	2	1	0	6	2

WALES

	P	W	D	L	F	A
Argentina	1	0	0	1	0	1
Austria	5	1	1	3	4	7
Belgium	6	3	1	2	12	8
Bulgaria	2	1	0	1	1	1
Brazil	7	1	1	5	5	12
Canada	2	1	0	1	3	2
Chile	1	0	0	1	0	2
Costa Rica	1	1	0	0	1	0
Cyprus	1	1	0	0	1	0

Scotland defeated the CIS 3–0 in the 1992 European Championship finals having never defeated the old Soviet Union. Here Kevin Gallacher takes on Dimitri Kuznetsov (Bob Thomas)

Wales centre-back Mark Aizlewood slides in to challenge Franky Van der Elst of Belgium in a World Cup qualifier at Cardiff in 1993 as Ryan Giggs looks on (Bob Thomas)

	P	W	D	L	F	A
Czechoslovakia	11	3	2	6	8	13
Denmark	5	2	0	3	5	5
England	97	14	21	62	90	239
Faroes	2	2	0	0	9	0
Finland	6	3	2	1	11	4
France	4	1	1	2	4	9
East Germany	4	1	0	3	7	8
West Germany	10	0	4	4	5	14
Greece	2	1	0	1	4	3
Holland	3	0	0	2	1	3
Hungary	8	3	2	3	11	13
Iceland	5	2	1	1	8	4
Iran	1	1	0	0	1	0
Japan	1	1	0	0	1	0
Northern Ireland	90	42	21	27	181	126
Republic of Ireland	7	5	0	3	11	10
Israel	4	2	2	0	7	3
Italy	4	1	0	3	3	9
Kuwait	2	0	2	0	0	0
Luxembourg	4	4	0	0	10	1
Malta	3	3	0	0	12	2
Mexico	2	0	1	1	2	3
Norway	5	1	2	2	4	6
Poland	3	1	1	1	2	3
Portugal	2	1	0	1	4	4
Romania	4	1	1	1	6	7
Saudi Arabia	1	1	0	0	2	1
Scotland	101	18	23	60	111	238
Spain	5	1	2	2	6	7
Sweden	4	0	1	3	3	10
Switzerland	2	1	0	1	3	6
Turkey	4	3	0	1	6	1
Rest of UK	2	1	0	1	3	3
Uruguay	1	0	1	0	0	0
USSR	5	1	2	2	3	6
Yugoslavia	7	0	3	4	10	18

NORTHERN IRELAND

	P	W	D	L	F	A
Albania	6	4	2	0	11	3
Algeria	1	0	1	0	1	1
Argentina	1	0	0	1	1	3
Austria	5	2	2	1	7	6
Australia	3	2	1	0	5	3
Belgium	2	1	0	1	3	2
Brazil	1	0	0	1	0	3
Bulgaria	4	2	1	1	4	3
Chile	1	0	0	1	0	1
Cyprus	4	3	0	1	11	1
Czechoslovakia	2	2	0	0	3	1
Denmark	6	1	1	3	4	9
England	96	6	16	74	80	319
Finland	2	1	0	1	2	2
France	7	0	3	4	4	17
Germany	1	0	1	0	1	1
West Germany	7	2	1	4	8	15
Greece	3	1	0	2	5	5
Holland	5	1	2	2	4	8
Honduras	1	0	1	0	1	1
Hungary	2	0	0	2	1	3
Iceland	2	1	0	1	2	1
Republic of Ireland	4	1	2	2	1	6
Israel	6	3	3	0	9	4
Italy	4	1	1	2	6	7
Latvia	1	1	0	0	2	1
Lithuania	2	1	1	0	3	2
Malta	2	2	0	0	5	0
Mexico	1	1	0	0	4	1
Morocco	1	1	0	0	2	1
Norway	3	1	0	1	4	2
Poland	4	2	1	0	5	1
Portugal	6	2	3	1	7	4
Romania	2	2	0	0	4	2
Scotland	91	15	16	60	81	253
Spain	12	1	4	7	7	23
Sweden	4	2	0	2	6	3
Switzerland	2	1	0	1	2	2
Turkey	8	5	2	1	12	3
Uruguay	2	2	0	0	4	0
USSR	4	0	2	2	1	4
Wales	90	27	21	42	126	181
Yugoslavia	7	1	1	3	2	6

REPUBLIC OF IRELAND

	P	W	D	L	F	A
Albania	1	1	0	0	2	0
Algeria	1	0	0	1	0	2
Argentina*	3	0	1	2	0	2
Austria	10	2	2	6	13	27

	P	W	D	L	F	A
Belgium	12	4	4	4	22	22
Brazil	3	1	0	2	2	9
Bulgaria	6	2	1	3	7	5
Chile	5	2	1	2	6	5
China	1	1	0	0	2	0
Cyprus	2	2	0	0	9	2
Czechoslovakia	12	4	1	7	14	29
Denmark	10	3	4	3	12	15
Ecuador	1	1	0	0	3	2
England	13	2	6	5	12	19
Egypt	1	0	1	0	0	0
Finland	3	1	2	0	5	2
France	11	4	3	4	13	15
Germany	3	1	1	1	7	6
West Germany	11	4	1	6	12	20
Holland	11	4	2	5	20	21
Hungary	10	2	3	5	16	23
Iceland	5	4	1	0	12	4
Iran	1	1	0	0	2	1
Northern Ireland	5	2	2	1	6	1
Israel	3	1	1	1	5	3
Italy	7	0	0	7	3	15
Latvia	2	2	0	0	6	0
Lithuania	1	1	0	0	1	0
Luxembourg	5	5	0	0	14	2
Malta	5	5	0	0	16	0
Mexico	1	0	1	0	0	0
Morocco	1	1	0	0	1	0
Norway	14	6	6	2	26	16
Poland	21	5	7	9	23	37
Portugal	6	2	0	4	5	9
Romania	2	1	1	0	2	0
Scotland	6	2	2	2	4	8
Spain	22	4	6	12	16	44
Sweden	6	1	1	4	7	14
Switzerland	11	7	1	3	15	5
Trinidad & Tobago	1	0	0	1	1	2
Tunisia	1	1	0	0	4	0
Turkey	9	5	3	1	23	10
Uruguay	2	0	1	1	1	3
USA	4	2	1	1	9	7
USSR	8	3	1	4	8	8
Wales	8	3	0	5	10	11
Yugoslavia	2	1	0	1	3	4

Includes 0–0 draw in 1979 not considered a full international.

INTERNATIONAL FACTS & FEATS

Billy Wright set a world record of 70 consecutive appearances for England which began against France on 3 October 1951 and ended against the USA on 28 May 1959. He captained England for the first time against Northern Ireland in October 1948 and remained as skipper until his last game against the Americans. He played in all but three of England's first 108 international matches after the Second World War. Moving from his original position of wing-half to centre-half for the game with Switzerland in June 1954, he played in that position thereafter. Wright made 105 international appearances.

Ireland had played 50 international matches before including a player from a Football League club in their team. In their 51st game on 4 March 1899 against Wales in Belfast, Archie Goodall (Derby County), Bill Taggart (Walsall) and Tom Morrison (Burnley) played in a 1–0 win.

Scotland first used a player from the Football League in their 59th international match on 4 April 1894 against England at Celtic Park. They had five Anglo-Scots in their side and won 2–1.

In the Wales v Northern Ireland match on 17 March 1937 at Wrexham, all the players from the Welsh team were drawn from clubs outside the country and all but two of the Irish team, Fulton and Banks, both amateurs, were similarly taken from outside their country. Wales won 4–1.

Before and just after the Second World War it was not unusual for Irish players to turn out for both the Republic and Northern Ireland. For example, Johnny Carey, when a Manchester United player, played against England in two full international matches within three days for different countries. He appeared for Northern Ireland in Belfast on 28 September 1946 and for the Republic of Ireland in Dublin on 30 September. Thirty-one players achieved such dual nationality.

Ladislav Kubala played for Hungary on three occasions followed by six games for Czechoslovakia. He was later naturalised by Spain and made 19 appearances for them in the 1950s and 1960s.

Hungary are the only continental side to have scored as many as six and seven goals in full international matches against England. They won 6–3 at Wembley on 25 November 1953 and 7–1 in Budapest on 23 May 1954.

The Hungarians completed an unbeaten run of 34 international matches after losing 5–3 to Austria on 14 May 1950 until they were beaten 3–2 in the World Cup final by West Germany on 4 July 1954. This sequence included winning the 1952 Olympic Games title in Helsinki when they defeated Yugoslavia 2–0. But two of the matches included in this run were of dubious origin. Both were played against a Moscow Selection on 25 and 28 May 1952 before the USSR returned to international competition. Hungary completed 13 years unbeaten at home, starting with a 2–0 win over Austria on 19 August 1945 and continuing until they lost 4–2 to Czechoslovakia on 20 May 1956.

Torino supplied ten off the Italian team against Hungary on 11 May 1947: Aldo Ballarin, Virgilio Maroso, Giuseppe Grezar, Mario Rigamonti, Eusebio Castigliano, Romeo Menti II, Ezio Loik, Guglielmo Gabetto, Valentino Mazzola and Pietro Ferraris II (captain). Odd man out was goalkeeper Lucidio Sentimenti IV of the other Turin club Juventus. Italy won 3–2.

When the Belgian goalkeeper Jean Trappeniers came on as a second-half substitute for his country against Holland on 30 September 1964 he joined Georges Heylens, Laurient Verbiest, Jean Plaskie, Jean Cornelis, Pierre Hanon, Joseph Jurion, Jacky Stockman, Johan Devrindt, Paul Van Himst and Wilfried Puis, all from Anderlecht, his own club. Belgium won 1–0.

Although Arsenal supplied seven players for the England team against Italy at Highbury on 14 November 1934, only five had originally been selected. George Male came in for the injured Tom Cooper (Derby County), who had been chosen to captain the team at right-back. At centre-forward Fred Tilson (Manchester City) was the first choice but also had to drop out with injury. His replacement was George Hunt (Tottenham Hotspur), but he, too, was forced to withdraw for a similar reason. The reserves selected were a right-half Tom Gardner (Aston Villa) and an inside-forward Raich Carter (Sunderland). Both Male and Hunt appeared in the official programme but it was Ted Drake who played at centre-forward, following the late withdrawal of Hunt. The other five Arsenal players were Frank Moss, Eddie Hapgood, Wilf

Copping, Ray Bowden, Cliff Bastin. England's trainer was Tom Whittaker of Arsenal. England won 3–2 against the World Cup holders.

During 1936–37, Arsenal had 14 international players on their books. In addition to the seven mentioned previously, Jack Crayston, Joe Hulme, Bernard Joy, Alf Kirchen and Herbie Roberts (all England), Alex James (Scotland) and Bob John (Wales) completed the set.

In 1973 Leeds United had 15 internationals on their staff. Paul Madeley, Terry Cooper, Allan Clarke, Jack Charlton, Norman Hunter, Paul Reaney and Mick Jones (all England), Peter Lorimer, Billy Bremner, David Harvey, Joe Jordan and Eddie Gray (Scotland), Gary Sprake and Terry Yorath (Wales) and Johnny Giles (Republic of Ireland).

On 20 November 1974, Leeds achieved the remarkable feat of providing ten of their players for full international matches on the same day. Madeley, Cooper and Clarke for England v Portugal; Harvey, Bremner, Lorimer, Jordan and McQueen for Scotland v Spain; Yorath for Wales v Luxembourg and Giles for the Republic of Ireland v Turkey.

Cardiff City had 17 players on their staff towards the end of the 1925–26 season, all of whom had been capped: nine for Wales, four for Scotland and four for Northern Ireland.

At the start of the 1992–93 season, AC Milan had 17 internationals on their staff, 11 of them Italian. The foreigners were: Zvonimir Boban (Croatia), Ruud Gullit (Holland), Jean-Pierre Papin (France), Frank Rijkaard (Holland), Dejan Savicevic (Yugoslavia) and Marco Van Basten (Holland).

In 1977–78, Manchester United had 18 full internationals: six from Scotland, five from England, five from Northern Ireland and two from the Republic of Ireland. In a period of just over seven years in the 1970s, United could claim 38 full international players with the club at one time or another: ten from England, eleven from Scotland, three from Wales, eight from Northern Ireland and six from the Republic of Ireland.

In the 1933–34 season, Aston Villa had 14 internationals, ten from England, three Scots and one Welshman. In 1932–33 Rangers had 13 international players on their books: ten Scots, and three for Ireland. In 1991–92 they had 13 again: seven from Scotland, three England, two USSR and one Holland.

Linfield supplied seven of the players in the Ireland team against Scotland on 25 March 1893 in Glasgow, but the Scots won 6–1.

England and Ireland's third meeting inside a year had a familiar outcome, 1–1. Niall Quinn equalises for the Irish at Wembley in 1991 despite the attentions of Tony Adams (Bob Thomas)

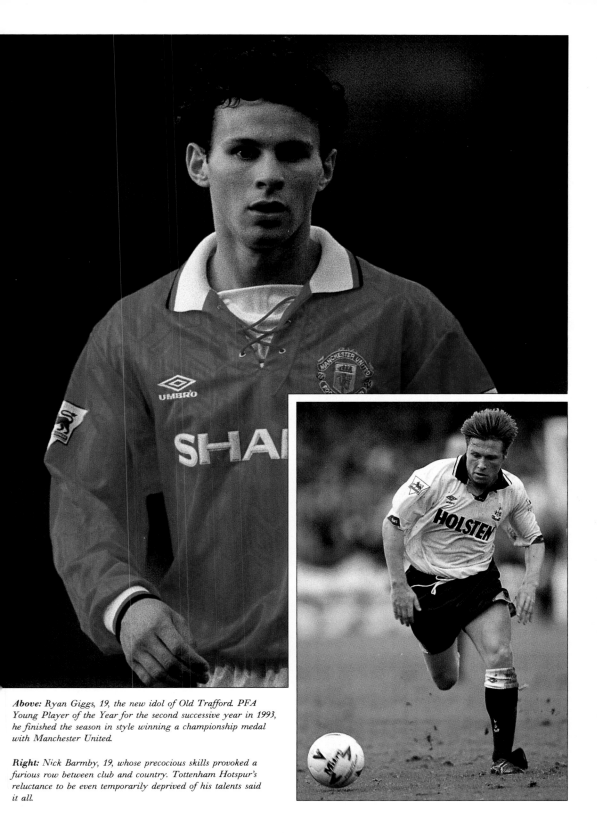

Above: Ryan Giggs, 19, the new idol of Old Trafford. PFA
Young Player of the Year for the second successive year in 1993,
he finished the season in style winning a championship medal
with Manchester United.

Right: Nick Barmby, 19, whose precocious skills provoked a
furious row between club and country. Tottenham Hotspur's
reluctance to be even temporarily deprived of his talents said
it all.

Left: Leeds' Scottish international midfielder Gary McAllister (10) gets the European Cup tie off to a sensational start as he volleys in a first-minute goal to stun the Ibrox crowd.

Above: Man of the match Iain Durrant of Rangers is challenged by Gary Speed.

Below: Leeds keeper John Lukic is helpless as Ally McCoist gleefully turns the ball in to put Rangers 2–1 up.

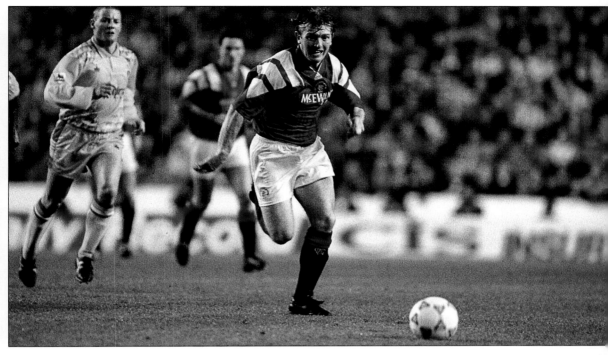

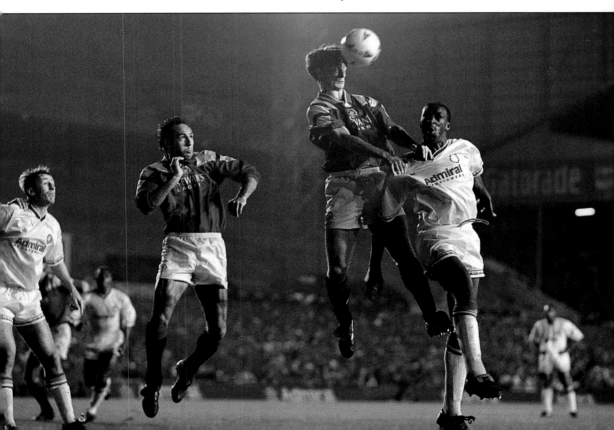

Above: Determination as ever on the face of Yorkshire-born Stuart McCall of Rangers as his opposite number David Batty looks on.

Below: Two weeks later Rangers defend heroically at Elland Road and clinch the title of Britain's Best with two outstanding goals. Here young left-back Davie Robertson gets the better of Chris Whyte.

Above: Chris Waddle (inset, out of main picture) kicks off FA Cup semi-final weekend with a stunning free-kick that has Alan Kelly in the Sheffield United goal well beaten.

Right: Young Wednesdayites and Unitedites enjoy Sheffield's day out at Wembley.

Below: Head to head, Danny Wilson (left) and Mitch Ward.

Bottom right: Wednesday boss Trevor Francis celebrates the Owls' 2–1 win with his Swedish international right-back Roland Nilsson.

Above: It's a tense affair the following day as North London rivals Arsenal and Spurs clash. Man of the match Paul Merson (right) tussles for possession with Steve Sedgley as Ray Parlour looks on.

Right: Sheer delight for Arsenal skipper Tony Adams after his header puts Arsenal in front with just ten minutes left on the clock.

Below: Ian Wright leads the celebration of the Gunners' 1–0 win while Spurs manager Doug Livermore (inset) is philosophical in defeat!

Above: England defeat San Marino 6–0 at Wembley and David Platt (seen here about to complete his hat-trick) follows Gary Lineker into the record books as the latest player to score four goals in a match for his country.

Below: Andy Townsend (left) stays ahead of Steve Morrow in the all-Ireland clash at Lansdowne Road. The Republic enjoyed a comfortable 3–0 victory over Northern Ireland to keep on course for the World Cup finals in the USA.

Above: It's the turn of John Barnes (10, white shirt) to spring a first-minute surprise at Wembley. He curls a free-kick past Dutch keeper Ed de Goey to give England the lead in the crucial World Cup qualifier which finished 2–2.

Below: Welsh national team boss Terry Yorath looks relaxed as he signs autographs before his side's 2–0 World Cup win over Belgium in front of an ecstatic home crowd at Cardiff Arms Park.

Above: Brian Clough (stripes) in action for Sunderland towards the end of a playing career in which he scored an amazing 251 goals in 264 League games.

Above: Perhaps the finest hour for the managerial partnership of Clough and Peter Taylor as they savour their first European Cup triumph with Nottingham Forest in 1979.

Above: Clough, now proclaimed by his rosette as the world's greatest Grandpa, meets the Prince of Wales on Cup Final day in 1991. The FA Cup was the one domestic honour which famously eluded him.

Left: Now then, young man . . . Clough in familiar pose as he charms the watching public with his straight talking.

There have been only two occasions this century when Scotland have not included a player from a Glasgow club in a full international match against England. It happened at Newcastle in April 1907 when they drew 1–1 and at Wembley in May 1979 when they lost 3–1. On only one other occasion since the Second World War have Scotland fielded a team in a British International Championship match that did not include a player from either Celtic or Rangers. On 2 April 1955 they lost 7–2 to England at Wembley, but they did have two players from Glasgow clubs Clyde and Partick Thistle in their team. Before the war the Scots team fielded no Glasgow-based players in October 1933 when they lost 3–2 to Wales. They had been unable to turn out a number of regular players owing to injuries and other causes.

The Scottish team which played Norway at Hampden Park on 25 October 1978 was composed entirely of Anglo-Scots. Scotland won 3–2. The Scottish team which played Holland at the same venue on 11 May 1966 was made up of players with Scottish League teams. Holland won 3–0.

The Scots included ten Anglos in their team which started the match against East Germany in East Berlin on 7 September 1977. Later they brought on two more Anglos as substitutes. The only Scottish League player in the team was Danny McGrain, the Celtic right-back.

When Nigel Clough was capped by England against Chile on 23 May 1989 at Wembley he emulated the achievement of George Eastham junior by following in his father's footsteps. Brian Clough had been capped twice in the 1959–60 season. George Eastham senior played once pre-war for England, his son 19 times afterwards.

Graham Taylor was appointed England team manager after the 1990 World Cup finals. The team remained unbeaten in his first season, winning nine and drawing three. The sequence began with a 1–0 win over Hungary at Wembley on 12 September 1990 and ended with a 1–0 defeat against Germany at Wembley on 11 September 1991.

England's most successful run came in the decade before the turn of the century. It began when they beat Wales 3–1 on 15 March 1890 and ended after they again defeated the Welsh 9–1 on 16 March 1896. A sequence of 20 matches, it comprised 16 wins and four draws and at one time produced nine successive wins.

After losing 3–1 to the USSR on 18 June 1988 in the European Championship, England remained unbeaten in 17 matches until losing 2–1 to Uruguay at Wembley on 22 May 1990. England won 10 and drew seven matches during this sequence.

During the 1980–81 and 1992–93 seasons, England had a run of six matches without a win. Between March and May 1981 they had five successive games at Wembley losing three, drawing the other two and scoring just one goal, in the first game of the sequence. In the period May to October 1958 they went seven games without a win, drawing five and losing two.

Scotland's most successful run came in the 1880s when they had 13 wins in a row, beating Wales six times, England five and Ireland twice. They actually completed 22 games without defeat from beating Wales 3–0 on 7 April 1879 until a 5–1 win over Wales on 10 March 1888.

Northern Ireland's best sequence of results began on 1 May 1957 against Portugal in a 3–0 win and ended after a 1–0 win against Czechoslovakia in the World Cup on 8 June 1958. It produced four wins and three draws.

Wales's best sequence of results began with a 1–1 draw against Scotland on 13 November 1957 and ended after a 2–1 win over Hungary on 17 June 1958 in the World Cup. It produced three wins and five draws.

In the 1890s there were three occasions when England were engaged in two international fixtures on the same day. The dates were: 15 March 1890, 7 March 1891 and 5 March 1892. England met Ireland and Wales on each day and won all six games. But the total number of internationals played by England during this period was only eight.

On 31 October 1974 all five countries in the British Isles won full international matches without conceding a goal: England 3 Czechoslovakia 0; Wales 2 Hungary 0; Scotland 3 East Germany 0; Sweden 0 Northern Ireland 2; Republic of Ireland 3 USSR 0.

MAJOR BRITISH RECORDS

Highest scores

FIRST CLASS MATCH

This century: Stirling Albion 20 Selkirk 0, Scottish Cup
Overall: Arbroath 36 Bon Accord 0, Scottish Cup 1st
Round, 12 Sep 1885

INTERNATIONAL

England 13 Northern Ireland 0, 18 Feb 1882

FA CUP

Preston North End 26 Hyde 0, 1st Round, 15 Oct 1897

LEAGUE CUP

West Ham United 10 Bury 0, 2nd Round, 2nd leg, 25
Oct 1983
Liverpool 10 Fulham 0, 2nd Round, 1st leg, 23 Sep 1986

PREMIER LEAGUE

Home: Blackburn Rovers 7 Norwich City 1, 3 Oct 1992
Away: Blackburn Rovers 2 Coventry City 5, 26 Jan 1993

*Alan Shearer scored the pick of the goals as Blackburn defeated
fellow Premier League pace-setters Norwich City 7–1 at Ewood
Park, a record victory for the new division (Allsport/Shaun Botterill)*

FOOTBALL LEAGUE

Division 1
Home: West Bromwich Albion 12 Darwen 0, 4 Apr 1892
Nottingham Forest 12 Leicester Fosse 0, 21 Apr 1909
Away: Newcastle United 1 Sunderland 9, 5 Dec 1908
Cardiff City 1 Wolverhampton Wanderers 9, 3 Sep 1955

Division 2
Home: Newcastle United 13 Newport County 0, 5 Oct
1946
Away: Burslem Port Vale 0 Sheffield United 10, 10 Dec
1892

Division 3
Home: Tranmere Rovers 9 Accrington Stanley 0, 18 Apr
1959
Brentford 9 Wrexham 0, 15 Oct 1963
Away: Halifax Town 0 Fulham 8, 16 Sep 1969
Brighton & Hove Albion 2 Bristol Rovers 8, 1 Dec 1973

Division 3 (South)
Home: Luton Town 12 Bristol Rovers 0, 13 Apr 1936
Away: Northampton Town 0 Walsall 8, 2 Feb 1947

Division 3 (North)
Home: Stockport County 13 Halifax Town 0, 6 Jan 1934
Away: Accrington Stanley 0 Barnsley 9, 3 Feb 1934

Division 4
Home: Oldham Athletic 11 Southport 0, 26 Dec 1962
Away: Crewe Alexandra 1 Rotherham United 8, 8 Sep
1973

Aggregate
Tranmere Rovers 13 Oldham Athletic 4, Div 3N, 26 Dec
1935

SCOTTISH LEAGUE

Premier Division
Home: Aberdeen 8 Motherwell 0, 26 Mar 1979
Away: Kilmarnock 1 Rangers 8, 20 Sep 1980

Division 1
Home: Celtic 11 Dundee 0, 26 Oct 1895
Away: Airdrieonians 1 Hibernian 11, 24 Oct 1950

Division 2
Home: East Fife 13 Edinburgh City 2, 11 Dec 1937
Away: Alloa Athletic 0 Dundee 0, 8 Mar 1947

Most goals in one match (individual)

FOOTBALL LEAGUE

10 goals, Joe Payne, Luton Town v Bristol Rovers,
Division 3S, 13 April 1936

Division 1
7 goals, Ted Drake, Arsenal v Aston Villa, 14 Dec 1935;
James Ross, Preston North End v Stoke City, 6 Oct
1888

FA CUP

9 goals, Ted MacDougall, Bournemouth v Margate, 20 Nov 1971

Preliminary rounds

10 goals, Chris Marron, South Shields v Radcliffe, 20 Sep 1947

LEAGUE CUP

6 goals, Frankie Bunn, Oldham Athletic v Scarborough, 25 Oct 1989

SCOTTISH LEAGUE

8 goals, Jimmy McGrory, Celtic v Dunfermline Athletic, 14 Jan 1928

SCOTTISH CUP

13 goals, John Petrie, Arbroath v Bon Accord, 5 Sep 1885

BRITISH INTERNATIONAL CHAMPIONSHIP

6 goals, Joe Bambrick, Ireland v Wales, 1 Feb 1930

Highest career goalscoring totals

FOOTBALL LEAGUE

434 goals, Arthur Rowley, West Bromwich Albion, Fulham, Leceister City and Shrewsbury Town, 1946–65

SCOTTISH LEAGUE

410 goals, Jimmy McGrory, Celtic and Clydebank, 1922–1938

Quickest goals

6 seconds, Albert Mundy, Aldershot v Hartlepool United, Division 4, 25 Oct 1958
6 seconds, Barrie Jones, Notts County v Torquay United, Division 3, 31 Mar 1962
6 seconds, Keith Smith, Crystal Palace v Derby County, Division 2, 12 Dec 1964

Fastest hat-tricks

3 goals in 2½ minutes, Ephraim 'Jock' Dodds, Blackpool v Tranmere Rovers, Wartime Regional League, 28 February 1943
Jimmy Scarth, Gillingham v Leyton Orient, Division 3S, 1 Nov 1952
4 goals in 5 minutes, John McIntyre, Blackburn Rovers v Everton, 16 Sep 1922
Billy 'Ginger' Richardson, West Bromwich Albion v West Ham United, 7 Nov 1931 (from the start of the game including three in 3 minutes)
6 goals in 21 minutes, Frank Keetley, Lincoln City v Halifax Town, Division 3N, 16 Jan 1932

IN INTERNATIONALS

3 goals in 3½ minutes, Willie Hall, England v Ireland, 16 Nov 1938

Fastest own goal

6 seconds, Pat Kruse, Torquay United v Cambridge United, 3 Jan 1977

Goalkeeping clean-sheet records

BRITISH RECORD (ALL COMPETITIVE GAMES)

Chris Woods, Rangers, 1196 minutes from 26 November 1986 to 31 January 1987

FOOTBALL LEAGUE

Steve Death, Reading, 1103 minutes from 24 March to 18 August 1979

INTERNATIONAL

Dino Zoff, Italy, unbeaten in 1142 minutes from September 1972 to June 1974

Most cup-winners medals

FA CUP

5 James Forrest (Blackburn Rovers) 1884–86, 1890–91
The Hon. Sir Arthur Fitzgerald Kinnaird, Kt (Wanderers) 1873, 1877–78, (Old Etonians) 1879, 1882
Charles H.R. Wollaston (Wanderers) 1872–73, 1876–78

SCOTTISH CUP

8 Charles Campbell (Queen's Park), 1874–76, 1880–82, 1884 and 1886

Most League appearances

FOOTBALL LEAGUE

991 Peter Shilton (286 Leicester City, 110 Stoke City, 202 Nottingham Forest, 188 Southampton, 175 Derby County, 30 Plymouth Argyle) 1966–
824 Terry Paine (713 Southampton, 111 Hereford United) 1957–77
797 Tommy Hutchison (165 Blackpool, 314 Coventry City, 46 Manchester City, 92 Burnley, 180 Swansea City) 1968– ; also 68 Alloa 1965–68
777 Alan Oakes (565 Manchester City, 211 Chester City, 1 Port Vale) 1959–84
770 John Trollope (all for Swindon Town) 1960–80
764 Jimmy Dickinson (all for Portsmouth) 1946–65
761 Roy Sproson (all for Port Vale) 1950–72
758 Billy Bonds (95 Charlton Athletic, 663 West Ham United) 1964–88
758 Ray Clemence (48 Scunthorpe United, 470 Liverpool, 240 Tottenham Hotspur) 1966–87
757 Pat Jennings (48 Watford, 472 Tottenham Hotspur, 237 Arsenal) 1963–86

757 Frank Worthington (171 Huddersfield Town, 210 Leicester City, 84 Bolton Wanderers, 75 Birmingham City, 32 Leeds United, 19 Sunderland, 34 Southampton, 31 Brighton & Hove Albion, 59 Tranmere Rovers, 23 Preston North End, 19 Stockport County) 1966–88

SCOTTISH LEAGUE
Division 1
626 Bob Ferrier (Motherwell) 1918–37

Most first-class appearances

1374 Peter Shilton (991 League, 125 internationals, 102 League Cup, 86 FA Cup, 13 Under-23, four Football League, 51 others – European Cup, UEFA Cup, World Cup Championship, Charity Shield, European Super Cup, Full Members Cup, Screen Sport Super Cup, Anglo-Italian Cup, Texaco Cup, Simod Cup and Zenith Data Systems Cup.

Youngest players

FOOTBALL LEAGUE DEBUT
Albert Geldard, 15 years 158 days, Bradford Park Avenue v Millwall, Division 2, 16 Sep 1929
Ken Roberts, 15 years 158 days, Wrexham v Bradford Park Avenue, Division 3N, 1 Sep 1951

FOOTBALL LEAGUE SCORER
Ronnie Dix, 15 years 180 days, Bristol Rovers v Norwich City, Division 3S, 3 March 1928

DIVISION 1 DEBUT
Derek Forster, 15 years 185 days, Sunderland v Leicester City, 22 Aug 1984

DIVISION 1 SCORER
Jason Dozzell, 16 years 57 days, as substitute for Ipswich Town v Coventry City, 4 Feb 1984

FA CUP
Andy Awford, 15 years 88 days as a substitute for Worcester City v Borehamwood, 3rd Qualifying Round, 10 Oct 1987

FA CUP PROPER
Scott Endersby, 15 years 288 days, Kettering v Tilbury, 1st Round, 26 Nov 1977

FA CUP FINAL
James Prinsep, 17 years 245 days, Clapham Rovers v Old Etonians, 1879
Wembley: Paul Allen, 17 years 256 days, West Ham United v Arsenal, 1980

FA CUP FINAL SCORER
Norman Whiteside, 18 years 18 days, Manchester United v Brighton & Hove Albion, 1983

FA CUP FINAL CAPTAIN
David Nish, 21 years 212 days, Leicester City v Manchester City, 1969

INTERNATIONALS
England
Pre-war: James Prinsep (Clapham Rovers) 17 years 252 days, 5 Apr 1879
Post-war: Duncan Edwards (Manchester United), 18 years 183 days, v Scotland, 2 Apr 1955
Northern Ireland
Norman Whiteside (Manchester United), 17 years 42 days, v Yugoslavia, 17 Jun 1982
Scotland
Johnny Lambie (Queen's Park), 17 years 92 days, v Ireland, 20 Mar 1886
Wales
John Charles (Leeds United), 18 years 71 days, v Ireland, 8 Mar 1950
Republic of Ireland
Jimmy Holmes, 17 years 200 days, v Austria, 30 May 1971

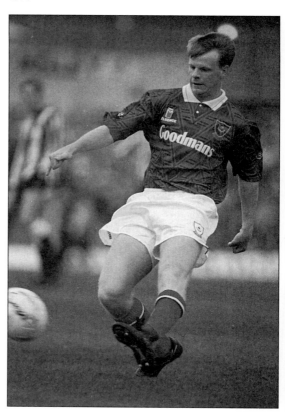

Andy Awford in familiar Portsmouth colours. In his non-league days with Worcester City he became the youngest ever player in the FA Cup at just 15 years 88 days (Allsport/Steve Morton)

Oldest players

FOOTBALL LEAGUE

Neil McBain, 52 years 4 months, New Brighton v Hartlepools United, Div 3N, 15 Mar 1957 (McBain was New Brighton's manager and had to play in an emergency)

DIVISION 1

Stanley Matthews, 50 years 5 days, Stoke City v Fulham, 6 Feb 1965

FA CUP FINAL

Walter Hampson, 41 years 8 months, Newcastle United v Aston Villa, 1924

FA CUP

Billy Meredith, 49 years 8 months, Manchester City v Newcastle United, 29 Mar 1924

INTERNATIONAL DEBUT

Leslie Compton, 38 years 2 months, England v Wales, 15 Nov 1950

INTERNATIONAL

Billy Meredith, 45 years 229 days, Wales v England, 15 Mar 1920

Highest attendances

INTERNATIONAL

149,547 Scotland v England, Hampden Park, Glasgow, 17 Apr 1937

EUROPEAN CUP

136,505 Celtic v Leeds United, semi-final, Hampden Park, Glasgow, 15 Apr 1970

FA CUP FINAL

160,000 (126,047 counted admissions) West Ham United v Bolton Wanderers, Wembley, 28 Apr 1923

SCOTTISH CUP FINAL

146,433, Celtic v Aberdeen, Hampden Park, Glasgow, 24 Apr 1937

PREMIER LEAGUE

44,619 Liverpool v Everton, Anfield 20 Mar 1993

FOOTBALL LEAGUE
Division 1
83,260, Manchester United v Arsenal, Maine Road, 17 Jan 1948
Division 2
68,029, Aston Villa v Coventry City, Villa Park, 30 Oct 1937

Division 3
49,309, Sheffield Wednesday v Sheffield United, Hillsborough, 26 Dec 1979
Division 3S
51,621, Cardiff City v Bristol City, Ninian Park, 7 Apr 1947
Division 3N
49,655, Hull City v Rotherham United, Boothferry Park, 25 Dec 1948
Division 4
37,774, Crystal Palace v Millwall, Selhurst Park, 31 Mar 1961

SCOTTISH LEAGUE
118,567, Rangers v Celtic, Ibrox Park, 2 Jan 1939

NON-LEAGUE
FA Amateur Cup Finals
100,000, Pegasus v Harwich and Parkeston, Wembley Stadium, 11 Apr 1953
GM Vauxhall Conference
9432, Lincoln City v Wycombe Wanderers, 2 May 1988
Southern League
29,786, Queen's Park Rangers v Plymouth Argyle, Park Royal, 25 Dec 1907

Lowest Attendances

BRITISH INTERNATIONAL

2315, Wales v Northern Ireland, Racecourse Ground, Wrexham, 27 May 1982

FOOTBALL LEAGUE

450, Rochdale v Cambridge United, Div 3, 5 Feb 1974
469, Thames v Luton Town, Div 3S, 6 Dec 1930
484, Gateshead v Accrington Stanley, Div 3N, 26 Mar 1952

PREMIER LEAGUE

3039, Wimbledon v Everton, 26 Jan 1993
Division 1 (post-war)
3121, Wimbledon v Sheffield Wednesday, 2 Oct 1991
NB Although the Stockport County v Leicester City Division 2 game at Old Trafford on 7 May 1921 was reported to have had an official attendance of only 13, contemporary reports estimated the crowd at 2000. Similarly, for the FA Cup third round second replay between Bradford City and Norwich City at Lincoln in 1915 the official attendance was nil, but although it was played behind closed doors so as not to interfere with war work in nearby factories, several hundred spectators gained admittance without paying.

SCOTTISH LEAGUE

32, East Stirling v Leith Athletic, Div 2, 15 April 1939

EUROPEAN FOOTBALL

EUROPEAN CHAMPIONSHIP

European Nations Cup 1960–68

Year	Winner		Runners up	Venue	Attendance	Referee	Entries	Top scorer (3 or more goals in final tournament)	
1960	USSR	2–1	Yugoslavia	Paris, France	17,966	Ellis, England	17	–	
1964	Spain	2–1	USSR	Madrid, Spain	120,000	Holland, England	29	–	
1968	Italy	1–1 2–0	Yugoslavia	Rome, Italy	60,000 75,000	Dienst, Switzerland	31	–	
1972	West Germany	3–0	USSR	Brussels, Belgium	43,437	Marschall, Austria	32	Gerd Muller (West Germany)	4
1976	Czechoslovakia (Czechs won 5–3 on penalties)	2–2*	West Germany	Belgrade, Yugoslavia	45,000	Gonella, Italy	32	Dieter Muller (West Germany)	4
1980	West Germany	2–1	Belgium	Rome, Italy	47,864	Rainea, Rumania	32	Klaus Allofs (West Germany)	3
1984	France	2–0	Spain	Paris, France	48,000	Christov, Czechoslovakia	33	Michel Platini (France)	8
1988	Holland	2–0	USSR	Munich, West Germany	72,308	Vautrot, France	33	Van Basten (Holland)	5
1992	Denmark	2–0	Germany	Gothenburg, Sweden	37,800	Galler, Switzerland	34	Four players	3

* after extra time

EUROPEAN CUP

REAL MADRID

Year	Score	Runners-up	Venue	Attendance
1956	4–3	Stade de Reims	Paris, France	38,000
1957	2–0	Fiorentina	Madrid, Spain	124,000
1958	3–2	AC Milan	Brussels, Belgium	67,000
1959	2–0	Stade de Reims	Stuttgart, W Germany	80,000
1960	7–3	Eintracht Frankfurt	Glasgow, Scotland	135,000
1966	2–1	Partizan Belgrade	Brussels, Belgium	55,000

Real Madrid's five successive European Cup titles have never been equalled. In 1956 they came back from 2–0 and 3–2 down to win 4–3 against Reims, with Alfredo di Stefano – the 'White Arrow' – acclaimed as the supreme architect of victory. A disputed penalty from Di Stefano and a memorable second goal from Francisco Gento disposed of ultra-cautious Fiorentina a year later. In 1958 Real again had to come from behind twice against AC Milan and only forced the winner through Gento in extra time. The following year Enrique Mateos put Real ahead in the first minute against Reims, who had only three survivors from the 1956 final. Though Raymond Kopa, appearing against his old club, was reduced to half-speed and Dominique Colonna saved a Mateos penalty, Real won easily.

They reached their peak in 1960 at Hampden Park; though Eintracht Frankfurt scored first in 18 minutes, it was over by half-time as a game but not as a spectacle. Individual skill, speed and devastating finishing produced a regal victory brilliantly forged, with the Germans playing no small part in the entertainment. Di Stefano's artistry, Ferenc Puskas' power and Luis Del Sol's organisation completed a memorable occasion. Real with a much younger all-Spanish team and only Enrique Pachin and Gento with winners' medals, were a goal down to Partizan Belgrade in 1966 but equalised and Francisco Serena won it six minutes from the end.

BENFICA

Year	Score	Runners-up	Venue	Attendance
1961	3–2	Barcelona	Berne, Switzerland	28,000
1962	5–3	Real Madrid	Amsterdam, Holland	65,000

Benfica's attempt to adopt the mantle of Real Madrid was not quite sustained. They conceded an early goal to Barcelona in 1961, but took full advantage of two errors by goalkeeper Antonio Ramallets to lead 2–1 and Mario Coluna added a third. The Spaniards hit the post before and after reducing the deficit. Benfica faced Real themselves the following season, an ageing Spanish side in unfamiliar blue. It was 'The night of the long shots', some spectacular and speculative efforts. Puskas became the first player to score hat-tricks in two finals but finished on the losing side. Real were 2–0 ahead and again at 3–2. Benfica only took the lead in the 63rd minute, but as the younger, fitter team deserved victory.

AC MILAN

Year	Score	Runners-up	Venue	Attendance
1963	2–1	Benfica	Wembley, England	45,000
1969	4–1	Ajax	Madrid, Spain	50,000
1989	4–0	Steaua Bucharest	Barcelona, Spain	97,000
1990	1–0	Benfica	Vienna, Austria	57,500

The Italians robbed Benfica of a hat-trick, despite Eusebio scoring in-off-a-post after accelerating past the AC Milan defence. Jose Altafini hit two goals to set a new individual record with 14 goals in the season as Milan were masterminded by Gianni Rivera in midfield. The Italian 'Golden Boy' provided the inspiration for a Pierino Prati hat-trick in 1969 against an Ajax team lacking in confidence. Ex-Partizan defender Velibor Vasovic scored from a penalty for them to become the first player to score in the final for different teams. Discipline, technique and double-Dutch strikes from Ruud Gullitt and Marco Van Basten revealed the Italians' superiority against the Romanian army team Steaua Bucharest in 1989 and a 67th minute goal from the third Dutchman Frank Rijkaard disposed of Benfica the following year.

INTERNAZIONALE

Year	Score	Runners-up	Venue	Attendance
1964	3–1	Real Madrid	Vienna, Austria	74,000
1965	1–0	Benfica	Milan, Italy	80,000

Precision defending under the direction of Helenio Herrera, the high priest of *catenaccio*, as Internazionale,

Milan's other team, frustrated Real Madrid at every turn in 1964, though the Spaniards hit the woodwork after Sandro Mazzola had scored. It was the last European Cup game for Di Stefano, Puskas and Jose Santamaria. Mazzola scored the Italians' third after Real had reduced the lead. The following year on their own ground and in heavy rain, Inter had everything in their favour. Alberto Costa Pereira, the Benfica goalkeeper, let Jair's shot through his legs and was later taken off with a leg injury, the limping Luis Germano having to go in goal.

CELTIC

Year	Score	Runners-up	Venue	Attendance
1967	2–1	Internazionale	Lisbon, Portugal	56,000

When Mazzola of Inter sent Ronnie Simpson the wrong way from a seventh minute penalty, it seemed that the Scots had a mountain to climb. But spurred on by 12,000 travelling fans, they threw everything into attack with controlled, ceaseless pressure and were rewarded with Tommy Gemmell's 25-yard strike in the 62nd minute. He later hit the bar but the winner came five minutes from time when the tireless Bobby Murdoch had his shot deflected in by Steve Chalmers.

MANCHESTER UNITED

Year	Score	Runners-up	Venue	Attendance
1968	4–1*	Benfica	Wembley, England	100,000

* After extra time

The advantage of playing at Wembley seemed to finely balance the experience of Benfica, appearing in their fifth final in eight years. United took the lead in the 52nd minute with a rare near-post header from Bobby Charlton, but Jaime Graca levelled the scores with 11 minutes remaining. But three goals in seven minutes – a George Best solo, one from Brian Kidd and another Charlton effort – again sealed a memorable evening in extra time.

FEYENOORD

Year	Score	Runners-up	Venue	Attendance
1970	2–1	Celtic	Milan, Italy	50,000

The Dutch showed tactical superiority against Celtic, though the Scots led from a Gemmell free-kick in the 29th minute. Feyenoord immediately equalised from another free-kick by Rinus Israel. Four minutes from the

Feyenoord's keeper Graafland punches clear during the 1970 European Cup final at the San Siro. The Dutch side won the match 2–1 in extra time (Popperfoto)

end of extra time, the referee allowed Ove Kindvall to run on and score after handball by Billy McNeill.

AJAX

Year	Score	Runners-up	Venue	Attendance
1971	2–0	Panathinaikos	Wembley, England	90,000
1972	2–0	Internazionale	Rotterdam, Holland	67,000
1973	1–0	Juventus	Belgrade, Yugoslavia	93,500

Rinus Michels marked his last game as Ajax coach with victory over Puskas' Panathinaikos. The Dutch were ahead in five minutes but had to wait until Johan Cruyff's sparkle on the wing provided a second goal for substitute Arie Haan three minutes from time to be sure of success. Romanian Stefan Kovacs took over and gave full rein to the 'total football' concept which dominated Dutch football during the era. Inter's blanket defence looked worn and outdated. Cruyff scored three minutes after half-time when the goalkeeper dropped the ball and headed a second in the 77th minute. Ajax had just one change in 1973, Johnny Rep coming in on the right wing and he scored with a far post header after only four minutes. But Juventus made the Dutch fight all the way from then on for their deserved hat-trick.

BAYERN MUNICH

Year	Score	Runners-up	Venue	Attendance
1974	1–1*	Atletico Madrid	Brussels, Belgium	65,000
Replay	4–0	Atletico Madrid	Brussels, Belgium	65,000
1975	2–0	Leeds United	Paris, France	50,000
1976	1–0	St. Etienne	Glasgow, Scotland	54,864

* After extra time

Bayern Munich equalled Ajax's three in a row, but were fortunate in the first final against Atletico Madrid who were leading 1–0 with the seconds dying away in extra time. Then Georg Schwarzenbeck crashed home a speculative drive from 30 yards to level the scores. Two days later with better tactics on the day, Bayern dominated over the older, tiring Spaniards. Uli Hoeness from the half-way line past two defenders scored the pick of their four goals. The following year Leeds United had all the play, Peter Lorimer had a volley disallowed for offside, but with Franz Beckenbauer marshalling the team fore and aft, the Germans survived two penalty appeals and Gerd Muller made it safe at the near post in the 83rd minute. Franz Roth, who had scored Bayern's first against Leeds, converted a free-kick against St Etienne in the 57th minute after the French had twice hit the woodwork and Muller had had a goal disallowed for offside at the opposite end.

LIVERPOOL

Year	Score	Runners-up	Venue	Attendance
1977	3–1	Moenchengladbach	Rome, Italy	57,000
1978	1–0	FC Bruges	Wembley, England	92,000
1981	1–0	Real Madrid	Paris, France	48,360
1984	1–1*	Roma	Rome, Italy	69,693

* Liverpool won 4–2 on penalties

Liverpool took the lead over Borussia Moenchengladbach after 27 minutes but Allan Simonsen equalised with a swerving shot from an angle in the 51st minute. A brilliant save by Ray Clemence from Uli Stielike five minutes later turned the match. Phil Neal's 11th penalty of the season sealed it. In 1978, Bruges goalkeeper Birger Jensen kept Liverpool out until the 65th minute when Kenny Dalglish committed him before chipping the only goal. The old and new masters were in opposition in 1981, Real Madrid bidding to recapture former glories, but Alan Kennedy's late effort with eight minutes remaining kept them from victory. In 1984 the decision went to penalty kicks after extra time. Neal had scored first for Liverpool in the 15th minute and Roberto Pruzzo back-headed the equaliser after 38 minutes. Despite Steve Nicol missing the first spot kick, Liverpool won 4–2 in the shoot-out with Alan Kennedy netting the decisive penalty.

NOTTINGHAM FOREST

Year	Score	Runners-up	Venue	Attendance
1979	1–0	Malmo	Munich, W Germany	57,500
1980	1–0	Hamburg	Madrid, Spain	50,000

Trevor Francis, in his first European Cup game, stretched himself at the far post for a spectacular winner in a disappointing final which was continuing the trend of matches being decided by a single goal. Forest retained the trophy the following year without Francis who had an achilles tendon injury. John Robertson with a right foot shot just outside the penalty area hit the inside of a post and watched it go in. In goal Peter Shilton frustrated Kevin Keegan and his Hamburg colleagues.

ASTON VILLA

Year	Score	Runners-up	Venue	Attendance
1982	1–0	Bayern Munich	Rotterdam, Holland	46,000

Despite losing goalkeeper Jimmy Rimmer early on, Nigel Spink – the first substitute goalkeeper in a European final – proved an able deputy and Villa's defence held firm. Peter Withe scored in a yawning goal in the 67th minute after neat approach work by Tony Morley. Bayern lost their first domestic and European final in 14 attempts.

HAMBURG

Year	Score	Runners-up	Venue	Attendance
1983	1–0	Juventus	Athens, Greece	75,000

In 1983 the sixth successive European Cup Final with just one goal separating the teams saw Felix Magath's ninth minute goal win another below-par final in which Ernst Happel's coaching strategy outwitted poor Juventus tactics.

JUVENTUS

Year	Score	Runners-up	Venue	Attendance
1985	1–0	Liverpool	Brussels, Belgium	58,000

The low-key Heysel final after the tragedy off the field was won by a Michel Platini penalty in the 57th minute, controversial in that Liverpool claimed it was outside the area when Gary Gillespie brought down Zbigniew Boniek.

STEAUA BUCHAREST

Year	Score	Runners-up	Venue	Attendance
1986	0–0*	Barcelona	Seville, Spain	70,000

* Steaua won 2–0 on penalties

The first club from Eastern Europe to win the trophy, the Romanian Army team had to thank goalkeeper Helmut Ducadam for ultimate success. He saved four post-match penalties against Barcelona. Only two of eight attempted in the entire shoot-out found the target.

PORTO

Year	Score	Runners-up	Venue	Attendance
1987	2–1	Bayern Munich	Vienna, Austria	59,000

The most rewarding final for a decade saw Porto produce flair and imagination in beating Bayern Munich, who took the lead in the 25th minute through Ludwig Kogl. The Portuguese left it late but goals from Algerian Rabah Madjer and Brazilian substitute Juary in four minutes gave them a win with nine minutes left. Madjer's back heel goal was probably the cheekiest seen in a final.

PSV EINDHOVEN

Year	Score	Runners-up	Venue	Attendance
1988	0–0*	Benfica	Stuttgart, W Germany	70,000

* PSV won 6–5 on penalties

It was back to no goals, little excitement and penalties in 1988, but this time the ultimate marksmanship was more accurate. It was not until the 12th kick from Benfica's Veloso – a weak effort – was stopped by Hans Van Breukelen in the Dutch goal, that one failed to hit its target.

RED STAR BELGRADE

Year	Score	Runners-up	Venue	Attendance
1991	0–0*	Marseille	Bari, Italy	56,000

* Red Star Belgrade won 5–3 on penalties

Neither the flair which Marseille had shown earlier nor the powerful finishing which Red Star Belgrade had revealed in previous rounds was in evidence in another sterile, unimaginative final which again needed a shoot-out to decide it. Manuel Amoros was the unfortunate who failed from the spot. Miodrag Belodedic became the first player to win medals with different teams, having won one in 1986 with Steaua.

BARCELONA

Year	Score	Runners-up	Venue	Attendance
1992	1–0	Sampdoria	Wembley	70,827

Barcelona, coached by Cruyff, at last won the European Cup which had eluded them throughout their history in a much more impressive final at Wembley which needed the extra period before a goal was scored. It was a typical Ronald Koeman free-kick in the 111th minute which divided the teams. Koeman had won a medal with PSV in 1988.

OLYMPIQUE MARSEILLE

Year	Score	Runners-up	Venue	Attendance
1993	1–0	AC Milan	Munich, Germany	64,400

The first ever French club triumph in a European competition and a victory for Marseille's wealthy owner Bernard Tapie over his Italian counterpart Silvio Berlusconi. Basile Boli headed the winning goal just before the interval after Milan had squandered opportunities at the other end.

Goalscorer Ronald Koeman (left) and Michael Laudrup celebrate Barcelona's first ever European Cup triumph after their 1–0 win over Sampdoria at Wembley in 1992 (Allsport/David Cannon)

CUP-WINNERS' CUP

FIORENTINA

Year	Score	Runners-up	Venue	Attendance
1961	2–0	Rangers (1)	Glasgow, Scotland	80,000
	2–1	Rangers (2)	Florence, Italy	50,000

ATLETICO MADRID

Year	Score	Runners-up	Venue	Attendance
1962	1–1	Fiorentina	Glasgow, Scotland	27,389
Replay	3–0	Fiorentina	Stuttgart, W Germany	45,000

TOTTENHAM HOTSPUR

Year	Score	Runners-up	Venue	Attendance
1963	5–1	Atletico Madrid	Rotterdam, Holland	25,000

SPORTING LISBON

Year	Score	Runners-up	Venue	Attendance
1964	3–3	MTK Budapest	Brussels, Belgium	9,000
1964	1–0	MTK Budapest	Antwerp, Belgium	18,000

WEST HAM UNITED

Year	Score	Runners-up	Venue	Attendance
1965	2–0	Munich 1860	Wembley, England	100,000

BORUSSIA DORTMUND

Year	Score	Runners-up	Venue	Attendance
1966	2–1*	Liverpool	Glasgow, Scotland	41,657

* After extra time

BAYERN MUNICH

Year	Score	Runners-up	Venue	Attendance
1967	1–0*	Rangers	Nuremberg, W Germany	69,480

* After extra time

AC MILAN

Year	Score	Runners-up	Venue	Attendance
1968	2–0	Hamburg	Rotterdam, Holland	60,000
1973	1–0	Leeds United	Salonika, Greece	45,000

SLOVAN BRATISLAVA

Year	Score	Runners-up	Venue	Attendance
1969	3–2	Barcelona	Basle, Switzerland	40,000

MANCHESTER CITY

| 1970 | 2–1 | Gomik Zabrze | Vienna, Austria | 10,000 |

CHELSEA

| 1971 | 1–1* | Real Madrid | Athens, Greece | 42,000 |
| Replay | 2–1 | Real Madrid | Athens, Greece | 24,000 |

* After extra time

RANGERS

| 1972 | 3–2 | Moscow Dynamo | Barcelona, Spain | 35,000 |

MAGDEBURG

| 1974 | 2–0 | AC Milan | Rotterdam, Holland | 5,000 |

DYNAMO KIEV

| 1975 | 3–0 | Ferencvaros | Basle, Switzerland | 13,000 |
| 1986 | 3–0 | Atletico Madrid | Lyon, France | 39,300 |

ANDERLECHT

| 1976 | 4–2 | West Ham United | Brussels, Belgium | 58,000 |
| 1978 | 4–0 | Austria/WAC | Amsterdam, Holland | 48,679 |

HAMBURG

| 1977 | 2–0 | Anderlecht | Amsterdam, Holland | 65,000 |

BARCELONA

1979	4–3*	Fortuna Dusseldorf	Basle, Switzerland	58,000
1982	2–1	Standard Liege	Barcelona, Spain	100,000
1989	2–0	Sampdoria	Berne, Switzerland	45,000

* After extra time

VALENCIA

| 1980 | 0–0* | Arsenal | Brussels, Belgium | 40,000 |

* Valencia won 5–4 on penalties

DYNAMO TBILISI

| 1981 | 2–1 | Carl Zeiss Jena | Dusseldorf, W Germany | 9,000 |

ABERDEEN

| 1983 | 2–1* | Real Madrid | Gothenburg, Sweden | 17,804 |

* After extra time

JUVENTUS

| 1984 | 2–1 | Porto | Basle, Switzerland | 60,000 |

EVERTON

Year	Score	Runners-up	Venue	Attendance
1985	3–1	Rapid Vienna	Rotterdam, Holland	30,000

AJAX

| 1987 | 1–0 | Lokomotive Leipzig | Athens, Greece | 35,000 |

MECHELEN

| 1988 | 1–0 | Ajax | Strasbourg, France | 39,446 |

SAMPDORIA

| 1990 | 2–0* | Anderlecht | Gothenburg, Sweden | 20,103 |

* After extra time

MANCHESTER UNITED

| 1991 | 2–1 | Barcelona | Rotterdam, Holland | 45,000 |

WERDER BREMEN

| 1992 | 2–0 | Monaco | Lisbon, Portugal | 16,000 |

PARMA

| 1993 | 3–1 | Royal Antwerp | Wembley, England | 37,393 |

Parma's opening goal in the 1993 Cup-Winners' Cup final at Wembley scored by Lorenzo Minotti (out of picture). They became the fifth Italian winners of the trophy (Allsport)

UEFA CUP

BARCELONA

Year	Score	Runners-up	Attendance
1955–58	2–2	London (A)	45,466
	6–0	London (H)	62,000
1958–60	0–0	Birmingham City (A)	40,500
	4–1	Birmingham City (H)	70,000
1965–66	0–1	Zaragoza (H)	70,000
	4–2	Zaragoza (A)	70,000

ROMA

1960–61	2–2	Birmingham City (A)	21,005
	2–0	Birmingham City (H)	60,000

VALENCIA

1961–62	6–2	Barcelona (H)	65,000
	1–1	Barcelona (A)	60,000
1962–63	2–1	Dynamo Zagreb (A)	40,000
	2–0	Dynamo Zagreb (H)	55,000

ZARAGOZA

1963–64	2–1	Valencia	50,000

FERENCVAROS

1964–65	1–0	Juventus	25,000

DYNAMO ZAGREB

1966–67	2–0	Leeds United (H)	40,000
	0–0	Leeds United (A)	35,604

LEEDS UNITED

Year	Score	Runners-up	Attendance
1967–68	1–0	Ferencvaros (H)	25,368
	0–0	Ferencvaros (A)	70,000
1970–71	0–0	Juventus (A)	65,000
		(abandoned 51 minutes)	
	2–2	Juventus (A)	65,000
	1–1	Juventus (H)	42,483
		(Leeds won on away goals)	

NEWCASTLE UNITED

1968–69	3–0	Ujpest Dozsa (H)	60,000
	3–2	Ujpest Dozsa (A)	37,000

ARSENAL

1969–70	1–3	Anderlecht (A)	37,000
	3–0	Anderlecht (H)	51,612

TOTTENHAM HOTSPUR

1971–72	2–1	Wolverhampton Wanderers (A)	45,000

Year	Score	Runners-up	Attendance
	1–1	Wolverhampton Wanderers (H)	48,000
1983–84	1–1	Anderlecht (A)	40,000
	1–1	Anderlecht (H)	46,258
		(Tottenham won 4–3 on penalties)	

LIVERPOOL

1972–73	3–0	Moenchengladbach (H)	41,169
	2–0	Moenchengladbach (A)	35,000
1975–76	3–2	FC Bruges (H)	56,000
		FC Bruges (A)	32,000

FEYENOORD

1973–74	2–2	Tottenham Hotspur (A)	46,281
	2–0	Tottenham Hotspur (H)	68,000

MOENCHENGLADBACH

1974–75	0–0	Twente (H)	45,000
	5–1	Twente (A)	24,500
1978–79	1–1	Red Star Belgrade (A)	87,500
	1–0	Red Star Belgrade (H)	45,000

JUVENTUS

1976–77	1–0	Athletic Bilbao (H)	75,000
	1–2	Athletic Bilbao (A)	43,000
1989–90	3–1	Fiorentina (H)	45,000
	0–0	Fiorentina (A)	32,000
1992–93	3–1	Borussia Dortmund (A)	37,000
	3–0	Borussia Dortmund (H)	60,000

PSV EINDHOVEN

1977–78	0–0	Bastia (A)	15,000
	3–0	Bastia (H)	27,000

EINTRACHT FRANKFURT

1979–80	2–3	Moenchengladbach (A)	25,000
	1–0	Moenchengladbach (H)	60,000
		(Eintracht won on away goals)	

IPSWICH TOWN

1980–81	3–0	AZ '67 (H)	27,532
	2–4	AZ '67 (A)	28,500

GOTHENBURG

1981–82	1–0	Hamburg (H)	42,548
	3–0	Hamburg (A)	60,000
1986–87	1–0	Dundee United (H)	50,023
	1–1	Dundee United (A)	20,911

ANDERLECHT

Year	Score	Runners-up	Attendance
1982–83	1–0	Benfica (H)	45,000
	1–1	Benfica (A)	80,000

REAL MADRID

1984–85	3–0	Videoton (A)	30,000
	0–1	Videoton (H)	98,300
1985–86	5–1	Cologne (H)	80,000
	0–2	Cologne (A)	15,000

BAYER LEVERKUSEN

1987–88	0–3	Espanol (A)	42,000
	3–0	Espanol (H)	22,000
		(Leverkusen won 3–2 on penalties)	

NAPOLI

1988–89	2–1	Stuttgart (H)	83,000
	3–3	Stuttgart (A)	67,000

INTERNAZIONALE

1990–91	2–0	Roma (H)	68,887
	0–1	Roma (A)	70,901

AJAX

1991–92	2–2	Torino (A)	65,377
	0–0	Torino (H)	40,000

SUPER CUP

Contested by the winners of the Champions' Cup and Cup-Winners Cup, played the following season.

Year	Winners	Runners-up	Scores
1972	Ajax	Rangers	3–1, 3–2
1973	Ajax	AC Milan	0–1, 6–0
1974	Not contested		
1975	Dynamo Kiev	Bayern Munich	1–0, 2–0
1976	Anderlecht	Bayern Munich	4–1, 1–2
1977	Liverpool	Hamburg	1–1, 6–0
1978	Anderlecht	Liverpool	3–1, 1–1
1979	Nottingham Forest	Barcelona	1–0, 1–1
1980	Valencia*	Nottingham Forest	1–2, 1–0
1981	Not contested		
1982	Aston Villa	Barcelona	0–1, 3–0
1983	Aberdeen	Hamburg	0–0, 2–0
1984	Juventus	Liverpool	2–0 (in Turin)
1985	Not contested		
1986	Steaua Bucharest	Dynamo Kiev	1–0 (in Monaco)
1987	Porto	Ajax	1–0, 1–0
1988	Mechelen	PSV Eindhoven	3–0, 0–1
1989	AC Milan	Barcelona	1–1, 1–0
1990	AC Milan	Sampdoria	1–1, 2–0
1991	Manchester U	Red Star Belgrade	1–0
1992	Barcelona	Werder Bremen	1–1, 2–1

*won on away goals

Inter, winners of the 1991 UEFA Cup in an all-Italian final against Roma (Allsport/Shaun Botterill)

EUROPEAN CLUB COMPETITION RECORDS

Highest Scores

14–0 Ajax v Red Boys, UEFA Cup 1st Round, 3 Oct 1984

12–2 Feyenoord v KR Reykjavik, European Cup 1st Round, 17 Sep 1969

11–0 Dinamo Bucharest v Crusaders, European Cup 1st Round, 3 Oct 1973

16–1 Sporting Lisbon v Apoel Nicosia, Cup Winners' Cup 1st Round, 13 Nov 1963

13–0 Cologne v Union Luxembourg, Fairs Cup 1st Round, 15 Oct 1965

HIGHEST SCORES INVOLVING BRITISH CLUBS

13–0 Chelsea v Jeunesse Hautcharage, Cup Winners' Cup, 29 Sep 1971

12–0 Derby County v Finn Harps, UEFA Cup, 15 Sep 1976

12–0 Swansea City v Sliema Wanderers, Cup Winners' Cup, 15 Sep 1982

11–0 Liverpool v Stromsgodset, Cup Winners' Cup, 17 Sep 1974

Goalscoring in European competitions

EUROPEAN CUP INDIVIDUAL AGGREGATE

49, Alfredo di Stefano (Real Madrid) 1955–56 to 1963–64

46, Eusebio (Benfica) 1961–62 to 1973–74

37, Gerd Muller (Bayern Munich) 1969–70 to 1976–77

36, Ferenc Puskas (Honved, Real Madrid) 1955–56 to 1963–64

31, Francisco Gento (Real Madrid) 1955–56 to 1969–70

Goals in a season

EUROPEAN CUP

14, Jose Altafini (AC Milan) 1962–63

CUP WINNERS' CUP

14, Lothar Emmerich (Borussia Dortmund), 1965–66

UEFA CUP

14, John Wark (Ipswich Town), 1980–81

Chelsea's 13–0 win over Jeunesse Hautcharage at Stamford Bridge is still a record for European club competition. Here Tommy Baldwin (8) scores his second (Popperfoto)

Top British marksmen in European competitions

LEADING SCORERS

30 goals Peter Lorimer (Leeds United) 1965–66 to 1976–77

28 goals Denis Law (Manchester United) 1963–64 to 1968–69

23 goals John Wark (Ipswich Town and Liverpool) 1978–79 to 1984–85

22 goals Martin Chivers (Tottenham Hotspur) 1971–72 to 1973–74

20 goals Kenny Dalglish (Celtic and Liverpool) 1972–73 to 1983–84

5 goals in one match

Ray Crawford (Ipswich Town) v Floriana, European Cup 1st Round 2nd leg, 25 Sep 1962

Peter Osgood (Chelsea) v Jeunesse Hautcharage, Cup Winners' Cup, 29 Sep 1971

Aggregate scores by individuals

11 goals, Stan Bowles (Queen's Park Rangers) UEFA Cup, 1976–77

7 goals in one tie (five in first leg) Kevin Hector (Derby County) UEFA Cup, 1976–77

4 goals on two occasions, Trevor Whymark (Ipswich Town) v Lazio, UEFA Cup, 24 Oct 1973; v Landskrona Bois, UEFA Cup 28 Sep 1977

BRITISH CLUBS IN EUROPE

* won on away goals counting double   *† won on penalties*   *‡ won on the toss of a coin*

Football League Clubs

ARSENAL

Season	Competition	Round	Date	Opponents (Country)	Venue	Result	Scorers
1963–64	Fairs Cup	1	25 Sep 63	Staevnet (Denmark)	A	W 7–1	Strong 3, Baker 3, MacLeod
			22 Oct 63		H	L 2–3	Skirton, Barnwell
		2	13 Nov 63	Liege (Belgium)	H	D 1–1	Anderson
			18 Dec 63		A	L 1–3	McCullough
1969–70	Fairs Cup	1	9 Sep 69	Glentoran	H	W 3–0	Graham 2, Gould
			29 Sep 69	(Northern Ireland)	A	L 0–1	
		2	29 Oct 69	Sporting Lisbon	A	D 0–0	
			26 Nov 69	(Portugal)	H	W 3–0	Radford, Graham 2
		3	17 Dec 69	Rouen (France)	A	D 0–0	
			13 Jan 70		H	W 1–0	Sammels
		QF	11 Mar 70	Dynamo Bacau	A	W 2–0	Sammels, Radford
			18 Mar 70	(Romania)	H	W 7–1	George 2, Sammels 2, Radford 2, Graham
		SF	8 Apr 70	Ajax (Holland)	H	W 3–0	George 2 (1 pen), Sammels
			15 Apr 70		A	L 0–1	
		F	22 Apr 70	Anderlecht (Belgium)	A	L 1–3	Kennedy
			28 Apr 70		H	W 3–0	Kelly, Radford, Sammels
1970–71	Fairs Cup	1	16 Sep 70	Lazio (Italy)	A	D 2–2	Radford 2
			23 Sep 70		H	W 2–0	Radford, Armstrong
		2	21 Oct 70	Sturm Graz (Austria)	A	L 0–1	
			4 Nov 70		H	W 2–0	Storey (pen), Kennedy
		3	2 Dec 70	Beveren (Belgium)	H	W 4–0	Graham, Kennedy 2, Sammels
			16 Dec 70		A	D 0–0	
		QF	9 Mar 71	FC Cologne*	H	W 2–1	McLintock, Storey
			23 Mar 71	(West Germany)	A	L 0–1	
1971–72	European Cup	1	15 Sep 71	Stromsgodset	A	W 3–1	Simpson, Marinello, Kelly
			29 Sep 71	(Norway)	H	W 4–0	Kennedy, Radford 2, Armstrong
		2	20 Oct 71	Grasshoppers	A	W 2–0	Kennedy, Graham
			3 Nov 71	(Switzerland)	H	W 3–0	Kennedy, George, Radford
		QF	8 Mar 72	Ajax (Holland)	A	L 1–2	Kennedy
			22 Mar 72		H	L 0–1	
1978–79	UEFA Cup	1	13 Sep 78	Lokomotive Leipzig	H	W 3–0	Stapleton 2, Sunderland
			27 Sep 78	(East Germany)	A	W 4–1	Brady (pen), Stapleton 2, Sunderland
		2	18 Oct 78	Hajduk Split	A	L 1–2	O'Leary
			1 Nov 78	(Yugoslavia)	H	W 1–0	Young
		3	22 Nov 78	Red Star Belgrade	A	L 0–1	
			6 Dec 78	(Yugoslavia)	H	D 1–1	Sunderland
1979–80	Cup-Winners' Cup	1	19 Sep 79	Fenerbahce (Turkey)	H	W 2–0	Sunderland, Young
			3 Oct 79		A	D 0–0	
		2	24 Oct 79	Magdeburg	H	W 2–1	Young, Sunderland
			7 Nov 79	(East Germany)	A	D 2–2	Price, Brady
		QF	5 Mar 80	Gothenburg (Sweden)	H	W 5–1	Sunderland 2, Price, Brady, Young
			19 Mar 80		A	D 0–0	

Season	Competition	Round	Date	Opponents (Country)	Venue	Result	Scorers
		SF	9 Apr 80	Juventus (Italy)	H	D 1–1	own goal
			23 Apr 80		A	W 1–0	Vaessen
		F	14 May 80	Valencia (Spain)†	N	D 0–0	
1981–82	UEFA Cup	1	16 Sep 81	Panathinaikos	A	W 2–0	McDermott, Meade
			30 Sep 81	(Greece)	H	W 1–0	Talbot
		2	20 Oct 81	Winterslag (Belgium)*	A	L 0–1	
			3 Nov 81		H	W 2–1	Hollins, Rix
1982–83	UEFA Cup	1	14 Sep 82	Moscow Spartak	A	L 2–3	Robson, Chapman
			29 Sep 82	(USSR)	H	L 2–5	Chapman, own goal
1991–92	European Cup	1	18 Sep 91	FK Austria	H	W 6–1	Linighan, Smith 4, Limpar
			2 Oct 91	(Austria)	A	L 0–1	
		2	23 Oct 91	Benfica	A	D 1–1	Campbell
			6 Nov 91	(Portugal)	H	L 1–3	Pates

ASTON VILLA

Season	Competition	Round	Date	Opponents (Country)	Venue	Result	Scorers
1975–76	UEFA Cup	1	17 Sep 75	Antwerp (Belgium)	A	L 1–4	Graydon
			1 Oct 75		H	L 0–1	
1977–78	UEFA Cup	1	14 Sep 77	Fenerbahce (Turkey)	H	W 4–0	Gray, Deehan 2, Little
			28 Sep 77		A	W 2–0	Deehan, Little
		2	19 Oct 77	Gornik Zabrze	H	W 2–0	McNaught 2
			2 Nov 77	(Poland)	A	D 1–1	Gray
		3	23 Nov 77	Athletic Bilbao	H	W 2–0	own goal, Deehan
			7 Dec 77	(Spain)	A	D 1–1	Mortimer
		QF	1 Mar 78	Barcelona (Spain)	H	D 2–2	McNaught, Deehan
			15 Mar 78		A	L 1–2	Little
1981–82	European Cup	1	16 Sep 81	Valur (Iceland)	H	W 5–0	Morley, Withe 2, Donovan 2
			30 Sep 81		A	W 2–0	Shaw 2
		2	21 Oct 81	Dynamo Berlin	A	W 2–1	Morley 2
			4 Nov 81	(East Germany)	H	L 0–1	
		QF	3 Mar 82	Dynamo Kiev	A	D 0–0	
			17 Mar 82	(USSR)	H	W 2–0	Shaw, McNaught
		SF	7 Apr 82	Anderlecht (Belgium)	H	W 1–0	Morley
			21 Apr 82		A	D 0–0	
		F	26 May 82	Bayern Munich	N	W 1–0	Withe
				(West Germany)			
1982–83	European Cup	1	15 Sep 82	Besiktas (Turkey)	H	W 3–1	Withe, Morley, Mortimer
			29 Sep 82		A	D 0–0	
		2	20 Oct 82	Dinamo Bucharest	A	W 2–0	Shaw 2
			3 Nov 82	(Romania)	H	W 4–2	Shaw 3, Walters
		QF	2 Mar 83	Juventus (Italy)	H	L 1–2	Cowans
			16 Mar 83		A	L 1–3	Withe
1982–83	Super Cup	F	19 Jan 83	Barcelona (Spain)	A	L 0–1	
			26 Jan 83		H	W 3–0	Shaw, Cowans, McNaught
1983–84	UEFA Cup	1	14 Sep 83	Vitoria Guimaraes	A	L 0–1	
			28 Sep 83	(Portugal)	H	W 5–0	Withe 3, Ormsby, Gibson
		2	19 Oct 83	Moscow Spartak	A	D 2–2	Gibson, Walters
			2 Nov 83	(USSR)	H	L 1–2	Withe
1990–91	UEFA Cup	1	19 Sep 90	Banik Ostrava	H	W 3–1	Platt, Mountfield, Olney

Season	Competition	Round	Date	Opponents (Country)	Venue	Result		Scorers
			3 Oct 90	(Czechoslovakia)	A	W	2–1	Mountfield, own goal
		2	24 Oct 90	Internazionale	H	W	2–0	Nielsen, Platt
			7 Nov 90	(Italy)	A	L	0–3	

BIRMINGHAM CITY

Season	Competition	Round	Date	Opponents (Country)	Venue	Result		Scorers
1955–58	Fairs Cup	Gp. D	15 May 56	Inter Milan (Italy)	A	D	0–0	
			17 Apr 57		H	W	2–1	Govan 2
			22 May 56	Zagreb (Yugoslavia)	A	W	1–0	Brown
			3 Dec 56		H	W	3–0	Orritt, Brown, Murphy
		SF	23 Oct 57	Barcelona (Spain)	H	W	4–3	Murphy 2, Brown, Orritt
			13 Nov 57		A	L	0–1	
			26 Nov 57		N	L	1–2	Murphy
1958–60	Fairs Cup		14 Oct 58	FC Cologne	A	D	2–2	Neal, Hooper
			11 Nov 58	(West Germany)	H	W	2–0	Larkin, Taylor
		QF	6 May 59	Zagreb (Yugoslavia)	H	W	1–0	Larkin
			25 May 59		A	D	3–3	Larkin 2, Hooper
		SF	7 Oct 59	Union St Gilloise	A	W	4–2	Hooper, Gordon, Barrett, Taylor
			11 Nov 59	(Belgium)	H	W	4–2	Gordon 2, Larkin, Hooper
		F	29 Mar 60	Barcelona (Spain)	H	D	0–0	
			4 May 60		A	L	1–4	Hooper
1960–61	Fairs Cup	1	19 Oct 60	Ujpest Dozsa	H	W	3–2	Gordon 2, Astall
			26 Oct 60	(Hungary)	A	W	2–1	Rudd, Singer
		QF	23 Nov 60	Copenhagen	A	D	4–4	Gordon 2, Singer 2
			7 Dec 60	(Denmark)	H	W	5–0	Stubbs 2, Harris, Hellawell, own goal
		SF	19 Apr 61	Inter Milan (Italy)	A	W	2–1	Harris, own goal
			3 May 61		H	W	2–1	Harris 2
		F	27 Sep 61	AS Roma (Italy)	H	D	2–2	Hellawell, Orritt
			11 Oct 61		A	L	0–2	
1961–62	Fairs Cup	1	bye					
		2	15 Nov 61	Espanol (Spain)	A	L	2–5	Bloomfield, Harris (pen)
			7 Dec 61		H	W	1–0	Auld

BURNLEY

Season	Competition	Round	Date	Opponents (Country)	Venue	Result		Scorers
1960–61	European Cup	Pr	bye					
		1	16 Nov 60	Reims (France)	H	W	2–0	Robson, McIlroy
			30 Nov 60		A	L	2–3	Robson, Connelly
		QF	18 Jan 61	SV Hamburg	H	W	3–1	Pilkington 2, Robson
			15 Mar 61	(West Germany)	A	L	1–4	Harris
1966–67	Fairs Cup	1	20 Sep 66	Stuttgart	A	D	1–1	Irvine
			27 Sep 66	(West Germany)	H	W	2–0	Coates, Lochhead
		2	10 Oct 66	Lausanne	A	W	3–1	Coates, Harris, Lochhead
			25 Oct 66	(Switzerland)	H	W	5–0	Lochhead 3, O'Neill, Irvine
		3	18 Jan 67	Napoli (Italy)	H	W	3–0	Coates, Latcham, Lochhead
			8 Feb 67		A	D	0–0	
		QF	4 Apr 67	Eintracht Frankfurt	A	D	1–1	Miller
			18 Apr 67	(West Germany)	H	L	1–2	Miller

CARDIFF CITY

Season	Competition	Round	Date	Opponents (Country)	Venue	Result		Scorers
1964–65	Cup-Winners' Cup	1	9 Sep 64	Esbjerg (Denmark)	A	D	0–0	
			13 Oct 64		H	W	1–0	King
		2	16 Dec 64	Sporting Lisbon	A	W	2–1	Farrell, Tapscott

Season	Competition	Round	Date	Opponents (Country)	Venue	Result		Scorers
			23 Dec 64	(Portugal)	H	D	0–0	
		QF	20 Jan 65	Real Zaragoza (Spain)	A	D	2–2	Williams, King
			3 Feb 65		H	L	0–1	
1965–66	Cup-Winners' Cup	1	8 Sep 65	Standard Liege	H	L	1–2	Johnston
			20 Oct 65	(Belgium)	A	L	0–1	
1967–68	Cup-Winners' Cup	1	20 Sep 67	Shamrock Rovers	A	D	1–1	King
			4 Oct 67	(Eire)	H	W	2–0	Toshack, Brown (pen)
		2	15 Nov 67	NAC Breda	A	D	1–1	King
			29 Nov 67	(Holland)	H	W	4–1	Brown, Barrie Jones, Clark, Toshack
		QF	6 Mar 68	Moscow Torpedo	H	W	1–0	Barrie Jones
			19 Mar 68	(USSR)	A	L	0–1	
			3 Apr 68		H	W	1–0	Dean
		SF	24 Apr 68	SV Hamburg	A	D	1–1	Dean
			1 May 68	(West Germany)	H	L	2–3	Dean, Harris
1968–69	Cup-Winners' Cup	1	18 Sep 68	Porto (Portugal)	H	D	2–2	Toshack, Bird (pen)
			2 Oct 68		A	L	1–2	Toshack
1969–70	Cup-Winners' Cup	1	17 Sep 69	Mjondalen (Norway)	A	W	7–1	Clark 2, Toshack 2, Lea, Sutton, King
			1 Oct 69		H	W	5–1	King 2, Allan 3
		2	12 Nov 69	Goztepe Izmir	A	L	0–3	
			16 Nov 69	(Turkey)	H	W	1–0	Bird
1970–71	Cup-Winners' Cup	1	16 Sep 70	Pezoporikos (Cyprus)	H	W	8–0	Toshack 2, Clark 2, Sutton, Gibson, King, Woodruff
			30 Sep 70		A	D	0–0	
		2	21 Oct 70	Nantes (France)	H	W	5–1	Toshack 2, Gibson, King, Phillips
			4 Nov 70		A	W	2–1	Toshack, Clark
		QF	10 Mar 71	Real Madrid (Spain)	H	W	1–0	Clark
			24 Mar 71		A	L	0–2	
1971–72	Cup-Winners' Cup	1	15 Sep 71	Dynamo Berlin	A	D	1–1	Gibson
			29 Sep 71	(East Germany)†	H	D	1–1	Clark
1973–74	Cup-Winners' Cup	1	19 Sep 73	Sporting Lisbon	H	D	0–0	
			3 Oct 73	(Portugal)	A	L	1–2	Vincent
1974–75	Cup-Winners' Cup	1	18 Sep 74	Ferencvaros	A	L	0–2	
			2 Oct 74	(Hungary)	H	L	1–4	Dwyer
1976–77	Cup-Winners' Cup	Pr	4 Aug 76	Servette (Switzerland)	H	W	1–0	Evans
			11 Aug 76		A	L	1–2*	Showers
		1	15 Sep 76	Dynamo Tbilisi	H	W	1–0	Alston
			29 Sep 76	(USSR)	A	L	0–3	
1977–78	Cup-Winners' Cup	1	14 Sep 77	Austria/WAC	H	D	0–0	
			28 Sep 77	(Austria)	A	L	0–1	
1988–89	Cup-Winners' Cup	1	7 Sep 88	Derry City (Eire)	A	D	0–0	
			5 Oct 88		H	W	4–0	McDermott, Gilligan 3
		2	26 Sep 88	Aarhus (Denmark)	H	L	1–2	Gilligan
			2 Nov 88		A	L	0–4	
1992–93	Cup-Winners' Cup	1	16 Sep 92	Admira Wacker	H	D	1–1	Pike
			29 Sep 92	(Austria)	A	L	0–2	

CHELSEA

Season	Competition	Round	Date	Opponents (Country)	Venue	Result	Scorers
1958–60	Fairs Cup	I	30 Sep 58	Frem Copenhagen (Denmark)	A	W 3–I	Harrison, Greaves, Nicholas
			4 Nov 58		H	W 4–I	Greaves 2, Sillett (P), own goal
		QF	29 Apr 59	Belgrade	H	W I–0	Brabrook
			13 May 59	(Yugoslavia)	H	L I–4	Brabrook
1965–66	Fairs Cup	I	22 Sep 65	AS Roma (Italy)	H	W 4–I	Venables 3, Graham
			6 Oct 65		A	D 0–0	
		2	17 Nov 65	Wiener SK (Austria)	A	L 0–I	
			I Dec 65		H	W 2–0	Murray, Osgood
		3	9 Feb 66	AC Milan (Italy)	A	L I–2	Graham
			16 Feb 66		H	W 2–I	Graham, Osgood
			2 Mar 66		A	D I–I‡	Bridges
		QF	15 Mar 66	Munich 1860	A	D 2–2	Tambling 2
			29 Mar 66	(West Germany)	H	W I–0	Osgood
		SF	27 Apr 66	Barcelona (Spain)	A	L 0–2	
			II May 66		H	W 2–0	own goals 2
			25 May 66		A	L 0–5	
1968–69	Fairs Cup	I	18 Sep 68	Morton (Scotland)	H	W 5–0	Osgood, Birchenall, Cooke, Boyle, Hollins
			30 Sep 68		A	W 4–3	Baldwin, Birchenall, Houseman, Tambling
		2	23 Oct 68	DWS Amsterdam	H	D 0–0	
			30 Oct 68	(Holland)‡	A	D 0–0	
1970–71	Cup-Winners' Cup	I	16 Sep 70	Aris Salonika	A	D I–I	Hutchinson
			30 Sep 70	(Greece)	H	W 5–I	Hutchinson 2, Hollins 2, Hinton
		2	21 Oct 70	CSKA Sofia	A	W I–0	Baldwin
			4 Nov 70	(Bulgaria)	H	W I–0	Webb
		QF	10 Mar 71	FC Bruges	A	L 0–2	
			24 Mar 71	(Belgium)	H	W 4–0	Houseman, Osgood 2, Baldwin
		SF	14 Apr 71	Manchester City	H	W I–0	Smethurst
			28 Apr 71	(England)	A	W I–0	Weller
		F	19 May 71	Real Madrid (Spain)	N	D I–I	Osgood
			21 May 71		N	W 2–I	Dempsey, Osgood
1971–72	Cup-Winners' Cup	I	15 Sep 71	Jeunesse Hautcharage (Luxembourg)	A	W 8–0	Osgood 3, Houseman 2, Hollins, Webb, Baldwin
			29 Sep 71		H	W13–0	Osgood 5, Baldwin 3, Hollins (pen), Hudson, Webb, Houseman, Harris
		2	20 Oct 71	Atvidaberg (Sweden)*	A	D 0–0	
			3 Nov 71		H	D I–I	Hudson

COVENTRY CITY

Season	Competition	Round	Date	Opponents (Country)	Venue	Result	Scorers
1970–71	Fairs Cup	I	16 Sep 70	Trakia Plovdiv	A	W 4–I	O'Rourke 3, Martin
			30 Sep 70	(Bulgaria)	H	W 2–0	Joicey, Blockley
		2	20 Oct 70	Bayern Munich	A	L I–6	Hunt
			3 Nov 70	(West Germany)	H	W 2–I	Martin, O'Rourke

DERBY COUNTY

Season	Competition	Round	Date	Opponents (Country)	Venue	Result	Scorers
1972–73	European Cup	I	13 Sep 72	Zeljeznicar	H	W 2–0	McFarland, Gemmill
			27 Sep 72	(Yugoslavia)	A	W 2–I	Hinton, O'Hare
		2	25 Oct 72	Benfica (Portugal)	H	W 3–0	McFarland, Hector, McGovern

Season	Competition	Round	Date	Opponents (Country)	Venue	Result	Scorers
			8 Nov 72		A	D 0–0	
		QF	7 Mar 73	Spartak Trnava	A	D 0–0	
			21 Mar 73	(Czechoslovakia)	H	W 2–0	Hector 2
		SF	11 Apr 73	Juventus (Italy)	A	L 1–3	Hector
			25 Apr 73		H	D 0–0	
1974–75	UEFA Cup	1	18 Sep 74	Servette (Switzerland)	H	W 4–1	Hector 2, Daniel, Lee
			2 Oct 74		A	W 2–1	Lee, Hector
		2	23 Oct 74	Atletico Madrid	H	D 2–2	Nish, Rioch (pen)
			6 Nov 74	(Spain)	A	D 2–2†	Rioch, Hector
		3	27 Nov 74	Velez Mostar	H	W 3–1	Bourne 2, Hinton
			11 Dec 74	(Yugoslavia)	A	L 1–4	Hector
1975–76	European Cup	1	17 Sep 75	Slovan Bratislava	A	L 0–1	
			1 Oct 75	(Czechoslovakia)	H	W 3–0	Bourne, Lee 2
		2	22 Oct 75	Real Madrid (Spain)	H	W 4–1	George 3 (2 pen), Nish
			5 Nov 75		A	L 1–5	George
1976–77	UEFA Cup	1	15 Sep 76	Finn Harps (Eire)	H	W 12–0	Hector 5, James 3, George 3, Rioch
			29 Sep 76		A	W 4–1	Hector 2, George 2
		2	20 Oct 76	AEK Athens (Greece)	A	L 0–2	
			3 Nov 76		H	L 2–3	George, Rioch

EVERTON

Season	Competition	Round	Date	Opponents (Country)	Venue	Result	Scorers
1962–63	Fairs Cup	1	24 Oct 62	Dunfermline Athletic	H	W 1–0	Stevens
			31 Oct 62	(Scotland)	A	L 0–2	
1963–64	European Cup	1	18 Sep 63	Inter Milan (Italy)	H	D 0–0	
			25 Sep 63		A	L 0–1	
1964–65	Fairs Cup	1	23 Sep 64	Valerengen (Norway)	A	W 5–2	Pickering 2, Harvey, Temple 2
			14 Oct 64		H	W 4–2	Young 2, Vernon, own goal
		2	11 Nov 64	Kilmarnock (Scotland)	A	W 2–0	Temple, Morrissey
			23 Nov 64		H	W 4–1	Harvey, Pickering 2, Young
		3	20 Jan 65	Manchester United	A	D 1–1	Pickering
			9 Feb 65	(England)	H	L 1–2	Pickering
1965–66	Fairs Cup	1	28 Sep 65	FC Nuremberg	A	D 1–1	Harris
			12 Oct 65	(West Germany)	H	W 1–0	Gabriel
		2	3 Nov 65	Ujpest Dosza	A	L 0–3	
			16 Nov 65	(Hungary)	H	W 2–1	Harris, own goal
1966–67	Cup-Winners' Cup	1	28 Sep 66	Aalborg (Denmark)	A	D 0–0	
			11 Oct 66		H	W 2–1	Morrissey, Ball
		2	9 Nov 66	Real Zaragoza	A	L 0–2	
			23 Nov 66	(Spain)	H	W 1–0	Brown
1970–71	European Cup	1	16 Sep 70	Keflavik (Iceland)	H	W 6–2	Ball 3, Royle 2, Kendall
			30 Sep 70		A	W 3–0	Royle 2, Whittle
		2	21 Oct 70	Borussia	A	D 1–1	Kendall
			4 Nov 70	Moenchengladbach	H	D 1–1†	Morrissey
				(West Germany)			
		QF	9 Mar 71	Panathinaikos	H	D 1–1	Johnson
			24 Mar 71	(Greece)	A	D 0–0	
1975–76	UEFA Cup	1	17 Sep 75	AC Milan (Italy)	H	D 0–0	
			1 Oct 75		A	L 0–1	

Season	Competition	Round	Date	Opponents (Country)	Venue	Result	Scorers
1978–79	UEFA Cup	1	12 Sep 78	Finn Harps (Eire)	A	W 5–0	Thomas, King 2, Latchford, Walsh
			26 Sep 78		H	W 5–0	King, Latchford, Walsh, Ross, Dobson
		2	18 Oct 78	Dukla Prague	H	W 2–1	Latchford, King
			1 Nov 78	(Czechoslovakia)	A	L 0–1	
1979–80	UEFA Cup	1	19 Sep 79	Feyenoord (Holland)	A	L 0–1	
			3 Sep 79		H	L 0–1	
1984–85	Cup-Winners' Cup	1	19 Sep 84	UCD (Eire)	A	D 0–0	
			2 Oct 84		H	W 1–0	Sharp
		2	24 Oct 84	Inter Bratislava	A	W 1–0	Bracewell
			7 Nov 84	(Czechoslovakia)	H	W 3–0	Heath, Sharp, Sheedy
		QF	6 Mar 85	Fortuna Sittard	H	W 3–0	Gray 3
			20 Mar 85	(Holland)	A	W 2–0	Reid, Sharp
		SF	10 Apr 85	Bayern Munich	A	D 0–0	
			24 Apr 85	(West Germany)	H	W 3–1	Gray, Sharp, Steven
		F	15 May 85	Rapid Vienna (Austria)	N	W 3–1	Gray, Sheedy, Steven

IPSWICH TOWN

Season	Competition	Round	Date	Opponents (Country)	Venue	Result	Scorers
1962–63	European Cup	Pr	18 Sep 62	Floriana (Malta)	A	W 4–1	Crawford 2, Phillips 2
			25 Sep 62		H	W 10–0	Crawford 5, Moran 2, Phillips 2, Elsworthy
		1	14 Nov 62	AC Milan (Italy)	A	L 0–3	
			28 Nov 62		H	W 2–1	Crawford, Blackwood
1973–74	UEFA Cup	1	19 Sep 73	Real Madrid (Spain)	H	W 1–0	own goal
			3 Oct 73		A	D 0–0	
		2	24 Oct 73	Lazio (Italy)	H	W 4–0	Whymark 4
			7 Nov 73		A	L 2–4	Viljoen (pen), Johnson
		3	28 Nov 73	Twente Enschede	H	W 1–0	Whymark
			12 Dec 73	(Holland)	A	W 2–1	Morris, Hamilton
		QF	6 Mar 74	Lokomotive Leipzig	H	W 1–0	Beattie
			20 Mar 74	(East Germany)†	H	L 0–1	
1974–75	UEFA Cup	1	18 Sep 74	Twente Enschede	H	D 2–2	Hamilton, Talbot
			2 Oct 74	(Holland)*	A	D 1–1	Hamilton
1975–76	UEFA Cup	1	17 Sep 75	Feyenoord (Holland)	A	W 2–1	Whymark, Johnson
			1 Oct 75		H	W 2–0	Woods, Whymark
		2	22 Oct 75	FC Bruges (Belgium)	H	W 3–0	Gates, Peddelty, Austin
			5 Nov 75		A	L 0–4	
1977–78	UEFA Cup	1	14 Sep 77	Landskrona (Sweden)	A	W 1–0	Whymark
			28 Sep 77		H	W 5–0	Whymark 4 (1 pen), Mariner
		2	19 Oct 77	Las Palmas (Spain)	H	W 1–0	Gates
			2 Nov 77		A	D 3–3	Mariner 2, Talbot
		3	23 Nov 77	Barcelona (Spain)†	H	W 3–0	Gates, Whymark, Talbot
			7 Dec 77		A	L 0–3	
1978–79	Cup-Winners' Cup	1	13 Sep 78	AZ67 (Holland)	A	D 0–0	
			27 Sep 78		H	W 2–0	Mariner, Wark (pen)
		2	18 Oct 78	SW Innsbruck (Austria)	H	W 1–0	Wark (pen)
			1 Nov 78		A	D 1–1	Burley
		QF	7 Mar 79	Barcelona (Spain)	H	W 2–1	Gates 2
			21 Mar 79		A	L 0–1	
1979–80	UEFA Cup	1	19 Sep 79	Skeid Oslo (Norway)	A	W 3–1	Mills, Turner, Mariner

Season	Competition	Round	Date	Opponents (Country)	Venue	Result		Scorers
			3 Oct 79		H	W	7–0	Muhren 2, McCall 2, Wark, Thijssen, Mariner
		2	24 Oct 79	Grasshoppers*	A	D	0–0	
			7 Nov 79	(Switzerland)	H	D	1–1	Beattie
1980–81	UEFA Cup	1	17 Sep 80	Aris Salonika	H	W	5–1	Wark 4 (3 pens), Mariner
			1 Oct 80	(Greece)	A	L	1–3	Gates
		2	22 Oct 80	Bohemians	H	W	3–0	Wark 2, Beattie
			5 Nov 80	(Czechoslovakia)	A	L	0–2	
		3	26 Nov 80	Widzew Lodz	H	W	5–0	Wark 3, Brazil, Mariner
			10 Dec 80	(Poland)	A	L	0–1	
		QF	4 Mar 81	St Etienne	A	W	4–1	Mariner 2, Wark, Brazil
			18 Mar 81	(France)	H	W	3–1	Butcher, Wark (pen), Mariner
		SF	8 Apr 81	FC Cologne	H	W	1–0	Wark
			22 Apr 81	(West Germany)	A	W	1–0	Butcher
		F	6 May 81	AZ67 (Holland)	H	W	3–0	Wark (pen), Thijssen, Mariner
			20 May 81		A	L	2–4	Thijssen, Wark
1981–82	UEFA Cup	1	16 Sep 81	Aberdeen (Scotland)	H	D	1–1	Thijssen
			30 Sep 81		A	L	1–3	Wark (pen)
1982–83	UEFA Cup	1	15 Sep 82	AS Roma (Italy)	A	L	0–3	
			29 Sep 82		H	W	3–1	Gates, McCall, Butcher

LEEDS UNITED

Season	Competition	Round	Date	Opponents (Country)	Venue	Result		Scorers
1965–66	Fairs Cup	1	29 Sep 65	Torino (Italy)	H	W	2–1	Bremner, Peacock
			6 Oct 65		A	D	0–0	
		2	24 Nov 65	Lokomotive Leipzig	A	W	2–1	Lorimer, Bremner
			1 Dec 65	(East Germany)	H	D	0–0	
		3	2F eb 66	Valencia (Spain)	H	D	1–1	Lorimer
			16 Feb 66		A	W	1–0	O'Grady
		QF	2 Mar 66	Ujpest Dosza	H	W	4–1	Cooper, Bell, Storrie, Bremner
				(Hungary)				
			9 Mar 66		A	D	1–1	Lorimer
		SF	20 Apr 66	Real Zaragoza	A	L	0–1	
			27 Apr 66	(Spain)	H	W	2–1	Johanneson, Charlton
			11 Mar 66		N	L	1–3	Charlton
1966–67	Fairs Cup	1	bye					
		2	18 Oct 66	DWS Amsterdam	A	W	3–1	Bremner, Johanneson, Greenhoff
				(Holland)				
			26 Oct 66		H	W	5–1	Johanneson 3, Giles, Madeley
		3	18 Jan 67	Valencia (Spain)	H	D	1–1	Greenhoff
			8 Feb 67		A	W	2–0	Giles, Lorimer
		QF	22 Mar 67	Bologna (Italy)	A	L	0–1	
			19 Apr 67		H	W	1–0†	Giles (pen)
		SF	19 May 67	Kilmarnock	H	W	4–2	Belfitt 3, Giles (pen)
			24 May 67	(Scotland)	A	D	0–0	
		F	30 Aug 67	Dynamo Zagreb	A	L	0–2	
			6 Sep 67	(Yugoslavia)	H	D	0–0	
1967–68	Fairs Cup	1	3 Oct 67	Spora Luxembourg	A	W	9–0	Lorimer 4, Greenhoff 2, Madeley, Jones, Bremner
				(Luxembourg)				
			17 Oct 67		H	W	7–0	Johanneson 3, Greenhoff 2, Cooper, Lorimer
		2	29 Nov 67	Partizan Belgrade	A	W	2–1	Lorimer, Belfitt
			6 Dec 67	(Yugoslavia)	H	D	1–1	Lorimer

Season	Competition	Round	Date	Opponents (Country)	Venue	Result	Scorers
		3	20 Dec 67	Hibernian (Scotland)	H	W 1–0	Gray (E)
			10 Jan 68		A	D 0–0	
		QF	26 Mar 68	Rangers (Scotland)	A	D 0–0	
			9 Apr 68		H	W 2–0	Lorimer, Giles (pen)
		SF	1 May 68	Dundee (Scotland)	A	D 1–1	Madeley
			15 May 68		H	W 1–0	Gray (E)
		F	7 Aug 68	Ferencvaros	H	W 1–0	Charlton
			11 Sep 68	(Hungary)	A	D 0–0	
1968–69	Fairs Cup	1	18 Sep 68	Standard Liege	A	D 0–0	
			23 Oct 68	(Belgium)	H	W 3–2	Charlton, Lorimer, Bremner
		2	13 Nov 68	Napoli (Italy)	H	W 2–0	Charlton 2
			27 Nov 68		A	L 0–2‡	
		3	18 Dec 68	Hanover 96	H	W 5–1	O'Grady, Hunter, Lorimer 2, Charlton
			4 Feb 69	(West Germany)	A	W 2–1	Belfitt, Jones
		QF	5 Mar 69	Ujpest Dozsa	A	L 0–1	
			19 Mar 69	(Hungary)	H	L 0–2	
1969–70	European Cup	1	17 Sep 69	Lyn Oslo (Norway)	H	W 10–0	Jones 3, Clarke 2, Giles 2, Bremner 2, O'Grady
			1 Oct 69		A	W 6–0	Belfitt 2, Hibbitt 2, Jones, Lorimer
		2	12 Nov 69	Ferencvaros	H	W 3–0	Giles, Jones 2
			26 Nov 69	(Hungary)	A	W 3–0	Jones 2, Lorimer
		QF	4 Mar 70	Standard Liege	A	W 1–0	Lorimer
			18 Mar 70	(Belgium)	H	W 1–0	Giles (pen)
		SF	1 Apr 70	Celtic (Scotland)	H	L 0–1	
			15 Apr 70		A	L 1–2	Bremner
1970–71	Fairs Cup	1	15 Sep 70	Sarpsborg (Norway)	H	W 1–0	Lorimer
			29 Sep 70		H	W 5–0	Charlton 2, Bremner 2, Lorimer
		2	21 Oct 70	Dynamo Dresden	A	W 1–0	Lorimer
			4 Nov 70	(East Germany)	A	L 1–2*	Jones
		3	2 Dec 70	Sparta Prague (Czechoslovakia)	H	W 6–0	Clarke, Bremner, Gray (E) 2, Charlton, own goal
			9 Dec 70		A	W 3–2	Gray (E), Clarke, Belfitt
		QF	10 Mar 71	Setubal (Portugal)	H	W 2–1	Lorimer, Giles (pen)
			24 Mar 71		A	D 1–1	Lorimer
		SF	14 Apr 71	Liverpool (England)	A	W 1–0	Bremner
			28 Apr 71		H	D 0–0	
		F	28 May 71	Juventus (Italy)	A	D 2–2	Madeley, Bates
			3 Jun 71		H	D 1–1*	Clarke
1971–72	UEFA Cup	1	15 Sep 71	Lierse (Belgium)	A	W 2–0	Galvin, Lorimer
			29 Sep 71		H	L 0–4	
1972–73	Cup-Winners' Cup	1	13 Sep 72	Ankaragucu (Turkey)	A	D 1–1	Jordan
			28 Sep 72		H	W 1–0	Jones
		2	25 Oct 72	Carl Zeiss Jena	A	D 0–0	
			8 Nov 72	(East Germany)	H	W 2–0	Cherry, Jones
		QF	7 Mar 73	Rapid Bucharest (Romania)	H	W 5–0	Giles, Clarke, Lorimer 2, Jordan
			23 Mar 73		A	W 3–1	Jones, Jordan, Bates
		SF	11 Apr 73	Hajduk Split	H	W 1–0	Clarke
			25 Apr 73	(Yugoslavia)	A	D 0–0	
		F	16 May 73	AC Milan (Italy)	N	L 0–1	
1973–74	UEFA Cup	1	19 Sep 73	Stromsgodset	A	D 1–1	Clarke
			3 Oct 73	(Norway)	H	W 6–1	Clarke 2, Jones 2, Gray (F), Bates

Above: *Lee Chapman in action for Leeds United during their brave 4–1 win over VfB Stuttgart at Elland Road in 1992–93, a match subsequently awarded to them 3–0 by UEFA which kept them in the tie (Allsport/Mike Hewitt)*

Left: *David Platt challenges Aldo Serena of Inter during Aston Villa's UEFA Cup clash with the Italians in 1990-91. Villa, 2–0 up from the first leg, lost 3–0 in Milan (Allsport/Richiardi)*

Season	Competition	Round	Date	Opponents (Country)	Venue	Result		Scorers
		2	24 Oct 73	Hibernian (Scotland)	H	D	0–0	
			7 Nov 73		A	D	0–0†	
		3	28 Nov 73	Setubal (Portugal)	H	W	1–0	Cherry
			12 Dec 73		A	L	1–3	Liddell
1974–75	European Cup	1	28 Sep 74	FC Zurich (Switzerland)	H	W	4–1	Clarke 2, Lorimer (pen), Jordan
			2 Oct 74		A	L	1–2	Clarke
		2	23 Oct 74	Ujpest Dozsa	A	W	2–1	Lorimer, McQueen
			6 Nov 74	(Hungary)	H	W	3–0	McQueen, Bremner, Yorath
		QF	5 Mar 75	Anderlecht (Belgium)	H	W	3–0	Jordan, McQueen, Lorimer
			19 Mar 75		A	W	1–0	Bremner
		SF	9 Apr 75	Barcelona (Spain)	H	W	2–1	Bremner, Clarke
			24 Apr 75		A	D	1–1	Lorimer
		F	28 May 75	Bayern Munich (West Germany)	N	L	0–2	
1979–80	UEFA Cup	1	19 Sep 79	Valletta (Malta)	A	W	4–0	Graham 3, Hart
			3 Oct 79		H	W	3–0	Curtis, Hankin, Hart
		2	24 Oct 79	Uni. Craiova	A	L	0–2	
			7 Nov 79	(Romania)	H	L	0–2	
1992–93	European Cup	1	16 Sep 92	Stuttgart (Germany)	A	L	0–3	
			30 Sep 92		H	W	4–1	Speed, McAllister (pen), Cantona, Chapman
			(UEFA declared 3–0 win for Leeds as Stuttgart fielded an ineligible player)					
			9 Oct 92		N	W	2–1	Strachan, Shutt
		2	21 Oct 92	Rangers (Scotland)	A	L	1–2	McAllister
			4 Nov 92		H	L	1–2	Cantona

N. B. Leeds met Barcelona in Spain on 22 Sep 71 in a match to determine who should hold the Fairs Cup trophy permanently. Barcelona, the first winners beat Leeds, the holders 2–1 (Jordan was the United scorer).

LEICESTER CITY

Season	Competition	Round	Date	Opponents (Country)	Venue	Result	Scorers
1961–62	Cup-Winners' Cup	1	13 Sep 61	Glenavon (Northern Ireland)	A	W 4–1	Walsh 2, Appleton, Keyworth
			27 Sep 61		H	W 3–1	Wills, Keyworth, McIlmoyle
		2	25 Oct 61	Atletico Madrid	H	D 1–1	Keyworth
			15 Nov 61	(Spain)	A	L 0–2	

LIVERPOOL

Season	Competition	Round	Date	Opponents (Country)	Venue	Result	Scorers
1964–65	European Cup	Pr	17 Aug 64	KR Reykjavik (Iceland)	A	W 5–0	Wallace 2, Hunt 2, Chisnall
			14 Sep 64		H	W 6–1	Byrne, St John 2, Graham, Hunt, Stevenson
		1	25 Nov 64	Anderlecht	H	W 3–0	St John, Hunt, Yeats
			16 Dec 64	(Belgium)	A	W 1–0	Hunt
		QF	10 Feb 65	FC Cologne	A	D 0–0	
			17 Mar 65	(West Germany)	H	D 0–0	
			24 Mar 65		N	D 2–2‡	St John, Hunt
		SF	4 May 65	Inter Milan (Italy)	H	W 3–1	Hunt, Callaghan, St John
			12 May 65		A	L 0–3	
1965–66	Cup-Winners' Cup	1	29 Sep 65	Juventus (Italy)	A	L 0–1	
			13 Oct 65		H	W 2–0	Lawler, Strong
		2	1 Dec 65	Standard Liege	H	W 3–1	Lawler 2, Thompson (P)
			15 Dec 65	(Belgium)	A	W 2–1	Hunt, St John
		QF	1 Mar 66	Honved (Hungary)	A	D 0–0	
			8 Mar 66		H	W 2–0	Lawler, St John
		SF	14 Apr 66	Celtic (Scotland)	A	L 0–1	
			19 Apr 66		H	W 2–0	Smith, Strong
		F	5 May 66	Borussia Dortmund (West Germany)	N	L 1–2	Hunt
1966–67	European Cup	1	28 Sep 66	Petrolul Ploesti	H	W 2–0	St John, Callaghan
			12 Oct 66	(Romania)	A	L 1–3	Hunt
			19 Oct 66		N	W 2–0	St John, Thompson (P)
		2	7 Dec 66	Ajax (Holland)	A	L 1–5	Lawler
			14 Dec 66		H	D 2–2	Hunt 2
1967–68	Fairs Cup	1	19 Sep 67	Malmo FF (Sweden)	A	W 2–0	Hateley 2
			4 Oct 67		H	W 2–1	Yeats, Hunt
		2	7 Nov 67	Munich 1860 (West Germany)	H	W 8–0	St John, Hateley, Thompson (P), Smith (pen), Hunt 2, Callaghan 2
			14 Nov 67		A	L 1–2	Callaghan
		3	28 Nov 67	Ferencvaros	A	L 0–1	
			9 Jan 68	(Hungary)	H	L 0–1	
1968–69	Fairs Cup	1	18 Sep 68	Athletic Bilbao	A	L 1–2	Hunt
			2 Oct 68	(Spain)‡	H	W 2–1	Lawler, Hughes
1969–70	Fairs Cup	1	16 Sep 69	Dundalk (Eire)	H	W 10–0	Evans 2, Smith 2, Graham 2, Lawler, Lindsay, Thompson (P), Callaghan
			30 Sep 69		A	W 4–0	Thompson (P) 2, Graham, Callaghan
		3	11 Nov 69	Setubal (Portugal)*	A	L 0–1	
			26 Nov 69		H	W 3–2	Smith (pen), Evans, Hunt

Season	Competition	Round	Date	Opponents (Country)	Venue	Result	Scorers
1970–71	Fairs Cup	1	15 Sep 70	Ferencvaros	H	W 1–0	Graham
			29 Sep 70	(Hungary)	A	D 1–1	Hughes
		2	21 Oct 70	Dinamo Bucharest	H	W 3–0	Lindsay, Lawler, Hughes
			4 Nov 70	(Romania)	A	D 1–1	Boersma
		3	9 Dec 70	Hibernian (Scotland)	A	W 1–0	Toshack
			22 Dec 70		H	W 2–0	Heighway, Boersma
		QF	10 Mar 71	Bayern Munich	H	W 3–0	Evans 3
			24 Mar 71	(West Germany)	A	D 1–1	Ross
		SF	14 Apr 71	Leeds United	H	L 0–1	
			28 Apr 71	(England)	A	D 0–0	
1971–72	Cup-Winners' Cup	1	15 Sep 71	Servette	A	L 1–2	Lawler
			29 Sep 71	(Switzerland)	H	W 2–0	Hughes, Heighway
		2	20 Oct 71	Bayern Munich	H	D 0–0	
			3 Nov 71	(West Germany)	A	L 1–3	Evans
1972–73	UEFA Cup	1	12 Sep 72	Eintracht Frankfurt	H	W 2–0	Keegan, Hughes
			26 Sep 72	(West Germany)	A	D 0–0	
		2	24 Oct 72	AEK Athens (Greece)	H	W 3–0	Boersma, Cormack, Smith (pen)
			7 Nov 72		A	W 3–1	Hughes 2, Boersma
		3	29 Nov 72	Dynamo Berlin	A	D 0–0	
			12 Dec 72	(East Germany)	H	W 3–1	Boersma, Heighway, Toshack
		QF	7 Mar 73	Dynamo Dresden	H	W 2–0	Hall, Boersma
			21 Mar 73	(East Germany)	A	W 1–0	Keegan
		SF	10 Apr 73	Tottenham Hotspur	H	W 1–0	Lindsay
			25 Apr 73	(England)	A	L 1–2*	Heighway
		F	10 May 73	Borussia	H	W 3–0	Keegan 2, Lloyd
			23 May 73	Moenchengladbach (West Germany)	A	L 0–2	
1973–74	European Cup	1	19 Sep 73	Jeunesse D'Esch	A	D 1–1	Hall
			3 Oct 73	(Luxembourg)	H	W 2–0	Toshack, own goal
		2	24 Oct 73	Red Star Belgrade	A	L 1–2	Lawler
			6 Nov 73	(Yugoslavia)	H	L 1–2	Lawler
1974–75	Cup-Winners' Cup	1	17 Sep 74	Stromsgodset (Norway)	H	W 11–0	Lindsay (pen), Boersma 2, Heighway, Thompson (PB) 2, Smith, Cormack, Hughes, Callaghan, Kennedy
			1 Oct 74		A	W 1–0	Kennedy
		2	23 Oct 74	Ferencvaros	H	D 1–1	Keegan
			5 Nov 74	(Hungary)*	A	D 0–0	
1975–76	UEFA Cup	1	17 Sep 75	Hibernian (Scotland)	A	L 0–1	
			30 Sep 75		H	W 3–1	Toshack 3
		2	22 Oct 75	Real Sociedad (Spain)	A	W 3–1	Heighway, Callaghan, Thompson (PB)
			4 Nov 75		H	W 6–0	Toshack, Kennedy 2, Fairclough, Heighway, Neal
		3	26 Nov 75	Slask Wroclaw	A	W 2–1	Kennedy, Toshack
			10 Dec 75	(Poland)	H	W 3–0	Case 3
		QF	3 Mar 76	Dynamo Dresden	A	D 0–0	
			17 Mar 76	(East Germany)	H	W 2–1	Case, Keegan
		SF	30 Mar 76	Barcelona (Spain)	A	W 1–0	Toshack
			14 Apr 76		H	D 1–1	Thompson (PB)
		F	28 Apr 76	FC Bruges (Belgium)	H	W 3–2	Kennedy, Case, Keegan (pen)
			19 May 76		A	D 1–1	Keegan
1976–77	European Cup	1	14 Sep 76	Crusaders	H	W 2–0	Neal (pen), Toshack

Season	Competition	Round	Date	Opponents (Country)	Venue	Result	Scorers
			28 Sep 76	(Northern Ireland)	A	W 5–0	Johnson 2, Keegan, McDermott, Heighway
		2	20 Oct 76	Trabzonspor (Turkey)	A	L 0–1	
			3 Nov 76		H	W 3–0	Heighway, Johnson, Keegan
		QF	2 Mar 77	St Etienne (France)	A	L 0–1	
			16 Mar 77		H	W 3–1	Keegan, Kennedy, Fairclough
		SF	6 Apr 77	FC Zurich	A	W 3–1	Neal 2 (1 pen), Heighway
			20 Apr 77	(Switzerland)	H	W 3–0	Case 2, Keegan
		F	25 May 77	Borussia Moenchengladbach (West Germany)	N	W 3–1	McDermott, Smith, Neal (pen)
1977–78	Super Cup	F	22 Nov 77	SV Hamburg	A	D 1–1	Fairclough
			6 Dec 77	(West Germany)	H	W 6–0	Thompson, McDermott 3, Fairclough, Dalglish
1977–78	European Cup	1	bye				
		2	19 Oct 77	Dynamo Dresden	H	W 5–1	Hansen, Case 2, Neal (pen), Kennedy
			2 Nov 77	(East Germany)	A	L 1–2	Heighway
		QF	1 Mar 78	Benfica (Portugal)	A	W 2–1	Case, Hughes
			15 Mar 78		H	W 4–1	Callaghan, Dalglish, McDermott, Neal
		SF	29 Mar 78	Borussia Moenchengladbach (West Germany)	A	L 1–2	Johnson
			12 Apr 78		H	W 3–0	Kennedy, Dalglish, Case
		F	10 May 78	FC Bruges (Belgium)	N	W 1–0	Dalglish
1978–79	Super Cup	F	4 Dec 78	Anderlecht (Belgium)	A	L 1–3	Case
			19 Dec 78		H	W 2–1	Hughes, Fairclough
1978–79	European Cup	1	13 Sep 78	Nottingham Forest	A	L 0–2	
			27 Sep 78	(England)	H	D 0–0	
1979–80	European Cup	1	19 Sep 79	Dynamo Tbilisi (USSR)	H	W 2–1	Johnson, Case
			3 Oct 79		A	L 0–3	
1980–81	European Cup	1	17 Sep 80	Oulun Palloseura	A	D 1–1	McDermott
			1 Oct 80	(Finland)	H	W10–1	Souness 3 (1 pen), Fairclough 2, McDermott 2, Dalglish, Lee, Kennedy (R)
		2	22 Oct 80	Aberdeen (Scotland)	A	W 1–0	McDermott
			5 Nov 80		H	W 4–0	Neal, Dalglish, Hansen, own goal
		QF	4 Mar 81	CSKA Sofia	H	W 5–1	Souness 3, Lee, McDermott
			18 Mar 81	(Bulgaria)	A	W 1–0	Johnson
		SF	8 Apr 81	Bayern Munich	H	D 0–0	
			22 Apr 81	(West Germany)	A	D 1–1*	Kennedy (R)
		F	27 May 81	Real Madrid (Spain)	N	W 1–0	Kennedy (A)
1981–82	European Cup	1	16 Sep 81	Oulun Palloseura	A	W 1–0	Dalglish
			30 Sep 81	(Finland)	H	W 7–0	Dalglish, McDermott 2, Kennedy (R), Johnson, Rush, Lawrenson
		2	21 Oct 81	AZ67 (Holland)	A	D 2–2	Johnson, Lee
			4 Nov 81		H	W 3–2	McDermott (pen), Rush, Hansen
		QF	3 Mar 82	CSKA Sofia	H	W 1–0	Whelan
			17 Mar 82	(Bulgaria)	A	L 0–2	
1982–83	European Cup	1	14 Sep 82	Dundalk (Eire)	A	W 4–1	Whelan 2, Rush, Hodgson
			28 Sep 82		H	W 1–0	Whelan

Season	Competition	Round	Date	Opponents (Country)	Venue	Result		Scorers
		2	19 Oct 82	HJK Helsinki	A	L	0–1	
			2 Nov 82	(Finland)	H	W	5–0	Dalglish, Johnston, Neal, Kennedy (A) 2
		QF	2 Mar 83	Widzew Lodz	A	L	0–2	
			16 Mar 83	(Poland)	H	W	3–2	Neal (pen), Rush, Hodgson
1983–84	European Cup	1	14 Sep 83	BK Odense (Denmark)	A	W	1–0	Dalglish
			28 Sep 83		H	W	5–0	Robinson 2, Dalglish 2, own goal
		2	19 Oct 83	Athletic Bilbao	H	D	0–0	
			2 Nov 83	(Spain)	A	W	1–0	Rush
		QF	7 Mar 84	Benfica (Portugal)	H	W	1–0	Rush
			21 Mar 84		A	W	4–1	Whelan 2, Johnston, Rush
		SF	11 Apr 84	Dinamo Bucharest	H	W	1–0	Lee
			25 Apr 84	(Romania)	A	W	2–1	Rush 2
		F	30 May 84	AS Roma (Italy)	N	D	1–1†	Neal
1984–85	Super Cup	F	16 Jan 85	Juventus (Italy)	A	L	0–2	
1984–85	European Cup	1	19 Sep 84	Lech Poznan (Poland)	A	W	1–0	Wark
			3 Oct 84		H	W	4–0	Wark 3, Walsh
		2	24 Oct 84	Benfica (Portugal)	H	W	3–1	Rush 3
			7 Nov 84		A	L	0–1	
		QF	6 Mar 85	FK Austria (Austria)	A	D	1–1	Nicol
			20 Mar 85		H	W	4–1	Walsh 2, Nicol, own goal
		SF	10 Apr 85	Panathinaikos	H	W	4–0	Wark, Rush 2, Beglin
			24 Apr 85	(Greece)	A	W	1–0	Lawrenson
		F	29 May 85	Juventus (Italy)	N	L	0–1	
1991–92	UEFA Cup	1	18 Sep 91	Kuusysi (Finland)	H	W	6–1	Saunders 4, Houghton
			2 Oct 91		A	L	0–1	
		2	23 Oct 91	Auxerre (France)	A	L	0–2	
			6 Nov 91		H	W	3–0	Molby (pen), Marsh, Walters
		3	27 Nov 91	Tirol (Austria)	A	W	2–0	Saunders 2
			11 Dec 91		H	W	4–0	Saunders 3, Venison
		QF	4 Mar 92	Genoa (Italy)	A	L	0–2	
			18 Mar 92		H	L	1–2	Rush
1992–93	Cup-Winners' Cup	1	16 Sep 92	Apollon (Cyprus)	H	W	6–1	Stewart 2, Rush 4
			29 Sep 92		A	W	2–1	Rush, Hutchison
		2	22 Oct 92	Spartak Moscow	A	L	2–4	Wright, McManaman
			4 Nov 92	(Russia)	H	L	0–2	

MANCHESTER CITY

Season	Competition	Round	Date	Opponents (Country)	Venue	Result		Scorers
1968–69	European Cup	1	18 Sep 68	Fenerbahce (Turkey)	H	D	0–0	
			2 Oct 68		A	L	1–2	Coleman
1969–70	Cup-Winners' Cup	1	17 Sep 69	Athletic Bilbao	A	D	3–3	Young, Booth, own goal
			1 Oct 69	(Spain)	H	W	3–0	Oakes, Bell, Bowyer
		2	12 Nov 69	Lierse (Belgium)	A	W	3–0	Lee 2, Bell
			26 Nov 69		H	W	5–0	Bell 2, Lee 2, Summerbee
		QF	4 Mar 70	Academica Coimbra	A	D	0–0	
			18 Mar 70	(Portugal)	H	W	1–0	Towers
		SF	1 Apr 70	Schalke 04	A	L	0–1	
			15 Apr 70	(West Germany)	H	W	5–1	Young 2, Doyle, Lee, Bell
		F	29 Apr 70	Gornik Zabrze	N	W	2–1	Young, Lee (pen)
				(Poland)				
1970–71	Cup-Winners' Cup	1	16 Sep 70	Linfield	H	W	1–0	Bell

Season	Competition	Round	Date	Opponents (Country)	Venue	Result	Scorers
			30 Sep 70	(Northern Ireland)	A	L 1–2*	Lee
		2	21 Oct 70	Honved (Hungary)	A	W 1–0	Lee
			4 Nov 70		H	W 2–0	Bell, Lee
		QF	10 Mar 71	Gornik Zabrze	A	L 0–2	
			24 Mar 71	(Poland)	H	W 2–0	Mellor, Doyle
			31 Mar 71		N	W 3–1	Young, Booth, Lee
		SF	14 Apr 71	Chelsea (England)	A	L 0–1	
			28 Apr 71		H	L 0–1	
1972–73	UEFA Cup	1	13 Sep 72	Valencia (Spain)	H	D 2–2	Mellor, Marsh
			27 Sep 72		A	L 1–2	Marsh
1976–77	UEFA Cup	1	15 Sep 76	Juventus (Italy)	H	W 1–0	Kidd
			29 Sep 76		A	L 0–2	
1977–78	UEFA Cup	1	14 Sep 77	Widzew Lodz	H	D 2–2	Barnes, Channon
			28 Sep 77	(Poland)*	A	D 0–0	
1978–79	UEFA Cup	1	13 Sep 78	Twente Enschede	A	D 1–1	Watson
			27 Sep 78	(Holland)	H	W 3–2	Kidd, Bell, own goal
		2	18 Oct 78	Standard Liege	H	W 4–0	Hartford, Kidd 2 (1 pen),
				(Belgium)			Palmer
			1 Nov 78		A	L 0–2	
		3	23 Nov 78	AC Milan (Italy)	A	D 2–2	Kidd, Power
			6 Dec 78		H	W 3–0	Booth, Hartford, Kidd
		QF	7 Mar 79	Borussia	H	D 1–1	Channon
			21 Mar 79	Moenchengladbach	A	L 1–3	Deyna
				(West Germany)			

MANCHESTER UNITED

Season	Competition	Round	Date	Opponents (Country)	Venue	Result	Scorers
1956–57	European Cup	Pr	12 Sep 56	Anderlecht (Belgium)	A	W 2–0	Viollet, Taylor (T)
			29 Sep 56		H	W10–0	Viollet 4, Taylor (T) 3, Whelan 2, Berry
		1	17 Oct 56	Borussia Dortmund	H	W 3–2	Viollet 2, Pegg
			21 Nov 56	(West Germany)	A	D 0–0	
		QF	16 Jan 57	Athletic Bilbao	A	L 3–5	Taylor (T), Viollet, Whelan
			6 Feb 57	(Spain)	H	W 3–0	Viollet, Taylor (T), Berry
		SF	11 Apr 57	Real Madrid (Spain)	A	L 1–3	Taylor (T)
			24 Apr 57		H	D 2–2	Taylor (T), Charlton
1957–58	European Cup	Pr	25 Sep 57	Shamrock Rovers (Eire)	A	W 6–0	Whelan 2, Taylor (T) 2, Berry, Pegg
			2 Oct 57		H	W 3–2	Viollet 2, Pegg
		1	20 Nov 57	Dukla Prague	H	W 3–0	Webster, Taylor (T), Pegg
			4 Dec 57	(Czechoslovakia)	A	L 0–1	
		QF	14 Jan 58	Red Star Belgrade	H	W 2–1	Charlton, Colman
			5 Feb 58	(Yugoslavia)	A	D 3–3	Viollet, Charlton 2
		SF	8 May 58	AC Milan (Italy)	H	W 2–1	Viollet, Taylor (E) (pen)
			14 May 58		A	L 0–4	
1963–64	Cup Winners' Cup	1	25 Sep 63	Willem II Tilburg	A	D 1–1	Herd
			15 Oct 63	(Holland)	H	W 6–1	Setters, Law 3, Charlton, Chisnall
		2	3 Dec 63	Tottenham Hotspur	A	L 0–2	
			10 Dec 63	(England)	H	W 4–1	Herd 2, Charlton 2
		QF	26 Feb 64	Sporting Lisbon	H	W 4–1	Law 3 (2 pens), Charlton
			18 Mar 65	(Portugal)	A	L 0–5	
1964–65	Fairs Cup	1	23 Sep 64	Djurgaarden (Sweden)	A	D 1–1	Herd

Season	Competition	Round	Date	Opponents (Country)	Venue	Result	Scorers
			27 Oct 64		H	W 6–1	Law 3 (1 pen), Charlton 2, Best
		2	11 Nov 64	Borussia Dortmund	A	W 6–1	Herd, Charlton 3, Best, Law
			2 Dec 64	(West Germany)	H	W 4–0	Charlton 2, Law, Connelly
		3	20 Jan 65	Everton (England)	H	D 1–1	Connelly
			9 Feb 65		A	W 2–1	Connelly, Herd
		QF	12 May 65	Strasbourg (France)	A	W 5–0	Connelly, Herd, Law 2, Charlton
			19 May 65		H	D 0–0	
		SF	31 May 65	Ferencvaros	H	W 3–2	Law (pen), Herd 2
			6 Jun 65	(Hungary)	A	L 0–1	
			16 Jun 65		A	L 1–2	Connelly
1965–66	European Cup	Pr	22 Sep 65	HJK Helsinki	A	W 3–2	Herd, Connelly, Law
			6 Oct 65	(Finland)	H	W 6–0	Connelly 3, Best 2, Charlton
		1	17 Nov 65	Vorwaerts Berlin	A	W 2–0	Law, Connelly
			1 Dec 65	(East Germany)	H	W 3–1	Herd 3
		QF	2 Feb 66	Benfica (Portugal)	H	W 3–2	Herd, Law, Foulkes
			9 Mar 66		A	W 5–1	Best 2, Connelly, Crerand, Charlton
		SF	13 Apr 66	Partizan Belgrade	A	L 0–2	
			20 Apr 66	(Yugoslavia)	H	W 1–0	own goal
1967–68	European Cup	1	20 Sep 67	Hibernians (Malta)	H	W 4–0	Sadler 2, Law 2
			27 Sep 67		A	D 0–0	
		2	15 Nov 67	Sarajevo (Yugoslavia)	A	D 0–0	
			29 Nov 67		H	W 2–1	Aston, Best
		QF	28 Feb 68	Gornik Zabrze	H	W 2–0	Kidd, own goal
			13 Mar 68	(Poland)	A	L 0–1	
		SF	24 Apr 68	Real Madrid (Spain)	H	W 1–0	Best
			15 May 68		A	D 3–3	Sadler, Kidd, Foulkes
		F	29 Apr 68	Benfica (Portugal)	N	W 4–1	Charlton 2, Best, Kidd
1968–69	European Cup	1	18 Sep 68	Waterford (Eire)	A	W 3–1	Law 3
			2 Oct 68		H	W 7–1	Stiles, Law 4, Burns, Charlton
		2	13 Nov 68	Anderlecht (Belgium)	H	W 3–0	Kidd, Law 2
			27 Nov 68		A	L 1–3	Sartori
		QF	26 Feb 69	Rapid Vienna (Austria)	H	W 3–0	Best 2, Morgan
			5 Mar 69		A	D 0–0	
		SF	23 Apr 69	AC Milan (Italy)	A	L 0–2	
			15 Apr 69		H	W 1–0	Charlton
1976–77	UEFA Cup	1	15 Sep 76	Ajax (Holland)	A	L 0–1	
			29 Sep 76		H	W 2–0	Macari, McIlroy
		2	20 Oct 76	Juventus (Italy)	H	W 1–0	Hill
			3 Nov 76		A	L 0–3	
1977–78	Cup-Winners' Cup	1	14 Sep 77	St Etienne (France)	A	D 1–1	Hill
			5 Oct 77		H	W 2–0	Pearson, Coppell
		2	19 Oct 77	Porto (Portugal)	A	L 0–4	
			2 Nov 77		H	W 5–2	Coppell 2, own goals 2, Nicholl
1980–81	UEFA Cup	1	17 Sep 80	Widzew Lodz*	H	D 1–1	McIlroy
			1 Oct 80	(Poland)	A	D 0–0	
1982–83	UEFA Cup	1	15 Sep 82	Valencia (Spain)	H	D 0–0	
			29 Sep 82		A	L 1–2	Robson
1983–84	Cup-Winners' Cup	1	14 Sep 83	Dukla Prague	H	D 1–1	Wilkins
			27 Sep 83	(Czechoslovakia)	A	D 2–2*	Robson, Stapleton

Season	Competition	Round	Date	Opponents (Country)	Venue	Result	Scorers
		2	19 Oct 83	Spartak Varna	A	W 2–1	Robson, Graham
			2 Nov 83	(Bulgaria)	H	W 2–0	Stapleton 2
		QF	7 Mar 84	Barcelona (Spain)	A	L 0–2	
			21 Mar 84		H	W 3–0	Robson 2, Stapleton
		SF	11 Apr 84	Juventus (Italy)	H	D 1–1	Davies
			24 Apr 84		A	L 1–2	Whiteside
1984–85	UEFA Cup	1	19 Sep 84	Raba Gyor (Hungary)	H	W 3–0	Robson, Muhren, Hughes
			3 Oct 84		A	D 2–2	Brazil, Muhren
		2	24 Oct 84	PSV Eindhoven	A	D 0–0	
			7 Nov 84	(Holland)	H	W 1–0	Strachan
		3	28 Nov 84	Dundee United	H	D 2–2	Strachan, Robson
			12 Dec 84	(Scotland)	A	W 3–2	Hughes, Muhren, own goal
		QF	6 Mar 85	Videoton (Hungary)†	H	W 1–0	Stapleton
			20 Mar 84		A	L 0–1	
1990–91	Cup-Winners' Cup	1	19 Sep 90	Pecsi Munkas	H	W 2–0	Blackmore, Webb
			3 Oct 90	(Hungary)	A	W 1–0	McClair
		2	23 Oct 90	Wrexham (Wales)	H	W 3–0	McClair, Bruce (pen), Pallister
			7 Nov 90		A	W 2–0	Robins, Bruce
		QF	6 Mar 91	Montpellier	H	D 1–1	McClair
			19 Mar 91	(France)	A	W 2–0	Blackmore, Bruce (pen)
		SF	10 Apr 91	Legia Warsaw	A	W 3–1	McClair, Hughes, Bruce
			24 Apr 91	(Poland)	H	D 1–1	Sharpe
		F	15 May 91	Barcelona (Spain)	N	W 2–1	Hughes 2
1991–92	Cup-Winners' Cup	1	18 Sep 91	Athinaikos	A	D 0–0	
			1 Oct 91	(Greece)	H	W 2–0	Hughes, McClair
		2	23 Oct 91	Atletico Madrid	A	L 0–3	
			6 Nov 91	(Spain)	H	D 1–1	Hughes
1991–92	Super Cup	F	19 Nov 91	Red Star Belgrade (Yugoslavia)	H	W 1–0	McClair
1992–93	UEFA Cup	1	16 Sep 92	Torpedo Moscow	H	D 0–0	
			29 Sep 92	(Russia)†	A	D 0–0	

NEWCASTLE UNITED

Season	Competition	Round	Date	Opponents (Country)	Venue	Result	Scorers
1968–69	Fairs Cup	1	11 Nov 68	Feyenoord (Holland)	H	W 4–0	Scott, Robson (B), Gibb1, Davies
			17 Nov 68		A	L 0–2	
		2	30 Oct 68	Sporting Lisbon	A	D 1–1	Scott
			20 Nov 68	(Portugal)	H	W 1–0	Robson (B)
		3	1 Jan 69	Real Zaragoza (Spain)	A	L 2–3	Robson (B), Davies
			15 Jan 69		H	W 2–1*	Robson (B), Gibb
		QF	12 Mar 69	Setubal (Portugal)	H	W 5–1	Robson (B) 2, Gibb, Davies, Foggon
			26 Mar 69		A	L 1–3	Davies
		SF	14 Apr 69	Rangers (Scotland)	A	D 0–0	
			22 May 69		H	W 2–0	Scott, Sinclair
		F	29 May 69	Ujpest Dozsa	H	W 3–0	Moncur 2, Scott
			11 Jun 69	(Hungary)	A	W 3–2	Moncur, Arentoft, Foggon
1969–70	Fairs Cup	1	15 Sep 69	Dundee United	A	W 2–1	Davies 2
			1 Oct 69	(Scotland)	H	W 1–0	Dyson
		2	19 Nov 69	Porto (Portugal)	A	D 0–0	
			26 Nov 69		H	W 1–0	Scott
		3	17 Dec 69	Southampton	H	D 0–0	
			13 Jan 70	(England)	A	D 1–1*	Robson (B)

Season	Competition	Round	Date	Opponents (Country)	Venue	Result	Scorers
		QF	11 Mar 70	Anderlecht (Belgium)*	A	L 0–2	
			18 Mar 70		H	W 3–1	Robson (B) 2, Dyson
1970–71	Fairs Cup	1	23 Sep 70	Inter Milan (Italy)	A	D 1–1	Davies
			30 Sep 70		H	W 2–0	Moncur, Davies
		2	21 Oct 70	Pecs Dozsa	H	W 2–0	Davies 2
			4 Nov 70	(Hungary)†	A	L 0–2	
1977–78	UEFA Cup	1	14 Sep 77	Bohemians (Eire)	A	D 0–0	
			28 Sep 77		H	W 4–0	Gowling 2, Craig 2
		2	19 Oct 77	Bastia (France)	A	L 1–2	Cannell
			2 Nov 77		H	L 1–3	Gowling

NEWPORT COUNTY

Season	Competition	Round	Date	Opponents (Country)	Venue	Result	Scorers
1980–81	Cup-Winners' Cup	1	16 Sep 80	Crusaders (Northern Ireland)	H	W 4–0	Gwyther, Moore, Aldridge, Bruton
			1 Oct 80		A	D 0–0	
		2	22 Oct 80	Haugar (Norway)	A	D 0–0	
			4 Nov 80		H	W 6–0	Gwyther, Lowndes, Aldridge, Tynan 2, Moore
		QF	4 Mar 81	Carl Zeiss Jena	A	D 2–2	Tynan 2
			18 Mar 81	(East Germany)	H	L 0–1	

NOTTINGHAM FOREST

Season	Competition	Round	Date	Opponents (Country)	Venue	Result	Scorers
1961–62	Fairs Cup	1	13 Sep 61	Valencia (Spain)	A	L 0–2	
			4 Oct 61		H	L 1–5	Cobb
1967–68	Fairs Cup	1	20 Sep 67	Eintracht Frankfurt	A	W 1–0	Baker
			17 Oct 67	(West Germany)	H	W 4–0	Baker 2, Chapman, Lyons
		2	31 Oct 67	Zurich (Switzerland)*	H	W 2–1	Newton, Moore (pen)
			14 Nov 67		A	L 0–1	
1978–79	European Cup	1	13 Sep 78	Liverpool (England)	H	W 2–0	Birtles, Barrett
			27 Sep 78		A	D 0–0	
		2	18 Oct 78	AEK Athens (Greece)	A	W 2–1	McGovern, Birtles
			1 Nov 78		H	W 5–1	Needham, Woodcock, Anderson, Birtles 2
		QF	7 Mar 79	Grasshoppers (Switzerland)	H	W 4–1	Birtles, Robertson (pen), Gemmill, Lloyd
			21 Mar 79		A	D 1–1	O'Neill
		SF	11 Apr 79	FC Cologne	H	D 3–3	Birtles, Bowyer, Robertson
			25 Apr 79	(West Germany)	A	W 1–0	Bowyer
		F	30 May 79	Malmo FF (Sweden)	N	W 1–0	Francis
1979–80	Super Cup		30 Jan 80	Barcelona (Spain)	H	W 1–0	George
			5 Feb 80		A	D 1–1	Burns
1979–80	European Cup	1	19 Sep 79	Oster (Sweden)	H	W 2–0	Bowyer, own goal
			3 Oct 79		A	D 1–1	Woodcock
		2	24 Oct 79	Arges Pitesti	H	W 2–0	Woodcock, Birtles
			7 Nov 79	(Romania)	A	W 2–1	Bowyer, Birtles
		QF	5 Mar 80	Dynamo Berlin	H	L 0–1	
			19 Mar 80	(East Germany)	A	W 3–1	Francis 2, Robertson (pen)
		SF	9 Apr 80	Ajax (Holland)	H	W 2–0	Francis, Robertson (pen)
			23 Apr 80		A	L 0–1	
		F	28 May 80	SV Hamburg (West Germany)	N	W 1–0	Robertson

Season	Competition	Round	Date	Opponents (Country)	Venue	Result	Scorers
1980–81	Super Cup	F	25 Nov 80	Valencia (Spain)*	H	W 2–1	Bowyer 2
			17 Dec 80		A	L 0–1	
1980–81	European Cup	1	17 Sep 80	CSKA Sofia	A	L 0–1	
			1 Oct 80	(Bulgaria)	H	L 0–1	
1983–84	UEFA Cup	1	14 Sep 83	Vorwaerts	H	W 2–0	Wallace, Hodge
			28 Sep 83	(East Germany)	A	W 1–0	Bowyer
		2	19 Oct 83	PSV Eindhoven	A	W 2–1	Davenport, Walsh (pen)
			2 Nov 83	(Holland)	H	W 1–0	Davenport
		3	23 Nov 83	Celtic (Scotland)	H	D 0–0	
			7 Dec 83		A	W 2–1	Hodge, Walsh
		QF	7 Mar 84	Sturm Graz (Austria)	H	W 1–0	Hart
			21 Mar 84		A	D 1–1	Walsh (pen)
		SF	11 Apr 84	Anderlecht (Belgium)	H	W 2–0	Hodge 2
					A	L 0–3	
1984–85	UEFA Cup	1	19 Sep 84	FC Bruges (Belgium)	H	D 0–0	
			3 Oct 84		A	L 0–1	

QUEEN'S PARK RANGERS

Season	Competition	Round	Date	Opponents (Country)	Venue	Result	Scorers
1976–77	UEFA Cup	1	15 Sep 76	Brann Bergen	H	W 4–0	Bowles 3, Masson
			29 Sep 76	(Norway)	A	W 7–0	Bowles 3, Givens 2, Thomas, Webb
		2	20 Oct 76	Slovan Bratislava	A	D 3–3	Bowles 2, Givens
			3 Nov 76	(Czechoslovakia)	H	W 5–2	Givens 3, Bowles, Clement
		3	24 Nov 76	FC Cologne	H	W 3–0	Givens, Webb, Bowles
			7 Dec 76	(West Germany)	A	L 1–4*	Masson
		QF	2 Mar 77	AEK Athens (Greece)	H	W 3–0	Francis 2 (2 pens), Bowles
			16 Mar 77		A	L 0–3†	
1984–85	UEFA Cup	1	18 Sep 84	KR Reykjavik	A	W 3–0	Stainrod 2, Bannister
			2 Oct 84	(Iceland)	H	W 4–0	Bannister 3, Charles
		2	24 Oct 84	Partizan Belgrade*	H	W 6–2	Gregory, Fereday, Stainrod, Neill, Bannister 2
			7 Nov 84	(Yugoslavia)	A	L 0–4	

SHEFFIELD WEDNESDAY

Season	Competition	Round	Date	Opponents (Country)	Venue	Result	Scorers
1961–62	Fairs Cup	1	12 Sep 61	Lyon (France)	A	L 2–4	Ellis, Young
			4 Oct 61		H	W 5–2	Fantham 2, Griffin, McAnearney (pen), Dobson
		2	29 Nov 61	AS Roma (Italy)	H	W 4–0	Fantham, Young 3
			13 Dec 61		A	L 0–1	
		QF	28 Feb 62	Barcelona (Spain)	H	W 3–2	Fantham 2, Finney
			28 Mar 62		A	L 0–2	
1963–64	Fairs Cup	1	25 Sep 63	DOS Utrecht (Holland)	A	W 4–1	Holliday, Layne, Quinn, own goal
			15 Oct 63		H	W 4–1	Layne 3 (1 pen), Dobson
		2	6 Nov 63	FC Cologne	A	L 2–3	Pearson 2
			27 Nov 63	(West Germany)	H	L 1–2	Layne
1992–93	UEFA Cup	1	16 Sep 92	Spora (Luxembourg)	H	W 8–1	Waddle, Anderson, Warhurst 2, Bart-Williams, Worthington
			1 Oct 92		A	W 2–1	Watson, Warhurst
		2	20 Oct 92	Kaiserslautern	A	L 1–3	Hirst
			4 Nov 92	(Germany)	H	D 2–2	Wilson, Sheridan

SOUTHAMPTON

Season	Competition	Round	Date	Opponents (Country)	Venue	Result	Scorers
1969–70	Fairs Cup	1	17 Sep 69	Rosenborg (Norway)	A	L 0–1	
			1 Oct 69		H	W 2–0	Davies, Paine
		2	4 Nov 69	Vitoria Guimaraes	A	D 3–3	Channon, Davies, Paine
			12 Nov 69	(Portugal)	H	W 5–1	Gabriel, Davies 2 (1 pen), Channon, own goal
		3	17 Dec 69	Newcastle United	A	D 0–0	
			13 Jan 70	(England)*	H	D 1–1	Channon
1971–72	UEFA Cup	1	15 Sep 71	Athletic Bilbao	H	W 2–1	Jenkins, Channon (pen)
			29 Sep 71	(Spain)	A	L 0–2	
1976–77	Cup-Winners' Cup	1	15 Sep 76	Marseille (France)	H	W 4–0	Waldron, Channon 2 (1 pen), Osgood
			29 Sep 76		A	L 1–2	Peach
		2	20 Oct 76	Carrick Rangers	A	W 5–2	Stokes, Channon 2, McCalliog, Osgood
			3 Nov 76	(Northern Ireland)	H	W 4–1	Williams, Hayes 2, Stokes
		QF	2 Mar 77	Anderlecht (Belgium)	A	L 0–2	
			16 Mar 77		H	W 2–1	Peach (pen), MacDougall
1981–82	UEFA Cup	1	16 Sep 81	Limerick (Eire)	A	W 3–0	Moran 2, Armstrong
			29 Sep 81		H	D 1–1	Keegan
		2	21 Oct 81	Sporting Lisbon	H	L 2–4	Keegan (pen), Channon
			4 Nov 81	(Portugal)	A	D 0–0	
1982–83	UEFA Cup	1	15 Sep 82	Norrkoping (Sweden)	H	D 2–2	Williams, Wright
			29 Sep 82		A	D 0–0	
1984–85	UEFA Cup	1	19 Sep 84	Hamburg	H	D 0–0	
			3 Oct 84	(West Germany)	A	L 0–2	

STOKE CITY

Season	Competition	Round	Date	Opponents (Country)	Venue	Result	Scorers
1972–73	UEFA Cup	1	13 Sep 72	Kaiserslautern	H	W 3–1	Conroy, Hurst, Ritchie
			27 Sep 72	(West Germany)	A	L 0–4	
1974–75	UEFA Cup	1	18 Sep 74	Ajax (Holland)*	H	D 1–1	Smith
			2 Oct 74		A	D 0–0	

SWANSEA CITY

Season	Competition	Round	Date	Opponents (Country)	Venue	Result	Scorers
1961–62	Cup-Winners' Cup	1	6 Sep 61	Motor Jena	H	D 2–2	Reynolds, Nurse (pen)
			18 Oct 61	(East Germany)	A	L 1–5	Reynolds
			(in Linz, Austria)				
1966–67	Cup-Winners' Cup	1	21 Sep 66	Slavia Sofia	H	D 1–1	Todd
			5 Oct 66	(Bulgaria)	A	L 0–4	
1981–82	Cup-Winners' Cup	1	16 Sep 81	Lokomotive Leipzig	H	L 0–1	
			30 Sep 81	(East Germany)	A	L 1–2	Charles
1982–83	Cup-Winners' Cup	Pr	17 Aug 82	Braga (Portugal)	H	W 3–0	Charles 2, own goal
			25 Aug 82		A	L 0–1	
		1	15 Sep 82	Sliema Wanderers (Malta)	H	W12–0	Charles 2, Loveridge 2, Irwin, Latchford, Hadziabdic, Walsh 3, Rajkovic, Stevenson

Season	Competition	Round	Date	Opponents (Country)	Venue	Result		Scorers
			29 Sep 82		A	W	5–0	Curtis 2, Gale 2, Toshack
		2	20 Oct 82	Paris St Germain	H	L	0–1	
			3 Nov 82	(France)	A	L	0–2	
1983–84	Cup-Winners' Cup	Pr	24 Aug 83	Magdeburg	H	D	1–1	Walsh
			31 Aug 83	(East Germany)	A	L	0–1	
1989–90	Cup-Winners' Cup	1	13 Sep 89	Panathinaikos	A	L	2–3	Raynor, Salako
			27 Sep 89	(Greece)	H	D	3–3	James (pen), Melville 2
1991–92	Cup-Winners' Cup	1	17 Sep 91	Monaco (France)	H	L	1–2	Legg
			1 Oct 91		A	L	0–8	

TOTTENHAM HOTSPUR

Season	Competition	Round	Date	Opponents (Country)	Venue	Result		Scorers
1961–62	European Cup	Pr	13 Sep 61	Gornik Zabrze	A	L	2–4	Jones, Dyson
			20 Sep 61	(Poland)	H	W	8–1	Blanchflower (pen), Jones 3, Smith 2, Dyson, White
		1	1 Nov 61	Feyenoord (Holland)	A	W	3–1	Dyson, Saul 2
			15 Oct 61		H	D	1–1	Dyson
		QF	14 Feb 62	Dukla Prague	A	L	0–1	
			26 Feb 62	(Czechoslovakia)	H	W	4–1	Smith 2, Mackay 2
		SF	21 Mar 62	Benfica (Portugal)	A	L	1–3	Smith
			5 Apr 62		H	W	2–1	Smith, Blanchflower (pen)
1962–63	Cup-Winners' Cup	1		bye				
		2	31 Oct 62	Rangers (Scotland)	H	W	5–2	White, Greaves, Allen, Norman, own goal
			11 Dec 62		A	W	3–2	Greaves, Smith 2
		QF	5 Mar 63	Slovan Bratislava	A	L	0–2	
			14 Mar 63	(Czechoslovakia)	H	W	6–0	Mackay, Smith, Greaves 2, Jones, White
		SF	24 Apr 63	OFK Belgrade	A	W	2–1	White, Dyson
			1 May 63	(Yugoslavia)	H	W	3–1	Mackay, Jones, Smith
		F	15 May 63	Atletico Madrid (Spain)	N	W	5–1	Greaves 2, White, Dyson 2
1963–64	Cup-Winners' Cup	1		exempt				
		2	3 Dec 63	Manchester United	H	W	2–0	Mackay, Dyson
			10 Dec 63	(England)	A	L	1–4	Greaves
1967–68	Cup-Winners' Cup	1	20 Sep 67	Hajduk Split	A	W	2–0	Robertson, Greaves
			27 Sep 67	(Yugoslavia)	H	W	4–3	Robertson 2, Gilzean, Venables
		2	29 Nov 67	Lyon (France)*	A	L	0–1	
			13 Dec 67		H	W	4–3	Greaves 2 (1 pen), Jones, Gilzean
1971–72	UEFA Cup	1	14 Sep 71	Keflavik (Iceland)	A	W	6–1	Gilzean 3, Coates, Mullery 2
			28 Sep 71		H	W	9–1	Chivers 3, Gilzean 2, Perryman, Coates, Knowles, Holder
		2	20 Oct 71	Nantes (France)	A	D	0–0	
			2 Nov 71		H	W	1–0	Peters
		3	8 Dec 71	Rapid Bucharest	H	W	3–0	Peters, Chivers 2
			15 Dec 71	(Romania)	A	W	2–0	Pearce, Chivers
		QF	7 Mar 72	UT Arad (Romania)	A	W	2–0	Morgan, England
			21 Mar 72		H	D	1–1	Gilzean
		SF	5 Apr 72	AC Milan (Italy)	H	W	2–1	Perryman 2
			19 Apr 72		A	D	1–1	Mullery
		F	3 May 72	Wolverhampton	A	W	2–1	Chivers 2
			17 May 72	Wanderers (England)	H	D	1–1	Mullery

Season	Competition	Round	Date	Opponents (Country)	Venue	Result	Scorers
1972–73	UEFA Cup	I	13 Sep 72	Lyn Oslo (Norway)	A	W 6–3	Peters, Pratt, Gilzean 2, Chivers 2
			27 Sep 72		H	W 6–0	Chivers 3, Coates 2, Pearce
		2	25 Oct 72	Olympiakos Piraeus	H	W 4–0	Pearce 2, Chivers, Coates
			8 Nov 72	(Greece)	A	L 0–1	
		3	29 Nov 72	Red Star Belgrade	H	W 2–0	Chivers, Gilzean
			13 Dec 72	(Yugoslavia)	A	L 0–1	
		QF	7 Mar 73	Setubal (Portugal)	H	W 1–0	Evans
			21 Mar 73		A	L 1–2*	Chivers
		SF	10 Apr 73	Liverpool (England)*	A	L 0–1	
			25 Apr 73		H	W 2–1	Peters 2
1973–74	UEFA Cup	I	19 Sep 73	Grasshoppers	A	W 5–1	Chivers 2, Evans, Gilzean 2
			3 Oct 73	(Switzerland)	H	W 4–1	Peters 2, England, own goal
		2	24 Oct 73	Aberdeen (Scotland)	A	D 1–1	Coates
			7 Nov 73		H	W 4–1	Peters, Neighbour, McGrath 2
		3	28 Nov 73	Dynamo Tbilisi (USSR)	A	D 1–1	Coates
			12 Dec 73		H	W 5–1	McGrath, Chivers 2, Peters 2
		QF	6 Mar 74	FC Cologne	A	W 2–1	McGrath, Peters
			20 Mar 74	(West Germany)	H	W 3–0	Chivers, Coates, Peters
		SF	10 Apr 74	Lokomotive Leipzig	A	W 2–1	Peters, McGrath
			24 Apr 74	(East Germany)	H	W 2–0	McGrath, Chivers
		F	21 May 74	Feyenoord (Holland)	H	D 2–2	England, own goal
			29 May 74		A	L 0–2	
1981–82	Cup-Winners' Cup	I	16 Sep 81	Ajax (Holland)	A	W 3–1	Falco 2, Villa
			29 Sep 81		H	W 3–0	Galvin, Falco, Ardiles
		2	21 Oct 81	Dundalk (Eire)	A	D 1–1	Crooks
			4 Nov 81		H	W 1–0	Crooks
		QF	3 Mar 82	Eintracht Frankfurt	H	W 2–0	Miller, Hazard
			17 Mar 82	(West Germany)	A	L 1–2	Hoddle
		SF	7 Apr 82	Barcelona (Spain)	H	D 1–1	Roberts
			21 Apr 82		A	L 0–1	
1982–83	Cup-Winners' Cup	I	15 Sep 82	Coleraine	A	W 3–0	Crooks 2, Archibald
			28 Sep 82	(Northern Ireland)	H	W 4–0	Crooks, Mabbutt, Brooke, Gibson
		2	20 Oct 82	Bayern Munich	H	D 1–1	Archibald
			3 Nov 82	(West Germany)	A	L 1–4	Hughton
1983–84	UEFA Cup		14 Sep 83	Drogheda (Eire)	A	W 6–0	Falco 2, Crooks, Galvin, Mabbutt 2
			28 Sep 83		H	W 8–0	Falco 2, Roberts 2, Brazil 2, Hughton, Archibald
		2	19 Oct 83	Feyenoord (Holland)	H	W 4–2	Archibald 2, Galvin 2
			2 Nov 83		A	W 2–0	Hughton, Galvin
		3	23 Nov 83	Bayern Munich	A	L 0–1	
			7 Dec 83	(West Germany)	H	W 2–0	Archibald, Falco
		QF	7 Mar 84	FK Austria (Austria)	H	W 2–0	Archibald, Brazil
			21 Mar 84		A	D 2–2	Brazil, Ardiles
		SF	11 Apr 84	Hajduk Split	A	L 1–2	Falco
			25 Apr 84	(Yugoslavia)	H	W 1–0*	Hazard
		F	9 May 84	Anderlecht (Belgium)	A	D 1–1	Miller
			23 May 84		H	D 1–1†	Roberts
1984–85	UEFA Cup	I	19 Sep 84	Sporting Braga	A	W 3–0	Falco 2, Galvin
			3 Oct 84	(Portugal)	H	W 6–0	Stevens, Hughton, Falco, Crooks 3
		2	24 Oct 84	FC Bruges (Belgium)	A	L 1–2	Allen
			7 Nov 84		H	W 3–0	Hazard, Allen, Roberts
		3	28 Nov 84	Bohemians	H	W 2–0	Stevens, own goal

Season	Competition	Round	Date	Opponents (Country)	Venue	Result		Scorers
			12 Dec 84	(Czechoslovakia)	A	D	1–1	Falco
		QF	6 Mar 85	Real Madrid (Spain)	H	L	0–1	
			20 Mar 85		A	D	0–0	
1991–92	Cup-Winners' Cup	Pr	21 Aug 91	Stockerau	A	W	1–0	Durie
			4 Sep 91	(Austria)	H	W	1–0	Mabbutt
		1	17 Sep 91	Hajduk Split	A	L	0–1	
			2 Oct 91	(Croatia)	H	W	2–0	Tuttle, Durie
		2	23 Oct 91	Porto	H	W	3–1	Lineker 2, Durie
			7 Nov 91	(Portugal)	A	D	0–0	
		QF	4 Mar 92	Feyenoord	A	L	0–1	
			18 Mar 92	(Holland)	H	D	0–0	

WATFORD

Season	Competition	Round	Date	Opponents (Country)	Venue	Result		Scorers
1983–84	UEFA Cup	1	14 Sep 83	Kaiserslautern	A	L	1–3	Gilligan
			28 Sep 83	(West Germany)	H	W	3–0	Richardson 2, own goal
		2	19 Oct 83	Levski Spartak	H	D	1–1	Rostron
			2 Nov 83	(Bulgaria)	A	W	3–1	Callaghan, Rostron, Richardson
		3	23 Nov 83	Sparta Prague	H	L	2–3	Rostron, Gilligan
			7 Dec 83	(Czechoslovakia)	A	L	0–4	

WEST BROMWICH ALBION

Season	Competition	Round	Date	Opponents (Country)	Venue	Result		Scorers
1966–67	Fairs Cup	1		bye				
		2	2 Nov 66	DOS Utrecht (Holland)	A	D	1–1	Hope
			9 Nov 66		H	W	5–2	Brown (T) 3 (1 pen), Clark, Kaye
		3	2 Feb 67	Bologna (Italy)	A	L	0–3	
			8 Mar 67		H	L	1–3	Fairfax
1968–69	Cup-Winners' Cup	1	18 Sep 68	FC Bruges (Belgium)	A	L	1–3	Hartford
			2 Oct 68		H	W	2–0*	Brown (T), Hartford
		2	13 Nov 68	Dinamo Bucharest	A	D	1–1	Hartford
			27 Nov 68	(Romania)	H	W	4–0	Lovett, Astle, Brown (T) 2 (1 pen)
		QF	15 Jan 69	Dunfermline Athletic	A	D	0–0	
			19 Feb 69	(Scotland)	H	L	0–1	
1978–79	UEFA Cup	1	13 Sep 78	Galatasaray (Turkey)	A	W	3–1	Robson, Regis, Cunningham
			27 Sep 78		H	W	3–1	Robson, Cunningham (pen), Trewick
		2	18 Oct 78	Sporting Braga	A	W	2–0	Regis 2
			1 Nov 78	(Portugal)	H	W	1–0	Brown (A)
		3	22 Nov 78	Valencia (Spain)	A	D	1–1	Cunningham
			6 Dec 78		H	W	2–0	Brown (T) 2 (1 pen)
		QF	7 Mar 79	Red Star Belgrade	A	L	0–1	
			21 Mar 79	(Yugoslavia)	H	D	1–1	Regis
1979–80	UEFA Cup	1	19 Sep 79	Carl Zeiss Jena	A	L	0–2	
			3 Oct 79	(East Germany)	H	L	1–2	Wile
1981–82	UEFA Cup	1	16 Sep 81	Grasshoppers	A	L	0–1	
			30 Sep 81	(Switzerland)	H	L	1–3	Robertson

WEST HAM UNITED

Season	Competition	Round	Date	Opponents (Country)	Venue	Result		Scorers
1964–65	Cup-Winners' Cup	1	23 Sep 64	La Gantoise (Belgium)	A	W	1–0	Boyce
			7 Oct 64		H	D	1–1	Byrne
		2	25 Nov 64	Sparta Prague	H	W	2–0	Bond, Sealey
			9 Dec 64	(Czechoslovakia)	A	L	1–2	Sissons
		QF	16 Mar 65	Lausanne	A	W	2–1	Dear, Byrne

Season	Competition	Round	Date	Opponents (Country)	Venue	Result	Scorers
			23 Mar 65	(Switzerland)	H	W 4–3	Dear 2, Peters, own goal
		SF	7 Apr 65	Real Zaragoza	H	W 2–1	Dear, Byrne
			28 Apr 65	(Spain)	A	D 1–1	Sissons
		F	19 May 65	Munich 1860	N	W 2–0	Sealey 2
				(West Germany)			
1965–66	Cup-Winners' Cup	1		bye			
		2	24 Nov 65	Olympiakos Piraeus	H	W 4–0	Hurst 2, Byrne, Brabrook
			1 Dec 65	(Greece)	A	D 2–2	Peters 2
		QF	2 Mar 66	Magdeburg	H	W 1–0	Byrne
			16 Mar 66	(East Germany)	A	D 1–1	Sissons
		SF	5 Apr 66	Borussia Dortmund	H	L 1–2	Peters
			13 Apr 66	(West Germany)	A	L 1–3	Byrne
1975–76	Cup-Winners' Cup	1	17 Sep 75	Lahden Reipas	A	D 2–2	Brooking, Bonds
			1 Oct 75	(Finland)	H	W 3–0	Robson (K), Holland, Jennings
		2	22 Oct 75	Ararat Erevan (USSR)	A	D 1–1	Taylor (A)
			5 Nov 75		H	W 3–1	Paddon, Robson (K), Taylor (A)
		QF	3 Mar 76	Den Haag (Holland)	A	L 2–4	Jennings 2
			17 Mar 76		H	W 3–1*	Taylor (A), Lampard, Bonds (pen)
		SF	31 Mar 76	Eintracht Frankfurt	A	L 1–2	Paddon
			14 Apr 76	(West Germany)	H	W 3–1	Brooking 2, Robson (K)
		F	5 May 76	Anderlecht (Belgium)	N	L 2–4	Holland, Robson (K)
1980–81	Cup-Winners' Cup	1	17 Sep 80	Castilla (Spain)	A	L 1–3	Cross
			1 Oct 80		H	W 5–1	Pike, Cross 3, Goddard
		2	22 Oct 80	Poli. Timisoara (Romania)	H	W 4–0	Bonds, Goddard, Stewart (pen), Cross
			5 Nov 80		A	L 0–1	
		QF	4 Mar 81	Dynamo Tbilisi	H	L 1–4	Cross
			18 Mar 81	(USSR)	A	W 1–0	Pearson

WOLVERHAMPTON WANDERERS

Season	Competition	Round	Date	Opponents (Country)	Venue	Result	Scorers
1958–59	European Cup	Pr		bye			
		1	12 Nov 58	Schalke 04	H	D 2–2	Broadbent 2
			18 Nov 58	(West Germany)	A	L 1–2	Jackson
1959–60	European Cup	Pr	30 Sep 59	Vorwaerts	A	L 1–2	Broadbent
			7 Oct 59	(East Germany)	H	W 2–0	Broadbent, Mason
		1	11 Nov 59	Red Star Belgrade	A	D 1–1	Deeley
			24 Nov 59	(Yugoslavia)	H	W 3–0	Murray, Mason 2
		QF	10 Feb 60	Barcelona (Spain)	A	L 0–4	
			2 Mar 60		H	L 2–5	Murray, Mason
1960–61	Cup-Winners' Cup	Pr		bye			
		QF	12 Oct 60	FK Austria (Austria)	A	L 0–2	
			30 Nov 60		H	W 5–0	Kirkham 2, Mason, Broadbent 2
		SF	29 Mar 61	Rangers (Scotland)	A	L 0–2	
			19 Apr 61		H	D 1–1	Broadbent
1971–72	UEFA Cup	1	15 Sep 71	Academica Coimbra	H	W 3–0	McAlle, Richards, Dougan
			29 Sep 71	(Portugal)	A	W 4–1	Dougan 3, McAlle
		2	20 Oct 71	Den Haag (Holland)	A	W 3–1	Dougan, McCalliog, Hibbitt
			3 Nov 71		H	W 4–0	Dougan, own goals 3
		3	24 Nov 71	Carl Zeiss Jena	A	W 1–0	Richards
			8 Dec 71	(East Germany)	H	W 3–0	Hibbitt, Dougan 2
		QF	7 Mar 72	Juventus (Italy)	A	D 1–1	McCalliog
			21 Mar 72		H	W 2–1	Hegan, Dougan

Season	Competition	Round	Date	Opponents (Country)	Venue	Result		Scorers
		SF	4 Apr 72	Ferencvaros	A	D	2–2	Richards, Munro
			19 Apr 72	(Hungary)	H	W	2–1	Bailey, Munro
		F	3 May 72	Tottenham Hotspur	H	L	1–2	McCalliog
			17 May 72	(England)	A	D	1–1	Wagstaffe
1973–74	UEFA Cup	1	26 Sep 73	Belenenses (Portugal)	A	W	2–0	Richards, Dougan
			3 Oct 73		H	W	2–1	Eastoe, McCalliog
		2	24 Oct 73	Lokomotive Leipzig	A	L	0–3	
			7 Nov 73	(East Germany)	H	W	4–1	Kindon, Munro, Dougan, Hibbitt
1974–75	UEFA Cup	1	18 Sep 74	Porto (Portugal)	A	L	1–4	Bailey
			2 Oct 74		H	W	3–1	Bailey, Daley, Dougan
1980–81	UEFA Cup	1	17 Sep 80	PSV Eindhoven	A	L	1–3	Gray
			1 Oct 80	(Holland)	H	W	1–0	Eves

WREXHAM

Season	Competition	Round	Date	Opponents (Country)	Venue	Result		Scorers
1972–73	Cup-Winners' Cup	1	13 Sep 72	Zurich (Switzerland)	A	D	1–1	Kinsey
			27 Sep 72		H	W	2–2	Ashcroft, Sutton
		2	25 Oct 72	Hajduk Split (Yugoslavia)*	H	W	3–1	Tinnion, Smallman, own goal
			8 Nov 72		A	L	0–2	
1975–76	Cup-Winners' Cup	1	17 Sep 75	Djurgaarden (Sweden)	H	W	2–1	Griffiths, Davis
			1 Oct 75		A	D	1–1	Whittle
		2	22 Oct 75	Stal Rzeszow (Poland)	H	W	2–0	Ashcroft 2
			5 Nov 75		A	D	1–1	Sutton
		QF	3 Mar 76	Anderlecht (Belgium)	A	L	0–1	
			17 Mar 76		H	D	1–1	Lee
1978–79	Cup-Winners' Cup	1	13 Sep 78	Rijeka (Yugoslavia)	A	L	0–3	
			27 Sep 78		H	W	2–0	McNeil, Cartwright
1979–80	Cup-Winners' Cup	1	19 Sep 79	Magdeburg	H	W	3–2	McNeil, Fox, Buxton
			3 Oct 79	(East Germany)	A	L	2–5	Vinter, Hill
1984–85	Cup-Winners' Cup	1	19 Sep 84	Porto (Portugal)	H	W	1–0	Steel
			3 Oct 84		A	L	3–4	King 2, Horne
		2	24 Oct 84	Roma (Italy)	A	L	0–2	
			7 Nov 84		H	L	0–1	
1986–87	Cup-Winners' Cup	1	17 Sep 86	Zurrieq (Malta)	A	W	3–0	Massey, Charles, Conroy
			1 Oct 86		H	W	4–0	Massey 2 (1 pen), Steel, Horne
		2	22 Oct 86	Zaragoza (Spain)*	A	D	0–0	
			5 Nov 86		H	D	2–2	Massey, Buxton
1990–91	Cup-Winners' Cup	1	19 Sep 90	Lyngby (Denmark)	H	D	0–0	
			3 Oct 90		A	W	1–0	Armstrong
		2	23 Oct 90	Manchester United	A	L	0–3	
			7 Nov 90	(England)	H	L	0–2	

SCOTTISH LEAGUE CLUBS

ABERDEEN

Season	Competition	Round	Date	Opponents (Country)	Venue	Result	Scorers
1967–68	Cup-Winners' Cup	I	6 Sep 67	KR Reykjavik (Iceland)	H	W 10–1	Munro 3, Storrie 2, Smith 2, McMillan, Petersen, Taylor
			13 Sep 67		A	W 4–1	Storrie 2, Buchan, Munro
		2	29 Nov 67	Standard Liege	A	L 0–3	
			6 Dec 67	(Belgium)	H	W 2–0	Munro, Melrose
1968–69	Fairs Cup	I	17 Sep 68	Slavia Sofia (Bulgaria)	A	D 0–0	
			2 Oct 68		H	W 2–0	Robb, Taylor
		2	23 Oct 68	Real Zaragoza (Spain)	H	W 2–1	Forrest, Smith
			30 Oct 68		A	L 0–3	
1970–71	Cup-Winners' Cup	I	16 Sep 70	Honved (Hungary)†	H	W 3–1	Graham, Harper, Murray (S)
			30 Sep 70		A	L 1–3	Murray (S)
1971–72	UEFA Cup	I	15 Sep 71	Celta Vigo (Spain)	A	W 2–0	Harper, own goal
			29 Sep 71		H	W 1–0	Harper
		2	27 Oct 71	Juventus (Italy)	A	L 0–2	
			17 Nov 71		H	D 1–1	Harper
1972–73	UEFA Cup	I	13 Sep 72	Borussia	H	L 2–3	Harper, Jarvie
			27 Sep 72	Moenchengladbach (West Germany)	A	L 3–6	Harper 2, Jarvie
1973–74	UEFA Cup	I	19 Sep 73	Finn Harps (Eire)	H	W 4–1	Miller (R), Jarvie 2, Graham
			3 Oct 73		A	W 3–1	Robb, Graham, Miller (R)
		2	24 Oct 73	Tottenham Hotspur	H	D 1–1	Hermiston (pen)
			7 Nov 73	(England)	A	L 1–4	Jarvie
1977–78	UEFA Cup	I	14 Sep 77	RWD Molenbeek	A	D 0–0	
			28 Sep 77	(Belgium)	H	L 1–2	Jarvie
1978–79	Cup-Winners' Cup	I	13 Sep 78	Marek Stanke	A	L 2–3	Jarvie, Harper
			27 Sep 78	(Bulgaria)	H	W 3–0	Strachan, Jarvie, Harper
		2	18 Oct 78	Fortuna Dusseldorf	A	L 0–3	
			I Nov 78	(West Germany)	H	W 2–0	McLelland, Jarvie
1979–80	UEFA Cup	I	19 Sep 79	Eintracht Frankfurt	H	D 1–1	Harper
			3 Oct 79	(West Germany)	A	L 0–1	
1980–81	European Cup	I	17 Sep 80	Austria Vienna	H	W 1–0	McGhee
			I Oct 80	(Austria)	A	D 0–0	
		2	22 Oct 80	Liverpool (England)	H	L 0–1	
			5 Nov 80		A	L 0–4	
1981–82	UEFA Cup	I	16 Sep 81	Ipswich Town	A	D 1–1	Hewitt
			30 Sep 81	(England)	H	W 3–1	Strachan (pen), Weir 2
		2	21 Oct 81	Arges Pitesti	H	W 3–0	Strachan, Weir, Hewitt
			4 Nov 81	(Rumania)	A	D 2–2	Strachan (pen), Hewitt
		3	25 Nov 81	SV Hamburg	H	W 3–2	Black, Watson, Hewitt
			9 Dec 81	(West Germany)	A	L 1–3	McGhee
1982–83	Cup-Winners' Cup	Pr	18 Aug 82	Sion (Switzerland)	H	W 7–0	Black 2, Strachan, Hewitt, Simpson, McGhee, Kennedy
			I Sep 82		A	W 4–1	Hewitt, Miller, McGhee 2
		I	15 Sep 82	Dynamo Tirana	H	W 1–0	Hewitt
			29 Sep 82	(Albania)	A	D 0–0	
		2	20 Oct 82	Lech Poznan (Poland)	H	W 2–0	McGhee, Weir
			3 Nov 82		A	W 1–0	Bell
		QF	2 Mar 83	Bayern Munich	A	D 0–0	
			16 Mar 83	(West Germany)	H	W 3–2	Simpson, McLeish, Hewitt
		SF	6 Apr 83	Waterschei (Belgium)	H	W 5–1	Black, Simpson, McGhee 2, Weir
			19 Apr 83		A	L 0–1	
		F	II May 83	Real Madrid (Spain)	N	W 2–1	Black, Hewitt
1983–84	Super Cup	F	22 Nov 83	SV Hamburg	A	D 0–0	

Season	Competition	Round	Date	Opponents (Country)	Venue	Result	Scorers
			20 Dec 83	(West Germany)	H	W 2–0	Simpson, McGhee
1983–84	Cup-Winners' Cup	1	14 Sep 83	IA Akranes (Iceland)	A	W 2–1	McGhee 2
			28 Sep 83		H	D 1–1	Strachan (pen)
		2	19 Oct 83	Beveren (Belgium)	A	D 0–0	
			2 Nov 83		H	W 4–1	Strachan 2 (1 pen), Simpson, Weir
		QF	7 Mar 84	Ujpest Dozsa	A	L 0–2	
			21 Mar 84	(Hungary)	H	W 3–0	McGhee 3
		SF	11 Apr 84	Porto (Portugal)	A	L 0–1	
			25 Apr 84		H	L 0–1	
1984–85	European Cup	1	19 Sep 84	Dynamo Berlin	H	W 2–1	Black 2
			3 Oct 84	(East Germany)†	A	L 1–2	Angus
1985–86	European Cup	1	18 Sep 85	IA Akranes (Iceland)	A	W 3–1	Black, Hewitt, Stark
			2 Oct 85		H	W 4–1	Simpson, Hewitt, Gray, Falconer
		2	23 Oct 85	Servette (Switzerland)	A	D 0–0	
			6 Nov 85		H	W 1–0	McDougall
		QF	5 Mar 86	IFK Gothenburg*	H	D 2–2	Miller (J), Hewitt
			19 Mar 86	(Sweden)	A	D 0–0	
1986–87	Cup-Winners' Cup	1	17 Sep 86	Sion (Switzerland)	H	W 2–1	Bett (pen), Wright
			1 Oct 86		A	L 0–3	
1987–88	UEFA Cup	1	15 Sep 87	Bohemians (Eire)	A	D 0–0	
			30 Sep 87		H	W 1–0	Bett (pen)
		2	21 Oct 87	Feyenoord*	H	W 2–1	Falconer, Miller (J)
			4 Nov 87	(Holland)	A	L 0–1	
1988–89	UEFA Cup	1	7 Sep 88	Dynamo Dresden	H	D 0–0	
			5 Oct 88	(East Germany)	A	L 0–2	
1989–90	UEFA Cup	1	13 Sep 89	Rapid Vienna* (Austria)	H	W 2–1	Robertson (C), Grant
			27 Sep 89		A	L 0–1	
1990–91	Cup-Winners' Cup	1	19 Sep 90	Famagusta (Cyprus)	A	W 2–0	Mason, Gilhaus
			3 Oct 90		H	W 3–0	Robertson (C), own goal, Jess
		2	24 Oct 90	Legia Warsaw (Poland)	H	D 0–0	
			7 Nov 90		A	L 0–1	
1991–92	UEFA Cup	1	18 Sep 91	B1903 Copenhagen	H	L 0–1	
			2 Oct 91	(Denmark)	A	L 0–2	

AIRDRIEONIANS

Season	Competition	Round	Date	Opponents (Country)	Venue	Result	Scorers
1992–93	Cup-Winners' Cup	1	15 Sep 92	Sparta Prague	H	L 0–1	
			30 Sep 92	(Czechoslovakia)	A	L 1–2	Black

CELTIC

Season	Competition	Round	Date	Opponents (Country)	Venue	Result	Scorers
1962–63	Fairs Cup	1	26 Sep 62	Valencia (Spain)	A	L 2–4	Carrol 2
			24 Oct 62		H	D 2–2	Crerand, own goal
1963–64	Cup-Winners' Cup	1	17 Sep 63	Basle (Switzerland)	A	W 5–1	Divers, Hughes 3, Lennox
			9 Oct 63		H	W 5–0	Johnstone, Divers 2, Murdoch, Chalmers
		2	4 Dec 63	Dynamo Zagreb	H	W 3–0	Chalmers 2, Hughes
			11 Dec 63	(Yugoslavia)	A	L 1–2	Murdoch
		QF	26 Feb 64	Slovan Bratislava	H	W 1–0	Murdoch (pen)
			4 Mar 64	(Czechoslovakia)	A	W 1–0	Hughes
		SF	15 Apr 64	MTK Budapest	H	W 3–0	Johnstone, Chalmers 2
			29 Apr 64	(Hungary)	A	L 0–4	
1964–65	Fairs Cup	1	23 Sep 64	Leixoes (Portugal)	A	D 1–1	Murdoch
			7 Oct 64		H	W 3–0	Murdoch (pen), Chalmers 2
		2	18 Nov 64	Barcelona (Spain)	A	L 1–3	Hughes
			2 Dec 64		H	D 0–0	
1965–66	Cup-Winners' Cup	1	29 Sep 65	Go Ahead Deventer (Holland)	A	W 6–0	Gallagher 2, Hughes, Johnstone 2, Lennox

Season	Competition	Round	Date	Opponents (Country)	Venue	Result	Scorers
			7 Oct 65		H	W 1–0	McBride
		2	3 Nov 65	Aarhus (Denmark)	A	W 1–0	McBride
			17 Nov 65		H	W 2–0	McNeill, Johnstone
		QF	12 Jan 66	Dynamo Kiev (USSR)	H	W 3–0	Gemmell, Murdoch 2
			26 Jan 66		A	D 1–1	Gemmell
		SF	14 Apr 66	Liverpool (England)	H	W 1–0	Lennox
			19 Apr 66		A	L 0–2	
1966–67	European Cup	1	28 Sep 66	Zurich (Switzerland)	H	W 2–0	Gemmell, McBride
			5 Oct 66		A	W 3–0	Gemmell 2 (1pen), Chalmers
		2	30 Nov 66	Nantes (France)	A	W 3–1	McBride, Lennox, Chalmers
			7 Dec 66		H	W 3–1	Johnstone, Lennox, Chalmers
		QF	1 Mar 67	Vojvodina (Yugoslavia)	A	L 0–1	
			8 Mar 67		H	W 2–0	Chalmers, McNeill
		SF	12 Apr 67	Dukla Prague	H	W 3–1	Johnstone, Wallace 2
			25 Apr 67	(Czechoslovakia)	A	D 0–0	
		F	25 May 67	Inter Milan (Italy)	N	W 2–1	Gemmell, Chalmers
1967–68	European Cup	1	20 Sep 67	Dynamo Kiev (USSR)	H	L 1–2	Lennox
			4 Oct 67		A	D 1–1	Lennox
1968–69	European Cup	1	18 Aug 68	St Etienne (France)	A	L 0–2	
			2 Oct 68		H	W 4–0	Gemmell (pen), Craig, Chalmers, McBride.
		2	13 Nov 68	Red Star Belgrade (Yugoslavia)	H	W 5–1	Murdoch, Johnstone 2, Lennox, Wallace
			27 Nov 68		A	D 1–1	Wallace
		QF	19 Feb 69	AC Milan (Italy)	A	D 0–0	
			12 Mar 69		H	L 0–1	
1969–70	European Cup	1	17 Sep 69	Basle (Switzerland)	A	D 0–0	
			1 Oct 69		H	W 2–0	Hood, Gemmell
		2	12 Nov 69	Benfica (Portugal)	H	W 3–0	Gemmell, Wallace, Hood
			26 Nov 69		A	L 0–3†	
		QF	4 Mar 70	Fiorentina (Italy)	H	W 3–0	Auld, Wallace, own goal
			18 Mar 70		A	L 0–1	
		SF	1 Apr 70	Leeds United	A	W 1–0	Connolly
			15 Apr 70	(England)	H	W 2–1	Hughes, Murdoch
		F	6 May 70	Feyenoord (Holland)	N	L 1–2	Gemmell
1970–71	European Cup	1	16 Sep 70	KPV Kokkola (Finland)	H	W 9–0	Hood 3, Wilson 2, Hughes, McNeill, Johnstone, Davidson
			30 Sep 70		A	W 5–0	Wallace 2, Callaghan, Davidson, Lennox
		2	21 Oct 70	Waterford (Eire)	A	W 7–0	Wallace 3, Murdoch 2, Macari 2
			4 Nov 70		H	W 3–2	Hughes, Johnstone 2
		QF	10 Mar 70	Ajax (Holland)	A	L 0–3	
			24 Mar 71		H	W 1–0	Johnstone
1971–72	European Cup	1	15 Sep 71	BK 1903 Copenhagen	A	L 1–2	Macari
			29 Sep 71	(Denmark)	H	W 3–0	Wallace 2, Callaghan
		2	20 Oct 71	Sliema Wanderers (Malta)	H	W 5–0	Gemmell, Macari 2, Hood, Brogan
			3 Nov 71		A	W 2–1	Hood, Lennox
		QF	8 Mar 72	Ujpest Dosza (Hungary)	A	W 2–1	Macari, own goal
			22 Mar 72		H	D 1–1	Macari
		SF	5 Apr 72	Inter Milan (Italy)†	A	D 0–0	
			19 Apr 72		H	D 0–0	
1972–73	European Cup	1	13 Sep 72	Rosenborg (Norway)	H	W 2–1	Macari, Deans
			27 Sep 72		A	W 3–1	Macari, Hood, Dalglish
		2	25 Oct 72	Ujpest Dozsa (Hungary)	H	W 2–1	Dalglish 2
			8 Nov 72		A	L 0–3	
1973–74	European Cup	1	19 Sep 73	Turun (Finland)	A	W 6–1	Callaghan 2, Hood, Johnstone, Connolly (pen), Deans

Season	Competition	Round	Date	Opponents (Country)	Venue	Result	Scorers
			3 Oct 73		H	W 3–0	Deans, Johnstone 2
		2	24 Oct 73	Vejle (Denmark)	H	D 0–0	
			6 Nov 73		A	W 1–0	Lennox
		QF	27 Feb 74	Basle (Switzerland)	A	L 2–3	Wilson, Dalglish
			20 Mar 74		H	W 4–2	Dalglish, Deans, Callaghan, Murray
		SF	10 Apr 74	Atletico Madrid (Spain)	H	D 0–0	
			24 Apr 74		A	L 0–2	
1974–75	European Cup	1	18 Sep 74	Olympiakos Piraeus	H	D 1–1	Wilson
			2 Oct 74	(Greece)	A	L 0–2	
1975–76	Cup-Winners' Cup	1	16 Sep 75	Valur Reykjavik (Iceland)	A	W 2–0	Wilson, McDonald
			1 Oct 75		H	W 7–0	Edvaldsson, Dalglish, McCluskey (P) (pen), Hood 2, Deans, Callaghan
		2	22 Oct 75	Boavista (Portugal)	A	D 0–0	
			5 Nov 75		H	W 3–1	Dalglish, Edvaldsson, Deans
		QF	3 Mar 76	Sachsenring Zwickau	H	D 1–1	Dalglish
			17 Mar 76	(East Germany)	A	L 0–1	
1976–77	UEFA Cup	1	15 Sep 76	Wisla Krakow (Poland)	H	D 2–2	McDonald, Dalglish
			29 Sep 76		A	L 0–2	
1977–78	European Cup	1	14 Sep 77	Jeunesse D'Esch (Luxembourg)	H	W 5–0	McDonald, Wilson, Craig 2, McLaughlin
			28 Sep 77		A	W 6–1	Lennox 2, Edvaldsson 2, Glavin, Craig
		2	19 Oct 77	SW Innsbruck (Austria)	H	W 2–1	Craig, Burns
			2 Nov 77		A	L 0–3	
1979–80	European Cup	1	19 Sep 79	Partizan Tirana	A	L 0–1	
			3 Oct 79	(Albania)	H	W 4–1	McDonald, Aitken 2, Davidson
		2	24 Oct 79	Dundalk (Eire)	H	W 3–2	McDonald, McCluskey, Burns
			7 Nov 79		A	D 0–0	
		QF	5 Mar 80	Real Madrid (Spain)	H	W 2–0	McCluskey, Doyle
			19 Mar 80		A	L 0–3	
1980–81	Cup-Winners' Cup	Pr	20 Aug 80	Diosgyor (Hungary)	H	W 6–0	McGarvey 2, McCluskey 2, Sullivan, own goal
			3 Sep 80		A	L 1–2	Nicholas
		1	17 Sep 80	Poli. Timisoara*	H	W 2–1	Nicholas 2
			1 Oct 80	(Romania)	A	L 0–1	
1981–82	European Cup	1	16 Sep 81	Juventus (Italy)	H	W 1–0	MacLeod
			30 Sep 81		A	L 0–2	
1982–83	European Cup	1	15 Sep 82	Ajax (Holland)	H	D 2–2	Nicholas, McGarvey
			29 Sep 82		A	W 2–1	Nicholas, McCluskey
		2	20 Oct 82	Real Sociedad (Spain)	A	L 0–2	
			3 Nov 82		H	W 2–1	MacLeod 2
1983–84	UEFA Cup	1	14 Sep 83	Aarhus (Denmark)	H	W 1–0	Aitken
			28 Sep 83		A	W 4–1	MacLeod, McGarvey, Aitken, Provan
		2	19 Oct 83	Sporting Lisbon	A	L 0–2	
			2 Nov 83	(Portugal)	H	W 5–0	Burns, McAdam, McClair, MacLeod, McGarvey
		3	23 Nov 83	Nottingham Forest	A	D 0–0	
			7 Dec 83	(England)	H	L 1–2	MacLeod
1984–85	Cup-Winners' Cup	1	19 Sep 84	Gent (Belgium)	A	L 0–1	
			3 Oct 84		H	W 3–0	McGarvey 2, McStay
		2	24 Oct 84	Rapid Vienna	A	L 1–3	McClair
			7 Nov 84	(Austria)	H	W 3–0	McClair, MacLeod, Burns
			(match ordered to be replayed by UEFA)				
			12 Dec 84		N	L 0–1	
1985–86	Cup-Winners' Cup	1	18 Sep 85	Atletico Madrid (Spain)	A	D 1–1	Johnston
			2 Oct 85		H	L 1–2	Aitken
1986–87	European Cup	1	17 Sep 86	Shamrock Rovers	A	W 1–0	MacLeod
			1 Oct 86		H	W 2–0	Johnston 2

Season	Competition	Round	Date	Opponents (Country)	Venue	Result		Scorers
		2	22 Oct 86	Dynamo Kïev (USSR)	H	D	1–1	Johnston
			5 Nov 86		A	L	1–3	McGhee
1987–88	UEFA Cup	1	15 Sep 87	Borussia Dortmund	H	W	2–1	Walker, Whyte
			20 Sep 87	(West Germany)	A	L	0–2	
1988–89	European Cup	1	7 Sep 88	Honved (Hungary)	A	L	0–1	
			5 Oct 88		H	W	4–0	Stark, Walker, McAvennie, McGhee
		2	26 Oct 88	Werder Bremen	H	L	0–1	
			9 Nov 88	(West Germany)	A	D	0–0	
1989–90	Cup-Winners' Cup	1	12 Sep 89	Partizan Belgrade*	A	L	1–2	Galloway
			27 Sep 89	(Yugoslavia)	H	W	5–4	Dziekanowski 4, Walker
1991–92	UEFA Cup	1	18 Sep 91	Ekeren (Belgium)	H	W	2–0	Nicholas 2 (1 pen)
			1 Oct 91		A	D	1–1	Galloway
		2	22 Oct 91	Neuchatel Xamax	A	L	1–5	O'Neil
			6 Nov 91	(Switzerland)	H	W	1–0	Miller
1992–93	UEFA Cup	1	15 Sep 92	Cologne (Germany)	A	L	0–2	
			30 Sep 92		H	W	3–0	McStay, Creaney, Collins
		2	20 Oct 92	Borussia Dortmund	A	L	0–1	
			3 Nov 92	(Germany)	H	L	1–2	Creaney

DUNDEE

Season	Competition	Round	Date	Opponents (Country)	Venue	Result		Scorers
1962–63	European Cup	Pr	5 Jun 62	FC Cologne (West Germany)	H	W	8–1	Gilzean 3, own goal, Wishart, Robertson, Smith, Penman
			26 Sep 62		A	L	0–4	
		1	24 Oct 62	Sporting Lisbon	A	L	0–1	
			31 Oct 62	(Portugal)	H	W	4–1	Gilzean 3, Cousin
		QF	6 Mar 63	Anderlecht (Belgium)	A	W	4–1	Gilzean 2, Cousin, Smith
			13 Mar 63		H	W	2–1	Cousin, Smith
		SF	24 Apr 63	AC Milan (Italy)	A	L	1–5	Cousin
			1 May 63		H	W	1–0	Gilzean
1964–65	Cup-Winners' Cup	1		bye				
		2	18 Nov 64	Real Zaragoza (Spain)	H	D	2–2	Murray, Houston
			8 Dec 64		A	L	1–2	Robertson
1967–68	Fairs Cup	1	27 Sep 67	DWS Amsterdam	A	L	1–2	McLean (G)
			4 Oct 67	(Holland)	H	W	3–0	Wilson (S), McLean 2 (1 pen)
		2	1 Nov 67	FC Liege (Belgium)	H	W	3–1	Stuart 2, Wilson (S)
			14 Nov 67		A	W	4–1	MacLean (G) 4
		3		bye				
		QF	27 Mar 68	Zurich (Switzerland)	H	W	1–0	Easton
			3 Apr 68		A	W	1–0	Wilson (S)
		SF	1 May 68	Leeds United	H	D	1–1	Wilson (R)
			15 May 68	(England)	A	L	0–2	
1971–72	UEFA Cup	1	15 Sep 71	Akademisk	H	W	4–2	Bryce 2, Wallace, Lambie
			29 Sep 71	Copenhagen (Denmark)	A	W	1–0	Duncan
		2	19 Oct 71	FC Cologne	A	L	1–2	Kinninmonth
			3 Nov 71	(West Germany)	H	W	4–2	Duncan 3, Wilson (R)
		3	24 Nov 71	AC Milan (Italy)	A	L	0–3	
			8 Dec 71		H	W	2–0	Wallace, Duncan
1973–74	UEFA Cup	1	19 Sep 73	Twente Enschede	H	L	1–3	Stewart
			3 Oct 73	(Holland)	A	L	2–4	Johnston, Scott (J)
1974–75	UEFA Cup	1	18 Sep 74	RWD Molenbeek	A	L	0–1	
			2 Oct 74	(Belgium)	H	L	2–4	Duncan, Scott (J).

DUNDEE UNITED

Season	Competition	Round	Date	Opponents (Country)	Venue	Result		Scorers
1966–67	Fairs Cup	1		bye				
		2	25 Oct 66	Barcelona (Spain)	A	W	2–1	Hainey, Seeman
			16 Nov 66		H	W	2–0	Mitchell, Hainey

Season	Competition	Round	Date	Opponents (Country)	Venue	Result	Scorers
		3	8 Feb 67	Juventus (Italy)	A	L 0–3	
			8 Mar 67		H	W 1–0	Dossing
1969–70	Fairs Cup	1	15 Sep 69	Newcastle United	H	L 1–2	Scott
			1 Oct 69	(England)	A	L 0–1	
1970–71	Fairs Cup	1	15 Sep 70	Grasshoppers	H	W 3–2	Reid (1), Markland, Reid (A)
			30 Sep 70	(Switzerland)	A	D 0–0	
		2	21 Oct 70	Sparta Prague	A	L 1–3	Traynor
			4 Nov 70	(Czechoslovakia)	H	W 1–0	Gordon
1974–75	Cup-Winners' Cup	1	18 Sep 74	Jiul Petrosani	H	W 3–0	Narey, Copland, Gardner
			2 Oct 74	(Romania)	A	L 0–2	
		2	23 Oct 74	Bursaspor (Turkey)	H	D 0–0	
			6 Oct 74		A	L 0–1	
1975–76	UEFA Cup	1	23 Sep 75	Keflavik (Iceland)	A	W 2–0	Narey 2
			30 Sep 75		H	W 4–0	Hall 2, Hegarty (pen), Sturrock
		2	22 Oct 75	Porto (Portugal)	H	L 1–2	Rennie
			5 Nov 75		A	D 1–1	Hegarty
1977–78	UEFA Cup	1	14 Sep 77	KB Copenhagen	H	W 1–0	Sturrock
			27 Sep 77	(Denmark)	A	L 0–3	
1978–79	UEFA Cup	1	12 Sep 78	Standard Liege	A	L 0–1	
			27 Sep 78	(Belgium)	H	D 0–0	
1979–80	UEFA Cup	1	19 Sep 79	Anderlecht (Belgium)	H	D 0–0	
			2 Oct 79		A	D 1–1*	Kopel
		2	24 Oct 79	Diosgyor (Hungary)	H	L 0–1	
			7 Nov 79		A	L 1–3	Kopel
1980–81	UEFA Cup	1	17 Sep 80	Slask Wroclaw	A	D 0–0	
			1 Oct 80	(Poland)	H	W 7–2	Dodds 2, Pettigrew 2, Stark, Hegarty, Payne (pen)
		2	22 Oct 80	Lokeren* (Belgium)	H	D 1–1	Pettigrew
			5 Nov 80		A	D 0–0	
1981–82	UEFA Cup	1	16 Sep 81	Monaco (France)	A	W 5–2	Bannon 2 (1 pen), Dodds 2, Kirkwood
			30 Sep 81		H	L 1–2	Milne
		2	20 Oct 81	Borussia	A	L 0–2	
			3 Nov 81	Moenchengladbach (West Germany)	H	W 5–0	Milne, Kirkwood, Sturrock, Hegarty, Bannon
		3	1 Dec 81	Winterslag	A	D 0–0	
			9 Dec 81	(Belgium)	H	W 5–0	Bannon, Narey, Hegarty, Milne 2
		QF	3 Mar 82	Radnicki Nis	H	W 2–0	Narey, Dodds
			17 Mar 82	(Yugoslavia)	A	L 0–3	
1982–83	UEFA Cup	1	15 Sep 82	PSV Eindhoven	H	D 1–1	Dodds
			29 Sep 82	(Holland)	A	W 2–0	Kirkwood, Hegarty
		2	20 Oct 82	Viking Stavanger	A	W 3–1	Milne 2, Sturrock
			3 Nov 82	(Norway)	H	D 0–0	
		3	24 Nov 82	Werder Bremen	H	W 2–1	Milne, Narey
			8 Dec 82	(West Germany)	A	D 1–1	Hegarty
		QF	2 Mar 83	Bohemians	A	L 0–1	
			16 Mar 83	(Czechoslovakia)	H	D 0–0	
1983–84	European Cup	1	14 Sep 83	Hamrun Spartans	A	W 3–0	Reilly, Bannon, Stark
			28 Sep 83	(Malta)	H	W 3–0	Milne, Kirkwood 2
		2	19 Oct 83	Standard Liege	A	D 0–0	
			2 Nov 83	(Belgium)	H	W 4–0	Milne 2, Hegarty, Dodds
		QF	7 Mar 84	Rapid Vienna (Austria)	A	L 1–2	Stark
			21 Mar 84		H	W 1–0*	Dodds
		SF	11 Apr 84	AS Roma (Italy)	H	W 2–0	Dodds, Stark
			24 Apr 84		A	L 0–3	
1984–85	UEFA Cup	1	19 Sep 84	AIK Stockholm	A	L 0–1	
			3 Oct 84	(Sweden)	H	W 3–0	Sturrock, Milne 2
		2	24 Oct 84	ASK Linz (Austria)	A	W 2–1	Kirkwood, Bannon (pen)

Season	Competition	Round	Date	Opponents (Country)	Venue	Result	Scorers
			7 Nov 84		H	W 5–1	Hegarty, Coyne 2, Gough, Beaumont
		3	28 Nov 84	Manchester United	A	D 2–2	Hegarty, Sturrock
			12 Dec 84	(England)	H	L 2–3	Dodds, Hegarty
1985–86	UEFA Cup	1	18 Sep 85	Bohemians (Eire)	A	W 5–2	Sturrock 3, Bannon 2
			2 Oct 85		H	D 2–2	Milne, Redford
		2	23 Oct 85	Vardar Skopje	H	W 2–0	Redford, Gough
			6 Nov 85	(Yugoslavia)	A	D 1–1	Hegarty
		3	27 Nov 85	Neuchatel Xamax	H	W 2–1	Dodds, Redford
			11 Dec 85	(Switzerland)	A	L 1–3	Redford
1986–87	UEFA Cup	1	17 Sep 86	Lens (France)	A	L 0–1	
			1 Oct 86		H	W 2–0	Milne, Coyne
		2	22 Oct 86	Uni. Craiova	H	W 3–0	Redford 2, Clark
			5 Nov 86	(Romania)	A	L 0–1	
		3	26 Nov 86	Hajduk Split	H	W 2–0	McInally, Clark
			10 Dec 86	(Yugoslavia)	A	D 0–0	
		QF	4 Mar 87	Barcelona (Spain)	H	W 1–0	Gallacher
			18 Mar 87		A	W 2–1	Clark, Ferguson
		SF	8 Apr 87	Borussia	H	D 0–0	
			22 Apr 87	Moenchengladbach	A	W 2–0	Ferguson, Redford
				(West Germany)			
		F	6 May 87	IFK Gothenburg	A	L 0–1	
			20 May 87	(Sweden)	H	D 1–1	Clark
1987–88	UEFA Cup	1	15 Sep 87	Coleraine	A	W 1–0	Sturrock
			30 Sep 87	(Northern Ireland)	H	W 3–1	Gallacher, Sturrock, Clark
		2	21 Oct 87	Vitkovice	H	L 1–2	Ferguson
			4 Nov 87	(Czechoslovakia)	A	D 1–1	own goal
1988–89	Cup-Winners' Cup	1	7 Sep 88	Floriana (Malta)	A	D 0–0	
			5 Oct 88		H	W 1–0	Meade
		2	26 Oct 88	Dinamo Bucharest	H	L 0–1	
			9 Nov 88	(Romania)	A	D 1–1	Beaumont
1989–90	UEFA Cup	1	13 Sep 89	Glentoran	A	W 3–1	Cleland, McInally Hinds
			27 Sep 89	(Northern Ireland)	H	W 2–0	Clark, Gallacher
		2	17 Oct 89	Antwerp (Belgium)	A	L 0–4	
			31 Oct 89		H	W 3–2	Paatelainen, O'Neill, Clark
1990–91	UEFA Cup	1	18 Sep 90	Hafnarfjordur	A	W 3–1	Jackson, Cleland, own goal
			3 Oct 90	(Iceland)	H	D 2–2	Connolly, own goal
		2	24 Oct 90	Vitesse	A	L 0–1	
			7 Nov 90	(Holland)	H	L 0–4	

DUNFERMLINE ATHLETIC

Season	Competition	Round	Date	Opponents (Country)	Venue	Result	Scorers
1961–62	Cup-Winners' Cup	1	12 Sep 61	St Patrick's Athletic (Eire)	H	W 4–1	Melrose, Peebles, Dickson, Macdonald
			27 Sep 61		A	W 4–0	Peebles 2, Dickson 2
		2	25 Oct 61	Vardar Skopje	H	W 5–0	Smith, Dickson 2, Melrose, Peebles
			8 Nov 61	(Yugoslavia)	A	L 0–2	
		QF	13 Feb 62	Ujpest Dozsa	A	L 3–4	Smith, Macdonald 2
			20 Feb 62	(Hungary)	H	L 0–1	
1962–63	Fairs Cup	1	24 Oct 62	Everton (England)	A	L 0–1	
			31 Oct 62		H	W 2–0	Miller, Melrose
		2	12 Dec 62	Valencia (Spain)	A	L 0–4	
			19 Dec 62		H	W 6–2	Melrose, Sinclair 2, McLean, Peebles, Smith
			6 Feb 63		N	L 0–1	
1964–65	Fairs Cup	1	13 Oct 64	Oergryte (Sweden)	H	W 4–2	McLaughlin 2, Sinclair 2
			20 Oct 64		A	D 0–0	
		2	17 Nov 64	Stuttgart	H	W 1–0	Callaghan (T)
			1 Dec 64	(West Germany)	A	D 0–0	
		3	27 Jan 65	Athletic Bilbao (Spain)	A	L 0–1	

Season	Competition	Round	Date	Opponents (Country)	Venue	Result	Scorers
			3 Mar 65		H	W 1–0	Smith
			16 Mar 65		A	L 1–2	Smith
1965–66	Fairs Cup	1		bye			
		2	3 Nov 65	KB Copenhagen	H	W 5–0	Fleming, Paton 2, Robertson, Callaghan (T)
			17 Nov 65	(Denmark)	A	W 4–2	Edwards, Paton, Fleming, Ferguson
		3	26 Jan 66	Spartak Brno	H	W 2–0	Paton, Ferguson (pen)
			16 Feb 66	(Czechoslovakia)	A	D 0–0	
		QF	16 Mar 66	Real Zaragoza (Spain)	H	W 1–0	Paton
			20 Mar 66		A	L 2–4	Ferguson 2
1966–67	Fairs Cup	1	24 Aug 66	Frigg Oslo (Norway)	A	W 3–1	Fleming 2, Callaghan (T)
			28 Sep 66		H	W 3–1	Delaney 2, Callaghan (T)
		2	26 Oct 66	Dynamo Zagreb*	H	W 4–2	Delaney, Edwards, Ferguson 2
			11 Nov 66	(Yugoslavia)	A	L 0–2	
1968–69	Cup-Winners' Cup	1	18 Sep 68	Apoel (Cyprus)	H	W 10–1	Robertson 2, Renton 2, Barry, Callaghan (W) 2, Gardner, Edwards, Callaghan (T)
			2 Oct 68		A	W 2–0	Gardner, Callaghan (W)
		2	13 Nov 68	Olympiakos Piraeus	H	W 4–0	Edwards 2, Fraser, Mitchell
			27 Nov 68	(Greece)	A	L 0–3	
		QF	15 Jan 69	West Bromwich Albion	H	D 0–0	
			18 Feb 69	(England)	A	W 1–0	Gardner
		SF	9 Apr 69	Slovan Bratislava	H	D 1–1	Fraser
			23 Apr 69	(Czechoslovakia)	A	L 0–1	
1969–70	Fairs Cup	1	16 Sep 69	Bordeaux (France)	H	W 4–0	Paton 2, Mitchell, Gardner
			30 Sep 69		A	L 0–2	
		2	5 Nov 69	Gwardia Warsaw	H	W 2–1	McLean, Gardner
			18 Nov 69	(Poland)	A	W 1–0	Renton
		3	17 Dec 69	Anderlecht (Belgium)*	A	L 0–1	
			14 Jan 70		H	W 3–2	McLean 2, Mitchell

HEARTS

Season	Competition	Round	Date	Opponents (Country)	Venue	Result	Scorers
1958–59	European Cup	Pr	3 Sep 58	Standard Liege	A	L 1–5	Crawford
			9 Sep 58	(Belgium)	H	W 2–1	Bauld 2
1960–61	European Cup	Pr	29 Sep 60	Benfica (Portugal)	H	L 1–2	Young
			5 Oct 60		A	L 0–3	
1961–62	Fairs Cup	1	27 Sep 61	Union St Gilloise	A	W 3–1	Blackwood, Davidson 2
			4 Oct 61	(Belgium)	H	W 2–0	Wallace, Stenhouse
		2	6 Nov 61	Inter Milan (Italy)	H	L 0–1	
			22 Nov 61		A	L 0–4	
1963–64	Fairs Cup	1	25 Sep 63	Lausanne	A	D 2–2	Traynor, Ferguson
			9 Oct 63	(Switzerland)	H	D 2–2	Cumming, Hamilton (J)
			15 Oct 63		A	L 2–3	Wallace, Ferguson
1965–66	Fairs Cup	1		bye			
		2	18 Oct 65	Valerengen (Norway)	H	W 1–0	Wallace
			27 Oct 65		A	W 3–1	Kerrigan 2, Traynor
		3	12 Jan 66	Real Zaragoza (Spain)	H	D 3–3	Anderson, Wallace, Kerrigan
			26 Jan 66		A	D 2–2	Anderson, Wallace
			2 Mar 66		A	L 0–1	
1976–77	Cup-Winners' Cup	1	15 Sep 76	Lokomotive Leipzig	A	L 0–2	
			29 Sep 76	(East Germany)	H	W 5–1	Kay, Gibson 2, Brown, Busby
		2	20 Oct 76	SV Hamburg	A	L 2–4	Park, Busby
			3 Nov 76	(West Germany)	H	L 1–4	Gibson
1984–85	UEFA Cup	1	19 Sep 84	Paris St Germain	A	L 0–4	
			3 Oct 84	(France)	H	D 2–2	Robertson 2
1986–87	UEFA Cup	1	17 Sep 86	Dukla Prague*	H	W 3–2	Foster, Clark, Robertson
			1 Oct 86	(Czechoslovakia)	A	L 0–1	

Season	Competition	Round	Date	Opponents (Country)	Venue	Result	Scorers
1988–89	UEFA Cup	1	7 Sep 88	St Patrick's Athletic	A	W 2–0	Foster (pen), Galloway
			5 Oct 88	(Eire)	H	W 2–0	Black, Galloway
		2	26 Oct 88	FK Austria (Austria)	H	D 0–0	
			9 Nov 88		A	W 1–0	Galloway
		3	23 Nov 88	Velez Mostar	H	W 3–0	Bannon, Galloway, Colquhoun
			7 Dec 88	(Yugoslavia)	A	L 1–2	Galloway
		QF	28 Feb 89	Bayern Munich	H	W 1–0	Ferguson
			15 Mar 89	(West Germany)	A	L 0–2	
1990–91	UEFA Cup	1	19 Sep 90	Dnepr (USSR)	A	D 1–1	Robertson
			3 Oct 90		H	W 3–1	McKinlay, Robertson (2, 1 pen)
		2	24 Oct 90	Bologna (Italy)	H	W 3–1	Foster 2, Ferguson (1)
			7 Nov 90		A	L 0–3	
1992–93	UEFA Cup	1	16 Sep 92	Slavia Prague	A	L 0–1	
			30 Sep 92	(Czechoslovakia)	H	W 4–2	Mackay, Baird, Levein, Snodin
		2	21 Oct 92	Standard Liege	H	L 0–1	
			4 Nov 92	(Belgium)	A	L 0–1	

HIBERNIAN

Season	Competition	Round	Date	Opponents (Country)	Venue	Result	Scorers
1955–56	European Cup	1	14 Sep 55	Rot-Weiss Essen	A	W 4–0	Turnbull 2, Reilly, Ormond
			12 Oct 55	(West Germany)	H	D 1–1	Buchanan (J)
		QF	23 Nov 55	Djurgaarden (Sweden)	H	W 3–1	Combe, Mulkerrin, own goal
			28 Nov 55		A	W 1–0	Turnbull (pen)
		SF	4 Apr 56	Reims (France)*	A	L 0–2	
			18 Apr 56		H	L 0–1	
1960–61	Fairs Cup	1		Lausanne (Switzerland)			
				Lausanne withdrew			
		QF	27 Dec 60	Barcelona (Spain)	A	D 4–4	McLeod, Preston, Baker 2
			22 Feb 61		H	W 3–2	Kinloch 2 (1 pen), Baker
		SF	19 Apr 61	AS Roma (Italy)	H	D 2–2	Baker, McLeod
			26 Apr 61		A	D 3–3	Baker 2, Kinloch
			27 May 61		A	L 0–6	
1961–62	Fairs Cup	1	4 Sep 61	Belenenses (Portugal)	H	D 3–3	Fraser 2, Baird (pen)
			27 Sep 61		A	W 3–1	Baxter 2, Stevenson
		2	1 Nov 61	Red Star Belgrade	A	L 0–4	
			15 Nov 61	(Yugoslavia)	H	L 0–1	
1962–63	Fairs Cup	1	3 Oct 62	Stavenet (Denmark)	H	W 4–0	Byrne 2, Baker, own goal
			23 Oct 62		A	W 3–2	Stevenson 2, Byrne
		2	27 Nov 62	DOS Utrecht	A	W 1–0	Falconer
			12 Dec 62	(Holland)	H	W 2–1	Baker, Stevenson
		QF	13 Mar 63	Valencia (Spain)	A	L 0–5	
			3 Apr 63		H	W 2–1	Preston, Baker
1965–66	Fairs Cup	1	8 Sep 65	Valencia (Spain)	H	W 2–0	Scott, McNamee
			12 Oct 65		A	L 0–2	
			3 Nov 65		A	L 0–3	
1967–68	Fairs Cup	1	20 Sep 67	Porto (Portugal)	H	W 3–0	Cormack 2, Stevenson
			4 Oct 67		A	L 1–3	Stanton (pen)
		2	22 Nov 67	Napoli (Italy)	A	L 1–4	Stein
			29 Nov 67		H	W 5–0	Duncan, Quinn, Cormack, Stanton, Stein
		3	20 Dec 67	Leeds United	A	L 0–1	
			10 Jan 68	(England)	H	D 1–1	Stein
1968–69	Fairs Cup	1	18 Sep 68	Ljubljana (Yugoslavia)	A	W 3–0	Stevenson, Stein, Marinello
			2 Oct 68		H	W 2–1	Davis 2 (2 pens)
		2	13 Nov 68	Lokomotive Leipzig	H	W 3–1	McBride 3
			20 Nov 68	(East Germany)	A	W 1–0	Grant
		3	18 Dec 68	SV Hamburg	A	L 0–1	
			15 Jan 69	(West Germany)	H	W 2–1	McBride 2

Season	Competition	Round	Date	Opponents (Country)	Venue	Result		Scorers
1970–71	Fairs Cup	I	16 Sep 70	Malmo FF (Sweden)	H	W	6–0	McBride 3, Duncan 2, Blair
			30 Sep 70		A	W	3–2	Duncan, McEwan, Stanton
		2	14 Oct 70	Vitoria Guimaraes	H	W	2–0	Duncan, Stanton
			28 Oct 70	(Portugal)	A	L	1–2	Graham
		3	9 Dec 70	Liverpool (England)	H	L	0–1	
			22 Dec 70		A	L	0–2	
1972–73	Cup-Winners' Cup	I	13 Sep 72	Sporting Lisbon	A	L	1–2	Duncan
			27 Sep 72	(Portugal)	H	W	6–1	Gordon 2, O'Rourke 3, own goal
		2	25 Oct 72	Besa (Albania)	H	W	7–1	Cropley, O'Rourke 3, Duncan 2, Brownlie
			8 Nov 72		A	D	1–1	Gordon
		QF	7 Mar 73	Hajduk Split	H	W	4–2	Gordon 3, Duncan
			21 Mar 73	(Yugoslavia)	A	L	0–3	
1973–74	UEFA Cup	I	19 Sep 73	Keflavik (Iceland)	H	W	2–0	Black, Higgins
			3 Oct 73		A	D	1–1	Stanton
		2	24 Oct 73	Leeds United	A	D	0–0	
			2 Oct 73	(England)†	A	D	0–0	
1974–75	UEFA Cup	I	18 Sep 74	Rosenborg (Norway)	A	W	3–2	Stanton, Gordon, Cropley
			2 Oct 74		H	W	9–1	Harper 2, Munro 2, Stanton 2, Cropley 2 (2 pens), Gordon
		2	23 Oct 74	Juventus (Italy)	H	L	2–4	Stanton, Cropley
			6 Nov 74		A	L	0–4	
1975–76	UEFA Cup	I	17 Sep 75	Liverpool (England)	H	W	1–0	Harper
			30 Sep 75		A	L	1–3	Edwards
1976–77	UEFA Cup	I	15 Sep 76	Sochaux (France)	H	W	1–0	Brownlie
			29 Sep 76		A	D	0–0	
			20 Oct 76	Osters Vaxjo	H	W	2–0	Blackley, Brownlie (pen)
			3 Nov 76	(Sweden)	A	L	1–4	Smith
1978–79	UEFA Cup	I	13 Sep 78	Norrkoping (Sweden)	H	W	3–2	Higgins 2, Temperley
			27 Sep 78		A	D	0–0	
		2	18 Oct 78	Strasbourg (France)	A	L	0–2	
			1 Nov 78		H	W	1–0	McLeod (pen)
1989–90	UEFA Cup	I	12 Sep 89	Videoton (Hungary)	H	W	1–0	Mitchell
			26 Sep 89		A	W	3–0	Houchen, Evans, Collins
		2	18 Oct 89	FC Liege (Belgium)	H	D	0–0	
			31 Oct 89		A	L	0–1	
1992–93	UEFA Cup	I	15 Sep 92	Anderlecht (Belgium)*	H	D	2–2	Beaumont, McGinlay
			29 Sep 92		A	D	1–1	Jackson

KILMARNOCK

Season	Competition	Round	Date	Opponents (Country)	Venue	Result		Scorers
1964–65	Fairs Cup	I	2 Sep 64	Eintracht Frankfurt	A	L	0–3	
			22 Sep 64	(West Germany)	H	W	5–1	Hamilton, McIlroy, McFadzean, McInally, Sneddon
		2	11 Nov 64	Everton (England)	H	L	0–2	
			23 Nov 64		A	L	1–4	McIlroy
1965–66	European Cup	Pr	8 Sep 65	Nendori Tirana	A	D	0–0	
			29 Sep 65	(Albania)	H	W	1–0	Black
		I	17 Nov 65	Real Madrid (Spain)	H	D	2–2	McLean (pen), McInally
			1 Dec 65		A	L	1–5	McIlroy
1966–67	Fairs Cup	I		bye				
		2	25 Oct 66	Antwerp (Belgium)	A	W	1–0	McInally
			2 Nov 66		H	W	7–2	McInally 2, Queen 2, McLean 2, Watson
		3	14 Dec 66	La Gantoise (Belgium)	H	W	1–0	Murray
			21 Dec 66		A	W	2–1	McInally, McLean
		QF	19 Apr 67	Lokomotive Leipzig	A	L	0–1	
			26 Apr 67	(East Germany)	H	W	2–0	McFadzean, McIlroy

Season	Competition	Round	Date	Opponents (Country)	Venue	Result	Scorers
		SF	19 May 67	Leeds United	A	L 2–4	McIlroy 2
			24 May 67	(England)	H	D 0–0	
1969–70	Fairs Cup	1	16 Sep 69	Zurich (Switzerland)	A	L 2–3	McLean (J), Mathie
			30 Sep 69		H	W 3–1	McGrory, Morrison, McLean (T)
		2	19 Nov 69	Slavia Sofia (Bulgaria)	H	W 4–1	Mathie 2, Cook, Gilmour
			26 Nov 69		A	L 0–2	
		3	17 Dec 69	Dynamo Bacau	H	D 1–1	Mathie
			13 Jan 70	(Romania)	A	L 0–2	
1970–71	Fairs Cup	1	15 Sep 70	Coleraine	A	D 1–1	Mathie
			29 Sep 70	(Northern Ireland)	H	L 2–3	McLean (T), Morrison

MORTON

Season	Competition	Round	Date	Opponents (Country)	Venue	Result	Scorers
1968–69	Fairs Cup	1	18 Sep 68	Chelsea (England)	A	L 0–5	
			30 Sep 68		H	L 3–4	Thorop, Mason, Taylor

MOTHERWELL

Season	Competition	Round	Date	Opponents (Country)	Venue	Result	Scorers
1991–92	Cup Winners' Cup	1	18 Sep 91	Katowice (Poland)*	A	L 0–2	
			3 Oct 91		H	W 3–1	Kirk 2, Cusack

PARTICK THISTLE

Season	Competition	Round	Date	Opponents (Country)	Venue	Result	Scorers
1963–64	Fairs Cup	1	16 Sep 63	Glentoran	A	W 4–1	Hainey, Yard 2, Wright
			30 Sep 63	(Northern Ireland)	H	W 3–0	Smith 2, Harvey (pen)
		2	18 Nov 63	Spartak Brno (Czechoslovakia)	H	W 3–2	Yard, Harvey (pen), Ferguson
			27 Nov 63		A	L 0–4	
1972–73	UEFA Cup	1	13 Sep 72	Honved (Hungary)	A	L 0–1	
			27 Sep 72		H	L 0–3	

RANGERS

Season	Competition	Round	Date	Opponents (Country)	Venue	Result	Scorers
1956–57	European Cup	Pr		bye			
		1	24 Oct 56	Nice (France)	H	W 2–1	Murray, Simpson
			14 Nov 56		A	L 1–2	Hubbard (pen)
			28 Nov 56		N	L 1–3	own goal
1957–58	European Cup	Pr	4 Sep 57	St Etienne (France)	H	W 3–1	Kichenbrand, Scott, Simpson
			25 Sep 57		A	L 1–2	Wilson
		1	27 Nov 57	AC Milan (Italy)	H	L 1–4	Murray
			11 Dec 57		A	L 0–2	
1959–60	European Cup	Pr	16 Sep 59	Anderlecht (Belgium)	H	W 5–2	Millar, Scott, Matthew, Baird 2
			24 Sep 59		A	W 2–0	Matthew, McMillan
		1	11 Nov 59	Red Star Belgrade (Czechoslovakia)	H	W 4–3	McMillan, Scott, Wilson, Millar
			18 Nov 59		A	D 1–1	Scott
		QF	9 Mar 60	Sparta Rotterdam	A	W 3–2	Wilson, Baird, Murray
			16 Mar 60	(Holland)	H	L 0–1	
			30 Mar 60		N	W 3–2	Baird 2, own goal
		SF	13 Apr 60	Eintracht Frankfurt	A	L 1–6	Caldow (pen)
			5 May 60	(West Germany)	H	L 3–6	McMillan 2, Wilson
1960–61	Cup-Winners' Cup	Pr	28 Sep 60	Ferencvaros	H	W 4–2	Davis, Millar 2, Brand
			12 Oct 60	(Hungary)	A	L 1–2	Wilson
		QF	15 Nov 60	Borussia	A	W 3–0	Millar, Scott, McMillan
			30 Nov 60	Moenchengladbach (West Germany)	H	W 8–0	Baxter, Brand 3, Millar 2, Davis, own goal
		SF	29 Mar 61	Wolverhampton	H	W 2–0	Scott, Brand
			19 Apr 61	Wanderers (England)	A	D 1–1	Scott
		F	17 May 61	Fiorentina (Italy)	H	L 0–2	
			27 May 61		A	L 1–2	Scott

Season	Competition	Round	Date	Opponents (Country)	Venue	Result	Scorers
1961–62	European Cup	Pr	5 Sep 61	Monaco (France)	A	W 3–2	Baxter, Scott 2
			12 Sep 61		H	W 3–2	Christie 2, Scott
		1	15 Nov 61	Vorwaerts	A	W 2–1	Caldow (pen), Brand
			23 Nov 61	(East Germany)	H	W 4–1	McMillan 2, Henderson, own goal
		QF	7 Feb 62	Standard Liege	A	L 1–4	Wilson
			14 Feb 62	(Belgium)	H	W 2–0	Brand, Caldow (pen)
1962–63	Cup-Winners' Cup	1	5 Sep 62	Seville (Spain)	H	W 4–0	Millar 3, Brand
			26 Sep 62		A	L 0–2	
		2	31 Oct 62	Tottenham Hotspur	A	L 2–5	Brand, Millar
			11 Dec 62	(England)	H	L 2–3	Brand, Wilson
1963–64	European Cup	Pr	25 Sep 63	Real Madrid (Spain)	H	L 0–1	
			9 Oct 63		A	L 0–6	
1964–65	European Cup	Pr	2 Sep 64	Red Star Belgrade	H	W 3–1	Brand 2, Forrest
			9 Sep 64	(Yugoslavia)	A	L 2–4	Greig, McKinnon
			4 Nov 64		N	W 3–1	Forrest 2, Brand
		1	18 Nov 64	Rapid Vienna (Austria)	H	W 1–0	Wilson
			8 Dec 64		A	W 2–0	Forrest, Wilson
		QF	17 Feb 65	Inter Milan (Italy)	A	L 1–3	Forrest
			3 Mar 65		H	W 1–0	Forrest
1966–67	Cup-Winners' Cup	1	27 Sep 66	Glentoran	A	D 1–1	McLean
			5 Oct 66	(Northern Ireland)	H	W 4–0	Johnston, Smith (D), Setterington, McLean
		2	23 Nov 66	Borussia Dortmund	H	W 2–1	Johansen, Smith (A)
			6 Dec 66	(West Germany)	A	D 0–0	
		QF	1 Mar 67	Real Zaragoza	H	W 2–0	Smith, Willoughby
			22 Mar 67	(Spain)	A	L 0–2‡	
		SF	19 Apr 67	Slavia Sofia	A	W 1–0	Wilson
			3 May 67	(Bulgaria)	H	W 1–0	Henderson
		F	31 May 67	Bayern Munich (West Germany)	N	L 0–1	
1967–68	Fairs Cup	1	21 Sep 67	Dynamo Dresden	A	D 1–1	Ferguson
			4 Oct 67	(East Germany)	H	W 2–1	Penman, Greig
		2	8 Nov 67	FC Cologne	H	W 3–0	Ferguson 2, Henderson
			28 Nov 67	(West Germany)	A	L 1–3	Henderson
		3		bye			
		QF	26 Mar 68	Leeds United	H	D 0–0	
			9 Apr 68	(England)	A	L 0–2	
1968–69	Fairs Cup	1	18 Sep 68	Vojvodina	H	W 2–0	Greig (pen), Jardine
			2 Oct 68	(Yugoslavia)	A	L 0–1	
		2	30 Oct 68	Dundalk (Eire)	H	W 6–1	Henderson 2, Ferguson 2, Greig, own goal
			13 Nov 68		A	W 3–0	Mathieson, Stein 2
		3	11 Jan 69	DWS Amsterdam	A	W 2–0	Johnstone, Henderson
			22 Jan 69	(Holland)	H	W 2–1	Smith, Stein
		QF	19 Mar 69	Athletic Bilbao (Spain)	H	W 4–1	Ferguson, Penman, Persson, Stein
			2 Apr 69		A	L 0–2	
		SF	14 May 69	Newcastle United	H	D 0–0	
			22 May 69	(England)	A	L 0–2	
1969–70	Cup-Winners' Cup	1	17 Sep 69	Steaua Bucharest	H	W 2–0	Johnston 2
			1 Oct 69	(Rumania)	A	D 0–0	
		2	12 Nov 69	Gornik Zabrze	A	L 1–3	Persson
			26 Nov 69	(Poland)	H	L 1–3	Baxter
1970–71	Fairs Cup	1	16 Sep 70	Bayern Munich	A	L 0–1	
			30 Sep 70	(West Germany)	H	D 1–1	Stein
1971–72	Cup-Winners' Cup	1	15 Sep 71	Rennes (France)	A	D 1–1	Johnston
			28 Sep 71		H	W 1–0	MacDonald
		2	20 Oct 71	Sporting Lisbon	H	W 3–2	Stein 2, Henderson

Season	Competition	Round	Date	Opponents (Country)	Venue	Result	Scorers
			3 Nov 71	(Portugal)	A	L 3–4*	Stein 2, Henderson
		QF	8 Mar 72	Torino (Italy)	A	D 1–1	Johnston
			22 Mar 72		H	W 1–0	MacDonald
		SF	5 Apr 72	Bayern Munich	A	D 1–1	own goal
			19 Apr 72	(West Germany)	H	W 2–0	Jardine, Parlane
		F	24 May 72	Dynamo Moscow (USSR)	N	W 3–2	Johnstone 2, Stein
1972–73	Super Cup	F	16 Jan 73	Ajax (Holland)	H	L 1–3	MacDonald
			24 Jan 73		A	L 2–3	MacDonald, Young
1973–74	Cup-Winners' Cup	1	19 Sep 73	Ankaragucu (Turkey)	A	W 2–0	Conn, McLean
			3 Oct 73		H	W 4–0	Greig 2, O'Hara, Johnstone
		2	24 Oct 73	Borussia	A	L 0–3	
			7 Nov 73	Moenchengladbach (West Germany)	H	W 3–2	Conn, Jackson, MacDonald
1975–76	European Cup	1	17 Sep 75	Bohemians (Eire)	H	W 4–1	Fyfe, Johnstone, O'Hara, own goal
			1 Oct 75		A	D 1–1	Johnstone
		2	22 Oct 75	St Etienne (France)	A	L 0–2	
			5 Nov 75		H	L 1–2	MacDonald
1976–77	European Cup	1	15 Sep 76	Zurich (Switzerland)	H	D 1–1	Parlane
			29 Sep 76		A	L 0–1	
1977–78	Cup-Winners' Cup	Pr	17 Aug 77	Young Boys	H	W 1–0	Greig
			31 Aug 77	(Switzerland)	A	D 2–2	Johnstone, Smith
		1	14 Sep 77	Twente Enschede	H	D 0–0	
			28 Sep 77	(Holland)	A	L 0–3	
1978–79	European Cup	1	13 Sep 78	Juventus (Italy)	A	L 0–1	
			27 Sep 78		H	W 2–0	MacDonald, Smith
		2	18 Oct 78	PSV Eindhoven	H	D 0–0	
			1 Nov 78	(Holland)	A	W 3–2	MacDonald, Johnstone, Russell
		QF	6 Mar 79	FC Cologne	A	L 0–1	
			22 Mar 79	(West Germany)	H	D 1–1	McLean
1979–80	Cup-Winners' Cup	Pr	21 Aug 79	Lillestrom (Norway)	H	W 1–0	Smith
			5 Sep 79		A	W 2–0	MacDonald(A), Johnstone
		1	19 Sep 79	Fortuna Dusseldorf	H	W 2–1	MacDonald(A), McLean
			3 Oct 79	(West Germany)	A	D 0–0	
		2	24 Oct 79	Valencia (Spain)	A	D 1–1	McLean
			7 Nov 79		H	L 1–3	Johnstone
1981–82	Cup-Winners' Cup	1	16 Sep 81	Dukla Prague	A	L 0–3	
			30 Sep 81	(Czechoslovakia)	H	W 2–1	Bett, McDonald(J)
1982–83	UEFA Cup	1	15 Sep 82	Borussia Dortmund	A	D 0–0	
			29 Sep 82	(West Germany)	H	W 2–0	Cooper, Johnstone
		2	20 Sep 82	FC Cologne	H	W 2–1	Johnstone, McClelland
			3 Nov 82	(West Germany)	A	L 0–5	
1983–84	Cup-Winners' Cup	1	14 Sep 83	Valletta (Malta)	A	W 8–0	Paterson, McPherson 4, McDonald, Prytz 2
			28 Sep 83		H	W 10–0	Mitchell 2, McDonald 3, Dawson, McKay, Davis 2, Redford
		2	19 Oct 83	Porto (Portugal)*	H	W 2–1	Clark, Mitchell
			2 Nov 83		A	L 0–1	
1984–85	UEFA Cup	1	18 Sep 84	Bohemians (Eire)	A	L 2–3	McCoist, McPherson
			3 Oct 84		H	W 2–0	Paterson, Redford
		2	24 Oct 84	Inter Milan (Italy)	A	L 0–3	
			7 Nov 84		H	W 3–1	Mitchell, Ferguson 2
1985–86	UEFA Cup	1	18 Sep 85	Osasuna (Spain)	H	W 1–0	Paterson
			2 Oct 85		A	L 0–2	
1986–87	UEFA Cup	1	17 Sep 86	Ilves (Finland)	H	W 4–0	Fleck 3, McCoist
			1 Oct 86		A	L 0–2	
		2	23 Oct 86	Boavista (Portugal)	H	W 2–1	McPherson, McCoist
			4 Nov 86		A	W 1–0	Ferguson

Above: *Rangers celebrate a goal by Iain Ferguson (far left) in the Champions' League game against CSKA Moscow in Bochum (Allsport/Ben Radford)*

Left: *Dundee United's European campaigns in the 1980s peaked with a UEFA Cup final appearance in 1987 when they lost 2–1 on aggregate to IFK Gothenburg (Popperfoto)*

Season	Competition	Round	Date	Opponents (Country)	Venue	Result		Scorers
		3	26 Nov 86	Borussia	H	D	1–1	Durrant
			10 Dec 86	Moenchengladbach (West Germany)*	A	D	0–0	
1987–88	European Cup	1	16 Sep 87	Dynamo Kiev (USSR)	A	L	0–1	
			30 Sep 87		H	W	2–0	Falco, McCoist
		2	21 Oct 87	Gomik Zabrze	H	W	3–1	McCoist, Durrant, Falco
			4 Nov 87	(Poland)	A	D	1–1	McCoist (pen)
		QF	2 Mar 88	Steaua Bucharest	A	L	0–2	
			16 Mar 88	(Romania)	H	W	2–1	Gough, McCoist (pen)
1988–89	UEFA Cup	1	7 Sep 88	Katowice (Poland)	H	W	1–0	Walters
			5 Oct 88		A	W	4–2	Butcher 2, Durrant, Ferguson
		2	26 Oct 88	FC Cologne	A	L	0–2	
			9 Nov 88	(West Germany)	H	D	1–1	Drinkell
1989–90	European Cup	1	13 Sep 89	Bayern Munich	H	L	1–3	Walters(pen)
			27 Sep 89	(West Germany)	A	D	0–0	
1990–91	European Cup	1	19 Sep 90	Valetta (Malta)	A	W	4–0	McCoist (pen), Hateley, Johnston
			2 Oct 90		H	W	6–0	Dodds, Spencer, Johnston 3 (1 pen), McCoist
		2	24 Oct 90	Red Star Belgrade	A	L	0–3	
			7 Nov 90	(Yugoslavia)	H	D	1–1	McCoist
1991–92	European Cup	1	18 Sep 91	Sparta Prague	A	L	0–1	
			2 Oct 91	(Czechoslovakia)*	H	W	2–1	McCall 2
1992–93	European Cup	2	16 Sep 92	Lyngby (Denmark)	H	W	2–0	Hateley, Huistra
			30 Sep 92		A	W	1–0	Durrant
		2	21 Oct 92	Leeds United	H	W	2–1	own goal, McCoist
			4 Nov 92	(England)	A	W	2–1	Hateley, McCoist
		SF	25 Nov 92	Marseille (France)	H	D	2–2	McSwegan, Hateley
			9 Dec 92	CSKA Moscow (Russia)	A	W	1–0	Ferguson
			3 Mar 93	FC Bruges (Belgium)	A	D	1–1	Huistra
			17 Mar 93		H	W	2–1	Durrant, Nisbet
			7 Apr 93	Marseille (France)	A	D	1–1	Durrant
			21 Apr 93	CSKA Moscow (Russia)	H	D	0–0	

ST JOHNSTONE

Season	Competition	Round	Date	Opponents (Country)	Venue	Result	Scorers
1971–72	UEFA Cup	1	15 Sep 71	SV Hamburg	A	L 1–2	Pearson
			29 Sep 71	(West Germany)	H	W 3–0	Hall, Pearson, Whitelaw
		2	20 Oct 71	Vasas Budapest	H	W 2–0	Connolly (pen), Pearson
			2 Nov 71	(Hungary)	A	L 0–1	
		3	24 Nov 71	Zeljeznicar	H	W 1–0	Connolly
			8 Dec 71	(Yugoslavia)	A	L 1–5	Rooney

ST MIRREN

1980–81	UEFA Cup	1	17 Sep 80	Elfsborg(Sweden)	A	W 2–1	Somner, Abercromby
			1 Oct 80		H	D 0–0	
		2	22 Oct 80	St Etienne (France)	H	D 0–0	
			5 Nov 80		A	L 0–2	
1983–84	UEFA Cup	1	14 Sep 83	Feyenoord (Holland)	H	L 0–1	
			28 Sep 83		A	L 0–2	
1985–86	UEFA Cup	1	17 Sep 85	Slavia Prague	A	L 0–1	
			2 Oct 85	(Czechoslovakia)	H	W 3–0	Gallagher, McGarvey 2
		2	23 Oct 85	Hammarby (Sweden)	A	D 3–3	Gallagher 3
			6 Nov 85		H	L 1–2	McGarvey
1987–88	Cup-Winners' Cup	1	16 Sep 87	Tromso (Norway)	H	W 1–0	McDowall
			30 Sep 87		A	D 0–0	
		2	21 Oct 87	Mechelen (Belgium)	A	D 0–0	
			4 Nov 87		H	L 0–2	

IRISH LEAGUE CLUBS

ARDS

1958–59	European Cup	Pr	17 Sep 58	Reims(France)	H	L 1–4	Lowry
			8 Oct 58		A	L 2–6	Lawther, Quee
1969–70	Cup-Winners' Cup	1	17 Sep 69	AS Roma (Italy)	H	D 0–0	
			1 Oct 69		A	L 1–3	Crothers
1973–74	UEFA Cup	1	12 Sep 73	Standard Liege	H	W 3–2	Cathcart, McAvoy (pen)
				(Belgium)			McAteer (pen)
			19 Sep 73		A	L 1–6	Guy
1974–75	Cup-Winners' Cup	1	18 Sep 74	PSV Eindhoven	A	L 0–10	
			2 Oct 74	(Holland)	H	L 1–4	Guy

BALLYMENA UNITED

1978–79	Cup-Winners' Cup	1	13 Sep 78	Beveren (Belgium)	A	L 0–3	
			27 Sep 78		H	L 0–3	
1980–81	UEFA Cup	1	17 Sep 80	Vorwaerts	H	W 2–1	McQuiston, Sloan
			1 Oct 80	(East Germany)	A	L 0–3	
1981–82	Cup-Winners' Cup	1	16 Sep 81	AS Roma (Italy)	H	L 0–2	
			30 Sep 81		A	L 0–4	
1984–85	Cup-Winners' Cup	1	19 Sep 84	Hamrun Spartans	H	L 0–1	
			26 Sep 84	(Malta)	A	L 1–2	Beattie
1989–90	Cup-Winners' Cup	1	13 Sep 89	Anderlecht	A	L 0–6	
			27 Sep 89	(Belgium)	H	L 0–4	

BANGOR

1991–92	UEFA Cup	1	18 Sep 91	Sigma Olomouc	H	L 0–3	
			2 Oct 91	(Czechoslovakia)	A	L 0–3	

CARRICK RANGERS

Season	Competition	Round	Date	Opponents (Country)	Venue	Result		Scorers
1966–77	Cup-Winners' Cup	I	15 Sep 76	Aris Bonnevoie	H	W	3–I	Prenter 2, Connor
			6 Oct 76	(Luxembourg)	A	L	1–2	Erwin
		2	20 Oct 76	Southampton	H	L	2–5	Erwin, Prenter
			3 Nov 76	(England)	A	L	1–4	Reid

CLIFTONVILLE

1979–80	Cup-Winners' Cup	I	20 Sep 79	Nantes (France)	H	L	0–I	
			3 Oct 79		A	L	0–7	

COLERAINE

1965–66	Cup-Winners' Cup	I	2 Sep 65	Dynamo Kiev (USSR)	H	L	1–6	Curley
			8 Sep 65		A	L	0–4	
1969–70	Fairs Cup	I	17 Sep 69	Jeunesse D'Esch	A	L	2–3	Curley, Murray
			I Oct 69	(Luxembourg)	H	W	4–0	Dickson 2, Wilson, Jennings
		2	II Nov 69	Anderlecht (Belgium)	A	L	1–6	Murray
			20 Nov 69		H	L	3–7	Dickson 2, Irwin
1970–71	Fairs Cup	I	15 Sep 70	Kilmarnock (Scotland)	H	D	1–I	Mullan
			29 Sep 70		A	W	3–2	Dickson 3
		2	20 Oct 70	Sparta Rotterdam	A	L	0–2	
			4 Nov 70	(Holland)	H	L	1–2	Jennings
1974–75	European Cup	I	18 Sep 74	Feyenoord (Holland)	A	L	0–7	
			2 Oct 74		H	L	1–4	Simpson
1975–76	Cup-Winners' Cup	I	16 Sep 75	Eintracht Frankfurt	A	L	1–5	Cochrane
			30 Sep 75	(West Germany)	H	L	2–6	McCurdy, Cochrane
1977–78	Cup-Winners' Cup	I	14 Sep 77	Lokomotive Leipzig	H	L	1–4	Tweed
			28 Sep 77	(East Germany)	A	D	2–2	Guy 2
1982–83	Cup-Winners' Cup	I	15 Sep 82	Tottenham Hotspur	H	L	0–3	
			28 Sep 82	(England)	A	L	0–4	
1983–84	UEFA Cup	I	14 Sep 83	Sparta Rotterdam	A	L	0–4	
			28 Sep 83	(Holland)	H	D	1–I	Healy
1985–86	UEFA Cup	I	18 Sep 85	Lokomotive Leipzig	H	D	1–I	Wade
			2 Oct 85	(East Germany)	A	L	0–5	
1986–87	UEFA Cup	I	17 Sep 86	Stahl Brandenburg	H	D	1–I	Healy (pen)
			I Oct 86	(East Germany)	A	L	0–I	
1987–88	UEFA Cup	I	16 Oct 87	Dundee United	H	L	0–I	
				(Scotland)	A	L	1–3	Edgar

CRUSADERS

1967–68	Cup-Winners' Cup	I	20 Sep 67	Valencia (Spain)	A	L	0–4	
			4 Oct 67		H	L	2–4	Trainor, Magill
1968–69	Cup-Winners' Cup	I	18 Sep 68	Norrkoping (Sweden)	H	D	2–2	Jamison, Parke
			2 Oct 68		A	L	1–4	McPolin
1973–74	European Cup	I	19 Sep 73	Dinamo Bucharest	H	L	0–I	
			3 Oct 73	(Romania)	A	L	0–11	
1976–77	European Cup	I	14 Sep 76	Liverpool (England)	A	L	0–2	
			28 Sep 76		H	L	0–5	
1980–81	Cup-Winners' Cup	I	16 Sep 80	Newport County	A	L	0–4	
			I Oct 80	(Wales)	H	D	0–0	

DERRY CITY

1964–65	Cup-Winners' Cup	I	9 Sep 64	Steaua Bucharest	A	L	0–3	

Season	Competition	Round	Date	Opponents (Country)	Venue	Result	Scorers
			16 Sep 64	(Rumania)	H	L 0–2	
1965–66	European Cup	Pr	31 Aug 65	Lyn Oslo (Norway)	A	L 3–5	Wood (R), Gilbert 2
			9 Sep 65		H	W 5–1	Wilson 2, Crossan, Wood (R), McGeough
		I	23 Nov 65	Anderlecht (Belgium)	A	L 0–9	
				Derry City withdrew			

DISTILLERY

Season	Competition	Round	Date	Opponents (Country)	Venue	Result	Scorers
1963–64	European Cup	Pr	25 Sep 63	Benfica (Portugal)	H	D 3–3	John Kennedy, Hamilton, Ellison
			2 Oct 63		A	L 0–5	
1971–72	Cup-Winners' Cup	I	15 Sep 71	Barcelona (Spain)	H	L 1–3	O'Neill
			29 Sep 71		A	L 0–4	

GLENAVON

Season	Competition	Round	Date	Opponents (Country)	Venue	Result	Scorers
1957–58	European Cup	Pr	11 Sep 57	Aarhus (Denmark)	A	D 0–0	
			25 Sep 57		H	L 0–3	
1960–61	European Cup	Pr		withdrew			
1961–62	Cup-Winners' Cup	I	13 Sep 61	Leicester City	H	L 1–4	Jones
			27 Sep 61	(England)	A	L 1–3	Wilson
1977–78	UEFA Cup	I	14 Sep 77	PSV Eindhoven	H	L 2–6	Malone (pen), McDonald
			28 Sep 77	(Holland)	A	L 0–5	
1979–80	UEFA Cup	I	18 Sep 79	Standard Liege	H	L 0–1	
			3 Oct 79	(Belgium)	A	L 0–1	
1988–89	Cup-Winners' Cup	I	7 Sep 88	Aarhus (Denmark)	H	L 1–4	McCann
			5 Oct 88		A	L 1–3	McConville
1990–91	UEFA Cup	I	18 Sep 90	Bordeaux (France)	H	D 0–0	
			2 Oct 90		A	L 0–2	
1991–92	Cup-Winners' Cup	I	17 Sep 91	Ilves Tampere	H	W 3–2	Ferguson, McBride (pen), Conville
			2 Oct 91	(Finalnd)*	A	L 1–2	McBride
1992–93	Cup-Winners' Cup	I	15 Sep 92	Antwerp (Belgium)+	H	D 1–1	Smith
			30 Sep 92		A	D 1–1	Farris

GLENTORAN

Season	Competition	Round	Date	Opponents (Country)	Venue	Result	Scorers
1962–63	Fairs Cup	I	26 Sep 62	Real Zaragoza (Spain)	H	L 0–2	
			10 Oct 62		A	L 2–6	Doherty 2
1963–64	Fairs Cup	I	16 Sep 63	Partick Thistle	H	L 1–4	Thompson
			30 Sep 63	(Scotland)	A	L 0–3	
1964–65	European Cup	Pr	16 Sep 64	Panathinaikos	H	D 2–2	Turner, Thompson
			30 Sep 64	(Greece)	A	L 2–3	Turner, Pavis
1965–66	Fairs Cup	I	28 Sep 65	Antwerp (Belgium)	A	L 0–1	
			6 Oct 65		H	D 3–3	Hamilton, Thompson 2
1966–67	Cup-Winners' Cup	I	27 Sep 66	Rangers (Scotland)	H	D 1–1	Sinclair
			5 Oct 66		A	L 0–4	
1967–68	European Cup	I	13 Sep 67	Benfica (Portugal)*	H	D 1–1	Colrain (pen)
			4 Oct 67		A	D 0–0	
1968–69	European Cup	I	18 Sep 68	Anderlecht (Belgium)	A	L 0–3	
			2 Oct 68		H	D 2–2	Morrow, Johnston
1969–70	Fairs Cup	I	9 Sep 69	Arsenal (England)	A	L 0–3	
			29 Sep 69		H	W 1–0	Henderson
1970–71	European Cup	I	16 Sep 70	Waterford (Eire)	H	L 1–3	Hall
			30 Sep 70		A	L 0–1	
1971–72	UEFA Cup	I	14 Sep 71	Eintracht Brunswick	H	L 0–1	
			28 Sep 71	(West Germany)	A	L 1–6	McCaffrey
1973–74	Cup-Winners' Cup	I	19 Sep 73	Chimea Ramnicu	A	D 2–2	Jamison, McCreary
			3 Oct 73	(Romania)	H	W 2–0	Jamison, Craig

Season	Competition	Round	Date	Opponents (Country)	Venue	Result		Scorers
		2	24 Oct 73	Brann Bergen	A	D	1–1	Feeney
			7 Nov 73	(Norway)	H	W	3–1	Feeney, Jamison 2
		QF	5 May 74	Borussia	H	L	0–2	
			20 May 74	Moenchengladbach (West Germany)	A	L	0–5	
1975–76	UEFA Cup	1	16 Sep 75	Ajax (Holland)	H	L	1–6	Jamison
			1 Oct 75		A	L	0–8	
1976–77	UEFA Cup	1	14 Sep 76	Basle (Switzerland)	H	W	3–2	Feeney 2, Dickenson
			29 Sep 76		A	L	0–3	
1977–78	European Cup	1	15 Sep 77	Valur (Iceland)	A	L	0–1	
			29 Sep 77		H	W	2–0	Robson, Jamison
		2	19 Oct 77	Juventus (Italy)	H	L	0–1	
			2 Nov 77		A	L	0–5	
1978–79	UEFA Cup	1	5 Sep 78	IBV Westman*	A	D	0–0	
			14 Sep 78	(Iceland)	H	D	1–1	Caskey (J)
1981–82	European Cup	1	16 Sep 81	Progres Niedercom	A	D	1–1	Cleary
			30 Sep 81	(Luxembourg)	H	W	4–0	Blackledge 2, Jameson, Manley
		2	21 Oct 81	CSKA Sofia (Bulgaria)	A	L	0–2	
			4 Nov 81		H	W	2–1	Cleary, Manley
1982–83	UEFA Cup	1	15 Sep 82	Banik Ostrava	H	L	1–3	Bowers
			29 Sep 82	(Czechoslovakia)	A	L	0–1	
1983–84	Cup-Winners' Cup	1	14 Sep 83	Paris St Germain	H	L	1–2	Jameson
			28 Sep 83	(France)	A	L	1–2	Mullan
1984–85	UEFA Cup	1	18 Sep 84	Standard Liege	H	D	1–1	Bowers
			3 Oct 84	(Belgium)	A	L	0–2	
1985–86	Cup-Winners' Cup	1	21 Sep 85	Fram (Iceland)	A	L	1–3	Bowers
			2 Oct 85		H	W	1–0	Mullan
1986–87	Cup-Winners' Cup	1	17 Sep 86	Lokomotive Leipzig	H	D	1–1	Cleary
			1 Oct 86	(East Germany)	A	L	0–2	
1987–88	Cup-Winners' Cup	1	16 Sep 87	Ropa Rovaniemi*	A	D	0–0	
			30 Sep 87	(Finland)	H	D	1–1	Caskey (W)
1988–89	European Cup	1	7 Sep 88	Moscow Spartak	A	L	0–2	
			5 Oct 88	(USSR)	H	D	1–1	Moore
1989–90	UEFA Cup	1	13 Sep 89	Dundee United	H	L	1–3	Jameson
			27 Sep 89	(Scotland)	A	L	0–2	
1990–91	Cup-Winners' Cup	1	19 Sep 90	Steaua Bucharest	H	D	1–1	Douglas
			3 Oct 90	(Romania)	A	L	0–5	
1992–93	European Cup	1	16 Sep 92	Marseille	H	L	0–5	
			30 Sep 92	(France)	A	L	0–3	

LINFIELD

Season	Competition	Round	Date	Opponents (Country)	Venue	Result		Scorers
1959–60	European Cup	Pr	9 Sep 59	Gothenburg (Sweden)	H	W	2–1	Milburn 2
			23 Sep 59		A	L	1–6	Dickson
1961–62	European Cup	Pr	30 Aug 61	Vorwaerts (East Germany)	A	L	0–3	
					Linfield withdrew			
1962–63	European Cup	Pr	5 Sep 62	Esbjerg (Denmark)	H	L	1–2	Dickson
			19 Sep 62		A	D	0–0	
1963–64	Cup-Winners' Cup	1		bye				
		2	13 Nov 63	Fenerbahce (Turkey)	A	L	1–4	Dickson
			11 Dec 63		H	W	2–0	Craig, Ferguson
1966–67	European Cup	1	7 Sep 66	Aris Bonnevoie	A	D	3–3	Hamilton, Pavis, Scott
			16 Sep 66	(Luxembourg)	A	W	6–1	Thomas 3, Scott, Pavis
		2	26 Oct 66	Valerengen (Norway)	A	W	4–1	Scott, Pavis, Thomas (pen), Shields
			8 Nov 66		H	D	1–1	Thomas
		QF	1 Mar 67	CSKA Sofia (Bulgaria)	H	D	2–2	Hamilton, Shields
			15 Mar 67		A	L	0–1	
1967–68	Fairs Cup	1	19 Sep 67	Lokomotive Leipzig	A	L	1–5	Pavis

			4 Oct 67	(East Germany)	H	W	1–0	Hamilton
1968–69	Fairs Cup	1	18 Sep 68	Setubal (Portugal)	A	L	0–3	
			9 Oct 68		H	L	1–3	Scott
1969–70	European Cup	1	17 Sep 69	Red Star Belgrade	A	L	0–8	
			1 Oct 69	(Yugoslavia)	H	L	2–4	McGraw 2
1970–71	Cup-Winners' Cup	1	16 Sep 70	Manchester City*	A	L	0–1	
			30 Sep 70	(England)	H	W	2–1	Millen 2
1971–72	European Cup	1	15 Sep 71	Standard Liege	A	L	0–2	
			29 Sep 71	(Belgium)	H	L	2–3	Magee, Lamour
1975–76	European Cup	1	17 Sep 75	PSV Eindhoven	H	L	1–2	Malone (P)
			1 Oct 75	(Holland)	A	L	0–8	
1978–79	European Cup	1	13 Sep 78	Lillestrom (Norway)	H	D	0–0	
			27 Sep 78		A	L	0–1	
1979–80	European Cup	Pr	29 Aug 79	Dundalk (Eire)	A	D	1–1	Feeney
			5 Sep 79	(in Haarlem, Holland)	H	L	0–2	
1980–81	European Cup	1	16 Sep 80	Nantes (France)	H	L	0–1	
			30 Sep 80		A	L	0–2	
1981–82	UEFA Cup	1	16 Sep 81	Beveren (Belgium)	A	L	0–3	
			29 Sep 81		H	L	0–5	
1982–83	European Cup	1	15 Sep 82	17 Nendori (Albania)	A	L	0–1	
			29 Sep 82		H	W	2–1	Gibson, Anderson
1983–84	European Cup	1	14 Sep 83	Benfica (Portugal)	A	L	0–3	
			28 Sep 83		H	L	2–3	Walsh, own goal
1984–85	European Cup	1	19 Sep 84	Shamrock Rovers	H	D	0–0	
			3 Oct 84	(Eire)	A	D	1–1*	Jeffrey
		2	24 Oct 84	Panathinaikos	A	L	1–2	Totten
			7 Oct 84	(Greece)	H	D	3–3	McGaughey 2 (1 pen), Maxwell
1985–86	European Cup	1	18 Sep 85	Servette	H	D	2–2	Anderson, McKeown
			2 Oct 85	(Switzerland)	A	L	1–2	Anderson
1986–87	European Cup	1	17 Sep 86	Rosenborg (Norway)	A	L	0–1	
			1 Oct 86		H	D	1–1	McKeown (pen)
1987–88	European Cup	1	16 Sep 87	Lillestrom (Norway)	A	D	1–1	Baxter
			30 Sep 87		H	L	2–4	McGaughey 2
1988–89	UEFA Cup	1	7 Sep 88	TPS Turun (Finland)	A	D	0–0	
			5 Oct 88		H	D	1–1*	O'Boyle
1989–90	European Cup	1	13 Sep 89	Dnepr (USSR)	H	L	1–2	Mooney (pen)
			27 Sep 89		A	L	0–1	

PORTADOWN

1962–63	Cup-Winners' Cup	1		bye				
		2	7 Nov 62	OFK Belgrade	A	L	1–5	Clements
			22 Nov 62	(Yugoslavia)	H	W	3–2	Burke, Jones, Cush
1974–75	UEFA Cup	1	18 Sep 74	Valur (Iceland)	A	D	0–0	
			1 Oct 74		H	W	2–1	MacFaul, Morrison (pen)
		2	23 Oct 74	Partizan Belgrade	A	L	0–5	
			6 Nov 74	(Yugoslavia)	H	D	1–1	Malcolmson
1990–91	European Cup	1	19 Sep 90	Porto (Portugal)	A	L	0–5	
			3 Oct 90		H	L	1–8	Fraser
1991–92	European Cup	1	17 Sep 91	Red Star Belgrade	A	L	0–4	
			2 Oct 91	(Yugoslavia)	H	L	0–4	
1992–93	UEFA Cup	1	16 Sep 92	Liege (Belgium)	A	L	0–5	
			29 Sep 92		H	D	0–0	

LEAGUE OF IRELAND CLUBS

ATHLONE TOWN

Season	Competition	Round	Date	Opponents (Country)	Venue	Result		Scorers
1975–76	UEFA Cup	1	18 Sep 75	Valerengen (Norway)	H	W	3–0	Martin, Davis 2
			1 Oct 75		A	D	1–1	Martin
		2	22 Oct 75	AC Milan (Italy)	H	D	0–0	
			5 Nov 75		A	L	0–3	
1981–82	European Cup	1	16 Sep 81	KB Copenhagen	A	D	1–1	O'Connor (M)
			30 Sep 81	(Denmark)	H	D	2–2	Davis 2
1983–84	European Cup	1	14 Sep 83	Standard Liege	H	L	2–3	Collins, Salmon
			28 Sep 83	(Belgium)	A	L	2–8	Salmon, Hitchcock

BOHEMIANS

Season	Competition	Round	Date	Opponents (Country)	Venue	Result		Scorers
1970–71	Cup-Winners' Cup	Pr	26 Aug 70	Gottwaldov	H	L	1–2	Swan (pen)
			2 Sep 70	(Czechoslovakia)	A	D	2–2	O'Connell, Dunne
1972–73	UEFA Cup	1	13 Sep 72	FC Cologne	A	L	1–2	Daly
			27 Sep 72	(West Germany)	H	L	0–3	
1974–75	UEFA Cup	1	18 Sep 74	SV Hamburg	A	L	0–3	
			2 Oct 74	(West Germany)	H	L	0–1	
1975–76	European Cup	1	17 Sep 75	Rangers (Scotland)	A	L	1–4	Flanagan
			1 Oct 75		H	D	1–1	O'Connor (T)
1976–77	Cup-Winners' Cup	1	15 Sep 76	Esbjerg (Denmark)	H	W	2–1	Ryan (B), own goal
			29 Sep 76		A	W	1–0	Mitten
		2	20 Oct 76	Slask Wroclaw	A	L	0–3	
			3 Nov 76	(Poland)	H	L	0–1	
1978–79	European Cup	1	13 Sep 78	Omonia Nicosia	A	L	1–2	O'Connor (P)
			27 Sep 78	(Cyprus)	H	W	1–0	Joyce
		2	18 Oct 78	Dynamo Dresden	H	D	0–0	
			1 Nov 78	(East Germany)	A	L	0–6	
1979–80	UEFA Cup	1	19 Sep 79	Sporting Lisbon	A	L	0–2	
			3 Oct 79	(Portugal)	H	D	0–0	
1984–85	UEFA Cup	1	18 Sep 84	Rangers (Scotland)	H	W	3–2	O'Brien 2, Lawless
			3 Oct 84		A	L	0–2	
1987–88	UEFA Cup	1	15 Sep 87	Aberdeen (Scotland)	H	D	0–0	
			30 Sep 87		A	L	0–1	
1992–93	Cup-Winners' Cup	1	16 Sep 92	Steaua Bucharest	H	D	0–0	
			29 Sep 92	(Romania)	A	L	0–4	

BRAY WANDERERS

Season	Competition	Round	Date	Opponents (Country)	Venue	Result		Scorers
1990–91	Cup-Winners' Cup	Pr	22 Aug 90	Trabzonspor	H	D	1–1	Nugent
			5 Sep 90	(Turkey)	A	L	0–2	

CORK CELTIC

Season	Competition	Round	Date	Opponents (Country)	Venue	Result		Scorers
1964–65	Cup-Winners' Cup	1	30 Sep 64	Slavia Sofia (Bulgaria)	A	D	1–1	Leahy
			7 Oct 64		H	L	0–2	
1974–75	European Cup	1		walkover				
		2	23 Oct 74	Ararat Erevan (USSR)	H	L	1–2	Tambling
			6 Nov 74		A	L	0–5	
1989–90	Cup-Winners' Cup	1	13 Sep 89	Moscow Torpedo	A	L	0–5	
			27 Sep 89	(USSR)	H	L	0–1	

CORK CITY

Season	Competition	Round	Date	Opponents (Country)	Venue	Result		Scorers
1991–92	UEFA Cup	1	18 Sep 91	Bayern Munich	H	D	1–1	Barry
			1 Oct 91	(Germany)	A	L	0–2	

CORK HIBS

Season	Competition	Round	Date	Opponents (Country)	Venue	Result		Scorers
1970–71	Fairs Cup	I	16 Sep 70	Valencia (Spain)	H	L	0–3	
			26 Sep 70		A	L	1–3	Wigginton
1971–72	European Cup	I	15 Sep 71	Borussia	H	L	0–5	
			29 Sep 71	Moenchengladbach (West Germany)	A	L	1–2	Dennehy
1972–73	Cup-Winners' Cup	I	10 Sep 72	Pezoporikos (Cyprus)	A	W	2–1	Lawson (pen), Sheehan
			13 Sep 72		H	W	4–1	Wallace, Lawson 2, Dennehy
		2	25 Oct 72	Schalke 04	H	D	0–0	
			8 Nov 72	(West Germany)	A	L	0–3	
1973–74	Cup-Winners' Cup	I	19 Sep 73	Banik Ostrava	A	L	0–1	
			3 Oct 73	(Czechoslovakia)	H	L	1–2	Humphries

DERRY CITY

Season	Competition	Round	Date	Opponents (Country)	Venue	Result		Scorers
1988–89	Cup-Winners' Cup	I	7 Sep 88	Cardiff City (Wales)	H	D	0–0	
			5 Oct 88		A	L	0–4	
1989–90	European Cup	I	13 Sep 89	Benfica (Portugal)	H	L	1–2	Carlyle
			27 Sep 89		A	L	0–4	
1990–91	UEFA Cup	I	19 Sep 90	Vitesse (Holland)	H	L	0–1	
			2 Oct 90		A	D	0–0	
1992–93	UEFA Cup	I	16 Sep 92	Vitesse (Holland)	A	L	0–3	
			29 Sep 92		H	L	1–2	Mooney

DROGHEDA

Season	Competition	Round	Date	Opponents (Country)	Venue	Result		Scorers
1983–84	UEFA Cup	I	14 Sep 83	Tottenham Hotspur	H	L	0–6	
			28 Sep 83	(England)	A	L	0–8	

DRUMCONDRA

Season	Competition	Round	Date	Opponents (Country)	Venue	Result		Scorers
1958–59	European Cup	Pr	17 Sep 58	Atletico Madrid	A	L	0–8	
			I Oct 58	(Spain)	H	L	1–5	Fullam (pen)
1961–62	European Cup	Pr	23 Aug 61	FC Nuremberg	A	L	0–5	
			13 Sep 61	(West Germany)	H	L	1–4	Fullam
1962–63	Fairs Cup	I	3 Oct 62	Odense BK 09	H	W	4–1	Dixon 2, Morrissey, McCann
			17 Oct 62	(Denmark)	A	L	2–4	Rice, Morrissey
		2	4 Dec 62	Bayern Munich	A	L	0–6	
			12 Dec 62	(West Germany)	H	W	1–0	Dixon
1965–66	European Cup	Pr	15 Sep 65	Vorwaerts	H	W	1–0	Morrissey
			22 Sep 65	(East Germany)	A	L	0–3	
1966–67	Fairs Cup	I	21 Sep 66	Eintracht Frankfurt	H	L	0–2	
			5 Oct 66	(West Germany)	A	L	1–6	Whelan

DUNDALK

Season	Competition	Round	Date	Opponents (Country)	Venue	Result		Scorers
1963–64	European Cup	Pr	11 Sep 63	Zurich (Switzerland)	H	L	0–3	
			25 Sep 63		A	W	2–1	Cross, Hasty
1967–68	European Cup	I	20 Sep 67	Vasas Budapest	H	L	0–1	
			11 Oct 67	(Hungary)	A	L	1–8	Hale
1968–69	Fairs Cup	I	11 Sep 68	DOS Utrecht (Holland)	A	D	1–1	Stokes
			I Oct 68		H	W	2–1	Stokes, Morrissey
		2	30 Oct 68	Rangers (Scotland)	A	L	1–6	Murray (pen)
			13 Nov 68		H	L	0–3	
1969–70	Fairs Cup	I	16 Sep 69	Liverpool (England)	A	L	0–10	
			30 Sep 69		H	L	0–4	
1976–77	European Cup	I	15 Sep 76	PSV Eindhoven	H	D	1–1	McDowell
			29 Sep 76	(Holland)	A	L	0–6	
1977–78	Cup-Winners' Cup	I	14 Sep 77	Hajduk Split	H	W	1–0	Flanagan

Season	Competition	Round	Date	Opponents (Country)	Venue	Result		Scorers
			28 Sep 77	(Yugoslavia)	A	L	0–4	
1979–80	European Cup	Pr	29 Aug 79	Linfield (Northern Ireland)	H	D	1–1	Devine
			5 Sep 79	(in Haarlem, Holland)	A	W	2–0	Muckian 2
		1	19 Sep 79	Hibernians (Malta)	H	W	2–0	Carlyle, Devine
			26 Sep 79		A	L	0–1	
		2	24 Oct 79	Celtic (Scotland)	A	L	2–3	Muckian, Lawlor
			7 Nov 79		H	D	0–0	
1980–81	UEFA Cup	1	16 Sep 80	Porto (Portugal)	A	L	0–1	
			1 Oct 80		H	D	0–0	
1981–82	Cup-Winners' Cup	1	16 Sep 81	Fram (Iceland)	A	L	1–2	Fairclough
			30 Sep 81		H	W	4–0	Flanagan (pen), Fairclough, Lawlor, Duff
		2	21 Oct 81	Tottenham Hotspur	H	D	1–1	Fairclough
			4 Nov 81	(England)	A	L	0–1	
1982–83	European Cup	1	14 Sep 82	Liverpool (England)	H	L	1–4	Flanagan
			28 Sep 82		A	L	0–1	
1987–88	Cup-Winners' Cup	1	16 Sep 87	Ajax (Holland)	A	L	0–4	
			30 Sep 87		H	L	0–2	
1988–89	European Cup	1	7 Sep 88	Red Star Belgrade	H	L	0–5	
			5 Oct 88	(Yugoslavia)	A	L	0–3	
1989–90	UEFA Cup	1	13 Sep 89	Wettingen	A	L	0–3	
			27 Sep 89	(Switzerland)	H	L	0–2	
1991–92	European Cup	1	18 Sep 91	Kispest Honved	A	D	1–1	McEvoy
			2 Oct 91	(Hungary)	H	L	0–2	

FINN HARPS

Season	Competition	Round	Date	Opponents (Country)	Venue	Result		Scorers
1973–74	UEFA Cup	1	19 Sep 73	Aberdeen (Scotland)	A	L	1–4	Harkin
			3 Oct 73		H	L	1–3	Harkin
1974–75	Cup-Winners' Cup	1	18 Nov 74	Bursaspor (Turkey)	A	L	2–4	Ferry, Bradley
					H	D	0–0	
1976–77	UEFA Cup	1	15 Sep 76	Derby County	A	L	0–12	
			29 Sep 76	(England)	H	L	1–4	own goal
1978–79	UEFA Cup	1	12 Sep 78	Everton (England)	H	L	0–5	
			26 Sep 78		A	L	0–5	

GALWAY UNITED

Season	Competition	Round	Date	Opponents (Country)	Venue	Result		Scorers
1985–86	Cup-Winners' Cup	1	18 Sep 85	Lyngby (Denmark)	A	L	0–1	
			2 Oct 85		H	L	2–3	Murphy, Bonner
1986–87	UEFA Cup	1	16 Sep 86	Groningen (Holland)	A	L	1–5	McGee (pen)
			1 Oct 86		H	L	1–3	Murphy
1991–92	Cup-Winners' Cup	Pr	21 Aug 91	Odense (Denmark)	H	L	0–3	
			3 Sep 91		A	L	0–4	

HOME FARM

Season	Competition	Round	Date	Opponents (Country)	Venue	Result		Scorers
1975–76	Cup-Winners' Cup	1	17 Aug 75	Lens (France)	H	D	1–1	Brophy
			1 Oct 75		A	L	0–6	

LIMERICK

Season	Competition	Round	Date	Opponents (Country)	Venue	Result		Scorers
1960–61	European Cup	Pr	31 Aug 60	Young Boys	H	L	0–5	
			5 Oct 60	(Switzerland)	A	L	2–4	Lynam, O'Reilly
1965–66	Cup-Winners' Cup	1	7 Oct 65	CSKA Sofia (Bulgaria)	H	L	1–2	O'Connor
			13 Oct 65		A	L	0–2	
1971–72	Cup-Winners' Cup	1	15 Sep 71	Torino (Italy)	H	L	0–1	
			29 Sep 71		A	L	0–4	

Season	Competition	Round	Date	Opponents (Country)	Venue	Result		Scorers
1980–81	European Cup	I	17 Sep 80	Real Madrid (Spain)	H	L	1–2	Kennedy
			I Oct 80		A	L	1–5	Kennedy
1981–82	UEFA Cup	I	16 Sep 81	Southampton	H	L	0–3	
			29 Sep 81	(England)	A	D	1–1	Morris
1982–83	Cup-Winners' Cup	I	15 Sep 82	AZ67 (Holland)	H	D	1–1	Nolan
			30 Sep 82		A	L	0–1	

SHAMROCK ROVERS

Season	Competition	Round	Date	Opponents (Country)	Venue	Result		Scorers
1957–58	European Cup	Pr	25 Sep 57	Manchester United	H	L	0–6	
			2 Oct 57	(England)	A	L	2–3	McCann, Hamilton
1959–60	European Cup	Pr	26 Aug 59	Nice (France)	A	L	2–3	Hamilton, Tuohy
			23 Sep 59		H	D	1–1	Hennessy
1962–63	Cup-Winners' Cup	I		bye				
		2	24 Oct 62	Botev Plovdiv	H	L	0–4	
			14 Nov 62	(Bulgaria)	A	L	0–1	
1963–64	Fairs Cup	I	18 Sep 63	Valencia (Spain)	H	L	0–1	
			10 Oct 63		A	D	2–2	O'Neill, Mooney
1964–65	European Cup	Pr	16 Sep 64	Rapid Vienna (Austria)	A	L	0–3	
			30 Sep 64		H	L	0–2	
1965–66	Fairs Cup	I		bye				
		2	17 Nov 65	Real Zaragoza (Spain)	H	D	1–1	Tuohy
			24 Nov 65		A	L	1–2	Fullam
1966–67	Cup-Winners' Cup	I	28 Sep 66	Spora (Luxembourg)	H	W	4–1	Fullam, Dixon, Kearin, O'Neill (pen)
			5 Oct 66		A	W	4–1	Kearin, Dixon 2, O'Neill
		2	9 Nov 66	Bayern Munich	H	D	1–1	Dixon
			23 Nov 66	(West Germany)	A	L	2–3	Gilbert, O'Neill
1967–68	Cup-Winners' Cup	I	20 Sep 67	Cardiff City (Wales)	H	D	1–1	Gilbert
			4 Oct 67		A	L	0–2	
1968–69	Cup-Winners' Cup	I	18 Sep 68	Randers Freja	A	L	0–1	
			2 Oct 68	(Denmark)	H	L	1–2	Fullam
1969–70	Cup-Winners' Cup	I	17 Sep 69	Schalke 04	H	W	2–1	Barber 2
			I Oct 69	(West Germany)	A	L	0–3	
1978–79	Cup-Winners' Cup	I	13 Sep 78	Apoel Nicosia	H	W	2–0	Giles, Lynex
			27 Sep 78	(Cyprus)	A	W	1–0	Lynex
		2	18 Oct 78	Banik Ostrava	A	L	0–3	
			I Nov 78	(Czechoslovakia)	H	L	1–3	Giles
1982–83	UEFA Cup	I	15 Sep 82	Fram (Iceland)	A	W	3–0	Murphy, Campbell, Gaynor
			30 Sep 82		H	W	4–0	O'Carroll, Buckley, Beglin, Gaynor
		2	21 Oct 82	Uni. Craiova	H	L	0–2	
			3 Nov 82	(Romania)	A	L	0–3	
1984–85	European Cup	I	19 Sep 84	Linfield*	A	D	0–0	
			3 Oct 84	(Northern Ireland)	H	D	1–1	Eccles
1985–86	European Cup	I	18 Sep 85	Honved (Hungary)	A	L	0–2	
			2 Oct 85		H	L	1–3	Coady
1986–87	European Cup	I	17 Sep 86	Celtic (Scotland)	H	L	0–1	
			I Oct 86		A	L	0–2	
1987–88	European Cup	I	16 Sep 87	Omonia Nicosia	H	L	0–1	
			30 Sep 87	(Cyprus)	A	D	0–0	

SHELBOURNE

Season	Competition	Round	Date	Opponents (Country)	Venue	Result		Scorers
1962–63	European Cup	Pr	19 Sep 62	Sporting Lisbon	H	L	0–2	
			27 Sep 62	(Portugal)	A	L	1–5	Hennessy
1963–64	Cup-Winners' Cup	I	24 Sep 63	Barcelona (Spain)	H	L	0–2	
			15 Oct 63		A	L	1–3	Bonham (pen)
1964–65	Fairs Cup	I	16 Sep 64	Belenenses (Portugal)	A	D	1–1	Barber
			14 Oct 64		H	D	0–0	

Season	Competition	Round	Date	Opponents (Country)	Venue	Result		Scorers
			28 Oct 64		N	W	2–1	Hannigan, Conroy (M)
		2	25 Nov 64	Atletico Madrid	H	L	0–1	
			2 Dec 64	(Spain)	A	L	0–1	
1971–72	UEFA Cup	1	15 Sep 71	Vasas Budapest	A	L	0–1	
			29 Sep 71	(Hungary)	H	D	1–1	Murray
1992–93	European Cup	Pr	19 Aug 92	Tavria Simferopol	H	D	0–0	
			2 Sep 92	(Ukraine)	A	L	1–2	Daly

SLIGO ROVERS

Season	Competition	Round	Date	Opponents (Country)	Venue	Result		Scorers
1983–84	European Cup	1	14 Sep 83	Haka Valkeakosken	H	L	0–1	
			28 Sep 83	(Finland)	A	L	0–3	

ST PATRICK'S ATHLETIC

Season	Competition	Round	Date	Opponents (Country)	Venue	Result		Scorers
1961–62	Cup-Winners' Cup	Pr	12 Sep 61	Dunfermline Athletic	A	L	1–4	O'Rourke
			27 Sep 61	(Scotland)	H	L	0–4	
1967–68	Fairs Cup	1	13 Sep 67	Bordeaux (France)	H	L	1–3	Hennessy
			11 Oct 67		A	L	3–6	Campbell 2, Ryan
1988–89	UEFA Cup	1	7 Sep 88	Hearts (Scotland)	H	L	0–2	
			5 Oct 88		A	L	0–2	
1990–91	European Cup	1	19 Sep 90	Dinamo Bucharest	A	L	0–4	
			3 Oct 90	(Romania)	H	D	1–1	Fenlon

UCD

Season	Competition	Round	Date	Opponents (Country)	Venue	Result		Scorers
1984–85	Cup-Winners' Cup	1	19 Sep 84	Everton (England)	H	D	0–0	
			2 Oct 84		A	L	0–1	

WATERFORD

Season	Competition	Round	Date	Opponents (Country)	Venue	Result		Scorers
1966–67	European Cup	Pr	31 Aug 66	Vorwaerts Berlin	H	L	1–5	Lynch
			9 Sep 66	(East Germany)	A	L	0–6	
1968–69	European Cup	1	18 Sep 68	Manchester United	H	L	1–3	Matthews
			2 Oct 68	(England)	A	L	1–7	Casey
1969–70	European Cup	1	17 Sep 69	Galatasaray (Turkey)	A	L	0–2	
			1 Oct 69		H	L	2–3	Buck, Morley
1970–71	European Cup	1	16 Sep 70	Glentoran	A	W	3–1	O'Neill, McGeough, Casey
			30 Sep 70	(Northern Ireland)	H	W	1–0	Casey
		2	21 Oct 70	Celtic (Scotland)	H	L	0–7	
			4 Nov 70		A	L	2–3	Matthews, own goal
1972–73	European Cup	1	13 Sep 72	Omonia Nicosia	H	W	2–1	Hale 2
			27 Sep 72	(Cyprus)	A	L	0–2	
1973–74	European Cup	1	19 Sep 73	Ujpest Dozsa	A	L	2–3	Kirby, O'Neill
			3 Oct 73	(Hungary)	A	L	0–3	
1979–80	Cup-Winners' Cup	1	19 Sep 79	Gothenburg (Sweden)	A	L	0–1	
			3 Oct 79		H	D	1–1	Keane
1980–81	Cup-Winners' Cup	1	17 Sep 80	Hibemians (Malta)	A	L	0–1	
			1 Oct 80		H	W	4–0	Kirk 2, Finucane, Fitzpatrick
		2	22 Oct 80	Dynamo Tbilisi	H	L	0–1	
			5 Nov 80	(USSR)	A	L	0–4	
1986–87	Cup-Winners' Cup	1	17 Sep 86	Bordeaux (France)	H	L	1–2	Synnott
			30 Sep 86		A	L	0–4	

WELSH NON-LEAGUE CLUBS

BANGOR CITY

Season	Competition	Round	Date	Opponents (Country)	Venue	Result		Scorers
1962–63	Cup-Winners' Cup	1	5 Sep 62	Napoli (Italy)	H	W	2–0	Matthews, Birch (pen)

Season	Competition	Round	Date	Opponents (Country)	Venue	Result		Scorers
			26 Sep 62		A	L	1–3	McAlister
			10 Oct 62		N	L	1–2	McAlister
1985–86	Cup-Winners' Cup	1	18 Sep 85	Fredrikstad	A	D	1–1	Williams (E)
			2 Oct 85	(Norway)	H	D	0–0*	
		2	24 Oct 85	Atletico Madrid	H	L	0–2	
			6 Nov 85	(Spain)	A	L	0–1	

BOROUGH UNITED

Season	Competition	Round	Date	Opponents (Country)	Venue	Result		Scorers
1963–64	Cup-Winners' Cup	1	15 Sep 63	Sliema Wanderers	A	D	0–0	
			3 Oct 63	(Malta)	H	W	2–0	Duffy, Pritchard (M)
		2	11 Dec 63	Slovan Bratislava	H	L	0–1	
			15 Dec 63	(Czechoslovakia)	A	L	0–3	

MERTHYR

Season	Competition	Round	Date	Opponents (Country)	Venue	Result		Scorers
1987–88	Cup-Winners' Cup	1	16 Sep 87	Atalanta (Italy)	H	W	2–1	Rogers, Ceri Williams
			30 Sep 87		A	L	0–2	

Representative Team

LONDON

Season	Competition	Round	Date	Opponents (Country)	Venue	Result		Scorers
1955–58	Fairs Cup	F	5 Mar 58	Barcelona (Spain)	H	D	2–2	Greaves, Langley (pen)
			1 May 58		A	L	0–6	

EUROPEAN FOOTBALLER OF THE YEAR

1956	Stanley Matthews (Blackpool)
1957	Alfredo Di Stefano (Real Madrid)
1958	Raymond Kopa (Real Madrid)
1959	Alfredo Di Stefano (Real Madrid)
1960	Luis Suarez (Barcelona)
1961	Omar Sivori (Juventus)
1962	Josef Masopust (Dukla Prague)
1963	Lev Yashin (Moscow Dynamo)
1964	Denis Law (Manchester United)
1965	Eusebio (Benfica)
1966	Bobby Charlton (Manchester United)
1967	Florian Albert (Ferencvaros)
1968	George Best (Manchester United)
1969	Gianni Rivera (AC Milan)
1970	Gerd Muller (Bayern Munich)
1971	Johan Cruyff (Ajax)
1972	Franz Beckenbauer (Bayern Munich)
1973	Johan Cruyff (Barcelona)
1974	Johan Cruyff (Barcelona)
1975	Oleg Blokhin (Dynamo Kiev)
1976	Franz Beckenbauer (Bayern Munich)
1977	Allan Simonsen (Borussia Moenchengladbach)
1978	Kevin Keegan (Hamburg)

Jean-Pierre Papin, European Footballer of the Year with Marseille in 1991, subsequently transferred to AC Milan in 1992 for a fee of £10 million (Allsport/Dan Smith)

1979	Kevin Keegan (Hamburg)	1986	Igor Belanov (Dynamo Kiev)
1980	Karl-Heinz Rummenigge (Bayern Munich)	1987	Ruud Gullit (AC Milan)
1981	Karl-Heinz Rummenigge (Bayern Munich)	1988	Marco Van Basten (AC Milan)
1982	Paolo Rossi (Juventus)	1989	Marco Van Basten (AC Milan)
1983	Michel Platini (Juventus)	1990	Lothar Matthaus (Internazionale)
1984	Michel Platini (Juventus)	1991	Jean-Pierre Papin (Marseille)
1985	Michel Platini (Juventus)	1992	Marco Van Basten (AC Milan)

THE GOLDEN BOOT

AWARDED TO EUROPE'S LEADING GOALSCORER

Season	Gold		Silver		Bronze	
1967–68	Eusebio (Benfica)	43	Antal Dunai (Ujpest Dozsa)	36	Bobby Lennox (Celtic)	32
1968–69	Petar Jekov (CSKA Sofia)	36	George Sideris (Olympiakos)	35	Helmut Kogelberger (FC Austria)	31
					Antal Dunai (Ujpest Dozsa)	31
1969–70	Gerd Muller (Bayern Munich)	38	Jan Devillet (Spora Lux)	31	Petar Jekov (CSKA Sofia)	31
1970–71	Josip Skoblar (Marseilles)	44	Salif Keita (St Etienne)	42	George Dedes (Panionios)	28
1971–72	Gerd Muller (Bayern Munich)	40	Antonis Antoniadis (Panathinaikos)	39	Joe Harper (Aberdeen)	33
					Slodogan Santrac (OFK Belgrade)	33
					Francis Lee (Man City)	33
1972–73	Eusebio (Benfica)	40	Gerd Muller (Bayern Munich)	36	Petar Jekov (CSKA Sofia)	29
1973–74	Hector Yazalde (Sporting Lisbon)	46	Hans Krankl (Rapid Vienna)	36	Gerd Muller (Bayern Munich	30
					Jupp Heynckes (Borussia Moenchengladbach)	30
					Carlos Bianchi (Reims)	30
1974–75	Dudu Georgescu (Dinamo Bucharest)	33	Hector Yazalde (Sporting)	30		
			Ruud Geels Ajax)	30		
			Delio Onnis (Monaco)	30		
1975–76	Sotiris Kaiafas (Omonia Nicosia)	39	Carlos Bianchi (Reims)	34	Peter Risi (Zurich)	33
1976–77	Dudu Georgescu (Dinamo Bucharest)	47	Bela Varadi (Vasas Budapest)	36	Ruud Geels (Ajax)	34
					Dieter Muller (FC Cologne)	34
1977–78	Hans Krankl (Rapid Vienna)	41	Carlos Bianchi (Paris SG)	37	Rudd Geels (Ajax)	34
1978–79	Kees Kist (AZ 67 Alkmaar)	34	Thomas Mavros (AEK)	31		
			Lazlo Fekete (Ujpest Dozsa)	31		
1979–80	Erwin Van Den Bergh (Lierse)	39	Laszlo Fazekas (Ujpest Dosza)	36	Walter Schachner (FK Austria)	34
1980–81	Georgi Slavkov (Trakia Plovdiv)	31	Tibor Nyilasi (Ferencvaros)	30	Karl-Heinz Rummenigge (Bayern Munich)	29
1981–82	Wim Kieft (Ajax)	32	Kees Kist (AZ 67 Alkmaar)	29	Allan Hansen (Odense BK)	28
			Delio Onnis (Tours)	29		
1982–83	Fernando Gomez (Porto)	36	Peter Houtman (Feyenoord)	30	Nikos Anastopoulos (Olympiakos)	29
					Charlie Nicholas (Celtic)	
1983–84	Ian Rush (Liverpool)	32	Marco Van Basten (Ajax)	28	Nico Claesen (Seraing)	27
1984–85	Fernando Gomez (Porto)	39	Martin McGaughey (Linfield)	34	Vahid Halilhodzic (Nantes)	28
1985–86	Marco Van Basten (Ajax)	37	Oleg Protasov (Dnepr)	36	Toni Polster (FK Austria)	33
					Tanju Colak (Samsunsport)	33
1986–87	Rodion Camataru (Dinamo Bucharest)	44	Toni Polster (FK Austria)	39	Nasko Sirakov (Vitosha)	36

Season	Gold		Silver		Bronze	
1987–88	Tanju Colak (Galatasaray)	39	John Eriksen (Servette)	36	Tommy Coyne (Dundee)	33
1988–89	Dorin Mateut (Dinamo Bucharest)	43	Baltazar (Atletico Madrid)	35	Aykut (Fenerbahce)	29
1989–90	Hugo Sanchez (Real Madrid)	38	Gerhard Rodax (Admira Wacker)	35	Christo Stoichkov (CSKA Sofia)	38
1990–91	Darko Pancev (Red Star Belgrade)	34	Tanju Colak (Galatasaray)	31	Vaclav Danek (Tirol)	29
1991–92	Ally McCoist (Rangers)	34	Ricky Owubokiri (Boavista)	30	Ian Wright (Crystal Palace/Arsenal)	29
					Zoran Ubavic (Olimpia Ljubljana)	29
1992–93	Ally McCoist (Rangers)	34	Vasilis Dimitriadis (AEK Athens)	33	Krystof Warzycha (Panathinaikos)	32

Ally McCoist, for two consecutive seasons the winner of the Golden Boot. In 1992–93 he achieved this despite breaking a leg with a month of the season still to run (Allsport/Steve Morton)

FOOTBALL IN OTHER CONTINENTS

SOUTH AMERICAN CHAMPIONSHIP

Copa America

Year	Venue	Teams	Matches	Goals	Champions	Pts
1916	Buenos Aires, Argentina	4	6	18	Uruguay	5
1917	Montevideo, Uruguay	4	6	21	Uruguay	6
1919	Rio de Janeiro, Brazil[1]	4	7	26	Brazil	7
1920	Valparaiso, Chile	4	6	16	Uruguay	5
1921	Buenos Aires, Argentina	4	6	14	Argentina	6
1922	Rio de Janeiro, Brazil[2]	5	11	23	Brazil	7
1923	Montevideo, Uruguay	4	6	18	Uruguay	6
1924	Montevideo, Uruguay	4	6	15	Uruguay	5
1925	Buenos Aires, Argentina[3]	3	6	26	Argentina	7
1926	Santiago de Chile, Chile	5	10	55	Uruguay	8
1927	Lima, Peru	4	6	37	Argentina	6
1929	Buenos Aires, Argentina	4	6	23	Argentina	6
1935	Lima, Peru*	4	6	18	Uruguay	6
1937	Buenos Aires, Argentina[4]	6	16	68	Argentina	10
1939	Lima, Peru	5	10	47	Peru	8
1941	Santiago de Chile, Chile*	5	10	32	Argentina	8
1942	Montevideo, Uruguay[5]	7	21	81	Uruguay	12
1945	Santiago de Chile, Chile*	7	21	89	Argentina	11
1946	Buenos Aires, Argentina*	6	15	61	Argentina	10
1947	Guayaquil, Ecuador	8	28	102	Argentina	13
1949	Rio de Janeiro, Brazil[6]	8	29	130	Brazil	14
1953	Lima, Peru[7]	7	21	67	Paraguay	10
1955	Santiago de Chile, Chile	6	15	73	Argentina	9
1956	Montevideo, Uruguay*	6	15	38	Uruguay	9
1957	Lima, Peru	7	21	101	Argentina	10
1959	Buenos Aires, Argentina	7	21	86	Argentina	11
1959	Guayaquil, Ecuador*	5	20	39	Uruguay	7
1963	La Paz & Cochabamba, Bolivia	7	21	91	Bolivia	11
1967	Montevideo, Uruguay	6	15	49	Uruguay	9
1975	(Reorganized	10	25	79	Peru	N/A
1979	on home and	10	25	63	Paraguay	N/A
1983	away basis)	10	24	55	Uruguay	N/A
1987	Argentina	10	13	33	Uruguay	N/A
1989	Brazil	10	26	56	Brazil	N/A
1991	Chile	10	26	73	Argentina	N/A
1993	Ecuador	12	26	66	Argentina	N/A

* extraordinary tournaments
[1] play-off; Brazil 1 Uruguay 0
[2] play-off; Brazil 3 Paraguay 1; Uruguay withdrew
[3] two legs were played (home and away)
[4] play-off; Argentina 2 Brazil 0
[5] Chile withdrew
[6] play-off; Brazil 7 Paraguay 0
[7] play-off; Paraguay 3 Brazil 2 (organized by the Paraguayan Football League)

SOUTH AMERICAN CUP

Copa Libertadores

Year	Winner	Entries	Matches	Goals	Year	Winner	Entries	Matches	Goals
1960	Penarol (Uruguay)	8	13	39	1988	Nacional	21	82	169
1961	Penarol	9	16	52	1989	Nacional (Colombia)	21	91	233
1962	Santos (Brazil)	10	25	101	1990	Olimpia	19	82	184
1963	Santos	9	19	63	1991	Colo Colo (Chile)	21	91	222
1964	Independiente (Argentina)	10	25	89	1992	Sao Paulo (Brazil)	21	99	242
1965	Independiente	10	27	72					
1966	Penarol	17	94	218					
1967	Racing (Argentina)	19	114	355					
1968	Estudiantes (Argentina)	21	93	232					
1969	Estudiantes	17	74	211					
1970	Estudiantes	19	88	253					
1971	Nacional (Uruguay)	21	73	196					
1972	Independiente	20	69	176					
1973	Independiente	19	66	190					
1974	Independiente	21	76	178					
1975	Independiente	21	76	208					
1976	Cruzeiro (Brazil)	21	77	211					
1977	Boca Juniors (Argentina)	21	75	152					
1978	Boca Juniors	21	75	181					
1979	Olimpia (Paraguay)	21	74	211					
1980	Nacional	21	75	160					
1981	Flamengo (Brazil)	21	77	220					
1982	Penarol	21	73	163					
1983	Gremio (Brazil)	21	74	179					
1984	Independiente	21	75	206					
1985	Argentios Juniors (Argentina)	21	71	181					
1986	River Plate (Argentina)	19	64	166					
1987	Penarol	21	76	207					

Argentina's Claudio Caniggia is challenged by Cabrera of Colombia in the final match of the 1991 Copa America tournament in Chile (Popperfoto)

AFRICA

From a modest beginning in 1957 with three competitors, the African Nations Cup has encompassed the entire continent and is now regularly held every two years, despite the handicap of political problems in various countries.

For the original tournament held in Khartoum, Egypt beat Sudan 2–1 and went on to defeat Ethiopia by four clear goals. Egypt retained their title in 1959 when the three teams played against each other.

The Confederation Africaine de Football (CAF) was established in 1956 and has progressed to such an extent that member countries have shown outstanding promise in the World Cup since the finals were extended to 24 teams in 1982. Indeed their performances in the final stages have outstripped representatives from Asia and Concacaf. For the 1994 World Cup there has been the provision for a third African finalist.

This situation is in no small measure due to the competitive nature of the African Nations Cup, which has given an impetus to the improving standards of play on the Dark Continent.

However, in order to reach this plateau, there were many problems to surmount. After the 1965 series in which Ghana retained their crown won two years earlier, there was a gap of three years before the competition was expanded.

Now the tournament takes 18 months to complete and the finals are held in the same year as the World Cup, though held before these finals take place.

There is now some form of professional football

in six African countries: Algeria, Egypt, Cameroon, Kenya, Morocco and Tunisia. Egypt has had the most consistent record in the African Nations Cup having appeared in more competitions than any other country.

Honours, too, have been spread around with no one nation managing to dominate. For the 18th championship held in Senegal in 1992, the Ivory Coast won the trophy for the first time in their history. They beat the favourites Ghana on a marathon penalty shoot-out 11–10 following a goalless draw. In the play-off for third place, World Cup quarter-finalists Cameroon lost 2–1 to Nigeria.

For the first time there was an increase to 12 teams in the final tournament and the closeness of the results pointed to a levelling of standards throughout a wide spread of competing countries, and the fact that fancied teams from Algeria, Morocco and Egypt were eliminated in group games showed a definite sign of the balance of power remaining elusive.

The 19th African Nations Cup will be held in Tunisia, staged in four towns: Tunis, where two grounds will be used, Bizerta, Sousse and Sfax. The admission of South Africa after years in the wilderness has opened up further exciting possibilities for the future of the game in Africa as a whole. Ghana have been the most successful national team with four wins, adding 1978 and 1982 to their earlier victories. Egypt won their third title in 1986 and overall there have been 11 different winners.

Interest in the African Nations Cup has been such that capacity crowds are almost guaranteed whenever an important match is staged under the banner of the competition.

But it was certainly 1990 which proved to be an exceptional year for African football. Cameroon qualified for the quarter-finals of the World Cup and Egypt also gave some memorable performances.

While African football dates back many years – Ghana's first football club was formed as long ago as 1903 – and Egypt were only just defeated 2–1 by Italy in the 1920 Olympics, it has been during the last 30 years with the development of the Nations Cup that the African game has been brought to the forefront of the world platform.

At club level, too, the start of the African Champions' Cup in 1965 and the African Cup Winners' Cup ten years later produced another dimension for playing standards to rise.

Then in 1970 an African country, Morocco, managed to qualify for the World Cup finals. Only Egypt in 1934 had previously figured in the competition's last stage.

In 1978 it was a 3–1 win by Tunisia over Mexico which provided Africa with its first success in the World Cup finals. In 1982 Africa did even better when Algeria beat West Germany and Chile, while Cameroon were eliminated on goal difference without actually losing a game in the final tournament.

Joel Tiehi (left) of the Ivory Coast gets his shot in ahead of Ghana's Anthony Baffoe in the African Nations Cup final in 1992. The Ivory Coast won 11–10 on penalties (Popperfoto)

Peter Ndlovu of Coventry City and Zimbabwe, a star performer in the Premier League in 1992–93 in between turning out in World Cup qualifying matches for his country (Bob Thomas)

In 1986 Morocco finished top of a group which included England, Poland and Portugal. It prompted the North African country to bid to stage the 1994 World Cup finals in their country.

Improvements in administration, discipline and application by the CAF itself have provided a more professional approach off the field which has assisted the growth of the game in Africa.

There remain the twin problems of poverty and political problems which beset some countries. There is also a lack of stability in the managerial ranks of clubs and associations which retards the full development in many areas.

But to underline the potential for further advancement on the field of play, Ghana's success in winning the 1st Under–17 World Championship in Italy during 1991, in which spirit, technical ability and sense of fair play predominated, augured well for the future of the game in the Dark Continent. Ghana also finished with the Bronze Medal at the 1992 Olympics and as impressive runners-up to Brazil in the 1993 World Under–20 Championship held in Australia.

USA & WORLD CUP 1994

The FIFA Executive Committee awarded the 1994 World Cup to the USA on American Independence Day, 4 July 1988. After abstentions by Joao Havelange, FIFA's President and Abilio d'Almedia, the Brazilian member of the Executive Committee, the USA received ten votes, Morocco seven and Brazil two. As a Brazilian, and with Brazil as one of the candidates, Havelange refrained from presiding over the meeting. Senior Vice-President Harry H. Cavan presided instead.

The USA should make a success of staging the finals, support for big names in soccer has never been a problem there. The North American Soccer League (NASL) collapsed largely because there was an insufficient number of star players. When Pele retired, followed by Franz Beckenbauer, there was a rapid decline of interest. Conversely, there is a grassroots revival of considerable proportion among several million young players of the game, of both sexes as well. It is estimated that there are 8.7 million youngsters up to High School level playing the game.

The 1984 Olympic Games football tournament in the US was a pronounced success. It attracted 1,421,627 paying spectators to the 32 matches and this was the best attended sporting discipline in the entire Games. The problem will not be finding fans, but producing a strong team.

Even for the Los Angeles Olympics there were astonishing problems in this area. According to official FIFA reports, for incomprehensible reasons, the United States team changed its formation three weeks ahead of the competition itself. But then the playing side has been a constant source of concern throughout the country's history.

However, once it was agreed to stage the 1994 World Cup in the USA, it was hoped that a national league could be created to build up interest in soccer as a spectator sport. There were ambitions for the American Soccer League (ASL) started in 1987 with some 60 per cent of the players of American stock.

The United States Soccer Federation introduced a plan in January 1989 to play 40 to 50 games over two years to give a possible squad for the World Cup every chance of togetherness.

Domestically, the other outdoor competition, the Western Soccer Alliance (WSL) was in its fifth season and there were talks about combining the WSL and the ASL. The Southwest Indoor Soccer League in the Mid-West decided to increase its coverage with an outdoor championship between May and August.

FIFA president Joao Havelange (left) pictured with Striker, the mascot for the 1994 World Cup finals, after inspecting the Rose Bowl in Pasadena, the venue for the final (Popperfoto)

Support for foreign teams visiting the country again underlined the potential for crowds. In September 1989 the USSR team Dnepr attracted a crowd of 43,356 to Philadelphia, then the highest attendance by the national team apart from the 1984 Olympics.

Linking the east coast ASL with the west coast WSL into the American Professional Soccer League would produce enormous problems of travel and expense.

In 1990 the Major Indoor Soccer league dropped the Indoor part of its title to show its expansion interest and the American Indoor Soccer Association became the National Professional Soccer League.

The national team which had been the youngest competing in the 1990 World Cup with an average age of 24 years, 2 months, had largely been dispersed around various parts of the world having turned professional.

But in July 1991 a new generation saw the squad win the Concacaf Championship on a penalty shoot-out after a 0–0 draw with Costa Rica. A crowd of 40,000 in the Coliseum in Los Angeles witnessed the triumph.

Later in the year the USA Women's team won the World Championship in China, to underline the progress made at this level of interest.

In April 1992 the USA Under–17s won a Youth tournament in France beating Czechoslovakia 2–0 in the final.

A Cup for the winners of all Confederations in the world saw the USA take third place beating the Ivory Coast 5–2 in 1992. Then along with Mexico, the United States found themselves admitted to the Copa America, the South American Championships, for the first time in 1993.

When the FIFA committee responsible for selecting suitable venues for the finals in 1994 met, there was no shortage of applications. Though there were many of suitable size, those with the required pitch measurements were fewer in number.

Eventually nine sites were chosen: Giants Stadium, New York; Robert F Kennedy Memorial Stadium, Washington; The Citrus Bowl, Orlando; Foxboro Stadium, Boston; Pontiac Silverdome, Detroit; Soldier Field, Chicago; The Cotton Bowl, Dallas; The Rose Bowl, Los Angeles and Stanford Stadium, San Francisco.

Alas, the MSL has folded after 17 years and the nationwide professional competition is now unlikely to start before the finals in 1994. Though these factors may

not adversely affect the World Cup, it has been a blow to those who wanted one in place for the finals.

This could change dramatically if the performance of the team representing the USA, succeeds in capturing the imagination of the American public. But history shows that this may prove a false premise. Remember in 1950 when the American team beat the cream of England's full-time professionals 1–0 in the World Cup in Belo Horizonte, it did nothing to popularise the game in the USA. Amazingly the Americans doubled the margin in 1993. It was no tea party for the Brits in Boston and at least the American media took more interest, hence headlines like Colonials 2 Redcoats 0.

Yet the circumstances of forty or more years ago have changed. The game has a sound footing as a sport played by young people of both sexes and the spectators have proved themselves interested in watching the top stars.

A four team tournament for the United States Cup involving the USA, Brazil, England and Germany was played in June 1993 and to show the need for stronger domestic competition, San Francisco Blackhawks, the 1991 APSL champions, expressed a desire to play in the Mexican championship.

Soldier Field, Chicago, the home of the Chicago Bears which will stage the opening game of the 1994 World Cup finals as world champions Germany, who played the USA in front of 53,549 here in 1993, begin the defence of their title (Allsport/Jonathan Daniel)

WORLD FOOTBALL

THE WORLD CUP

Year	Final	Venue	Attendance	Referee
1930	Uruguay 4 Argentina 2	Montevideo, Italy	90 000	Langenus, Belgium
1934	Italy 2 Czechoslovakia 1 (aet)	Rome, Italy	50 000	Eklind, Sweden
1938	Italy 4 Hungary 2	Paris, France	45 000	Capdeville, France
1950	Uruguay 2 Brazil 1	Rio de Janeiro, Brazil	199 854	Reader, England
1954	West Germany 3 Hungary 2	Berne, Switzerland	60 000	Ling, England
1958	Brazil 5 Sweden 2	Stockholm, Sweden	49 737	Guigue, France
1962	Brazil 3 Czechoslovakia 1	Santiago, Chile	68 679	Latychev, USSR
1966	England 4 West Germany 2 (aet)	Wembley, England	93 802	Dienst, Switzerland
1970	Brazil 4 Italy 1	Mexico City, Mexico	107 412	Glockner, East Germany
1974	West Germany 2 Holland 1	Munich, West Germany	77 833	Taylor, England
1978	Argentina 3 Holland 1 (aet)	Buenos Aires, Argentina	77 000	Gonella, Italy
1982	Italy 3 West Germany 1	Madrid, Spain	90 080	Coelho, Brazil
1986	Argentina 3 West Germany 2	Mexico City, Mexico	114 580	Filho, Brazil
1990	West Germany 1 Argentina 0	Rome, Italy	73 603	Codesal, Mexico

WINNERS' RECORDS

Year	Winners	P	W	D	L	F	A	Players used	Year	Winners	P	W	D	L	F	A	Players used
1930	Uruguay	4	4	0	0	16	3	15	1966	England	6	5	1	0	11	3	15
1934	Italy	5	4	1	0	12	3	17	1970	Brazil	6	6	0	0	19	7	15
1938	Italy	4	4	0	0	15	5	14	1974	West Germany	7	6	0	1	13	4	18
1950	Uruguay	4	3	1	0	15	5	14	1978	Argentina	7	5	1	1	15	4	17
1954	West Germany	6	5	0	1	25	14	18	1982	Italy	7	4	3	0	12	6	15
1958	Brazil	6	5	1	0	16	4	16	1986	Argentina	7	6	1	0	14	5	18
1962	Brazil	6	5	1	0	14	5	12	1990	West Germany	7	5	2	0	15	5	17

GATES AND GOALS

Year	Aggregate attendances	Average attendance	Matches	Goals	Average	Top Scorer	Goals
1930	434 500	24 193	18	70	3.88	Guillermo Stabile (Argentina)	8
1934	395 000	23 235	17	70	4.11	Angelo Schiavio (Italy)	4
						Oldrich Nejedly (Czechoslovakia)	
						Edmund Cohen (Germany)	
1938	483 000	26 833	18	84	4.66	Leonidas Da Silva (Brazil)	8
1950	1 337 00	60 772	22	88	4.00	Ademir (Brazil)	9
1954	943 000	36 270	26	140	5.38	Sandor Kocsis (Hungary)	11
1958	868 000	24 800	35	126	3.60	Just Fontaine (France)	13
1962	776 000	24 250	32	89	2.78	Drazen Jerkovic (Yugoslavia)	5
1966	614 677	50 458	32	89	2.78	Eusebio (Portugal)	9
1970	1 673 975	52 312	32	95	2.96	Gerd Muller (West Germany)	10
1974	1 774 002	46 685	38	97	2.55	Grzegorz Lato (Poland)	7
1978	1 610 215	42 374	38	102	2.68	Mario Kempes (Argentina)	6
1982	2 064 364	38 816	52	146	2.81	Paolo Rossi (Italy)	6
1986	2 441 731	46 956	52	132	2.53	Gary Lineker (England)	6
1990	2 515 168	48 368	52	115	2.21	Salvatore Schillaci (Italy)	6

URUGUAY

In 1930, Uruguay's strength was built around the half-back line of Jose Andrade, Lorenzo Fernandez and Alvaro Gestido, known as 'la costilla metallica' – the iron curtain. They had the nucleus of their 1924 and 1928 Olympic-winning teams. Uruguay scored in 12 minutes through Pablo Dorado but were 2–1 behind at the interval with Argentina goals from Peucelle and Stabile, the latter's effort being claimed offside by the Uruguayans. In the second half, territorial advantage and the edge in technique produced Uruguay goals for Pedro Cea, Santos Iriarte and Hector Castro with a long-range drive.

In 1950, there was no actual final, but a final pool of four teams. The crucial match saw Brazil as 10–1 on favourites, a samba entitled 'Brazil the Victors' had already been recorded. The Brazilians put the well-organised Uruguayan defence under pressure from the start and Friaca put them ahead shortly after the interval. Throwing caution away, Uruguay took command with the industrious Rodriguez Andrade, accurate distribution from Obdulio Varela and individual skill of Juan Schiaffino assuming control. Schiaffino hit 'Chico' Ghiggia's cross first time for the equaliser and 11 minutes from time, Ghiggia drove in low for the winner inside Barbosa's near post.

ITALY

In 1934, Italy included Luisito Monti from Argentina's 1930 team, but their ace was Giuseppe Meazza. Yet it was Czechoslovakia's neat, short-passing game which surprised them. Twenty minutes from the end of an undistinguished match, the crowd was stunned when Antonin Puc put Czechoslovakia ahead following a corner, much to the delight of visiting supporters. Possibly through over-eagerness, the Czechs missed two further chances, one hitting a post. The Italians switched their forwards in desperation and eight minutes from the final whistle Raimondo Orsi hit a swerving shot of speculative origin to equalise. In extra time Italy at last revealed their tactical skill and strategy and Angelo Schiavio scored the winner.

In 1938, Italy swept aside the delicate Hungarians. Luigi Colaussi scored after six minutes, only for Hungary's persistence and close-passing game to produce an equaliser. Italy roared back with goals from Colaussi and Silvio Piola before half-time. In the second-half, Hungary gained a hold in midfield and made it 3–2 before Piola drove in Italy's fourth goal ten minutes from the end. Another triumph for Vittorio Pozzo the extrovert manager. In 1982, the Italians shrugged off the indifference and ineffectiveness of the early rounds but were unable to turn their superiority in the final into a goal until Paolo Rossi struck in the 56th minute. Antonio Cabrini had even become the first player to miss a penalty in a final after 24 minutes. Marco Tardelli added a second in the 69th minute and Altobelli made it 3–0 with ten minutes remaining. Paul Breitner's goal three minutes later was but a consolation for West Germany. Dino Zoff at 40 was the oldest captain to accept the trophy and the first goalkeeping skipper since Giampiero Combi in 1934 so to do. Manager Enzo Bearzot's attempts to rid Italy of its negative psychology had paid off.

WEST GERMANY

In 1954 Hungary stormed into the lead, Ferenc Puskas pouncing on a deflection after six minutes and Zoltan Czibor capitalising on a defensive error two minutes later. But the Germans refused to be unsettled; swinging the ball about and using their fast-raiding wingers on the slippery surface changed the complexion of the match completely. They had been able to get back into the game a minute after Hungary's second goal when Max Morlock scored from another deflection. By the 18th minute they were level, Helmut Rahn driving in a left-wing corner when goalkeeper Gyula Grosics failed to clear. Hungary came back to hit the woodwork twice and their goalkeeper Toni Turek was in inspired form. The Germans counter-attacked and six minutes from time Rahn took advantage of a defensive mistake for his second goal. Puskas equalised immediately but was controversially given offside by English referee Bill Ling from Welsh linesman Mervyn Griffith's flag.

In 1974 there were two penalties awarded inside the first half-hour. Holland kicked off and were awarded the first within a minute of play, without a German touching the ball. Johan Cruyff was brought down inside the area and John Neeskens hit the spot kick straight at goal while goalkeeper Sepp Maier was diving to his right. Referee Jack Taylor, applauded for that decision, was criticised for his next when Wim Jansen was adjudged to have clipped the legs of Bernd Holzenbein in the 26th minute. Paul Breitner equalised. Two minutes from the break, Rainer Bonhof raided on the right and pulled the ball back slightly behind Gerd Muller, who checked, turned and scored superbly. For all their commendable 'total' football, the Dutch were unable to find a goal. The Germans, though past their peak, again showed the danger of underestimating them.

In 1990, West Germany won the poorest final of all. They attacked constantly in the first half though without much guile. In the second half the Argentines hung on for penalty kicks as the game, which began badly enough, fell away. Pedro Monzon became the first player to be sent off in a World Cup Final and near the end Gustavo Dezotti the second. This came after Roberto Sensini allegedly brought down Rudi Voller and Andreas Brehme converted the penalty to end the whole misery.

BRAZIL

In 1958 Nils Liedholm contrived an opening for himself after only four minutes, but the Brazilians showing style and discipline were level three minutes later. Garrincha, the 'Little Bird' flying on the wing, destroyed Sweden's left flank. His acceleration, swerving runs and accurate crosses gave Vava the equaliser and then the chance to put Brazil ahead. After the break, Pele, with a memorable control, overhead flick and finish, then Mario Zagalo put Brazil 4–1 in front. Agne Simonsson pulled one back for Sweden, but Pele headed a fifth for Brazil's triumph of instinctive innovation.

In 1962 Adolf Scherer put the Czechs ahead, splitting the Brazilian defence for Josef Masopust to run in. Amarildo, Pele's replacement, equalised, squeezing the ball inside Wilhelm Schroif's near post from a seemingly impossible angle. Amarildo centred for Zito to head Brazil into a second-half lead and 13 minutes from time, Schroif erred again, flapping at a high cross to allow Vava to slot Brazil's third, in an easily forgotten final. In 1970, Brazil's improvisation and supreme individuality overcame Italy's *catenaccio* defence. It was a real contest for 17 minutes until Pele, in irresistible form, powerfully headed in a teasing cross from Rivelino. Careless defending presented Boninsegna with an equaliser 20 minutes later and it was not until the 65th minute that Brazil regained the lead. Gerson's strong, long-range, left-foot drive finally broke down Italy's resistance and Pele again laid on goals for Jairzinho six minutes later and for Carlos Alberto with three minutes remaining. Tostao, playing despite only recently recovered from a detached retina and forbidden to head the ball, and hard-working Clodoaldo were Brazil's other gems.

ENGLAND

In 1966 the Germans led when Helmut Haller snapped up Ray Wilson's rare mistake in the 12th minute. Seven minutes later, England levelled when Bobby Moore's free-kick was headed in by Geoff Hurst. But it was not until the 78th minute that England regained the lead, Martin Peters stabbing the ball in following a corner and a blocked shot from Hurst. In the dying seconds Wolfgang Weber equalised. A dubious free-kick bounced agonisingly around, hit a defender, was prodded at by Siggi Held, appeared to be handled by Karl-Heinz Schnellinger and was finally knocked over the line by Weber.

The controversial third goal saw Alan Ball pull a centre back for Hurst to turn on it, hitting the underside of the bar with a snap shot as he fell back. The ball bounced down in a split second and came out for Weber to head over for a corner. Referee Rudolf Dienst immediately appealed to Soviet linesman Tofik Bakhramov, who had been 10 yards from the line, but still signalled a goal. Finally, Bobby Moore hit a long ball up to Hurst unmarked, three youths rushed on to the pitch on the opposite side, Hurst stumbled on and scored from an angle in the 119th minute.

ARGENTINA

In 1978, Argentina had three outstanding individuals: defence organiser Daniel Passarella, midfield genius Ossie Ardiles who was at the hub of almost every attack and Mario Kempes, a rakish striker and dangerous in the penalty area. Argentina made the most of almost every opening while the below-par Dutch squandered half-chances. Kempes scored after 38 minutes and it was not until substitute Dirk Nanninga equalised with just eight minutes left, that they appeared vulnerable. In extra time, Kempes' powers of penetration led to him scoring again after 105 minutes and making the opening for Daniel Bertoni to make it 3–1 eleven minutes later.

In 1986 Argentina overcame a typically determined fight-back by the Germans when all seemed beyond them. The virtuoso performances by Diego Maradona were for once subdued in the needs of the

Brazil's World Cup winning team in 1958, featuring the great Pele (front, third from left). Behind him, skipper Bellini holds the Jules Rimet trophy (Popperfoto)

team. After 22 minutes a free-kick by Jorge Burruchaga was misjudged by goalkeeper Toni Schumacher, enabling Jose Luis Brown to head firmly into goal. Counter-attacking cleverly, Argentina kept the Germans at full stretch and in the 56th minute Maradona found Enrique. Valdano collected his pass out on the left and shot right-footed diagonally beyond the goalkeeper's reach. With 17 minutes remaining Karl-Heinz Rummenigge ran the ball in after Rudi Voller had headed on a corner. A repeat set-piece from Andreas Brehme's flag kick eight minutes later, headed back by Berthold, was nodded in by Voller from three yards. But Maradona had the last word, unleashing a short pass to Jorge Burruchaga who raced 50 yards, drew the goal-keeper and scored the winner past Schumacher in the 84th minute.

WORLD CLUB CHAMPIONSHIP

Year	Winners		Runners-up	Venue	Attendance	Referee
1960	Real Madrid	0–0	Penarol	Montevideo	75 000	Praddaude (Argentina)
		5–1		Madrid	125 000	Aston (England)
1961	Penarol	0–1	Benfica	Lisbon	55 000	Ebert (Switzerland)
		5–0		Montevideo	57 358	Nay Foino (Argentina)
		2–1		Montevideo	62 300	Praddaude (Argentina)
1962	Santos	3–2	Benfica	Rio de Janeiro	90 000	Ramirez (Paraguay)
		5–2		Lisbon	75 000	Schwinte (France)
1963	Santos	2–4	AC Milan	Milan	80 000	Harbseliner (Austria)
		4–2		Rio de Janeiro	150 000	Brozzi (Argentina)
		1–0		Rio de Janeiro	121 000	Brozzi (Argentina)
1964	Internazionale	0–1	Independiente	Buenos Aires	70 000	Armando Marques (Brazil)
		2–0		Milan	70 000	Geroe (Hungary)
		1–0		Madrid	45 000	De Mendibil (Spain)
1965	Internazionale	3–0	Independiente	Milan	70 000	Krietlein (West Germany)
		0–0		Buenos Aires	70 000	Yamasaki (Peru)
1966	Penarol	2–0	Real Madrid	Montevideo	70 000	Vicuna (Chile)
		2–0		Madrid	70 000	Lo Bello (Italy)
1967	Racing Club	0–1	Celtic	Hampden Park	103 000	Gardeazabal (Spain)
		2–1		Buenos Aires	80 000	Esteban Marino (Spain)
		1–0		Montevideo	65 172	Osorio (Paraguay)
1968	Estudientes	1–0	Manchester United	Buenos Aires	65 000	Miranda (Paraguay)
		1–1		Old Trafford		
1969	AC Milan	3–0	Estudiantes	Milan	80 000	Machin (France)
		1–2		Buenos Aires	65 000	Massaro (Chile)
1970	Feyenoord	2–2	Estudiantes	Buenos Aires	65 000	Glockner (East Germany)
		1–0		Rotterdam	70 000	Tejada (Peru)
1971	Nacional	1–1	Panathanaikos	Athens	60 000	
		2–1		Montevideo	70 000	
1972	Ajax	1–1	Independiente	Buenos Aires	65 000	Bakhramov (USSR)
		3–0		Amsterdam	65 000	Romey (Paraguay)
1973	Independiente	1–0	Juventus	Rome	35 000	Belcourt (Belgium)
1974	Atletico Madrid	0–1	Independiente	Buenos Aires	60 000	Corver (Holland)
		2–0		Madrid	45 000	Robles (Chile)
1975	Independiente and Bayern Munich could not agree on dates to play					
1976	Bayern Munich	2–0	Cruzeiro	Munich	22 000	Pestarino (Argentina)
		0–0		Belo Horizonte	114 000	Partridge (England)
1977	Boca Juniors	2–2	Moenchengladbach	Buenos Aires	50 000	Doudine (Bulgaria)
		3–0		Karlsruhe	21 500	Cerullo (Uruguay)
1978	Not contested; Liverpool declined to play					
1979	Olimpia	1–0	Malmo	Malmo	4 811	Partridge (England)
		2–1		Asuncion	35 000	Cardellino (Uruguay)
1980	Nacional	1–0	Nottingham Forest	Tokyo	62 000	Klein (Israel)
1981	Flamengo	3–0	Liverpool	Tokyo	62 000	Vasquez (Mexico)

Year	Winners		Runners-up	Venue	Attendance	Referee
1982	Penarol	2–0	Aston Villa	Tokyo	62 000	Siles (Costa Rica)
1983	Gremio	2–1	Hamburg	Tokyo	62 000	Vautrot (France)
1984	Independiente	1–0	Liverpool	Tokyo	62 000	Filho (Brazil)
1985	Juventus	2–2*	Argentinos Juniors	Tokyo	62 000	Roth (West Germany)
(Juventus won 4–2 on penalties)						
1986	River Plate	1–0	Steaua Bucharest	Tokyo	62 000	Bazan (Uruguay)
1987	Porto	2–1*	Penarol	Tokyo	45 000	Wohrer (Austria)
1988	Nacional	2–2*	PSV Eindhoven	Tokyo	62 000	Palacio (Colombia)
(Nacional won 7–6 on penalties)						
1989	AC Milan	1–0*	Nacional (Colombia)	Tokyo	62 000	Fredriksson (Sweden)
1990	AC Milan	3–0	Olimpia	Tokyo	62 000	Wright (Brazil)
1991	Red Star Belgrade	3–0	Colo Colo	Tokyo	60 000	Rothlisberger (Switzerland)
1992	Sao Paulo	2–1	Barcelona	Tokyo	80 000	Loustau (Argentina)

*after extra time

WORLD GOALSCORING RECORDS

For club

16 goals, Stephan Stanis (Stanikowski) and sometimes known as Dembicki), Racing Club Lens v Aubry-Asturies, French Cup, 13 Dec 1942.

International matches

10 goals, Sofus Nielsen, Denmark v France, 1908 Olympics
Gottfried Fuchs, Germany v Russia (as Russia), 1912 Olympics.

World career records

1329 goals, Artur Friedenreich, in Brazilian football, 1910–30
1216 goals, Edson Arantes do Nascimento (Pele) 1956–74, in Brazilian football, later in USA for New York Cosmos and then after farewell performances 1285
1006 goals, Franz 'Bimbo' Binder, in Austrian football, 1921–50

Most international goals

Pele (Brazil)	97*	1957–71
Ferenc Puskas (Hungary)	83	1945–56
Sandor Kocsis (Hungary)	75	1948–56
Gerd Muller (West Germany)	68	1966–74

* Includes matches against non-international teams

Over thirty years after his first World Cup, Pele turns out in a special celebration match in Milan for his 50th birthday. He still holds the record for international goals (Allsport/Richiardi)

INTERNATIONAL TEAM COACHES

Antigua	Micah Samuel
Argentina	Alfio Basile
Australia	Eddie Thomson
Austria	Dieter Constantini
Bangladesh	Mohammed Kaikobad
Belgium	Paul Van Himst
Benin	Peter Schnittger
Brazil	Carlos Alberto Parreira
Bulgaria	Dimitar Penev
Byelorussia	Mikhail Vergeenko
Canada	Bob Lenarduzzi
Chile	Arturo Salah
China	Klaus Schlappner
Croatia	Martin Novoselac
Cyprus	Andreas Michaelides
Czechoslovakia	Milan Macala
Denmark	Richard Moller-Nielsen
Dominican Republic	Francisco Ramirez
England	Graham Taylor
Estonia	Lino Piir
Faroes	Pall Gudlaugsson
Finland	Jukka Vakkila
France	Gerard Houllier
Gambia	Ebrima Bajong
Georgia	Anatoli Norakize
Germany	Berti Vogts
Ghana	Otto Pfister
Greece	Alketas Panagoulias
Guinea	Serge Deveze
Guinea Bissau	Armando Miranda
Holland	Dick Advocaat
Hungary	Imre Jenei
Northern Ireland	Billy Bingham
Republic of Ireland	Jack Charlton
Israel	Shlomo Scharf
Italy	Arrigo Sacchi
Japan	Marius Johan Ooft
Jordan	Neef Matouf Abdelgader
Korea	Ho Kim
Kuwait	Valmir Louruz
Latvia	Janis Gillis
Lithuania	A. Liubinskas
Luxembourg	Paul Philipp
Malaysia	Kenneth Joseph Worden
Maldivia	Miklos Temesvari
Mauritius	Mukesh Ramrhaka
New Zealand	Ian Marshall
Norway	Egil Olsen
Pakistan	Mohammad Aslam
Papua New Guinea	Ludwig W. Peka
Paraguay	Sergio Markarian
Peru	Vladimir Popovic
Poland	Andrzej Strejlau
Portugal	Carlos Manuel de Brito Leal Queiroz

Puerto Rico	Oscar Rosa Lugardo
Romania	Cornel Dinu
Scotland	Andy Roxburgh
Singapore	N. N. Sivati
Slovenia	Bojan Prasnikar
Spain	Vicente Miera Campos
Sweden	Tommy Svensson
Switzerland	Roy Hodgson
Taiwan	Jong Chien Wu
Tunisia	M'rad Mahjoub
Turkey	Sepp Piontek
Uruguay	Luis Cubilla
USA	Bora Milutinovic
Venezuela	Ratomir Dujkovic
Vietnam	Tran Binh Su
Wales	Terry Yorath

Jack Charlton, manager of Ireland since 1986 and by far the most successful in their history. His sights are now firmly set on World Cup success in 1994 (Bob Thomas)

INTERNATIONAL APPEARANCES

After 1953, one cap only was awarded for the British International Championship as a whole rather than for separate matches. This obviously reduced the total number of such caps to any particular player. But since the short three-letter word for international appearances was merely a convenience, it did produce a confusion which really did not exist.

On a worldwide scale, each country had a different interpretation of what constituted a full international appearance. The norm in most South American countries was to include all matches played by the national team whether against other countries or club sides either at home or abroad. In Eastern Europe, matches involving Olympic Games often featured in the total of a full international player.

However FIFA, the world governing body, decreed from 6 September 1990 that only games contested by the foremost national squad of each of the National Associations concerned can be classified as 'A' internationals, with matches against club sides and other non-national teams not qualifying.

Much of the discussion concerning the quality of matches under discussion came during the World Cup when a gathering of interested parties questioned whether Peter Shilton with 125 appearances for England was the most 'capped' player of all time or whether the honour went to Soon-Ho Choi of South Korea, with 132.

Investigation by FIFA discovered that with his three appearances in the World Cup finals and four in the First Asian Dynasty Cup tournament, the Korean's legitimate total was 102, thus becoming the first non-European player to be sanctioned with a century of full international appearances.

In April 1990, FIFA published a list of 19 players who had qualified for 100 appearances. They were all from European countries. At the time Pat Jennings of Northern Ireland was top with 119. He was subsequently overtaken by Peter Shilton.

However in October 1990, FIFA amended their list after the South American Confederation announced that two other internationals had qualified for the '100 club'. They were the Peruvian centre-back Hector Chumpitaz with 104 appearances between April 1965 and December 1981 and Djalma Santos with exactly 100 for Brazil, his first being awarded against Peru in April 1952 and the last in June 1968 v Uruguay.

However Djalma Santos was the subject of a full list of appearances in the 1984 edition of *Soccer Facts and Feats*. Of the 107 matches listed no fewer than ten were against clubs! Should his total be 97?

FIFA again listed an amended version of the centurions with 22 players qualifying.

Peter Shilton (England)	125
Pat Jennings (Northern Ireland)	119
Bjorn Nordqvist (Sweden)	115
Dino Zoff (Italy)	112
Oleg Blokhin (USSR)	109
Ladislau Boloni (Romania)	108
Bobby Moore (England)	108
Bobby Charlton (England)	106
Billy Wright (England)	105
Heinz Hermann (Switzerland)	105
Hector Chumpitaz (Peru)	104
Grzegorz Lato (Poland)	104
Torbjorn Svenssen (Norway)	104
Franz Beckenbauer (West Germany)	103
Soon-Ho Choi (South Korea)	102
Kenny Dalglish (Scotland)	102
Kazimierz Denya (Poland)	102
Morten Olsen (Denmark)	102
Joachim Streich (East Germany)	102
Joszef Bozsik (Hungary)	100
Djalma Santos (Brazil)	100
Hans-Jurgen Dorner (East Germany)	100

Peter Shilton's 125 international caps are now officially recognised by FIFA as the all-time record. Three of the top four international centurions are goalkeepers (Allsport/David Cannon)

Since then, Heinz Hermann has taken his total of appearances for Switzerland to 117 before retiring from the international arena. Lothar Matthaus (Germany) also reached three figures in 1993.

Again the figures quoted for Bozsik of Hungary are likely to be the cause of further argument. He was featured in the 1978 edition of *Facts and Feats*. On 25 May 1951 Hungary played one of two matches against Moscow Selection, and Bozsik's total includes this game. But the USSR did not restart international fixtures until 1952.

Interestingly enough, the first player to make 100 actual international appearances was Billy Wright of England who completed his century in 1958 and ended his international career the following year.

Another point worth noting is that Pele who was listed with 111 appearances for Brazil, made 19 of these against non-national teams, leaving him with 92. But at the grand old age of 50 he played part of a game for Brazil against Italy on 8 October 1990 in Milan and is credited by FIFA as playing in his 95th match!

The debate continues . . .

WORLD FOOTBALLER OF THE YEAR

From *World Soccer* magazine

1982	Paolo Rossi (Italy)
1983	Zico (Brazil)
1984	Michel Platini (France)
1985	Michel Platini (France)
1986	Diego Maradona (Argentina)
1987	Ruud Gullit (Holland)
1988	Marco Van Basten (Holland)
1989	Ruud Gullit (Holland)
1990	Lothar Matthäus (West Germany)
1991	Jean-Pierre Papin (France)
1992	Marco Van Basten (Holland)

FIFA FAIR PLAY AWARD

1987 Dundee United and supporters for their conduct in European football.

1988 Frank Ordenewicz, German player for persuading referee to give a penalty against his own team.

1989 Trinidad & Tobago FA for the exemplary conduct of the national team and supporters after narrowly failing to qualify for the 1990 World Cup finals.

1990 Gary Lineker awarded £20,000 for never having been sent off or cautioned during his career with Leicester City, Everton, Barcelona, Tottenham and England.

1991 Jorginho, Brazilian international, with Bayern Munich.

1992 The Belgian FA for a scheme helping deprived children in Toluca, Mexico.

Gary Lineker shows off his FIFA Fair Play Award. Lineker was also a member of the England team which picked up the team award for Fair Play at the 1990 World Cup (Bob Thomas)

RULES

The International Football Association Board is the only authority to effect changes and amendments to the Laws of the Game. In 1882, the English Football Association proposed that there should be a meeting between the four British Associations, to agree on the Laws.

A meeting was held at the Queen's Hotel in Manchester on 6 December 1882 and was attended by two members each of the four Associations of England, Scotland, Ireland and Wales. It was an immediate success.

After nearly twenty years of struggle and growth and of varied opinion as to technical points of Law, the first step had been taken towards the establishment of a uniform code of rules.

Since the Manchester Conference, no change has been made in the Laws without the consent of the four home countries, the International Board being formed later in 1886, for the purpose of considering and sanctioning if approved, any changes thought necessary.

The International Board became the highest authority in the world for the control of the Laws of the Game and though its constitution was later broadened by the election of two (now four) representatives of the Federation Internationale de Football Association (FIFA) to its executive control, that constitution has effectively altered little over the years from the points originally framed in 1886. The International Board is hosted in turn by one of the member Associations.

In recent years attempts have been made to eliminate foul play, curtail time-wasting tactics and encourage goalscoring ratios.

The so-called 'professional foul' – a deliberately unfair tackle by a defending player on an opponent with a clear sight of goal – was the subject of a crack down by the Football League during 1982–83. It resulted in a then record number of sendings-off amounting to 242 (211 in the League alone).

There was such an outcry following this situation that there was an easing of the enforcement, but for the 1990–91 season, the professional foul was outlawed by FIFA. Ironically, in 1991–92 the Football League had its worst season for discipline, with 278 dismissals of which 245 were in the League, the rest in various senior cup competitions.

In 1990 the Board made the professional foul a sending-off offence and this applied to players handling the ball to prevent a goal. At the same time the offside law, which had remained untouched since the amendment in 1925 requiring two not three players to be goal-side of an attacker when the ball is played forward, was changed to allow players level with the opposition as stated previously, to remain onside.

Most of the legislation concerning time-wasting and a lack of goalscoring came from the statistics from various World Cup competitions, which have seen a gradual reduction in the number of goals registered in final competitions. The average number of goals per game in World Cup final tournaments had been healthy enough until reaching a peak in 1954 in Switzerland when the average was 5.3 goals per game. In 1974 it touched a new low at 2.5, but there was a slight improvement in the next two competitions until dropping back to 2.5 in Mexico for 1986. However, in 1990 the finals in Italy saw a further slump to 2.21.

This produced a variety of extreme ideas to combat the lack of goalscoring. They included wider goals, fewer players and the elimination of offside.

When the International Board met in Wales in May 1992 five amendments were made to the Laws to take effect from July 25. In an attempt to curb time-wasting, FIFA's proposal was approved that the goalkeeper shall no longer handle the ball when a player deliberately kicks it back to him. If he does, an indirect free-kick was to be given where the handling occurred. If the offence took place in the goal-area, the free-kick was to be taken from the edge of the six-yard line. Goalkeepers were still to be allowed to catch the ball if it was headed or chested to them.

In other measures to speed up the game, a goal-kick or free-kick awarded to the defending team inside the goal-area could be taken from either side of the area.

Players without shin-guards or boots were to be ordered from the field of play and not allowed to return without them. When a player is sent off for a second caution, the referee was to show both yellow and red cards, to make clear that the dismissal was for the double caution.

In major championships, two substitutes were to be used from up to nine players on the bench, instead of two from five. This was already in place during the 1992 European Championship finals.

Erik Thorstvedt of Spurs was one of the first to concede a goal directly as a result of the new rule which prevented keepers handling passes from team-mates (Allsport/Shaun Botterill)

The most important change clearly involved the pass to the goalkeeper by a defending player. In recent years this had become an attacking feature with the ball often being passed back from the half-way line to the goalkeeper for him to launch a long, aerial attack unhindered by any opposing player.

From evidence during the 1992–93 season it was difficult to make any definite statement whether the new measure was as successful as it had been expected to be. In the Premier League, slightly fewer goals were scored but there was a noticeable increase in the three Football League divisions.

However this might well have been the result of the elimination of goal difference in the League itself, with the number of goals scored taking priority when teams were level on points.

TACTICS

Tactics can be all things to all men and often like beauty, they lie in the eyes of the beholder. But since it became normal around the 1860s for only 11 players to be used in a team, there have been trends brought about by circumstances, which cannot be refuted. And the accompanying diagrams of some of the more obvious systems make it clear that almost without exception, these have resulted in the increase in the number of midfield and defensive players at the expense of attacking ones.

The one undeniable weakness of tactics is that they are based on a known or expected response from the opposition. The quality of players will often tip the balance in favour of one side or another, regardless of the system used.

The late 1980s produced a degree of flexibility in tactics without any retreat from the premise that defence was the safest form of survival. The alternatives of a flat back-four or employing a sweeper behind them were supplemented with a sweeper behind *and* in front, the forward player acting as a deep-lying midfield operator as well.

This inevitably reduced the midfield and forward options to just four players and invariably left an isolated striker with three in midfield, leaving a 1-4-1-3-1 formation.

There has yet to be a satisfactory nomination of the actual positions on the field. When lost for words, observers often refer to 'inside-left channels' and 'on the wing'. In simple terms, there remain five attacking positions on the field, two wide, one central, two down the channels.

The five-man midfield has had its admirers, but it requires an industrious striker, able to function in isolation and keep possession until reinforcements arrive. This usually manifests itself as 4-5-1.

The Diamond has also developed with a sweeper behind two central defenders and full-backs operating in a definite wide-midfield capacity. Two more central midfield players thus complete a virtual four-man midfield, while the attacking pattern can either be a forward who plays behind two strikers, or two forwards operating behind a pure target man.

Of all the various systems, the most difficult to pinpoint for obvious reasons was the total football offered by Holland in the mid-1970s. It was based on three facts: firstly, when in possession, that player attacked and was supported by his teammates. Secondly, when he did not have the ball, he attempted to tackle the opponent in possession and lastly, when this failed, everyone placed themselves behind the ball.

In the years preceding the Second World War, Karl Rappan's Bolt system was in Switzerland one of the forerunners of *catenaccio*, developed to negative perfection by Helenio Herrera in Italian football in the 1960s.

At the time of Real Madrid's fifth European Cup success in 1960, the two most common systems operating in Spain were 3-3-4 and 4-2-4, the latter popularised by Brazil in winning the 1958 World Cup.

In 1992 Italy played 12 international matches, employing varying formations according to the opposition and requirements of a particular match. In every match they used two full-backs and two central defenders. The variations occurred in other departments. In four games there were twin strikers, only in four games did they use just one wide player up front. In seven matches there were two central midfield players, and so on, which revealed the flexible and complex nature of approaching tactics at the highest level.

With any defensive system, there are two major options: man-to-man marking or zonal defence where the players largely retain their allotted positions and refrain from being pulled out of formation.

However, there is no substitute for applying a system which suits the players in question, rather than imposing one of them which might be unworkable.

The next variation might well be the Pyramid, with four defenders three in midfield, two withdrawn forwards and a central striker. This would be 4-3-2-1.

In summary one can identify twelve major tactical progressions in the history of the game as follows:

1 The early dribbling game of organised football with seven forwards and sometimes even as many as eight used.

2 Scotland's successful withdrawal to a stronger midfield and a passing game in the 1870s.

3 The 2-3-5 of the 1880s and a defensive drift.

4 The 'WM' formation of the 1930s with a defensive centre back introduced.

5 The 4-2-4 formation developed by Hungary and Brazil in the 1950s using an extra central defender.

6 Italy's ultra defensive *catenaccio* system from the 1960s

with a 'libero' (free-back) or sweeper at the back of four defenders.

7 The 4-3-3 wingless wonders style popular after England's 1966 World Cup success. Only by comparison with *catenaccio* was it an adventurous system.

8 The 4-4-2 system with its heavily populated midfield area from the 1970s.

9 Extra insurance in defence and midfield with a 1-4-1-3-1 formation and sweepers behind and in front of the back four defenders in the 1980s and 1990s.

10 Reinforced midfield of five players leaving one isolated striker.

11 A move towards more flexibility with the Diamond. Full-backs used more as wide midfield players and a triangle of forwards.

12 Another variation of the Diamond with one central striker backed by two withdrawn forwards and a move towards the Pyramid.

TRANSFERS

Transfer fees are a grey area. In 1922 the Football League decided that they should be treated as private and confidential. But this cloak of secrecy applies on a worldwide scale even now, when exact figures are almost impossible to determine.

Attempts to limit fees have been largely unsuccessful, though UEFA, the European governing body, have attempted to regularise those involving players who are out of contract with the club holding their registration.

As long ago as 1899, the Football Association suggested to the Football League that there should be a transfer ceiling of £10. But it was not until 1908 that a limit of £350 was imposed. It lasted only four months, the regulation being removed by the FA's annual meeting.

The first four-figure transfer saw Alf Common move from Sunderland to Middlesbrough for £1,000 in February 1905. Since then there has been a continual increase and worldwide transfer fees have escalated in recent years.

When Diego Maradona was transferred from Barcelona to Napoli in 1984 the original figure quoted for his move was £6.9 million, but over the years the figure has been scaled down. But Roberto Baggio joined Juventus from Fiorentina in 1990 for £7.7 million to establish another record.

The first £100,000 deal involving a British player saw Denis Law leave Manchester City for Torino in 1961 a year after his record £55,000 move from Huddersfield Town. A year later he came back to England and Manchester United for £115,000, a record fee for a British club.

The first 'million pound' player was Johan Cruyff who went to Barcelona from Ajax for £922,300.

Kevin Keegan's transfer from Liverpool to Hamburg for £500,000 in 1977 was the highest fee involving a British club and the first £1 million transfer concerning British clubs saw Trevor Francis move from Birmingham City to Nottingham Forest in 1979. It was also the first seven-figure fee.

When Juventus agreed to pay £3.2 million for Ian Rush the Liverpool striker, another milestone was reached for a British player. The move was arranged in 1986 and took effect from 1987. The domestic record was broken when Gary Pallister joined Manchester United from Middlesbrough in 1989 for £2.3 million. But in 1991 Dean Saunders cost Liverpool £2.9 million from Derby County. Then in 1992 the transfer of Alan Shearer from Southampton to Blackburn Rovers put the figure up to £3.6 million.

However in the summer of 1992 the continent also produced a new high and the significant eight-figure barrier was breached three times, all by Italian clubs. Gianluigi Lentini, a wide-playing forward, cost £13 million when AC Milan secured his transfer from Torino. The same club paid £10 million for Jean-Pierre Papin, the Marseille striker. Gianluca Vialli moved from Sampdoria to Juventus for £12 million.

The highest fee paid for a British player had been the £4.5 million paid by Marseille for Chris Waddle of Tottenham Hotspur. But David Platt then joined the exodus to Italy in 1991 when Bari paid £5.5 million for his services. Platt stayed just one season there before going to Juventus in a £7 million deal. Paul Gascoigne,

The latest big money transfer from Holland to Italy, Dennis Bergkamp left Ajax for Inter in 1993. By contemporary standards the fee was a modest £6 million (Allsport/Shaun Botterill)

who had originally been the subject of a similar bid from Lazio before his injury in the 1991 FA Cup Final, finally left Italy in 1992 at £5.5 million.

The record fee for a Scottish club is £5 million paid by Marseille to Rangers for Trevor Steven in 1991. Steven made the reverse journey a year later. In fact the same player had set a record for a deal between English and Scottish clubs when Rangers bought him from Everton for £1.5 million in 1989.

In recent years transactions have been further complicated by the addition of VAT and other built-in sums which have made the exact identification of a particular fee impossible to track down. Part-exchange deals have provided further complications.

When Arsenal finally persuaded Bolton Wanderers to part with David Jack for £10,890 in 1928 after 11 hours of negotiation, it was the first four figure fee and 50 per cent higher than any previously paid. But to illustrate the conflicting view of transfers even that long ago, Bolton's version is that they sold him for £10,340.

Arsenal ten years later beat the record again when paying £14,500 for Bryn Jones, the Wolverhampton Wanderers inside-forward. In 1947 came the first £20,000 move when Tommy Lawton transferred to Notts County from Chelsea.

Arsenal had also been involved in another unique signing. They paid £2,000 for Charlie Buchan from Sunderland in 1925 and agreed to pay the Roker Park club an extra £100 for each goal Buchan scored during his first season. He scored 21 goals.

It was from Chelsea that Jimmy Greaves moved to AC Milan in Italy for an unhappy few months prior to being rescued by Tottenham Hotspur. The fee was deliberately put at £99,999 so as not to break the six-figure mark.

Not all transfers are at the extreme end of the market. There have been many far more modest ones. In 1979 the Uruguayan First Division club Rentistas wanted to sign Daniel Allende from Second Division Central Espanol but had no money. Their president owned a slaughter house and he agreed to allow Espanol to receive 550 beef steaks for the player at the rate of 25 a week plus 30 percent of any subsequent transfer fee.

Manchester United persuaded Stockport County to allow amateur wing-half Hughie McLenahan join them in 1927 for three freezers of ice cream, Gillingham signed Tony Cascarino from Crockenhill in 1981–82 for a set of tracksuits and in pre-war times Jimmy Skelton was transferred from Moss End Celtic to Holytown United for 30 corrugated sheets of iron urgently required for the Moss End ground. A far cry from AC Milan's San Siro stadium and the dealings of millionaire president Silvio Berlusconi.

EXTRA TIME

LOWLAND GATHERING

When East Stirling met Leith Athletic on 15 April 1939 the match clashed with the Scotland v England game at Hampden Park. Only 32 spectators turned up for the Division Two encounter.

ONE UNDER THE EIGHT

During the 1990–91 and 1991–92 seasons, Southend United missed seven consecutive penalty kicks awarded to them.

TIES IN A KNOT

In 1985–86 seven of the eight FA Cup fifth round ties needed replays. In 1992–93 all eight were won by the home team.

LANGUAGE BARRIER

When Norwich City signed Paddy Sloan from Brescia for 7 million Lire (£4,000) in December 1951, transfer talks were held in a Paris hotel. The sellers spoke Italian, German and French but no English. The buyers spoke only English plus the Italian colloquialisms of the Player (Irish). The Bank Manager (French) spoke English, Spanish and of course French, but no Italian. The Interpreter spoke French and Italian but no English. After that he (Sloan) made only six League appearances.

SCHOLASTIC ENDEAVOUR

Harry Stapley, an amateur centre-forward and schoolmaster, was Glossop's leading goalscorer in Division Two for four seasons between 1908–12, a Football League record for consecutive years for a non-professional. Stapley scored 67 goals in 135 appearances during this period and in the three preceding seasons he had topped West Ham United's scoring charts in their Southern League days.

WALTZING REEL?

At the end of the 1951–52 season Stranraer entertained their only continental opposition when they were beaten 3–2 by Graz AK of Austria.

GERD-A-GOAL

Gerd Muller not only scored 68 international goals for West Germany but registered 68 in cup goals for Bayern Munich in European competitions.

DUNDEE DUMPED

In 1937–38 Dundee began with six successive wins but then slumped. However on 5 February 1938 they beat Rangers 6–1 at Dens Park. Unfortunately the next 11 games produced only seven points and they were relegated.

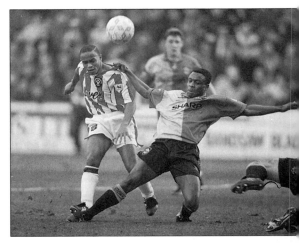

When Sheffield United pulled off a surprise win against Manchester United in the fifth round of the FA Cup in 1993, it completed a round in which every tie was won by the home team at the first attempt (Allsport/Mike Hewitt)

'BLUES' WHITEWASHED

When Scotland met the USSR in an international at Hampden Park in 1967, they wore an all-white strip, the Soviets winning 2–0.

ECONOMY-SIZE VALLEY

Charlton Athletic played 304 consecutive away games during a seven-year exile from The Valley. They returned on 5 December 1992 and beat Portsmouth 1–0 in a Division One match in front of a capacity crowd of 8,337, nearly a tenth of the size of the old stadium.

A SWITCH IN TIME

When Barnet beat Newport County 6–1 in an FA Cup first round tie in the 1970–71 season, it was the heaviest defeat suffered by a Football League club against non-league opposition in the competition. By 1991–92 Barnet had become members of the League while Newport were no longer in existence under their former title.

NOT THE WORST

Crewe Alexandra's 7–4 win at Barnet on 17 August 1991 was the highest aggregate score involving a club making its Football League debut. Crewe had lost their first League game 7–1 at Burton Swifts on 3 September 1892.

THE 'N' FACTOR

During the 1969–70 season Rangers had 18 players on their staff with names ending in the letter 'n', but they never managed to field 11 in one team. John Greig was the one who did not fall into this category on the six occasions where there were ten such others.

UNIQUE TREBLE

At the end of the 1930–31 season Bill Bocking played for Stockport County in a Division Three (North) match before being transferred to Everton, for whom he appeared in their last Division Two match when they achieved promotion. His next home game was in Division One at the start of 1931–32.

CORNER-SHOPPED

Sheffield United forced 28 corners in a Division Two match at home to West Ham United on 14 October 1989. West Ham won 2–0.

OH! BROTHERS

On 6 December 1952, Torquay United introduced centre-forward Albert Calland and left-winger Ted Calland, brothers of defender Ralph Calland, in a friendly against Bournemouth. Torquay won 3–0 with both newcomers scoring once.

INTERNATIONAL RESORT

Newcastle United's FA Cup-winning team of 1910 included nine internationals. The team was: Lawrence; McCracken, Carr, Veitch, Low, McWilliam, Rutherford, Howie, Shepherd, Higgins, Wilson. Only Lawrence and Low had not been previously capped but they were so honoured the following season.

FORT FOR DEFENCE

Millwall was the first Third Division club to have one of its players capped for England. Jack Fort, right-back and captain, was chosen against Belgium on 21 May 1921 in Brussels. England won 2–0.

A fine view of the return of League football to The Valley, Charlton Athletic's home. On the near side of the ground is what remains of the huge terrace of old (Allsport/Shaun Botterill)

ELEVEN-A-SIDE

On 24 October 1925 Manchester City beat Burnley 8–3 at home. Two days later they were beaten 8–3 at Sheffield United.

RELATIVELY LOCAL

When Southport lost their Football League status, two Jones twins Mick and Mark aged 17 still had six months of their apprenticeship to be completed. They went to Wigan Athletic, Southport's replacement, playing in a reserve side with three other ex-Southport lads.

RUINED BY A FOWLER

The best start to a season by any Football League goalkeeper was achieved by Tom Newton of Portsmouth in 1922–23. He kept a clean sheet for the first eight games before being beaten by a first-minute goal by Plymouth Argyle's Jack Fowler in a 2–1 defeat at Fratton Park.

EARLY CUP SHOOT-OUT

Birmingham City were the first club to be involved in a penalty shoot-out in an FA Cup game. On 5 August 1972 at St Andrews against Stoke City in a play-off for third place held over from the previous season, Birmingham won 4–3 after a goalless draw.

TWO AND TWO MAKE FOUR

Ipswich Town scored two goals within two minutes of the start of the Division Three (South) match v Brentford on 22 September 1956 and York City equalled the feat at Norwich City in a Division Two match on 18 January 1975.

EXORCISE OR EXERCISE?

A curse has supposedly hung over Priestfield Stadium, the home of Gillingham, since the 1940s when a motor accident involving the then manager of the club resulted in the death of a young gypsy girl in a nearby street. In November 1992 the club appointed Kevin McElhinney a 29-year-old Catholic priest and supporter. Gillingham won their next three home games.

BOYS FROM THE BLACK STUFF

Airdrieonians midfield player Kenny Black arrived home to find two burglars ransacking his home. They took off – but in the player's car. The following night, when Airdrie played Partick Thistle, Black's team were 2–1 ahead with a minute remaining but he was sent off for a foul on the edge of the penalty area and from the resulting free-kick Thistle equalised. It happened on 9 March 1993.

SWANUPPING

On 15 August 1992, Swansea City lost 1–0 at Burnley in a Division Two match, to equal their worst run of 12 games without a win, set in 1937–38 and 1988–89.

DOUBLE-EDGED RESPONSE
When Walsall won 4–3 at Carlisle United on 15 August 1992 in a Division Three match, George Oghani (Carlisle) and Ron McDonald (Walsall) each scored for both teams.

DYET MENU
Jim Dyet scored eight goals when King's Park beat Forfar Athletic in Division Two on 2 January 1930 during a 12–2 win.

LATIN LOSER
When Lazio met Roma during 1978–79, Paolo Ammoniaci was sent off after 25 seconds of appearing as a last minute substitute. As the players were arguing over a free-kick, Ammoniaci was brought on by Lazio but ordered off for pretending he had been kicked.

YOU CANNOT BE SERIE A
Perugia were unbeaten in the Italian Division One (Serie A) during 1978–79 with 11 wins and 19 draws. But they could only finish runners-up to AC Milan; the champions were three points ahead despite losing three times.

LEAST SAID, SOUNESS MENDED
Graeme Souness played part of only one first team game for Tottenham Hotspur. It was as a substitute for Alan Mullery against Keflavik in the UEFA Cup on 14 September 1971. Spurs won 6–1.

CELL-BY DATE
Bobby McKinlay and Doug Fraser, both former Nottingham Forest defenders, had spent their footballing careers trying to keep opponents out. They became prison warders in Nottingham, were they were required to keep them in.

FATHERLY ADVICE PAYS OFF
George Thompson senior, a former York City goalkeeper, watched his sons George (25) and Des (23) play respectively in goal for Scunthorpe United and York on 17 January 1952. The match ended happily enough for father, a 1–1 draw.

WARTIME EXPERIENCE
Scott Duncan, signed by Rangers from Newcastle United in 1913, played two games as a guest player for Celtic while on Army leave during the 1914–18 war.

BOUNCY REWARD
When Everton met Grimsby Town on 12 April 1930, both teams were struggling at the bottom of the Division One table. Everton dropped Dixie Dean, but the crowd laughed when the Grimsby forward Robson bounced onto the pitch rather in the style of a long-jumper before the kick-off. But the laughter had

subsided by the end of the game because Grimsby won 4–2 and Joe Robson scored four times. Yet before the game he had felt unwell and did not want to play until a director told him to sit with him in the stand and watch a *real* centre-forward Dixie Dean play. Everton were relegated.

LAVA SURVIVOR
In 1973 IB Vestmann's ground sank under the lava from a volcano in Iceland. Two years later it was dug out safely and used again.

TWO ON A PLATE
River Plate toyed with the idea of running two 'first teams' in 1978. One would play in the Argentine domestic competitions, the other on foreign tours to bring in extra revenue.

PARK IN SPACE
When Hamilton Academical beat Dunfermline Athletic 6–1 on 29 February 1936, John Park scored four goals including three penalties.

YOU CANNOT BE SIRIUS
A Swedish cup match between Sirius and Oddewold in 1967 was ordered to be replayed. Thirty seconds from the end, Sirius brought on a substitute too quickly and had 12 players on the field. Sirius won the replay, all three goals being scored by the previous 12th man.

LUIGI, WET AND DRY
During Italy's international with Belgium on 21 May 1922 in Milan, Luigi Burlando headed a goal from 45 yards in the 71st minute. Italy won 4–2. Burlando had competed for Italy in the 1920 Olympics at football and water polo.

TWO BLANK CZECHS
On 21 February 1993, West Ham United drew 0–0 with Newcastle United in a Division One match at Upton Park. The respective goalkeepers were Ludek Miklosko and Pavel Srnicek, both Czechs who had previously played for Banik Ostrava in their home country.

IBROX INTERNATIONAL
At one period during the summer of 1991, Rangers had three international goalkeepers on their staff: Andy Goram (Scotland), Chris Woods (England) and Bonni Ginzburg (Israel).

FRENCH CONNECTION
At the end of the 1909–10 season, Swindon Town and Barnsley were invited to play a match in Paris, the winners to be awarded the Dubonnet Cup. During the game the cup was guarded by two armed soldiers with rifle and fixed bayonet. Swindon won 2–1 with Harold Fleming scoring twice.

SEASICK AS PARROTS
Southend United Supporters Club organised a boat trip through the General Steam Navigation Company for their Good Friday visit to Gillingham in 1930. The team lost 1–0.

NOT ROCKY ROKER
Between Christmas Day 1925 and 30 December 1961, no Football League or FA Cup tie was called off at Sunderland's Roker Park because of the weather.

MERSEY BEAT
Edward Bainbridge had the distinction of being a director of both Liverpool and Everton at the same time before the First World War. Despite the obvious strain from such conflict of interests, he survived until 1927 when he died at the age of 92.

AMATEUR SUCCESS
Crewe Alexandra were the last amateur club to reach the semi-finals of the FA Cup, losing 4–0 to Preston North End in February 1888. The previous year they had won their first trophy – the Crewe and District Cup.

FIVE INTO NINE DIDN'T GO
In the first half of their record-breaking goalscoring season of 1928–29 which produced 128 League goals,

Newcastle United's Pavel Srnicek, who faced his fellow country-man and goalkeeper Ludek Miklosko of West Ham at Upton Park in 1992–93 (Bob Thomas)

Bradford City tried five different players at centre-forward before signing Albert Whitehurst from Liverpool in February. He scored 24 goals in the last 15 games including seven against Tranmere Rovers, four against Barrow and a hat-trick against Wrexham.

EARLY FROST
David Frost's boyhood ambition was to play for Newcastle United because he liked their black and white stripes. He almost signed for Nottingham Forest as a youth but went to Cambridge University instead.

WHISTLER'S FORERUNNER
Prior to 1878 when the whistle was introduced in a game between Nottingham Forest and Sheffield, referees had to shout decisions to the players.

RESERVED OCCUPATION
In a Pontins Central League match Everton Reserves were beaten 10–3 by Derby County on 25 February 1993. The Everton team included senior players Paul Rideout, Andy Hinchcliffe, Robert Warzycha, Stuart Barlow and Mark Ward.

BAR THE DAI
Welsh international goalkeeper Dai Davies was refused permission to fly to Kuwait in September 1977, because his passport had an Israeli stamp on it.

GOALS GALORE
At the end of the 1978–79 season teams from the villages of Ilinden and Debarce were neck and neck in the race for a place in Yugoslavia's Macedonian Regional League. On the last day it was merely a matter of which team scored more than the other, providing they won the match. The results were: Gradinar 0 Debarce 88; Ilinden 134 Mladost 1. All four teams were suspended.

SLIPPED DISC
Kevin Keegan made a record in the 1970s called 'Five Years'. It failed to reach the charts.

NO COTTAGERS INDUSTRY?
Lord Grosvenor, one of Britain's richest men in the late 1970s, had been a keen player at Harrow and was once offered a trial by Fulham.

NO PULLING POWER
The Dental Cup in 1928 was not a financial success, the final between Partick Thistle and Rangers being watched by only 5000 spectators. Partick won 2–0.

MONARCHS' PLAYGROUND?
King George V visited Stamford Bridge three times in 14 months: Chelsea v Leicester City, FA Cup 3rd rd, 21 February 1920; Chelsea v Arsenal, Division 1, 4 December 1920; Tottenham Hotspur v Wolverhampton Wanderers, FA Cup Final, 23 April 1921.

TERRACE TALK
Morton was founded in 1874 by local Greenock lads living in the area around Morton Terrace.

HEARTS ARE TRUMPS
On December 1936, Hearts gave Rangers a two goals start in only six minutes but still beat them 5–2.

CHERCHEZ LA FEMME
In the late 1940s, Stirling Albion became the first Scottish club to use female turnstile operators.

TICKET TOUTING
When Wrexham were about to meet Manchester United in an FA Cup-tie a crowd of 18,069 turned up for a reserve match against Winsford United in the Cheshire League because tickets were available for the cup game. It happened on 19 January 1957.

TIMELY GIFTS
Over Christmas 1938 Swindon Town beat Newport County 8–0 at home and lost 6–4 to them away.

EXTENUATING CIRCUMSTANCES
Celtic were beaten 8–0 by Motherwell on 30 April 1937 but finished the match with nine men. Goalkeeper Joe Kennaway was injured after only 30 minutes and Willie Buchan took over in goal. Later they were deprived of the services of left-back Ian Morrison.

ON THE SPOT
On 22 April 1957, Queen's Park were leading Rangers 4–1 when they were awarded a penalty. Bert Cromar missed from the spot and Rangers went on to win 6–4.

TREBLE SHOOTERS
Prior to gaining election to the Football League in 1960, Peterborough United had won the Midland Counties League championship three years in succession.

RELATIVE VALUES
Nick Ross of Preston North End scored a hat-trick against Burnley on 28 September 1889 and his brother Jimmy scored three times the following week on 5 October against West Bromwich Albion. Nick Ross then scored three goals against Bolton Wanderers on 12 October.

TWO CHOICES
Queen's Park are the only first-class club in either England or Scotland to have two home grounds: Hampden Park and New Lesser Hampden.

LATE FOR STRIKERS
When Newcastle United were waiting to play an away fixture in Division Two against Walsall Town Swifts on 29 December 1894, the home players refused to take the field because they had not been paid. They finally did so, but so late that the game had to be abandoned through bad light with Newcastle leading 3–2. The score was allowed to stand.

HEART OF THE AFFAIR
Right-half Tom Helsby played for Rhyl Athletic, Wigan Borough, Runcorn and Cardiff City before joining Bradford City in May 1931 where he was diagnosed as having heart trouble. A local doctor made him fit and he continued his career with Swindon Town, Hull City and Newport County.

MOORE THE MERRIER
Paddy Moore was born in Ireland, played for a Welsh club and one in England without much success but developed with a Scottish club and is one of few players to have scored as many as four goals in a World Cup game. He was signed by Cardiff City from Mullingar in June 1929 and made his debut in the opening game of the following season. He did not play for Cardiff again in the League and after four games for Tranmere Rovers moved to Aberdeen in 1931.

FORD TRANSIT
When Jimmy Greaves took part in the 1970 World Cup Rally, his co-driver was Tony Ford and they competed in a Ford Escort.

AFFINITY FOR THE LIONS' DEN
On 14 September 1946, Jimmy Constantine scored a hat-trick for Manchester City at Millwall on his League debut in a 3–1 win. His next appearance at The Den was for Bury and he scored another hat-trick in a 7–1 win on 21 February 1948. Millwall signed him in May 1948.

WHAT'S IN A NAME?
Alf Earl made his debut for West Ham United at left-back against Aston Villa on Christmas Day 1925. Though the Hammers won 5–2, his first appearance was overshadowed by Stan Earle scoring a hat-trick.

NO BILL OF FARE
When officials from Alloa signed brothers John and Bob in their father's miner's home in Glenbuck, a younger brother asked them to come back for him. They did not and so lost out on Bill Shankly.

McSTAYING POWER
At the end of the 1937–38 season, Alloa sacked all 16 professionals and appointed a new manager in Jimmy McStay. They won promotion the following season.

ROVERS RETURN
Albion Rovers won the Division Two championship by beating Dumbarton 2–0 on 22 April 1989, with goals from Ally Graham and Jim Chapman.

LEST WE FORGET

Ayr United won their initial League game on 20 August 1910 against Port Glasgow Athletic at Somerset Park. The honour of scoring their first goal went to Archie Campbell their outside-left in the 2–0 success. He was killed in the First World War.

A REEL BEGINNING

A group of young men who attended a dance club in the Canongate area of Edinburgh formed a football team who played in the East Meadows. The dance club was called Heart of Midlothian.

ROBBING THE SAINTS

When Barnsley were still known as Barnsley St Peters and were competing in the Sheffield and District League and playing in chocolate and white shirts, they beat Clinton 13–0 in a January fixture. Six of their goals came in the first 30 minutes. But Clinton withdrew from the competition and their record was expunged along with Barnsley's highest ever score.

FEE FOR BURY

Port Vale beat off a late bid from Tranmere Rovers to take Leeds City's place in the Football League in 1919. But five of the Vale first team were ineligible for the competition and transfers had to be negotiated. But Bury demanded a fee for Harry Pearson and he never played for Port Vale again.

FRETWELL FRETS WELL

Quickest own goal in the FA Cup was recorded by David Fretwell of Bradford City against Luton Town. He put through his own goal after 20 seconds of the FA Cup, fourth round tie on 26 January 1974 after Luton had kicked off.

METROPOLIS ATTRACTION

Robert Turnbull was Dumbarton born but spent most of his senior career as a player with London clubs. At Arsenal he was converted from full-back to centre-forward and subsequently played for Charlton Athletic, Chelsea, Clapton Orient and Crystal Palace.

PAYING THE PENALTY

When Crewe Alexandra played Bradford Park Avenue in a Division Three (North) match on 8 March 1924, John Doran of Crewe had a penalty kick saved. He shot wide from a second such award before William Goodwin hit the bar with effort number three. Doran then scored from a fourth in a 1–1 draw.

BATTEN DOWN – UNDER

Plymouth Argyle inside-left Bert Batten scored six goals for the FA touring team v South Australia at Adelaide on 16 May 1925 and five against Australia on 11 July.

OWLS BY A WINK

On the last day of the 1949–50 season, Sheffield United had already finished their programme. Their neighbours and close rivals Sheffield Wednesday drew 0–0 with Tottenham Hotspur. But had the game ended at 1–1 there would have been a tie with United on goal average which would have required a play-off the following Monday. Wednesday won promotion to Division One by .008 of a goal.

ALMOST HOLY ORDERS

Ian St John joined Motherwell from Douglas Water Thistle in 1957 and subsequently signed for the registrar's department as a benedict.

DARWEN'S THEORETICAL PRACTICE

In 1898–99, Darwen used the services of 45 players. No one was an ever present, but only five made just one appearance.

LOYAL LLOYD

In the New Year's Honours List in 1992, the British Empire Medal was awarded to Fred Lloyd, an 82-year-old retired steel worker, who had helped part-time for Walsall since 1924, overseeing gate stewards, paying turnstile operators and referees expenses.

THREE-IN-ONE

Three FA Cup third round ties in 1991–92 were played on the same ground with different home clubs involved. The Farnborough v West Ham United match was switched to Upton Park on police advice and finished 1–1. The following day, Charlton Athletic who were still using the ground as their home beat Barnet 3–1, while West Ham won their replay with Farnborough 1–0 ten days later.

RACING CERTAINTY

On 3 December 1962, Mansfield Town purchased the Hurst Park Grandstand at an auction when the racecourse was sold off.

POINT TAKEN

Rotherham United won their first 20 home matches in Division Three (North) in 1946–47 and drew the last one on 7 June.

RIGHTEOUS INDIGNATION

St Johnstone played Hibernian on 30 November 1991 and had the match ball supplied by the Church of Scotland. But Hibs won 1–0.

CHARLIE WAS THEIR DARLING

Hereford United's first most prolific scoring player was Charlie Thompson, centre-forward signed from Sheffield United in 1947. In over 450 Southern League games for the club he scored 184 goals up to 1958, despite often playing at centre-half. He scored eight when Hereford beat Thynnes 11–0 in an FA Cup qualifying round game on 13 September 1947.

THE NAME'S THE SAME

At least two players of the same surname appeared with Dumbarton from 1968–69 to 1988–89 inclusive. The longest surviving with them were the brothers Joe and Tom Coyle from 1978–79 to 1985–86 inclusive. In 1985–86 they were joined by another brother Owen. Tom and Owen were left on their own for the last two seasons involved.

ELEVEN OF THE BEST

When East Fife won the Scottish Cup in 1938 they played 11 matches: one each against Airdrie and Dundee United, two each against Aberdeen and Raith, three in the semi-final with St Bernards and two in the final with Kilmarnock.

TWO-WHEELED BAN

Northampton Town banned its players from indulging in motor cycling during the season in 1924, because it had led to many accidents.

SCARBOROUGH FARE

Scarborough playing away to Crewe Alexandra in a Division Four match on 19 October 1991 were losing 3–0 with four minutes remaining and down to ten men having had a player sent off. They drew 3–3.

QUEEN'S TRUMP IT

On October 1930, Queen's Park were entertaining Celtic at Hampden Park but losing 3–2 when the referee prematurely ended the game with two minutes still remaining for play. He recalled the teams for the miscalculation to be redressed and J. B. McAlpine succeeded in equalising from a penalty in the 3–3 draw.

TIME TRAVELLERS

On 5 September 1992, Wimbledon's John Fashanu scored in the 81st minute against Arsenal, while at the same time his brother Justin was being sent off for Torquay against Cardiff City.

BAPTISM OF FIRE

Hereford United took part in an FA Cup tie only a week after their first competitive match. On 6 September 1924 they were beaten 7–2 away at Kidderminster Harriers in an Extra Preliminary round game, seven days after losing 3–2 to Atherstone Town in the Birmingham Combination.

DING-DONG AFFAIR

On 27 August 1952 during a Division One match between Middlesbrough and Cardiff City at Ayresome Park, the Middlesbrough right-half Harry Bell hit a

high ball out of defence from near his own goal-line. It bounced near the Cardiff goalkeeper who became distracted by the oncoming Boro centre-forward Neil Mochan and allowed the ball to enter the net. Bell scored another goal in the match which Middlesbrough won 3–1.

FORREST FIREPOWER

Jim Forrest once scored all seven goals for Rangers Reserves against St Mirren on 1 September 1962 in a 7–3 win. He made his League debut v Falkirk at Brockville on 17 November 1962.

FOUR-PLAY SCORES

In January 1961 Brazil named 110 players for World Cup training. They were split into four camps of 18–20 each and subsequently sent on tour, the A team to Europe, the B side to South America, the C squad to the Far East and the D party to the Middle East. In 1962 Brazil retained the World Cup trophy.

BREAK IN TRADITION

After seven years of winning the opening match of the season, Liverpool lost their first game 1–0 at Nottingham Forest in the Premier League on 16 August 1992, though the match was played a day later than the others in the division. On the day before, Wolverhampton Wanderers had beaten Brentford 2–0 away in the Barclays Division One, their first opening day success since 1982. They remained unbeaten for 12 games.

HONESTY PAYS?

In 1935 the Falkirk manager Robert Orr successfully persuaded an Ayr United player not to play in a crucial relegation match between the two clubs. The player admitted this and the game was ordered to be replayed. Falkirk forfeited four points and were relegated. Ayr's nickname is The Honest Men.

BONE OF CONTENTION

In a match against Arbroath on 1 April 1939, Jimmy Delaney the Celtic right-winger sustained a severe fracture of the right arm which led to two years out of action. There was a reluctance to insure him because it was feared that he was brittle boned and the Scottish Football Association was not anxious to have to pay out a large sum in compensation. The matter was resolved at the end of the war and Delaney scored the winning goal in the Victory International against England at Hampden Park in 1946.

THE JONES JOY

The 1935 FA Cup replay between Everton and Sunderland at Goodison Park was not a game for defenders to remember as Everton won 6–4, but Jack

Jones, the Everton left-back who had succeeded Warney Cresswell in the position, was eventually signed by Sunderland. He later acted as coach at Roker Park.

CONSISTENT LOSERS

Between 1980 and 1992 Luxembourg completed 67 international matches without a win. It included two other unwanted records: 32 consecutive games without avoiding defeat and failing to score in nine successive matches. Luxembourg's previous win was in May 1980 when they beat South Korea 3–2.

TARTAN RECORD-BREAKER

On 2 February 1993 Graeme Armstrong made his 563rd Scottish League appearance in a match for Stenhousemuir v Alloa in Division Two. His previous clubs had been Meadowbank Thistle and Berwick Rangers. His total established a record in the competition.

Paul Stewart moves forward on his League debut for Liverpool, the opening fixture of the 1992–93 season away at Nottingham Forest. It ended in a 1–0 reverse for the Reds, breaking their run of seven consecutive opening wins (Allsport/Shaun Botterill)

AHEAD OF HIS TIME

Herbert Chapman, the first £2,000 a year football manager with Arsenal, was a visionary, experimenting with a white ball, artificial playing surfaces and advocating promotion and relegation of half the teams in each division.

SPINNING JIMMY

Jim Forrest was the only Blackburn Rovers player to appear in all five of the club's FA Cup successes in the late 19th century. He was a tape-sizer in the cotton trade.

SUNDAY DE-NOMINATION!

Ron Greenwood's first connection with football was as ball boy to two church teams, one Wesleyan, another Church of England. Though they called it a Sunday League, the teams played on Saturday. Greenwood, later a player and manager at the highest level, was originally a sign-writer at Wembley Stadium.

FEMALE INTUITION

Pegasus, the famous Amateur Club of the post-war period were formed in 1948. Their name was given to them by the former Miss Grace Penelope Stradling, an Oxford classics scholar who married Dr. H. W. 'Tommy' Thompson before the war. She derived the club's name from the Oxford Centaur (headed horse) and Cambridge Falcon (bird), the two undergraduate football clubs at the respective universities. Dr. Ben Brown, goalkeeper in the 1953 Amateur Cup Final, presented his winning medal to her.

IN THE REDS

Arsenal began the 1946–47 season with debts of £200,000, a colossal sum at the time. Seven years in which their Highbury ground had been out of use by them because of the war, when the Gunners shared White Hart Lane with Tottenham Hotspur, had brought them to a financial crisis.

INDEX

Page references in italics denote illustrations, those in bold colour illustrations.

Abercorn 106
Aberdare Athletic 5
Aberdeen 107, *107*, 200–1
Accrington Stanley 5
Adams, Tony **5c**, *160*
Africa 228–30
African Nations Cup 228–9, *229*
Airdrieonians 108, 201
Aitken, Roy *142*
Aizlewood, Mark *158*
Ajax 168
Albion Rovers 108–9
Aldershot 5–6
Alloa 109–10
Anglo-Italian Cup 106
Arbroath 110
Ards 214
Armadale 111
Argentina *228*, 234–5
Arsenal **5c**, 6–7, *7*, *87*, 100, *100*, 175–6
Arthurlie 111
Ashington 7
Aston Villa 7–8, *8*, 95–6, 169, 176–7, *184*
Athlone Town 219
Autoglass Trophy 105–6
Awford, Andy *164*
Ayr Parkhouse 111
Ayr United 111–12

Baldwin, Tommy *174*
Ballymena United 214
Bangor 214
Bangor City 150, 223
Barcelona 170, *170*
Barmby, Nick **1c**
Barnes, John **7c**
Barnet 9
Barnsley 9, 99
Barrow 9–10
Bathgate 112
Batty, David **3c**
Bayern Munich 168
Benfica 167
Bergkamp, Dennis *243*
Berwick Rangers 112–13
Birmingham City 10–11, 177
Blackburn Olympic 95
Blackburn Rovers 11–12, *84*, 95, *162*
Blackpool 12–13, 101
Bodin, Paul *73*
Bohemians 219

Bolton Wanderers 13–14, 99
Bo'ness 113
Bootle 14
Borough United 150, 224
Bournemouth, AFC 14
Bradford City 14–15, 98–9
Bradford Park Avenue 15–16
Bray Wanderers 219
Brazil 234, *234*
Brechin City 113
Brentford 16
Brighton & Hove Albion 17
Bristol City 17–18
Bristol Rovers 18–19
British football
    fastest hat-tricks in 163
    fastest own goal in 163
    goalkeeping records in 163
    highest attendances in 165
    highest scores in 162
    lowest attendances in 165
    most appearances in 163–4
    most career goals in 163
    most cup-winners medals in 163
    most goals in one match 162–3
    oldest players in 165
    quickest goals in 163
    youngest players in 164
Broxburn United 113
Burnley 19–20, *19*, 99, 177
Burton Swifts 20
Burton United 20
Burton Wanderers 20
Bury 20–1, 97

Cambridge United 21
Cambuslang 113
Cardiff City 21–2, 100, 149–50, *150*, 117–8
Carlisle United 22–3
Carrick Rangers 215
Celtic 114–15, *114*, *143*, *148*, 167, 201–4
Chapman, Lee *184*
Charlton Athletic 23, 101, *245*
Charlton, Jack *237*
Chelsea 23–4, *24*, 101, *105*, *174*, 179
Chester City 24–5
Chesterfield 25–6
Clackmannan 115
Clapham Rovers 95
Cliftonville 215
Clough, Brian **8c**, *30*
Clyde 115–16
Clydebank 116
Colchester United 26

Coleraine 215
Copa America *see* South American Championship
Copa Libertadores *see* South American Club Cup
Cork Celtic 219
Cork City 219
Cork Hibs 220
Coventry City 26–7, 102, 179
Cowdenbeath 116–17
Cowlairs 117
Crewe Alexandra 27–8
Crusaders 215
Crystal Palace 28

Darlington 28–9
Darwen 29
Derby County 29–30, *30*, 100, 179–80
Derry City 215–16, 220
Distillery 216
Dixon, Kerry *24*
Docherty, John *50*
Doncaster Rovers 30–1
Drogheda 220
Drumcondra 220
Dumbarton 117–18
Dundalk 220–1
Dundee 118–19, 204
Dundee Hibernians 119
Dundee United 119–20, 204–6, *213*
Dundee Wanderers 120
Dunfermline Athletic 120, 206–7
Durham 31
Durrant, Iain **2c**

East Fife 120–1
East Stirlingshire 121–2
Edinburgh City 122
England
    international results 156–7
    in World Cup **6–7c**, 234
European Championship 166
European club competitions
    British clubs results in 175–224
    highest scores in 174
    most career goals in 174
    top British scorers in 174
European Cup
    winners 166–70
European Cup-Winners Cup
    winners 170–1
European Footballer of the Year 224–5
European Super Cup 173
Everton 31–2, *86*, 98, 180–1
Exeter City 32–3

FA Charity Shield 106
FA Cup
    facts and feats 102–3
    winners 94–102
Fair Play Award 239
Falkirk 122–3
Ferguson, Iain *147*
Feyenoord 167–8, *168*
Finn Harps 221
Football League
    best starts 93–4
    champions 82–4
    fewest goals conceded in season 93
    fewest goals scored in season 92–3
    fewest wins in season 88–9
    most defeats in season 89–90
    most draws in season 89
    most goals conceded in season 92
    most goals scored in season 91–2
    most wins in season 88
    sequences 90–1
Forfar Athletic 123
Francis, Gerry *61*
Francis, Trevor **4c**
Fulham 33–4
Full Members Cup 105

Gainsborough Trinity 34
Gallacher, Kevin *157*
Galway United 221
Gateshead 34
Giggs, Ryan **1c**
Gillingham 34–5
Glenavon 216
Glentoran 216–17
Glossop North End 35
goalscoring 153–4, 236
Golden Boot award 225–6
Graham, George *156*
Grimsby Town 35–6

Halifax Town 36–7
Hamburg SV 169
Hamilton Academical 123–4
Hartlepool United 37
Havelange, Joao *230*
Heart of Midlothian 124–5, 207–8
Hereford United 38
Hibernian 125–6, 208–9
Hoddle, Glenn *73*
Home Farm 221
Huddersfield Town 38, 99
Hughes, Mark *84*
Hughes, Michael *151*
Hull City 39

Ipswich Town 39–40, *40*, 101–2, 181–2
international football
    appearances 238–9

facts and feats 159–61
Internazionale 167, *173*, *184*
Ireland
    international results 158–9
    in World Cup **6c**
Irish Cup 150–1
Irish League 150–1
Italy 233

Johnstone 126
Juventus 169

Keane, Roy *152*
Keegan, Kevin *52*
Kelly, Alan **4c**
Kilmarnock 126–7, *127*, 209–10
King's Park 127–8
Kiwomya, Chris *40*
Klinsmann, Jurgen *4*
Konica League of Wales 149

League Cup
    facts and feats 104–5
    winners 103–4
League of Ireland 152–3
Leeds United **2–3c**, 40–1, *41*, 101, 182–5, *184*
Leicester City 41–2, 185
Leith Athletic 128
Leyton Orient 42–3
Limerick 221–2
Lincoln City 43
Lineker, Gary *239*
Linfield 217–18
Linthouse 128
Livermore, Doug **5c**
Liverpool 44–5, *44*, 101, 168, 185–8, *251*
Lochgelly 128
London XI 224
Loughborough 45
Lukic, John **2c**
Luton Town 45

McAllister, Gary **2c**
McCall, Stuart **3c**, *142*
McCoist, Ally **2c**, *226*
McLintock, Frank *50*
Maidstone United 45–6
managers 155–6, 237
Manchester City 46–7, *46*, 97–8, 188–9
Manchester United 47–8, *48*, *84*, 98, 189–91, *244*
Mansfield Town 48
Maskell, Craig *73*
Meadowbank Thistle 128–9
Mercer, Joe *46*
Merson, Paul **5c**
Merthyr Town 48, 149–50, 224

Middlesbrough 49
Middlesbrough Ironopolis 49
Milan AC 167
Millwall 49–50, *50*
Montrose 129
Morrow, Steven **6c**
Morton 129–30, 210
Motherwell 130–1, *147*, 210

Ndlovu, Peter *229*
Nelson 50
Nevin, Pat *24*
New Brighton 50–1
Newcastle United 51–2, *52*, 98, 191–2
Newport County 52, 149, 192
Nilsson, Roland **4c**
Nithsdale Wanderers 131
Northampton Town 53
Northern 131
Northern Ireland
    international results 158
    in World Cup **6c**
Northwich Victoria 53
Norwich City 53–4
Nottingham Forest 54–5, 97, *104*, 169, 192–3
Notts County 55–6, 97

Old Carthusians 95
Old Etonians 95
Oldham Athletic 56–7, *57*
Olympique Marseille 170
Oxford United 57
Oxford University 95

Papin, Jean-Pierre *224*
Parma AC *171*
Partick Thistle 131–2, 210
Pele *236*
Peterborough United 57
Platt, David **6c**, *184*
Plymouth Argyle 58
Port Glasgow Athletic 132
Port Vale 59–60
Portadown 218
Porto 169
Portsmouth 59, *59*, 100
Preston North End 60–1, 96
PSV Eindhoven 169

Queen of the South 132–3
Queen's Park 133–4
Queens Park Rangers 61–2, *61*, 193
Quinn, Niall *160*

Raith Rovers 134–5
Rangers **2–3c**, 135–6, *136*, *142*, *148*, 210–13, *213*

Reading 62
Real Madrid 166
Red Star Belgrade 169–70
Renton 136
Revie, Don *41*
Robertson, Davie **3c**
Rochdale 62–3
Rotherham United 63–4
Royal Engineers 95
rules 239–40
Rush, Ian *153*

St Bernards 136
St Johnstone 136–7, 214
St Patrick's Athletic 223
St Mirren 137–8, *147*, 214
Scarborough 64
Scotland
  international results 157
Scottish Cup
  winners 145–7
  facts and feats 147–8
Scottish League
  champions 141–2
  fewest defeats in season 143
  fewest goals conceded in season
    145
  fewest goals scored in season 144–5
  fewest wins in season 142–3
  most defeats in season 143
  most draws in season 144
  most goals conceded in season 144
  most goals scored in season 144
  most points in season 143–4
  most wins in season 142
  sequences 144
Scottish League Cup
  winners 148–9
  facts and feats 149
Scunthorpe United 64
Sedgley, Steve **5c**
Serena, Aldo *184*

Shamrock Rovers 222
Shearer, Alan *162*
Sheffield United **4c**, 64–5, 97, *244*
Sheffield Wednesday **4c**, 65–6, 97, 193
Shelbourne 222–3
Shilton, Peter *238*
Shrewsbury Town 66–7
Sligo Rovers 223
Small, Mike *87*
South American Championship 227
South American Club Cup 228
Southampton 67, 101, 194
Southend United 67–8
Southport 68–9
Speed, Gary **2c**
Srnicek, Pavel *247*
Stalybridge Celtic 69
Steaua Bucharest 169
Stenhousemuir 138–9
Stewart, Paul *251*
Stirling Albion 139
Stockport County 69–70
Stoke City 70–1, *70*, 194
Strachan, Gordon *107*
Stranraer 139–40
Sunderland 71, 100
Swansea City 72, 149–50, 194–5
Swindon Town 72–3, *73*

tactics 241–2
Taylor, Peter **8c**, *30*
Taylor, Shaun *73*
Thames 73
Third Lanark 140
Thistle 140
Thorstvedt, Erik *240*
Torquay United 73–4
Tottenham Hotspur **5c**, 74–5, *74*, 99,
  195–7
Townsend, Andy **6c**
Tranmere Rovers 75
transfers 242–3

UCD 223
UEFA Cup
  winners 172–3
Uruguay 233
USA 230–1

Vale of Leven 140–1

Waddle, Chris **4c**
Wales
  international results 157–8
  in World Cup **7c**
Walsall 75–6
Wanderers 94
Ward, Mitch **4c**
Waterford 223
Watford 76–7, 197
Welsh Cup 149–50
West Bromwich Albion 77–8, 96, *96*,
  197
West Germany *4*, 233–4
West Ham United 78–9, *87*, 101,
  197–8
Whittingham, Guy *154*
Whyte, Chris **3c**
Wigan Athletic 79
Wigan Borough 79
Wilson, Danny **4c**
Wimbledon 79, 102
Wolverhampton Wanderers 79–80,
  80, 96–7, 198–9
Workington 80–1
World Club Championship 235–6
World Cup **6–7c**, 230–1, 232–5
World Footballer of the Year 239
Wrexham 81, 159, 199
Wright, Ian **5c**

Yorath, Terry **7c**
York City 81–2